A trooper of the 17th Lancers equipped for battle. Cologne, 11 June 1919. Photograph courtesy of the Imperial War Museum, London. (Negative number: Q 7723)

DOCTRINE AND REFORM IN THE BRITISH CAVALRY 1880–1918

A prevalent view among historians is that both horsed cavalry and the cavalry charge became obviously obsolete in the second half of the nineteenth century in the face of increased infantry and artillery firepower, and that officers of the cavalry clung to both for reasons of prestige and stupidity. It is this view, commonly held but rarely supported by sustained research, that this book challenges. It shows that the achievements of British and Empire cavalry in the First World War, although controversial, are sufficient to contradict the argument that belief in the cavalry was evidence of military incompetence. It offers a case study of how in reality a practical military doctrine for the cavalry was developed and modified over several decades, influenced by wider defence plans and spending, by the experience of combat, by Army politics, and by the rivalries of senior officers.

Debate as to how the cavalry was to adjust its tactics in the face of increased infantry and artillery firepower began in the mid nineteenth century, when the increasing size of armies meant a greater need for mobile troops. The cavalry problem was how to deal with a gap in the evolution of warfare between the mass armies of the later nineteenth century and the motorised firepower of the mid twentieth century, an issue that is closely connected with the origins of the deadlock on the Western Front. Tracing this debate, this book shows how, despite serious attempts to 'learn from history', both European-style wars and colonial wars produced ambiguous or disputed evidence as to the future of cavalry, and doctrine was largely a matter of what appeared practical at the time.

About the author

Stephen Badsey is Reader in Conflict Studies at the University of Wolverhampton. He was educated at King Edward's School Birmingham and Cambridge University, where he was awarded a PhD in 1982; and he was elected a Fellow of the Royal Historical Society in 1995. Further information can be found at his website www.stephenbadsey.com

To My Parents
Leonard George Badsey, born 1925
Joan Badsey née Davies, born 1926
The children of another war

Doctrine and Reform in the British Cavalry 1880–1918

STEPHEN BADSEY
University of Wolverhampton, UK

LONDON AND NEW YORK

Birmingham Studies in First World War History

Series Editor

John Bourne
The University of Birmingham, UK

The First World War is a subject of perennial interest to historians and is often regarded as a watershed event, marking the end of the nineteenth century and the beginning of the 'modern' industrial world. The sheer scale of the conflict and massive loss of life means that it is constantly being assessed and reassessed to examine its lasting military, political, sociological, industrial, cultural and economic impact. Run in conjunction with the *Centre for First World War Studies* at the University of Birmingham, this new series offers a platform for the publication of international research on all aspects of the Great War. Whilst the main thrust of the series is on the military aspects of the conflict, other related areas (including cultural, political and social) can also addressed. Books published will be aimed primarily at a post-graduate academic audience, furthering exciting recent interpretations of the war, whilst still being accessible enough to appeal to a wider audience of educated lay readers.

Also in this series

*British Generalship during the Great War
The Military Career of Sir Henry Horne (1861–1929)*
Simon Robbins

*Arming the Western Front
War, Business and the State in Britain 1900–1920*
Roger Lloyd-Jones and M.J. Lewis

First published 2008 by Ashgate Publishing

2 Park Square, Milton Park, Abingdon, Oxon OX14 4RN
711 Third Avenue, New York, NY 10017, USA

Routledge is an imprint of the Taylor & Francis Group, an informa business

First issued in paperback 2016

Copyright © 2008 Stephen Badsey

Stephen Badsey has asserted his moral right under the Copyright, Designs and Patents Act, 1988, to be identified as the author of this work.

All rights reserved. No part of this book may be reprinted or reproduced or utilised in any form or by any electronic, mechanical, or other means, now known or hereafter invented, including photocopying and recording, or in any information storage or retrieval system, without permission in writing from the publishers.

Notice:
Product or corporate names may be trademarks or registered trademarks, and are used only for identification and explanation without intent to infringe.

British Library Cataloguing in Publication Data
Badsey, Stephen
    Doctrine and reform in the British cavalry 1880–1918. – (Birmingham studies in First World War history) 1. Great Britain. Army – Cavalry – History
    I. Title
    357.1'84'0941'09034

Library of Congress Cataloging-in-Publication Data
Badsey, Stephen.
    Doctrine and reform in the British cavalry 1880–1918 / By Stephen Badsey.
      p. cm. – (Birmingham Studies in First World War history)
    Includes bibliographical references and index.
    ISBN 978-0-7546-6467-3 (alk. paper)
  1. Great Britain. Army–Cavalry–History. I. Title.

UA654.B34 2008
357'.184094109034—dc22

2007045483

ISBN 978-0-7546-6467-3 (hbk)
ISBN 978-1-138-25362-9 (pbk)

Contents

Series Editor's Introduction		*xi*
List of Illustrations		*xiii*
Preface		*xv*
1	Doctrine and the Cavalry 1880–1918	1
2	The Wolseley Era 1880–1899	35
3	The Boer War 1899–1902	81
4	The Roberts Era 1902–1905	143
5	The Haldane Era 1905–1914	191
6	The First World War 1914–1918	239
Conclusion		303
Appendix British and Imperial Cavalry Regiments 1914–1918		*309*
Bibliography		*315*
Index		*341*

Series Editor's Introduction

The British Army of the Great War has been the subject of much criticism and abuse over the years. In sections of the British press and in the numerous popular accounts of the war, the army remains unrehabilitated. Its generals are dismissed as callous butchers, its soldiers sentimentalised or despised as passive victims. But in academic circles there has been a transformation. This was begun by Bidwell & Graham's *Firepower* (1982), which abandoned the sterile debate about the alleged professional and moral failings of senior British commanders and inaugurated the analysis of the British army as an institution. This resulted in a greater understanding of how the army confronted and eventually overcame the challenges of the Great War. There is now general acceptance that the army underwent a 'learning curve', though 'learning process' might be a more appropriate phrase. Although there remains debate and disagreement over the cause, pace and effectiveness of the process, much of it focused on the still-controversial record of Sir Douglas Haig, there is a measure of agreement that the army was transformed from the small colonial police force of 1914 – arguably at least – into the best army in the world by the second half of 1918. The army's training, equipment, command and control, tactical evolution, logistics, artillery, discipline, leadership and morale, and eventual 'all arms co-operation' have been the subject of revisionist studies. One branch of the army, however, remains unredeemed by this new orthodoxy, the British cavalry.

Cavalry, even in the writings of otherwise revisionist scholars, still functions as shorthand for the amateurism and traditionalism that the army was forced to abandon during the war. The cavalry could never be part of this process because it was useless and irrelevant on the modern, industrialised battlefield. For too long the principal challenge to these views has been found in Dr Stephen Badsey's Cambridge PhD thesis 'Fire and Sword: The British Army and the *Arme Blanche* Controversy, 1871–1921' (1982). When Dr Badsey accepted my invitation to become a Member of the Birmingham Centre for First World War Studies, I queried why his thesis had never been published. When no satisfactory answer was forthcoming I said that I should like to publish it as the first of the *Birmingham Studies in First World War History* series. Dr Badsey happily agreed, went away to revisit his text, extending and updating it in the light of subsequent research. The resulting book is a *tour de force*. Its focus is on the reform of the British cavalry in the years before the outbreak of the Great War and its continued utility during the war. Badsey's scholarship establishes the cavalry as a centre of professionalism and innovation with a clear understanding of the 'firepower revolution'. It will no longer be possible to airbrush the cavalry out of the operational history of the Great War or to use it as a prop to sustain discredited 'incompetence myths'. Read on.

John Bourne
Director of the Centre for First World War Studies
The University of Birmingham

List of Illustrations

Frontispiece: A trooper of the 17th Lancers equipped for battle. Cologne, 11 June 1919. Photograph courtesy of the Imperial War Museum, London. (Negative number: Q 7723)   i

1. A mounted trooper of the 18th Bengal Lancers, 1897. Photograph by F.W. Bremner. National Army Museum, London (Negative number: 23640). Courtesy of the Council of the National Army Museum London   131

2. A sergeant of a Mounted Infantry detachment on Home Service, 1896. Plate 71 from G. Tylden, *Horses and Saddlery* (London: J.A. Allen & Co. in association with Army Museums Ogilby Trust, 1965)   132

3. An Australian mounted rifleman on an Indian country-bred troop horse serving in South Africa in 1899. Plate 90 from G. Tylden, *Horses and Saddlery* (London: J.A. Allen & Co. in association with Army Museums Ogilby Trust, 1965)   133

4. Figure 20 from page 270 of *Cavalry Training 1912* (HMSO), illustrating how a cavalry squadron should attack by combining a mounted charge with firepower   134

5. A Lancer regiment, either 5th Lancers or 16th Lancers, on the march, Western Front, September 1914. Photograph courtesy of the Imperial War Museum, London. (Negative number: Q 56308)   135

6. The Deccan Horse in Carnoy Valley, 7th Division Area, 14 July 1916. Photograph courtesy of the Imperial War Museum, London. (Negative number: Q 823)   136

7. The Royal Gloucestershire Hussars during the advance towards Damascus, 2 October 1918. Photograph courtesy of the Imperial War Museum, London. (Negative number: Q 12386)   137

8. Cavalry Hotchkiss gun team practising coming into action. Near Querrieu, (Fourth Army H.Q.) 29 July 1916. Photograph courtesy of the Imperial War Museum, London. (Negative number: Q 4067)   138

9. This controversial picture is now widely accepted as a genuine photograph of the actual charge at Beersheba as it took place on 31 October 1917. Australian War Memorial Negative Number A02684   139

10. Canadian cavalry watering their horses in the River Authie near Aix le Chateau, 17 September 1918. Photograph courtesy of the Imperial War Museum, London. (Negative number: Q 9311)   140

11. Haig and Joffre with Lloyd George at XIV Corps headquarters Mesaulte, 12 September 1916. This is the picture described by Lloyd George on page 270. Photograph courtesy of the Imperial War Museum, London. (Negative number: Q 1177)   141

Preface

There is an affectation current in the writing of prefaces for the author to begin with an account of the profound spiritual, and otherwise highly personal, journey that brought him to the point of writing. In lieu of this, I offer the opening to Sir Frederick Ponsonby's *Recollections of Three Reigns*, to whose views I entirely subscribe (except possibly the last sentence):

> The early lives of great men are tiresome enough in all conscience, but the adolescence of a mere chronicler of interesting events would be quite unreadable. The intimate details of my early life must be assumed because they differed in no way from those of the rest of my generation. Nor do I intend to weary the reader with any account of my ancestors, although many writers of autobiographies seem to think that details about their ancestry must be of absorbing interest. Suffice it to say that my youth was no more idiotic than that of most of my contemporaries.[1]

I believe it to be instead the proper purpose of a preface, as well as a matter of pleasure and good manners, for me to acknowledge and thank the people who helped this book into existence.

This book owes its origins to a thesis successfully submitted for the degree of Doctor of Philosophy at Cambridge University in 1982, entitled 'Fire and the Sword: The British Army and the *Arme Blanche* Controversy 1871–1921'. This thesis was an attempt to redress a false conception in history, and as is common in such attempts I overstated my case somewhat; but I still regard its basic findings as sound, and I have retained its final conclusion word for word. I wish to thank my thesis supervisor Correlli Barnett of Churchill College – now Dr Correlli Barnett CBE – and my examiners, Dr Hew Strachan, now Chichele Professor of the History of War at All Souls, Oxford University, and Dr Richard Holmes, now Professor of Military and Security Studies at Cranfield University. I also wish to repeat my thanks to Professor Richard Holmes, Professor Edward Spiers and Dr Philip Towle for the use of information from their own doctoral theses, and to add my thanks for this book to Dr Jean Bou, Dr Bryn Hammond, and Dr Graham Winton. I also wish to thank David Kenyon whose doctoral thesis for Cranfield University, on British cavalry on the Western Front, was due for examination as this book was going into proofs, with expectations that a book version of his thesis will appear shortly in this series.

I wish to repeat the thanks that I gave in my doctoral thesis to the late Brigadier Shelford Bidwell, to Susan Coaker of the Sherburton Pony Stud on Dartmoor for answering certain questions regarding horses, to Professor Derek Beales, to Sylvia Smither for typing the thesis professionally, and particularly to Phil Barker and Sue Laflin-Barker of the Wargames Research Group, whose contributions to military

---

1 Ponsonby, *Recollections of Three Reigns*, p. 1.

history, including inspiring and encouraging military historians of all ages and abilities, are sadly under-recognised.

This book is one of the new series of Birmingham Studies in First World War History. I am grateful to Dr John Bourne as series editor for suggesting its publication, and to Thomas Gray and Emily Ruskell of Ashgate Publishing as my editors for bringing this book to completion; my thanks also to Jonathan Hoare for compiling the index. I am grateful to The National Archives of Great Britain for those British official documents which are Crown Copyright and which I have quoted from or cited in this book, and to the Council of the Australian War Memorial for Australian official documents and some private papers. I am also grateful to those individuals and institutions that have allowed me to quote from collections of private papers, and given me access to their collections of books and journals. This includes thanks to the Brenthurst Library, Johannesburg, for the diary of Sir John French, Earl of Ypres; to Mr Richard Chauvel for the Chauvel Papers; to Earl Haig for the Haig Papers; to Mr Johnnie Pakington for the Lord Hampton Papers; to Mr Andrew Rawlinson for the First World War papers of General Lord Rawlinson; to the Bodleian Library, Oxford; to the British Library, London; to the Cambridge University Library; to the Master, Fellows, and Scholars of Churchill College and the Churchill Archives Centre, Cambridge; to Hove Library of Brighton and Hove City Library Services; to the Trustees of the Imperial War Museum, London; to the Library of the Joint Services Command and Staff College Shrivenham; to the Trustees of the Liddell Hart Centre for Military Archives, Kings College, London; to the Light Dragoons (15th/19th Kings Royal Hussars) Museum Collection; to Dr Alan Guy, Dr Alastair Massie and the National Army Museum, London; to Andrew Orgill, the Librarian at the Royal Military Academy Sandhurst and his staff; and to the Library of the Royal United Services Institute for Defence and Security Studies, London. Material from *Arms and the Man* by George Bernard Shaw is reproduced by permission of the Society of Authors on behalf of the Bernard Shaw Estate; material from *Charge To Glory!* by James Lunt by permission of the author and publisher, Heinneman Ltd; material from *The Fire of Life* by George Barrow by permission of The Random House Group Ltd for Hutchinson; and material from *My Political Life Volume One: England Before the Storm 1896–1914* by L.S. Amery by permission of David Higham Associates. Material from the published writings of Winston Churchill is reproduced by permission of Curtis Brown Ltd on behalf of the estate of Winston S. Churchill. Every reasonable effort has been made to trace the owners of copyright materials quoted in this book. The author and publisher would be glad to receive information leading to more complete acknowledgements in any subsequent printings, and in the meantime I extend my apologies for any omissions that may exist.

My next thanks go to almost two generations of gifted and hard-working military historians whose publications have done so much to transform our broader understanding of the British Army before and during the First World War, and of how that war was fought. In this book I have on occasions perched quite readily on the shoulders of these giants, my contemporaries, confident in the strength of their knowledge. For many years I enjoyed a professional correspondence with the Marquis of Anglesey, and my debt to his eight volume work *A History of the British Cavalry 1816–1919* is evident, although this present book is in no sense an attempt to tell the same story. Similarly, this book deals with wars and battles which have been the subject of much scholarly controversy and re-interpretation in recent years; in each case I have followed the thread of cavalry doctrine, while acknowledging that this is only one part of a more complex tapestry.

I am grateful to colleagues who have read all or part of this book in draft form and saved me from several errors: these include Dr John Bourne, Professor Ian F.W. Beckett, Dr Elizabeth Greenhalgh, Dr Matthew Hughes, and especially Professor Gary Sheffield. It would be bad mannered of me not to thank Professor Richard Holmes, for a third time, for his insights and help over several years. Others that I wish to thank for advice, assistance, inspiration and support that led (sometimes by indirect paths) to the publication of this book include my wife Dr Phylomena Badsey, Professor Christopher Bellamy, Professor Brian Bond, the late Rose E.B. Coombs, Professor David French, Ken Gillings, Dr Paddy Griffith, Dr J.P. Harris, Vivian John, Professor Greg Kennedy, Professor John Laband, John Lee, Chris McCarthy, Dr Stephen Miller, Dr Gervase Phillips, the late Dr John Pimlott, Professor Fransjohan Pretorius, Dr Christopher Pugsley, Professor Peter Simkins, Roger B.N. Smither, Professor Edward Spiers, Dr Simon Trew, Dr Bruce Vandervort, Professor Andrew Wiest; and Professor Brian Holden Reid for a few quiet words of sound advice.

The writing style of a book is a matter of personal choice and publishing conventions, but its only purpose should be to help the reader understand the author's meaning. Although it deals with history, this book is written in the English of my own time, using words from other languages or other periods as little as possible. The arcane British military terminology of this period, including both military and social rank and titles, was intended as a trap to expose and humiliate the outsider, and I have done my best to mitigate the effects of this form of snobbery. When I have quoted from a foreign language I have translated the quotation, placing the original in a footnote; and I have glossed any expressions that I believe might be misunderstood. Personal names, proper names, names of wars and battles, names of military units and names of places have been given in the version most common at the time. If another version has come to dominate modern usage, my choice has been explained by a gloss. I am aware that in describing peoples, races, and classes, exactly what names and descriptions others might find offensive can change quickly and without warning. I have used the expressions of my own time and culture, although in quotations I have kept the expressions used as they stand. If any future reader of this book finds any of its language or indeed its views offensive, then this was not my intention. Anyone who feels that they are offended by war, or the thought of war, has missed one of the points of this book.

To avoid anachronisms and maintain consistency, most measurements, including distances, weapons calibres, and prices, have been given as they appeared in the original documents or publications, mostly those in use by the British Empire in 1880–1918. For those unfamiliar with these measurements, there are three feet to a yard, a yard is just a little shorter than a metre, and a mile (1,760 yards) is just over 1600 metres; in measuring weights, a pound (lb) is just less than half a kilogram and a stone (st) is 14 pounds. Given the problems involved in making any modern comparisons it is best to regard a pound Sterling (£) and its subdivisions into shillings and pence as just units of money.

Otherwise, any errors of fact in this book, and any historical ideas, opinions and judgements that it contains, are mine. In accordance with both politeness and convention I take full responsibility for both this book and its contents.

Stephen Badsey
University of Wolverhampton
September 2007

Chapter 1

Doctrine and the Cavalry 1880–1918

'In what manner the cavalry of the twentieth century will differ from the hussars and cuirassiers of the nineteenth century is undoubtedly, from a military point of view, one of the most interesting and momentous questions of the day', so wrote Lieutenant Colonel G.F.R. Henderson in 1902, in one of his last published pieces before his premature death in the following March.[1] As Professor of Military History at the Army Staff College Camberley 1891–1899, and head of the Intelligence branch of the staff under Field Marshal Lord Roberts VC during the Boer War of 1899–1902, Henderson was widely regarded as the British Army's principal military theorist of his time, and his concerns over the future of cavalry reflected a profound debate within the Army that was to continue up to the First World War and beyond.[2]

The origins of this debate may be traced back to before the middle of the nineteenth century, driven by the impact of the industrial revolution on land warfare, including increases in the effectiveness of firearms and artillery, and in Europe and North America at least by the potential for considerable increases in the size of armies provided by the rapid growth of urban populations.[3] The extent to which European land warfare was transformed between the early nineteenth century and early twentieth century almost cannot be overstated. The Battle of Waterloo in 1815 was fought in a single day, with fewer than 200,000 soldiers actively engaged, using linear tactics on a battlefield of a few square miles, mostly obscured in clouds of smoke produced by smoothbore muskets with effective ranges of barely 100 yards and smoothbore cannon with ranges of 1,000 yards, both with rates of fire rarely greater than two or three rounds a minute. There could hardly be a more complete contrast between this and the Battle of the Somme in 1916, fought over five months on a frontage of more than twenty miles by several hundred thousand soldiers in rotation, armed with magazine rifles and machine-guns whose maximum ranges and rates of fire exceeded practical ammunition resupply capabilities; protected by barbed wire, earth and concrete; and supported both by artillery using indirect fire at ranges

---

1   Henderson, *The Science of War*, p. 51.
2   The Boer War has also been known as the South African War, the Anglo-Boer War, the Second Boer War, the English War, and the Second War of Independence (or Liberation); its present official title, as stipulated by the government of South Africa, is the 'South African Anglo-Boer War'.
3   See Strachan, *European Armies and the Conduct of War*, pp. 60–149; Addington, *The Patterns of War Since the Eighteenth Century*, pp. 43–171; Jones, *The Art of War in the Western World*, pp. 387–488; Bond, *War and Society in Europe 1870–1970*, pp. 13–134; van Creveld, *Supplying War*, pp. 75–108; and, still valuable for some facts and insights, Fuller, *The Conduct of War 1789–1961*, pp. 77–182 and Falls, *The Art of War*, pp. 60–112.

of several miles and by primitive aircraft and tanks.[4] As early as the 1850s, it seemed scarcely credible that a target as large and vulnerable as a horseman could survive on a battlefield when faced by the new firepower, and well before the century's end it was a commonplace assumption that any cavalry charge was doomed. In George Bernard Shaw's play *Arms and the Man* of 1894 (set during a war in Bulgaria in 1885), the leading character proclaimed, 'Well come! Is it professional to throw a regiment of cavalry on a battery of machine guns, with the dead certainty that if the guns go off not a man or horse will get to within fifty yards of the fire?'[5]

One option open to cavalry in the face of increased firepower was to find some way of improving the effectiveness of their mounted charge. A suggestion examined in the 1860s and 1870s was to maintain a flat-out gallop for a mile or more to reduce the time spent under fire; but although adopted in German cavalry regulations in 1875, this was largely rejected by the British as impractical.[6] Another option was to remain mounted, but to fire back in some way (known as 'saddle fire') either as part of a charge or some other mounted manoeuvre such as a retreat. Another option was for the cavalry to dismount with a firearm and turn themselves temporarily into infantry. It seemed likely, and turned out to be the case, that any practical solution would require some or all these options in combination. Accompanying this was the issue of whether a single type of cavalry could be trained both to charge and to fight dismounted, or whether two different types of horse soldier were possible or necessary. If there was to be only one type of cavalry, then they would need to be good enough to charge successfully against enemy firepower, and yet also good enough shoot down an enemy mounted charge, and to know which, or which combination, of these options to chose in any given tactical situation.

The British cavalry's doctrinal response to these issues was one of qualified success, as the cavalry adjusted its composition, its weapons and its tactics to provide a viable and sometimes valuable role in warfare up to the end of the First World War, including the use of mounted charges.[7] While there was much continuity in the composition of British cavalry regiments and the military functions that they performed, both the cavalry trooper and the cavalry regiment of 1918 looked very different from their predecessors of 1880, as well as being markedly superior in weaponry, tactics and fighting abilities.[8] But the story of the debate over British cavalry doctrine is also linked with the much wider story of the reform and restructuring of the British Army, and the way that it fought the First World War, over which the cavalry debate exercised a significant and not always benign influence.

---

4   Waterloo is compared with the first day of the Somme in Keegan, *The Face of Battle*, pp. 117–284.

5   The character Bluntschli in Shaw, *Plays Pleasant*, p. 30.

6   See 'Military Studies, Number 3, Cavalry', *Colburn's United Service Magazine*, 1863 Part III, p. 17; 'Tactics on the Battle-Field', *Colburn's United Service Magazine*, 1875 Part II, pp. 371–5; von Schmidt, *Instructions for the Training, Employment and Leading of Cavalry*.

7   For a summary of current views see Phillips, 'Scapegoat Arm', pp. 37–74.

8   For a good summary of the cavalry in 1914 see Holmes, *Riding the Retreat*, pp. 26–42 and pp. 58–66. The title 'trooper' was commonly used to describe a cavalry soldier of this period, but strictly the official title of the rank was 'private' until 1902 in the Household and 1922 in the line cavalry.

Not all those who believed that cavalry had a future were cavalrymen: Colonel F.N. Maude, who played an important role in encouraging cavalry reform, was an engineer and Henderson an infantryman.[9] Nor was the debate restricted to soldiers: from time to time it involved some of the most senior figures in the British government, and provoked interest and sometimes major rows in public and in the press. The debate also considerably affected the careers of several British officers who held high rank in the First World War, colouring their attitudes to each other and to the way that they thought about their profession. As might be expected, these included officers who began their military service in cavalry regiments and are often regarded as 'cavalry generals', such as Sir John French and Sir Douglas Haig, both of whom either witnessed or participated in successful cavalry charges early in their careers. But the debate also affected other officers whose careers are not normally associated with the cavalry, including Sir Horace Smith-Dorrien, Sir Henry Wilson, Sir Henry Rawlinson, and Sir Ian Hamilton. This was a doctrinal issue on which every senior British Army officer of 1914 had, and was expected to have, an opinion.

The idea of what is meant by a military doctrine was well understood in the British Army of the period, although the term 'doctrine' was itself only rarely used. Deriving appropriately from the language of religious belief, military doctrine means the prescriptive setting out of the courses of action that armed forces should follow, and in its widest sense it is an all-embracing concept, covering all aspects of their existence and function. One recent definition by the British Army is that 'Military doctrine is a formal expression of military knowledge and thought, that the Army accepts as being relevant at a given time, which covers the nature of current and future conflicts, the preparation of the Army for such conflicts and the methods of engaging in them to achieve success.'[10] Some definitions of military doctrine stress its formal and written nature, and it has been argued that since the Army of 1880–1918 had no central written text it did not have 'doctrine' as such but only 'ethos'.[11] But while the Army rejected some forms of written doctrine as over-prescriptive, this is not a distinction that it would have understood or accepted. Written doctrine, in the form of drill books, training manuals, and books set for officers to study, certainly increased both in number and in importance for the British Army before the First World War. But mostly these doctrinal writings followed the terminology established early in the nineteenth century by the Swiss-French theorist Henri Jomini, by avoiding the term 'doctrine' and elaborating instead on 'principles' or 'fundamentals' of war in discursive paragraphs. It was only during and after

---

9   From his first anonymous publication as a captain in 1888, Maude contributed frequently to the debate about cavalry as well as other issues as a newspaper critic well into the First World War, by which time he was satirised as the opinionated 'Major Taude BC'; see *The Wipers Times*, p. 142; Luvaas, *The Military Legacy of the Civil War*, p. 118.

10 *Design for Military Operations: The British Military Doctrine*, p. 1–1; the original phrasing and punctuation have been retained.

11 The first work to point out that the Army of this period had no doctrine in the narrow prescriptive sense was Bidwell and Graham, *Fire-Power*, p. 295. Recently Palazzo, *Seeking Victory on the Western Front*, pp. 8–17 has argued that the British Army of the First World War substituted 'ethos' for 'doctrine', seeing them as opposites rather than one as an aspect of the other.

the First World War that a new fashion emerged, established chiefly by Lieutenant Colonel J.F.C. Fuller, for reducing principles of war to checklists of single words and doctrinal statements to short sentences; and it was not until the end of the twentieth century that the belief that doctrine should be largely centralised and written down came to dominate British military thinking.[12]

Rather than being expressed in any formal manner, much military doctrine throughout the centuries has fallen within the wider concept of military ethos or culture, and has been inherent in the conscious and unconscious behaviour of armed forces as institutions. The control and definition of doctrine has also been a fundamental part of institutional military power, so that while there were many *theories* in this era on what the future of cavalry should be, the doctrines actually adopted by the British Army were determined chiefly by where power and authority within the Army lay at the time. Any lack of a centralised and authoritative written British military doctrine before the First World War was the product of the social and organisational structure of the Army and of its officer corps, including the formal and informal power of the regiments, and of prominent generals.

Part of the military thought of the age was that a study of military history was believed to yield 'lessons' directly relevant to serving officers. Major General Michael W. Smith (late of the 3rd Dragoon Guards), saw nothing odd in opening his book on 'modern tactics' for the cavalry, published in 1869, with a discourse on Xenophon and Alexander the Great, and he was far from being an isolated case.[13] Henderson, writing at the end of the nineteenth century, summarised the value of this use of military history for doctrinal purposes:

> Theory is of two kinds. First there is speculative theory, which in default of great campaigns fought with modern materiel endeavours, from a study of ballistics, of new inventions, of results on the ranges, of the incidents of manoeuvres and field days, to forecast the fighting of the future. Second, there is theory based on the actual experiences of war; theory which does not neglect to consider the modifications which new arms and appliances may produce, but puts in the fore-ground the conditions which ruled the last great battles between civilised armies... If we would learn what men can do, and what they cannot do, under the stress of fire, then we must turn to history.[14]

Part of the reasoning behind this belief was that the horse, sword and lance had not changed in any fundamental way for millennia, and neither had many of the basic duties of cavalry. Historically, the role of light cavalry was to carry out scouting duties away from the battlefield, to bring back information on the enemy's location and movements, and to deny the enemy the same information; although by the nineteenth century this role had been divided by military terminology into a number of largely self-explanatory functions, such as patrol work, outpost work, protection,

---

12 For Fuller's criticisms see Holden Reid, *J.F.C. Fuller: Military Thinker*, pp. 27–9, and Trythall, *'Bony' Fuller*. For a discussion and some definitions of military doctrine as understood in the later twentieth century see Badsey, 'The Doctrines of the Coalition Forces', pp. 57–80.

13 Smith, *Modern Tactics of the Three Arms*, p. 1.

14 Henderson, Introduction to *The Battle of Woerth* (no pagination).

and pursuit. These were themselves dangerous and demanding roles for mounted troops. Lord Roberts, writing in 1910 of his own experiences in India and Afghanistan many years earlier, claimed that 'I have taken part in Cavalry combats, and have frequently had occasion to scout and reconnoitre with two, three or perhaps half a dozen Cavalry soldiers, at a time when capture by the enemy meant certain death. And I have no hesitation in saying that scouting and reconnoitring try the nerves far more seriously than charging the enemy.'[15] A further widely-discussed form of independent cavalry action was the 'cavalry raid', with antecedents stretching back at least to the mediaeval *chevauchée*, in which a large body of mounted troops rode through enemy territory aiming to inflict economic and structural damage, while avoiding major battles.[16] In these cases, cavalry were expected to fight without the support of infantry and artillery (although they might be accompanied by their own 'horse artillery'), usually skirmishing against the enemy's cavalry in an effort to obtain superiority and to reach important objectives. Light cavalry's main strength was in their speed of movement over long distances, requiring smaller men and horses that were lightly equipped, although they might still be expected to charge when needed. On the battlefield, the charge required a different kind of heavy cavalry, bigger men (perhaps wearing partial armour) on bigger horses, used in co-ordination with infantry and artillery to break through enemy cavalry and infantry formations. Cavalry charges against artillery had always been seen as highly dangerous, with a low chance of success unless delivered under unusual circumstances.

In practice, by the later nineteenth century the British Army had ceased to distinguish separate roles for its light and heavy cavalry. There were so few British regular cavalry regiments of the line, divided between so many tasks and locations around the Empire, that as early as 1844 a War Office regulation stipulated that all regiments should be capable of carrying out any functions, including both scouting and charging.[17] Although minor differences in the size of both men and horses were maintained between heavy, medium and light British cavalry regiments, until the 1880s the weight of the rider and equipment carried by all British cavalry horses was about 22 stones, proverbially more than the weight of a mediaeval knight in plate armour; a load that strenuous efforts at reform reduced only to 20 stones by 1899.[18]

There were 31 regular British cavalry regiments in 1880, a number that did not alter until after the First World War. The structure and organisation of these regiments were both different from those of the infantry, and they were largely unaffected by the two periods of Army reorganisation under the Liberal Secretaries of State for War Edward Cardwell 1868–1874, and Hugh Childers 1880–1882. Cardwell and Childers each made some attempt to reform the cavalry, but in both cases the first tentative change met with so much opposition that no further effort was made. Unlike the infantry regiments, the cavalry retained their regimental numbers throughout the Cardwell–Childers reforms, although some accompanying titles changed before the First World War, often to reflect royal patronage such as the 17th Lancers (Duke

---

15 Roberts, preface to Childers, *War and the Arme Blanche*, p. xv.
16 Lynn, *Battle*, pp. 73–110.
17 Tylden, *Horses and Saddlery*, p. 20.
18 Ibid., p. 20 and p. 46.

of Cambridge's Own).[19] Cavalry regiments were single battalions with a strength varying between 400 and 600 officers and men in peacetime, divided into eight troops and later in the period into three or four squadrons, with no part-time or volunteer affiliates equivalent to the militia battalions of the infantry. Regiments were recruited nationally rather than regionally, except in practice for regiments with strong regional affiliations such as the 5th (Royal Irish) Lancers. Unofficial affiliations could also develop between some regiments, such as between the 2nd Dragoons (Royal Scots Greys) and the 6th Inniskilling Dragoons, or between the 2nd Life Guards and the 10th Hussars, regiments that jokingly called each other their '2nd Battalion'.[20]

The Household Cavalry, the mounted equivalent of the Foot Guards and considered the pinnacle of social exclusivity in the Army, consisted of three regiments of cuirassiers (with steel breast-and-backplates and helmets, not worn when campaigning overseas), designated as the 1st and 2nd Life Guards and the Royal Horse Guards.[21] These regiments did not normally serve overseas before the First World War, but instead contributed troops to form a temporary composite 'Household Cavalry Regiment'. Of the 28 cavalry regiments of the line, in 1880 ten were heavy cavalry (without cuirasses), seven of which were Dragoon Guards and three of which were Dragoons, although by 1888 only the 1st (Royal) Dragoons and the 2nd Dragoons (Royal Scots Greys) remained heavy cavalry, the rest having been converted to medium cavalry.[22] The 'dragoon' titles of these regiments came from their origins, which (very confusingly) had been chiefly as light infantry mounted on horses for reasons of mobility and equipped with a short firearm known as a 'dragon', or in the case of the 6th Dragoon Guards (Carabiniers) as a 'carabine'. The five regiments of Lancers were classed as medium cavalry, increased to six regiments in 1897 when the 21st Hussars were converted to become the 21st Lancers. The 12 regiments of light cavalry were all Hussars, a title of Hungarian origin reflected in their distinctive parade dress. Line cavalry served by rotation either overseas or at home in the United Kingdom including Ireland, with typically between six and nine regiments serving in India, and after the middle 1880s up to four in either South Africa or Egypt.

For weapons, all cavalry troopers carried swords, lancers also carried a light ash or bamboo lance, and all troopers by the 1880s used a type of short-barrelled rifle

---

19 For the regiments and their title changes see Ascoli, *A Companion to the British Army 1660–1983*; for their structure and organisation see Goodenough and Dalton, *The Army Book for the British Empire*, pp. 190–213; Grierson, *Scarlet into Khaki*, pp. 43–50. Grierson's book was originally written and published in German in 1897 when he was British military attaché in Berlin, and in English in 1899 under the title *The British Army – by a Lieutenant Colonel in the British Army*.

20 Woodham Smith, *The Reason Why*, pp. 227–8, Brander, *The 10th Royal Hussars*, p. 73.

21 See Dundonald, *My Army Life*, pp. 5–14 for the social experience and expenses of a junior officer in the Life Guards on the cusp of the abolition of purchase in 1871.

22 The 4th and 5th Dragoon Guards were re-designated as medium cavalry in 1888; see Goodenough and Dalton, *The Army Book for the British Empire*, p. 192.

known as a carbine.[23] The largest cavalry formations with a permanent existence were brigades, usually consisting of two regiments before 1899 and three regiments after that. A cavalry division was not normally a peacetime formation, but was formed for war on three occasions: for the Egyptian expedition in 1882, the Boer War in 1899, and the British Expeditionary Force (BEF) in 1914. The main firepower support for the cavalry was provided by the Royal Horse Artillery or RHA, regarded as the social and technological elite of the Royal Artillery, with gun calibres that increased from 9-pounders in 1880 to 13-pounders in 1914.[24] The major change in the cavalry's armament came on either side of the Boer War, with the issue to cavalrymen first of magazine carbines and then magazine rifles identical to those of the infantry, together with machine-guns, and improved 13-pounder quick-firing (QF) guns for their horse artillery. A cavalry or mounted brigade included artillerymen and members of other branches of the Army, and had its own considerable intrinsic firepower.

Most, but not all, cavalry regiments were regarded as socially 'smart' or 'fashionable', terms that are largely self-explanatory. The Army's unofficial hierarchy of smartness was headed by the Household Cavalry and the Foot Guards, after which the order of smartness between regiments was largely a matter of peer-group recognition, and not necessarily related to their position in the 'Order of Precedence', an official list based largely on the date of foundation of the regiments. Just as officers (except those commissioned from the ranks) were expected to be gentlemen by birth, status and lifestyle, so smartness involved the level of conspicuous display by a regiment's officers, and its ability to attract high-status officers and patrons.[25] Allowing for an inevitable degree of subjectivity, at the end of the nineteenth century the 10th Hussars headed the list of smart line cavalry regiments, closely followed by the 1st (Royal) Dragoons, the 9th Lancers and the 13th Hussars. Although most cavalry regiments ranked above most infantry regiments in smartness, the 21st Lancers was distinctly lacking in status, while smart infantry regiments included the two 'Rifle' regiments, confusingly named the Rifle Brigade and the Kings Royal Rifle Corps, and also some of the Highland and Lowland Scots regiments. As noted, the Royal Horse Artillery was regarded as smart, but not the rest of the Royal Artillery.[26]

---

23 Rogers, *The Mounted Troops of the British Army 1066–1945*, pp. 211–44; Goodenough and Dalton, *The Army Book for the British Empire*, pp. 190–213; Grierson, *Scarlet into Khaki*, pp. 43–50 and pp. 124–5; Barnes, *The British Army of 1914*, pp. 17–41 and pp. 109–12.

24 It is a source of confusion that the Royal Regiment of Artillery contained fighting formations also called 'regiments'; these were larger than 'batteries' which were the basic tactical units of four to eight guns, and which in turn might be larger than or identical to 'troops' of artillery depending on the context. In 1914 the Royal Regiment of Artillery had two branches: the Royal Garrison Artillery and the Royal Field Artillery, of which the Royal Horse Artillery was a sub-branch.

25 French, *Military Identities*, pp. 164–7; Mason, *The English Gentleman*, pp. 181–206.

26 Cairnes, *Social Life in the British Army*, pp. 35–6; Cairnes's book was published anonymously as 'by a British officer'. French, *Military Identities*, pp. 166–7 offers a quantitative model of smartness over an extended period 1910–1950; the results broadly match subjective assessments, but place the Royal Scots, one of the smartest regiments in the Army, in the 'unsmart' category.

Particularly important for patronage was the system of regimental colonels, a title deriving from a previous age when a lieutenant colonel was the deputy for the colonel who raised and effectively owned the regiment. A regimental colonelcy was an appointment offered as an honour to a senior officer, sometimes of royal or noble birth, in return for which he acted as the unpaid titular head of the regiment, representing its interests in politics, in society, and at the War Office. An even greater honour was the appointment of a 'colonel-in-chief', a practice which became more common after the First World War, but in this period was limited to a few royal appointments. The Duke of Cambridge was made colonel-in-chief of the 60th Rifles (later the King's Royal Rifle Corps) in 1869, and the Prince of Wales (the future Edward VII) was colonel-in-chief of the Rifle Brigade 1868–1880 before becoming colonel in-chief of all three Household Cavalry regiments; he was also made colonel of the 10th Hussars in 1868. Apparently the only case of a line cavalry regiment with a royal colonel-in-chief in this period was the appointment of the Duke of Connaught to the 6th (Inniskilling) Dragoons in 1897.[27]

Commissioned officers of the cavalry were volunteers drawn chiefly from privileged social classes. Before the abolition of the purchase of officers' commissions in 1871, about two-thirds of all cavalry officers purchased their commissions, compared to about half of all infantry officers (purchase was almost universal in the Foot Guards and Household Cavalry, and did not exist in the Royal Artillery or the Royal Engineers).[28] In 1899 about two-thirds of senior officers in all British Army regiments came from the aristocracy, the gentry, and from military families, and the proportion was much higher in cavalry regiments, whose officers were mostly regarded as being socially superior to those of other arms, with some exceptions on both sides.[29] Despite the high status of most cavalry regiments, both promotion from the ranks and the existence of gentleman rankers appear to have been more common in the cavalry than in other arms.[30] A sample of the years 1871–1893 shows that of 2,625 officers commissioned into infantry regiments, only 70 or 2.66 per cent came from the ranks, while in cavalry regiments the figure was 31 out of 424 or 7.3 per cent (excluding riding masters and quartermasters, normally also commissioned from the ranks).[31] Horses, uniforms and equipment for troopers, non-commissioned officers and warrant officers (collectively the 'other ranks') were provided by the Army, but officers were expected to pay for their own uniforms and kit, and for civilian clothes made by a suitably expensive tailor, and to provide at least two riding horses, (sometimes doubling as suitable mounts for hunting), one of which had to be a cavalry charger of an appropriate breed. Almost all British Army cavalry horses

---

27 French, *Military Identities*, pp. 79–80; Heathcote, *The British Field Marshals 1736–1997*, pp. 27, 106, 143 and 327–9; Bidwell and Graham, *Fire-Power*, pp. 190–91.

28 Glover, 'The Purchase of Commissions', p. 235; Woodhall, 'The Abolition of Purchase in the British Army', pp. 676–84.

29 Spiers, *The Late Victorian Army 1868–1902*, pp. 93–4.

30 Anglesey, *A History of the British Cavalry 1816–1919, Volume 3: 1872–1898*, pp. 85–7. This is the first reference in this book to Anglesey's multi-volume history. Hereafter, the following convention will be observed: Anglesey, *A History of the British Cavalry Volume 3*, pp. 85–7.

31 Skelley, *The Victorian Army at Home*, p. 200.

of this period were bred in Ireland, and in 1887 an Army Remount Department was created, accompanied by a register of civilian owners of horses suitable for military use and an annual purchase of some 2,500 horses, which established a degree of uniformity in the types used by each branch of the Army. Most cavalry officers bought their horses from the Remount Department, at a regulation cost of £52 per horse for the cavalry of the line and £63 per horse for the Household Cavalry.[32]

Contrary to the views of many critics of the cavalry, being a wealthy and privileged officer in a cavalry regiment was not in itself proof of military incompetence, any more than of military ability. Wealth and gentlemanliness in officers, and smartness and patronage in regiments, were in this period fully compatible with military professionalism and competence as well as with bravery, although a regiment that was fashionable or of high status but not militarily efficient would be more likely to earn the description 'traditional'.[33] Indeed, reforming lieutenant colonels in smart regiments often had considerable advantages over their less smart equivalents in implementing changes, because of the institutional freedom their money and status provided. For example, in 1874 the 10th Hussars introduced their own system of regimental dismounted work whereby one man in four acted as a horseholder; this worked in the Second Afghan War of 1878–1880, and was copied by the rest of the cavalry.[34]

Cavalry troopers were also volunteers, like all soldiers in the regular British Army, serving by 1914 for seven years with the colours, followed by five years in the reserve.[35] While the Army continued to draw its recruits from the lower classes of society, the cavalry with its rather higher social cachet had less difficulty in attracting and retaining good recruits. A survey in 1851 showed that two-thirds of cavalry troopers came from cities rather than smaller towns or the countryside, and they were considered more alert and intelligent than their counterparts in other arms.[36] 'Many men are attracted by the uniform and the swagger', explained the colonel in charge

---

32 HPL Wolseley Papers W/Mem/1: Memorandum by Wolseley, 20 April 1885 and W/Mem/2: Memorandum by Wolseley, 19 October 1886; Tylden, *Horses and Saddlery*, pp. 25–8; Goodenough and Dalton, *The Army Book for the British Empire*, pp. 182–4. The definitive study of the horse supply is Winton, 'Horsing the British Army 1878–1923'. For lieutenants a third horse was required in war, captains and majors had to provide three horses in peace or war, and lieutenant colonels to provide four horses in peace and three in war; see Grierson, *Scarlet into Khaki*, pp. 247–8.

33 Strachan, *The Politics of the British Army*, p. 14; Cannadine, *The Decline and Fall of the British Aristocracy*, pp. 264–79; Bourne, *Patronage and Society in Nineteenth Century England*, pp. 176–8; Lee, *A Soldier's Life*, p. 9. A similar system of appointing eighteenth-century Royal Navy officers based on patronage and competence is described by Rodger, *The Wooden World*, pp. 273–302.

34 Brander, *The 10th Royal Hussars*, p. 57; Heathcote, *The Afghan Wars 1839–1919*, pp. 103–12.

35 The total length of service for the cavalry, including time spent in the reserve, remained constant at 12 years from 1870 onwards, but the proportion of this time spent with the colours varied from six years to eight.

36 Skelley, *The Victorian Army at Home*, pp. 290–94; Strachan, *Wellington's Legacy*, p. 89.

of the Canterbury cavalry depot in 1891, 'and this accounts in a great measure for the better class of recruits who join the cavalry.'[37] Until 1897 regiments were completely autonomous in their recruiting, and other ranks could not be transferred out of their regiment except voluntarily; thereafter limited transfers were permitted.

The ethos of uniqueness and closeness in a regiment was meant to be an important factor in its fighting abilities as well as its institutional existence, idealised as a paternalistic relationship between officers and men. But the social gulf that existed in the peacetime Army makes generalisations about the men's attitudes towards the officers difficult. 'How can any ill come to our beloved country as long as the Shires produce such men?' enthused gentleman ranker Private Frances Maitland of the 19th Hussars just before the First World War, 'Has any writer, philosopher, psychologist ever properly placed these young men who officer the proud British Army?'[38] Private P.Y. Grainger of the 9th Lancers, in his diary in 1904, preferred to describe his officers as 'our Blue Blooded bacon driers, cheese mongers and pork butchers that are in command and have money'.[39]

In addition to learning the basics of soldiering, cavalry troopers also had to learn to ride and to care for their horses, the horses had to be trained, and together they had to master the various skills and tactical evolutions required for mounted combat, a process which took on average at least a year, considerably longer than training an infantryman.[40] The predominantly urban recruits to the cavalry had to be taught not just horsemanship but 'horsemastership' (or sometimes 'horse management'), a mixture of basic veterinary science and country wisdom aimed at keeping horses in good condition. An important part of horsemastership was the care that came from an emotional bond that was encouraged between mounted soldiers and their horses, particularly on active service. It is not unusual to find the memoirs of cavalrymen of the First World War referring to their horses with considerable affection.[41]

Other than the regular cavalry regiments, the British Empire's chief source of cavalry was the Indian Army, which took over the light and irregular native cavalry regiments of the East India Company after 1857. Indian cavalry brigades usually consisted of one British regiment and two Indian regiments, serving in India or more rarely overseas. There were 40 Indian cavalry regiments in 1893, reduced to 39 by 1914 after a major re-organisation in 1901–1903 including changes in regimental titles.[42] Some of these titles remained quite simple, such as the 16th Cavalry or the 28th Light Cavalry, but others were a combination of the regiment's original name (used for everyday purposes) with a more elaborate official name, such as the 10th Duke of Cambridge's Own Lancers (Hodson's Horse). The most elaborate title belonged to Queen Victoria's Own Corps of Guides (Frontier Force) (Lumsden's)

---

37 Quoted in Spiers, *The Late Victorian Army 1868–1902*, p. 124.

38 Maitland, *Hussar of the Line*, p. 37.

39 NAM Grainger Papers: Diary entry, 9 April 1903. See also Baynes, *Morale*, and Sheffield, *Leadership in the Trenches*.

40 Wood, 'Mounted Riflemen', Royal United Service Institution Pamphlet, p. 5.

41 Hatton, *The Yarn of a Yeoman*, p. 82; Maitland, *Hussar of the Line*, p. 26.

42 See Bowling, *Indian Cavalry Regiments 1880–1914*, for a full list of the regiments and their titles; Heathcote, *The Indian Army*, pp. 38–40; Goodenough and Dalton, *The Army Book for the British Empire*, pp. 453–4.

Cavalry, in practice only ever known as 'the Guides', which was unique in having no regimental number.[43] Indian cavalry regiments were organised, equipped and trained in much the same way as the regular British cavalry, but with some important differences. In the time of the East India Company the practice had been for British cavalry regiments to be reserved for the battlefield charge, while Indian cavalry were employed for scouting, and this distinction continued to form part of their respective ethos. Indian cavalry troopers were drawn from a much higher class or caste within their own society than their British equivalents, and by 1914 all but three of the Indian cavalry regiments used the *silladar* or *silladari* ('contractor', probably from the old Persian) system of recruitment and discipline, inherited from the East India Company's irregular cavalry. Under this system, on recruitment the trooper handed over to his regiment a sum of money for his horse and equipment, for which he then took responsibility, and he was entitled to the money back on his retirement. This made the relationship between troopers and their regiments different from the obligations demanded of British soldiers, and produced a very relaxed and independently minded regimental system.[44] At least one attempt was made before the First World War to introduce the officer–man ethos of the *silladar* system into a British cavalry regiment, in the 4th Hussars in 1913 by a commanding officer and second-in-command with Indian experience.[45]

By the later nineteenth century, earlier prejudices among British Army officers against 'Indian' officers as being of lower social status had largely disappeared, but service in the Indian cavalry remained less socially prestigious than in the British cavalry, and also significantly less expensive. Even so, King Edward VII was colonel-in-chief of the Guides, which could be considered socially smart even by British regimental standards, and of four other Indian cavalry regiments.[46] Indian cavalry regiments had some officers of Indian nationality, broadly equivalent in rank and function to British warrant officers, and by 1918 they could hold commissions. Otherwise, commissioned officers were all British, broadly from the same social classes as their British cavalry equivalents, and officers could be loaned or transfer between British and Indian regiments, such as Lieutenant William Birdwood of the 12th Lancers, who transferred to the 11th Bengal Lancers (later 11th Prince of Wales's Own Lancers) while stationed in India in 1886; or Lieutenant John Shea, who transferred from the Royal Irish Regiment to the 15th Bengal Lancers (later 15th Lancers) in 1891.[47]

A smaller but important source of cavalry was the Egyptian Army, constitutionally belonging to an independent Egypt but trained by British officers on loan using

---

43 Goodenough and Dalton, *The Army Book for the British Empire*, pp. 455–6; Tylden, *Horses and Saddlery*, pp. 166–7; the Corps of Guides also included an infantry component.

44 Birdwood, *Khaki and Gown*, pp. 43–5; Barrow, *The Fire Of Life*, pp. 12–15; Heathcote, *The Indian Army*, pp. 38–40; Holmes, *Sahib*, pp. 359–73.

45 Sheffield, *Leadership in the Trenches*, pp. 26–7.

46 Heathcote, *The British Field Marshals 1736–1997*, p. 107.

47 Birdwood, *Khaki and Gown*, pp. 36–9; Heathcote, *The Indian Army*, pp. 135–46. Strictly, British officers were transferred to the Indian Army Staff Corps, and were then assigned to Indian regiments. The first places for native Indian officer cadets at the Royal Military College Sandhurst were created in 1917.

Egyptian ranks, and often employed together with British troops in combat. Anglo-Egyptian armies under *Sirdar* (Commander-in-Chief) Sir Evelyn Wood VC in 1882–1885, and later under *Sirdar* Sir Herbert Kitchener in the reconquest of the Sudan in 1896–1898, included several officers who would later hold high rank in the First World War, among them Captain Douglas Haig, who gained his first combat experience in 1898 with the Egyptian cavalry that he had helped train.[48] Particularly from 1899 onwards, the mounted troops of Canada, Australia, and New Zealand also played an important part in the story, partly through interaction with the British Army as part of the wider issue of Imperial defence. The Union of South Africa, which was established in 1910, included several mounted units in its armed forces before the First World War, but unlike their predecessors these had little influence on British mounted doctrine.

The cavalry equivalent of the militia in Great Britain was the 'Yeomanry' (a title of some antiquity suggesting the better-off rural peasantry), volunteers who were paid only for the 20 to 30 days a year that they met to train, including an annual regimental camp of 8 to 14 days, and who could be called out for home service in case of civil disorder or foreign invasion. The yeomanry were regionally recruited, mostly on a county basis with titles to match, including regiments of 'dragoons' or 'hussars', so called for historical reasons, and other more exotic titles such as the Royal 1st Devon Yeomanry, or the City of London Yeomanry (Rough Riders), formed for the Boer War. Yeomanry regiments varied in size, the smallest regiments in 1880 having fewer than 100 troopers, increasing to a standard size of 450–500 troopers by 1914.

Armed for most of this period with swords and carbines, the yeomanry resembled the regular cavalry in general appearance, but by the 1880s their ceremonial and social functions were seen as more significant than their military value. Military standards improved by 1899, when newly commissioned yeomanry officers were required to serve for a month with a regular cavalry regiment and receive a certificate of competence. Commissions in yeomanry regiments granted considerable social status, and a few regiments aspired to smartness, including the Oxfordshire Yeomanry (Queen's Own Oxfordshire Hussars), of which Edward VII was colonel-in-chief. Although yeomanry officers received some remuneration, in practice they paid for the privileges of their rank, an estimated average of £100 a year in costs and expenses.[49] About half the yeomanry's officers, according to an assessment in 1899, were 'retired cavalry officers, landed proprietors, and enthusiastic fox-hunters'.[50] Some yeomanry regiments also enjoyed strong political connections, such as the West Kent Yeomanry, which in the 1880s included among its number six members of parliament and two peers.[51]

---

48 Charteris, *Field Marshal Earl Haig*, pp. 16–17; Judd, *Empire*, pp. 96–7; Spiers, *Sudan: The Reconquest Reappraised*.

49 Beckett, *The Amateur Military Tradition 1558–1945*, p. 188; Grierson, *Scarlet into Khaki*, pp. 189–90; Heathcote, *The British Field Marshals 1736–1997*, p. 107.

50 Quoted in Sheffield, *Leadership in the Trenches*, p. 15.

51 Beckett, *The Amateur Military Tradition 1558–1945*, p. 187.

Yeomanry troopers of the later nineteenth century were typically small farmers, owners of livery stables, coach proprietors and others who could provide their own horses.[52] In 1893 the commanding officer of the Cheshire Yeomanry (Earl of Chester's) served notice to quit on one of his tenants on the grounds that he was apparently unwilling to serve in the yeomanry (and also to observe the Anglican faith).[53] Part of the rationale for keeping the yeomanry institutionally separate from the cavalry was that they recruited their troopers from completely different social classes.[54] The yeomanry as a force of tolerably well-off volunteers that met only occasionally to train had a quite different approach to discipline and officer–man relations than the regular Army. A distinct yeomanry ethos continued into the First World War, fostered in other units by officers who had served in the peacetime yeomanry; and this was often considered more appropriate to a citizen Army than pre-war regular officer behaviour.[55]

Unlike the regular cavalry, the number of yeomanry regiments changed after 1880 as regiments were created or disbanded, and the yeomanry were incorporated into the Territorial Force on its creation before the First World War. There were 38 yeomanry regiments in 1899 and 57 yeomanry or territorial mounted regiments in 1914, including a few anomalies that were part of the Special Reserve such as King Edward's Horse.[56] The part-time 'Rifle Volunteer' movement begun in 1860 also included a few mounted companies, designated either as 'mounted rifles' or as 'light horse'. One of these mounted companies, the 1st Hampshire Light Horse Volunteers formed by Lieutenant Colonel J. Bower, ('Bower's Hants Horse') popularised the deep Namaqua rifle bucket, originally from Cape Colony, which was later widely used.[57] In 1883 Major Edward 'Curly' Hutton of the King's Royal Rifle Corps proposed unsuccessfully a scheme for a permanent brigade of what he called Mounted Infantry Volunteers to the War Office.[58] But most of the mounted volunteer companies became defunct in the 1880s, and the last remaining units had transferred to the yeomanry by the start of the twentieth century.[59]

The same titles of 'mounted rifles' and 'light horse' were also used throughout the British Empire for locally raised volunteer mounted units, most of which had only a temporary existence before the start of the twentieth century, the most significant exception being the Cape Mounted Rifles, which dated (with some gaps in its lineage) back to the 1840s.[60] Like the yeomanry, the chief advantage of these

---

52 Grierson, *Scarlet into Khaki*, p. 29.
53 Beckett, *The Amateur Military Tradition 1558–1945*, p. 190.
54 Goodenough and Dalton, *The Army Book for the British Empire*, p. 100.
55 Sheffield, *Leadership in the Trenches*, pp. 15–18 and pp. 156–9; Baynes, *Morale*, pp. 164–79.
56 James, *British Regiments 1914–18*, pp. 15–34; Grierson, *Scarlet into Khaki*, p. 88.
57 Carman, *Light Horse and Mounted Rifle Volunteers*, pp. 159–63; Tylden, *Horses and Saddlery*, p. 99.
58 BL Hutton Papers Add. 50078: Alison to Hutton, 21 March 1883. Lieutenant General Sir Archibald Alison was Adjutant General in 1883.
59 Carman, *Light Horse and Mounted Rifle Volunteers 1860–1901*, pp. 1–3.
60 Strachan, *From Waterloo to Balaclava*, pp. 86–90; Anglesey, *A History of the British Cavalry Volume 3*, pp. 168–79.

mounted riflemen was that they could be less well trained and at less cost, with the inevitable consequence that they were seen as inherently both second-rate and second-class, militarily and socially, when compared to cavalry. Later nineteenth-century commanders on campaign also had the option of providing horses (or mules, or even camels and elephants) for their infantry as a means of transport only, and if these formations managed more than a brief existence they often became known as 'mounted infantry'. Mounted companies of regular infantry were used in the Cape Frontier Wars of the 1830s to the 1870s, sometimes alongside cavalry and colonial mounted forces, all of which in practice fought as mounted riflemen.[61] A small force of mounted infantry was also used in the Indian Mutiny of 1857–1859 by Captain Sir Henry 'Harry' Havelock VC, son of the more famous general.[62] A War Office study in 1880 concluded that 'To be able to keep his seat over rough ground, and not to roll about in his saddle sufficiently to give his horse a sore back, is about the extent of horsemanship that would be required of a mounted infantry soldier.'[63] Sore backs were caused by the saddle rubbing against the horse's hide, through poor riding skills or loss of weight by the horse due to poor feeding and exertion, and were a persistent problem on campaign; they could render a horse useless for riding until it recovered.

While there was no comparison between the often expert horsemen of some mounted rifle units and a mounted infantry unit improvised simply by giving an infantryman a horse, the terms 'mounted infantry' and 'mounted rifles' were often used loosely and interchangeably when discussing cavalry, resulting in sometimes unnecessary confusion. As one cavalry officer wrote in 1878:

> If the duties of cavalry are in the future to be confined to scouting and outpost work, and the collection of intelligence, infinitely important as they are, the days of cavalry proper would be numbered, as such duties may be as well or better performed by mounted infantry… a far cheaper arm, and one that can be turned to a variety of uses.[64]

This confusion was understandable, as although mounted infantry soldiers were not supposed to be trained for mounted manoeuvres of any kind, in reality any distinction between mounted riflemen and mounted infantry could and did break down, either over some years during peace, or very quickly with the demands of campaigning. Well before the end of the nineteenth century there were cases of both mounted riflemen and mounted infantry making charges on horseback, sometimes improvising by using bayonets as swords, or even makeshift lances. Further, not all troops described as 'mounted riflemen' actually carried rifles instead of carbines.

---

61 The (Eastern) Cape Frontier Wars, fought against (and sometimes between) the African peoples of the eastern Cape by British and African forces, were usually known at the time as the Kaffir Wars, a term that was offensive then, and remains so; see Lock and Quantrill, *Zulu Victory*, authors' note at the start of the book.

62 Luvaas, *The Military Legacy of the Civil War*, p. 109; Strachan, *From Waterloo to Balaclava*, pp. 84–90; David, *The Indian Mutiny*, p. 250 and p. 331.

63 TNA WO 33/37 A855 'Memorandum on Mounted Riflemen by Colonel C.F. Clery', 1 March 1880, in 'Précis on Mounted Infantry', (1881).

64 [Anon], *Notes on Cavalry Tactics, Organisation etc, by a Cavalry Officer*, p. 1.

An early nineteenth-century cavalry carbine was an altogether inferior weapon to an infantry rifle (whether muzzleloading or breechloading), but from the 1860s onwards carbines came into service with which dismounted cavalry stood a reasonable chance of out-shooting infantry at closer ranges, and by the 1880s there was little to distinguish a carbine such as the British Martini-Henry from the equivalent infantry rifle except the length of the barrel.

The most important distinction in tactics between the cavalry (including the Indian cavalry and the yeomanry) and mounted rifles or light horse was not always one of charging, or even fighting mounted. The critical distinction was that cavalry training included the close order or 'knee-to-knee' charge, sometimes simply just known as 'the charge', in which the enemy was faced with an apparently solid wall of onrushing horsemen. British cavalry training manoeuvres sometimes culminated in a final mass charge, known as the 'cavalry fight', made in these close formations by up to an entire division of 6,000 or more troopers against rival cavalry, pulling up just short of actual contact, although this spectacle was frowned upon by cavalry reformers as representing a tactical situation unlikely to occur on a real battlefield. In 1894 an article in *The Times*, taking its lead from the reforming Inspector General of Cavalry, Lieutenant General James Keith Fraser, commented:

> It is only in peace manoeuvres that cavalry attack each other merely for the sake of a fight. In war the cavalry fight, if it comes off, does so because the commanders, being entrusted with the carrying out of some mission, regard the fight as indispensable for its performance. If they can execute that mission without a fight, a fight is worse than useless.[65]

The power of a mounted charge, whether knee-to-knee or in more open formation, came from a combination of the speed of the horses and the skill of their riders in maintaining a straight line, so that they all struck the enemy at once: about three-quarters of a ton of horse and rider moving at a gallop of over seven yards a second (440 yards a minute in British regulations). This kind of charge, hard to learn and execute, was seen as the pinnacle of the cavalry's achievements, and was critical to cavalry ethos and doctrine. As Brian Bond has very accurately observed, for the British cavalry of this era '"the charge" connoted not merely a tactical movement but a whole way of life'.[66] Many contemporaries treated the cavalry and the charge as inseparable, and confused the wide variety of charging tactics available to the cavalry with this single spectacular manoeuvre. The reciprocal of this argument was that, on various occasions when cavalry charges succeeded, critics of the cavalry would argue that this had not been a 'real' charge, since a knee-to-knee charge was by definition expected to fail in the face of the new firepower. One fine example of this is Lord Roberts's commentary on the open-order charge supported by artillery made

---

65 NLS Haig Papers 6f: Cutting from *The Times*, 4 October 1894. The British upper class habit of the era of using multiple surnames has resulted in some doubt over whether to render this officer's surname as Fraser, Keith Fraser or Keith-Fraser; none of the versions appears to be inherently more correct than the others. The title of Inspector General of Cavalry sometimes appeared in official documents of this period as Inspector of Cavalry.

66 Bond, 'Doctrine and Training in the British Cavalry 1870–1914', p. 99.

by the Cavalry Division under Sir John French at Klip Drift on 15 February 1900 during the Boer War, which broke through a long skirmish line of enemy riflemen:

> General French's admirable movement at Klip Drift was essentially a rapid advance of fighting men carried out at extended intervals. It was a rapid advance of warriors who possessed the ability, by means of horses and rifles (not swords and lances) to place their enemy *hors de combat*. It was an ideal Cavalry operation, but it was not a 'Cavalry charge', as this term is generally understood.[67]

This contrasts with the view of a participating young lancer officer, who had no doubt that his regiment had 'made a magnificent charge'.[68] In the writings of some critics of the cavalry, there seem to be almost no convolutions that would not be attempted, rather than admitting the modest claim that both cavalry and the occasional mounted charge continued to have some military value into the twentieth century. The British Army's official historian of the First World War, Sir James Edmonds, was a particular opponent of the cavalry, arguing that in 1914–1918 cavalry charges had only succeeded against weakened enemy forces, including those already subject to infantry and artillery attack, or that a victory could hypothetically have been achieved without the use of cavalry.[69] The obvious objection to such arguments is that co-ordination with other arms and attacking only weakened enemies was the whole basis of cavalry tactics of the period. It is something of a commonplace to contrast the First World War on the Western Front, which for most of its duration was dominated by the tactics of artillery and combat engineering, with the war on other fronts, notably Palestine where mobility and cavalry often dominated. But just as it is an exaggeration to call the Palestine campaign 1917–1918 a 'cavalry war', so it is a historical error to omit the cavalry's contribution to the Western Front.[70]

The Klip Drift charge, which succeeded completely for negligible losses to the cavalry, was the last occasion in the history of the British Army of a mounted charge made by a cavalry division moving as a single body. From then on, although British divisions manoeuvred and even charged mounted, they did so using tactical mobility

---

67 Roberts, preface to Childers, *War and the Arme Blanche*, p. x.

68 NAM Bellew Papers: Diary entry, 15 February 1900.

69 This is the first reference in this book to the British Army's official history of the First World War, overseen by James (later Sir James) Edmonds. The referencing apparatus given for this multi-volume work in the British Library catalogue, and appropriate to this particular reference, is Edmonds, *History of the Great War Based on Official Documents: Military Operations: France and Belgium 1918, Volume V*, pp. 195–6 and p. 256; hereafter a widely accepted shortened form will be used: Edmonds, *Official History France and Belgium 1918, Volume V*, pp. 195–6 and p. 256; Other references will follow the same convention; in cases in which individual volumes were written by contributors other than Edmonds, this will be made clear, e.g. McMunn and Falls (ed. Edmonds), *Official History Egypt and Palestine, Volume I*. See also Phillips, 'Scapegoat Arm', pp. 37–74; Wawro, *The Austro-Prussian War*, p. 269; Spiers, *The Late Victorian Army 1868–1902*, pp. 317–18; Hughes, *Allenby and British Strategy in the Middle East 1917–1919*, pp. 55–9.

70 Review of Woodward, *Hell in the Holy Land*, in the *Journal of Military History*, Volume 70, Number 3, July 2006, p. 855; Badsey, 'Cavalry and the Development of the Breakthrough Doctrine', pp. 162–3.

within the division, and combinations of mounted and dismounted action. Although charges involving thousands of troopers had featured in battles of the Napoleonic Wars, from the middle nineteenth century onwards most charges were affairs of a few hundred, taking advantage of ground and opportunity. The charge of the Light Brigade at the Battle of Balaklava in 1854 involved fewer than 700 horsemen. The Prussian 'Death Ride' charge of two regiments under von Bredow at Mars-la-Tour in August 1870 during the Franco-Prussian War, equally famous and even more successful, involved only 750 men; and as British officers regularly visited the battlefield for training purposes they could see that the charging Prussians had succeeded by exploiting a fold of ground to cover their approach; Henry Wilson as Commandant of the Staff College in 1909 used to make his students run the route of the charge on foot.[71] The clash of French and Prussian cavalry later in the day at Mars-la-Tour was probably the last large entirely mounted 'cavalry fight' to take place in western Europe, although certainly far from being the last cavalry charge of that or any other war.

Most non-military contemporaries, if they had any view on what a charge involved, envisaged something like Lady Butler's painting of the charge of the Scots Greys at Waterloo, 'Scotland Forever', first exhibited in 1881, showing a solid clump of horses and riders.[72] But even in the 'cavalry fight', long before 1914 British doctrinal orthodoxy for cavalry was not simply to hurl a large charging mass frontally towards the enemy. One key to the evolution of British tactics was the 'squadron system', based on a squadron of between 100 and 200 men and horses as the unit for tactical manoeuvre, which was used informally well before 1880, and was officially introduced in 1892. In close or open order, a charge by British regular cavalry was made by a formation two deep, with the second echelon five or six yards behind the first, together forming a single 'line'.[73] Yeomanry and mounted rifles were trained to manoeuvre in the simpler single-rank or 'rank entire' formation, and were often employed in dispersed formations and small numbers. As practised in the decades before 1914, the British charging formation used three such lines, with the intervals between them depending on the size of the formation charging, working up from 150–200 yards deep for a regiment to deeper formations for a brigade or division. For a divisional charge the front line consisted of two brigades each of three regiments (or 12 squadrons in total) with a second line of one brigade about 300 yards behind it, and a third reserve line of one brigade another 200 yards behind that. Spread out like this, the whole formation of a divisional charge occupied a considerable area of ground; by 1916 squadrons were taught to manoeuvre using a variable frontage of up to a mile.[74] Tactical manoeuvre by squadrons was always encouraged, so that

---

71 Woodham Smith, *The Reason Why*, p. 259; Wood, *Achievements of Cavalry*, p. 225; Bond, *The Victorian Army and the Staff College*, p. 250. The present author has led battlefield tours and staff rides to Mars-la-Tour.

72 Lady Butler's painting, which has been often reproduced, hangs at present in Leeds Art Gallery. For criticisms of its historical accuracy in depicting a cavalry charge see Keegan, *The Face of Battle*, p. 176 photograph caption 6.

73 Goodenough and Dalton, *The Army Book for the British Empire*, p. 195.

74 AWM 4 151 War Diary 1st Australian Light Horse Brigade, Training Schedule, 6 February 1916.

the outer squadrons of the first line and all the squadrons of the remaining two lines might strike the enemy in the flank or rear rather than frontally. As summarised by Lieutenant Colonel James 'Jimmy' Grierson in his semi-official account in 1899, British cavalry tactical doctrine was that all mounted attacks including the 'cavalry fight' were to be supported by fire from artillery, machine-guns, and dismounted troops (a role for which mounted infantry were seen as particularly suitable); enemy artillery were always to be attacked in loose order and from a flank; and skirmishing enemy infantry were also to be attacked in loose order. As for the charge against close-order bodies of infantry:

> If the enemy's infantry is in close order and unshaken, the attack must be made in close order by regiments or squadrons following each other at intervals of 150 to 200 yards, *and from different directions*. The nature of the ground is to be utilised in every way, so as to take the enemy by surprise; but if circumstances are not favourable for such a manoeuvre compensation must be secured by rapidity of execution. At a distance of 1000 yards or more the gallop must commence, and the pace quickened as much as possible. It will always be advantageous to commence the advance in loose order, or at large intervals, and to form close formations when near to the enemy.[75]

It was considered vital to support a cavalry charge against infantry by firepower. But such charges, although practised in training, were recognised as unlikely to occur in any future war.

Practising the knee-to-knee charge had a further function for the cavalry, which was to enhance its prestige. 'A cavalry charge is a cavalry charge', wrote Major General Sir George Younghusband, describing his experience leading a charge of the Guides, 'and there is nothing on earth to equal it.'[76] So great was the prestige involved that, despite the danger, it was not unknown for officers to attach themselves to charging regiments purely out of a desire to participate, the most famous being Captain Lewis Nolan, who joined the charge of the Light Brigade at Balaklava. When two cavalry brigades, one British and one Indian, charged at the Battle of Kassassin in Egypt in September 1882, Major Alexander Tulloch of the staff joined the 19th Hussars with the words 'Oh, Colonel, do let me join your charge. I have always longed for such a chance all through my soldiering.'[77] Lieutenant Winston Churchill of the 4th Hussars attached himself to the 21st Lancers at the Battle of Omdurman in September 1898, for a charge that was widely considered to have little tactical purpose, and to have been undertaken for prestige by a junior cavalry regiment previously without battle honours. Haig, who was an eyewitness, 'feared this all along, for the regiment was here to do something, and meant to charge something before the show was over'.[78]

---

75 Grierson, *Scarlet into Khaki*, pp. 146–7 and preface by P.S. Walton pp. v–vii, emphasis added; see also von Schmidt, *Instructions for the Training, Employment and Leading of Cavalry*; see also *Cavalry Drill Volume II*, p. 207.

76 Younghusband, *A Soldier's Memories in Peace and War*, p. 64.

77 Quoted in Anglesey, *A History of the British Cavalry Volume 3*, p. 294.

78 Scott (ed.), *Douglas Haig: The Preparatory Prologue: Diaries and Letters 1861–1914*, p. 102. The originals of these letters are in the NLS Haig Papers, and in keeping with the practices of this book while a published edition has been used, wherever possible it has been checked against the original documents. See also Spiers, *The Late Victorian Army*, p. 293.

In the same way that a cavalry regiment could raise its social prestige by a charge, a main reason that troops raised as mounted rifles or mounted infantry would take to charging mounted was that, in addition to its tactical value, a successful charge was also a very effective way of raising their self-esteem. Haig wrote in April 1898 to his chief confidante about his Army career before his marriage, his elder sister Henrietta Jameson, describing the charges and manoeuvres by his Egyptian cavalry brigade in the approach to the Battle of Atbara:

> Had the Dervish horsemen been all that the papers say of them, we would never have got away. Fortunately, they ran away the moment we showed a bold front, and only came on when we turned our backs. Our casualties were pretty severe, 30 [wounded] and 10 killed. We had over 20 horses shot and many wounded. The cavalry did very well, I think, and the Sirdar [Kitchener] came out and met the squadrons as they returned and complimented some of them. This I hear is the *first time* the Gyppe [sic] Cavalry has ever had anything in the way of fighting to do. This accounts for the delight at Headquarters in discovering that they don't run away.[79]

Ideally, cavalry charges were not expected to result in a collision, but in the enemy turning in flight, so that relatively low numbers of enemies killed or wounded with swords and lances were taken as evidence of success rather than failure. One participant at the Battle of Mahsama in Egypt in 1882 described the sight of an approaching charge of three squadrons of British heavy cavalry supported by artillery and dismounted fire as 'too much for the Egyptian warriors, for they bolted, leaving us in possession of the entire camp baggage, hundreds of arms, and tons of ammunition, seven breech-loading Krupp guns (beautiful weapons) and last but not least, a train load of stores etc'.[80]

The combination of the physical force of the charge striking home against the enemy with the psychological threat of such an impact was often described by cavalrymen as 'shock', a term which otherwise had no very precise definition. Many defenders of the cavalry charge argued that despite the increased range and effectiveness of firepower, the impact of shock would still allow the charge to succeed. But since there was little way of determining the likelihood of success before the charge was launched, cavalry charges increasingly came to resemble a lethal mass version of what a later motor-driving age would call a game of chicken, embarked upon at very high risk for possible high gain. If the enemy did not run from the charge, then heavy casualties for the cavalry were almost inevitable. Churchill's account of the charge of the 21st Lancers at Omdurman against Dervish footsoldiers carrying only spears, swords and obsolete firearms showed how dangerous such a charge could be, how much courage it required, and how very quickly psychological reaction set in afterwards:

---

79 Cooper, *Haig*, Volume I, p. 58; emphasis in the original; 'Gyppe' or 'Gippy' was a slang abbreviation for 'Egyptian'.

80 Private Robert Gamble of the 7th Dragoon Guards, quoted in Spiers, *The Victorian Solider in Africa*, p. 82; see also Maurice, *Military History of the Campaign of 1882 in Egypt*, pp. 50–51.

It is very rare that stubborn and unshaken infantry meet equally stubborn and unshaken cavalry. Usually, either the infantry run away and are cut down in flight, or they keep their heads and nearly destroy all the horsemen by musketry. In this case the two living walls crashed together with a mighty collision... The [cavalry] regiment broke completely through the line everywhere, leaving sixty Dervishes dead and many wounded in their track. A hundred and fifty yards away they halted, rallied, and in less than five minutes were reformed and ready for a second charge. The men were anxious to cut their way back through their enemies. But some realisation of the cost of that wild ride began to come to all of us. Riderless horses galloped across the plain. Men, clinging to their saddles, lurched hopelessly about, covered in blood from perhaps a dozen wounds... In one hundred and twenty seconds five officers, sixty-six men, and one hundred and nineteen horses out of three hundred had been killed or wounded.[81]

Rather than launch a second charge, the regiment dismounted and opened fire with carbines to disperse their enemies.

Despite criticisms made of the charge of the 21st Lancers at Omdurman, the regimental commander was unrepentant, 'If cavalry are going to wait first to calculate the strength of the foe', he argued, 'and are only to attack if they find him weak enough, what is the use of them on the field of battle?'[82] Reformers within the cavalry had to contend not only with critics who argued for a different kind of mounted arm altogether, but also with a solid base of cavalry reactionaries whose solution to almost any tactical problem was to charge mounted, and see what happened. Colonel Maude complained in the 1890s that such an officer 'picks up from some text-book instances in which the cavalry has been successful, never stops to enquire the cause of the success, but jumps to the conclusion that if they ride home they will always be equally fortunate'.[83] This attitude continued into the First World War: the history of the 20th Deccan Horse, written by one of its majors, described the regiment's transfer to Palestine in 1918 as 'Our tactics were the same as those which had invariably proved successful in France, viz: to charge at the gallop, no matter what disparity of force there might be.'[84] A disconcerting problem, for reformers and critics of the cavalry alike, was that such tactics sometimes worked. From the 1880s onwards there were only two sets of circumstances in which a cavalry charge was bound to fail without doubt. One of these was when the charge was launched over genuinely impossible terrain, and the other was when it encountered a large swathe of uncut barbed wire, which – after all – had been invented to restrict the movements of animals. In the Boer War scouts with wirecutters led British cavalry advances, and by the First World War wirecutters were standard equipment, 'Never move without nippers in the Sam Browne belt!' as a cavalry officer wrote in 1914.[85] Otherwise, cavalry charges were subject to the same vagaries of success and failure as any other battlefield tactic.

---

    81   Woods, *Young Winston's Wars*, pp. 159–60.
    82   Quoted in Spiers, 'Campaigning under Kitchener', p. 72.
    83   Maude, 'The Rise, Decay and Revival of the Prussian Cavalry', *Journal of the Royal United Service Institution*, Volume 38, p. 20.
    84   Tennant, *The Royal Deccan Horse in the Great War*, p. 68.
    85   Captain Valentine Fleming MP of the Queen's Own Oxfordshire Hussars, quoted in Brown, *The Imperial War Museum Book of the Western Front*, p. 29.

The heart of the charge, and of a cavalry regiment's doctrine and ethos, was 'cavalry spirit', a term so often used that it was hardly felt to need definition. Writing in 1961, Major General James Lunt, a former commander of a British cavalry regiment converted to tanks, described how 'A great cavalry soldier, General Sir Hubert Gough, once defined that spirit as a combination of independence of thought, quickness in decision, and boldness in action. I would choose to add one more quality – that gaiety of spirit which the French prefer to call élan – or even panache.'[86] A further component to cavalry spirit, emphasised by General Sir Henry Beauvoir de Lisle, who commanded a mounted infantry unit in the Boer War and a cavalry regiment before the First World War, was that 'mounted troops should only act on instruction and not on orders', or that cavalry should be taught when the situation arose to disregard their formal orders and act as they thought best, which usually meant with aggression rather than with hesitation, and which demanded a style of command based on high levels of mutual confidence.[87] This style of command became extremely fashionable in military doctrine in the later twentieth century under the German name of Auftragstaktik, or 'mission command', and it has been commonplace to contrast the superiority of this German style on the Western Front with British failings.[88] But if the British Cavalry did not use the same terminology, the same command style was inherent in cavalry spirit and central to their doctrine long before 1914.

Cavalry spirit as a tactical doctrine fitted particularly well in this period with cavalry spirit as a social ethos within the regiments. As the 1904 edition of the *Cavalry Training* manual expressed it, 'The "cavalry spirit" of enterprise and dash, which is equally necessary to success in war, though it cannot be taught by theory, must be regularly ingrained into every officer and man by practical exercises, and by the highly personal example of the leaders themselves.'[89] One way in which the cavalry benefited from the Cardwell reforms was that after 1870 a regimental commander and his officers became actually, rather than nominally, responsible for their men, horses and equipment.[90] From regimental commanders to troopers, the progressive adoption of the squadron system, together with the cavalry's sense of being a social elite, the generally greater intelligence of cavalry recruits, and possibly the example of the Indian *silladar* system, all gave the cavalry (together with the horse artillery), a great sense of confidence and independence that promoted tactical flair, while at the same time also promoting resistance to any authority's intrusion into their regimental affairs.

This combination meant that cavalry spirit was not always seen as an unalloyed positive attribute. From at least the early nineteenth century, British cavalrymen and their horses were often judged to be of very high quality, but their officers were

---

86 Lunt, *Charge To Glory!* p. ix; Lunt commanded the 16th/5th Lancers 1957–1959, Gough had commanded the 16th Lancers, 1912–1914.

87 de Lisle, *Reminiscences of Sport and War*, p. 26.

88 van Creveld, *Command in War*, pp. 155–88; Samuels, *Command or Control?* See also Badsey, 'The Doctrines of the Coalition Forces', pp. 69–70.

89 *Cavalry Training 1904*, p. 19.

90 Smith, *A History of the Royal Army Veterinary Corps*, pp. 171–2.

seen as brave but brainless, obsessed with the idea of the mounted charge. An often-quoted observation by the Duke of Wellington about the Peninsula War summed up the prevailing view in the middle nineteenth century:

> I consider our cavalry so inferior to the French for want of order, although I consider one squadron a match for two French squadrons, I should not have liked to see four British squadrons opposing four French... It is occasioned entirely by the trick our officers of cavalry have acquired of galloping at everything, and their galloping back as fast as they gallop at the enemy.[91]

This perception was reinforced during the Crimean War, in particular by the popular attention given to the Light Brigade at Balaklava, including through Lord Tennyson's famous poem, rather than the successful charge of the Heavy Brigade shortly beforehand, or the more successful charge of the 16th Lancers at the Battle of Aliwal in 1846 during the First Sikh War.[92] It was a commonplace of the era to see Lord Cardigan of Light Brigade fame as representative of all cavalry generals, and to take the affectations of languor and gentlemanly indifference expected of mid-nineteenth-century cavalry officers at face value.[93] Beliefs that officers, particularly in the more expensive cavalry regiments, were hostile to professionalism and staff training persisted into the First World War, and an often repeated joke concerned a cavalry officer who was 'so stupid that even his brother officers noticed!'[94]

The cavalry could adopt a defensive tone to these criticisms, but some officers enjoyed playing up to their image of studied amateurism and contempt for officialdom. The Honourable Sidney Peel, who served as an officer with the Bedfordshire Yeomanry on the Western Front (and previously as a volunteer gentleman ranker in the Boer War), recorded a prime example of a respected but unambitious major of the 19th Hussars responding to a peremptory question by a general:

> 'How many squadrons have you up here now?' He thought for some time, and then turning to his regimental sergeant major drawled slowly: 'How many squadrons have we up here now, Mr. Johnson?' 'Two and a half, sir.' Turning back to the general and gravely saluting he repeated with great deliberation: 'Two and a half, sir'.[95]

The same manner was employed by Sir Philip Chetwode, known as 'The Bart' (he was a baronet), which led to his being described by Cyril Falls as 'superficially,

---

91 Quoted in Haythornthwaite, *The Armies of Wellington*, p. 106.

92 For the impact of Tennyson's famous poem on the charge of the Light Brigade see the entry 'Crimean War' in Cull, Culbert and Welch (eds), *Propaganda and Mass Persuasion*; see also Woodham Smith, *The Reason Why*, pp. 224–59; Bruce, *Six Battles for India*, pp. 158–72.

93 Woodham Smith, *The Reason Why*, p. 7.

94 Quoted as one of the stories that 'my father never tired of telling' by Ismay, *The Memoirs of General The Lord Ismay*, p. 4; Hastings 'Pug' Ismay was commissioned into the Indian 21st Cavalry in 1907, his father was Sir Stanley Ismay, a member of the Viceroy's Legislative Council and later chief judge of the Mysore Court. See also Baynes, *Morale*, p. 249.

95 Peel, *O.C. Beds Yeomanry*, p. 28.

Chetwode was all that Americans most dislike in Britons and that many Britons dislike in their own countrymen'.[96] Both Chetwode and his fellow cavalryman Hubert Gough were the subjects of anecdotes (possibly misunderstood) reflecting their indifference to authority.[97] In Gough's case this backfired after his dismissal from command of Fifth Army following the German Kaiserschlacht offensive of March 1918. Gough commented sourly in his memoirs on newspaper reports that:

> Being a cavalry officer I knew nothing about the handling of all arms, and had only one idea, which was to charge about the field and hurl my cavalry at the enemy. 'With this end in view' – so one correspondent who was explaining 'how we lost the battle' actually asserted – I 'had all the wire on my army front pulled up in order to enable my cavalry to charge unhampered by obstacles!!!'[98]

Despite their best efforts to portray themselves as reformers and thinking soldiers, not even the most professional and energetic of cavalry generals could ever quite overcome this stereotype.

The idea of the stupid cavalry general has been repeatedly evoked as an explanation for the wider performance of the British Army on the Western Front, often as a substitute for more profound analysis. Implicit in this evocation is that the Army would have done much better without cavalrymen in high command, and also without cavalry at all. In fact very few contemporary participants in the debate over the future of cavalry ever argued for its complete abolition, in the sense of having the Army dispense with all soldiers who rode horses. From the later nineteenth century onwards the cavalry's scouting role increased in importance as armies grew larger. The real debate was over what kind of horse soldiers the Army needed. If the battlefield charge was obsolete, then this implied an entire restructuring of the cavalry to optimise itself for the scouting role, all the way down to the size and breed of the horses, together with the immensely significant loss of any arm of breakthrough and exploitation as part of the battle; and possibly the institutional trauma of disbanding the cavalry regiments.

A further powerful reason that the abolition of the cavalry was rarely suggested between 1880 and 1899 was that the argument for abolition had already been made during the wars of the previous generation, and had been firmly discredited. Among modern historians, a debate exists over the wars in Europe and North America between the 1850s and 1870s, which are seen by some as pointing towards the future deadlock on the Western Front and by others as retaining many of the characteristics of the Napoleonic Wars.[99] This in turn is a reflection of a disagreement in the historical

---

96 Quoted in Woodward, *Hell in the Holy Land*, p. 53; see also Hill, *Chauvel of the Light Horse*, p. 106.

97 Gardner, *Trial By Fire*, pp. 19–20; Anglesey, *A History of the British Cavalry Volume 7*, p. 79.

98 Gough, *Soldiering On*, p. 176.

99 Claims for the 'first modern war' stretch back to the Crimean War, and for the 'last Napoleonic war' forward to the American Civil War; generally, claims that the early breechloaders transformed warfare are more common from American historians than their British and European colleagues. Compare Beckett, *The Victorians at War*, pp. 161–78;

sources, and of a dispute that took place during the nineteenth century itself about the lessons to be learned about any one war or weapon. A particular issue was whether early rifles provided the infantry with an advance in firepower that was revolutionary or only incremental when compared with smoothbore muskets. Remarkable claims were made first for muzzleloading rifles using the new Minié ammunition, versions of which equipped most armies from the 1840s onwards, and then even more remarkable claims for the breechloaders which replaced them.[100] In 1859, at the Royal United Service Institution in Whitehall, one British officer proclaimed that no troops in battle would be safe from the Enfield .577 rifled musket, which used Minié-type ammunition, at any range up to half a mile (880 yards), while another argued that the Enfield was 'effective at 1,000 yards'; and in the *United Service Magazine* in 1869 yet another officer predicted that with the new Snider breechloading rifle, 'if an infantry regiment reserve their fire till advancing cavalry are within 500 yards' (just over a minute's gallop), 'and aim always low, they may pour in a storm of bullets numbering at least thirty per man'.[101] Some officers proposed that cavalry should be replaced by a new highly trained light infantry, capable of fast rates of march and of tactical manoeuvre on the battlefield, presenting a smaller target than a horseman, and armed with rifles for very accurate long range fire. The first troops created to fulfil this role were the French Army's Chasseurs à Pied of the 1830s, the doctrinal ancestors of the Confederate 'foot cavalry' of the American Civil War of 1861–1865, and ultimately of the hard-marching, sharp-shooting infantry of the BEF of 1914.[102]

Accounts of real ranges and rates of fire in combat are hard to interpret for infantry rifles of this period, but broadly, earlier breechloaders such as the Prussian Dreyse 'needle gun' or the Snider had a rate of fire of three or four rounds a minute and an effective range of about 300–400 yards, only slightly better than a Minié rifle, although the breechloader could be used more easily from cover or lying down.[103]

Griffith, *Forward Into Battle*, pp. 43–74; Griffith, *Rally Once Again*, pp. 189–92; Grimsley, 'Surviving Military Revolution: The US Civil War', pp. 74–91; Showalter, 'The Prusso-German RMA 1840–1871', pp. 92–113; Hagerman, *The American Civil War and the Origins of Modern Warfare*; Förster and Nagler (eds), *On the Road to Total War*.

100 For dates and a description of the introduction of successive types of infantry firearm see Derry and Williams, *A Short History of Technology*, pp. 500–502.

101 Tyler, 'The Rifle and the Spade, or the Future of Field Operations', *Journal of the Royal United Service Institution*, Volume 3, p. 173; 'The Dragoon, His Horse and Their Training', *Colburn's United Service Magazine*, 1864 Part III, p. 330; see also 'The Newly Proposed Service Arm, or the Martini-Henry Rifle', *Colburn's United Service Magazine*, 1869 Part II, p. 106.

102 Griffith, *Forward Into Battle*, pp. 52–7; and Griffith, *Military Thought in the French Army 1815–51*, pp. 125–30. The American Civil War has also been known as the War of Secession, the War of Rebellion, and sometimes as the War for the Southern Confederacy. *Chasseurs* ('Hunters') was a French designation for infantry or cavalry suggesting elite skirmishing troops; *Chasseurs à Pied* means literally 'hunters on foot'.

103 Majendie, 'Military Breechloading Small Arms', *Journal of the Royal United Service Institution*, Volume 12, p. 196; 'The Newly Proposed Service Arm, or, the Martini Henry Rifle', *Colburn's United Service Magazine*, 1869 Part III, p. 109; Younghusband, *A Soldier's Memories in Peace and War*, p. 50; Hozier, *The Seven Weeks' War*, Volume I, p. 221; [Anon],

Later breechloaders such as the French Chassepôt or the British Martini-Henry were much more accurate, with combat ranges and rates of fire up to about 600 yards and six rounds a minute (about half their maximum range and rate of fire).[104] But although in these wars infantry and artillery firepower increased, successful cavalry charges still took place, and battles had far more of the characteristics of Waterloo than the Somme.[105] This may have been because the new weapons failed to function as well as predicted, or because reactionary generals failed to adjust their tactics to new weapons, or because politicians and peoples were reluctant to embrace ever more destructive forms of warfare, or quite possibly because of a combination of all these factors together with others. One important consequence was that, having been told so firmly and so wrongly that both cavalry and the charge were obsolete, British cavalry officers became highly critical of such claims. In 1871 one wrote that 'It might be supposed that a cavalry attack would be attended with fearful losses, but such in reality is not the case', and another in 1878 that:

> It has been frequently denied that cavalry can [any longer be effective in battle] and too often this dictum is acquiesced in by cavalry officers themselves, who accepting without examination what is termed 'the logic of facts' are content to see their arm relegated to what is, however we may seek to deny it, a position of inferiority.[106]

Having been once bitten, most theorists developed a strong immunity to claims that the cavalry was obsolete. But it was while the debate over cavalry doctrine was at its height from the 1880s onwards that an indisputably revolutionary change in battlefield weaponry did take place, with the introduction of the new generation of magazine rifles, practical machine-guns, and quick-firing artillery using new explosives and smokeless propellants.[107] Together with the potential for much larger armies, these represented a significantly greater change to European warfare than all the changes which had gone before them, as became apparent in 1914.[108]

The British Army's cavalry doctrines were also shaped by the fact that, while it did not fight a major land war in Europe between 1856 and 1914, it was almost constantly involved in colonial warfare. The development and transfer of technology played an important part in these colonial wars, including the new firepower provided first by breechloading rifles and later by magazine rifles and machine-

---

Notes on Cavalry Tactics, Organisation etc, by a Cavalry Officer, p. 37; von Wright and Hozier (trans), *The Campaign of 1866 in Germany*, p. 140.

104 [Anon], *Notes on Cavalry Tactics, Organisation etc, by a Cavalry Officer*, p. 9; Henderson, *The Science of War*, p. 372; Laband, *The Transvaal Rebellion*, p. 77; Wawro, *The Franco-Prussian War*, pp. 52–4.

105 Still by far the best modern account of the campaigns and battles of the Franco-Prussian War is Howard, *The Franco-Prussian War*. For recent accounts see Wawro, *The Franco-Prussian War*, and Stone, *First Reich*, and for a short account see Badsey, *The Franco-Prussian War 1870–1871*.

106 [Anon], *Notes on Cavalry Tactics, Organisation etc, by a Cavalry Officer*, p. 76; Spencer, 'The German Cavalry', *Colburn's United Service Magazine*, 1873 Part I, p. 220.

107 Derry and Williams, *A Short History of Technology*, pp. 500–502.

108 Sheffield, 'The Impact of Two Revolutions 1789–1898', pp. 1–20; Badsey, 'The Road to Stalemate 1899–1914', pp. 21–43.

guns.[109] But for the British the circumstances of individual wars and battles could far outweigh any broad principles or doctrines laid down for the conduct of battle, and the tactics needed for one war could be utterly different from the next. In an often-quoted passage, General Sir Neville Lyttelton reflected on his personal experiences of the Battle of Omdurman in September 1898 followed by the Battle of Colenso in December 1899: 'Few people have seen two battles in succession in such startling contrast as Omdurman and Colenso. In the first, 50,000 fanatics streamed across the open regardless of cover to certain death, while at Colenso I never saw a Boer all day till the battle was over, and it was our men who were the victims.'[110] With such a wide range of tactical conditions that they might face, and so few cavalry regiments, it was virtually inevitable that British cavalry doctrine was to train for almost any eventuality.

The only influential senior British officer of the First World War who persistently championed the view that cavalry might be entirely replaced by fast-moving infantry sharpshooters was Ian Hamilton, who advanced this belief in his book *The Fighting of the Future* of 1885 and never entirely abandoned it, although he later came to include the possibility of sharpshooters who were mobile on horses. Like French and Haig, Hamilton had personal experiences to support his views. Very early in his career he had absorbed the new rifle doctrine of the School of Musketry at Hythe, and had been made his battalion's musketry instructor. Then in January 1881, his left wrist was permanently shattered by a bullet from a Boer dismounted sharpshooter during the Battle of Majuba Hill, the decisive British defeat of the Transvaal War of 1880–1881, which the British lost because they were tactically out-shot.[111]

While the Army rightly valued both combat experience and courage, the way in which this kind of early personal experience shaped opinions on doctrine also created problems, because such experiences could vary considerably in such a wide variety of campaigns. Like the study of history or theory, personal experience could lead to enlightened reflection or to dogmatism, depending on the abilities and predisposition of the individual officer. Shortly after the Boer War, Colonel Maude complained acidly that 'The hardest task of all is to convince a man who has seen a good deal of active service that the scope of his personal impressions and opportunities is not in itself sufficient to provide him with brains if he has none, or to over-ride the experience of thousands of others who have gone before him.'[112]

Despite attempts at the time to learn from personal experiences and from history, even the most basic facts about what happened in a cavalry charge were extremely hard to establish, and in almost all cases the most important evidence has now been lost. It was nothing unusual for two honest, experienced officers who took part in

---

109 Headrick, *The Tools of Empire*, pp. 83–128; Fergusson, *Empire*, pp. 221–93.
110 Lyttelton, *Eighty Years*, p. 212.
111 Hamilton, *The Fighting of the Future*; Lee, *A Soldier's Life*, pp. 11–16; Laband, *The Transvaal Rebellion*, pp. 204–9; Griffith, *Forward Into Battle*, p. 53. The Transvaal War of 1880–1881 is also known variously as the Transvaal Rebellion and as the First Boer War.
112 Maude, *Cavalry: Its Past and Future*, p. 158.

the same charge to give radically different accounts of it later.[113] There was even some debate as to whether the final impetus to ride the enemy down came from the rider keeping a reluctant horse going straight, or from a horse almost crazed by the experience of the charge carrying the rider along. Writing in 1897, Evelyn Wood, who began his military career in the 17th Lancers and had commanded irregular mounted riflemen, backed the second of these views, but the matter was never resolved with any certainty.[114] There was also little understanding of why some cavalry charges succeeded despite the theoretical firepower available to stop them. One of the most surprising findings from the 1890s and early 1900s, confirmed by repeated veterinary tests, was that wounds particularly from the smaller calibre bullets introduced for the new generation of magazine rifles and machine-guns had much less penetrating and stopping power against horses than had been expected: a rifle bullet hitting a charging horse even at 50 yards would not bring it down unless it hit a major bone or organ, and a charge would cover that distance in about seven seconds; it was common for horses to collapse from wounds after a charge was completed, but not before.[115]

Although much of the debate about the cavalry was concerned with what weapons they should carry and how to use them, there was no obvious connection between the physical and psychological shock generated by an onrushing charge and the weapons carried. In fact an individual weapon was not essential: Lord George Paget, commanding the second line in the charge of the Light Brigade at Balaklava, kept his hands on his reins, only drawing his sword at the last moment (he also smoked a cigar for most of the charge); the regimental commander of the 21st Lancers at Omdurman also chose not to draw his weapon in the charge, as did at least one French cavalry commander at Mars-la-Tour.[116] But on both sides of the tactical debate, swords and lances were seen not only as weapons but as symbols of the philosophy of the charge and of cavalry spirit. The term often used for a sword or lance was the French 'arme blanche', meaning roughly 'cold steel' and sometimes rendered into English as 'the white arm'. Although this expression was stretched by some writers to include infantry bayonets and swords, the association with the mounted charge was so strong that arme blanche was often used as a synonym for the cavalry itself. Writing in 1895 about the Zulu War of 1879, the British war correspondent Archibald Forbes expected his readers to understand without further explanation his comment on the charge of the 17th Lancers at the Battle of Ulundi, 'It did one good to see the glorious old "white arm" reassert again its pristine prestige.'[117]

The visible threat of the arme blanche in a charge was often considered as important as its actual use, a view that again persisted into the First World War.

---

113 Anglesey, *A History of the British Cavalry 1816–1919, Volume 3: 1872–1898*, p. 295.

114 Wood, *Achievements of Cavalry*, p. 242; Lunt, *Charge to Glory!*, p. 22.

115 Smith, 'The Effect of the Lee-Metford Bullet on the Bones of Horses', *Journal of the Royal United Service Institution*, Volume 38, p. 51–60; TNA WO 33/463, 'Reports on Experiments with Various Bullets against Animals' (1908).

116 Woodham Smith, *The Reason Why*, pp. 237–50; Woods, *Young Winston's Wars*, p. 160; Wood, *Achievements of Cavalry*, p. 219.

117 Forbes, *Memories and Studies of War and Peace*, p. 44.

In 1917 in Palestine, Major General Sir Henry Hodgson, the British cavalryman (15th Hussars) commanding the Australian Mounted Division, whose light horse regiments were armed with rifles and bayonets but not swords, issued a divisional order that 'To manoeuvre and attack mounted an *arme-blanche* weapon is necessary. The Divisional Commander suggests that the bayonet is equally as good as the sword, if used as a sword for pointing only; it has the same moral effect as the sword as it glitters in the sun and the difference could not be detected by the enemy.'[118] Although recent historical studies of behaviour in combat have largely concentrated on infantry soldiers in the twentieth century, they provide some help in understanding the nature of such a charge.[119] At least, later accounts of deaths in combat from edged weapons such as knives and bayonets are consistent with the claims of cavalrymen about the effect of a sword or lance. In the words of one late twentieth-century American combat veteran, 'The thought of cold steel sliding into your guts is more horrific and real than the thought of a bullet doing the same – perhaps because you can see the steel coming.'[120]

Cavalry charges were extremely stressful experiences, often lasting for minutes rather than seconds, inducing in the riders very high levels of emotion, including in some cases fear or a sadistic blood lust that were for all practical purposes indescribable, followed by a rapid emotional reaction. But this was an era in which open displays or discussion of emotion by officers and gentlemen were regarded as socially unacceptable, and officers were often reticent in their descriptions of charges. Other ranks could be more forthcoming, such as the anonymous non-commissioned officer of the 17th Lancers who described the regiment's charge at Ulundi:

> Presently the infantry commenced cheering like mad, and 'Mount the 17th' was shouted all round. As we left the [protection of the British infantry] square the infantry ceased firing and gave us a rattling cheer, then we were off and among the Zulus. You should have seen us. With tremendous shouts of 'Death! Death!' we were on them. They tried lying down to escape, but it was no use, we had them anyhow, no mercy or quarter from the 'Old Tots'. We only stopped when we could go no further and the horses were completely done up, then we stopped a little while, after which we went on to Ulundi, which we burnt. It was a splendid sight.[121]

This professional non-commissioned officer's attitude to a successful charge was a combination of satisfaction and regimental pride.

---

118 AWM 4 957 General Staff HQ Australian Mounted Division, Preliminary Instruction Number 1, 26 September 1917. 'Moral' used in this sense, and usually pronounced with a long 'a', was the common English spelling of the French word 'morale'.

119 The recent literature on this issue is considerable, if of variable quality; see Ellis, *The Sharp End of War*, pp. 97–112; Holmes, *Firing Line*, pp. 136–75; Fergusson, *The Pity of War*, pp. 357–66; Griffith, *Forward Into Battle*; Bourke, *An Intimate History of Killing*; Grossman, *On Killing*; Dean, *Shook Over Hell*.

120 'Bob McKenna', quoted in Grossman, *On Killing*, p. 121.

121 Quoted in Knight and Castle, *The Zulu War Then and Now*, p. 197; 'Old Tots' was a regimental nickname deriving from the German word 'Totenkopf' or death's-head, a reference to the skull-and-crossed-lances regimental crest of the 17th Lancers.

Descriptions of what it was like to face a cavalry charge, whether successful or not, are very rare, partly because the experience itself was inherently terrifying and even shaming if the survivors ran away. One charge that was quite well documented from both sides came early in the Boer War, when at the culmination of the Battle of Elandslaagte in October 1899 a retreat by Boer mounted riflemen was intercepted and repeatedly charged into and over by one squadron each of the 5th Dragoon Guards and the 5th Lancers ('the charge of the two Fifths'). Major Douglas Haig, who interviewed Boer prisoners, was deeply impressed by their expressions of loathing for the British use of lances as 'butchery, not war'; and the memory of the lancer charge at Elandslaagte also stayed with the man who ordered it, Lieutenant General John French.[122] Among the survivors was the future Boer general, B.J. 'Ben' Viljoen, whose impressions, recorded in imperfect English, were, 'I could see their long assegais [lances]; I could hear the snorting of their unwieldy horses, the clattering of their swords. These unpleasant combinations were enough to strike terror into the heart of any ordinary man.'[123] The cavalrymen involved in these repeated charges gave only laconic judgements of 'most excellent pig-sticking', and 'we just gave them a good dig as they lay'.[124]

The combination of the extreme danger and violence of a charge and the reluctance to describe the experience in detail continued into the First World War. Captain A.C. Allan-Williams of the 1/1st Warwickshire Yeomanry provided (from his hospital bed some weeks later) a description of the mounted charge by his squadron at Huj in Palestine in November 1917 against an enemy rearguard consisting of an Austrian field artillery battery protected by machine-guns and about 200 Turkish infantry, but chose in his letter not to describe the moment of contact or beyond. Allan-Williams's squadron manoeuvred using the cover of dead ground to charge the Austrian battery frontally (which was not ideal tactics), while a reinforced squadron of the 1/1st Worcestershire Hussars Yeomanry charged into the Turkish infantry from a flank:

> The Colonel gave Val [Captain R. Valentine, the squadron commander] the order to form 'column of half squadrons, draw swords & charge'. Before we had time to actually move off, the Turks who had of course seen us, shortened their fuses & burst a salvo of shrapnel six feet from the ground & right among us. Over the top we went & in a cloud of dust & a shout went straight at them. The reception they gave us was like riding into hell. Men & horses going the most awful losses I have ever seen anybody go [sic]. Some killed outright and others wounded. I was conscious of having been hit but could hold onto the reins alright. The shells tore through the air so close one could almost feel them. The crack of machine-gun bullets was terrific. I won't describe in too much detail what happened when the guns were reached but suffice to say that the gun teams were killed or captured to a man.[125]

---

122 Scott (ed.), *Douglas Haig: The Preparatory Prologue: Diaries and Letters 1861–1914*, p. 132; Holmes, *The Little Field Marshal*, pp. 11–14.

123 Quoted in Anglesey, *A History of the British Cavalry Volume 4*, p. 57.

124 Quoted in Packenham, *The Boer War*, pp. 169–70. 'Assegai' in this context is a word of Zulu origin meaning 'spear'; pig sticking was the typically humorous British term for the sport of hunting wild boars on horseback in India using a short lance or 'hog spear', a pastime which carried a real chance of injury and sometimes death.

125 Quoted in Woodward, *Hell in the Holy Land*, p. 125.

A highly impressionistic account of what happened when a cavalry charge struck home was given by one British veteran in 1985, also describing a charge (possibly the same one) against the Turks:

> By the time I got there the whole mass of cavalry was in line, and it so coincided that the alarm had already been sounded by the trumpeters. My mount, of course, being a cavalry charger, became imbued with the excitement of the time and the electric atmosphere – he joined in.
>
> The strength of a charge is in the straightness of the line. Once the alarm had sounded – draw swords. At that very moment the charge sounded. It was like riding into hell. The guns boomed, batteries, smoke everywhere. Matter of fact, half the time you were blinded by the smoke of the guns, and not only the shells exploding, the guns themselves, we were up amongst them!
>
> Anyway, right through that line they broke. Germans, Bulgarians, Turks, it didn't matter who they were, they were smashed, sundered, slaughtered. It was carnage, absolutely.
>
> Sword: slash – slash – slash – slash, see? Then someone appears, [sword] over the horse's head, dig in, out again – then that one appears over there, you simply reverse it [the sword], twist your wrist and slice at him! – and then that side! And of course everybody's doing the same thing, you see, so you have to be careful you're not wounding your next-door neighbour![126]

In this case, although the veteran had long forgotten the date and circumstances of the charge, the experience remained.

Although such descriptions convey something of the drama and confusion of a cavalry charge, even eyewitness accounts do not necessarily help in determining the actual events. If horsemen vanished into dust and smoke accompanied by bursting shells, observers could assume that the charge had been shot down or wiped out, simply because it had disappeared from sight. Recalling an episode after more than 60 years, a British artillery lieutenant gave this account of the charge at High Wood on the Western Front on 14 July 1916 by squadrons of the 7th Dragoon Guards and the 20th Deccan Horse:

> It was an incredible sight, and unbelievable sight, they galloped up with their lances and with pennants flying, up the slope to High Wood and straight into it. Of course they were falling all the way... the German machine-guns were going for the infantry [sic] and the shells were falling all over the place. I've never seen anything like it! They simply galloped through all that and horses and men dropping on the ground, with no hope against the machine-guns, because the Germans up on the ridge were firing down into the valley where the soldiers were. It was an absolute rout. A magnificent sight. Tragic.[127]

---

126 Hari 'Quagga' Williams, interviewed in Birmingham for the British documentary television programme *Soldiers: Cavalry*, first transmitted on BBC1 television on 25 September 1985. As shown in the unedited version of the interview, Williams believed this charge took place at Kut al-Amara, a siege in Mesopotamia 1915–1916, although there is no doubt that he served in Palestine and was describing events in 1917–1918. The author worked as a researcher on this programme.

127 2nd Lieutenant F.W. Beadle, quoted in Macdonald, *Somme*, pp. 137–8.

There seems to be no doubt that this veteran was present at the event that he described. But the cavalry did not charge into High Wood but across open ground which lay to the south, and the charge itself, far from being routed in massacre, was successful in temporarily capturing a piece of critical ground; British and Indian cavalry losses for the whole day were 14 men dead and 60 wounded, plus 112 horse casualties, most of them suffered in the aftermath of the charge (also, British and Indian cavalry had not carried pennants on their lances in war since 1898).[128] Further confusion comes from the assessment made in August 1916 by the defending German IV Corps, 'The frontal attacks over open ground against a portion of our unshaken infantry, carried out by several English cavalry regiments, which had to retire with heavy losses, give some indication of the tactical knowledge of the Higher Command.'[129] In fact the two squadrons at High Wood made the only British cavalry charge in the Battle of the Somme up to the end of August. It is possible that the Germans misinterpreted other British actions (such as the movement of transport horses) as cavalry charges, or that their tales of the charge at High Wood grew with the telling.

A particularly enduring impression of cavalry charges was that they were wiped out or shot down by machine-gun fire. This issue is part of the larger historical debate on the effectiveness of the machine-gun on the Western Front, which has assumed even greater importance in the history of memory and of culture.[130] There is no dispute that both heavy tripod-mounted and lighter bipod-mounted machine-guns were very effective infantry weapons. But like the clouds of shellfire into which cavalry apparently vanished to destruction, the effect of bursts of machine-gun fire on a cavalry charge left a sometimes misleading impression on witnesses, who assumed that a few horse casualties meant a disaster. The Battle of Amiens on 8 August 1918 included several successful British cavalry charges against German defenders, including machine-gunners, as part of much larger cavalry advances. In a comment reflected throughout the Army, Brigadier General Archibald 'Sally' Home, the chief staff officer of the Cavalry Corps, wrote that 'All our objectives were gained', and that 'the absolute necessity of good and well trained cavalry was proved'.[131] In contrast, the German official account of the battle quoted a defending soldier in terms which suggest complete failure for the British cavalry:

> In a matter of minutes, the mounted attack collapsed in the face of our fire, which was extraordinarily violent, especially from our light and heavy machine-guns. I shall never forget the sight – how the cavalry pushed forward, and was converted in an instant into a

---

128 Anglesey, *A History of the British Cavalry Volume 8*, pp. 51–8; Norman, *The Hell They Called High Wood*, pp. 99–106.

129 'Experiences of the IV German Corps in the Battle of the Somme during July, 1916', issued by General Headquarters (Intelligence) 30 September 1916, p. 5.

130 Terraine, *The Smoke and the Fire*, pp. 130–42; Fussell, *The Great War and Modern Memory*, pp. 144–54; Ellis, *The Social History of the Machine Gun*.

131 Home, *The Diary of a World War I Cavalry Officer*, p. 179. The original of Home's diary is held in the Imperial War Museum; the published version has been used in this book but checked against the original. Like many upper-class Anglo-Scots, Home pronounced his surname as 'Hume'.

mass of horses, weltering [sic] in their blood, hobbling on shattered limbs, or galloping riderless through our lines of infantry.[132]

That the sight of dead and mutilated horses was a horrible one is confirmed by accounts from many periods of warfare. But this does not justify the often-quoted statement, 'You can't have a cavalry charge until you have captured the enemy's last machine-gun', attributed by Edmonds to an anonymous US Army officer shortly before Amiens.[133] In fact, British cavalry both charged successfully and captured machine-guns at Amiens, including a notable charge by the 7th Dragoon Guards that captured 'a large number of Maxims [machine-guns] and close on a hundred prisoners'.[134]

A last illustration of the problem of interpreting what actually happened in a cavalry charge comes from one of the better documented charges on the Western Front, and illustrates the tactics used by cavalry late in the First World War. This was a brigade attack using dismounted firepower in conjunction with small mounted charges which took place at Moreuil Wood near Amiens on the morning of 30 March 1918, when German forces threatened to break through and capture Amiens from the British as the culmination of the Kaiserschlacht offensive. Moreuil ridge with its woods and village protected an important river crossing, and the battle took the form of an encounter between the advancing troops of 23rd (Saxon) Infantry Division and 243rd (Württemberg) Infantry Division and the arriving defenders of the Canadian Cavalry Brigade (then part of the British 3rd Cavalry Division but temporarily serving under the 2nd Cavalry Division) under Brigadier General J.E.B. 'Galloper Jack' Seely. The three understrength Canadian cavalry regiments each of about 300 troopers were significantly outnumbered by elements of at least four German infantry battalions, each of 300 to 400 men accompanied by machine-guns, and by two batteries each of six 76mm or 150mm guns.

The battle began as both sides attempted to pass through Morieul Wood at about the same time from opposite directions, with the Germans slightly in advance of the Canadians. Believing at first that the wood was largely clear of enemy, Seely ordered one of his regiments, the Royal Canadian Dragoons, to send a mounted squadron (about 100 men) round each side, while the regiment's third squadron rode through it, after which Seely's second regiment, Lord Strathcona's Horse, would follow up and clear the wood dismounted, while the Fort Garry Horse remained in reserve. On entering the wood the middle squadron of the Royal Canadian Dragoons came under fire, whereupon they dismounted and attacked with fixed bayonets, driving about 300 Germans out of the other side. Meanwhile to the south the squadron attempting to skirt the wood came unexpectedly under heavy fire from a German battalion supported by machine-gun and artillery, and turned into the wood to take refuge. According to German official records, 'In a few minutes one could only see a few riderless horses heading towards our gun lines. The greatest part of the riders

---

132 *Schlachten des Weltkrieges XXXVI*, p. 186, quoted in Guderian, *Achtung – Panzer!*, p. 123.

133 Edmonds, *Official History France and Belgium, Volume V*, p. 196.

134 Quoted in Anglesey, *A History of the British Cavalry Volume 8*, p. 233, and see pp. 220–49 for cavalry operations in the battle.

lay dead or wounded on the ground.'[135] The squadron of Royal Canadian Dragoons attempting to skirt the wood from the north suffered a similar experience at the hands of another German battalion, and also took refuge in the wood.

Lord Strathcona's Horse now came up and advanced into the northern part of the wood with two dismounted squadrons. The regiment then received new orders from Seely for its reserve squadron, C Squadron under Lieutenant Gordon Flowerdew, to ride round the wood from the north and attack mounted into the enemy rear, while the rest of the regimental advance continued through the wood dismounted. Coming round the wood and seeing Germans only 300 yards away, Flowerdew's weak squadron of about 75 men charged a German front line consisting of a company of the Saxon 101st Grenadier Regiment, with a short distance behind them the Württemberg 1st Battalion of 122nd Fusilier Regiment with a machine-gun company and an artillery battery. The fire of five infantry companies with machine-guns and artillery effectively wiped out the charging Canadian squadron: 24 men were killed, 15 later died of wounds including Lieutenant Flowerdew, and only one man is known to have survived the day unharmed.

This much is common ground between the German and Canadian accounts. But the official account of this episode by 101st Grenadier Regiment described the charge as a complete failure, 'the last horses collapsed 200 metres in front of our company. Only one horse and two wounded troopers reached our line', meaning the first German line.[136] This cannot in any way be reconciled with Lieutenant Flowerdew's Victoria Cross citation, which reads in part:

> The squadron (less one troop) passed over both [enemy] lines, killing many of the enemy with the sword; and wheeling about galloped on them again. Although the squadron had lost about 70 per cent of its members, killed and wounded from rifle and machine-gun fire directed on it from the front and both flanks, the enemy broke and retired.[137]

Brigadier General Seely's personal account was that, 'It was recorded that seventy Germans were killed by sword thrust alone outside the wood. I saw perhaps another two or three hundred lying there, who had been killed by [Canadian] machine-gun fire.'[138]

After the charge, the Fort Garry Horse came up to reinforce the Canadian attack, joined later by artillery support and by the British 3rd Cavalry Brigade, which used the same tactics as the Canadians by galloping mounted onto the ridge until they came under heavy fire, then dismounting to resume the advance. For the rest of the day the two cavalry brigades contested the woods with the Germans, preventing them from advancing to secure the river crossing. The Canadian casualties for the day's fighting were 305 men and at least 800 horses; the two German divisions recorded higher losses over a period of several days. The delay imposed at Moreuil Wood was

---

135 Quoted in Grodzinski and McNorgan, 'It's a Charge, Boys, It's a Charge!', p. 260; the account of Moreuil Wood given here draws particularly on this work and on Anglesey, *A History of the British Cavalry Volume 8*, pp. 198–214.
  136 Quoted in Grodzinski and McNorgan, 'It's a Charge, Boys, It's a Charge!', p. 265.
  137 Quoted in Anglesey, *A History of the British Cavalry Volume 8*, pp. 205–6.
  138 Seely, *Adventure*, p. 304.

an important factor in the defeat of the German offensive, and both eyewitnesses and historians attributed the German failure to press their attack to their anxiety, after Flowerdew's charge, that cavalry might once again appear behind them. In this sense, whether or not the small Canadian charge against greatly superior numbers succeeded tactically is much less important than its wider impact upon the enemy's behaviour.

Faced with these problems of evidence and interpretation of cavalry combats, the only possible choice is to shift the perspective away from the tactical event to its verifiable consequences. The charge at High Wood had no long term or major consequences for either side, but clearly it did not result in the futile massacre of the troops involved. The charge at Huj was a minor tactical success which helped maintain the momentum of a much greater British victory, and a validation of the tactical doctrine employed. The Canadian action at Moreuil Wood, including the mounted charges it involved, was a significant success, and also a validation of the tactical doctrine employed.

Such assessments form a yardstick whereby the success of the cavalry, its doctrine and its reforms before and during the First World War may reasonably be judged. The story of the cavalry – including the yeomanry and the cavalry and mounted troops of the Empire – on the battlefield is an emotional and dramatic one of courage, death, and occasionally of black farce, and no account of war can afford to ignore these elements. But British cavalry doctrine in the First World War was also shaped by high politics, by social and economic issues of which most cavalry officers were only vaguely aware if at all, by the actions of a formidable series of military personalities, and by a debate that had begun many, many years before.

Chapter 2

The Wolseley Era 1880–1899

For several decades before the 1880s, the British Army's concerns about the future and doctrines of cavalry were chiefly a matter for a few military theorists, predominantly retired officers or their intelligent and ambitious juniors. In 1859 a Prussian quarterly journal gave its opinion that Prussia and the rest of Germany produced 50 per cent of all didactic military literature, France 25 per cent, and Great Britain perhaps one per cent, a reflection both of the lack of formal or written doctrine in British military thinking, and of a strong German sense of their own superiority in such matters.[1] The British Army had considerable experience of the role of cavalry and other mounted troops in colonial warfare, as well as observing wars fought in Europe and North America. But it was the political changes, from the 1870s onwards, in the way that Great Britain and its Empire was defended, together with a re-structuring of the Army to conform to these changes, which made the future role and value of the cavalry such an important issue.[2] In particular, the actions and views of Sir Garnet Wolseley (Lord Wolseley from 1882) played a significant part in determining cavalry doctrine, and in shaping the debate. Affectionately known at the time as 'our only general', Wolseley's reputation has fluctuated over time; but he was widely recognised by contemporaries as the Army's leading reformer, and the unofficial leader of the 'Wolseley Ring' of heroic officers, first formed in the Ashanti War of 1873–1874 and otherwise known as the 'Ashanti Ring', or to its denigrators as 'The Mutual Admiration Society'.[3]

Following the Indian Mutiny and the 1858 Government of India Act, the British government assumed formal control over the Indian Army, the cost of which was borne by Indian taxpayers. From then on, the central issue for the British Army was to provide enough troops, on a voluntary basis and at a cost acceptable to the Treasury, to garrison Great Britain and Ireland (including actions in 'aid to the civil power' and as a defence against rebellion), and also to garrison India with a preferred ratio of about one British battalion to every three Indian battalions, while leaving enough troops over for the Army's remaining functions; as a result, by 1893 about a third of the British Army's fighting strength was stationed in India.[4] Achieving this balance between garrisoning India and all the other requirements of British

---

1 *Deutsches Vierteljahrschrift* 1859, Number 2, p. 69, quoted in Vagts, *A History of Militarism*, p. 226.
2 For an overview of Imperial defence in the period 1856–1956 see Kennedy (ed.), *Imperial Defence*.
3 Kochanski, *Sir Garnet Wolseley*, pp. 109–98 and pp. 213–56. The Ashanti War is sometimes known as the Asante War.
4 Goodenough and Dalton, *The Army Book for the British Empire*, p. 41.

defence within a stringent budget was the chief objective of every reform undertaken by successive Secretaries of State for War, from Edward Cardwell in 1870–1872 through to Richard Burdon Haldane in 1905–1912.[5]

The Cardwell reforms were prompted partly by the Army's weaknesses as exposed in the Crimean War, in particular the lack of any substantial trained reserves, and partly by the Prussian victories in the Austro-Prussian War of 1866 ('the Seven Weeks' War'), and in the Franco-Prussian War. Cardwell's most important reforms introduced short service for the other ranks (initially six years with the colours and six with the reserve), and under the Localisation Act of 1872 linked regular infantry battalions together in pairs based in sub-districts of the United Kingdom, with the intention that one battalion should serve overseas and the other at home, also linking the local militia and volunteer battalions to these regiments to provide the basis for a larger reserve. The process was continued by Hugh Childers in 1880–1882, transforming the linked infantry battalions into regiments based mostly on county recruiting areas, typically giving each regiment a new title, two regular battalions, a militia battalion, and one or more volunteer battalions. The regiments of the British Army already had considerable autonomy and institutional pride, and an important part of the reasoning behind this new structure was to encourage recruiting and retention, by promoting regimental *espirit de corps* still further and minimising cross-posting between regiments. By 1882 about two-thirds of all regular British soldiers served in infantry regiments that were notionally structured in this way, although practical necessity and some resistance within the Army meant that there were several exceptions and anomalies.[6]

These reforms to the infantry contrasted with the lack of any equivalent reforms to the cavalry, (or to the artillery, in which cross-posting between batteries and regiments was normal), and the lack of any official attempt to link the cavalry institutionally with the yeomanry. The British cavalry of 1870–1880 was badly in need of reform, with obsolete firearms and equipment, shortages of horses with few regiments able to field more than 300 mounted troopers, and repeated claims by experienced officers that the cavalry was unfit for war.[7] But both Cardwell and Childers saw the infantry as their priority, and neither they nor their successors made any attempt to address the cavalry in the same radical fashion. Even the modest reform of officially introducing squadrons rather than troops, attempted in 1869, was withdrawn after a year.[8] An attempt under Childers to link cavalry regiments

---

5 French, *Military Identities*, pp. 10–58; Spiers, *The Late Victorian Army*, pp. 2–24; Barnett, *Britain and Her Army*, pp. 299–324; Strachan, *The Politics of the British Army*, pp. 44–117; Bond, *The Victorian Army and the Staff College*; French and Holden Reid (eds), *The British General Staff: Reform and Innovation 1890–1939*; Gooch, *The Plans of War*; Hamer, *The British Army*; Harries-Jenkins, *The Army in Victorian Society*; Spiers, *Haldane*.

6 French, *Military Identities*, pp. 10–30; Spiers, *The Late Victorian Army*, pp. 2–24.

7 Verner, *The Military Life of H.R.H. George Duke of Cambridge*, Volume II, p. 41; 'Horses and Horsemen for the British Army', *Colburn's United Service Magazine*, 1872 Part I, p. 370; Baker, 'Organisation and Employment of Cavalry', *Journal of the Royal United Service Institution*, Volume 17, pp. 375–97; [Anon], *Notes on Cavalry Tactics, Organisation etc, by a Cavalry Officer*, p. 252.

8 Rogers, *The Mounted Troops of the British Army 1066–1945*, pp. 215–16.

together was also abandoned because of regimental opposition.[9] This failure to carry out reforms of the cavalry's structure and recruiting methods resulted in serious problems for the Army over the next two decades, culminating in an acute shortage of cavalry in the Boer War.[10]

By 1871, as part of Cardwell's plans, all regular British Army combat troops had been withdrawn from Canada, Australia, and New Zealand, leaving the deterrent power of the Royal Navy as their principal defence. The colonies were also encouraged to help pay for their own defence, and to develop their own forces, which included a few permanent cavalry regiments, such as the Royal Canadian Dragoons, founded in 1883, and in Australia the New South Wales Lancers, founded in 1894.[11] In South Africa, where British regular forces continued to be stationed, there were already part-time volunteer mounted rifle regiments such as the Natal Carbineers, founded in 1855, and the Natal Mounted Police, a permanently embodied paramilitary unit; although an attempt between 1878 and 1881 to augment the Cape Mounted Rifles with a much cheaper volunteer yeomanry ended in failure.[12] Throughout the Empire, for more than 40 years, the repeated requirement was for 'men who could ride and shoot' to serve as volunteers, but with very limited results. By the end of the nineteenth century, Natal's mounted forces numbered 1,601 volunteers and 659 police, while Cape Colony was only slightly better off with 1,066 full time regulars, 3,672 volunteers of all kinds, and 1,061 men in mounted rifle clubs, compared to an estimated English-speaking population of 190,000 in both colonies.[13]

From the Carnarvon Commission of 1879 onwards, the idea of a coherent grand strategy and a structure for Imperial defence developed slowly over the next two decades, including the view that the colonies might provide volunteer contingents for service outside their own borders. The prototype of these contingents was a small force sent by New South Wales to Suakin in the Sudan in 1885, and its culmination

---

9 French, *Military Identities*, pp. 29–30.

10 Goodenough and Dalton, *The Army Book for the British Empire*, p. 100.

11 Kennedy, *The Rise and Fall of British Naval Mastery*, pp. 177–202; Grey, *A Military History of Australia*, p. 22 and p. 38; Morton, *A Military History of Canada*, pp. 85–93; Belich, *The New Zealand Wars*. The New South Wales Lancers began as the New South Wales Cavalry Reserves in 1885 and were converted to lancers in 1894. The Canadian Militia Act of 1883 established the Canadian militia and a small number of regular units including a single cavalry regiment which, after a number of name changes, became the Royal Canadian Dragoons in 1893; the regiment officially dates its foundation to 1883. A second Canadian regular cavalry regiment was formed in 1909 as Lord Strathcona's Horse (Royal Canadians), a title derived from Strathcona's Horse, the mounted rifle regiment formed for the Boer War and later disbanded.

12 Morris, *The Washing of the Spears*, p. 301; Lock and Quantrill, *Zulu Victory*, pp. 42–4; Anglesey, *A History of the British Cavalry Volume 3*, p. 179. Originally raised as the Natal Carabiniers in 1855, the regiment's name went through several changes after about 1905 before becoming officially the *Natal Carbineers* in about 1925, and briefly the *Royal Natal Carbineers* 1934–1961; the version *Natal Carbineers* was in common use from the later nineteenth century.

13 Maurice, *History of the War in South Africa 1899–1902*, Volume I, p. 94; Lock and Quantrill, *Zulu Victory*, p. 29; Spence, 'To Shoot and to Ride', pp. 115–28; Wessels, 'Afrikaners at War', p. 73.

was the extensive Empire volunteer movement of the Boer War.[14] This was also a period of considerable British emigration overseas: departures for Australia and New Zealand peaked in 1879, but continued to rise for North America including Canada, and for various parts of Africa, up to the start of the First World War. Many of the colonial volunteers were first-generation immigrants born in the United Kingdom, and some had previous military experience with the British Army.[15]

The period of Army reorganisation in the 1870s and 1880s overlapped with considerable British Imperial military expansion, involving the dispatch of expeditionary forces from Great Britain and from India for sizeable colonial wars, from the Ashanti War of 1873–1874 to the Third Burmese War of 1885–1886, without any corresponding increase in the Army's size.[16] There is little evidence of any consistent British government policy behind this great upsurge of Imperial expansion.[17] At least part of the motivation was a response to a decline in British agriculture and traditional industries between 1873 and 1896, once described as 'the great depression', which also affected the recruiting base of the yeomanry.[18] Political and financial orthodoxy held that the Empire was a source of wealth rather than an expense, and that its expansion and upkeep should be as inexpensive as possible. In consequence, British Army doctrine in the 1880s was that any force sent to fight in Europe would almost certainly consist of regular troops, but that home defence against invasion (should the Royal Navy fail) would involve the militia, rifle volunteers and yeomanry; and that for colonial warfare British regular troops ('Imperial' soldiers in this context) would form a reliable core augmented by Indian or colonial forces, including troops recruited locally or temporarily and led by British officers. Garnet Wolseley's 'Ring' was only the most prominent of a number of unofficial groupings of officers who supported each other in finding places on these colonial expeditions as a way of enhancing their careers. Wolseley met several of his future Ring members during the Red River Expedition in Canada in 1870, for which he also successfully formed an experimental corps of mounted infantry.[19]

Other than the Second Afghan War of 1878–1880, all British wars of the period up to 1914 that needed mounted troops in significant numbers took place either in Egypt and the Sudan, or in southern Africa. Until the 1880s, training the cavalry was entirely

---

14 Bou, 'The Evolution and Development of the Australian Light Horse, 1860–1945', pp. 38–50; Grey, *A Military History of Australia*, pp. 45–62; Badsey, 'New Wars, New Press, New Country?' pp. 34–46.

15 Pooley and Turnbull, *Migration and Mobility in Britain Since the 18th Century*, pp. 279–80; Grey, *A Military History of Australia*, pp. 53–62; see also Morton, *When Your Number's Up*, pp. 277–9.

16 Farwell, *Queen Victoria's Little Wars*, pp. 190–294; Bond (ed.), *Victorian Military Campaigns*; Stewart, *The Pagoda War*.

17 See Judd, *Empire*, pp. 104–29; Hobsbawm, *The Age of Empire 1875–1914*, pp. 56–83; Kiernan, *Colonial Empires and Armies 1815–1960*, pp. 123–78; Kennedy, *The Rise and Fall of British Naval Mastery*, pp. 181–2; Spiers, *The Late Victorian Army*, pp. 272–4.

18 Searle, *A New England?*, pp. 183–6; Beales, *From Castlereagh to Gladstone*, pp. 221–9.

19 Hutton, *Five Lectures on Mounted Infantry*, Lecture Four, pp. 25–6; Beckett, *The Victorians at War*, pp. 8–9.

the responsibility of the Inspector General of Cavalry in London, rather than that of the general commanding any peacetime all-arms formation that included cavalry, such as at Aldershot; and there was no automatic reason for a British infantry general to have studied the uses of cavalry, or of artillery or engineering.[20] For colonial wars, any problems caused by a shortage of scouting troops, and by lack of information about the enemy, were expected to be offset by the tactical superiority of British infantry and artillery once the enemy was found. One of the most influential British military works, *Small Wars: Their Principles and Practice* by Charles Callwell of the Royal Artillery (which went through three editions between 1896 and 1906), summarised this prevailing doctrinal position:

> The strategical conditions in small wars favour the enemy... Strategy is not, however, the final arbiter in war. The battle-field decides, and on the battle-field the advantages pass over to the regular army. Superior armament, the force of discipline, a definite and acknowledged chain of responsibility, spirit de corps [sic], the moral force of civilisation, all these work together to give the trained and organised army an incontestable advantage from the point of view of tactics.[21]

British forces (meaning a cocktail of nationalities with Imperial troops as the main ingredient) were meant to invade hostile territory with confidence, and then when attacked in retaliation they were expected to destroy the enemy with disciplined firepower. As a matter of policy and racial ideology, the British before 1914 would not use Indian combat troops against Europeans or white people in general, particularly excluding them from the Transvaal War and the Boer War, and their tactics and training reflected this. Otherwise the Indian Army was increasingly used to provide troops for campaigns outside India, including for Egypt in 1882 and 1884–1885, and for the reconquest of the Sudan in 1896–1898.[22]

The result of this combination of Imperial expansion, military reorganisation, and severe financial restriction at home was that in the course of the 1880s the Army became severely overstretched. The Cardwell–Childers system of linked battalions and localised recruiting for the infantry broke down almost as soon as it was established, and major political rows were coupled with demands for further reforms.[23] Despite the utterly different strategic circumstances faced by Great Britain and the newly unified Germany, it was still hard for critics to understand how Germany could mobilise 19 Army Corps for war for an equivalent cost of £19,300,000 a year, while the British Army, which cost £14,600,000 a year, could not guarantee to field one such Corps.[24] These were also years of high unemployment and popular unrest in which the need for troops to control rioting at home loomed large, culminating in November 1887 in the suppression of the 'Bloody Sunday' riot

---

20 Robertson, *Soldiers and Statesmen 1914–1918*, Volume I, p. 3; French, *The Life of Field Marshal Sir John French*, pp. 29–30.

21 Callwell, *Small Wars*, p. 90.

22 Judd, *Empire*, pp. 77–8; Nasson, *Britannia's Empire*, pp. 186–7; Searle, *A New England?* pp. 252–8.

23 French, *Military Identities*, pp. 57–8; Hamer, *The British Army*, pp. 80–82.

24 Hamer, *The British Army*, p. 111.

in Trafalgar Square.[25] As complaints mounted, in 1888 Wolseley as Adjutant General gave an unprecedented speech in the House of Lords challenging the viability of government policy towards the Army; and in 1891 the demands for reform produced the Hartington Commission and the first steps towards creating a proper General Staff.[26] It was this much larger political debate, including the dominating issue of cost, which drove the British Army's subsidiary debate over its cavalry and mounted forces.

In December 1886, the renewed possibility of either a French invasion or a war in Europe produced a new Army mobilisation scheme, principally authored by Colonel Sir Henry Brackenbury as Director of Military Intelligence, under which the home Army would form two Corps and a cavalry division, either for home defence (with an additional Corps composed partly of militia and volunteers), or for dispatch overseas. In June 1891 the 'Stanhope Memorandum' authored by Secretary of State for War Edward Stanhope, confirmed Brackenbury's scheme, identifying military aid to the civil power in Great Britain and Ireland as the Army's first priority, followed by the garrisoning of India and the colonies, and then providing a force of two Corps and a cavalry division, for home defence or for dispatch overseas if needed. According to Stanhope, the size and nature of this force was not based on any calculation of grand strategy or military requirement, but purely 'how we could get the maximum result out of the existing force with the minimum of change and expense'.[27] Brackenbury's scheme for an expeditionary force of two Corps and a cavalry division (plus a third Corps in reserve) remained the standard for the British Army up to 1914. But the new plan also exposed the lack of attention paid to the cavalry by Cardwell and Childers, when Brackenbury discovered that there was little chance of mobilising even one Corps because of a shortage of horsed troops to carry out the critical roles of scouting and protection for the infantry and artillery, known as 'divisional cavalry' roles, with enough cavalry remaining to form a cavalry division as well.[28] The Duke of Cambridge, the Commander-in-Chief of the Army (C-in-C), minuted Wolseley in January 1887 that 'We have absolutely not got the full complement of cavalry for the two proposed Army Corps, and then there is nothing left to fall back on as a reserve for the absolute requirements in Ireland and England should the Army Corps be required to take the field.'[29] When the Treasury offered to permit some extra horses for Corps transport and for creating some mounted infantry, as long as an equal number was taken from the cavalry, Cambridge as C-in-C and Wolseley as Adjutant General, the professional heads of the Army of the greatest Empire in the world, found themselves agonising over whether the cavalry could spare just 240 horses.

---

25 Searle, *A New England?*, p. 156 and pp. 183–4; Babington, *Military Intervention in Britain*, pp. 121–2.

26 Kochanski, *Sir Garnet Wolseley*, pp. 181–2; Hamer, *The British Army*, pp. 92–147.

27 Hamer, *The British Army*, p. 107; Dunlop, *The Development of the British Army 1899–1914*, p. 307; Beckett, *The Victorians at War*, pp. 151–60.

28 Gooch, *The Plans of War*, p. 8.

29 HPL Wolseley Papers W/Mem/1: Memorandum from Cambridge to Wolseley, [no day] January 1887. Technically Cambridge's official title became Commander-in-Chief only in 1887; see Heathcote, *The British Field Marshals 1736–1997*, pp. 141–3.

Wolseley minuted that to discuss reducing the cavalry was a waste of time, and that the removal of even a single horse would seriously impair the Army's efficiency.[30]

All these factors – the discovery that Brackenbury's two Corps' scheme could not work because of a shortage of cavalry, the already existing debate including the experiments with mounted infantry, the aspiration that the colonies might provide mounted troops for future wars, and the likelihood of continuing colonial wars involving a combination of regular cavalry with other kinds of mounted troops – combined to give the issue of the future and doctrine of cavalry its considerable importance from the 1880s until the outbreak of the First World War.

The British Army's orthodoxy for cavalry tactical doctrine was set out for a generation of officers in Colonel Francis Clery's standard subaltern's textbook *Minor Tactics* of 1875, 'The force of cavalry lies in the combined action of man and horse. This is represented in its fullest form by the shock of collision with the enemy. Hence, although cavalry is armed with fire and hand-to-hand weapons, the latter remains always the principal, the former being the accessory.'[31] Cavalry were not meant to fight infantry except by charging them, and they were not meant to charge without firepower support. Although cavalry drill allowed for firing mounted, the prevailing British belief was that saddle fire was largely ineffective, and that so was any pistol or revolver fire beyond point-blank range, mounted or dismounted.[32] But the institutional power of the regiments meant that in practice they were allowed to choose their own tactics, including their use of firearms. As early as 1838, a hussar regiment and a dragoon guard regiment were sent to Canada equipped with new percussion carbines and trained in fighting dismounted; and another dragoon guard regiment was sent to the Cape in 1843 trained and equipped with infantry rifles and bayonets.[33] Before the introduction of the new Martini-Henry .45-inch breechloading carbine in 1877–1878, the only firearm carried by troopers in lancer regiments (except for a few carbine-equipped skirmishers in each troop) was an obsolete muzzleloading pistol.[34] While some regiments welcomed the introduction of the Martini-Henry, a story went round the Army in the 1880s that one lancer regiment had ceremonially dumped their newly issued carbines on the regimental midden.[35] The Martini-Henry was also issued to the Indian cavalry in 1888, replacing the Snider .577-inch breechloading carbine, and was in its turn replaced in 1892 in

---

30 HPL Wolseley Papers W/Mem/1: Memorandum from Wolseley, 12 November 1885, and W/Mem/1: Memorandum from Wolseley 14 March 1887, p. 12.

31 Clery, *Minor Tactics*, p. 87; the same view is given in *Regulations for the Instruction and Movement of Cavalry 1876*, pp. 142–7.

32 'The Dragoon, His Horse and His Training', *Colburn's United Service Magazine*, 1864 Part III, p. 333; Baker, 'Organisation and Employment of Cavalry', *Journal of the Royal United Service Institution*, Volume 17, pp. 375–97; Smith, *Drill and Manoeuvres of Cavalry*, p. 269.

33 Havelock, *Three Main Military Questions of the Day*, p. 56; Beckett, *The Amateur Military Tradition 1558–1945*, p. 171; Strachan, *From Waterloo to Balaclava*, pp. 84–90.

34 Robertson, *From Private to Field Marshal*, p. 15.

35 This story was first published 1912 in Rimington, *Our Cavalry*, p. 17, who wrote that it was generally known when he joined the Army; he was commissioned into the 6th (Inniskilling) Dragoons in 1881.

British and Indian regiments by the .303-inch Martini-Metford carbine, followed in 1896 by the .303-inch Lee-Enfield and Lee-Metford magazine carbines.[36]

The introduction of effective carbines for the cavalry was accompanied by a search for recent historical examples of how cavalry had made use of such weapons. This led to a surprisingly acrimonious debate, based on conflicting interpretations of the nature of mounted troops in the American Civil War of 1861–1865, a matter on which by the 1890s some senior British officers were ready almost to come to blows with each other.[37] The greatest British interest in the Civil War had occurred during its first two years, when it seemed most likely that Great Britain might intervene militarily in the war, and most British officers, including Wolseley (who visited the rival armies), openly sympathised with the Confederacy.[38] But although British interest in the Civil War fell off because of the Franco-Prussian War, it was revived in the early 1890s especially through Henderson's influence at the Staff College, culminating in his book *Stonewall Jackson and the American Civil War* in 1898. Needing to include militia and volunteers in their mobilisation scheme, the British were interested in how American citizen soldiers had fought; and they also sought inspiration from Henderson in the manoeuvring skill of Major General Thomas 'Stonewall' Jackson's fast moving Confederate infantry (nicknamed the 'foot cavalry') in the Shenandoah Valley campaign of 1862, as a model for how a small number of elite divisions, such as their own regular forces, might fare in European war.[39]

In an indirect fashion, the British Army also became the inheritors of a breakthrough in cavalry doctrine that took place during the Civil War. The experience of American mounted troops in their wars with Native American Indians and on the Mexican frontier was broadly comparable to that of the British mounted forces in South Africa. US Army cavalry doctrine, based on European influences, officially acknowledged the primacy of the mounted charge, but in practice the small United States' mounted forces (two regiments entitled 'cavalry', two of 'dragoons' and one of 'mounted rifles') all adopted essentially the same tactics of fighting dismounted with carbines, and charging mounted only very occasionally.[40] Where the Americans differed most from the British was in preferring pistols to swords for the charge, and believing that saddle fire could be effective. All these practices were carried over

---

36   Anglesey, *A History of the British Cavalry Volume 3*, pp. 402–3.

37   The best account of British interest in the Civil War is still Luvaas, *The Military Legacy of the Civil War*, although his interpretation of views of the cavalry must now be seen as out of date, especially in the light of the three-volume work by Starr, *The Union Cavalry in the Civil War*. For an essential corrective to Luvaas on the cavalry issue see also Phillips, 'Scapegoat Arm', pp. 62–3.

38   Luvaas, *The Military Legacy of the Civil War*, pp. 100–118; Holden Reid, *The Origins of the American Civil War*, pp. 368–95.

39   Henderson, *Stonewall Jackson and the American Civil War*; Luvaas, *The Education of an Army*, pp. 225–9; Luvaas, *The Military Legacy of the Civil War*, pp. 170–202; Bond, *The Victorian Army and the Staff College*, p. 157 and p. 306.

40   Starr, *The Union Cavalry in the Civil War*, Volume I, pp. 53–4; Hagerman, *The American Civil War and the Origins of Modern Warfare*, pp. 20–21; Urwin, *The United States Cavalry*, pp. 90–106.

into the greatly expanded mounted forces of both the Union and Confederate armies in the Civil War.

In its first years, the Civil War saw very few mounted combats, and those mounted charges that did take place were on a small scale and usually unsuccessful.[41] Also, for the first time for many years in a major war, infantry in the Civil War were not usually trained to form square to receive cavalry, but to try to drive them off with firepower. The earliest British reactions were that the troopers and horses on both sides were undertrained, and that the American preference for dismounted fighting was a consequence of their military unpreparedness. Captain C.C. Chesney, Professor of Military History at the Staff College in 1864, described the cavalry on both sides as 'dragoons' in the original meaning of the word as mounted infantry, writing that 'Improvements in the organisation of armies have caused this arm of the service to disappear' in Great Britain and Europe.[42] This led rapidly to the argument that 'the Americans had no real cavalry', in the British or European sense.[43] By shortly after the Civil War's end, it had become doctrinal orthodoxy in the US Army that the cavalry of both sides had been mounted infantry who never fought, or sought to fight, except on foot. In 1866 Major General William Hopkins Morris, who had commanded an infantry brigade in the Army of the Potomac, told the Royal United Service Institution that 'It is scarcely conceivable that cavalry will ever again charge infantry in order.'[44] A decade later, a semi-official US Army account of the Russo-Turkish War of 1877–1878 confidently asserted:

> The employment of large bodies of cavalry on the field of battle belongs to the order of 'shock tactics' whose day is wholly past.... The true use of cavalry in modern warfare was developed in our civil war, viz. in scouting and reconnaissance, in independent raids against lines of communication and supply, in following up a retreat, and in doing its fighting always on foot. Since 1865 there has been nothing new on the subject.[45]

The view that cavalry in the Civil War fought only on foot, entirely rejecting the mounted charge, has carried over into modern historical studies as part of the wider debate on how far the Civil War should be seen as a precursor of the First World War, being interpreted as a deliberate and forward-looking response to the modernisation and industrialisation of warfare, rather than a failure in cavalry training and preparedness. This in turn is linked to the extent to which industrialisation of the

---

41 Griffith, *Rally Once Again*, pp. 179–80 calculates that in the years 1861–1863 there were just five charges made in major battles by the cavalry of the Army of the Potomac, a total of 1,300 Union cavalrymen who suffered 365 casualties for no verifiable result; see also Hagerman, *The American Civil War and the Origins of Modern Warfare*, pp. 56–7.

42 Chesney, *A Military View of the Recent Campaigns in Virginia and Maryland*, Volume 2, p. 227; see also Rawley (ed.), *The American Civil War: An English View*, p. 44; and Fremantle, *Three Months in the Southern States*, p. 308.

43 Lieutenant Thompson (7th Hussars) in his introduction to Bonie, *The French Cavalry in 1870*, p. vii.

44 General William H. Morris, 'On the best method of arming, equipping and manoeuvring infantry', address to the Royal United Service Institution, 20 April 1866, reported in the *Journal of the Royal United Service Institution*, Volume 10, 1867, pp. 216–17.

45 Greene, *Report on the Russian Army and Its Campaigns in Turkey 1877–8*, p. 453.

battlefield took place both before and during the First World War, and the extent to which technological determinism constitutes an appropriate methodology for understanding the relationship between these wars.[46]

The Civil War caused particular interest in Canada, where in the later 1860s two military writers set out the basic positions that would form the substance of the British cavalry debate for the next half century. In 1867, Colonel Sir Harry Havelock VC, the Assistant Quartermaster General in Canada (and Indian Mutiny veteran), published a book of essays on *Three Main Military Questions of the Day*, which he considered to be the issue of Army reservists, the military defence of India, and thirdly 'cavalry as affected by breech-loading arms'. In a passage printed in block capitals for emphasis, Havelock wrote that 'INCREASED PRECISION, AND NOTABLY AND ESPECIALLY THE RAPID FIRE OF BREECHLOADERS, HAVE, ONCE AND FOR EVER, SET ASIDE THE SWAY THAT THE LANCE AND SABRE FORMERLY HELD.'[47] His model for the future was what he described as mounted infantry, mentioning particularly the 1st Hampshire Light Horse Volunteers. Havelock was quite scathing about the cavalry, writing that he expected opposition from 'all but the more enlightened, reflecting and observant of the cavalry officers of the old school', while laughing at 'the British lancer with his flag and pole'.[48]

Havelock's book had some influence on Wolseley, and was part of the inspiration for a much more influential work, *Modern Cavalry* published in 1868 by Lieutenant Colonel George Denison, commander of the Governor General of Canada's Bodyguard, who had first met Wolseley during the Fenian invasion scare of 1866. Denison's men were trained as mounted riflemen, and Wolseley considered that 'no similar number of regular cavalry could have done that duty as effectively'.[49] Getting his information chiefly from former Confederate cavalrymen who had fled to Canada (so giving him a very poor opinion of Union forces), Denison argued that in future cavalry should once more consist of two distinct arms. One of these would be heavy cavalry, equipped solely with the arme blanche (and perhaps also a pistol) and trained only to charge, so that 'the moral effect of this training would have a wonderful effect, not only on themselves, but on the enemy', and they would be able to charge through any opposition, apparently even steady infantry.[50] For his second type of horsemen, which he intended to form the considerable majority, Denison's terminology was extremely loose, describing them as 'dragoons', as 'mounted riflemen', or sometimes as 'light horse'. He intended troops like these to be used for scouting, and to be armed with rifles or carbines, with revolvers, and with a sword carried on the horse for the rare occasions that it might be needed. Denison

---

46 See Hagerman, *The American Civil War and the Origins of Modern Warfare*, pp. 56–7; Phillips, 'The Obsolescence of the *Arme Blanche* and Technological Determinism in British Military History', pp. 39–59; Luvaas, *The Military Legacy of the Civil War*.

47 Havelock, *Three Main Military Questions of the Day*, p. 35; capitals as in the original; Kochanski, *Sir Garnet Wolseley*, p. 38; Luvaas, *The Military Legacy of the Civil War*, pp. 109–11.

48 Havelock, *Three Main Military Questions of the Day*, p. 38.

49 Wolseley, *The Story of a Soldier's Life*, Volume II, pp. 148–9; Luvaas, *The Military Legacy of the Civil War*, pp. 111–13.

50 Denison, *Modern Cavalry*, p. 73 and p. 163.

offered the fact that these soldiers would not be as well trained as charging cavalry as a benefit, since 'the same time is not required to create the same skill in the use of the rifle', as the sword, 'and under any circumstances it is not as important'.[51] He repeated and expanded on these ideas in a further book, *A History of Cavalry from the Earliest Times*, written in 1877 in response to a prize offered by the Czar of Russia, which was also translated into German and published in Berlin in 1879. This book may have had some influence on Russian cavalry, and later on twentieth-century Soviet and American doctrines of manoeuvre.[52]

Neither Havelock nor Denison specified exactly how their proposed changes would relate to the existing British Army or to the defence of the Empire. Havelock's confident view that the cavalry charge was obsolete and that mounted infantry were the only future was actually quite reactionary for the time, looking back to the beliefs and attitudes of the 1850s. Denison's book looked forward to the idea of well trained cavalry supported by a much larger body of under-trained or improvised mounted riflemen, and he may well have hoped that these would include an expanded Canadian mounted militia. But his view that the cavalry should be taught nothing but the arme blanche charge was also reactionary. Even the notoriously conservative Duke of Cambridge told the Royal United Service Institution in 1865 that 'There should be masses of light cavalry. Probably the day of heavy cavalry has somewhat passed by', although adding that they might still be needed 'at a critical moment'.[53] The idea of two separate mounted arms, one of cavalry trained for the arme blanche charge and the other of mounted riflemen, was also described approvingly in the standard textbook *Operations of War* by Colonel Edward Hamley, Professor of Military History at the Staff College in 1866, although like many others Hamley left open the issue of whether the arme blanche cavalry should also carry a firearm and be prepared to fight dismounted.[54]

As more evidence on the Civil War became available in the later nineteenth century, the interpretation that Civil War cavalry were mounted infantry (either by choice or necessity) was challenged in Great Britain, particularly by Henderson, whose views have largely been confirmed by Stephen Z. Starr's monumental study of the Union cavalry.[55] Although mounted infantry were used as a temporary expedient, cavalry commanders on both sides, including J.E.B. 'Jeb' Stuart and Philip Sheridan, trained their men as cavalry rather than mounted rifles, and expected them to fight mounted. Both Wolseley and Henderson thought that the major factors in there being few cavalry charges at the start of the war were the heavily wooded country of the

---

51   Ibid., p. 394, and also pp. 20–29.

52   Denison, *A History of Cavalry From the Earliest Times*, pp. ix–x; see also Bellamy, *The Evolution of Modern Land Warfare*, p. 128. The author is grateful to Professor Christopher Bellamy for this reference.

53   Cambridge in the discussion of Chesney, 'Sherman's Campaign in Georgia', *The Journal of the Royal United Service Institution*, Volume 9, p. 220.

54   Hamley, *Operations of War*, pp. 433–6; Bond, *The Victorian Army and the Staff College*, pp. 83–9; Luvaas, *The Education of an Army*, pp. 130–68.

55   Starr, *The Union Cavalry in the Civil War*, especially Volume I, pp. 366–96 and Volume II, pp. 589–94.

South, and lack of training.[56] But small-scale charges became more common as the war progressed, sometimes by cavalrymen armed only with pistols, and these were used as part of manoeuvres by increasingly larger formations.[57] Sheridan deliberately encouraged the mass use of cavalry and of mounted tactics in order to dominate the enemy cavalry.[58] By the last year of the war, the Union cavalry in particular, armed with Spencer repeating carbines as well as swords, had evolved a very effective new style of tactics combining mobility with mounted and dismounted fighting.[59]

In 1902, in one of his last pieces of writing, Henderson admiringly summarised the new British interpretation of the Union and Confederate cavalry achievement, in a passage that set the later Civil War cavalry as the standard to which British cavalry reformers should aspire:

> Their cavalry, in the beginning, was formed, as far as possible, on the European model. But before long it became a new type. It could manoeuvre sufficiently well for all practical purposes. It was exceedingly mobile. It could charge home with sabre or the revolver. In addition, it was so equipped that it could fight on foot as readily as in the saddle, and it was so armed and trained that when dismounted it was little inferior to the infantry… The instances of cavalry charging infantry are so numerous as to disprove the common belief that the American horsemen were merely mounted infantry. The truth is that the Americans struck the balance between shock and dismounted tactics. They were prepared for both, as the ground and the situation demanded; and, more than this, they used fire and *l'arme blanche* in the closest and most effective combination, against both cavalry and infantry. Due respect was paid to individualism. The veteran trooper, when in the last years of the war he attained the proficiency at which his great leaders had always aimed, was a good shot, a skilful skirmisher, a good horseman, and a useful swordsman.[60]

While the predictions of previous decades had been that infantry firepower would make cavalry obsolete, the interpretation of the 1890s and 1900s was that cavalry using firepower in combination with the charge could even defeat infantry, and so act with much greater independence. British cavalrymen were particularly impressed by the cavalry raids deep behind enemy lines that were a feature of the Civil War on both sides. By the First World War, to have 'done a regular Jeb Stuart ride' with cavalry deep into the enemy rear positions was the aspiration of every British and Imperial cavalry commander.[61]

Why after the Civil War the US Army largely failed to acknowledge its own accomplishment in developing this cavalry tactical doctrine is a question that has yet to be answered. One possible explanation is that after 1865 the US Cavalry reverted to being a small all-volunteer force engaged in Indian wars, fighting mostly or entirely on foot, with the occasional rare pistol charge in loose order, and virtually

---

56 Henderson, *The Science of War*, pp. 246–7.

57 Duke, *A History of Morgan's Cavalry*, p. 181; Gilmore, *Four Years in the Saddle*, p. 145; Mosby, *The Memoirs of Colonel John S. Mosby*, p. 152.

58 Sheridan, *The Personal Memoirs of P.H. Sheridan*, Volume I, p. 354 and p. 453.

59 Starr, *The Union Cavalry in the Civil War*, Volume I, pp. 3–46.

60 Henderson, *The Science of War*, pp. 55–6.

61 Hill, *Chauvel of the Light Horse*, p. 171; see also Jones, *The Art of War in the Western World*, pp. 409–19.

gave up carrying swords.[62] Often their tactics were determined by the poor quality of their horses and equipment, and sometimes of their recruits.[63] But whereas European powers like France and Germany saw no need for mounted riflemen, and the British openly expected their mounted riflemen to accept an inferior status, the US Cavalry adopted a position of American exceptionalism, claiming their dismounted tactics as a mark of superiority over the sword-wielding Europeans. Instead of being transmitted in a coherent fashion by the Americans to the rest of the world, the idea of a newly versatile cavalry, combining manoeuvre, firepower and mounted shock through the interaction of small units, evolved slowly in British military thought, to be fully rediscovered over three decades later in the Boer War.

Between 1865 and about 1890 British interest in the Civil War was temporarily eclipsed by the Prussian victories in the Austro-Prussian War and again in the Franco-Prussian War. Study of these wars in considerable detail became a staple of British Army officer training, together with extensive reading of German and French military writers.[64] But for most British military theorists, the cavalry's performance was again a secondary issue. The Austro-Prussian War was fought by the Prussians with Dreyse breechloaders against the Austrians with muzzleloading rifles (Prussia's allies including Italy also used muzzleloaders); while the Franco-Prussian War was the first major war fought with infantry breechloaders on both sides, plus rifled breechloading cannon for the Prussians. The main British concerns were to understand the difference made to war by these weapons, and to learn the techniques of staffwork by which the Prussians had controlled and moved their new mass armies.

On all sides in both Prussian wars, the cavalry were believed to have done badly in scouting and on the battlefield; but in the light of earlier claims most theorists were surprised to find that there was any role for the cavalry at all, and that the battlefield charge had not proved completely obsolete. In the Austro-Prussian War, a massed cavalry charge at Stresetice, at the end of the Battle of Könniġrätz, enabled the defeated Austrians to retreat in reasonable order from the battlefield by inflicting a delay on the advancing Prussians; and there were a handful of smaller mounted combats.[65] Austrian cavalry also made some charges at the Battle of Custoza, but these were controversial actions against poor quality Italian infantry with muzzleloaders, who repulsed them only by forming square.[66] In the Franco-Prussian War the cavalry charges at Mars-la-Tour, which led to the Battle of Gravelotte and the trapping of the main French field army in the siege of Metz, received the greatest attention.[67] One grim lesson taken from these charges was that cavalry might have to charge against

---

62 Rickey, *Forty Miles a Day on Beans and Hay*, pp. 270–300.
63 Urwin, *The United States Cavalry*, pp 138–63; Leckie, *The Buffalo Soldiers*.
64 Luvaas, *The Education of an Army*, especially pp. 176–81.
65 von Wright and Hozier (trans.), *The Campaign of 1866 in Germany*, pp. 284–8; Chesney and Reeve, *The Military Resources of France and Prussia*, p. 122; Wood, *Achievements of Cavalry*, pp. 163–75. The Battle of Könniġrätz was also known as the Battle of Sadowa.
66 Wood, *Achievements of Cavalry*, pp. 141–62; see also Wawro, *The Austro-Prussian War*, pp. 104–7.
67 Wood, *Achievements of Cavalry*, pp. 205–38; Howard, *The Franco-Prussian War*, pp. 144–82.

apparently hopeless odds, for the greater good of an army that was already in peril, or to create the chance for a decisive victory.[68]

The greatest criticism levelled at cavalry in both wars, by British and European commentators, was that they had been held back rather than carrying out effective scouting and raiding, in contrast to the Civil War cavalry. The French cavalry were thought to have performed particularly badly: out of 65,160 Prussian and allied casualties in the Franco-Prussian War, losses from swords and lances – and clubbed rifles – were just six killed and 218 wounded.[69] In the Austro-Prussian War the Prussians had cavalry brigades but no independent cavalry divisions, something that they rectified in the Franco-Prussian War; but even so at Gravelotte and Sedan, just as at Custoza and Königgrätz, the mass armies appeared to blunder into one another.[70] Now the predictions of cavalry obsolescence in the 1850s were seen as being self-fulfilling: all sides had made poor use of their cavalry because they already believed cavalry to be useless, and changes in doctrine, weapons and tactics were expected to rectify this. Henderson later wrote that for cavalry 'the climax of incompetency [sic] may have been said to have been reached during that cycle of European warfare which began with the Crimea and ended with the Russo-Turkish conflict of 1877–78', and that the tactics of the Union cavalry of 1865 could have stopped the Prussian cavalry divisions of 1870 on the French frontier.[71]

The increasing independence required from cavalry also brought it into conflict with isolated infantry detachments, so that scouting Prussian cavalry facing French troops or franc-tireurs in 1870–1871 either took to carrying infantry rifles, or had battalions of Jäger light infantry attached to them for fire support. Major General Carl von Schmidt, one of the principal authors of the German Cavalry Regulations of 1875, argued, in a work translated (perhaps a little clumsily) by the War Office Intelligence Department in 1881, that:

> We must have more thorough independence for our arm resulting from the possession of a good long-range firearm, and from careful instruction in its use and in dismounted service; this will enable us to perform every kind of duty, which it is impossible to do on horseback. There is no occasion whatever to fear that this will impair the true cavalry spirit; indeed, it can only gain from it, as our arm will be able to accomplish the object in all situations, and will not always have to retreat before every occupied village, defile, &c., which would certainly deteriorate the spirit of the arm. I even go so far as to assert, that if cavalry is not able to fight effectively on foot under all circumstances, it is not up to its work, and not worth the sacrifices that the State makes to maintain it.[72]

---

68 Lehautcourt, 'Studies in Applied Cavalry Tactics', *Journal of the Royal United Service Institution*, Volume 52, pp. 236–1359 (serialised).

69 Childers, *German Influence on British Cavalry*, p. 6. Prussia led what was officially the Army of the North German Federation, with the Bavarians as allies, up to the declaration of the German Empire in January 1871.

70 von Wright and Hozier (trans.), *The Campaign of 1866 in Germany*, p. 205 and p. 301; Hozier, *The Seven Weeks' War*, Volume I, p. 207; Kraft, *Letters on Cavalry*, p. 95; Bonie, *The French Cavalry in 1870*, p. 33.

71 Henderson, *The Science of War*, pp. 52–3.

72 von Schmidt, *Instructions for the Training, Employment and Leading of Cavalry*, p. 121, see also translator's preface; the German original appeared in 1875. 'Franc-tireur' (free-

Von Schmidt followed up this endorsement of dismounted action with arguments that agreed very much with Henderson:

> It is then at least required of it, that we should be in a position to overcome the opposition dismounted cavalry. Moreover, weak infantry detachments should not be able to say to us, "*So far you may come, but no further*". In the next place, we must of course be able to provide for the security of our cantonments and defend them against attack; we must be able to occupy rapidly with dismounted men any important and distant points, and to hold them against the enemy until the infantry can arrive.[73]

Although later German cavalry doctrine included the provision for fighting on foot, their prevailing argument was that their conscript system did not allow enough training time for cavalry to learn dismounted fighting properly, and that combining cavalry with Jäger infantry was the better solution, despite the loss of mobility involved.[74]

The two main lessons for mounted troops taken by the British from the wars of 1861 to 1871 were that mounted scouting had increased considerably in importance, and that although firepower had increased it did not yet prevent horsed soldiers from playing a part in war, and even from charging mounted in battle. This was the start of a gradual revival in belief in the effectiveness of the cavalry. The British Army's official doctrine, as reflected in Clery's *Minor Tactics*, remained generally pessimistic:

> Modern warfare has reduced the role of cavalry on a battlefield to very insignificant proportions. It has ceased to be used in great masses, or rather the attempts to use it in this manner have yet scarcely produced satisfactory results. Employed in small bodies it can seldom produce effects other than temporary and indecisive.[75]

But this was increasingly challenged by another view that, as a Royal Engineer officer put it in 1871, 'To say that the day of cavalry on the field of battle is past, is merely another way of saying that the knowledge of how to use it is wanting.'[76]

In developing these ideas, the British still looked to German military analysts for guidance. Von Schmidt was among the first to argue that by using squadron columns and concealment offered by the ground, a force as large as a cavalry division might be able to execute a mounted attack over a distance of at least a mile, with the squadrons

---

shooter) was a French term for an irregular or guerrilla fighter; 'Jäger' or 'Jaeger'(hunter) was comparable to the French 'Chasseur', and was a distinction that by 1870 had only historical meaning.

73 Ibid., p. 187; emphasis in the original.

74 Chenevix-Trench, 'Progress in Developing the Capabilities of Cavalry', *Journal of the Royal United Service Institution*, Volume 21, p. 998; Kraft, *Letters on Cavalry*, pp. 242–4.

75 Clery, *Minor Tactics*, p. 145.

76 Major Home, Royal Engineers, quoted in [Anon], *Notes on Cavalry Tactics, Organisation etc, by a Cavalry Officer*, p. vi.

arriving from more than one direction at once.[77] He was also adamant that 'Infantry will always be attacked only in flank, and by several successive lines.'[78] Part of the British inspiration also came from *Letters on Cavalry* by General Prince Karl August Kraft zu Hohenlohe-Ingelfingen, translated in 1889, together with his equivalent musings on infantry and artillery. Prince Kraft was one of several writers to suggest that holding a large mass of cavalry back beyond enemy artillery range would mean that they would take too long to reach the point at which they were needed, and that one solution was to keep small formations concealed behind cover as far forward as possible, much as the Prussian 'Death Ride' troopers had been concealed at Mars la Tour.[79] By the late 1880s, the thinking was already in place for the major change in British cavalry tactical doctrine that was to follow in the next decade. The same ideas were to be revived by the British cavalry in 1915, consciously or not, to help solve the tactical problems of the Western Front.

While something resembling a British cavalry reform movement was gaining in strength, reform of the British Army at its highest level demanded by politicians in the late 1880s meant the progressive removal of informal or prerogative power from the sovereign, as represented by the Duke of Cambridge as C-in-C. Part of Cambridge's dislike of reform was that he saw the regiments and their traditions as the very heart of the Army, and he opposed the amalgamations introduced by Cardwell and Childers. In return, the regiments believed that they had the right to lobby or petition the sovereign independently of the military chain of command. Cambridge was replaced in 1895 by Wolseley (with reduced powers), rather than by Queen Victoria's son the Duke of Connaught as she had hoped, and continuing pressure for reform led to the abolition of the post of C-in-C in 1904.[80] But up to the First World War and beyond, most regimental officers saw their loyalty as being to the sovereign rather than the government, while several senior officers maintained close connections with the royal household.[81]

Among the unintended longer-term consequences of the Cardwell–Childers reforms was that they greatly increased the unofficial power of the regiments, increased the patronage power of some senior officers, and weakened the central authority of the General Staff even as it was being created. Cardwell's chief motive in ending the purchase of commissions was to aid the restructuring of the infantry regiments by removing the perception that each regiment was the property of its colonel.[82] But one great advantage of purchase in combination with patronage was

---

77 von Schmidt, *Instructions for the Training, Employment and Leading of Cavalry*, pp. 73–4 and pp. 120–34.

78 Ibid., p. 156.

79 Kraft, *Letters on Cavalry*, pp. 71–7; [Anon], *Notes on Cavalry Tactics, Organisation etc, by a Cavalry Officer*, pp. 27–41; 'Tactics on the Battle-field', *Colburn's United Service Magazine*, 1875 Part II, p. 374.

80 Strachan, *The Politics of the British Army*, pp. 92–122; Spiers, *The Late Victorian Army*, pp. 153–6; Hamer, *The British Army*, pp. 148–73.

81 Strachan, *The Politics of the British Army*, pp. 63–6 and pp. 201–2; Stewart, *The Ulster Crisis*, p. 108; Beckett, 'King George V and His Generals', pp. 247–64; Williams, *Byng of Vimy*, p. 18.

82 Barnett, *Britain and Her Army*, pp. 307–8.

that it had helped the rapid promotion of brave and talented officers, including Wolseley. These officers did not necessarily buy their next promotion, but they could exchange between regiments, moving to wherever an officer of the next highest rank was about to sell out and leave the Army, or to a regiment that was marked to take part in a forthcoming war. As the impoverished son of a deceased former officer, Wolseley received his first commission through the patronage of the C-in-C, and by exploiting this system rose to brevet lieutenant-colonel at the age of 25, transferring between four regiments without once needing to purchase.[83] Evelyn Wood won a commission in the 13th Light Dragoons (the future 13th Hussars) in 1855 in the Crimea, transferring from the Royal Navy, and served in four different regiments on his way to becoming a lieutenant colonel by 1873.[84] But Cardwell's reforms largely confined officers to their existing regiments, making transfers much more difficult, and also made seniority within the regiment the chief criterion for promotion rather than seniority within the Army as a whole.[85] Promotion examinations for junior officers, introduced in 1871, were dismissed by Wolseley as a 'farce', and although a selection board for senior officers headed by the C-in-C was created at the War Office in 1891, this was also a subject for satire rather than an effective instrument.[86] An effort was made in 1875 to prevent officers remaining in any one rank for too long, but this was mainly aimed at retirement rather than accelerated promotion, and also favoured the power of the regiments.[87] The importance of the Staff College was increasing both as a centre of doctrine and as part of the career path of successful officers, but most of this increase came after Cambridge's removal: in 1890, Staff College graduates were just one group or faction among many within the Army, accounting for only seven per cent of serving generals, a number that rose steeply to 39 per cent by 1910.[88] This produced a distinction in the First World War between a majority of senior officers who had attended the Staff College, including Haig, Henry Wilson, and William 'Wully' Robertson, and those only a few years older who had not, including French and Kitchener.

After the abolition of purchase, the most reliable route left for ambitious officers to get accelerated promotion was the informal one of obtaining the patronage of a high ranking officer, usually in order to secure a prominent position in a colonial campaign. This in turn created an unnatural but mutually beneficial relationship

---

83 Kochanski, *Sir Garnet Wolseley*, p. 3.

84 Wood, *From Midshipman to Field Marshal*, Volume I, pp. 115–254.

85 Spiers, *The Late Victorian Army*, pp. 90–94; Heathcote, *The Indian Army*, pp. 117–19; Anglesey, *A History of the British Cavalry Volume 3*, pp. 89–95.

86 HPL Wolseley Papers SSL 10/1, p. xxxvi manuscript. This is the unpublished manuscript of the unfinished portion of Wolseley's memoirs, *The Story of a Soldier's Life*, the first two volumes of which were published in 1909; see also Beckett, *The Victorians at War*, p. 8.

87 Anglesey, *A History of the British Cavalry Volume 3*, pp. 88–90; Spiers, *The Late Victorian Army*, pp. 90–94.

88 French, *Military Identities*, pp. 168–9; Bond, *The Victorian Army and the Staff College*, pp. 116–211. 'Serving generals' here means major generals, lieutenant generals, generals and field marshals on the active list, excluding royal appointments, medical officers etc.

between successful generals such as Wolseley and war reporters for the new popular newspapers that also emerged in the 1880s, as public reputation became an important factor for any general who hoped to secure a command.[89] Successful generals of this era also could not ignore the increasing power of the regiments, which had extended to the highest levels of the Army. In 1901, Lord Kitchener, a Royal Engineer officer by origin and to some extent outside the influence of the regimental system, questioned the Secretary of State for War:

> Has it ever occurred to you that when Mr Cardwell carried out the great reform amongst officers of the Army by the abolition of purchase…the reform went only half way and left the personal regimental rights of officers, called the regimental system, still existing. I cannot help thinking that the immense improvement in the training of officers caused by Mr Cardwell's reform points to the corollary that a change or abolition of the regimental system would give you far more efficient officers in the higher ranks, by teaching them throughout their career that the Army is their profession, not the narrow groove of any regiment which seems to contract their minds, dwarf their intellect and from the bright young man who joins the regiments turns out the present unsatisfactory senior officer.[90]

Cardwell's attachment of the militia to the regular infantry gave many regiments politically influential patrons in the form of the county Lords Lieutenant, since after the Regulation of the Forces Act ended their direct control of the militia, many simply became colonels of their county regiments instead. A similar if indirect link was established for the cavalry regiments through their increased informal connections with the county yeomanry. By 1881, out of 122 Lords Lieutenant, 37 had served in the Army at some point in their lives.[91] Smart regiments particularly benefited from the new arrangements, since their officers were much more likely to regard military service as a temporary step along their career paths, and go on to influential positions in the wider world. In 1885 there were 132 members of the House of Lords with military experience (or about 27 per cent of the peerage), ranging from career soldiers like Cambridge and Wolseley to those peers who had served only briefly in smart regiments; a number that increased to 182 (35 per cent) in 1898.[92] In the same year, there were 37 Conservative members of the House of Commons with a military background, 17 Liberals (a number which declined shortly afterwards) and five from the Home Rule Party. Usually known collectively as the 'service members', this group had associations and influence that extended well beyond the Army, and its members could form a powerful bloc of unofficial support for the regiments in any dispute with the War Office.[93]

---

89 Badsey, 'The Impact of Communications and the Media on the Art of War since 1815', pp. 79–80; McLaughlin, *The War Correspondent*, pp. 54–7; Wilkinson-Latham, *From Our Special Correspondent*.

90 TNA PRO 30/57/22 Official Papers of Lord Kitchener, Kitchener to St John Brodrick, 28 June 1901.

91 Spiers, *The Late Victorian Army*, p. 159. The Lords Lieutenant retained the right after 1871 of nomination for first commissions only in the militia; the author is grateful to Professor Ian F.W. Beckett for this point.

92 Harries-Jenkins, *The Army in Victorian Society*, pp. 218–19.

93 Ibid, pp. 240–42; Spiers, *The Late Victorian Army*, pp. 168–70.

The colonial campaigns which took place alongside the Cardwell–Childers reforms were important both for ambitious generals, and as a test of the new doctrines on how the Empire was to be defended. The first major British campaign of the breechloader era to feature cavalry in significant numbers was the Second Afghan War of 1878–1880, which also marked the emergence of Sir Frederick 'Bobs' Roberts as Wolseley's main rival. In doctrinal terms, Roberts was an exponent of the importance of musketry in tactics, and of the superiority of Indian Army methods over those of the British Army.[94] Although Wolseley understood how to negotiate with newspapers, Roberts was also the first British wartime commander of the era to use an overt system of privileges and restrictions in order to manipulate the press and to promote his own reputation. From his first successes in Afghanistan, Roberts had a reputation as a political general who played up to the press and indulged heavily in favouritism when making appointments, particularly for peers or their sons in need of staff positions.[95]

The proportion of British and Indian cavalry taking part in the original British invasion of Afghanistan in 1878 was low by the standards of European warfare, partly because of problems of supply, which usually dominated in colonial campaigns. The hills and mountains of Afghanistan were suitable for horsemen, but not for massed mounted charges, and the Afghan cavalry were usually not prepared to face British or Indian cavalry in a charge. But the Afghans were enough of a threat to small parties of scouts to make the British carry out their reconnaissance in troop or squadron strength. The requirement to drive off the Afghan cavalry led the British and Indians to employ the new tactics of combining mounted and dismounted action, and a very clear description of how these tactics works has been left by the commanding officer of the 5th Punjab Cavalry (the future 25th Cavalry) working in co-operation with the 10th Hussars in a skirmish in January 1879:

> I immediately took advantage of a low detached hill… We dismounted a troop and opened fire at 400 yards, on which the enemy retired towards the high hills, keeping possession of one or two low hills at their base on which they planted their standards. Leaving a few men in this position to protect our right, I moved the remainder round to the left and taking advantage of some broken ground under fire of dismounted men, attempted to drive the enemy from a low hill. Aided by the fire of the 10th Hussars, the enemy were driven to the far side of it, but seeing their standards still flying there, I collected together the 4th Troop and went up the hill at a gallop, and rapidly dismounting half the men drove the enemy with a quick fire off the hill towards the high range.[96]

Lieutenant Colonel Baker Russell, a Wolseley Ring member commanding the 13th Hussars in this campaign, went further than most for the time in arguing after

---

94 Roberts, *Forty One Years in India*, pp. 499–500.
95 Forbes, 'War Correspondents and the Authorities', *The Nineteenth Century*, Volume VIII pp. 185–97; Roberts, *Forty One Years in India*, p. 374; Strachan, *The Politics of the British Army*, pp. 92–6; Heathcote, *The Afghan Wars 1839–1919*, pp. 103–41; James, *The Life of Lord Roberts*, pp. 150–64.
96 Quoted in Anglesey, *A History of the British Cavalry Volume 3*, p. 219.

using these tactics that cavalry should be 'able to act on foot as well as the best infantry'.[97]

In Afghanistan the British cavalry wore khaki like the Indian troopers, who were themselves sometimes barely distinguishable from their Afghan opponents at first sight. The arrival later in the campaign of the 9th Lancers, 'all shaved and pipeclayed as in cantonments' caused some amusement, but as Roberts noted they too soon adapted to the tactical situation. The regiment had just been issued with its new Martini-Henry carbines, and, in an example of low-level doctrinal improvisation, it had devised its own carbine sling to allow the carbine to be carried across the man's back with the sword carried on the horse. The sword being carried on the horse and the carbine either slung on the man or carried in a saddle bucket became standard for the cavalry in 1891, one of a number of cavalry reforms codified that decade.[98]

The next two major colonial wars followed in rapid succession after the peaceful British annexation in 1877 of the Transvaal Republic: the Zulu War of 1879 and the Transvaal War of 1880–1881, both of which exposed the limitations of depending on local volunteer mounted troops, and the problems inherent in moving cavalry regiments from Great Britain or India to a distant theatre of war.[99] The stony hills and grasslands of Zululand were excellent for horsemen, particularly when facing foot warriors who could move as fast as the Zulu; but just as in Afghanistan, the initial British invasion was made with a very small number of mounted men: barely more than 1,000 horsemen of greatly varying quality and experience to accompany a total force of 16,000 troops in five separated columns. These horsemen were described in informal correspondence as 'cavalry', but there were no British cavalry regiments in South Africa at the war's start, and there was a severe problem in finding suitable substitutes.[100] The part-time citizen soldiers of Natal were not obliged to serve outside its borders and only a few volunteered to do so; even the Natal Mounted Police were required to volunteer as individuals. Two troops of Imperial mounted infantry were formed (about 120 men in total), who Evelyn Wood as a column commander found to be alarmingly poor riders and horsemasters, and there were a few local irregular mounted units of which the largest was the high-quality Frontier Light Horse commanded by Redvers Buller, and some small volunteer groups of Boers.[101] About a quarter of the mounted force came from the Natal Native Horse,

---

97 Quoted in Baden-Powell, *Cavalry Instruction*, p. 128.

98 Roberts, *Forty One Years in India*, p. 437. See also TNA WO 33/37 'Report of Committee on Musketry Instruction in the Army (1881)'; WO 33/38 'Report of Cavalry Organisation Committee (1882)'; WO 33/42 'Proposals Submitted to the Secretary of State on Cavalry Reorganization (1882)'; WO 33/43 'Reports and Proceedings of Special Committee on Cavalry Swords and Scabbards (1884–5)'; WO 33/45 'Committee on Saddlery (1886)'.

99 The name 'Transvaal Republic' was and is habitually used for the South African Republic / Zuid Afrikaansche Republiek or ZAR, established north of the River Vaal between 1857 and 1864.

100 Letter from Colonel Anthony Durnford, late Royal Engineers, quoted in Lock and Quantrill, *Zulu Victory*, p. 91.

101 Different numbers of mounted Natal volunteers appear in different sources, but they appear to have been between 150 and 300 men; for the mounted forces available to Chelmsford see TNA WO 33/36 'General Report of Veterinary Department in the Zulu War'

but many of these were left behind in reserve when the invasion started. Rather than a hoard of light cavalry scouts tracking and harassing the Zulu forces from the start of the invasion, the British commander Lord Chelmsford advanced into Zululand with only a handful of horsemen with his central column, and no idea of the enemy's location. This failure in mounted scouting, together with an over-estimation of the firepower of the Martini-Henry rifle, was the principal cause of the British defeat and massacre at the Battle of Isandlwana.[102]

After the collapse of Chelmsford's first invasion attempt, reinforcements were sent to Natal including two cavalry regiments from Great Britain, the 17th Lancers and the 1st (King's) Dragoon Guards. Wolseley, who was sent out to replace Chelmsford for the end of the campaign, gave his opinion that Zululand did not provide enough grass to sustain an invading army except between May and August, and that 'lancers are simply useless' for fighting the Zulu.[103] This turned out to be half correct: a persistent problem was that horses could not be exercised on board ship and so arrived after a long sea voyage in a 'soft' condition, requiring several weeks' acclimatisation. Although the 17th Lancers delivered the decisive charge at Ulundi in July, the horses of the 1st (King's) Dragoon Guards were unable to keep up with Zulu retreating on foot, and used saddle fire instead.[104] Otherwise, in Chelmsford's second invasion and Wolseley's subsequent pursuit of the remaining Zulu, the cavalry and mounted riflemen were employed mainly as scouts, and some mounted riflemen took to carrying lances or assegais to make mounted charges against isolated groups of Zulu.[105] Chelmsford was also forced to solve his supply problems by cutting back severely on the cavalry horses' grain ration in late May, and the resulting deaths and sicknesses linked to starvation meant that by September the 17th Lancers gave up their horses to keep the 1st (King's) Dragoon Guards mounted. The problems of transporting cavalry horses, letting them acclimatise and then keeping them supplied were singled out by the Veterinary Department report on the war, which emphasised that 'in future wars in southern Africa it will have to be borne in mind that, in order to maintain the health and efficiency of British horses, it is imperative that they be liberally fed on suitable food'.[106] These words would come back to haunt the British in the Boer War.

In October 1880 the 1st (Kings) Dragoon Guards went home, and when the Transvaal War broke out two months later there were again no regular British cavalry in South Africa. The Transvaal rose in revolt at the end of December 1880, with the

---

(1880); Wood, *From Midshipman to Field Marshal*, Volume I, p. 318 and Volume II, p. 24; Knight and Castle, *Zulu War*, pp. 29–59; Lock and Quantrill, *Zulu Victory*, pp. 36–50 and 91–3; Morris, *The Washing of the Spears*, pp. 301–6.

102 There have been many theories about the British defeat at Isandlwana; Lock and Quantrill, *Zulu Victory* provides a discussion. The obvious explanation, that Chelmsford was criminally complacent and incompetent, appears to be making a comeback.

103 HPL Wolseley Papers CYP 1: Wolseley to Stanley, 16 February 1879.

104 Spiers, *The Victorian Soldier in Africa*, pp. 52–3.

105 HPL Wolseley Papers SA2: Wolseley to Cambridge, 18 July 1879; Morris, *The Washing of the Spears*, pp. 501–2; Callwell, *Small Wars*, p. 414.

106 TNA WO 33/36 'General Report of Veterinary Department in the Zulu War', (1880) p. 4; HPL Wolseley Papers SA2: Wolseley to Cambridge, 28 September 1879.

Boers laying siege to the small British garrisons within the country. Major General George Pomeroy-Colley (also of the Wolseley Ring) was ordered to relieve these sieges and suppress the rebellion, planning to advance into the Transvaal directly from northern Natal through the hill country at Laing's Nek. Pomeroy-Colley needed to move quickly, and felt unable to wait for reinforcements, but declined to ask Cape or Natal colonists to volunteer to serve against the Boers, fearing the long-term implications of a white-race civil war in South Africa.[107] For these political reasons, Pomeroy-Colley advanced against the Boers with no local mounted riflemen except the Natal Mounted Police.

The Boers were rightly regarded by the British as a unique military force. Mainly the descendents of Dutch colonists, they were farmers, cattle-workers and hunters who lived in the saddle and had evolved a burgher or citizen militia under what was known as the 'commando' system. Chiefly mobilised to fight rival cattle-owning black African tribes who fought as charging foot warriors, the tactics of the commandos were based on the techniques of game shooting, on skirmishing as mounted riflemen, or on using a wagon laager for defence. Just after the Transvaal War, a report by the Quartermaster General's department gave them high praise:

> The Boers are an enemy different from any with which we have had hitherto to contend. Mounted upon active, hardy little horses, provided with the best firearms.... They combine the rapidity of Asiatic Cavalry with more than the precision fire of the most highly-trained European Infantry. They always move on horseback but they invariably dismount to fight. They are thus probably the most perfect Mounted Infantry in the world.[108]

The Boers of the Transvaal provided a valuable model for the continuing British interest in mounted infantry. Edward Hutton gained his first experience with mounted infantry in South Africa at this time, together with Edwin Alderson of the Queen's Own (Royal West Kent) Regiment, who served under Hutton in further campaigns including the Boer War.

Without cavalry for the small column of just under 1,500 soldiers with which he planned to march into the Transvaal, Pomeroy-Colley improvised a mounted contingent from the Natal Mounted Police, supplemented by a 'mounted squadron' of 70 recently retired or convalescent Imperial troops, chiefly dragoon guards and mounted infantry (plus men of the Army Service Corps who presumably knew how to ride). His innovative orders were that if faced by the Boers this squadron should charge mounted as an unexpected tactic, and they were armed with swords for that purpose. At the little battle of Laing's Nek in January 1881, the mounted squadron did charge uphill, and may have come close to success before being repulsed with 17 men and 32 horses killed or wounded. The success or failure of the armed might of the British Empire had come down to this *ad hoc* unit of 70 horsemen. Pomeroy-

---

107 Laband, *The Transvaal Rebellion*, pp. 127–45; Bennett, *A Rain of Lead*.

108 TNA WO 32/7806 'Memorandum and Observations on proposal to advance on the Transvaal', (1881), p. 2; Hallam Parr, *The Further Training and Employment of Mounted Infantry and Yeomanry*, pp. 32–3; see also van der Waag, 'South Africa and the Boer Military System', pp. 45–69; Laband, *The Transvaal Rebellion*, pp. 59–67; Lehman, *The First Boer War*, pp. 104–13.

Colley blamed his problems on his shortage of mounted troops, and was convinced that regular cavalry would have won the battle for him.[109] A Boer comment recorded shortly afterwards was that 'if only you had four hundred men like that, with swords, who would gallop at us without caring if a few were shot, we should never have risen'.[110] For the British Army to launch a campaign like this, without proper mounted troops, was a stark indication of the structural weakness of its cavalry forces.

As part of the reinforcements for Pomeroy-Colley, four cavalry regiments were sent from Great Britain and India at their war strength of nearly 550 men and horses each, but to achieve this meant that other regiments had to be depleted: the 6th (Inniskilling) Dragoons took 164 horses from four different regiments, while other regiments sailed without their horses and took mounts provided at the Cape. Despite recommendations that the horses needed at least three weeks' acclimatisation, the first half-squadron of the 15th Hussars was rushed to Pomeroy-Colley in late February almost off the ships, while some new horses at first refused the unfamiliar local grain and grazing.[111] The delay meant that the cavalry played no part in Pomeroy-Colley's catastrophic defeat at the Battle of Majuba Hill, after which the British government capitulated and restored the Transvaal's independence. Arriving in Cape Town to find that peace had been made, Frederick Roberts, sent out to take command, vowed on board ship to adopt an abstemious lifestyle so as to live long enough to avenge the 'Majuba surrender', a vow which would have important consequences.[112] For the second time in two years in South Africa, a British advance into hostile territory made without adequate cavalry had resulted in disaster.

The British cavalry that would have taken part in the Transvaal War, had it lasted longer, were starting to change significantly from those that had fought in the Zulu War, as the cavalry reform movement began to have its impact. Taking part in a parade that accompanied the peace negotiations following Majuba, Troop Sergeant Major Mole of the 14th Hussars reflected on the changes made by their new reforming lieutenant colonel:

> We wore serge coats and *khaki* pants, with Indian *puttees*, or long strips of cloth bound round and round the leg, in lieu of jackboots: they were far more comfortable and supporting. Our helmets and belts were rubbed with red clay to harmonise with the colour of the ground, and our steel was all dulled. The squadrons of the Inniskillings and the 15th Hussars adopted quite a different style; they were as spick and span as could be, with helmets and gloves white and clean, and steel and brass work all sparkling in the sun. It

---

109 HPL Wolseley Papers Autograph Pomeroy-Colley 3: Pomeroy-Colley to Wolseley, 21 February 1881; and SSL 8/2 p. clcxxxi manuscript; Verner, *The Military Life of H.R.H. George Duke of Cambridge*, Volume II, p. 190; Laband, *The Transvaal Rebellion*, pp. 149–51; Lehman, *The First Boer War*, pp. 151–2.

110 'The Boers at Home: Jottings from the Transvaal', *Blackwood's Magazine*, Volume 130, p. 768; see also Duxbury, *David and Goliath*, pp. 20–22.

111 Jackson, *The Inniskilling Dragoons*, p. 189; Compton, *A King's Hussar*, pp. 238–55; Wood, *From Midshipman to Field Marshal*, Volume III, pp. 111–14.

112 Lehman, *The First Boer War*, p. 281.

was a queer contrast altogether, and represented two widely different schools of military opinion.[113]

In fact the 15th Hussars, which had come from recent fighting in the Second Afghan War, had arrived ready to go into action wearing khaki, but had smartened up for the parade.[114] Khaki became general wear on campaign in 1885 and official overseas dress in 1897, but as with so many British reforms of this period its adoption varied between regiments. William Birdwood remembered the 12th Lancers in India adopting in 1887 'a curious get-up consisting of khaki coat, white helmet with khaki cover and neck-pad, long brown boots like a Life Guardsman's, and gold-laced blue pantaloons'.[115] Wider reform was also still very much a matter for individual regiments. In 1883 Wolseley abolished the post of musketry instructor in the cavalry regiments in the belief that all troop officers should be competent to train their men in shooting, but this was not always the case in practice.[116] At about the same date, in an Indian cavalry regiment, the commanding officer was telling his men not to march in step when on foot, as this infantry habit destroyed their value as cavalry.[117]

The problems facing the British cavalry and other mounted troops in these colonial campaigns did not come largely from poor tactics or a tendency to charge wildly, but from the inadequacies of British defence policy for the Empire. The two campaigns in South Africa showed the practical limitations of raising local forces of mounted riflemen or improvising mounted infantry, while the combination of a voyage from Great Britain or India with the time needed for the horses to recover greatly limited their value on arrival. The weight that these big horses had to carry, and the exertions required of them, also posed problems of supply that in practice had no solution. The daily feed for a cavalry horse at home was ten pounds of oats, twelve pounds of hay and eight pounds of straw; and while on campaign an oat ration (often reduced) was provided, it was assumed the balance could be obtained by grazing, which in hostile territory was not automatically true.[118] Tactical doctrine and what weapons a horseman carried mattered very little if his horse was starving and he did not know how to keep it alive, and reducing the weight on the horse and improving horsemastership became not only critical military matters but also common ground among all British Army reformers.

The issue of sending large horses intended to charge on European battlefields into colonial campaigns was raised yet again in the next campaigns in Egypt and the Sudan. Wolseley's expedition to Egypt in 1882 to suppress the Arabi Revolt used a Corps of two divisions with the 19th Hussars as divisional cavalry, together with a cavalry division composed of a heavy cavalry brigade (including the composite

---

113 Compton, *A King's Hussar*, p. 285.
114 Laband, *The Transvaal Rebellion*, p. 182.
115 Birdwood, *Khaki and Gown*, p. 31.
116 Robertson, *From Private to Field Marshal*, p. 26.
117 Western, *Reminiscences of an Indian Cavalry Officer*, p. 247.
118 Grierson, *Scarlet into Khaki*, p. 237; Verner, *The Military Life of H.R.H. George Duke of Cambridge*, Volume II, p. 267.

Household Cavalry), and a brigade of three Indian cavalry regiments.[119] This was the fourth war in four years for which British regular cavalry regiments had been sent overseas, and to bring them up to strength the remaining home regiments had to be completely denuded of trained men and horses.[120] Throughout the 1880s and 1890s numerous minor changes were made in this way to the 'establishment' (official strengths) in men and horses for cavalry regiments at home and overseas, adding to the disruption of the regimental system while doing nothing to overcome the problem that there were simply not enough horses and men to go round.[121]

Following the various uses of mounted infantry in previous wars, special attention was paid in the 1882 Egyptian campaign to the role of mounted infantry. A contingent mostly with prior mounted experience in South Africa, including their commander Edward Hutton, was equipped with horses by the Khedive himself.[122] The cavalry and these mounted infantry co-operated well together in battle, with the mounted infantry providing dismounted fire rather than the cavalry having to dismount (although the mounted infantry also joined in at least one mounted charge). Charges by British heavy cavalry proved extremely effective against Arabi's Egyptian infantry and cavalry, including the spectacular 'charge by moonlight' of the Household Regiment at the Battle of Kassassin, together with the charge and pursuit by both cavalry brigades at the Battle of Tel-el-Kebir.[123]

The biggest problem facing the cavalry was that the British horses were unable to cope with the heat, lack of food, and shortage of water on campaign, and 'melted away', according to one veterinary officer, 'like ice in a summer sun'.[124] While the cavalry's horses were unfit after the sea voyage and suffered feeding difficulties, the mounted infantry used smaller native ponies already acclimatised to the country.[125] Following the 1882 campaign, Cambridge recommended that every British infantry battalion should keep available a full company for mounted infantry duties.[126] As already recounted, a proposal was also made to link the cavalry regiments together in threes in the same manner as Cardwell's linked infantry battalions, but the power of the regiments proved too great and Cambridge halted the scheme.[127] Anxieties

---

119 The leader of the 1882 revolt was known as Said Ahmed Arabi, Arabi Pasha, or Colonel Arabi to the British; some modern accounts give his name as Colonel Urabi; see Kochanski, *Sir Garnet Wolseley*, p. 133.

120 Maurice, *Military History of the Campaign of 1882 in Egypt*, pp. 112–21; Goodenough and Dalton, *The Army Book for the British Empire*, p. 193; Chenevix-Trench, *Cavalry in Modern War*, p. 39.

121 Anglesey, *A History of the British Cavalry Volume 3*, pp. 122–5.

122 Maurice, *Military History of the Campaign of 1882 in Egypt*, p. 12.

123 'Notes of an Egyptian Campaigner', *Blackwood's Magazine*, Volume II, pp. 150–51; Arthur, *The Letters of Lord and Lady Wolseley*, p. 75; Maurice, *Military History of the Campaign of 1882 in Egypt*, pp. 62–6 and pp. 88–99; Barthorp, *Blood-Red Desert Sand*, p. 60 and p. 68; Spiers, *The Victorian Soldier in Africa*, p. 84.

124 Quoted in Smith, *A Veterinary History of the War in South Africa*, p. 235.

125 Maurice, *Military History of the Campaign of 1882 in Egypt*, pp. 50–51.

126 Verner, *The Military Life of H.R.H. George Duke of Cambridge*, Volume II, p. 302.

127 TNA WO 33/42 'Proposals Submitted to the Secretary of State on Cavalry Reorganization', (1882); 'Cavalry Reorganisation', *Colburn's United Service Magazine*, 1882

even at the slightest suggestion of cavalry reform reached such levels that in 1885 Colonel James Keith Fraser, late the commanding officer of the 2nd Life Guards and a prominent cavalry reformer, felt obliged to deny in print a rumour that he had chaired a committee to convert the cavalry into mounted infantry.[128]

A partial solution was found to the cavalry's problems of acclimatisation when in 1884 the British dispatched troops to Egypt to oppose the rising in the Sudan by Mohammed Ahmed 'the Mahdi'. The 19th Hussars returned to Egypt, and were joined by the 10th Hussars from India, both regiments taking over trained and acclimatised Egyptian horses when they arrived, smaller than their usual troop horses but better able to stand the desert conditions.[129] At the Battle of El Teb both regiments charged and used dismounted carbine fire successfully, although finding that Mahdist foot warriors flung themselves to the ground to avoid their swords they also took to carrying lances; when the 20th Hussars arrived in 1885 they felt also felt that a charge with lances was much more effective against Arab footsoldiers than with swords.[130] One noteworthy participant in the campaign was Lieutenant Julian Byng of the 10th Hussars, who took part in his regiment's repeated charges at El Teb and had his horse killed underneath him at the Battle of Tamai.[131]

For the Gordon Relief Expedition of 1884–1885, as well as forming a battalion of mounted infantry under Hutton, Wolseley provided yet another improvisation: a camel corps for his Flying Column consciously made up of troops from the Army's smartest regiments, including the Household and Foot Guards, the cavalry and rifle regiments, (plus a contingent of Royal Marines), for which some 28 regiments and battalions provided 40 men and 2 officers each. Although the camel corps was not an outright failure, the men had little time to learn how to ride, many of the camels died from overwork and underfeeding, and the expedition failed to save Gordon.[132] Cambridge complained that all this was contrary to the regimental system, and that he would have preferred to send Wolseley an extra infantry battalion and a full-strength hussar regiment.[133] But after so many years of borrowing horses and men within the cavalry there were no full strength regiments left. As Wolseley noted in the following year, of 16 cavalry regiments in the British home establishment, 8 should have been on the 'higher establishment' (still short of war strength) of 542 trained men and 400 horses, but in fact just two cavalry regiments were on the higher

---

Part II, p. 399; Verner, *The Military Life of H.R.H. George Duke of Cambridge*, Volume II, p. 305.

    128 Editor's Note, *Colburn's United Service Magazine*, 1885 Part I, p. 78; Hills, *The Life Guards*, p. 80.

    129 French, *The Life of Field Marshal Sir John French*, p. 28; Rogers, *The Mounted Troops of the British Army 1066–1945*, pp. 216–18.

    130 NAM Fergusson Papers: Fergusson to his parents, 21 March 1885.

    131 Williams, *Byng of Vimy*, pp. 11–14.

    132 Wood, *From Midshipman to Field Marshal*, Volume II, p. 175; Spiers, *The British Army in Africa*, pp. 116–17.

    133 Verner, *The Military Life of H.R.H. George Duke of Cambridge*, Volume II, p. 267.

establishment, while in one regiment 169 men had less than a year's service and were for practical purposes untrained.[134]

The commander of the contingent of 2nd Life Guards (Keith Fraser's regiment) for the camel corps was Lord Cochrane, the future Earl of Dundonald. As another example of how an early personal experience shaped an officer's attitude towards the cavalry debate, at the Battle of Abu Klea in January 1885 Dundonald and his men fought dismounted as part of a large British square that repulsed repeated attempts by the Sudanese to break through it. For this campaign the Household were armed not with carbines but with semi-obsolescent Remington single-shot breechloading rifles. Dundonald later wrote that:

> Some fifty of the enemy who were mounted made straight for the part of the square where the Household Cavalry were, but were all shot down. It was here, armed as we were with the old high-trajectory Remington rifle, that I formed the opinion that if men on foot armed with a magazine rifle do not flinch, men on horseback with cold steel have but a poor chance of success against them in the attack, unless under very special circumstances, not likely often to occur. From this opinion, formed on this day, I have never varied, and gave expression to it at times when few held it.[135]

Other officers recorded their impressions that the Household's shooting was 'very wild', that they made poor footsoldiers, and that the Mahdists came close to success in their charges.[136] But whatever the merits of his analogy, Dundonald's view of the likelihood of unsupported cavalry successfully charging frontally against steady infantry with magazine rifles was much less contentious than he described. When in 1885, as part of a printed course of official lectures given to all cavalry and yeomanry, Captain Robert 'Stephe' Baden-Powell as adjutant of the 13th Hussars wrote that 'cavalry attacking good infantry formed up to receive them cannot do much without help from artillery or infantry; as a rule, however, they would never be required to do so', he was repeating a long-standing doctrinal truism.[137] Both the British mounted infantry and the cavalry did well, including the use of the cavalry to manoeuvre and provide flanking fire dismounted at the Battle of Tamai, and the critical role played by the 19th Hussars as the rearguard to the retreat of the Flying Column after Gordon's death, in which John French made his reputation as a rising young cavalry officer.[138]

In the Suakin Field Force of 1884–1885, based at the last British outpost in the Sudan before withdrawal at the end of the campaign, the three cavalry regiments (one of them Indian) and the mounted infantry battalion again all did well in combat.

---

134 HPL Wolseley Papers W/Mem/1: Memorandum by Wolseley, 20 April 1885 and W/Mem/2: Memorandum by Wolseley, 19 October 1886.

135 Dundonald, *My Army Life*, p. 39.

136 Spiers, *The Victorian Soldier in Africa*, p. 117.

137 Baden-Powell, *Cavalry Instruction*, p. 59. Baden-Powell was known to friends as 'Stephe', pronounced 'Stevie' and himself composed the following doggerel on his surname: 'Man, matron, maiden, please say it Baden / As for the Powell, rhyme it with Noel' (like 'pole' rather than the Christmas 'Noël').

138 Chevenix-Trench, *Cavalry in Modern War*, p. 191; Holmes, *The Little Field Marshal*, pp. 34–40.

The Suakin mounted infantry battalion was by then a veteran formation, commanded for most of its existence by Hutton, and composed of selected men from 35 different units (including the Royal Marines once more), mostly of soldiers with previous mounted infantry experience.[139] It was also no small consideration that each cavalry regiment cost £28,000 to maintain at Suakin, while the mounted infantry battalion (on a calculation based only on the extra cost of their horses and equipment) cost just £12,000.[140] Egypt and the Sudan showed that both cavalry charges and dismounted fire could be effective, that mounted infantry could be valuable if composed of picked troops and given long enough to train, that cavalry and mounted infantry could co-operate together tactically, and (reinforcing the lesson from South Africa) that the key to the value of any mounted force was acclimatised horses that were properly fit and properly fed.

This was the situation facing Wolseley as Adjutant General in 1887 when he set out to find enough mounted troops for Brackenbury's mobilisation scheme. On paper the Army was not actually short of cavalry, with just under 14,000 troopers serving in the ranks, and the proportion of cavalry in the Army at just under ten per cent was virtually identical to that of the armies of Germany and France.[141] The cavalry shortage was largely due to the British practice, for financial reasons, of keeping their cavalry regiments well below full strength, particularly in horses.[142] Another factor was that the organisation of the British cavalry into 31 understrength regiments with no official reserves of militia or volunteers was too inflexible for the Army's needs, and habitually left the cavalry short of trained troopers. But while Wolseley's own reputation and authority had been weakened by the failure of the Gordon Relief Expedition, the power of the regiments was still increasing, strongly supported by Cambridge, and no radical reorganisation of the cavalry seemed possible.

Wolseley's solution to this problem was an ingenious expedient. In addition to establishing the Remount Department, in February 1888 he created a Mounted Infantry School at Aldershot under Hutton, one of three such schools created over the subsequent decade in the United Kingdom (including one at the Curragh in Ireland) together with schools in Egypt and India. The purpose of this Aldershot school was to train a section of 32 first class shots plus an officer from every line battalion in the Army as mounted infantry.[143] On mobilisation, these picked sections would come together for the first time to form two mounted infantry battalions each about 1,000 men strong, one for each of the two planned Corps, chiefly as a substitute for their divisional cavalry. Trainees included officers from the militia and rifle volunteers,

---

139 HPL Wolseley Papers Autograph Stephenson: Stephenson to Wolseley, 6 May 1884; Smith-Dorrien, *Memories of Forty Eight Years' Service*, p. 55.

140 Hutton, 'Mounted Infantry', *Journal of the Royal United Service Institution*, Volume 30, p. 697; figures derived from TNA WO 112 Army Estimates 1880/81 to 1890/91. There were two British cavalry regiments with the Suakin Field Force, the 5th Lancers and 20th Hussars, plus the 9th Bengal Cavalry (the future 9th Hodson's Horse).

141 Chenevix-Trench, *Cavalry in Modern War*, p. 19; figures derived from TNA WO 112 Army Estimates 1880/81 to 1890/91.

142 Goodenough and Dalton, *The Army Book for the British Empire*, pp.73–7; HPL Wolseley Papers W/Mem/2: Memorandum by Wolseley, 19 October 1886.

143 Grierson, *Scarlet into Khaki*, p.42.

and colonial officers, as well as regular soldiers. The *Regulations and Field Service Manual for Mounted Infantry* appeared in January 1889. The scheme cost only £700 a year to maintain, and before leaving Aldershot in 1892 Hutton had trained almost 4,000 men, more than enough for Wolseley's needs.[144] In establishing the scheme permanently Evelyn Wood, who commanded at Aldershot, made a threefold case for the new mounted infantry:

> 1. As an adjunct to the cavalry, so long as our cavalry continue in their present system and training solely upon the model of the German and French cavalry.
> 2. As an improvised substitute for cavalry in colonial expeditions, when no cavalry are available...
> 3. As an extra mobile infantry.[145]

Clearly, a plan which required two mounted infantry battalions to come together on mobilisation from 64 different infantry battalions, each supposedly giving up some of its best men, was driven by cost and necessity rather than sound military policy. It was always Hutton's ideal to have the mounted infantry fully trained, and he would have preferred a smaller but better trained force.[146] But early reports on the value of the 'MI', as these regular British mounted infantry rapidly became known, all stressed savings in cost as their principal advantage; as a report in 1881 candidly put it, 'We have no experience of Mounted Infantry opposed to a well-trained cavalry', and this remained true throughout the MI's existence until their final abolition just before the First World War.[147] As part of the cost saving it was policy that they should be undertrained as riders, partly in an attempt to prevent their converting themselves into cavalry. The MI training period was just ten weeks, and for its first three years the Aldershot MI School was dependent on horses loaned by cavalrymen on leave.[148]

Despite this, and inevitably considering that the MI were picked men from British infantry battalions, within a very few years MI commanders would be claiming that they could perform all the tasks that cavalry could perform, if not actually perform them better. The MI attracted ambitious young officers, partly because each section provided an independent command at a junior level, and partly because a polo pony made an ideal MI officer's mount.[149] The establishment of the MI on an official basis was also important to an argument about tactics that was made increasingly by the infantry from the middle 1880s onwards: that the perfect small all-arms formation, at least for colonial warfare, was the augmented infantry battalion. As one theorist expressed it, 'With two machine-guns, the regimental engineers and a squad of mounted infantry, which could be easily and quickly organised, a battalion, if detached, would be complete in itself and independent of the other branches of

---

144 Goodenough and Dalton, *The Army Book for the British Empire*, pp. 172–6.
145 BL Hutton Papers Add. 50086: Memorandum on Mounted Infantry at Aldershot by Sir Evelyn Wood, December 1891.
146 Ibid., Wood to Hutton, 3 August 1897.
147 TNA WO 33/37 'Précis on Mounted Infantry', (1881).
148 Goodenough and Dalton, *The Army Book for the British Empire*, p. 174.
149 Tylden, *Horses and Saddlery*, p. 24.

the service.'[150] This argument was greatly strengthened by the introduction of the new .303-inch Lee-Metford and Lee-Enfield rifles, and by increasingly practical machine-guns, culminating in the Maxim with an effective rate of fire of 250 rounds a minute.[151] Many infantry officers were convinced that this new firepower really did mean the end of cavalry on the battlefield. A typical claim made in 1890 was that:

> In future wars guns will be able to destroy the enemy's cavalry if it is halted under their fire 3,000 or even 4,000 yards away, while experiments made at Aldershot with the magazine rifle in 1888 proved that infantry can hit a mark smaller than a cavalry division with every other shot at 2,000 yards, and every fourth shot at 2,600 yards.[152]

A more realistic test, using a firing party of 32 average infantry shots and a Maxim shooting for one minute each at 700 yards, at a target representing 100 infantry and an artillery gun crew, scored 19 hits for the infantry and nine for the machine-gun.[153] But the British chiefly lacked practical battlefield experience of these weapons. They did not encounter enemies armed with the new rifles on any scale until fighting on the Afghan frontier in the Tirah Expedition of 1897, and were themselves shocked by the devastation wrought by their own firepower, from rifles, artillery and machine-guns, at Omdurman in 1898.

Increasingly into the 1880s, this infantry and mounted infantry view came into conflict with the cavalry's argument for a greater and more independent role, also based on the value of its new firearms, and by 1890 openly described as 'the cavalry revival'.[154] Led by their new Inspector General of Cavalry, now Lieutenant General Sir James Keith Fraser, ambitious and reforming cavalry officers argued that the cavalry, acting well in advance or on the flanks of the main body of the Army, could use a combination of mounted charges and dismounted fire from their new carbines, backed by machine-guns and horse artillery, to overcome enemy infantry, or to clash with like-minded enemy cavalry in a critical duel to decide cavalry superiority. For the first time, in 1890 a cavalry division of two brigades was assembled under Keith Fraser for brigade and regimental manoeuvres on the Berkshire Downs, and

---

150 Knollys, 'Suggestions – II', *United Service Magazine*, 1886 Part I, pp. 105–6; TNA WO 33/48 'Report of a Committee on Magazine and Small Bore Rifles', (1888) p. 10.

151 The distinctions between the long Lee-Metford and Lee-Enfield were slight, chiefly that the Lee-Metford was capable of firing some older types of ammunition. A belt of 250 rounds a minute was the standard rate of rapid fire for the Maxim (and later Vickers-Maxim) which was normally fired in tactical situations in short bursts; sustained fire at the gun's cyclical rate of 600 rounds a minute rapidly damaged the barrel.

152 Altham, 'The Cavalry Revival: A Plea for Infantry', *United Service Magazine*, Volume II, New Series, p. 27.

153 Anstruther-Thomson, 'Machine Guns with Cavalry', *Journal of the Royal United Service Institution*, Volume 38, p. 629; '"Ajax" (pseudonym), Machine Guns: their Use and Abuse', *United Service Magazine*, Volume XVII, New Series, p. 512.

154 Altham, 'The Cavalry Revival: A Plea for Infantry', *United Service Magazine*, Volume II, New Series, p. 17; Moreland, The Mounted Infantry Regiment as an Integral Part of the Cavalry Division', *United Service Magazine*, Volume XII, New Series, p. 532.

in 1891 and 1892 the two brigades manoeuvred together as a complete division.[155] A reflection of where the doctrinal debate stood in the British Army is that in 1891 the examination papers on tactics for the senior division of the Royal Military College Sandhurst included the question 'Under what circumstances may a Cavalry charge against Infantry be effective?' Clearly, a range of well-argued answers to this question was possible.[156]

This cavalry revival would also inevitably clash with Wolseley's sponsorship of the new mounted infantry. At the end of his career, Hutton wrote that 'Looking back, it is a continual source of wonder that we – MI officers – were able to carry out to a very successful issue a system which was so fraught with difficulties and in the face of such fiery criticism from the cavalry and others.'[157] What is surprising is that the clash partly took the form of a historical argument over the cavalry of the American Civil War. Between 1885 and 1895 Hutton gave or published at least 15 talks and articles for the Royal United Service Institution and similar bodies, sponsored by Wolseley and Evelyn Wood, the main theme of which was that the mounted operations of the Civil War owed their success to the horsemen being mounted infantry, and that this provided a model for the new MI, while the cavalry should continue solely with the charge as Denison had recommended back in 1867.[158] In his new post as C-in-C Ireland in 1891, Wolseley summed up this position after chairing a lecture Hutton gave in Dublin, 'I certainly do not believe that you can get a good cavalry soldier to be a good infantry soldier at the same time. My idea is that he is intended to fight on horseback. If you intend to make him fight on foot, well, you will make him into a very bad mongrel, to [sic] a bad dragoon.'[159] With such impressive patronage, Hutton's lectures received considerable attention. But at nearly every occasion on which he spoke, at question time a senior cavalry officer would rise to explain that Hutton was wrong, and that the successful American horsemen had been cavalry. For Wolseley these arguments were intolerable; not only was he being openly defied, but to argue that cavalry and mounted infantry had separate and distinct roles was the only way that he could preserve both against the depredations of the Treasury and keep Brackenbury's mobilisation scheme alive. At the Dublin meeting in 1891 tempers were lost completely, with Keith Fraser insisting that the Americans 'always charged', while Wolseley replied that the very idea of their charging was 'ridiculous'. The real issue was broached when Keith Fraser invited Hutton to transfer the MI to

---

155 French, 'Cavalry Manoeuvres', *Journal of the Royal United Service Institution*, Volume 39, pp. 561–5; Goodenough and Dalton, *The Army Book for the British Empire*, p. 204; Chenevix-Trench, *Cavalry in Modern War*, p. 69; Spiers, *The Late Victorian Army*, pp. 258–9.

156 NAM Gough Papers 375 has a complete set of the eight senior division examination papers for December 1891 taken by Hubert Gough and forwarded to his father. The Royal Military College Sandhurst taught potential infantry and cavalry officers; the Royal Military Academy Woolwich taught potential artillery and engineer officers, although there were other ways to obtain a commission.

157 BL Hutton Papers Add 50114: Marginal note by Hutton in the index to his own papers, compiled in about 1915, p. 36.

158 Ibid., List of talks and publications in the index to Hutton's papers, pp. 42–6.

159 Wolseley quoted in Hutton, *Five Lectures on Mounted Infantry*, Lecture Five, p. 26.

the cavalry, and Hutton replied that 'We prefer our own arm.' Wolseley summed up the meeting angrily and accurately: 'I see, even from what has occurred here today, that there is a tendency on the part of cavalry officers to imagine that when men lecture them on the uses of mounted infantry that it is a sort of personal attack on the cavalry service.'[160] A year later Keith Fraser wrote to Evelyn Wood at Aldershot:

> The Federal cavalry, so called 'mounted infantry', which ultimately numbered about 80,000 men, was armed with sword, carbine and pistol. *It never carried a rifle from the beginning to the end of the war.* If our Mounted Infantry are prepared to play the role of the American cavalry... the sooner they are similarly armed the better, and then indeed they will be useful (as an increase of trained cavalry seems to be an impossibility) in swelling the number of men in our attenuated cavalry division, whereas at present with their horses (which are only to be used, as I understand, as a means of conveyance from one place to another) they would be, I fear, a heavy encumbrance to it.[161]

These suggestions from Keith Fraser and the cavalrymen that dismounted cavalry could fight on foot as well as infantry, or that the MI should be taken from the infantry and trained as cavalry, were almost as great an affront to the British infantry regiments as Hutton's claims were to the cavalry.

On leaving the Aldershot MI School in 1892, Hutton was sent overseas to promote the idea of Imperial defence, for which his experience with mounted infantry seemed ideal, first in 1893 as commandant of the militia of New South Wales, where in 1895 he issued a new drill book, *Mounted Drill – Australia*.[162] In 1898 he became commandant of the militia of Canada, where he found an ally for his reforms in an old friend and fellow MI enthusiast, Major Viscount 'Rowly' Melgund (Scots Guards), now Earl Minto and Governor General of Canada. Hutton was seen in both Australia and Canada as energetic but abrasive, insensitive to local concerns and politics. His promotion of a mounted infantry approach for the Australians and Canadians also provoked some controversies, which would not be fully resolved even in the First World War.[163]

In 1893, two Royal Artillery officers published *The Army Book for the British Empire*, an invaluable work of reference on the organisation of the Army, drawing on the advice of a number of prominent officers, although no reforming cavalrymen. Their view of cavalry, based chiefly on Prussian successes in the Franco-Prussian War, was summarised in a passage that would echo into the future.

> Decried as it has been, and deemed superfluous after the successive introduction of archers, of gunpowder, of firearms, and of rifled ordnance, we have yet to learn that cavalry, even in the face of the magazine rifle, has met its match, and that the speed of the charge and the suddenness of the attack will not, as heretofore, obtain glorious success.[164]

---

160 Ibid., Lecture Four, pp. 23–6.
161 NLS Haig Papers 14: Keith Fraser to Wood, 21 July 1892, emphasis in the original, copy in Haig's 'Cavalry Notes', Staff College Notebooks.
162 BL Hutton Papers Add. 50114: Note by Hutton in the index to his papers, p. 64.
163 Grey, *A Military History of Australia*, pp. 51–2; Morton, *A Military History of Canada*, pp. 111–15.
164 Goodenough and Dalton, *The Army Book for the British Empire*, p. 191.

It is instructive to compare the phrasing of this passage with the 1907 edition of the *Cavalry Training* manual. But for advice on mounted infantry the authors approached Hutton, and their resulting passage showed that the debate between reforming cavalrymen and mounted infantrymen, like that between reforming and traditionalist cavalrymen, would not be over without a further fight:

> Reading aright the lessons of the American war, leading military opinions in this country have long acknowledged the importance of this new departure on the part of the Americans, and have recognised that while modern cavalry must be trained to act on foot if required, effective fire action can never be expected from cavalry as such.[165]

Keith Fraser was still arguing against this point shortly before his retirement in 1895, when he was succeeded by Lieutenant General Sir George Luck (15th Hussars), who had previously served as Inspector General of Cavalry in India since 1887.[166]

What gave the cavalry debate its particular intensity for the British Army was that, from Wolseley's decision in 1887 onwards, the term 'Mounted Infantry' had an official meaning, as well as its older unofficial meaning of almost any mounted troops who were not cavalry. The infantry regiments had both an institutional and a social stake in promoting their new MI, while henceforth the threat of conversion to mounted infantry was a nightmare even for reforming cavalrymen, who interpreted the loose use of terms like 'mounted riflemen' in association with cavalry to mean the destruction of their regiments by their absorption into the infantry. The debate about the future of mounted troops in the British Army was also an institutional struggle for scarce men and resources between the infantry and cavalry regiments, made all the more complex and intense by their considerable unofficial influence and power.

The abolition of purchase in the Cardwell reforms had never been intended as socially revolutionary, and successive British governments continued to prefer the majority of officers to be the sons of officers, or gentry, or both. Officers who had purchased their commissions before 1870 were entitled to compensation or a pension on retiring from the Army, the last such payment did not take place until 1908, and the money involved caused the War Office some difficulties.[167] In addition to the costs of purchasing a commission, the prevailing British military culture meant that a private income was for most cavalry and infantry officers a necessity, especially at the start of their careers. These expenses had little or nothing to do with the actual costs of soldiering, they were the product of a culture of conspicuous display and consumption, including the belief that an officer should aspire to live just a little beyond his means, with junior officers in particular being subject to mess costs including 'subscriptions to the polo team, the regimental coach, the regimental hounds', not to mention the regimental band and various arbitrary fines and forfeits.[168]

---

165 Ibid., p. 173.
166 Moreland, 'The Mounted Infantry Regiment as an Integral Part of the Cavalry Division', *United Service Magazine*, Volume XII, New Series, p. 530.
167 TNA WO 32/8644 'Report of the Army Purchase Commission on the Abolition of Purchase in the Army'(1909); Spiers, *The Late Victorian Army*, pp. 92–3.
168 Cairnes, *Social Life in the British Army*, pp. 65–9.

Most ambitious career officers feared living on 'half pay', (in fact a much smaller fraction of their full salary), a device used when the War Office had no available post for them, or as an unsubtle hint that they should resign.

Service in India, or even in South Africa, was popular since the lower living costs allowed the junior officer of the 1880s to live on a private income of about £100 a year in addition to his pay; and special allowances were made in mess customs and behaviour for officers promoted from the ranks, including Wully Robertson.[169] One lieutenant serving in India with the 7th Hussars (Haig's regiment) in 1887 recorded his annual mess bill as £187, or about £70 more than his salary.[170] But among the smart regiments, whatever prestige was felt to have been lost by the abolition of purchase was rapidly regained by a considerable increase in the conspicuous display required of officers. While in the 1870s an average private income of £300 a year in the cavalry had been adequate, by the 1890s some £400–£600 was needed and £1,000 was not unusual, while even the least fashionable infantry regiments required at least £150.[171] A few years later, Evelyn Wood sought to decline an offered regimental colonelcy in the Royal Horse Guards, on the grounds that he could not afford the dress uniform.[172] By the 1890s, the levels of display among officers were such that, in the smart regiments at least, purchase in an unofficial form actually reappeared, whereby an officer would be asked his 'terms', a cash transaction, to exchange with another. Henry Wilson was pleased to be offered an exchange as a major without terms ('exchange if you like for nothing') between two battalions of the Rifle Brigade in 1893.[173] While Winston Churchill of the 4th Hussars recalled an incident in 1898:

> An officer of the Fourth Dragoon Guards had telegraphed to one of our Captains in the ordinary routine of the service, saying, 'Please state your lowest terms for an exchange into the Fourth Dragoon Guards'. To which our Captain had gaily replied '£10,000, a Peerage, and a free kit'. The Dragoon Guards had taken umbrage at this and thought it was a reflection upon the standing of their regiment.[174]

By way of further comparison, according to the 1899 pay scales the salary of a second lieutenant joining a cavalry regiment was just over £122 per year (and £96 for his equivalent in the infantry), while his regimental commander received £392 per year.[175] In other words, a newly arrived second lieutenant in an average cavalry regiment on home service was expected to have a private income at least greater

---

169 Robertson, *From Private to Field Marshal*, pp. 31–2; Gardiner, *Allenby*, pp. 8–10.

170 NAM Carew Papers: Diary entry, 4 October 1887; the exact figure give by Lieutenant Carew was '£187-11-8d' (eleven shillings and eight pence).

171 TNA CSC 3/319 'Report of Mr Akers-Douglas' Committee on the Education and Training of Army Officers', (1902) Appendix 42, p. 143; Cairnes, *Social Life in the British Army*, p. xi; Hillcourt, *Baden-Powell*, p. 40; Vaughan, *Cavalry and Sporting Memories*, p. 3.

172 French, *The Life of Field Marshal Sir John French*, p. 40; Wood accepted the colonelcy in 1907; see Heathcote. *The British Field Marshals 1736–1997*, p. 316.

173 IWM Wilson Papers: Diary entry, 28 May 1893; in the event Wilson took a staff position instead.

174 Churchill, *My Early Life*, p. 135.

175 Grierson, *Scarlet into Khaki*, pp. 223–8.

than his commanding officer's annual salary. (In order to place these amounts in some kind of context: in 1885 a working man's lodgings in London could be rented for the equivalent of just over £5 a year, in 1901 a reasonable income for a farm labourer was £25 a year, and in 1913 in the Lambeth district of London the income of a respectable working class man with a family ranged from about £45 to £75 a year.)[176]

While clothing and other expenses, including arbitrary penalties, were a factor in the mounting costs of being an officer in a smart regiment, there was in practice only so much bad champagne that even the most unbuttoned officers' mess could drink; it was horseriding, foxhunting and especially polo that offered the perfect vehicle for conspicuous display. Although polo had originated long before in India, at the first inter-regimental match played in 1871 between the 10th Hussars and the 9th Lancers it was so unfamiliar that it was reported as 'hockey on horseback'.[177] Its popularity bloomed among British regiments in India in the 1880s chiefly through the achievements of Beauvoir de Lisle, an outstanding horseman and athlete serving with the unfashionable Durham Light Infantry, who by introducing team tactics and training led his team to many notable victories.[178] Polo also allowed officers of different regiments to socialise with each other, particularly forging connections between the infantry (only the smarter regiments being really able to afford playing) and the cavalry, while as the opportunities for display increased, the cost in India of a good polo pony rose from £8 in 1880 to £22 by 1884, and as much as £80 by 1888.[179] If the cost of officers' expenses troubled reformers, then particularly after the Boer War the cost of polo became the most prominent aspect of this concern.

Largely unintentionally, this considerable increase in officers' expenses in smart regiments may have aided Army reform. It meant that such regiments remained likely to attract the sons of wealthy and influential men, while with the Army's budget kept so tight, reforming officers in smart regiments could still by-pass official channels to promote reform unofficially. In 1886 the commanding officer of the 10th Hussars organised a three-day 'cavalry raid' exercise for his regiment and bought one of the new Nordenfeldt machine-guns for it to try; a year later, after watching a demonstration organised by Baden-Powell, Wolseley authorised one of these new guns for every cavalry regiment. In 1895 Lord Dundonald, now commanding the 2nd Life Guards, organised an officers' subscription to pay privately for increased musketry training for his troopers.[180]

The prevailing attitude among officers meant that those who were well-enough born and adequately financed, but also professional in their approach and eager to

---

176 Beales, *From Castlereagh to Gladstone 1815–1885*, preface 'a note on money values'; Mason, *The English Gentleman*, p. 196; Pember Reeves, *Round About a Pound a Week*, pp. 2–3; Cook and Stevenson, *The Longman Handbook of Modern British History 1714–1980*, pp. 181–6.

177 Brander, *The 10th Royal Hussars*, p. 51.

178 McGregor, *Officers of the Durham Light Infantry, 1758–1968*, p. 89.

179 Younghusband, *Forty Years a Soldier*, p. 156; Maurice, *The Life of General Lord Rawlinson of Trent*, p. 8.

180 Dundonald, *My Army Life*, p. 80; Brander, *The 10th Royal Hussars*, pp. 72–3; Hillcourt, *Baden-Powell*, p. 77.

make the Army a career, had a much better chance of gaining responsibility and promotion in a smart regiment than elsewhere. Connections and influence (or, in the language of the time, 'friends' and 'interest') would help get an ambitious officer into a smart regiment and perhaps attract the attention of a patron, and after that he would have the opportunity to display his talents. On joining his battalion of the King's Royal Rifle Corps in India in 1884, the young Second Lieutenant Henry Rawlinson wrote home to his father the baronet, 'When I have established my position with the regiment and learned my job, your influence with the swells at the top of the tree will be invaluable.'[181] In contrast, Captain Wully Robertson, serving in an Indian Army staff appointment, complained despairingly that, 'I have no friends, no interest, and not a bob in the world, and what becomes of me after this job God alone knows!'[182] Robertson obtained recognition only when spotted by Henderson as a student at the Staff College in 1897–1898. When Roberts requested Henderson for his staff for the Boer War, Henderson used the opportunity to bring Robertson with him, marking the start of his career in the General Staff.[183]

An unofficial but valid distinction was made by most contemporary commentators about this kind of patronage. For a general to be made aware of a capable young officer and promote his career was seen as necessary and legitimate. But abuse of the practice, by a general promoting the career of a less capable officer out of 'friendship' or obligation to his family and associates, was not. Sometimes promotion and future fame depended simply on a regimental connection. Baker Russell of the Wolseley Ring spotted Baden-Powell as a capable young officer of his own regiment, the 13th Hussars, and in 1883 took him as his brigade major.[184] Herbert Plumer owed an appointment he received in 1890 to Garnet Wolseley, probably because his brother George Wolseley had served with Plumer in the same battalion of the unfashionable Yorkshire and Lancashire Regiment.[185] But by far the best way for a junior officer to win attention and promotion was by military competence and bravery, either through staff work or through the command of a small but independent formation like a detached cavalry squadron or mounted infantry company. This sense of personal loyalty to a prominent patron added yet another layer of complexity and animosity to the cavalry debate. Ian Hamilton of the Gordon Highlanders first gained the attention of Roberts through his personal bravery in Afghanistan in 1879, was rewarded by Roberts with an attachment as a staff officer to a cavalry brigade, and in fact Hamilton took part in a fire-and-charge attack by the 5th Punjab Cavalry.[186] Hamilton went on to become the most prominent of the younger members of the Roberts Ring, and the most outspoken in his criticisms of Roberts's opponents, writing in 1887 that 'all the difference between amateur and professional separates England and India' in

---

181 Quoted (admiringly) in Maurice, *The Life of General Lord Rawlinson of Trent*, p. 8.
182 Quoted in Younghusband, *A Soldier's Memories in Peace and War*, p. 237.
183 Robertson, *From Private to Field Marshal*, pp. 102–5; Bond, *The Victorian Army and the Staff College*, pp. 158–9.
184 Hillcourt, *Baden-Powell*, pp. 56–60.
185 Harington, *Plumer of Messines*, p. 3; Powell, *Plumer*, pp. 14–22.
186 Hamilton, *The Happy Warrior*, pp. 38–46; Lee, *A Soldier's Life*, pp. 12–13.

military matters.[187] Henry Rawlinson was given a post on Roberts's staff in 1885 at the entreaty of his father.[188] Rawlinson became close friends with Henry Wilson of the Rifle Brigade when both men commanded patrols in the same mounted infantry battalion in Burma in 1886–1887 hunting dacoit bandits (in the course of which Wilson was nearly killed), and introduced Wilson to Roberts at a cricket march in England in 1893.[189] Roberts displayed considerable paternal care for these men, including support for Rawlinson to enter the Staff College as a student in 1891 despite what Rawlinson himself confessed was his poor staff work (Rawlinson transferred into the Coldstream Guards in 1892).[190]

What may be described as the second generation of the Wolseley Ring was a more informal grouping than the Roberts Ring, and was largely represented by the protégés of Evelyn Wood and Redvers Buller rather than Wolseley himself. Captain Horace Smith-Dorrien (whose experiences included surviving Isandlwana) caught Wood's attention in Egypt in 1884, when by scouring Alexandria for horses and equipment he improvised a small troop of mounted infantry in two days.[191] As already mentioned, French made his reputation in 1885 with Redvers Buller, who commanded the retreat of the Flying Column after the Gordon Relief Expedition; Buller became French's patron, and they remained friends through life.[192] Haig took the first important steps in his career through his association with Keith Fraser as his aide de camp for the 1894 manoeuvres. Notoriously better on paper than when speaking, Haig also attracted Evelyn Wood's attention through his written reports; the two men met in 1895, and Wood (like Haldane a decade later) turned out to be one of those rare individuals to whom Haig could talk on military matters with clarity and pleasure. 'I told you that we got on very well together', Haig wrote to his sister, 'Sir E.W. is a capital fellow to have upon one's side as he always gets his own way.'[193] In 1898 Wood as Adjutant General selected Haig to serve in the reconquest

---

187 BL Dilke Papers Add. Mss. 43908: Hamilton to Lady Dilke, 5 July 1887.

188 NAM Roberts Papers 60: Rawlinson (senior) to Roberts, 27 March 1885; Maurice, *The Life of General Lord Rawlinson of Trent*, pp. 11–12.

189 IWM Wilson Papers: Diary entry, 27 May 1893; Callwell, *Field Marshal Sir Henry Wilson*, Volume I, pp. 5–7; Maurice, *The Life of General Lord Rawlinson of Trent*, pp. 14–17; Jeffrey, *Field Marshal Sir Henry Wilson*, pp. 13–14.

190 NAM Roberts Papers 61: Rawlinson to Roberts, 9 January 1890.

191 Wood, *From Midshipman to Field Marshal*, Volume II, pp. 150–51; Smith-Dorrien, *Memories of Forty Eight Years' Service*, pp. 37–9.

192 Holmes, *The Little Field Marshal*, pp. 39–42.

193 NLS Haig Papers 6b: Haig to his sister, 4 July 1895; Cooper, *Haig*, Volume I, pp. 39–44; see also Terraine, *Douglas Haig: The Educated Soldier*, pp. 54–5; Sheffield and Bourne (eds), *Douglas Haig: War Diaries and Letters 1914–1918*, p. 17. Haig's diary for 1914–1919 was not usually written as a day-to-day diary but as a summary, and after the war a typed version with attached documents was prepared. In addition to the original manuscript and typed versions held as part of the Haig Papers in the National Library of Scotland, copies of the typed version are held in other archives including The National Archives. Two editions of these diaries have been published, Blake (ed.), *The Private Papers of Douglas Haig 1914–1919* in 1952, and Sheffield and Bourne (eds), *Douglas Haig: War Diaries and Letters 1914–1918* in 2005. Following the practice of this book, references to a published edition have been given when possible, but checked against the unpublished version.

of the Sudan and to report back his impressions; French also confirmed to Haig 'that Sir E.W. is "a good friend of mine"', in the Sudan.[194] Other officers who rose to prominence in the First World War were connected in this way at a more junior level, including Philip Chetwode who served in the 19th Hussars under French, Cecil 'Cis' Bingham, who served as French's aide de camp with the Cavalry Division in South Africa 1899–1900, and Beauvoir de Lisle who served in the Suakin Field Force mounted infantry under Smith-Dorrien.[195] French made a point of advancing Chetwode's career after the Boer War by insisting on his appointment to a staff position even though he had not passed through the Staff College, making Chetwode his military secretary in 1906.[196]

Throughout this period, British cavalry reformers were highly conscious that while fighting colonial wars under varied conditions of climate, terrain and tactics, they might be called upon in any year to fight a major war in Europe or against invading European troops. To supplement their personal experience of colonial war, British cavalrymen continued to look for advice and inspiration to the Germans as the dominant military power in Europe, and to a lesser extent to the French. The most visible British cavalry imitation of German practice was the decision in 1891 to introduce lances into dragoon guard and dragoon regiments for the front rank only of the two-rank charging formation (although even then lances had been used by dragoon guards and dragoons for training since 1817).[197] Indian cavalry regiments, together with British dragoon guard and dragoon regiments stationed in India, adopted a slightly different approach by having one out of their four squadrons equipped with lances. The list of leading modern writers on cavalry compiled by Haig for his studies at the Staff College in 1896–1898 consisted of seven German and French authors, but none from Great Britain, or any other country.[198] Haig's own views, recorded early in his career in 1890, were typical of reforming British cavalrymen of the period:

> Every cavalry soldier must thoroughly understand that his proper place is on horseback, his proper mode of action the charge. Only in cases where cavalry cannot obtain its object by executing a charge, should the men be dismounted in order to use the carbine… [But] unless a cavalry force is by instruction and practice ready to fight on foot its usefulness will be curtailed and it cannot be considered efficient.[199]

---

194 NLS Haig Papers 6b: Haig to his sister, 21 April 1898.

195 French, *The Life of Field Marshal Sir John French*, p. 41; Smith-Dorrien, *Memories of Forty Eight Years' Service*, p. 62; Vaughan, *Cavalry and Sporting Memories*, p. 81.

196 French, *The Life of Field Marshal Sir John French*, pp. 139–40.

197 Evans, *The Story of the Fifth Inniskilling Dragoon Guards*, p. 90; the 6th (Inniskillings) amalgamated with the 5th Dragoon Guards to produce this regiment; Goodenough and Dalton, *The Army Book for the British Empire*, pp. 208–9.

198 NLS Haig Papers 14: Staff College Notebooks, 'Cavalry Notes'; see also Howard, 'Men Against Fire: The Doctrine of the Offensive in 1914', pp. 510–26.

199 NLS Haig Papers 14: Staff College Notebooks, 'Cavalry Notes'; 6a: Paper by Captain Douglas Haig, 'The Dismounted Action of Cavalry', 15 November 1890.

The reformers expected their cavalry normally to fight mounted, but if the circumstances called for dismounted shooting then they expected them to be very good at it. As a troop officer with the 7th Hussars, Haig's troop could score 98 per cent hits with their carbines at 300 yards.[200]

While neither the Germans nor the French adopted the mounted infantry or the squadron sized fire-and-charges of the British, the Germans did practise dismounted fire for their cavalry, and French and German cavalry manoeuvres were virtually the only occasions on which British observers could witness the charge of more than one cavalry division in close order. In keeping with the wider French Army doctrine of the offensive, French cavalry laid a particularly heavy stress on the mass charge. As an observer of the 1893 French cavalry manoeuvres, Haig recorded that the sword was carried on the saddle and the carbine on the man, but that a cloth cover wrapped round the carbine's firing mechanism made it impossible to use without some delay; this was, Haig noted with characteristic dryness, 'not altogether satisfactory'.[201] In the 1897 French cavalry manoeuvres, the troopers were told by their commander that 'The best reconnoitring cavalry will be one which is dashing and bold, sceptical of mathematical calculations, a cavalry whose men dream of the naked sword and the charge.'[202] Since in the 1890s the French were the most likely British enemy in a future continental war, the British were obliged to take these views seriously. However, in a way that was to be repeated throughout the British Army's debate over the future of cavalry, even first-hand observers tended to see what they wanted to see in these manoeuvres, depending on their pre-existing beliefs. Haig formed a high opinion of the German cavalry after watching their 1895 manoeuvres, whereas Lord Roberts, an observer at the same manoeuvres, had nothing but criticisms.[203]

The most important centre for British cavalry reform was Aldershot, where Evelyn Wood took over command in 1889, and it was at his instigation that two years later Keith Fraser was able to train the cavalry division called for in Brackenbury's mobilisation scheme as a complete formation.[204] Wood was very dissatisfied with the system of manoeuvres that he found, later writing that 'It was assumed that the effects of rifle-fire on service nearly equalled that obtained on the ranges', and that 'we over-estimated the value of artillery practice when guns were laid up on moving targets'.[205] Or, as Haig bluntly put it, 'Umpires always decide against cavalry.'[206] Wood's own views were that while cavalry should not dismount 'too often', and

---

200 Ibid., 1e: Diary entry, 5 February 1889.

201 Ibid., 6g: 'Report on French Cavalry Manoeuvres (1893)'.

202 De Négrier, quoted in Talbot, 'Manoeuvres in France of Two Divisions of Cavalry and an Army Corps, September 1897', *Journal of the Royal United Service Institution*, Volume 42, p. 1358.

203 NLS Haig Papers 74: 'Notes on German Cavalry Compiled by Captain Douglas Haig (1896)', especially p. 35; NAM Roberts Papers 107: Roberts to Cambridge, 7 October 1895.

204 French, 'Cavalry Manoeuvres', *Journal of the Royal United Service Institution*, Volume 39, pp. 561–5.

205 Wood, *Achievements of Cavalry*, p. v; Wood, *From Midshipman to Field Marshal*, Volume II, p. 192.

206 NLS Haig Papers 14: Staff College Notebooks, 'Cavalry Notes', 'Notes on the Skill Required of Cavalry Leaders', p. 40.

perfection of both mounted and dismounted skills was an impossibility, the cavalry should still consider shooting a vital skill.[207] The four British Army categories for rifle shooting were marksman followed by first, second, and third-class shot. Over his first three years at Aldershot Wood reduced the percentage of third-class shots in the cavalry from a half to a quarter, the same average percentage as in the infantry.[208] In the informal manner in which British cavalry reform spread through the regiments, Wood allowed French, commanding the 19th Hussars at Aldershot, to introduce the squadron system of command in his regiment in 1889, three years before it was officially introduced throughout the cavalry.[209] Hutton also later remembered how at Aldershot he and French had discussed 'Boer tactics' together with other officers.[210]

This was only one of a number of cavalry reforms introduced while Wood was in command at Aldershot District 1889–1897, in conjunction with Keith Fraser as Inspector General of Cavalry 1891–1895. In 1893 another attempt at rationalisation by grouping the regiments together as Household, dragoons, lancers and hussars to allow cross postings was made, but was abandoned after much resistance.[211] This was followed in 1897 by the closing of the cavalry depot at Canterbury previously used by all cavalry regiments serving overseas (and sometimes based at Colchester instead), followed by the successful introduction of a version of the system first proposed in 1882 of linking the regiments in threes (although falling far short of anything resembling amalgamation).[212] In the same year it was established that for home service regiments only three squadrons should serve in war, with the fourth forming a depot squadron, and the notional higher establishment for peacetime for the six home regiments standing first for overseas service was raised to 682 officers and men with 410 horses.[213] British cavalry regiments serving in India remained at four slightly smaller squadrons to conform to Indian Army practice.

For the 1894 manoeuvres, Sir Redvers Buller as Adjutant General brought French back from half pay to command the Aldershot cavalry brigade, apparently at Keith Fraser's instigation. But at both these manoeuvres and those of 1895, the last before he retired, Keith Fraser was dissatisfied with the cavalry's performance. The root of the problem was seen as the need to establish a system of consistent training. As Haig, who served as one of Keith Fraser's aides in the 1895 manoeuvres, noted, attempting divisional or even brigade drill before the squadrons were properly trained was like trying to run before walking.[214] This determination to reform the cavalry led to the inevitable grumble from the Duke of Cambridge, also serving in his last year as C-in-C, who 'congratulated the cavalry very highly on their efficiency, and told them

---

207 Wood, *Achievements of Cavalry*, p. 241; Wood in discussion in Hutton, *Five Lectures on Mounted Infantry*, Lecture Two, p. 22.
208 Wood, *From Midshipman to Field Marshal*, Volume II, p. 208.
209 Holmes, *The Little Field Marshal* pp. 44–5; Wood, *From Midshipman to Field Marshal*, Volume II, pp. 207–8.
210 BL Hutton Papers Add. 50096: Hutton to Marshall, 20 January 1900.
211 Goodenough and Dalton, *The Army Book for the British Empire*, p. 100.
212 Anglesey, *A History of the British Cavalry Volume 3*, pp. 122–3.
213 Goodenough and Dalton, *The Army Book for the British Empire*, p. 197.
214 NLS Haig Papers 1i: Diary entry, 15 August 1895.

that whatever people might say to the contrary he could not agree with them'.[215] The incoming Inspector General of Cavalry Sir George Luck, although regarded as much less of a reformer than his predecessor, gave French the task of re-writing the *Cavalry Drill* book in two volumes, bringing in Haig to complete the work in August 1895 when French became Assistant Adjutant General under Buller.[216] These actions helped secure the future careers of French and Haig, the two men who would play the central role on the cavalry reformers' side in the debate over the cavalry's future, and of course in much else.

The new *Cavalry Drill Volume II 1896* (reissued with amendments two years later as *Cavalry Drill Volume II 1898*), encapsulated the reformed cavalry thinking as endorsed by Wolseley and his Ring members, and provided the basis for a coherent programme of cavalry training. In terms of tactics it set out that cavalry charges against infantry should only be attempted in loose order, from close-in and launched from behind cover or dead ground, and always from a flank. Failing this only, a charge could be started from 1,000 yards away if the infantry could be clearly seen to be shaken, which at that distance meant in obviously panicked retreat. As for cavalry charges against cavalry, the drill book stipulated that 'in close country (like most parts of England)' mounted infantry would be of the greatest value since 'the mounted action of cavalry will be confined to conflicts between small bodies (probably not even the strength of a squadron on both sides) which may endeavour to make sudden dashes at one another down roads or across country'. But, with echoes of von Bredow at Mars-la-Tour, *Cavalry Drill Volume II 1896* also laid own that as a principle 'the cavalry division may be called upon to sacrifice itself entirely or partially for the general welfare of the Army', and the large-scale charge was retained for such rare eventualities.[217] Cavalry charges of larger than squadron size also continued to be seen as of obvious value in colonial warfare. Dismounted fighting occupied 11 pages of the manual, reflecting the cavalry's official eight days a year spent on shooting; although in practice shooting went on throughout the year including range firing and tactical training.[218]

An important part of Brackenbury's mobilisation scheme was the planned third Corps made up partly from militia and volunteers, including mounted troops. By 1887 the Mounted Rifle Volunteers had only three corps of light horse and one corps of mounted rifles left, and some of these had started to carry swords as well as rifles; although some infantry units of Volunteers also included a number of horsemen (and by 1899 some men with bicycles) of which no official record was ever kept.[219] These

---

215 Ibid., 1i: Press cutting preserved in diary for 28 August 1895.
216 Ibid., 1i: Diary entry, 31 August 1895; Ibid., 6b: Letter from Haig to his sister, 4 July 1895; Ibid., 6f: Cutting from *The Times*, 6 October 1894 and Cutting from M.A.P. 3 March 1900; Holmes, *The Little Field Marshal*, pp. 49–51; French, *The Life of Field Marshal Sir John French*, p. 35, Duff Cooper, *Haig*, Volume I, pp. 39–46. Volume I of *Cavalry Drill 1896* dealt with administration and organisation, Volume II with drill and manoeuvres, and miscellaneous matters.
217 *Cavalry Drill Volume II 1896*, the quotations are from p. 205 followed by p. 185.
218 Goodenough and Dalton, *The Army Book for the British Empire*, p. 202.
219 Carman, *Light Horse and Mounted Rifle Volunteers 1860–1901*, p. 4; Grierson, *Scarlet into Khaki*, pp. 91–2; 'The Best Arm for Volunteers', *United Service Magazine*, Volume I,

mounted riflemen were far cheaper than their equivalent in the yeomanry, which like the regular cavalry suffered from poor use of the little funding they were given. At a conference held with yeomanry commanders in 1882 Wolseley set out the problem: while each rifle volunteer footsoldier cost the country £1 13s 1d a year, each yeoman (even although he provided his own horse) cost a remarkable £6 7s 5¼d; and while there were 14,000 yeomanry on the muster rolls, the real figure of those who mustered for training each year fell between 8,000 and 10,000, a pattern that did not change significantly for the remainder of the century. Wolseley proposed to the gathering that the yeomanry should be converted to 'mounted riflemen', arguing that this was their natural role, on the (perhaps not very accurate) analogy of the Boers of South Africa, but the lieutenant colonels expressed a 'general and decided disinclination' to be converted.[220] Even so, as cavalry officers retired from active service and joined their local yeomanry, or as regular officers were attached to yeomanry regiments as adjutants, and as yeomanry officers served on attachment with the regular cavalry, so about a decade behind the cavalry the yeomanry began to take to shooting seriously.[221] In one yeomanry regiment shooting was started for the first time with the arrival of a new adjutant in 1882, and in other regiments commanding officers actively petitioned the War Office to equip some or all of their men with rifles rather than the shorter carbines.[222] By the start of the 1890s the emphasis on shooting had become general within the yeomanry, so that Cambridge advised Wolseley that 'I am fully prepared to do all in my power to induce the present yeomanry regiments to attend more to their carbines, but don't attempt to make Mounted Infantry out of them; that would simply destroy the force, and completely take the heart out of them.'[223] In 1888 the yeomanry regiments were made liable for service anywhere in Great Britain rather than only in their own regions, and in 1893 a major reform took place: regiments were reorganised into squadrons of a hundred troopers, those that failed to produce at least two squadrons were disbanded, and the surviving regiments mostly brigaded in pairs; although a requirement for brigade training every two years proved too optimistic, and was officially abandoned in 1898.[224]

A persistent concern about the yeomanry was that their recruiting base was fast diminishing as British agriculture declined from the 1870s onwards. For the Army, nothing emphasised the change in British society from the rural to the urban more than the creation in 1887 of cyclist companies for the Volunteers, as well as cyclists appearing in the ranks of the yeomanry. Against the cost of a suitable horse for a

---

New Series, p. 305

220 TNA WO 32/7237 'Proceedings of meetings to discuss state of Yeomanry Cavalry: proposal to convert Yeomanry into mounted riflemen', (1882).

221 Grierson, *Scarlet into Khaki*, pp. 189–90.

222 Adderley, *History of the Warwickshire Yeomanry Cavalry*, p. 94; Goodenough and Dalton, *The Army Book for the British Empire*, p. 374.

223 Verner, *The Military Life of H.R.H. George Duke of Cambridge*, Volume II, p. 363.

224 Crighton, 'Yeomanry and Its Future', *Journal of the Royal United Service Institution*, Volume 35, pp. 661–93; Goodenough and Dalton, *The Army Book for the British Empire*, pp. 37–57; Frewen, 'The Yeomanry Force and the New Army Warrant', *United Service Magazine*, Volume VII, New Series, pp. 830–35; Verdin, *The Cheshire (Earl of Chester's) Yeomanry 1898–1967*, p. 5.

yeoman of £35 and a further £45 a year to stable and keep it, a bicycle suitable for military purposes in 1890 cost no more than £12, and £3 a year in maintenance.[225] Increasingly, arguments were made that the Army must find at least part of its cavalry from India, and its volunteer mounted troops from the colonies, where a rural familiarity with horses was believed still to prevail.

In India there was neither the same shortage of cavalry, nor the need to find an expeditionary force, that had led to the formation of the MI at Aldershot. As C-in-C India 1885–1893, Roberts's view was firmly that both Indian cavalry regiments and British cavalry regiments in India should be able to fight on foot, although he was content to keep the cavalry armed with a carbine rather than a rifle.[226] In 1887, Roberts had appointed Luck as the first Inspector General of Cavalry in India. As Roberts himself remembered it, 'Just at first British officers were apprehensive that their sowars [troopers] would be turned into dragoons, but they soon found out that there was no intention of changing any of their traditional characteristics.'[227] Smith-Dorrien, who had taken a staff position in India on Evelyn Wood's recommendation, remembered that Luck 'had large ideas of the powers of cavalry' and that his manoeuvres were elaborate affairs covering much ground.[228] This was a mounted infantryman's view, not shared by Haig, who took part with the 7th Hussars in these manoeuvres. 'We go mooning on in close formation', Haig complained, 'no reconnoitring, no reserve, no patrols to approaches or flanks'.[229] Two of Haig's contemporaries on the same manoeuvres, also members of the emerging school of reforming cavalrymen, shared his views. George 'Billy' Barrow of the Indian 4th Lancers, who later played a small but important part in the cavalry reform debates, thought that Luck had little knowledge of 'the employment of cavalry masses in the higher sphere of strategy and tactics', while Captain Hubert Gough of the 16th Lancers condemned Luck's obsession with set-piece work rather than 'problems we were likely to meet in real war'.[230] Whatever the tactical competence of the Indian cavalry when facing non-European opponents, cavalry reformers believed that they lagged behind the British cavalry.

Allowing for differences of opinion that were well within the boundaries of a common doctrine, by about 1895 cavalry dismounted action, the squadron as the basic tactical unit for mounted combat, and the close co-operation of machine-guns and artillery with cavalry were among the most fashionable British military ideas of the day, endorsed by Lord Roberts, Evelyn Wood, Redvers Buller, James Keith Fraser, Baker Russell, and John French. For the cavalry reformers, practising these new tactics was entirely compatible with continuing to practise the mass knee-to-knee cavalry charge, and the two were closely related in training terms. As Keith Fraser himself put it, in agreement with French, 'the real object of manoeuvres is to

---

225 'The Best Mounted Arm for Volunteers', *United Service Magazine*, Volume I, New Series, pp. 308–9.
226 NAM Roberts Papers 110: Roberts to Lockyer, 27 December 1895.
227 Roberts, *Forty One Years in India*, p. 528.
228 Smith-Dorrien, *Memories of Forty Eight Years' Service*, p. 73.
229 NLS Haig Papers 2b: Diary entry, 29 January 1890.
230 Barrow, *The Fire of Life*, p. 34; Gough, *Soldiering On*, p. 43.

accustom the cavalry to act together in masses', and recent experience showed that mass charges in brigade strength or more might be needed.[231]

Once Wolseley's MI were accepted as part of the Army he was also able to change his previous view that cavalry should be kept only for the charge, (which is strong evidence that he had held this view chiefly for financial rather than military reasons). In 1895, soon after becoming C-in-C, Wolseley told a yeomanry regiment that he was inspecting:

> If any of you will take the trouble to examine the maps of the country lying between the coast and London you will find that there is no spot where cavalry can charge for a quarter of a mile [440 yards]. It is not likely that the invader would be so kind as to move to Salisbury Plain to oblige us in order that we with our large cavalry force and they without any cavalry to speak of might show how good were our horses and how gallant the men who rode them.... Now that means that for the 12,000 cavalry and 9,000 yeomanry to be of real service in defending England they must learn to shoot well and fight on foot. Cavalry relying on swords in a close country like England can do no useful fighting.[232]

The idea of using dismounted cavalry was so popular with junior officers of other arms that in 1891 the promotion examiners complained that 'dismounted cavalry are frequently used, when infantry are available, in a way calculated to dishearten mounted troops'.[233] From 1896 onwards the cavalry and some of the yeomanry regiments were issued with the Lee-Enfield and Lee-Metford magazine carbines, and taught to shoot and skirmish with them at 600 yards, which was their effective battlefield range, plus an issue of the new Maxim machine-guns to each regiment. By the end of the century the requirements for shooting standards in the cavalry were only slightly lower than in the infantry, and there were occasional instances of cavalry regiments winning shooting competitions against infantry battalions.[234]

Since 1878, wherever the cavalry had fought, they had been a tactical success. Their problems still came chiefly from the Empire's wider defence policy. There simply were not enough of them to go round, and to send cavalry regiments on colonial campaigns was an expensive and lengthy business. An invasion of Great Britain remained very unlikely, except for a raid or small landing by enemy infantry, and reform of the yeomanry was hardly a great military priority. If the British Army was to deploy to Europe (and Great Britain was not bound by any treaty or alliance to do so) then problems of cavalry transport by sea and acclimatisation would be much reduced. In colonial war, mounted infantry had shown their military value if given enough time to train and acclimatise; attempts to recruit mounted riflemen

---

231 Quoted in Spiers, *The Late Victorian Army*, p. 259.

232 HPL Wolseley Papers W/W1/14: Speech in Wolseley's handwriting, not dated but presumably 1895.

233 CUL Official Publications Room: 'Reports on the examination of officers of the regular forces, militia and volunteers', November 1892, p. 7; no cavalry or yeomanry officers took this particular examination.

234 Reynolds, *The Lee-Enfield Rifle*, p. 50; Grierson, *Scarlet into Khaki*, p. 50; Evans, *The Story of the Fifth Royal Inniskilling Dragoon Guards*, p. 94; Malet, *The Historical Memoirs of the XVIII Hussars*, p. 228.

locally as a substitute had been shown to be inadequate for a war of any size, and the whole concept of volunteer mounted riflemen was largely unproven.

Roberts had returned from India in 1895 to take over as C-in-C Ireland, and as the crisis with the Transvaal Republic deepened in 1897 he began pressing for the command in South Africa if war broke out. Although Wolseley himself was increasingly seen as physically no longer up to the strain of campaigning, the rivalry between the two Rings (which had been joined by other associations of officers, including Kitchener with his 'Egyptians' after the Sudan campaign), was far from over; Rawlinson in particular told Roberts that 'The Wolseley Ring will do their utmost to suppress your name' as a candidate for command in South Africa.[235] This continued rivalry of the Rings was to have a major impact on the Boer War, with consequences that would transform the debate on cavalry doctrine into a major national and public affair.

---

235 NAM Roberts Papers 61: Rawlinson to Roberts, 24 and 26 April 1897.

Chapter 3

The Boer War 1899–1902

The event which did most to shape the British Army's debate on cavalry doctrine and reform between 1880 and 1918 was not an advance in military thinking or written doctrine, but a campaign. It began on 11 February 1900, led by Field Marshal Lord Roberts to relieve the siege of Kimberley, and ended at the battle of Diamond Hill exactly five months later.[1] This campaign transformed the fortunes of both sides in the Boer War, which since its start on 11 October 1899 had seen a succession of British defeats (although far from an unbroken one) culminating in the triple defeat of 'Black Week' in December. Roberts's campaign led to the relief of Kimberley and continued with his triumphal entry on 13 March into Bloemfontein, capital of the Orange Free State. The British advance resumed on 3 May towards Johannesburg, and Pretoria, capital of the Transvaal Republic, which was reached on 5 June. The Orange Free State was annexed to the British Crown on 24 May under the name Orange River Colony, and the Transvaal was annexed on 25 October as Transvaal Colony.[2] Roberts proclaimed victory, and the Conservative government called and won a general election, widely known as the 'Khaki Election'. On 29 November, Roberts was succeeded by Lord Kitchener in South Africa and returned to London to succeed Wolseley as C-in-C of the Army. Talks to end the fighting began on 28 February 1901, leading to just over a year of guerrilla war that was frustrating for both sides, and culminating in the surrender of the remaining Boers in return for moderate peace terms, agreed at Vereeniging in the Transvaal on 31 May 1902 and ratified in Pretoria on the same day.

Despite the eventual British victory, the problems encountered both at the war's start and in the protracted efforts to achieve victory produced clamours for Army reform and a Royal Commission, chaired by Lord Elgin, which reported in 1903.[3] The war was also accompanied by literally scores of books, including multi-volume histories of which the most important were the *Times History of the War in South Africa*, edited by Leopold Amery who served as *The Times*'s senior correspondent in South Africa during the war, and the War Office's own official *History of the War*

---

1   The terminology of the Boer War can still excite controversy. The terms 'Boer' (meaning 'farmer') and 'burghers' used in this chapter are strictly inaccurate in describing all combatants against the British, but they were the terms almost universally used by the British at the time. For a discussion of problems of naming and identity in the war see Wessels, 'Afrikaners at War', pp. 73–6.

2   To be precise the annexation of the Orange Free State and its change of name took place over the period 24–8 May 1900.

3   Cd 1789 *Report [and Cd 1790–91 Minutes of Evidence and Appendices] of His Majesty's commissioners appointed to inquire into the military preparations and other matters connected with the war in South Africa*; hereafter *Elgin Commission Report*.

in South Africa, begun by Henderson and continued under Sir Frederick Maurice.[4] After 1910, almost nothing was published specifically about the Boer War for almost 50 years, when it began to attract the interest of political and social historians.[5] The war's centenary became the occasion for several historical studies and helped a reviving interest in the wider history of the British Empire.[6] But as with much of the military history of the Empire, books dealing with the Boer War still mostly take their interpretation of its military events from the versions that appeared in its immediate aftermath.[7]

Soon after its end, it became a cliché in British military circles that the Boer War had been so unusual as to make it difficult to draw any firm lessons. 'All wars are abnormal', John French commented in 1910, 'because there is no such thing as a normal war', reflecting the government policy of sending the Army to fight almost anywhere in the world.[8] Certainly there are difficulties in separating out the role of any one arm like the cavalry from the wider context of the war and its accompanying battles.[9] But the Boer War was uniquely important as a major test of cavalry doctrine. Twenty of the line cavalry regiments (plus the composite Household Regiment) fought in South Africa, most of them almost from its start to its end.[10] Even more important to the debates that followed was how the events of the war were interpreted by participating individuals and factions within the Army (and by the news reporters who accompanied them), and how relationships and antagonisms formed under the pressure of the fighting.

The major problem in British planning for the Boer War arose from a separation between political and military authority left unresolved by Wolseley's appointment

---

4   Amery (ed.), *The Times History of the War in South Africa* (seven volumes); Maurice (ed.), *History of the War in South Africa 1899–1902* (four volumes and four map volumes), due to illness Maurice's name did not appear on the third and fourth volumes; see also Amery, *My Political Life Volume One*, pp. 133–200; Beckett, 'British Official History and the South African War', pp. 33–42.

5   Packenham, *The Boer War* in 1979 has been claimed as the first study of the Boer War in English since the First World War, but was pre-dated by Pemberton, *Battles of the Boer War* in 1964, Selby, *The Boer War* in 1969, and Belfield, *The Boer War* in 1975; see also Price, *An Imperial War and the British Working Class*; Koss (ed.), *The Pro-Boers*, and for a commentary on these studies Miller, 'In Support of the "Imperial Mission"?', pp. 691–711.

6   For example Nasson, *The South African War 1899–1902*; Judd and Surridge, *The Boer War*; and Marix Evans, *The Boer War: South Africa 1899–1902*; Gooch (ed.), *The Boer War*. See also Judd, *Empire*; Nasson, *Britannia's Empire*, and Fergusson, *Empire*.

7   Exceptions being the invaluable Pretorius, *Life on Commando during the Anglo-Boer War, 1899–1902*, and Miller, *Lord Methuen and the British Army*. No modern general history of the Boer War combines the recent findings of military historians with wider analysis.

8   French in preface to Bernhardi, *Cavalry in War and Peace*, p. viii.

9   A short summary of the arguments on British cavalry doctrine and the war can be found in Badsey, 'The Boer War (1899–1902) and British Cavalry Doctrine: A Re-Evaluation', pp. 75–98. Although inevitably that article and this chapter cover some of the same issues and draw on some of the same evidence, they are intended as complementary to each other rather than as duplications.

10 Stirling, *Our Regiments in South Africa*, pp. 398–462; Hall, *The Hall Handbook of the Anglo-Boer War*, pp. 71–9.

as C-in-C in 1895.[11] The war was far from unexpected, particularly after the Jameson Raid of December 1895–January 1896. This was followed by the further war scare in 1897, leading the Transvaal to rearm, including purchasing 25,000 new German 7mm Mauser Model 93 magazine rifles with 10,000,000 cartridges.[12] Wolseley's assessment was that the Orange Free State as well as the Transvaal would have to be conquered, and that this would need a strong Corps of three divisions or 47,000 men sent from Great Britain. The distances involved and the conditions in South Africa meant that the British would need about three months from the first decision to mobilise until they were ready to start an invasion of the Boer republics. Negotiations with the Transvaal and the Orange Free State broke down on 5 June 1899, Redvers Buller was advised that he would command the Corps, which would include a cavalry division, and Wolseley pressed for mobilisation. But for domestic political reasons the British government declined to give the order, although in September it sent some reinforcements to South Africa from India, including a British cavalry brigade, together with a few troops and special service officers from home. Among those sent out was French (with Haig as his chief staff officer), on the assumption that he would command the Cavalry Division (two cavalry brigades plus a mounted infantry battalion and two horse artillery batteries, or about 6,700 soldiers), when it arrived.[13]

A squadron of the New South Wales Lancers was training at Aldershot in 1899 and mostly volunteered to serve with the Cavalry Division.[14] Further offers of volunteers were made by the dominions and by the yeomanry at home, but the British government seriously underestimated the military difficulties of conquering both Boer republics and the need for mounted troops (also, the yeomanry regiments were constitutionally forbidden to serve overseas, even in Ireland). In July 1899 Joseph Chamberlain, the Colonial Secretary, sent a telegram asking the dominions for volunteers:

[Formed] in units suitable for military requirements: Firstly, units should be about 125 men; secondly, may be Infantry, Mounted Infantry, or Cavalry. In view of numbers already available, Infantry most, Cavalry least serviceable; thirdly, all should be armed with .303 rifles or carbines, which can be supplied by Imperial [British] government, if necessary;

---

11 Surridge, *Managing the South African War, 1899–1902*, pp. 1–56; Hamer, *The British Army*, pp. 168–200; Kochanski, *Sir Garnet Wolseley*, pp. 234–45; Kochanski, 'Planning for War in the Final Years of the *Pax Britannica*, 1889–1903', pp. 16–21; Strachan, *The Politics of the British Army*, pp. 121–2.

12 Pretorius, *Life on Commando during the Anglo-Boer War, 1899–1902*, p. 80; strictly, 'Mauser 7mm' was a popular rather than official name for the Model 93, also sometimes known as the 'Spanish Mauser'.

13 Holmes, *The Little Field Marshal*, pp. 53–4; Goodenough and Dalton, *The Army Book for the British Empire*, p. 504.

14 Grey, *A Military History of Australia*, p. 53. As Australian historians like to point out, the Lancers were training at Aldershot at their own expense. Although strictly it is an anachronism, troops from Australia, Canada, and New Zealand are called 'dominion' troops in this chapter, to distinguish them from 'colonial' troops recruited in South Africa itself.

fourthly, must provide own equipment and Mounted troops their own horses; fifthly, not more than one captain and three subalterns to each unit.[15]

No distinction was made between mounted troops armed with carbines and with longer-range rifles, despite this being held up as a critical difference between MI and other mounted troops. There were later claims that Chamberlain had given priority to infantry from the dominions intending their conversion to mounted infantry with local horses on their arrival. In fact dominion infantry were very useful in the war, and the first Canadian contingent, modelled on a plan from Hutton, was an infantry battalion with attached machine-guns and mounted infantry ('dragoons'), very much in keeping with British MI doctrine. Of 7,368 Canadians who volunteered and served in the Boer War, only about 2,300 were mounted troops.[16]

The British government's decision to send the Corps under Buller to South Africa was made on 29 September, and the first troop transports sailed two weeks later.[17] But British plans and preparations were pre-empted by an ultimatum from the Transvaal and the Orange Free State on 9 October, and a Boer offensive which began within two days. There were probably at least 45,000 burghers under arms in the Orange Free State and the Transvaal in 1899. As a citizen army with some professional artillery, their great advantage over the British was their mobility on ponies that were fully acclimatised to the conditions of the *veldt* (grassland or steppe), and able to survive on about eight pounds of grain or oats a day and some grazing.[18] In contrast the British had just over 27,000 troops in South Africa when war was declared, including 14,500 horse soldiers consisting of the two regular cavalry regiments stationed there, the brigade of three regular regiments being rushed from India, about 5,000 permanently embodied or volunteer mounted riflemen such as the Natal Carbineers, and the remainder a mixture of recently raised colonial mounted rifle corps, including the South African Light Horse under Byng, and the Rhodesia Regiment under Plumer.[19]

The Orange Free State and the Transvaal lay mostly on the high veldt, a grassland plateau 3,000 to 6,000 feet above sea level, separated to the south from Cape Colony and the mountain kingdom of Basutoland by an escarpment which rose as it continued eastward to become the Drakensberg mountain range, further separating the Transvaal from northern Natal where the invasion route crossed the grain of hills and steep river valleys. Otherwise, the rolling grasslands of the veldt ranged from open pastures in the east to dusty red semi-desert in the west, broken only by characteristic flat-topped rocky hills like islands, known evocatively as *kop* or *kopje* ('head'). With a total area of 1,360,000 square miles, the scale of this theatre of war

---

15 *Elgin Commission Report*, Evidence Volume I, p. 341; Packenham, *The Boer War*, p. 305.

16 Miller, *Painting the Map Red*, pp. 50–51; Hall, *The Hall Handbook of the Anglo-Boer War*, p. 84.

17 Dunlop, *The Development of the British Army 1899–1914*, p. 73.

18 Rogers, *The Mounted Troops of the British Army 1066–1945*, pp. 227–8.

19 Maurice, *History of the War in South Africa 1899–1902*, Volume I, pp 1–3 and p. 94; Hall, *The Hall Handbook of the Anglo-Boer War*, pp. 84–5; Williams, *Byng of Vimy*, pp. 28–30; Harington, *Plumer of Messines*, pp. 32–5; Powell, *Plumer*, pp. 55–85.

posed much greater problems for the British in supply and transport – 'logistics' in more recent military terminology – than their previous campaigns in South Africa. From the southern frontiers to as far north as the Johannesburg area with its *rands* or transverse ridges the major rivers all flowed westerly, following the slope of the veldt down to the southern Atlantic, and making them natural barriers across the British advance. The only practical invasion routes followed the three single-track rail lines built from south to north. In what became the western theatre of the war the line from Cape Town mounted the escarpment, reached the railhead at De Aar Junction, crossed the Orange River and then ran northwards to the diamond town of Kimberley and on to Mafeking, both just to the west of the border with the Orange Free State. In the midlands theatre the lines from the coastal ports joined together above the escarpment near Colesburg before running north-easterly through Bloemfontein and on to Johannesburg and Pretoria. In the eastern or Natal theatre the rail line from Durban on the coast ran north across the Tugela River at Colenso on to Ladysmith, then up past Laing's Nek and Majuba Hill through the Drakensberg mountains and north-west to Johannesburg. The British were dependent on these railway lines to supply themselves in all three theatres, as were the Boers in Natal.[20]

The rare combination of the altitude, clear air and open spaces of the high veldt made it possible to see and shoot for well over 2,000 yards, up to the maximum ranges of the new magazine rifles, but even in the hills of northern Natal the longer range and greater accuracy of these new weapons was deadly, and with smokeless powder concealment amid the rocks and gullies was easy. Some British officers had recent experience of fighting enemies armed with the new rifles, especially those who had served in the Tirah Expedition in 1897, including Lieutenant General Lord Methuen, Ian Hamilton, and William Birdwood.[21] For both sides, field artillery proved much less effective than had been expected, particularly against earth entrenchments, and co-ordination between artillery and infantry was primitive; but in the early battles the horse artillery with the Cavalry Division, which included Major Henry Horne among its officers, was very effective in providing supporting fire in the open.[22]

The laws of the Orange Free State and the Transvaal governing the raising of Boer commandos for war differed in detail, but essentially all able bodied citizens of military age were required to muster with their horses and rifles and with supplies for a few days, after which their provisioning became the government's responsibility, but neither state's commissariat was equipped to supply a large force for an extended campaign.[23] Commandos assembled and were named based on their local towns or regions, officers were elected, and decision by *krijsraad* ('council of war') was

---

20 Hall, *The Hall Handbook of the Anglo-Boer War 1899–1902*, pp. 227–37; Maurice, *History of the War in South Africa 1899–1902*, Volume I, pp. 54–67; van der Waag, 'South Africa and the Boer Military System', pp. 51–4.

21 Miller, *Lord Methuen and the British Army*, pp. 55–9; Lee, *A Soldier's Life*, pp. 40–41; Birdwood, *Khaki and Gown*, pp. 77–81.

22 Cooper, *Haig*, Volume I, pp. 380–81; Wessels (ed.), *Lord Roberts and the War in South Africa 1899–1902*, p. 54 and p. 59; Robbins, 'Henry Horne', pp. 98–9.

23 Hall, *The Hall Handbook of the Anglo-Boer War 1899–1902*, pp. 1–33; Pretorius, *Life on Commando during the Anglo-Boer War, 1899–1902*, pp. 25–34; van der Waag, 'South Africa and the Boer Military System', pp. 54–69; Wessels, 'Afrikaners at War', pp. 76–82.

common, although the upper echelons of command were dominated by a quasi-aristocracy of old established families. A common practice was for the men 'on commando' to be accompanied by their families and retainers with ox-wagons, partly for supplies and partly for mutual protection, although the traditional Boer wagon laager was little used as being too vulnerable to British artillery. The informal nature of Boer military service meant that only general estimates are possible for their numbers; the size of a commando was usually between 300 and 3,000 men, and it is unlikely that the Boer forces in any one battle numbered more than 15,000 rifles. Volunteers from around the world, some of them fighting in national 'brigades', lent political support to the Boers and some colour to the early part of the war, but were of little military value or importance.[24] Estimates of the total Boer forces under arms during the war have ranged from 60,000 to 87,000, supported by up to 10,000 African *agterryers* ('after-riders' or retainers) and an unknown number of youngsters known as *penkoppe*, while 20,779 burghers surrendered at its end.[25] As Colonel Maude put it, without too much exaggeration, the British advance on Pretoria was the equivalent of a campaign from Vienna to Saint Petersburg opposed by 20 Cossack divisions.[26]

Although the Boers had been known to carry out assaults on African strongholds, their preferred style was to take up a good defensive or ambush position, invite the enemy to attack, and prepare to escape if combat threatened to become hand-to-hand.[27] They saw no virtue in a heroic last stand, and attached no stigma to avoiding a particular battle. The most famous of the Boer commando leaders, Christiaan de Wet, recounted how on the day of one crucial engagement eight burghers presented him with medical exemption certificates issued that morning.[28] Some Boers were equipped with militarily obsolescent but reliable rifles like the Martini-Henry, but most favoured the Mauser 7 mm, which was slightly superior at ranges above 2,000

---

24 These included two Irish 'brigades' as well as contingents from Scandinavia, Austria-Hungary and Russia; see McCracken, *MacBride's Brigade*; Davidson and Filatova, *The Russians and the Anglo-Boer War*; Judd and Surridge, *The Boer War*, pp. 247–51.

25 See Reitz, *Commando*; Deneys Reitz was 17 when the war began in 1899. Under the commando laws all men aged 16–60 were liable to serve, but usually only those 18–50 were called out. *Penkoppe*, literally 'quill-pen heads' and referring to young buffalo when they sprout their first horns, was applied as a term to Boers under 20 years old; some who served on commando may have been as young as eight. See also Pretorius, *Life on Commando during the Anglo-Boer War, 1899–1902*, pp. 237–41; Labuschagne, *Ghostriders of the Anglo-Boer War 1899–1902*, pp. 45–51; van der Waag, 'South Africa and the Boer Military System', pp. 45–69; Hall, *The Hall Handbook of the Anglo-Boer War*, pp. 1–33.

26 Maude, *Cavalry: Its Past and Future*, p. 271. From Cape Town to Pretoria is just over 800 miles compared to just under 1,000 miles from Vienna to Saint Petersburg; a Cossack division at this date would normally be more than 4,000 soldiers. By February 1900, the British Army in South Africa was the equivalent of eight infantry divisions, a cavalry division, and a division of irregulars and auxiliaries.

27 Laband, *The Transvaal Rebellion*, p. 64.

28 de Wet, *Three Years War*, p. 80; Pretorius, *Life on Commando during the Anglo-Boer War, 1899–1902*, pp. 145–6.

yards to the British Lee-Metford, although later in the war they became dependent on captured British weapons and ammunition.[29]

There is some dispute as to how far the Boer leadership devised a coherent strategy for the war, but their expectations in declaring war on the British while Buller's troops were still on the high seas were based on their past success in the Transvaal War, coupled with recognition of what was possible for their citizen army. After some preliminary battles in northern Natal the Boers laid siege to Ladysmith and Kimberley, and also to Mafeking in the far north-west (defended by Baden-Powell with much publicity), correctly expecting the British to advance and relieve all three sieges, and planning to defeat the relief columns as at Majuba, which they expected to lead to another humiliating British capitulation.[30] Some more aggressive or idealistic Boer leaders, including Jan Christiaan Smuts, argued that the republics should mount a general invasion of Natal and Cape Colony, provoking a mass uprising among the majority Afrikaans-speaking white population there. In the course of the war repeated small Boer invasions of Cape Colony and Natal were mounted in pursuit of this mass rebellion, but despite Boer hopes and British fears only small risings occurred.[31]

This Boer seizure of the initiative distorted British strategy for several months, leaving them little choice but to react to the Boer sieges, while virtually all the British problems of the war stemmed from their initial failure to co-ordinate their political and military warplanning. The average sea journey time to Cape Town for a British troopship was 23 days, and the last troops of Buller's corps did not reach South Africa until 29 December. Buller committed much of his forces to the Natal theatre and the relief of Ladysmith (defended by Lieutenant General Sir George White), while a division-sized force under Lord Methuen in the western theatre attempted to relieve Kimberley. As the British encountered further problems and suffered defeats, the equivalent of a second Corps was sent out, followed later by more reinforcements. The War Office coped surprisingly well with the demands for men, supplies and equipment for a war on this scale. In the course of the war, over 379,000 soldiers were transported by ship to South Africa, and only 220 arrived unfit for service. But this was not true of the demand for horses, especially for the cavalry; the tiny Remount Department, which expected to expand only from buying 2,500 horses a year in peacetime to buying 25,000 a year, became a scandalous failure as demands far exceeded this figure.[32] As on previous deployments, horses could not be exercised on board ship, and they mostly sailed for long distances from the northern to the southern hemisphere and so from winter to summer conditions.[33] For

---

29 van der Waag, 'South Africa and the Boer Military System', pp. 62–4; Pretorius, *Life on Commando during the Anglo-Boer War, 1899–1902*, pp. 80–95.

30 Wessels, 'Afrikaners at War', pp. 82–6.

31 Hancock and van der Poel (eds), *Selections from the Smuts Papers Volume I June 1886–May 1902*, pp. 313–29; Hancock, *Smuts: Volume I: The Sanguine Years 1870–1919*, pp. 107–17.

32 *Elgin Commission Report*, p. 98; Spiers, *The Late Victorian Army 1899–1902*, pp. 319–20.

33 Seely, *Adventure*, p. 56, whose memoirs are not entirely reliable, claimed to have exercised his horses on the voyage (it would be enlightening to know how) and to have lost

practical purposes all British Army horses reached South Africa unfit, and some did not survive the journey. Of 339,329 horses shipped to South Africa, 13,000 or four per cent died in transit, together with 2,000 out of 103,000 mules.[34] Some regiments coming out in 1899 were particularly badly hit: Edmund Allenby's squadron of the 6th (Inniskilling) Dragoons lost 26 horses out of 130 from pneumonia, injuries, and 'sheer seasickness and exhaustion'; while the 10th Hussars lost 18 horses early in the voyage from 'rough seas', followed by almost two-thirds of their horses in a shipwreck.[35]

An authoritative study of horses in the Boer War was undertaken by Major General Frederick Smith of the Army Veterinary Corps, first published with the journal *Veterinary Record* 1912–1914, and then in book form as *A Veterinary History of the War in South Africa 1889–1902*, although publication was delayed until 1919.[36] In Smith's judgement nine weeks' acclimatisation and recovery time was required for British horses after their arrival in South Africa, but this was very much a command decision weighing the needs of the horses against other factors; Kitchener, Hutton and Haig all thought that between two and four weeks were enough.[37] In practice, how much acclimatisation and training both individual horses and mounted units got before being sent into action varied from a few weeks to a few days. Having survived the voyage, the horses were transported by rail under equally poor conditions. The 500-mile rail journey from Cape Town up to De Aar Junction, 4,000 feet above sea level, took on average 33 hours, described by Allenby as 'we curved and crawled through passes among rocky hills, pulled by one engine and pushed by another', and by a sergeant major of the 7th Dragoon Guards, who reached Cape Town on 1 March 1900 and was sent to the front less than two weeks later, as 'This is awful travelling for the horses, they are put into trucks, packed like sardines, not tied up, it's positively cruel, we have lost two already, and ever so many kicked and knocked about.'.[38] Even when they arrived in the theatre, the unacclimatised and weakened horses were vulnerable, since in 1898 financial pressure had led to the deletion of a 'sick horse hospital' from the Army mobilisation scheme, and sick horses were mixed with healthy replacements in the same locations, virtually guaranteeing a pandemic of horse diseases.[39] All these issues of transport and horse care were part of the

---

'only' seven out of 300, or just over two per cent.

34 Brander, *The 10th Royal Hussars*, pp. 75–6; Hall, *The Hall Handbook of the Anglo-Boer War*, pp. 225–8; Spiers, *The Late Victorian Army 1868–1902*, pp. 320–21.

35 LHCMA Allenby Papers 1/2: Allenby to his wife, 16 November 1899.

36 Smith, *A Veterinary History of the War in South Africa 1889–1902*; Rimington, *The Horse in Recent War*, pp. 3–8; Tylden, *Horses and Saddlery*, pp. 28–30 and pp. 58–63.

37 Smith, *A Veterinary History of the War in South Africa 1899–1902*, pp. 189–90; NLS Haig Papers 2b: Diary entry, 13 October 1899; Wessels (ed.), *Lord Kitchener and the War in South Africa 1899–1902*, pp. 23–4.

38 LHCMA Allenby Papers 1/2: Allenby to his wife, 15 December 1899; NAM Cobb Papers: Cobb to his home, 13 March 1900; Hall, *The Hall Handbook of the War in South Africa 1899–1902*, p. 230.

39 Smith, *A History of the Royal Army Veterinary Corps 1796–1919*, pp. 208–10; Baker, *Battles and Battlefields of the Anglo-Boer War 1899–1902*, p. 238.

conditions of the campaign, but they were also matters for trained staff officers, of which there was a serious shortage throughout the war.[40]

The first battles, in which the commandos invaded northern Natal and threatened to invade Cape Colony through the midland route, showed that at least some British cavalry regiments had absorbed pre-war doctrine and used mounted and dismounted tactics in combination. These lessons were passed on to arriving cavalry regiments, so that the 16th Lancers, who would lead the Klip Drift charge in February 1900, spent their first squadron exercises a week after arrival in December 1899 practising 'dismounted and open order work'.[41] But correct peacetime doctrine did not automatically produce victory on the battlefield. At the Battle of Talana Hill in the Natal theatre on 20 October 1899, the 18th Hussars placed themselves dismounted with their machine-guns in a perfect position to shatter a Boer advance with firepower; but their commanding officer abandoned this for an ambitious advance that led to most of the regiment being cut off behind Boer lines, dismounting, and surrendering.[42] In contrast, at Elandslaagte next day French defeated his Boer opponents by combining a widely-spaced infantry attack with dismounted firepower from his colonial mounted riflemen, and the spectacular 'charge of the two Fifths' to end the battle. The infantry assault was commanded by Ian Hamilton, and as an early British success Elandslaagte was claimed by all schools of thought as their triumph. Although French made good use of dismounted firepower, after Elandslaagte he was convinced of the effect of mounted charges on Boer morale. Defending the Colesburg area in the midlands against possible Boer incursions, he improvised a cavalry force by training the New Zealand Mounted Rifles to charge mounted with fixed bayonets, noting that 'they should be armed with swords'.[43]

Next month Haig drew up a memorandum on these October battles and their lessons, stressing the number of times that cavalry (using the term to include colonial mounted riflemen) had acted dismounted with success, arguing that 'these operations have shown clearly the greatly increased power of action possessed by Cavalry, now that it is armed with a good carbine', and that cavalry needed even more training dismounted. Haig's overall assessment for British prospects in the eastern theatre was:

> We must conclude then, that for offensive warfare in Natal the offensive power of Infantry is limited. Infantry is essential for the assault on positions which the Boers hold as pivots, but about half the attacking force should consist of mounted troops in order to secure the flanks of the attacking Infantry column, and outmanoeuvre the Boers.[44]

---

40 Bond, *The Victorian Army and the Staff College 1854–1914*, pp. 181–211.
41 NAM Bellew Papers: Diary entries, 26–7 January 1900.
42 Marling, *Rifleman and Hussar*, pp. 243–5; Anglesey, *A History of the British Cavalry Volume 4*, pp. 38–46.
43 IWM French Papers: Diary entry, 4 December 1899; NLS Haig Papers 325b: New Zealand Rifle Association to Lady Haig, 4 March 1937.
44 Cooper, *Haig*, Volume I, pp. 377–82.

Haig was very critical of the MI: the ten-week training period was simply not enough to produce good horsed soldiers. In November 1899 he wrote to his sister Henrietta Jameson:

> The one thing required here is *Cavalry*! I think the country ought to be alive now to the fact (which we have already pointed out) that we don't keep up enough of this arm in peacetime. This Mounted Infantry craze is now I trust exploded. So far they have proved useless, and are not likely to be of use *until they learn to ride*. You had better not give these views to Sir Evelyn [Wood], for both he and Lord Wolseley are the parents of the Mounted Infantry. I am very sorry for the latter, for they are the best of officers and men but they feel they are no use and can't get about on their horses.[45]

This and other letters written during the campaign suggest that Haig was using his sister, who with her husband was well-connected socially, to communicate unofficially with Wood. In his memorandum, Haig stressed the value of good mounted riflemen such as the recently raised colonials of the Imperial Light Horse as 'essentially Cavalry, being organised as such and trained and led by Cavalry Officers, while there is a considerable proportion [sic] of old Cavalry soldiers in the ranks'.[46] This was in contrast with the view taken by Henry Wilson, serving on the staff of an infantry brigade in Natal in April 1900, 'What we want is a lot of MI, but Buller in the last five months has only raised 200 which are always kept in [the] rear. Our regular Cav[alry] are quite useless.'[47]

Once Buller attempted to relieve Ladysmith, he found his army in northern Natal suffering from the same severe transport and supply problems that had beset campaigning in Zululand and Natal in earlier wars, but on a much greater scale. On 6 November 1899, against the later protests of his Principal Veterinary Officer at Cape Town, Buller issued a standing order for the whole of the Army in South Africa limiting rations for horses to 12 pounds of oats a day, the entire ration to be reduced by up to a maximum of one-third if hay or grazing was available. In practice this meant that about eight pounds of oats a day became the expected British ration for cavalry and artillery horses, rising to ten pounds by the second half of the war.[48] This was enough for an acclimatised pony ridden by an accomplished Boer horsemaster, but little short of starvation for a British troop horse. Despite the efforts of the previous decades, British horses were still overladen; it took two men to lift a saddle with all its accoutrements onto the horse, and the regulation bit and breast-strap made it impossible for the horse to graze properly unless it was unsaddled; some replacement saddles also fitted badly.[49] By the war's end the weight

---

45 Scott (ed.), *Douglas Haig: The Preparatory Prologue: Diaries and Letters 1861–1914*, p. 147, emphasis in the original.

46 Cooper, *Haig*, Volume I, pp. 377–8.

47 IWM Wilson Papers: Diary entry, 11 April 1900; Wilson's estimate of only 200 mounted infantry raised under Buller's command is inexplicably low.

48 Smith, *A Veterinary History of the War in South Africa 1899–1902*, pp. 14–15 and pp. 185–6.

49 Tylden, *Horses and Saddlery*, p. 29; NLS Haig Papers 34: Cavalry Division War Diary entry 3 February 1900.

carried on the horse had been reduced in most British mounted corps to 17 stones, but this was still too much for underfed and unacclimatised horses. The quality of grass on the veldt varied considerably, and offsaddling or grazing horses was a dangerous option in the face of enemy superiority in mounted men. Major Michael Rimington of the 6th (Inniskilling) Dragoons, who was thought the Army's best horsemaster in South Africa, and for much of the war commanded his own volunteer mounted rifle regiment of Rimington's Guides – more often known as Rimington's Tigers from the strips of big cat fur that they wore as hatbands – recalled one officer telling him that 'If I graze my horses I should be likely to lose some, for which the responsibility would fall on me; whereas if they starve they do so in accordance with regulations, and I have no responsibility.'[50] Replacing this peacetime attitude with one in which officers were encouraged to take responsibility was in keeping with the traditions of cavalry spirit, and was one of the lessons that the British took from this war. Overloaded, underfed horses rapidly lost weight and condition and suffered sore backs from saddle slippage; the choice was then between resting the horses to recover, or forcing them to carrying on in pain and an increasingly weakened state, usually described as 'exhaustion'. At the altitude of the veldt, many underfed horses collapsed in the heat or died of cold at night in the southern winter, and before a veterinary hospital was established at Bloemfontein in March 1900 it was policy to shoot horses rather than leave them to suffer, so that many horses that could have recovered were destroyed, increasing the overall demand.[51]

This horse and supply problem was never solved for the duration of the war; according to the painfully detailed official calculations, of 518,794 horses and 150,781 mules and donkeys in British service, 326,073 horses, and 51,339 mules and donkeys, died – a loss of 66 per cent almost entirely from starvation, disease, and maltreatment, including an average of more than a thousand animals a week destroyed.[52] One later estimate was that the cost of horses, at £22,000,000, was about one-tenth of the cost of the war for the British.[53] Major General Smith argued that the horse population of South Africa in 1899 was enough to have met the Army's needs, but these were almost all smaller 'Cape Horse' types, thought suitable by the British for mounted riflemen rather than a charge. Also, the Cape Colony Dutch were unwilling to sell these horses to the British, and the Boer forces quickly commandeered most of those available.[54]

Victory in battle could have negated or at least disguised all British shortcomings in classic *Small Wars* style, but for the Boers the basic assumption behind this British way of colonial war – that the enemy would oppose an invasion by attacking in battle and so be destroyed by British firepower – did not apply, and the British were

---

50 Rimington, *The Horse in Recent War*, p. 19.
51 HPL Wolseley Papers Autograph Roberts 9: Roberts to Wolseley, 1 July 1900; Marling, *Rifleman and Hussar*, p. 276.
52 Smith, *A Veterinary History of the War in South Africa 1899–1902*, p. 226; Hall, *The Hall Handbook of the Anglo-Boer War 1899–1902*, pp. 236–7; Baker, *Battles and Battlefields of the Anglo-Boer War 1899–1902*, pp. 238–9; Maurice, *History of the War in South Africa 1899–1902*, Volume IV, p. 650.
53 Rogers, *The Mounted Troops of the British Army 1066–1945*, p. 227.
54 Baker, *Battles and Battlefields of the Anglo-Boer War 1899–1902*, p. 238.

obliged to attack on the battlefield in their efforts to reach Ladysmith and Kimberley. The typical battle of November–December 1899 consisted of the British advancing with infantry against a Boer firing line, after an inadequate reconnaissance due to the shortage or incapacity of their mounted troops, the infantry taking heavy casualties sometimes without seeing the enemy, and either driving them away or being repulsed. This culminated in 'Black Week' in December 1899 when three British columns, one on each of the main invasion routes, were defeated in turn. It was the nature rather than the scale of these defeats, and similar battles such as Modder River in November 1899 and Spion Kop in January 1900, which caused such a shock: they were defeats for British generalship and staffwork. The immediate reaction was that Roberts was sent out to South Africa to take command, with Kitchener as his chief staff officer, together with more reinforcements from Britain and around the Empire. A further four regular cavalry regiments reached South Africa by the end of March 1900, bringing the total in the country to 17 regiments.

After the first defeat of Black Week, suffered by Lieutenant General Sir William Gatacre's force at Stormberg on 10 December 1899 in the midlands theatre, Haig wrote to his sister that 'If we only had sufficient cavalry on *fit* horses we could do what we like with the Boers. It is because self-advertising men like Gatacre push on without realising the value of a well-found cavalry that we have been checked at so many points.'[55] The same lack of reconnoitring troops handicapped Lord Methuen's advance along the western railway towards Kimberley, leading to his repulse at Magersfontein on 11 December, the second defeat of Black Week. Methuen had defeated his Boer opponents in two previous battles, at Belmont on 22 November and Graspan (or Enslin) on 25 November, but been unable to exploit the victory with a mounted charge as French had done at Elandslaagte. 'My guns played on the masses of [retreating] horsemen', Methuen wrote after Graspan, 'but my few cavalry, dead beat, were powerless, and for a second time I longed for a Cavalry Brigade and a H[orse] A[rtillery] Battery to let me reap the fruits of a hard fought action.'[56] After Magersfontein, French offered to send Methuen the equivalent of a strong mounted brigade, but Methuen declined since his supply line through to Modder River could not provide enough food to sustain so many horses.[57] The third and final defeat of Black Week fell on Buller's army in Natal on 15 December at Colenso, in another battle marked by British infantry advancing against heavy fire from a largely unlocated enemy.

To add to these problems, the few British regular cavalry regiments had been spread between the theatres at the start of the war, and the resulting improvised mounted brigades had no common tactical doctrine. At Colenso, Buller's mounted brigade of 1,800 men under Lord Dundonald (until recently commanding officer of the 2nd Life Guards) consisted of a battery of field artillery, the 1st (Royal) Dragoons and two squadrons of the 13th Hussars, and four newly raised colonial mounted rifle

---

55 NLS Haig Papers 6b: Haig to his sister, 12 December 1899, emphasis in the original; Maurice, *History of the War in South Africa*, Volume I, pp. 288–303.

56 Quoted in Miller, *Lord Methuen and the British Army*, p. 102.

57 Amery, *The Times History of the War in South Africa 1899–1902*, Volume III, pp. 370–71; Miller, *Lord Methuen and the British Army*, pp. 123–59.

regiments: Bethune's Mounted Infantry, Thorneycroft's Mounted Infantry, part of the South African Light Horse; and a composite regiment made up of two companies of Imperial MI, a squadron of the Imperial Light Horse, and a combined squadron of Natal Carbineers and Natal Mounted Police. Dundonald's staff also included Hubert Gough of the 16th Lancers and William Birdwood of the 11th Bengal Lancers, while among the officers of the Imperial Light Horse was G.T.M. 'Tom' Bridges, then of the Royal Field Artillery.[58] In keeping with his own earlier experiences and with practicality, Dundonald made no effort either to standardise doctrine in his brigade or to encourage mounted tactics.[59]

On 16 December 1899, the day after Colenso, Buller telegraphed to Lord Lansdowne, the Secretary of State for War, with a request for more mounted troops that has seldom been quoted in full:

> Would it be possible for you to raise 8,000 irregulars in England, organised not in regiments but in companies of 100 each? They should be equipped as Mounted Infantry, be able to shoot as well as possible and ride decently. I would amalgamate them with colonists [colonials]. A party of the West Kent Yeomanry Cavalry are among the best irregulars I have here. Mounted men are absolutely necessary to finish this war, or indeed to hold our own. Infantry cannot cover the distances, with them one is always obliged to attack a prepared position, the very thing which ought not to be done, and the water difficulty is tremendous.[60]

Clearly, Buller wanted reinforcements to be amalgamated into his existing locally raised 'colonial' mounted regiments, which served brigaded with the cavalry, and his use of the term 'mounted infantry' rather than 'mounted rifles' was a matter of words only. Buller's telegram was nevertheless understood by Lansdowne to exclude the yeomanry regiments and any regular troops. Dr Arthur Conan Doyle took up the call, writing to *The Times* on 18 December that 'England is full of men who can ride and shoot', which he further defined as 'riding after foxes or shooting pheasants', and who were anxious to serve their country.[61] The same argument was used by Lansdowne's parliamentary under-secretary, George Wyndham, himself a yeomanry officer, who had been approached by yeoman friends in the county gentry and aristocracy. 'They are men of affairs', Wyndham told Lansdowne, 'and as masters of foxhounds, they are in touch with the young riding farmers and horse-masters of

---

58 Bridges, *Alarms and Excursions*, pp. 17–18.

59 Bethune's and Thorneycroft's Mounted Infantry were raised and commanded respectively by Lieutenant Colonel Edward Bethune of the 16th Lancers and Lieutenant Colonel Alec Thorneycroft of the Royal Scots Fusiliers.

60 NAM Roberts Papers 114: Printed South African War Confidential Telegrams, telegram number 56 (SA91) from Buller to Lansdowne, 16 December 1899, pp. 25–6. The reference to the West Kent Yeomanry, which is puzzling, is usually omitted when this passage is quoted. Buller was presumably referring to the contingent of 11 men from their sister regiment, the Royal East Kent Yeomanry, who served as volunteers with the South African Light Horse from October 1899 until the arrival of the Imperial Yeomanry; see Mollo, *The Kent Yeomanry*, p. 28.

61 Letter by Dr Arthur Conan Doyle to *The Times*, 18 December 1899.

this country.'[62] A precondition was that this new mounted force must raise and equip itself, since the War Office undertook to provide only arms, ammunition, tents, and a capitation grant of £25 (plus £40 for each horse).[63]

This was the haphazard origin of the Imperial Yeomanry or IY, a force of volunteer mounted infantry led by the gentry. The IY were formed by royal warrant on 24 December 1899; the committee of home force yeomanry officers which oversaw their creation met informally from 19 December onwards, became officially established by the War Office on 4 January 1900, and worked until May when the War Office took over and ended IY recruiting. Lansdowne expected to be able to send Roberts about 4,000 IY; in fact the response was just over 11,000 volunteers, organised into companies each of 131 all ranks, plus staffs and supernumeries.[64] From the call for recruits on 18 December, the first IY sailed from Great Britain on 27 January and arrived in South Africa on 21 February, while the last of the contingent sailed on 14 April and arrived on 3 May.[65] It was a remarkable achievement, except that there was little if any time for training in military skills, and nothing resembling a tactical doctrine. On 28 December Wolseley protested to Lansdowne that:

> I am very anxious to supply the GOC [General Officer Commanding] in South Africa with 8,000 *trained men accustomed to some sort of discipline*; but to go to the highways and byways and pick up any civilians who will volunteer to go to South Africa quite regardless of whether they have ever learnt even the rudiments of discipline and to form them into companies or battalions in the proportion of three of each to every one of the very imperfectly drilled and disciplined yeomanry men who volunteer is, according to my knowledge of war, a dangerous experiment.[66]

Lansdowne dismissed Wolseley's warning with the barbed quip that 'The Boers are not, I suppose, very highly drilled and disciplined.'[67] Behind the insult, and the political near-impossibility of Lansdowne declining the offer of the IY, was the belief that, although it took a year or more to train cavalry, a mounted infantryman could be created almost from nothing, and that men from rural areas who could ride, shoot and hunt would somehow become natural mounted riflemen in war.

The connection of the IY with the home service yeomanry regiments was both indirect and confusing. Officially the 78 IY companies that were raised were organised into 20 battalions, but despite official strictures some IY preferred to use the yeomanry

---

62 Quoted in Bennett, *Absent Minded Beggars*, p. 12.

63 The best short description of the official and constitutional issues involved in forming the Imperial Yeomanry remains Dunlop, *The Development of the British Army 1899–1914*, pp. 104–18.

64 Ibid., pp. 75–6 and pp. 104–12. Exact figures for the Imperial Yeomanry vary between sources, but a useful list of battalions, companies and totals has been compiled by Bennett, *Absent-Minded Beggars*, pp. 226–34.

65 Dunlop, *The Development of the British Army 1899–1914*, pp. 109–10; Maurice, *History of the War in South Africa*, Volume I, p. 414.

66 TNA WO 32/7866 'Raising of the Imperial Yeomanry, 1899', Marginal note by Wolseley, 28 December 1899; emphasis in the original.

67 Ibid., Marginal note by Lansdowne, 30 December 1899.

and cavalry terminology of regiments and squadrons.[68] The future commander of the Canadian Cavalry Brigade, 'Galloper Jack' Seely, at that date a yeomanry captain, was adamant that his 41st IY Company was actually the 'first squadron of the Hampshire Yeomanry'.[69] Twenty companies were raised from areas that had no yeomanry regiments, including 'special corps' such as the 18th 'Sharpshooters' and 20th 'Rough Riders' IY Battalions, predominantly from London, parts of Scotland, and Ireland; otherwise the companies were mostly raised by the county yeomanry organisations.[70] Although only four battalion commanders were yeomanry officers, all were former regular officers, and the yeomanry rarely provided fewer than half the officers and non-commissioned officers for each battalion.

Like the yeomanry, the IY carried considerable political weight: of 62 peers and members of parliament recorded as serving in South Africa by April 1900, 44 served with the IY, including some in the ranks. Anecdotes featuring gentlemen rankers who paid for themselves and their horses or donated their pay to charity were common, while the majority of the IY were described as middle class, in contrast to the lower middle-class or working-class character of many of the 108,849 British volunteers who served in the war.[71] A fifth of the IY came from yeomanry regiments, or about 2,200 troopers compared with the peacetime yeomanry strength of 8,829, and the proportion appears to have been much higher in several companies.[72]

Volunteer mounted rifle contingents were also sent out to South Africa from the dominions, either in response to Black Week or earlier in the war. As with the IY, British expectations of these troops (and their own countries' views of them) were partly shaped by a belief that the volunteers from Canada, Australia and New Zealand were ranchers or farmers or backwoodsmen, rather than products of an urban society like many British volunteers. Despite British request for autonomous companies of mounted infantry, the Canadians continued to send out all-arms contingents, including in December 1899 two small mounted regiments based on the Canadian militia cavalry, in which 76 per cent of the men had some previous military experience.

---

68 These companies were numbered 1st to 79th; the 8th IY and 16th IY Battalions each had three companies only, and there was no 64th Company raised.

69 Seely, *Adventure*, p. 55.

70 The Sharpshooters and Roughriders were recruited principally in London. For the origins of the Scottish IY companies from a mixture of yeomanry and non-yeomanry sources see McFarland, '"Empire-Enlarging Genius"', pp. 302–6.

71 Miller, 'In Support of the "Imperial Mission"?' pp. 691–711; Beckett, *The Amateur Military Tradition 1558–1945*, pp. 201–5; Maurice, *History of the War in South Africa 1899–1902*, Volume IV, p. 679.

72 These included Seely's 41st (Hampshire) Company, the 40th (Oxfordshire) Company, the 37th and 38th (Buckinghamshire) Companies raised through the Royal Bucks Hussars, and the 9th (Yorkshire Hussars) and 11th (Yorkshire Dragoons) Companies raised through the Yorkshire Dragoons, in which about a quarter were farmers, grooms, or men of 'no occupation' (almost certainly meaning of private means). *Elgin Commission Report*, pp. 70–77 and Evidence Volume I, pp. 310–12; Seely, Adventure, p. 54; Peel, *Trooper 8008 IY*, p. 2; Anglesey, *A History of the British Cavalry Volume 4*, pp. 91–2; Bennett, *Absent Minded Beggars*, pp. 16–22; Beckett, *The Amateur Military Tradition 1558–1945*, pp. 202–4; Dunlop, *The Development of the British Army 1899–1914*, p. 53 and pp. 109–10.

These were respectively the Royal Canadian Dragoons, recruited predominantly from the young urban professionals of eastern Canada (and including members of the home service Royal Canadian Dragoons, in a relationship similar to that of the IY and the yeomanry), and the Canadian Mounted Rifles, recruited from the west and including a high proportion of North West Mounted Police ('Mounties'). A third mounted regiment recruited from the western plains, Strathcona's Horse, left Canada for South Africa in March 1900. Like other dominion contingents, all three Canadian regiments were armed with Lee-Enfield rifles and sword-bayonets, and trained to act as mounted riflemen.[73] The Australians were more compliant with British requests, dispatching company-sized contingents which, other than the New South Wales Lancers, were either sent as, or converted into, mounted riflemen. Partly because they served in so many different units, estimating the number of Australians who fought in the war is problematic, but there were certainly over 10,000, together with over 6,000 New Zealanders.[74] Including the IY with these dominion contingents, by March 1900 more than 15,000 mounted riflemen of various levels of training and experience were arriving in South Africa from all over the Empire.

Roberts reached Cape Town as C-in-C South Africa on 10 January 1900, together with Kitchener. At 67 years old this would be Roberts's last fighting command, and his opportunity to avenge both the 'Majuba surrender' of 1881 and the loss of his only son Freddie, who had died of wounds winning a Victoria Cross at the Battle of Colenso. In putting his name forward after Black Week, Roberts had intimated to Lansdowne that the Wolseley Ring would rather see Great Britain defeated than let him take over, and in turn Lansdowne had appointed Roberts to command without reference to Wolseley (or to Queen Victoria, who would have preferred Wolseley himself to go out).[75] Roberts reported by cipher telegram and occasional letter only to Lansdowne, not to Wolseley as C-in-C.

Although Kitchener was sent from Egypt as Roberts's chief staff officer, neither man had any experience of Staff College procedures, and both saw command and staff relationships in personal terms. In practice Kitchener acted as a deputy commander for the aging and sometimes sick Roberts, using his position and reputation as the victor of the Sudan rather than his relatively junior Army rank of major general. Among those who complained about this (in private or in their memoirs) were two members of Roberts's staff, Wully Robertson, who arrived in Cape Town on 20 January, and Henry Rawlinson, who joined the quartermaster's department under Grierson in March. Grierson had studied the German General Staff when military

---

73 Wessels (ed.), *Lord Kitchener and the War in South Africa 1899–1902*, pp. 23–4; Miller, *Painting the Map Red*, pp. 155–65 and pp. 289–97; Morton, *A Military History of Canada*, pp. 116–17. The Royal Canadian Dragoons were originally (and officially) the 1st Canadian Mounted Rifles, and the Canadian Mounted Rifles were the 2nd Canadian Mounted Rifles, the titles changing in August 1900; Strathcona's Horse was privately raised and was officially a temporary unit of the British Army rather than of the Canadian Militia.

74 Grey, *A Military History of Australia*, pp. 54–62; Hall, *The Hall Handbook of the Anglo-Boer War*, pp. 80–83. The total number of Australians was about 16,000 including re-enlistments.

75 Wessels (ed.), *Lord Roberts and the War in South Africa 1899–1902*, p. 15; Surridge, *Managing the South African War 1899–1902*, pp. 66–9.

attaché in Berlin, and introduced Roberts's staff to some of its methods before leaving for China in June. 'As soon as this war is over', Rawlinson wrote, 'we must set about getting a staff system which shall be the same in peace as in war.'[76] The importance of this South African experience and Grierson's role in trying to reform Roberts's staff has been neglected in the evolution of the General Staff, perhaps as a result of Roberts's success in deflecting criticism away from himself and towards others.

Most British generals, including Buller, did not have the automatic authority to appoint their own subordinates and staff officers, but Roberts on his arrival in South Africa was able to recreate something of his old Ring by bringing together trusted officers who had served on his staff in India, including Major General George 'Prettyboy' Pretyman, Major General William 'Old Nick' Nicholson as his military secretary, and Major General Reginald 'Polly' Pole-Carew, later governor of Bloemfontein.[77] Roberts's staff also introduced a system of rewards and sanctions in order to control the British reporters with his headquarters, who generally admired Roberts and the imperial mission, and who would come to include such famous figures as Rudyard Kipling and Arthur Conan Doyle as well as Leopold Amery and Winston Churchill.[78] But Roberts was missing Ian Hamilton and Henry Rawlinson, both still trapped in Ladysmith until its relief on 28 February; it became important for later events that neither Hamilton nor Rawlinson was an eyewitness to the relief of Kimberley and the advance to Bloemfontein.

On 15 January, less than a week after his arrival at Cape Town, Roberts wrote to Lansdowne that 'Large bodies of Mounted Infantry are what are chiefly required. Those that are coming from the colonies and from England, as well as the Imperial Yeomanry, will be most useful, and I am doing all I can to raise more in this country.'[79] Roberts ordered every British infantry battalion in or arriving in South Africa to produce one MI company each in order to create eight new MI battalions.[80] He also approved Buller's plans to sanction the raising of more local mounted riflemen, who as the war progressed came to number about 10,000 troopers. As a special mark of favour, two of the new formations were named Kitchener's Horse and Roberts's Horse, and included in the forces for the relief of Kimberley.[81]

Unlike the IY, the MI were at least trained regular infantrymen, but they suffered the same problems as novice riders. Most of the men got their mounts only in the first week of February; some went into combat still wearing their infantry uniforms including trousers (and kilts), and more than one MI commander admitted that most

---

76 Quoted in Maurice, *The Life of General Lord Rawlinson of Trent*, p. 63; Robertson, *From Private to Field Marshal*, pp. 112–15.

77 James, *The Life of Lord Roberts*, pp. 302–3; Dundonald, *My Army Life*, p. 90.

78 Badsey, 'War Correspondents in the Boer War', pp. 187–202; Judd and Surridge, *The Boer War*, pp. 251–6.

79 NAM Roberts Papers 110: Roberts to Lansdowne, 15 January 1900. By 'colonies', Roberts presumably included the dominions.

80 Maurice, *History of the War in South Africa*, Volume I, pp. 414–15.

81 Hall, *The Hall Handbook of the Anglo-Boer War*, p. 85.

of his men did not know how to saddle a horse properly.[82] Robertson's description of the MI may be quoted at length as representative of many others:

> The infantry battalion on board the ship which had conveyed me was met on reaching port by a staff officer with orders to despatch one company that evening to De Aar, where it would find horses and saddlery, and thereupon would become a mounted infantry company. Three weeks later this same company, with others equally untrained, was sent forward to meet the enemy... Many of the men crossed a horse that day for the first time in their lives, and in the darkness of the night the horses often stumbled, many of the riders fell, and when camp was reached at daybreak next morning a considerable number were absent, having been left lying on the ground while their mounts went on with the column. Later in the war the mounted infantry performed excellent work, but at first they could not manoeuvre under fire, and by their bad riding galled both their horses and themselves. The need for mounted troops was obvious enough, but a mounted infantryman who can neither ride nor properly look after his horse is not of much fighting value, and he is decidedly expensive in the matter of horseflesh. No more unfortunate animal ever lived than the horse of the mounted infantryman during the early period of the march from the Modder to Pretoria.[83]

Kipling, who arrived in March as a journalist and unofficial propagandist at Roberts's headquarters, described the MI in an irresistibly quotable poem as 'the beggars that got / Three days "to learn equitation", an' six months o' bloomin' well trot!'[84] Rimington would later tell the Elgin Commission that an MI trooper had told him that he did not know whether to feed his horse on beef or mutton.[85] Rimington also wrote the second of two sets of notes issued from Roberts's headquarters in late January and early February, containing much good advice on caring for their horses, dismounting whenever possible, and reducing surplus equipment, and stressing the importance of grazing: 'they must have a bellyful; I graze whenever safe (and sometimes when doubtful)'.[86] Kitchener's prejudices during the First World War against sending untrained or partly trained troops into battle are sometimes attributed to his experiences as a volunteer medical orderly in the Franco-Prussian War. But there is nothing to suggest that he opposed or warned against the early use of these novice MI and IY, and it is hard to believe that the resulting experience made no impression on him.[87]

With hindsight, it would have been better for Roberts to *reduce* the number of mounted corps being formed, in order to provide increased food supplies for the

---

82 Childers, *War and the Arme Blanche*, p. 94; the idea of riding in trousers did not seem a problem to Buller as the Boers did so; see Packenham, *The Boer War*, p. 309.

83 Robertson, *From Private to Field Marshal*, p. 105; see also de Lisle, *Reminiscences of Sport and War*, pp. 90–92. De Aar Junction was the British rear assembly area for the western theatre of the war.

84 Kipling, 'MI (Mounted Infantry of the Line)' in *The Five Nations*, p. 166.

85 *Elgin Commission Report*, p. 97, and Evidence Volume II, p. 31.

86 Ibid., Evidence Volume I, pp. 531–2, Appendix, C.O.S. Circular Memos 5 and 8, 26 January and 5 February 1900.

87 Magnus, *Kitchener*, pp. 8–9 and pp. 279–80; Simkins, *Kitchener's Army*, p. 41.

cavalry and some of the better colonial mounted rifles. But in the same letter of 15 November, Roberts informed Lansdowne that:

> I have gone carefully into the important question of supplies and transport. In the matter of food and forage there would seem to be no cause for anxiety, as sufficient arrangements have apparently been made to meet the heavy demand which 150,000 men and some 60,000 animals will make on the Commissariat Department.[88]

Roberts did not yet understand the horse transport and supply nightmare that he had inherited, but on 20 January, after the situation had been brought properly to his attention, orders were issued attempting to establish a hay ration at between five and eight pounds a day, along with an oat ration of ten pounds a day, or slightly more than Buller's figures.[89] Roberts later blamed his chief supply officer, Colonel Wodehouse Richardson of the Army Service Corps, describing to Lansdowne how he 'nearly broke my heart – I had to do his work as well as my own and the strain tried me more than I can describe'.[90] But adding to his problems, in the same letter Roberts told Lansdowne that he and Kitchener had agreed to change the existing system of wagon transport used by the British Army, whereby individual regiments had their own attached transport. Instead, Kitchener would centralise the transport, the method with which Roberts was familiar from India and Kitchener from Egypt.[91] Whatever its suitability for the long term, this decision to change the Army's wagon transport system simultaneously with launching a major offensive produced a level of disorganisation that attracted considerable criticism, although it also distracted attention away from the wider issue of the decision to increase the number of untrained mounted troops.[92] As Major General Smith later wrote, after Roberts's arrival 'the operations which followed were carried out by partly starved animals'.[93]

In the summer heat of the virtual desert near the Modder River, in conditions that Methuen had felt could not support an additional cavalry brigade, Roberts concentrated a force of 37,000 men, 14,000 horses, 12,000 mules and 10,000 oxen. The re-formed Cavalry Division under French consisted of three cavalry brigades as planned (eight regiments including the composite Household Regiment and a second composite regiment with the New South Wales Lancers squadron). The intention was for the division to include two mounted brigades composed of the new MI, the colonial mounted rifles, and some dominion mounted troops; but the MI were not ready for the start of operations on 11 February, and the Cavalry Division moved with only one improvised mounted brigade. Later estimates of the Cavalry Division's strength varied from 8,000 to 5,500 or lower, but since new troops were arriving and horses were falling sick or dying daily the calculation is effectively

---

88 NAM Roberts Papers 110: Roberts to Lansdowne, 15 January 1900.
89 Smith, *A Veterinary History of the War in South Africa 1899–1902*, p. 29.
90 NAM Roberts Papers 124: Confidential reports by Roberts to Lansdowne on senior officers, August 1900.
91 Ibid., 110: Roberts to Lansdowne, 15 January 1900.
92 Amery, *My Political Life Volume One*, p. 126.
93 Smith, *A Veterinary History of the War in South Africa 1899–1902*, p. 30.

impossible.[94] What is certain is that Roberts's column far outnumbered all the Boer forces opposed to it, including the largest commando under Commandant Piet Cronjé in its position at Modder River blocking the way to Kimberley. As infantry, most of Roberts's troops were less mobile than the Boers, while Cronjé's force, which was accompanied by families and ox-wagons, was less mobile than the mounted troops of either side.

Relations between Roberts and French, the two men who between them would dominate the debate on cavalry doctrine for the next decade, suffered a bad start. French first met Roberts in Cape Town on 29 January and came away with the impression that he had only persuaded Roberts with some effort to reform the Cavalry Division for the relief of Kimberley, and to give him command of it.[95] Roberts preferred to give informal verbal orders supported by a few written notes (a style of command that had been popular in his youth), and although French had not attended the Staff College he was used to more formal procedures. Another problem was that Roberts, exerting his authority on his arrival, began to make changes in the cavalry, sometimes without French's agreement. The right or authority of a theatre C-in-C to appoint and remove officers was ill-defined, and most of Wolseley's formal letter appointing Roberts to command in South Africa was taken up with reminding Roberts that his authority was limited.[96] But in practice, the immense political prestige given to Roberts by the circumstances of his appointment gave him virtually a free hand. French, an acting lieutenant general, was only a substantive colonel, and any officer who fell foul of Roberts and was removed from his post would revert to his substantive rank, if not to half-pay.[97] Just before the operation to relieve Kimberley started, Roberts caused ill feeling by removing one of French's brigade commanders and a protégé of the Wolseley Ring, Colonel James Babington (late of the 16th Lancers), an action attributed by Haig to 'Pole-Carew's evil tales'.[98] French requested the removal of a second cavalry brigade commander, Major General Sir John Brabazon, the colourful 'Brab', a friend of the Prince of Wales and once Churchill's commanding officer in the 4th Hussars, who had served with distinction as a lieutenant under Roberts in Afghanistan, but who at 58 was too old for a cavalry command.[99] Of French's three new cavalry brigade commanders, two joined their brigades on the day the move to relieve Kimberley began (one of them straight off the ship from India), and the third not until the relief had been accomplished. French had also expected to keep Haig

---

94 Hall, *The Hall Handbook of the Anglo-Boer War*, pp. 59–62; Childers, *War and the Arme Blanche*, pp. 94; these numbers are disputed by Anglesey, *A History of the British Cavalry Volume 4*, p. 127 and pp. 503–5.

95 Holmes, *The Little Field Marshal*, pp. 83–4.

96 Wessels (ed.), *Lord Roberts and the War in South Africa 1899–1902*, pp. 19–20.

97 At this time British Army divisions were usually commanded by lieutenant generals and brigades by major generals, often as an acting or temporary rank; by the First World War the practice was for divisions to be commanded by substantive major generals and brigades by substantive colonels holding the appointment of brigadier general.

98 NLS Haig Papers 6b: Haig to his sister, 26 December 1900.

99 NAM Roberts Papers 110: Roberts to Lansdowne, 5 March 1900; Churchill, *My Early Life*, pp. 71–6; Roberts, *Forty One Years in India*, p. 362 and p. 385; Robson (ed.), *Roberts in India*, p. 435.

as his chief staff officer, with Captain John Vaughan (also 7th Hussars) as Haig's deputy. But on Wolseley's recommendation, Roberts had promised an appointment to Colonel the Earl of Erroll, late of Luck's staff as Inspector General of Cavalry, and he insisted on appointing Erroll as French's chief staff officer, with Haig as his deputy.[100] French simply ignored Erroll and continued to work through Haig.[101]

It would be unhistorical in the extreme to deny the drama, for all who took part, of the few weeks' fighting that began on 11 February at Modder River. After the shock of Black Week, the stability and even the survival of the British Empire seemed at risk; Queen Victoria expressed her concern over the effects of these defeats on British prestige, while *The Times* made comparisons with the Indian Mutiny.[102] A swift and decisive victory seemed essential to restore the situation. For senior officers such as Roberts, Kitchener and French, this was what the years of peacetime thinking and training were for, and it was an experience that coloured their views about warfare, and about each other, for ever.

French began his Cavalry Division's march to relieve Kimberley on the morning of 11 February, making a bold flanking sweep away from Cronjé's commando defending the Modder River crossings and the railway, planning to hook to the east to cross the Riet River and then the Modder River further north. There were several other Boer commandos in the area, including those maintaining the siege around Kimberley, and some just looking for opportunities, including a commando under Christiaan de Wet.[103] Kitchener, speaking in Roberts's name, impressed on French and his officers 'the risk to the Empire generally if Kimberley was not relieved' and that that this must be done at all costs.[104] Kitchener's personal note to Colonel Robert Broadwood (12th Lancers) commanding the 2nd Cavalry Brigade conveys the atmosphere well:

You will have an excellent brigade. What I want to impress upon you is the *great, very great* importance of the mission given to the cavalry. They must ride hard and *straight*

---

100 The title 'chief staff officer' used in this book was often employed, and is an accurate description of the post and its function. The actual title of the appointment for the senior staff officer of a division at this date was AAG (for Assistant Adjutant General) and DAAG (Deputy Assistant Adjutant General) for a lower appointment. The title 'Chief of Staff' has connotations of an authority and a relationship with a commander which did not exist in the British Army of this period, and the title itself was only rarely used, becoming more common by the First World War, by which period the title for a chief staff officer of a division was GSO1 (General Staff Officer 1st Grade), BGGS (Brigadier General, General Staff) for a Corps and MGGS (Major General, General Staff) for higher headquarters.

101 HPL Wolseley Papers Autograph Roberts 8: Roberts to Wolseley, 20 December 1899; Scott (ed.), *Douglas Haig: The Preparatory Prologue: Diaries and Letters 1861–1914*, pp. 161–2; Cooper, *Haig*, Volume I, pp. 79–80.

102 Wessels (ed.), *Lord Roberts and the War in South Africa 1899–1902*, p. 25; Miller, 'Slogging Across the Veldt', p. 159.

103 The number of Boers remains a matter of dispute, but the summary in Childers, *War and the Arme Blanche*, pp. 92–3, giving Cronjé's force as 12,000 men and 20 guns, is a reasonable place to start any discussion.

104 NLS Haig Papers 34: Cavalry Division War Diary, entries 10 and 11 February 1900; Cooper, *Haig*, Volume I, p. 80; Anglesey, *A History of the British Cavalry Volume 4*, p. 128.

to see this matter through. I am sure I need not say more to you. French will tell you everything.[105]

One version of these events had Roberts himself telling the cavalry brigade and regimental commanders that he was giving them the greatest chance that cavalry ever had, and that they must relieve Kimberley even at the cost of half their numbers, ending 'The enemy is afraid of the British cavalry, and I hope when you get them into the open you will make an example of them.'[106] If Roberts did say this, then it may not have reflected his real views of the relative merits of British cavalry and Boer mounted riflemen, but it was exactly what the British senior commanders needed their troopers to believe if they were to ride straight through the Boer lines.

With Rimington's Tigers leading as scouts, the Cavalry Division began its march with five days' forage distributed throughout the column, with the infantry following in their wake. Many cavalry regiments had no corn sacks, and as the spare horses became needed to replace riding horses that had fallen sick, some of the corn was simply dumped on the sandy veldt.[107] The march was slowed by heat, dust storms, and the five hours needed each evening to feed and water the horses; while mistakes by Roberts's staff prevented supplies from getting through to French, and created a traffic jam as the infantry tried to follow the cavalry across the Riet. On the first three days, 460 horses died or dropped out of the Cavalry Division's advance; on the third day two or three days' feed was issued, the last before Kimberley. Meanwhile, to add to the British problems, an enterprising commando raid led by Christiaan de Wet (in true Jeb Stuart style) avoided the mounted troops scouting for Roberts's infantry columns and intercepted the main British supply convoy to the south at Waterval Drift. Rather than send troops back to retrieve the situation, Roberts chose to abandon the convoy, losing 176 wagons and the corn that they were carrying, which was enough to have fed the Cavalry Division's horses for a week.[108] But despite the problems Roberts was very pleased, telegraphing to Lansdowne on 14 February that 'French's performance is brilliant considering the excessive heat and a blinding dust storm which raged during the latter part of the day'.[109]

Early on 15 February the Cavalry Division crossed the Modder River at Klip Drift (*drift* means ford), the last natural obstacle before Kimberley. Advancing northwards

---

105 NAM Broadwood Papers: Kitchener to Broadwood, 10 February 1900; emphasis in original.

106 French, *The Life of Field Marshal Sir John French*, pp. 69–70; Goldmann, *With General French and the Cavalry in South Africa*, p. 74; Selby, *The Boer War*, p. 168.

107 NLS Haig Papers 34: Cavalry Division War Diary, entries for 11–15 February 1900; Goldmann, *With General French and the Cavalry in South Africa*, p. 81.

108 Anglesey, *A History of the British Cavalry Volume 4*, pp. 132–3; Maurice, *History of the War in South Africa 1899–1902*, Volume II, pp. 73–8 and Smith, *A Veterinary History of the War in South Africa, 1899–1902*, p. 33. Both give the amount lost as '38,792 grain rations' as well as other foodstuffs. It is not clear in this context what a 'ration' constitutes, but taking it to be enough to feed one horse for one day, then for perhaps 5–6,000 horses in the Cavalry Division it represented about a week's supply.

109 NAM Roberts Papers 110: Cipher Telegram Roberts to Lansdowne, 14 February 1900.

for three miles, at about 10.30 a.m. the division came under fire from an unknown number of Boers under Commandant C.C. Froneman, later estimated at about 900 rifles and some artillery, holding the arc of low hills across the front of the advance between Klip Drift and Abon's Dam. The leading British cavalry dismounted and returned fire while the horse artillery came into action. The direct route to Abon's Dam and Kimberley lay northwards across a plain leading to a low *nek* or saddle, but the gentle slopes provided a natural glacis for the Boer riflemen, who would be firing on the advance from three sides. The cavalry had been ordered to ride straight for Kimberley; it was time for the sacrifice that French had written into *Cavalry Drill 1896* himself. Sending ahead scouts with wirecutters, French called for covering fire from five of his seven artillery batteries, and ordered his men to open out to five yard intervals between files. Then with four lancer squadrons in front, French took his division in a charge through the Boer positions and over the nek without stopping.

Haig's careful staffwork has meant that the Klip Drift charge was better documented than many other British charges, but much about it was a mystery at the time and has remained so. The leading brigade commander judged the pace as about 14 miles an hour (a slow gallop rather than a flat-out charge, all the weakened horses could manage), and the division spent roughly four minutes under Boer crossfire at ranges of 1,200 yards or less; as the lancers came over the nek they impaled a few of the Boer defenders in front of them, the rest ran. When the division collected itself miles beyond the nek, they found on a first count that their casualties were four men wounded and two horses killed, and the way to Kimberley was open; later counts put the casualties at one man dead and eleven wounded, plus more horses that were chiefly the victims of collapse and exhaustion, rather than bullets.[110]

This episode was utterly contrary to so many theories about the effects of the new firepower; the cavalrymen had been ready to die and they were still alive, but they did not know how they had done it. The reaction was such that Haig could not resist including in the divisional diary a suggestion that it was unfortunate the leading squadron had not been left in close order to improve the shock of the charge as they broke through over the nek![111] The accomplishment of a divisional charge in war was also seen as a vindication of training cavalry as a division to manoeuvre at the gallop. 'I think you will agree with me', Haig wrote to his sister (and through her probably to Evelyn Wood) 'that I have not been mistaken as to the power of cavalry when led with determination even in spite of modern guns!'[112] Among the personal wartime experiences that shaped the attitudes of officers, those who were at Klip Drift – including French, Haig, Allenby, Rimington, Vaughan and Bingham – found later arguments that rifle fire had made cavalry charges obsolete very unconvincing.

---

110 NLS Haig Papers 34: Cavalry Division War Diary, 15 February 1900; Anglesey, *A History of the British Cavalry Volume 4*, pp. 134–6. Other accounts put the British loss as 20 men or so; the point is that it was very low.

111 NLS Haig Papers 34: Cavalry Division War Diary, 15 February 1900; the same suggestion appears in Goldmann, *With General French and the Cavalry in South Africa*, pp. 83–4.

112 NLS Haig Papers 6c: Haig to his sister, 22 February 1900.

French relieved Kimberley that evening, although his supply problems were still severe, he was out of contact with Kitchener who was following up with four infantry divisions, and the strain of the march together with the Klip Drift charge had severely weakened the cavalry; an officer of the 16th Lancers described the horses as being in 'a desperate state' on 16 February.[113] Operations that day proved controversial: anxious to catch the besieging Boers who had fled on his division's approach, French sent out most of his troopers to scour the countryside to the north of Kimberley, with even greater losses to the horses from exhaustion. But French kept a reinforced 2nd Brigade in reserve under Broadwood, and when communications with Kitchener were re-established this was able to play another vital role. Cronjé's commando had been caught by surprise by the British flank manoeuvre, and was retreating eastwards along the Modder with Kitchener's infantry in pursuit; late on 16 February a galloper reached French with a letter from Kitchener stating that 'Our mounted infantry and field artillery are too sticky for words and the Boers fight an excellent rearguard action', and that the cavalry were badly needed.[114] Early next morning French accompanied Broadwood's brigade of about 1,500 horsemen on a ride 30 miles eastward to get ahead of Cronjé in a blocking position on the Modder at Paardeberg Drift. When Broadwood's horse artillery and dismounted men opened fire on Cronjé from the east, the Boers assumed that the British infantry had got round them, and entrenched along the riverbanks, dooming themselves to be eventually surrounded. It was later recounted that during his arguments with Kitchener in 1914 and 1915 French would recall with tears in his eyes how he had ridden that day with Broadwood's men to Kitchener's aid.[115]

Cronjé and his wagons were trapped, but there followed a chaotic ten-day combination of assault and siege, for which Kitchener was heavily criticised for his command style and Roberts's headquarters staff for their continuing failures; it was also during this battle that Henderson was invalided out with malaria and exhaustion. In another controversial episode on 18 February, orders from Kitchener to make a mounted charge against Cronjé's position reached Colonel Ormelie Hannay, commanding the 1st Mounted Brigade. In a reflection of the way that mounted troops could absorb the cavalry ethos, Hannay apparently interpreted a phrase in these orders, 'Gallop up, if necessary, and fire into laager', which would have been orthodox MI tactics, as an insult suggesting that he was afraid to charge home.[116] His charge with about 50 horsemen got only to within 400 yards of Cronjé's position, and Hannay himself was killed. One of the few British mounted charges of the Boer War to be shot down had been made by MI rather than by cavalry.[117]

---

113 NAM Bellew Papers: Diary entry, 16 February 1900.
114 Quoted in Holmes, *The Little Field Marshal*, pp. 94–5.
115 Magnus, *Kitchener*, pp. 162–70.
116 Quoted in ibid., p. 168.
117 Hannay's charge was a controversial episode about which many details are conjectural; compare the very dramatic version in Packenham, *The Boer War*, p. 418, with Maurice, *History of the War in South Africa 1899–1902*, Volume II, pp. 130–33. Hannay's 1st Mounted Brigade at Paardeberg consisted of 1st MI, 3rd MI, 5th MI and 7th MI, the New South Wales Mounted Rifles, Roberts's Horse, Kitchener's Horse, Rimington's Guides, and

Cronjé's surrender on 27 February (the anniversary of Majuba) gave Roberts his victory to go with the relief of Kimberley. Christiaan de Wet ascribed every Boer defeat for the next two months to the impact of this episode on their morale.[118] For the reforming cavalrymen, the combination of Klip Drift, the relief of Kimberley and Paardeberg Drift was a vindication of their beliefs: Haig wrote home that 'the idea of MI alone is to my mind quite exploded. Why have we, the cavalry, had success against the Boers? Because we can charge in the open as well as act dismounted.'[119] But since Roberts had sent Kitchener on ahead to command in his name (in part because he was suffering from illness) he never grasped the extent of the cavalry's achievement, and there is no mention of the Klip Drift charge in his letters to Lansdowne.[120]

Roberts caught up with the main body of his army at Paardeberg Drift on 19 February, where a series of quarrels between his headquarters and the Cavalry Division soured what should have been a mutual triumph. First, Roberts left Kitchener in command of the fighting, although Kitchener was only a substantive major general and French was the senior of three acting lieutenant generals present. Then on the night of 21 February, in an episode from which some parts of the evidence are clearly missing, French moved one of his brigade commanders to another position, returned a second brigade commander to his regiment, and gave Haig command of one of the brigades. By next evening both brigade commanders had been re-instated, but Haig had been made the Cavalry Division's chief staff officer and the Earl of Erroll had been given the new task of escorting Cronjé into captivity when he surrendered, (leaving, so French and Haig solemnly recorded, because of his ill health).[121] Even worse, while both Roberts and Kitchener had hoped for a swift victory over Cronjé and a lightning dash eastward towards Bloemfontein, French's division was no longer an effective mobile force. According to Haig's careful records (kept in his personal diary rather than the divisional war diary) from 17 to 19 February the Cavalry Division received no supplies for their horses, and an average of six pounds of oats per horse over the next four days, or something close to their inadequate usual rations. By this date few horses could move at any speed above a walk, and the division's total strength was down to 4,500 men with 4,200 horses, despite having received some remounts.[122]

---

the Grahamstown Volunteer Mounted Infantry; see also Baker, *Battles and Battlefields of the Anglo-Boer War 1899–1902*, p. 242.

118 de Wet, *Three Years War*, pp. 61–8.

119 NLA Haig Papers 334e: Haig to an unidentified recipient, 2 March 1900.

120 NAM Roberts Papers 110: Roberts to Lansdowne, 16 February 1900.

121 NLS Haig Papers 6c: Haig to his sister, 22 February 1900; Ibid., 38e: Haig personal diary entry, 22 February 1900; TNA WO 105/25 Papers of Lord Roberts as C-in-C South Africa, General French's Reports on Major General Brabazon/Colonel the Earl of Erroll/Colonel Babington, 27 February 1900. Reid, *Architect of Victory: Douglas Haig*, p. 97 suggests that the negotiation over Erroll took place between Kitchener and French's aide de camp Sir John Laycock.

122 NLS Haig Papers 38e: Haig personal diary entries, 15–23 February 1900, and Cavalry Division War Diary entries, 15–23 February 1900; IWM French Papers: Diary entry, 23 February 1900; Goldmann, *With General French and the Cavalry in South Africa*, p. 116.

In his letters to Lansdowne, Roberts attributed the problems in overcoming Cronjé at Paardeberg to supply problems rather than Kitchener's command style, writing on 22 February that 'We are experiencing extreme difficulties about supplies. None are available locally, and owing to the drought water is rarely found except in rivers. In most places there is little or no grazing for animals and it is impossible to carry forage for them.'[123] In addition to starvation and sickness among the horses, cases of cholera among the troops (known at the time as 'enteric' fever, or 'Peshawar' fever to Indian veterans) increased greatly. On 24 February a cavalry raid eastward had to be cancelled because of the state of the horses, and four days later Roberts told Lansdowne that 'we should have pushed on from here ere this had it not been that our Artillery and Cavalry are quite unequal to any prolonged effort without rest and an opportunity of grazing'.[124] A few days later, Roberts wrote to Cecil Rhodes that 'Even if I were not detained here by Cronjé, I should be unable to move on account of the crippled state of my horses. For several days they were hard worked, with no grain, and with very little else to eat. Several of them are too weak for a prolonged effort, and I have sent for all available remounts to get the cavalry division in working order.'[125]

But Roberts had already started to look for other justifications for why his campaign was not running smoothly. Haig, at Roberts's headquarters on a routine visit on 24 February, was told by Roberts something that he recorded in his diary and underlined in sheer disbelief, nearly breaking his pencil. '*He said he considered cavalry officers did not sufficiently look after their horses!*' Haig wrote, 'General French also, *to be hard on his horses.*'[126] Roberts had a point, in that overloading and poor horsemastership were factors in the weakness of the cavalry's horses. Vaughan was particularly critical of this, writing that as an experienced horsemaster and polo player, 'I had a mackintosh, a tooth brush and a razor in my saddlebag, and that was all my kit till we got to Bloemfontein.'[127] But the cavalry horses' starvation diet was clearly the responsibility of Roberts and his staff, and one that could not be simply wished away by issuing orders. Nevertheless, on the same day Roberts telegraphed to Cape Town for all available MI who had horses to be sent to the front at once. The number of novice MI and improvised mounted rifle contingents with the army at Paardeberg continued to grow to four large mounted brigades.[128]

On 26 February, a further incident put a final frost on Roberts's relationship with French and the cavalry. By this date the Cavalry Division numbered 3,500 effectives, after receiving a large number of poor quality remounts. Because of the supply and transport problems Roberts had made a personal appeal to the cavalry to

---

123 NAM Roberts Papers 110: Telegram from Lord Roberts to Lord Lansdowne, 22 February 1900.

124 Wessels (ed.), *Lord Roberts and the War in South Africa 1899–1902*, p. 58.

125 Quoted in Maurice, *History of the War in South Africa 1899–1902*, Volume III, p. 29.

126 NLS Haig Papers 38e: Haig personal diary entry, 24 February 1900; emphasis in original.

127 Vaughan, *Cavalry and Sporting Memories*, p. 77.

128 Maurice, *History of the War in South Africa 1899–1902*, Volume II, p. 605 and Volume III, p. 33.

put up with inadequate supplies for their horses, but he was told by Richardson, his chief supply officer, that the cavalry horses' rations had been considerably exceeded. Amery of *The Times*, who had joined Roberts's army at Paardeberg, remembered that 'this time the Little Chief [Roberts] let himself go and gave the Cavalry a real dressing down for not playing the game'.[129] French recorded in his diary that he was summoned by Roberts to his headquarters for 'a tremendous row' with his staff over the forage issue; although when French 'tackled him about what he had said to Haig' on 24 February, Roberts 'rather gave in'.[130] But the fault had once more been with Roberts's staff: as the cavalrymen pointed out with frigid politeness, they were drawing food for their sick horses, not just for those shown on the returns as fit for service. One estimate was that the 1st Cavalry Brigade had 1,200 sick horses compared with 300 effectives.[131] Amery wrote that 'The Cavalry never forgave' Roberts's behaviour.[132]

On 2 March Haig wrote to Colonel Sir Lonsdale Hale, military correspondent for *The Times*, describing French's relief of Kimberley and recalling Roberts's and Kitchener's orders. 'You will I think agree with me that the Cavalry – the *despised* cavalry I should say, has saved the Empire', Haig told Hale, adding 'I trust you to insist on a large and efficient cavalry being kept up in time of peace. *At least two divisions complete.*'[133] Haig's judgement that two cavalry divisions were needed in peacetime would later take on greater significance through his involvement in the creation of the BEF.

Roberts's victory at Paardeberg was accompanied by Buller finally relieving the siege of Ladysmith on 28 February, led by Lord Dundonald's mounted troops. Dundonald's handling of his brigade (the title and composition of which changed more than once in the campaign) won him a considerable public reputation. But even years later Hubert Gough, who commanded Dundonald's composite regiment in the relief and was first to reach Ladysmith with his troops, denounced Dundonald as 'hesitating, vacillating and vain' and his reputation as entirely the product of the press; other officers nicknamed him 'Lord Dundoodle', while Henry Wilson described him as 'a suspect fool and *useless*'.[134] According to Gough, whose account is supported by others, Dundonald arrived some hours after Ladysmith had been relieved, rushing to get there accompanied by a few staff officers including Birdwood, and by Churchill reporting for the *Morning Post*. Churchill, who had left the Army a year earlier

---

129 Amery, *My Political Life Volume One*, pp. 131–2.
130 IWM French Papers: Diary entry, 26 February 1900.
131 NAM Davies-Cook Papers: Diary entry for 28 February 1900; Davies-Cook was an officer of the Nottinghamshire Yeomanry serving with Allenby's detached squadron of the 6th (Inniskilling) Dragoons in 1st Cavalry Brigade; he was gazetted into the 10th Hussars in May 1900.
132 Amery, *My Political Life Volume One*, p. 132; NLS Haig Papers 38e: Haig personal diary entry, 28 February 1900, and Ibid., 34: Cavalry Division War Diary entry, 28 February 1900.
133 NLS Haig Papers 334e: Haig to Hale, 2 March 1900; emphasis in the original.
134 Gough, *Soldiering On*, p. 70 and pp. 75–81; IWM Wilson Papers: Diary entry, 11 April 1900, emphasis in the original; Jeffrey, *Field Marshal Sir Henry Wilson*, p. 36 reads this as 'perfect fool', which does not much alter the sense.

to establish a reputation and earn enough money from journalism and writing to stand for parliament, had been given a temporary (and highly irregular) commission in the South African Light Horse by Byng, and been taken on by Dundonald as a staff officer while still employed as a reporter; Churchill and his family also lobbied hard for him to receive a medal for his exploits in South Africa, and Dundonald supported this. Churchill's account of the relief of Ladysmith gave the credit entirely to Dundonald, and was written as if he had been an eyewitness to Dundonald leading the relief column into the town, a mild deception that was common among reporters of the era, but was deeply resented by Gough.[135]

The final controversial episode which would shape the debate over the cavalry until Roberts's death in 1914 came as Roberts began his delayed main advance towards Bloemfontein on 6 March. Appointed as Vice-Commandant-General of the Orange Free State, Christiaan de Wet assembled his remaining commandos to block the British advance at another line of hills at Poplar Grove. Roberts's plan for the battle next day was for a deep flanking sweep by the cavalry from the south to get behind the Boers, and to trap them against the Modder River once more as at Paardeberg. Roberts intended this as his decisive final battle of the campaign, and gave his orders in a rousing speech that evening, followed by a huddle of generals and staff officers, and a brief written order that French's cavalry should advance so as to threaten the enemy line of communication and 'avoid coming under enemy fire' until it had done so.[136] No written start times were given, and French came away with the belief that his Cavalry Division, by this time down to 2,800 fit horses, should move at 3.00 a.m. next morning, while the general commanding the supporting infantry division (French's good friend Lieutenant General Thomas Kelly-Kenny) believed that his troops should move an hour earlier, but behind the cavalry. The resulting delays meant that, by shortly after daybreak on 7 March when the British artillery opened fire on the Boer positions, the cavalry had barely got level with the enemy's southern flank.[137]

De Wet's burghers on their hill positions could see French's cavalry coming to envelop them from the south. More than three months' fighting had involved at first some bloody victories, but these had been followed by a string of defeats, and there

---

135 Gough, *Soldiering On*, p. 70, Birdwood, *Khaki and Gown*, pp. 106–8; Dundonald, *My Army Life*, pp. 147–52; Amery, *My Political Life Volume One*, p. 117; Churchill, *My Early Life*, pp. 313–21; Woods, *Young Winston's Wars*, p. 246; Packenham, *The Boer War*, p. 344 and pp. 453–5; Badsey, 'War Correspondents in the Boer War', pp. 192–8; Sandys, *Churchill Wanted Dead or Alive*, pp. 133–48.

136 Maurice, *History of the War in South Africa 1899–1902*, Volume II, pp. 190–92.

137 For differing perspectives on this very controversial sequence of events see Maurice, *History of the War in South Africa 1899–1902*, Volume II, pp. 185–206; Amery (ed.), *The Times History of the War in South Africa*, Volume III, pp. 553–70; James, *The Life of Lord Roberts*, pp. 297–8; Holmes, *The Little Field Marshal*, pp. 98–101; Packenham, *The Boer War*, pp. 464–6. So many different versions of what happened at Poplar Grove came into circulation after the war that Packenham's comment (p. 464) 'It is easy to say what went wrong, hard to apportion responsibility' seems the fairest judgement, although Robertson, *From Private to Field Marshal*, pp. 115–16, that the fault was entirely one of poor staff procedures, is the most historically significant.

was nothing in their culture or tactical doctrine to make them wait to be surrounded. De Wet himself described their response:

> A panic had seized my men. Before the English had even got near enough to shell our positions to any purpose, the wild flight began. Soon every position was evacuated. There was not even an attempt to hold them, though some of them would have been almost impregnable. It was a flight such as I had never seen before, and shall never see again.[138]

Roberts telegraphed to Lansdowne that 'the turning movement was necessary owing to the nature of the ground, and the cavalry and horse artillery are much done up. The fighting was practically confined to the Cavalry Division which as usual did exceedingly well', adding next day that the Boers had fled so quickly that they had left their cooked meals behind them, and on the following day that 'the rout, however, was complete, the men declaring that they could not stand against British artillery and such a formidable force of cavalry'.[139] French recorded in his diary for 8 March 'Interviewed [sic] the F[ield] M[arshal] at Poplar Grove last night. He expressed great satisfaction with the work down by the cavalry'.[140] But, partly because of de Wet's skilful defence using dismounted rearguards, the exhausted cavalry was largely unable to catch the retreating Boers. Smith-Dorrien, commanding an infantry brigade in the battle, later recalled that the cavalry were unable even to raise a trot from their horses, and had to stop and rest them several times.[141] In a further telegram on 9 March, Roberts explained the position on horses to Lansdowne:

> Owing to the absence of forage, and hard work, a good many [horses] have been lost during the past month. Five hundred and fifty eight were either killed, died or went missing during the relief of Kimberley, and on the 7th Inst [at Poplar Grove] 54 were killed, 47 wounded, 62 died from exhaustion and 116 other were reported unfit for work. It must be remembered that the sickly season is approaching... The artillery and Household cavalry consider the English horses suit them best, but the artillery would gladly take well-bred Walers such as are in use by batteries in India. The rest of the cavalry prefer Indian country breeds, Argentines, or any good stamp of small horses, such as have already been sent from India, or even smaller ones and Burma ponies are required for Mounted Infantry. The success of the campaign depends so materially on the mounted troops being efficient.[142]

Rimington's view was that the big English troop horses of the cavalry would have still been the best horses for them in South Africa, if only they could get enough food, but that the Cape Horse was suitable as a remount.[143] As in Egypt and the

---

138 de Wet, *Three Years War*, p. 69.
139 NAM Roberts Papers 110: Cipher Telegram Number 254, Roberts to Lansdowne, 7 March 1900, Cipher Telegram Number 259, Roberts to Lansdowne, 8 March 1900, and Cipher Telegram Number 266, Roberts to Lansdowne, 9 March 1900.
140 IWM French Papers: Diary entry, 8 March 1900.
141 Smith-Dorrien, *Memories of Forty Eight Years' Service*, p. 166.
142 NAM Roberts Papers 110: Cipher Telegram Number 271, Roberts to Lansdowne, 9 March 1900. 'Walers' were horses originally from New South Wales, first brought by the British to India in the middle nineteenth century; see Tylden, *Horses and Saddlery*, pp. 53–5.
143 Rimington, *The Horse in Recent War*, pp. 3–8.

Sudan in the 1880s, supply problems and poor horse care were forcing the British to take smaller breeds as remounts, but in the absence of an enemy on big horses likely to make a mounted charge this was not necessarily a drawback. The main complaint remained that the horses were being starved into sickness and death, or given sore backs from being ridden too badly or too hard, and very few soldiers knew how to address or ease any of these problems.

It was only on the day after Poplar Grove that Roberts discovered what a chance had been missed: joining de Wet that day had been President Paul Kruger of the Transvaal, and Roberts's information was that President Marthinus Steyn of the Orange Free State had accompanied him; to have captured all three men in a cavalry envelopment would have been an immense defeat for the Boers, possibly enough to have ended the war.[144] Instead, after further inconclusive skirmishes, Roberts's troops entered Bloemfontein unopposed on 13 March, with the triumphant press corps leading. Roberts's advance was stalled for six weeks at Bloemfontein by disease, supply and transport problems, and the need to reorganise his forces, while he issued proclamations trying to convince the Boers of the Orange River Colony that the war was over and that they should return home. But even this period of rest did not extend to the cavalry, which were needed for numerous small operations. On 16 March a furious Haig wrote to his sister:

> I have never seen horses so beat as ours this day. They have been having only 8 lbs [pounds] of oats a day, and practically starving since we left Modder River on February 11th. So many colonial Skallywag corps have been raised that the horses of the whole force could not have a full ration. The colonial corps raised in Cape Colony are quite useless, so are the recently raised Mounted Infantry. They can't ride, and they know nothing of their duties as mounted men. Roberts's Horse and Kitchener's Horse are only good for looting and the greater part of them disappear the moment a shot is fired or there is the prospect of a fight. You will see then that the success of the Cavalry Division has been in spite of these ruffians and notwithstanding the short rations.[145]

Vaughan echoed these sentiments in his memoirs, writing that 'if we had had a possibility of keeping our horses fit to gallop after the Relief of Kimberley, the Boers would have collapsed much more quickly than they did'.[146]

By coincidence, it was also on 16 March that Roberts wrote to Lansdowne with his own version of Poplar Grove and the failure to accomplish a second Paardeberg, 'The cavalry horses were, no doubt, done up, but we should have had a good chance of making the two Presidents prisoners if French had carried out my orders of making straight for the Modder river, instead of wasting valuable time by going after small parties of the enemy.'[147] It was at this time that Roberts was joined by Ian Hamilton

---

144 de Wet, *Three Years War*, pp. 67–73 does not mention the presence of President Steyn with President Kruger on his visit to the front; however, Steyn frequently accompanied de Wet's commando.

145 NLS Haig Papers 6c: Haig to his sister, 16 March 1900.

146 Vaughan, *Cavalry and Sporting Memories*, p. 74.

147 NAM Roberts Papers 110: Roberts to Lansdowne, 16 March 1900; this letter has been logged with the cipher telegrams rather than recorded in the letter book, and appears to be of a

and Rawlinson following the relief of Ladysmith. (Later, when Roberts's advance reached Pretoria, Rawlinson was joined on the staff by Wilson.) Hamilton had been through a dreadful experience in the siege followed by a bout of cholera; but as soon as he recovered he wrote to Roberts, and also to the military correspondent Spencer Wilkinson of the *Morning Post*, denouncing Buller in the strongest terms. Travelling to Bloemfontein by way of Cape Town, Hamilton gave vent to more of his opinions to Wilkinson and to Amery.[148]

During the weeks of the campaign from Modder River to Bloemfontein, the mounted volunteers who had set out to such public acclaim in the aftermath of Black Week started to arrive in South Africa, adding to the general strain on the supply system. The first to see action were the two MI companies of the City Imperial Volunteers (CIV) on 15 February, the same day as the cavalry's relief of Kimberley.[149] Roberts became colonel of the CIV, and arranged for their MI to be Cronjé's escort into captivity under Lord Erroll.[150] Roberts began by creating several large IY brigades of between four and six battalions each in April, giving commands to Brabazon, Erroll, and Lord Chesham who had been one of their founders. But although this first IY organisation appeared in the British *Official History* (and has been repeated in other accounts), it appears never to have actually existed in practice. Instead, very abruptly in May Roberts backed Lansdowne's decision to halt all IY recruiting, and broke up the IY to use them as Buller had originally intended, as companies to augment the existing colonial mounted corps, deploying them to subsidiary fronts away from the main British axis of advance.[151] Roberts instead found several noble IY officers positions on his own staff, including the Duke of Marlborough (Churchill's cousin) and the Duke of Norfolk, where they joined the Earl of Kerry, Lord Stanley (the future Earl of Derby) and also Lord Lansdowne's youngest son. Brabazon joined Roberts's headquarters as Commandant of the IY, but later complained that in dealings with Roberts he was ignored and bypassed by noble officers with 'family interest'.[152]

Before this redeployment could take full effect, the British suffered a considerable political and social, as well as military, disaster when the most exclusive of all the IY battalions, the 13th 'Millionaires Own' IY, was cut off and forced to surrender by the Boers at Lindley on 31 May.[153] This victory played a considerable part in restoring Boer morale, and was one of several small Boer victories at this time which led to

---

particularly confidential nature, also dealing with matters such as the dismissal of Babington and Brabazon from their commands.

148 LHCMA Ian Hamilton Papers 2/2/5: Hamilton to Roberts, 10 March 1900; Lee, *A Soldier's Life*, p. 58; Maurice, *The Life of General Lord Rawlinson of Trent*, pp. 61–3.

149 The City Imperial Volunteers consisted of an infantry battalion, two mounted infantry companies, and an artillery battery, raised and paid for by the City of London (the financial district); see Bennett, *Absent-Minded Beggars*, pp. 25–30.

150 Ibid., pp. 44–5.

151 Maurice, *History of the War in South Africa 1899–1902*, Volume III, p. 34; Bennett, *Absent Minded Beggars*, pp. 54–6.

152 Bennett, *Absent Minded Beggars*, pp. 53–4.

153 Lindley was a bizarre episode, not only for the events themselves but the fact that later enquiries exonerated everyone involved. For differing accounts see Bennett, *Absent Minded*

their decision to fight on. At a council of war at Kroonstadt on 17–20 March the Boer leadership had agreed to start abandoning the older style of ox-wagon trains for their commandos in favour of smaller formations moving entirely on horseback, with an emphasis on guerrilla tactics and raids against the British rather than set-piece battles, although this decision took some time to take effect. After evading capture by the British for the previous two months, in September de Wet made a thorough reorganisation of his forces, returning to commando many who had accepted the British occupation and gone home. From then on about 30,000 '*bitterender*' Boers fought their guerrilla war in small commandos usually named after their leaders.[154]

It is hard to escape the conclusion that in breaking up the IY Roberts quickly realised that they were a liability if used on their own, and that they must be distributed among more experienced formations. In a sentiment repeated throughout the IY, one corporal ruefully assessed his company's level of training as 'the men know nothing about horses. They are a helpless looking lot.'[155] Acclimatisation and training for the IY had averaged between four and ten days before they were sent to the front.[156] They were also seriously overloaded, one newly arrived IY gentleman-ranker describing his horse's load as starting with 'a heavy saddle with high arched pommels and cantle', topped off with 'huge balls of hay in a net strung across the horse's withers', adding how 'after a few months' experience we carried most of the impedimenta in wagons'; in June 1900 another IY trooper wrote home that 'I should like you to see us sometimes, with half a sheep hanging from our saddles and half a tree in front to cook it with.'[157]

Much to their own surprise, British commanders also thought the dominion troops who were arriving in South Africa to be poor horsemasters. Dundonald, whose brigade included Strathcona's Horse, felt that as plainsmen they were too used to having good horses readily available.[158] The truth was that not even the dominion troops had magical skills to overcome the basic problems of underfed, unacclimatised, overloaded horses. Strathcona's Horse arrived in South Africa with 90 per cent of their horses unfit for service.[159] Captain Henry 'Harry' Chauvel of the Queensland Mounted Infantry (which despite its name carried carbines), which arrived in South Africa in mid-December 1899 and served under Roberts, wrote home in early 1900 that the regiment did not have 20 horses fit to ride, and that

---

Beggars, pp. 110–22; Anglesey, *A History of the British Cavalry Volume 4*, pp. 176–82; Maurice, *History of the War in South Africa 1899–1902*, Volume III, pp. 115–20.

154 de Wet, *Three Years War*, pp. 79–80; Pretorius, *Life on Commando during the Anglo-Boer War, 1899–1902*, pp. 87–8; Wessels (ed.), *Lord Roberts and the War in South Africa 1899–1902*, p. 35; Hall, *The Hall Handbook of the Anglo-Boer War 1899–1902*, pp. 135–7; Pretorius, *The Great Escape of the Boer Pimpernell*.

155 NAM Paterson Papers: Scrapbook/Diary, April 1900.

156 Miller, 'Slogging Across the Veldt', p. 161.

157 Private Cosmo Rose-Innes (a London barrister) of 19th 'Paget's Horse' IY quoted in Bennett, *Absent Minded Beggars*, p. 54; NAM Britten Papers: Britten to his father, 29 June 1900.

158 Dundonald, *My Army Life*, p. 164; Birdwood, *Khaki and Gown*, pp. 113–14.

159 Wessels (ed.), *Lord Roberts and the War in South Africa 1899–1902*, pp. 108–11.

horses were dying at the rate of five a day.[160] By June 1900, after three months in South Africa, the Canadian Mounted Rifles had exactly six horses fit for service.[161]

On 3 April at Bloemfontein, Roberts formed a new Mounted Infantry Division under Ian Hamilton, elevated from substantive major to acting lieutenant general. Hamilton's division had two brigades, each of four 'corps' which on paper were the equivalent of strong mounted brigades (although in reality much weaker), consisting of a regular MI battalion of four or five companies plus between one and three irregular mounted rifle regiments. Almost all the Australian, Canadian and New Zealand mounted regiments joined the MI of Hamilton's 1st Mounted Brigade, now commanded by Hutton (one of Hutton's corps was led by de Lisle, another by Alderson). Fresh to the campaign, Hutton believed that the time had come for him to prove his mounted infantry theories beyond doubt, writing to Minto that 'I hear that [French's] Cavalry Division is practically *horseless*, and until they are provided with fresh horses we have no cavalry. The brunt of the mounted work therefore falls on the Mounted Infantry and local Mounted Corps.'[162] Recalling Hutton's command of the New South Wales militia, Chauvel expressed the disgust of his Queenslanders at his command style, writing that 'we hate him already', while the Canadians recorded with pleasure that many British officers also considered him 'a bit of a crank and somewhat impractical' in his views, and retaliated by stealing his personal saddle horse.[163] Oblivious to this, Hutton was convinced that he alone understood both colonial troops and mounted warfare. He wrote to Minto in April that, 'If God wills it our [Hamilton's] fine force of 11,000 Mounted Infantry should be able to make such an impression on the campaign as to establish the value of Mounted Troops, armed and equipped as ours are, above all cavil or argument.'[164]

Roberts's reorganisation left French's Cavalry Division consisting, again on paper, of four regular cavalry brigades (plus some Australians) each with a horse artillery battery and a machine-gun section. Haig, whose view of the MI could hardly have been more different to Hutton's, wrote to his sister:

> The mounted infantry have been formed into a division by themselves and are no longer under French. We don't regret this, for the MI are a useless lot, and seem as soon as mounted to cease to be good infantry. You will have seen of [sic] a force of infantry and MI being surrounded at Reddersburg and surrendering! Has ever anyone heard of *mounted* troops being surrounded? Cavalry never suffer themselves to be surrounded.[165]

---

160 Hill, *Chauvel of the Light Horse*, p. 20.

161 Miller, *Painting the Map Red*, p. 247.

162 BL Hutton Papers Add. 50080: Hutton to Minto, 3 April 1900; emphasis in the original.

163 Hill, *Chauvel of the Light Horse*, p. 23; Miller, *Painting the Map Red*, pp. 231–2; Maurice, *History of the War in South Africa*, Volume III, pp. 33–4 and p. 528;

164 BL Hutton Papers Add. 50080: Hutton to Minto, 14 April 1900.

165 Scott (ed.), *Douglas Haig: the Preparatory Prologue: Diaries and Letters 1861–1914*, p. 168; emphasis in the original. At Reddersburg (otherwise known as Mostertshoek or Mozar's Hoek) on 4 April half a British infantry battalion with two companies of MI took up a defensive position on a kopje, were surrounded by de Wet's commando, and forced to surrender; see Maurice, *History of the War in South Africa 1899–1902*, Volume III,

Haig had either forgotten about the 18th Hussars at Talana Hill, or took the view that their mistake was to dismount and seek cover. But whatever the force structure on paper, in reality Roberts introduced a quite different organisation for his army's mounted troops. French's Cavalry Division stayed as three cavalry brigades, plus Hutton's mounted brigade. This was similar to the pre-war structure for the division and reflected doctrinal orthodoxy by supplementing the mobility of the cavalry with the greater firepower of the MI. On 6 April, French recorded a conversation with Roberts:

> I asked him what he thought of MI He said he was a great advocate of their use but he was sure they could never in any sense replace cavalry. He has a strong [strange?] idea that the value of their fire is much greater than that of cavalry. I think we ought to combat this idea very strongly. The Boer Mauser carbine is our strong argument.[166]

Patrolling out frequently from Bloemfontein, by early April the Cavalry Division was down to only 1,073 fit horses, and French was very angry to find that Hutton, rather than accept that routine duties were an MI task to let the cavalry rest, had tried to get his men relieved by the cavalry to share the duties equally. Hutton wrote to Minto on 23 April:

> We MI are as usual treated as hewers of wood and drawers of water for the cavalry and everybody else. The first into action and the last out! As for our cavalry, they have so far done little enough in the campaign and are likely to do still less. They have lost nearly all their original horses and are being remounted on Argentine ponies, which have no breeding, no pace, and have no reasonable qualifications whatever for cavalry remounts.[167]

Hutton's pride in his own command did not stop him from being a good officer, or getting on well with French. Roberts noted later in the campaign that 'I believe that his troops do not like him, but they trust him as a commander. He is inordinately conceited and talks too much, but is still a valuable officer.'[168] He at least agreed about horses with Haig, who had complained that 'Whenever there is an alarm Lord R[oberts] at once orders out French and the Cavalry. I don't know what we'll do for horses. Only wretched beasts and Argentine ponies are arriving, and very few of them.'[169]

Stuck in Bloemfontein, by the time that Roberts wrote his next letter to Lansdowne on 24 April he had turned completely not only against French but towards the view

---

pp. 300–310; de Wet, *Three Years War*, pp. 95–101; Baker, *Battles and Battlefields of the Anglo-Boer War 1899–1902*, p. 177.

166 Quoted in Holmes, *The Little Field Marshal*, p. 102. Although a shorter carbine version of the Mauser did exist, it is hard to follow French's reasoning here.

167 BL Hutton Papers Add. 50080: Hutton to Minto, 14 April 1900. The phrase 'hewers of wood and drawers of water', meaning manual slaves, is from the King James version of the Bible, Joshua Chapter 9 Verse 23; it had proverbial status at the time.

168 Wessels (ed.), *Lord Roberts and the War in South Africa 1899–1902*, p. 130.

169 Scott (ed.), *Douglas Haig: The Preparatory Prologue: Diaries and Letters 1861–1914*, p. 167; Smith, *A Veterinary History of the War in South Africa 1889–1902*, pp. 52–4; Holmes, *The Little Field Marshal*, p. 102.

that all British problems in South Africa were due to the inadequacies of the cavalry and its commanders, and that the antidote was mounted infantry in all its forms:

> I think we might have done better on more than one occasion if our cavalry had been judiciously handled. French will never make a great cavalry leader, he is wanting in initiation [initiative] and has no idea of how to take care of his horses. He carried out the relief of Kimberley in a satisfactory manner because he acted in accordance with the instructions I gave him. But the following day, instead of giving his horses a much needed rest, he worked them from daylight until dark without any injury to the enemy or advantage to ourselves. I have never been able to get a complete return of the horse casualties on that occasion, but a large number of men had to be left at Kimberley as they had no horses to ride. At Poplar Grove French started late and allowed himself to be beguiled into fighting a series of rearguard actions, instead of giving them a wide berth and placing himself on the Boers' line of retreat. They were thus able to carry off their guns, and Kruger and Steyn effected their escape! ... Our mounted infantry has much improved of late, and I intend to see whether their employment in large bodies will not bring about more satisfactory results.[170]

The thinking behind Roberts's greatly increased support for the MI may have been Ian Hamilton's, although what exactly passed between them at the time was not recorded. But as a result of the great increase in the MI and the distribution of the IY throughout the army, any system for remounts and forage, and any proper organisation to enable the staff to address the problem, had simply collapsed, and there was also a shortage of trained officers to lead them.[171] Major General Smith later argued that this collapse of the British horse supply and remount system prevented a swift end to the war in 1900.[172]

For the advance from Bloemfontein, which began on 3 May, Roberts rather than using the Mounted Infantry Division as a fighting formation instead gave Hamilton a divisional sized 'column', a potentially tactically innovative formation consisting of a cavalry brigade, a mounted infantry brigade, and two infantry brigades (one of them commanded by Smith-Dorrien), each with an artillery battery and a machine-gun section, plus two additional field artillery batteries.[173] 'Hamilton's Column' marched most of the way to Pretoria in parallel with Roberts's main column, acting as a flank guard to the south, such a classic cavalry role as to leave no doubt about Roberts's view of French and the Cavalry Division, which he kept with his own column to cover his northern flank. Hamilton was guaranteed plaudits by Churchill, allowed by Roberts to join his forces after he had made it clear that he expected his co-operation as a reporter. Churchill's laudatory accounts of Hamilton's exploits

---

170 NAM Roberts Papers 110: Roberts to Lansdowne, 24 April 1900.

171 Smith, *A Veterinary History of the War in South Africa 1899–1902*, pp. 54–5; Maurice, *History of the War in South Africa 1899–1902*, Volume III, pp. 35–6.

172 Smith, *A Veterinary History of the War in South Africa 1899–1902*, p. 30, see also pp. 42–53 and pp. 131–41; see also Smith, *A History of the Royal Army Veterinary Corps 1796–1919*, pp. 200–205; Tylden, *Horses and Saddlery*, pp. 26–33.

173 The actual organisation of Hamilton's column is in an appendix to the official history, see Maurice, *History of the War in South Africa 1899–1902*, Volume III, p. 538.

were published in book form by the end of the year as *Ian Hamilton's March*.[174] In fact Hamilton's performance was a controversial one, particularly his failings in what became known as the 'first great de Wet hunt' of July–August 1900 after the fall of Pretoria.[175]

Amery, disregarding his own considerable role in these matters both during and after the Boer War, drew a picture in his memoirs of Roberts's mistakenly losing his temper with the cavalry over their grain supplies at Paardeberg as the trivial and accidental insult from which all else had flowed, including the mercurial French sulking before Poplar Grove, and privately refusing to co-operate with Roberts's plan.[176] While Amery acknowledged that up to this date French and Haig had both promoted flexible cavalry tactics, he argued that the further insult of Hamilton's appointment to command the Mounted Infantry Division, together with Roberts and Hamilton insisting on the superiority of mounted riflemen, led French and Haig – out of pure spite – to abandon their progressive position and espouse the opposing view that 'only the old knee to knee cavalry charge with lance and sword would decide the wars of the future', so that 'when the World War came the one idea dominating our two successive commanders-in-chief in France was the creation of a gap through which the great cavalry charge was to take place'.[177] Amery's account is a parody of the actual events of the cavalry debate after the Boer War, but it prevailed for many years, from its origins in Roberts's letter to Lansdowne on 24 April 1900, through its development in the war's aftermath, by Roberts himself, by Ian Hamilton, by Churchill, and by Amery's *Times History*, reaching its final form in Erskine Childers's book *War and the Arme Blanche*, published in 1910 with Roberts's patronage.

One of the contributing authors for Amery's *Times History*, Childers made his reputation as a novelist in 1903 with the best-selling thriller *Riddle of the Sands*. He served in South Africa as a driver with the artillery battery of the CIV between March and October 1900, chiefly as part of a column under Major General A.H. Paget.[178] In yet another example of how individual experience of war shaped attitudes towards the cavalry debate, Childers's defining moment came on 3 July 1900 in the small battle of Bakenlop, when 38th Royal Field Artillery took casualties from Boer rifle fire after the IY defending the battery withdrew.[179] That evening Childers found an artillery sergeant beside a camp fire, evidently deep in shock:

> I asked something, and he began a long rambling soliloquy about things in general, in a low thick voice, with his beard almost in the fire, scarcely aware of my presence. I can't

---

174 Churchill, *Ian Hamilton's March*; Lee, *A Soldier's Life*, pp. 58–60; James, *The Life of Lord Roberts*, pp. 318–20; Churchill, *My Early Life*, pp. 342–68; Sandys, *Churchill Wanted Dead or Alive*, pp. 186–208; Badsey, 'War Correspondents in the Boer War', pp. 197–9.

175 Pretorius, *The Great Escape of the Boer Pimpernel*, p. 200.

176 A suggestion given credence by James, *The Life of Lord Roberts*, pp. 298–301.

177 Amery, *My Political Life Volume One*, p. 132. The first of these quotations was repeated, without firm attribution to Amery, as representing French's and Haig's true views, as late as 1959; see Luvaas, *The Military Legacy of the Civil War*, p. 199.

178 Childers held a House of Commons Clerkship, a more important post than it sounds, marking him out as a rising man.

179 Maurice, *History of the War in South Africa*, Volume III, pp. 287–90.

reproduce it faithfully, because of the language, but it dealt with the war, which he thought would end next February, and the difference between Boer and British methods, of how our cavalry go along, heels down, toes in, arms close to side, eyes front, all according to regulation, keeping distance regardless of ground, while the Boer cares nothing as long as he gets there and does his work.[180]

Childers knew almost nothing about the wider circumstances of the battle, or that the mounted troops in his column were Australians, IY, and some Cape Colony irregulars, rather than cavalry. He returned to London convinced that the cavalry and their approach to warfare were the explanation for all the British Army's problems, views which Roberts would find valuable almost a decade later.

Once Roberts reached Pretoria on 5 June, and any need for a scapegoat for a failed campaign receded, he easily backed away from his original accusations made against French and the cavalry, confident that the war would end victoriously within a few months. On 2 August he wrote to Lansdowne that 'French has been doing very well lately. He lost his head a little after all the praise heaped upon him for the relief of Kimberley, but has now recovered and is of great use.'[181] By the end of August, he placed French alongside Ian Hamilton as 'one of the three or four I would entrust with a difficult business', and a few weeks later described French as 'an excellent cavalry commander'.[182] In a confidential assessment of senior officers submitted to Lansdowne in August 1900, he described Ian Hamilton as 'quite the most brilliant commander I have serving under me', and French in terms of guarded praise, 'I think he has improved immensely during the past few months, and although he has the great defect in a cavalry commander of not understanding how to take care of his horses, he is the only man except Broadwood whom I could trust to use a body of cavalry with dash and intelligence.'[183]

Roberts's behaviour (together with that of his staff), in espousing a particular military doctrine, and then exploiting political contacts and the press to promote this doctrine along with his own career, was a product of the entire nature of the British Army at the start of the twentieth century. Roberts may have been, in the language of the time, an intriguer and a self-advertiser, but although – like Henry Wilson later on – he bent the unofficial rules a little further than his opponents and victims felt was comfortable, he neither broke them nor invented them. From Roberts's perspective, French and the cavalry were welcome to share his glory as loyal subordinates, so long as they acknowledged that any failings in the early stages of his triumphal march from Modder River to Pretoria had been due to their errors as tacticians and horsemasters, and not to himself or his staff. Roberts, and Kitchener who succeeded him in South Africa at the end of 1900, took the view that the problems of supply were

---

180 Childers, *In the Ranks of the C.I.V.*, p. 120.

181 NAM Roberts Papers 110: Cipher Telegrams, Roberts to Lansdowne, 2 August 1900; see also Wessels (ed.), *Lord Roberts and the War in South Africa 1899–1902*, pp. 80–83.

182 NAM Roberts Papers 110: Cipher Telegrams, Letters from Roberts to Lansdowne, 29 August 1900 and 17 September 1900.

183 Wessels (ed.), *Lord Roberts and the War in South Africa 1899–1902*, pp. 129–30. Roberts's high opinion of Broadwood conflicts with his general condemnation as responsible for the minor British defeat at Sannah's Post (or Sannapos) on 31 March 1900.

part of the circumstances of the campaign, and that it was the responsibility of the cavalry to overcome them and produce horses and horsemen fit for combat. Roberts and his men were absolutely not an anti-cavalry conspiracy. When Rawlinson joined Roberts's staff in Bloemfontein he dined with French and Haig, and recorded that 'their dash to Kimberley was excellent'.[184] When Roberts returned to London at the end of 1900 taking Ian Hamilton with him as his military secretary, Haig wrote to his sister that Hamilton 'is a friend of mine and will, I know, do his best for me when he gets home. He promised French that I would be offered the first regiment which was in need of a commanding officer from the outside.'[185] Equally, French and the cavalry were far from being the innocent victims of Roberts's malice. French had his own powerful connections within the Army, including Buller, Haig's indirect communications with Evelyn Wood, and also his own compliant journalist in Goldmann of the *Standard*, who accompanied the Cavalry Division and was allowed privileged access to its records for his book *With General French and the Cavalry in South Africa*.[186] Later in the war, when Roberts was C-in-C and Ian Hamilton was back in South Africa as Kitchener's chief staff officer, Hamilton wrote to Roberts a carefully phrased letter about French:

> There is one point about General French which you ought to know, and which I hesitate the less [sic] to tell you as you are aware of my great admiration for him and how I prefer serving under him to almost anyone else. What I want you to know about him is his inclination to surround himself with personal friends, irrespective of their value as trained staff officers.[187]

Presumably Hamilton was oblivious to Roberts's own habit of employing 'friends', especially aristocrats, as staff officers, or hoped that Roberts would not make the comparison. But the cavalry certainly needed better commanding officers when Roberts took command in South Africa: French was quoted as saying that 'most of my cavalry commanders lost their heads in a crisis and were like old fussed

---

184 NAM Rawlinson Papers: Boer War Diary, Volume II, entry 27 March 1900. A note is needed here to avoid confusion. There are three deposits of General Lord [Henry] Rawlinson's papers held in different archives in Great Britain. That in the National Army Museum contains papers related mainly to his early career; that in the Churchill Archive Centre contains his personal diary for the First World War; that in the Imperial War Museum is a copy of the Fourth Army War Diary 1916–1918 originally given to the library at the Army Staff College Camberley in Rawlinson's memory by former members of his staff on his death, and which contains documents not extant in the copy of the Fourth Army War Diary held at The National Archives.

185 NLS Haig Papers 6c: Haig to his sister, 7 December 1900.

186 Goldmann, *With General French and the Cavalry in South Africa*; Badsey, 'War Correspondents in the Boer War', pp. 189–91. Sydney Goldmann later changed his name slightly to C.S Goldman, and then changed the style again to Charles S. Goldman when he became editor of *The Cavalry Journal*.

187 LHCMA Hamilton Papers 2/3/8: Ian Hamilton to Roberts, 16 December 1901. This was written after Haig had ceased to serve on French's staff.

hens', and Roberts had to replace five of them.[188] The cavalry's horsemastership also needed improvement, and it did improve considerably as a result of the war. What took place between Roberts with his supporters on one side and French with his supporters on the other was only one example – perhaps a little larger, more self-contained and better documented than most – of the way that doctrine was formed and campaigns were conducted in the British Army of this period, including the impact of personalities and institutional politics. Rawlinson recorded in March 1900 how 'Buller is crabbed [sic] by everyone including his own staff. The divisional leaders all crab one another', and 'the fact is that they are all at loggerheads'.[189] Buller himself (although hardly an impartial witness) described how on reaching Pretoria, 'I found Roberts sitting in one building with his Hindu [sic] staff, Kitchener in another with his Egyptian staff, and Kelly-Kenny in a third with an English staff, all pulling against each other.'[190]

When Roberts began his advance from Bloemfontein towards Johannesburg and Pretoria on 3 May he left French's Cavalry Division behind, still recovering from its exertions and assimilating remounts. But on 8 May, Roberts ordered French to move up his leading two brigades 60 miles in one day. The cavalry were needed for the battle of Zand River on 10 May, a tactical position similar to Poplar Grove with the Boer forces deployed along a line of kopjes. Although Zand River was altogether a harder fight than Poplar Grove, the Boers once more simply retreated in the face of the British mounted advance rather than allow themselves to be surrounded, in a battle that set the pattern for the next few weeks. Roberts's frustration was evident, as Haig wrote to his sister a few days later:

> I hear from several sources that the infantry is *quite jealous* of the success of the cavalry. The poor creatures merely carry their guns without a chance of loosing off! In fact they simply wear out their boots to no purpose!!...
>
> The Field Marshal [Roberts] was in a bad temper yesterday and opened upon [sic] French because so many men were missing! But what can you expect to happen if horses stop from exhaustion and one covers 60 or more miles in 2 days![191]

Once more Hutton provided a contrasting interpretation in his next letter to Lord Minto:

---

188 NLS Haldane Papers Mss. 5901–6109: Sworn deposition of Lieutenant Colonel Stephen Frewen, 16th Lancers; TNA WO 105/24 Papers of Lord Roberts as C-in-C South Africa, Confidential Reports, Case of Lieutenant Colonel Henry Page-Henderson 6th (Inniskilling) Dragoons, Case of Lieutenant Colonel Stephen Frewen 16th Lancers; NAM Roberts Papers 122: Roberts to Mr Sanders, 12 January 1905.

189 NAM Rawlinson Papers: Boer War Diary, Volume II, entry 3 March 1900.

190 Quoted in Beckett, 'Buller and the Politics of Command', p. 55. This use of 'Hindu' as a synonym for 'Indian', meaning staff officers associated with Roberts from service in India, was not unusual at the time; likewise 'Egyptian' meant officers who had served under Kitchener with the Egyptian Army, etc.

191 Scott (ed.), *Douglas Haig: The Preparatory Prologue: Diaries and Letters 1861–1914*, p. 169; emphasis in the original.

The whole campaign is a collaboration [confirmation] of the facts which your Excellency and I have been preaching for the last twenty years. It is a strange irony that the Indian School of soldiers, who always scoffed at our efforts to create a mobile infantry from our regular infantry battalions, are the very men who are now profiting from our determination and foresight. As for the cavalry, it is safe to say that the effect which they have had upon the war has been almost entirely moral. Their presence upon the flank or rear of the enemy has been in itself sufficient to divert the enemy's attention, and eventually to cause him to retreat. The actual effect of the cavalry, their killing power, has been trivial compared to that of the Mounted Infantry and infantry.[192]

What was beyond doubt was the continued effect on the horses. By 21 May French's three cavalry brigades had 184 effectives out of 2,270 (plus 678 men without horses), and his MI brigade had 190 effectives out of 3,327 (plus 113 men without horses).[193]

Zand River was the first battle at which both French and Ian Hamilton had served together since Elandslaagte, and a battle from which they took very different memories. Ten years later, Hamilton wrote to Erskine Childers that it was Zand River that destroyed his last remaining faith in the arme blanche, as he witnessed the failure of the cavalry's charging tactics to make headway against Boer dismounted riflemen. 'The horses were fresh', Hamilton told Childers, 'after several days' complete rest', but could not overcome the skilful Boer tactics as they retreated. 'I do not blame the cavalry personnel', Hamilton continued, 'no finer fellows serve in the British, or any other, Army'; rather he blamed 'the false training which had taught them in peace tactics palpably impractical for war'.[194] Writing in the same year, French took the exactly opposite view, recounting how at Zand River he had ordered the 8th Hussars to charge a Boer position:

> I galloped from the kopje to the outer brigade with the thought that either every idea which I had ever formed in my life as to the efficacy of shock action against mounted riflemen was utterly erroneous, or this was the moment to show that it was not... The Boers realised what was coming. Their fire became wild, and the bullets started to fly over our heads. Directly the advance began, the Boers hesitated, and many rushed to their horses. We pressed forward, with all the moderate speed of tired horses, whereupon the whole Boer force retired in the utmost confusion and disorder, losing in a quarter of an hour more ground than they had gained in three or four hours of fighting.[195]

Hamilton and French each saw what they wanted to see in this episode: for Hamilton it was a demonstration of how a controlled retreat using accurate long-range rifle fire could check advancing cavalry from charging; for French it was a demonstration of how even a slow charge by exhausted cavalry could drive mounted riflemen out of a good defensive position. Vaughan, an eyewitness to the 8th Hussars' charge, recalled with some amusement the Boers mounting up and retreating before 'the terrifying

---

192 BL Hutton Papers Add. 50080: Hutton to Minto, 14 May 1900.
193 NAM Rawlinson Papers: Boer War Diary, Volume III, entry 21 May 1900.
194 LHCMA Ian Hamilton Papers 7/3/15: Hamilton to Childers, 30 October 1910; Hamilton sent copies of this letter to Roberts and Churchill.
195 French, preface to Bernhardi, *Cavalry in War and Peace*, p. xi.

spectacle of 200 men flogging their horses with the flat of their blunt swords'.[196] Some cavalrymen preferred to call this kind of charge to take ground 'galloping' an enemy position.

Zand River set the pattern for many small engagements on Roberts's march to Pretoria (one estimate has been 26 such battles), mostly consisting of Boer forces taking up blocking positions across the British line of march and being driven off by mounted troops after firing a few shots, with the British incapable of effective pursuit.[197] It is difficult to determine how much, or how often, this Boer behaviour represented deliberate tactics, and how much it was the product of their inherent reluctance to face charging cavalry, and of low morale. On reaching Pretoria the four cavalry brigades had between them only 1,900 troopers and horses, just 230 of them combat effective, but they were still quite prepared to charge Boer positions frontally, even at a slow trot.[198]

What was almost the last set-piece battle of the war lasted for two days starting on 11 June at Diamond Hill east of Pretoria, where the remaining Boers spread themselves over 25 miles of hills and were driven off by the British, who were once again unable to pursue effectively. On the first day there were at least two notable cavalry charges, in both cases undertaken by troopers of 2nd Cavalry Brigade under Ian Hamilton's command, and reported upon by Churchill for the *Morning Post*. In the first of these, made by the 12th Lancers, the regiment employed the cavalry tactics of an earlier generation by rallying back slowly after they had driven the Boers from their position, and lost more men from enemy fire into their backs while rallying than while attacking. But next to charge was the composite Household Regiment, which halted on the Boer position to hold it dismounted. In Churchill's description:

> Delighted at the unlooked-for, unhoped-for opportunity the Life Guardsmen scrambled back into their saddles, thrust their hated [sic] carbines into the buckets, and drawing their long swords, galloped straight at the enemy. The Boers, who in this part of the field very considerably outnumbered the cavalry, might very easily have inflicted severe losses on them. But so formidable was the sight of these tall horsemen cheering and flogging their gaunt horses with the flat of their swords, that they did not abide, and running to their mounts, fled in a cowardly haste, so that, though eighteen horses were shot, the Household Cavalry sustained no losses in men.[199]

Successful charges like this were not limited to cavalry regiments. De Lisle, whose mounted troops had been the first into Pretoria, later described how on the second day at Diamond Hill he ordered his West Australian Mounted Infantry attacking a Boer position 'to gallop the hill under covering fire of two pom-poms', (quick-

---

196 Vaughan, 'Cavalry Notes', *Journal of the Royal United Service Institution*, Volume 45, p. 452.

197 Anglesey, *A History of the British Cavalry Volume 4*, pp. 167–9.

198 NAM Rawlinson Papers: Boer War Diary, Volume III, entry 15 June 1900 showing returns for 9 June 1900.

199 Quoted in Woods, *Young Winston's Wars*, p. 407; see also Anglesey, *A History of the British Cavalry Volume 4*, pp. 182–5, which puts the Household's losses at one man and twenty one horses.

firing light artillery), adding that 'On arriving near the crest they left their horses unattended, and soon the crackle of rifle fire was heard' as they carried the crest and the Boers retreated.[200] In the doctrinal debate after the war, distinctions would be made over whether these had been 'charges' or 'gallops', whether the enemy had fled or retreated, where exactly the horsemen had dismounted, and whether these were the tactics of cavalry or of mounted rifles; but at the time these distinctions scarcely mattered even if they could have been accurately determined.

For traditionalist cavalrymen such charges were proof, which they scarcely felt they needed, that a good charge would always succeed. Brabazon, after telling the Elgin Commission that 'the Boers were Yeomanry' (presumably in the sense that they were mounted riflemen), gave his evidence on this point with conviction, explaining that 'Both the Cavalry and the Yeomanry (for the Yeomanry were used as Cavalry) were doing a thing which certainly Cavalry were never taught to do, and that was, always attacking fortifications; there is no fortification in this world as a Boer kopje.'[201] Rather more soberly, cavalry reformers including French and Haig recognised that cavalry used in this way against Boer mounted riflemen could take and hold ground in a way that had not been seen since the American Civil War.

The campaign that had begun at Modder River on 11 February ended at Diamond Hill on 12 June with many fixed opinions regarding the doctrine and future of the cavalry, and several demonstrations of its strengths and weaknesses, but little consensus and much that was the product of the unique circumstances of the veldt. The fall of Pretoria also largely marked the end of the conventional phase of the Boer War, since Mafeking had been relieved on 17 May. Most of the influential reporters left South Africa soon afterwards, including Amery and Churchill, and when Roberts returned home a few months later it was widely assumed that the war was over. As set-piece battles gave way to guerrilla warfare, all the various types of mounted troops used by the British, as they learned to deal better with the conditions of the veldt, were reorganised into 'columns' of 500 to 2,000 horsemen plus artillery (mounted brigades in all but name) in order to pursue the remaining *bitterenders*. With the Boers unwilling to attack other than under the most favourable circumstances, and the British still suffering great problems with their horses, the typical column battle became a small-scale exchange of dismounted fire at 1,000 yards or more, with low combat casualties on both sides. It was particularly noted that the IY contingent suffered only two per cent combat deaths in more than a year that it spent in South Africa.[202]

While French continued to command mounted forces with some distinction, several rising cavalry officers who later achieved high rank in the First World War were given column commands, including Allenby, Byng and Gough, while Horne as an artilleryman served with several columns.[203] From May 1901 onwards Haig

---

200 de Lisle, *Reminiscences of Sport and War*, p. 96. The West Australian Mounted Infantry were part of de Lisle's 2nd Corps MI under Hutton.

201 *Elgin Commission Report*, Evidence Volume I, pp. 293–4.

202 Dunlop, *The Development of the British Army 1899–1914*, pp. 111–12.

203 Wavell, *Allenby*, pp. 90–109; Williams, *Byng of Vimy*, pp. 43–6; Gough, *Soldiering On*, pp. 82–90; Robbins, 'Henry Horne', p. 98.

in Cape Colony had an independent command of between three and six columns (including 'Byng's Column'), increasing at one point to elements of 18 columns totalling almost 19,000 mounted men, 1,000 footsoldiers, 49 guns, and 14 machine-guns. These are episodes in Haig's career to which little attention has been paid, quite possibly because he had not yet fully learned the importance of publicity: Ian Hamilton wrote to Roberts in his assessment of February 1902 that Haig 'does not seem able to bring off any "coup", and, as far as fame goes, he might as well have been in winter quarters with his men, but I have heard nothing against him'.[204]

Looking back later on the Boer War from the perspective of the outbreak of the First World War, Haig recorded what he claimed were his views of French's generalship at this time, 'His military ideas often shocked me when I was his Chief of Staff during the South African War. In those days, with only mounted troops under him, he fortunately could not put into practice some special theories which he told me he had deduced from Hamley's *Operations of War*.'[205] There is nothing among Haig's writings, or any other records of the Boer War, to support this retrospective view, and in fact both French and Haig had infantry and artillery under their respective commands in the guerrilla period of the war. French, who commanded in Cape Colony for most of the guerrilla war, never expressed the same antipathy to MI as Haig. In this period French also found an ally on mounted tactics in Edward Hutton, who he told in March 1901 that 'I am still very closely wedded to the ideas that I have expressed to you so often – viz. – to possess several new regiments of mounted rifles as part and parcel of the cavalry.'[206] In the same month Hutton wrote to Minto describing an article that he had recently published on mounted troops, 'You will see in it the views and proposals which French and I are agreed upon as regards the future development of this subject.'[207] In May 1901 French further told Hutton:

> I was much afraid at one time that the cavalry principle in England was getting to be at a lamentable and most dangerous discount. But I am very pleased to observe signs of a great change of emphasis in that respect. The 'morale', the 'cavalry *spirit*' is of such *vital* importance in all mounted troops (heavies, lancers, hussars, dragoons, mounted riflemen and mounted infantry) and it is in such danger of being lost sight of in these matters of reconnaissance etc.[208]

What French was describing were the tactically adept mounted riflemen of the columns out on the veldt. If Haig – and probably French also – traced their doctrinal origins to the reformed cavalry, and Hutton traced them to the MI, then in wartime this scarcely mattered: Hutton noted that 'our views were absolutely in accord in

---

204 LHCMA Hamilton Papers 2/3/16: Hamilton to Roberts, 8 February 1902; Cooper, *Haig*, Volume I, p. 86; Maurice, *History of the War in South Africa 1899–1902*, Volume IV, pp. 179–80.

205 Sheffield and Bourne (eds), *Douglas Haig: War Diaries and Letters 1914–1918*, p. 58.

206 BL Hutton Papers Add. 50086: French to Hutton, 30 March 1901.

207 Ibid., Add. 50081: Hutton to Minto, 27 March 1901.

208 Ibid., French to Hutton, 28 May 1901; emphasis in the original.

this period', and remained so for another five years.[209] In December 1901 French specifically asked Kitchener for a Guards MI battalion that was just arriving in South Africa.[210]

Since the mounted columns included troops other than cavalry, and there was a shortage of good commanders, column commands also went to officers who would otherwise never have commanded cavalry brigades. These included de Lisle, who developed a close affection for his 6th MI, and Plumer, who after the Rhodesia Regiment was disbanded in October 1901 continued to command brigade-sized colonial mounted contingents.[211] Smith-Dorrien also commanded a mounted column numbering 3,000 men under French before leaving for India later in 1901.[212] Rawlinson returned to London with Roberts, but came back in March 1901 to take command of a column consisting of the 2nd MI and 8th MI, augmented by some IY and by elements of Kitchener's Horse and Roberts's Horse. Rawlinson's command in South Africa was as controversial as his later career, and shortly before the end of the war Roberts wrote to Hamilton, who had returned to South Africa, 'If you come across Rawly, tell him that I hope to hear of him as being one of the most dashing leaders in the Army. It grieves me terribly to hear doubts about him.'[213] Birdwood left the staff of Dundonald's mounted brigade to serve on Kitchener's staff until the end of the war. The only Army commander on the Western Front in the First World War who gained no experience at all with mounted troops in South Africa was Charles Monro, who served on the staff of an infantry division before returning home in early 1901.[214] Robertson and Wilson also missed the experience of commanding a mounted column; both returned with Roberts at the end of 1900 to take up staff appointments.[215]

In February 1901, after the first negotiations to end the war had failed, Kitchener wrote to the new Secretary of State for War, St John Brodrick, that 'I wish I could make some kind of estimate of the duration of the war, but it seems quite impossible to do so.'[216] The state of the British mounted forces was only one of the many problems of the guerrilla war, but it remained of great importance. The composite Household Cavalry regiment returned home in November 1900, but two further cavalry regiments were sent to South Africa in early 1901, and two more at

---

209 Ibid., Add 50114: Note by Hutton in the index to his papers, p. 165.

210 NAM Roberts Papers 33: Kitchener to Roberts, 13 December 1901.

211 LHCMA Hamilton Papers 2/3/10: Hamilton to Roberts, 1 January 1902; de Lisle, *Reminiscences of Sport and War*, pp. 190–19; Harington, *Plumer of Messines*, pp. 38–52. Both Plumer and Byng were given home leave to rest by Kitchener shortly before the war's end.

212 Maurice, *History of the War in South Africa 1899–1902*, Volume IV, pp. 111–27.

213 NAM Roberts Papers 122: Roberts to Ian Hamilton, 27 March 1902; Maurice, *The Life of General Lord Rawlinson of Trent*, pp. 66–76. 'Rawly' is of course a diminutive of 'Rawlinson' and a common nickname for him.

214 Bourne, 'Charles Monro', pp. 122–4; Birdwood, *Khaki and Gown*, pp. 118–30.

215 Robertson, *From Private to Field Marshal*, pp. 125–6; Callwell, *Field Marshal Sir Henry Wilson*, Volume I, pp. 42–3; Jeffrey, *Field Marshal Sir Henry Wilson*, pp. 39–41.

216 TNA PRO 30/57/22 Official Papers of Lord Kitchener, Kitchener to Brodrick, 16 February 1901.

the end of the year. Between December 1900 and July 1901 most of the mounted volunteers also returned home, including many of the most experienced dominion troops, and most of the IY; and often green troops recruited in a hurry had to replace them.[217] A second contingent of just under 17,000 IY was raised in Great Britain, known to most veterans as the 'new yeomanry', followed later in the year by a third contingent of 7,000 that was mostly still training at home when the war ended.[218] Recruited centrally by the War Office rather than through the yeomanry associations, the second IY contingent was the subject of almost universal derision when it arrived in South Africa. A veteran British infantryman described them in August 1901 as 'an awe-inspiring lot. They make one tremble to look at them (for fear they may tumble out of the saddle). They will want a terrible knocking into shape before they are fit for anything.'[219] In a war in which the Boers were increasingly reliant on raiding the British for supplies and equipment, it became proverbial that a new IY company was so likely to get itself cut off and surrounded as to constitute little more than a free gift to the enemy. The routine of the guerrilla war, including farm burning and rounding up animals and people, may also have affected the morale of volunteers more than that of professional soldiers. Kitchener wrote to Roberts on 19 July that 'a good many have shown they have no heart. Want of training, want of riding and shooting, I admit. But when they surrender without an attempt or firing a shot, they do so much harm that they are dangerous to have with us.'[220] In the guerrilla phase of the war the British also started to employ Africans more openly as mounted riflemen, to the alarm and fury of some Boer commanders, although some of the Boer commando *agterryer* retainers also carried weapons and fought.[221]

At the height of the guerrilla war Kitchener had 90 or more mounted columns, containing many different types of troops including even Royal Artillery MI ('The Mounted Artillinfantry'), manoeuvring across the veldt in attempts to track down the last of the commandos. Unlike Roberts, Kitchener never expressed any particular view on arme blanche cavalry when compared with mounted riflemen or MI during his period of command. But Kitchener did share Roberts's views on horse management:

---

217 Miller, *Painting the Map Red*, pp. 277–88 and pp. 358–67; Hall, *The Hall Handbook of the Anglo-Boer War*, pp. 81–4; Dunlop, *The Development of the British Army 1899–1914*, pp. 110–12.

218 Maurice, *History of the War in South Africa*, Volume I, p. 414.

219 Private Alfred Burrows, quoted in Jenkins, 'One of the Human Atoms', p. 13. Private Burrows served in South Africa with the 1st Battalion, The Leicestershire Regiment from 1895 until his discharge at the end of the war in 1902.

220 NAM Roberts Papers 33: Kitchener to Roberts 19 July 1901; see also Gardner, *Allenby*, p. 50; Miller, 'Slogging Across the Veldt', pp. 162–3 and pp. 166–7.

221 Evidence for the use of armed black African troops on both sides tends to be sketchy, but the issue has attracted great attention. See Lee, *To the Bitter End*, pp. 200–202; Nasson, 'Africans at War', pp. 138–40; Nasson, *The South African War 1899–1902*, pp. 282–3; Labuschagne, *Ghostriders of the Anglo-Boer War 1899–1902*, pp. 45–58; TNA WO 32/7958 'Correspondence between Lord Kitchener etc. and Boers concerning treatment of non-combatants and wounded. Allegations as to use of armed natives by British', especially the letter of complaint about the British use of armed Africans from Christiaan de Wet to Kitchener, 18 March 1901.

he had issued orders that the horses of the mounted columns should be fit and well, and in his view it was the responsibility of the column commanders to make this happen. In March 1901 he complained to Brodrick of 'the reckless loss of horses by mobile columns', warning that 'I shall have to make an example by removing an officer from his command for neglect of orders if it goes on much longer.'[222] The problems faced by the British in hunting down the *bitterenders* were greatly increased by the fact that the problems of horse supply, feeding and exhaustion had still not been solved, and had so distorted the entire British conduct of the war that no solution seemed possible. In November 1901 Kitchener wrote a long explanation of the situation to Brodrick:

> The loss in horses, both in columns in the field and in the veterinary hospitals, has always been very serious especially during the [southern] winter months when grazing is not procurable. We have done our best to rest horses after their sea voyage, only the fittest landed are issued [to the columns] after an average rest of three weeks or a month.... The mounted troops we employ are some of them very bad in the care of horses. Colonials are terrible, Yeomanry and Mounted Infantry are bad, and column commanders and officers have the greatest trouble in getting moderate care taken of the animals. I tried fitting out columns with extra horses, as the Boers have, but the loss through want of care was so terrible I had to give up the plan. Where Boer ponies thrive, our horses simply die. A number of our men are now mounted on rough Boer ponies, but what will carry a Boer who has two or three spare ponies well, fails in most cases to carry the colonial or cavalry soldier. The work our mounted troops have to do in finding the Boers is also so much greater than that of the Boers who remain in hiding.[223]

The day after Kitchener wrote this letter, Ian Hamilton returned from the War Office to act as his chief staff officer until the end of the war. Hamilton, with the connivance of the rest of the staff, took to hiding the existence of some columns from Kitchener, in an effort to rest the horses.[224] But Kitchener never abandoned the idea that the responsibility lay with the column commanders and not with himself. 'If a column commander is not successful', he wrote to Roberts in February 1902, 'it is the first excuse that the horses were no good.'[225]

As part of the historical debate over technological determinism, a case can be made that if the Boer War had taken place even five years later its guerrilla phase would have been much shorter, and correspondingly less controversial. For 15 months after the fall of Pretoria the British attempted unsuccessfully to hunt down a relatively small number of mounted Boers in the vast spaces of the veldt. This experience may be compared with the much smaller Boer rebellion, led by Christiaan de Wet on the outbreak of war in Europe in 1914, inspired by hope of German support. De Wet, who evaded capture throughout the Boer War, was hunted down across the veldt with his commandos in 1914 and captured in a matter of weeks,

---

222 TNA PRO 30/57/22 Official Papers of Lord Kitchener, Kitchener to Brodrick, 29 March 1901.
223 TNA PRO 30/57/22 Official Papers of Lord Kitchener, Kitchener to Brodrick, 29 November 1901.
224 LHCMA Hamilton Papers 2/3/9: Hamilton to Roberts, 24 December 1901.
225 NAM Roberts Papers 33: Kitchener to Roberts, 7 February 1902.

chiefly by the use of troops in motor lorries which maintained a slow but relentless mechanical pursuit, giving the commandos' horses no time to rest and leading to their collapse from exhaustion.[226] The guerrilla phase of the Boer War would also have been radically different if the British had possessed aircraft for observation, and the Wright brothers' first flight took place in December 1903, not even two years after the war ended.[227] Just as both technological change and a technological hiatus have been used to explain the stalemate on the Western Front, so the same argument may be extended back to the Boer War. Within a few years of its end new technology was making the value of horsed cavalry increasingly questionable, just at the time that enthusiasts such as Haig were proclaiming the increasing value of cavalry now that it had its own effective firepower.[228]

Before Roberts left South Africa, the cavalry and other mounted troops had exchanged their carbines for longer-barrelled rifles in order to cope with the change to guerrilla warfare, and discarded as much weight as possible; while a brutal form of natural selection on campaign meant that smaller breeds of horse were being used, and horse management was improving. One issue was whether the cavalry should give up their lances and swords as part of this weight saving. Some column commanders took a very firm line on this: Smith-Dorrien gave the 5th Lancers, who were part of his column, the choice of leaving their swords and lances or themselves being left behind when the column moved off.[229] In contrast, Haig later gave evidence to the Elgin Commission that Jan Christiaan Smuts had told him that British columns giving up the arme blanche was their biggest mistake of the war.[230] After making a general enquiry among his commanders Roberts did not issue an actual order forbidding the arme blanche, and some regiments kept their swords and lances until the war's end.[231] Also, giving up swords did not necessarily mean giving up the mounted charge; at least one charge was contrived by a troop of the 18th Hussars in July 1901 using rifles and fixed bayonets, while Rawlinson described to Roberts how in an action on 13 December 1901 his 8th MI had charged mounted to contact with a small party of Boers, 'the more the Boers fired the more the MI cheered and galloped on and the stand cost the Boers sixteen killed'.[232]

In early 1901 the Boer commandos started to change their tactics again, augmenting their ambushes and long-range rifle skirmishes with mounted charges, in response to which Rawlinson's column turned once more to the arme blanche, stipulating in its standing orders for April 1901 that 'O[fficers] C[ommanding] mounted units

---

226 See Sampson, *The Capture of De Wet* for the British perspective on this campaign; being able to give a book that title must have given Sampson great satisfaction.

227 Buckley, *Air Power in the Age of Total War*, p. 16; the same point is made by Amery, *My Political Life Volume One*, p. 161.

228 Sheffield, *Forgotten Victory*, pp. 98–103; Terraine, *White Heat*, pp. 142–51.

229 Smith-Dorrien, *Memories of Forty Eight Years' Service*, pp. 260–61.

230 *Elgin Commission Report*, Evidence Volume II, p. 411.

231 TNA WO 105/29 Papers of Lord Roberts as C-in-C South Africa, 'Opinions as to the arming of the cavalry with the long rifle'; NAM Roberts Papers 122: Roberts to Ian Hamilton, 4 April 1902; LHCMA Hamilton Papers 24/7/10: Hamilton to Roberts, 30 April 1902.

232 NAM Roberts Papers 47: Rawlinson to Roberts, 15 December 1901; Marling, *Rifleman and Hussar*, p. 278.

will be good enough to ensure that their men are able, readily, to fix bayonets both mounted and dismounted. The act of doing so may be found useful where the enemy employs charging tactics.'[233] Next month at Vlakfontein a surprise Boer charge led by General J.C.G. Kemp, using a mixture of mounted and dismounted firing, inflicted 179 casualties on a British column.[234] Making a charge or assault on foot was a Boer tactic dating back to before the Transvaal War, and carried over into the guerrilla phase of the Boer War.[235] But the Boers had also begun riding up and then dismounting at close rifle range to advance on foot leading their horses, a tactic which they employed particularly successfully at Bakenlaagte on 30 October 1901. Next month, while on board ship for South Africa to take over as Kitchener's chief staff officer, Ian Hamilton gave Roberts his interpretation of these new tactics:

> To blaze away at a Boer galloping across the veldt, without knowing where your bullet goes, is no better practice than firing blank cartridges.... Several recent actions seem to me to show that the Boers are learning that they can gallop in on our fellows, and their bad, unpractised shooting, without much risk to themselves. You will remember how very strong I have always been on the point, that if they can gallop in to within 80 yards of our men [and dismount] they are our masters, owing to their style of snap-shooting, like jack-in-the-boxes, without aligning their sights on the object.[236]

Hamilton's interpretation of these Boer tactics, which he had not seen at first hand, may have been mistaken, particularly about their use of cover (although some of their charges were masked by smoke-screens generated by setting fire to the veldt). But as before, he remained convinced that the best rifle-shots would always win.

The new Boer tactics also included another form of mounted charge, a charge to contact in open order, sometimes firing from the saddle, that was virtually indistinguishable from an equivalent British cavalry charge. A particular study was made of these Boer 'rifle charges' by Childers for his book *War and the Arme Blanche*.[237] At Blood River Poort (also known as Scheepers Nek) on 17 September 1901, a column of about 250 MI led by Hubert Gough galloped forward and dismounted to engage 200 Boers, and were then charged over from the flank and encircled, with Gough and his entire command becoming prisoners.[238] Allenby led the party to rescue Gough, who he held responsible for falling into the Boer trap, and

---

233 NAM Rawlinson Papers 8: Orders and States, Rawlinson's Column, March 1901 to January 1902, Standing Order Number 4 of 27 April 1901.

234 Anglesey, *A History of the British Cavalry Volume 4*, p. 266.

235 Laband, *The Transvaal Rebellion*, pp. 59–67; Pretorius, *Life on Commando during the Anglo-Boer War*, p. 144.

236 LHCMA Hamilton Papers 2/3/1: Hamilton to Roberts, 13 November 1901.

237 Childers, *War and the Arme Blanche*, particularly pp. 239–60, and the evidence gathered by Childers in the NAM Roberts Papers files 221 to 224.

238 Blood River Poort is another controversial and disputed episode; Kitchener decided that Gough had fallen for a trap and was not to blame; see NAM Roberts Papers 33: Kitchener to Roberts, 27 September 1901. Differing versions may be found in Gough, *Soldiering On*, pp. 84–6; Anglesey, *A History of the British Cavalry Volume 4*, pp. 264–5; Maurice, *History of the War in South Africa 1899–1902*, Volume IV, pp. 217–18.

this has been suggested as the origin of the animosity between them.[239] As in earlier colonial wars, these small column engagements were important for the careers and later attitudes towards each other of the commanders involved. Writing in November 1914 on the Western Front, 'Sally' Home of the 11th Hussars commented:

> There seems to be a good deal of mistrust about – it has ever been thus in our army. It is the natural result of small wars, in which personal ambition may be satisfied by some feat of arms – South Africa was the worst case, a lot of small columns with each operating on its own and the reputation of the commander depending on those operations. This must lead to jealousy and the situation of the personal factor when put in contradistinction to the whole.[240]

A similar episode, in which a dismounted British column was enveloped from one or both flanks by charging Boers, took place at Onverwacht (or Bankkop) on 4 January 1902. Altogether there were at least nine large charges, each involving hundreds of mounted men, made by Boer commandos against British columns between September 1901 and May 1902, including a frontal charge made on 7 March at Tweebosch by the commando under General J.H. 'Koos' de la Rey that wounded and captured Lord Methuen. 'That was a magnificent charge', Methuen told de la Rey after his capture, 'If those are going to be your tactics in future, you still have a chance to win the war!'[241] A Boer charge at Boschmanskop on 1 April turned into a running mounted fight between a commando and the considerably outnumbered 2nd Dragoon Guards (Queen's Bays), supported by a squadron of the 7th Hussars. The British cavalry successfully extricated themselves, withdrawing by alternate squadrons in what may have been the only occasion in the war in which both sides intentionally charged and countercharged each other mounted, using either swords, bayonets or saddle fire at point-blank ranges.[242] The last Boer charge of all, made by Kemp at Rooiwal in the western Transvaal on 11 April, involved at least 800 charging Boers and was barely repulsed by British fire at close range. The defending British column numbered well over 1,000 men, including some very raw IY, plus artillery and machine-guns, but inflicted barely 90 casualties on the Boers.[243] In all these charges, Boer losses were much lower than the theoretical firepower directed against them would have predicted, and Kitchener was particularly critical of the poor shooting and morale of the new IY contingents when facing them.[244]

The lessons of the Boer War for tactical doctrine were that, both at its start and over its course, both sides needed to modify their pre-war doctrines, but neither side found it necessary or possible to modify them very much. Throughout, the dominant

---

239 Gardner, *Allenby*, p. 49; Wavell, *Allenby*, p. 89.
240 Home, *The Diary of a World War I Cavalry Officer*, p. 42.
241 Quoted in Miller, *Lord Methuen and the British Army*, p. 229.
242 Childers, *War and the Arme Blanche*, p. 247; Stirling, *Our Regiments in South Africa*, pp. 408–9. There is some dispute as to whether the two British cavalry regiments carried swords in this action.
243 The best summary of these charges is in Anglesey, *A History of the British Cavalry Volume 4*, pp. 258–75; as might be expected, even first hand accounts differ in detail.
244 NAM Roberts Papers 33: Kitchener to Roberts, 9 March 1902.

consideration for mounted troops on both sides was the fitness of their horses, and it was this that largely determined both their tactics and their value in battle. But on the British side, matters of mounted tactics were overlaid with considerations of politics, both in the sense of internal Army rivalries and power and also – for the first time in the controversy – much wider political and public matters, affecting both Great Britain and the Empire. It was these public and political forces that shaped the next part of the cavalry's story.

1 A mounted trooper of the 18th Bengal Lancers, 1897. Photograph by F.W. Bremner. National Army Museum, London (Negative number: 23640). Courtesy of the Council of the National Army Museum London

2   A sergeant of a Mounted Infantry detachment on Home Service, 1896. Plate 71 from G. Tylden, *Horses and Saddlery* (London: J.A. Allen & Co. in association with Army Museums Ogilby Trust, 1965)

3   An Australian mounted rifleman on an Indian country-bred troop horse serving in South Africa in 1899. Plate 90 from G. Tylden, *Horses and Saddlery* (London: J.A. Allen & Co. in association with Army Museums Ogilby Trust, 1965)

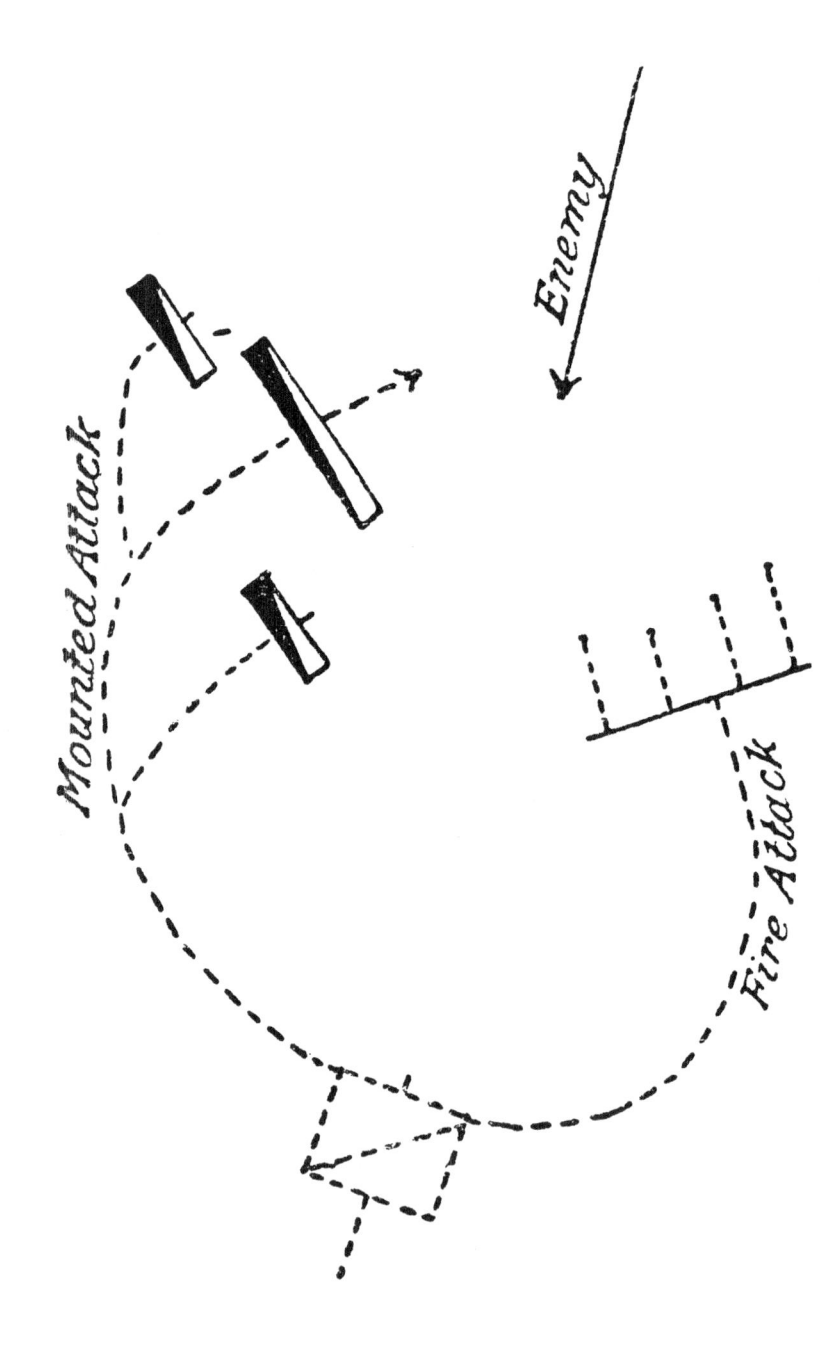

4   Figure 20 from page 270 of *Cavalry Training 1912* (HMSO), illustrating how a cavalry squadron should attack by combining a mounted charge with firepower

5 A Lancer regiment, either 5th Lancers or 16th Lancers, on the march, Western Front, September 1914. Photograph courtesy of the Imperial War Museum, London. (Negative number: Q 56308).

6 The Deccan Horse in Carnoy Valley, 7th Division Area, 14 July 1916. Photograph courtesy of the Imperial War Museum, London. (Negative number: Q 823)

7 The Royal Gloucestershire Hussars during the advance towards Damascus, 2 October 1918. Photograph courtesy of the Imperial War Museum, London. (Negative number: Q 12386).

8 Cavalry Hotchkiss gun team practising coming into action. Near Querrieu, (Fourth Army H.Q.) 29 July 1916. Photograph courtesy of the Imperial War Museum, London. (Negative number: Q 4067)

9 This controversial picture is now widely accepted as a genuine photograph of the actual charge at Beersheba as it took place on 31 October 1917. Australian War Memorial Negative Number A02684

10　Canadian cavalry watering their horses in the River Authie near Aix le Chateau, 17 September 1918. Photograph courtesy of the Imperial War Museum, London. (Negative number: Q 9311)

11 Haig and Joffre with Lloyd George at XIV Corps headquarters Mesaulte, 12 September 1916. This is the picture described by Lloyd George on page 270. Photograph courtesy of the Imperial War Museum, London. (Negative number: Q 1177)

Chapter 4

The Roberts Era 1902–1905

While stationed with his regiment at Rawalpindi in India 1903–1904 Private P.Y. Grainger of the 9th Lancers kept a diary, through which he exercised the traditional British soldier's prerogative of recording his dissatisfaction with the Army and with life in general. On 10 July 1903 Grainger found something new to complain about, writing that, 'Orders had come out no more to do with [the] lance, as they talk of doing away with them. I imagine that is some smart government official's work, making out that he is saving the expense of buying lances, to put the money in his own pocket. So it seems I have been on the last guard done with a lance. But I fancy we shall bring them on guard peachy (presently).'[1]

For once, the private soldier's reflex of blaming all his problems on the Treasury or on military bureaucracy was wrong; the order to abolish the lance came from Lord Roberts as C-in-C of the Army. Otherwise Private Grainger was quite right, but not for the reason that he believed: four days later, as he noted in his diary, the 9th Lancers 'went on parade with sword and lance'.[2] Roberts's order had allowed for lancer regiments to carry the lance on parades for inspection, although not for training, a subtlety not passed on to the other ranks. This *apparent* defiance of Roberts by the cavalry marked a very public, and very bad-tempered, high point in the debate over cavalry doctrine following the Boer War.

The start of Roberts's period as C-in-C coincided with the war's protracted ending. It was a difficult and unhappy time when wartime decisions, many of them made on horseback at a second's glance with shells and bullets in the air, were to be analysed and argued over, second-guessed and given meaning, until an agreed Army doctrine emerged on what changes if any had to be made. It was a time that could, and did, make and break careers as surely as the war itself. But it was also a time of great opportunity. On Roberts's return, Wolseley gave a dignified professional analysis of his successor's chances:

> Above all things, remember, I have no grievance and you and I must be most careful as to what we say of my little Hindoo [sic] successor and his old Cooley [sic] wife. With all the country at his back he can now do the Army and therefore the nation an enormous amount of good in reforming War Office administration and carrying out to completion the army system that I did so much to establish. I am afraid that he is such a popularity hunter and such a snob as regards Dukes and Earls etc that he will give way to society prejudices and pressure. He has of course everything to learn about an Army [in which] he has never

---

1   NAM Grainger Papers: Diary entry, 10 July 1903; the gloss of 'presently' for 'peachy' is in the original. As C-in-C Roberts had direct authority over the British Army in India, although not automatically over the Indian Army, which came under the C-in-C India.
2   Ibid., Diary entry, 14 July 1903.

served and to whose traditions and prejudices he is a stranger. But still I look to him for great improvement and for being able to face down opposition in a way that only a man returning home from the command of a successful war can ever hope to do.[3]

Roberts took up his position set on the reforms that he intended to mark the culmination of his career. Almost his first action was to press for greater powers for his office with less political interference, similar to those which he had enjoyed as C-in-C India.[4] Indeed, one plausible explanation for Roberts's subsequent behaviour towards the cavalry is that he failed to appreciate that his powers as C-in-C were more limited than they had been in the past.

Roberts was also immediately embroiled in the plans for reform and reorganisation of the Army put forward by Brodrick as the new Secretary of State for War, meant to make much greater use of volunteers and auxiliary forces in order to produce six Corps, three of them to be available for dispatch abroad, although accompanied by only one cavalry division.[5] The context for the debate over cavalry reform between 1901 and 1905 was this much wider issue of the future structure and purpose of the Army. Broderick's scheme included a requirement for every infantry battalion to produce an MI company, and Roberts supported a proposal to attach an MI battalion to every cavalry brigade in peacetime.[6] In a way almost calculated to annoy the cavalry, Roberts also made a point of putting forward the commanders of MI battalions in South Africa (including Rawlinson) for special or double decorations, as having 'borne the brunt of the fighting'.[7] Brodrick's successor after a government reshuffle in 1903, H.O. Arnold-Forster, went even further by proposing a two-track Army, of long-service troops for garrisoning India and short-service troops for Great Britain, including a 'Striking Force' for overseas wars based at Aldershot.[8] In the same period, the Army was subject to numerous investigative committees which challenged and changed everything from its weapons and uniforms to its most fundamental hierarchy and structure, starting with the creation of the Committee for Imperial Defence (CID) in 1902, then the Elgin Commission of 1902–1903, and in 1904 the radical reforms of the Esher Committee, which abolished Roberts's post as C-in-C. But even while these changes were implemented, other political voices argued for retrenchment. Roberts was told in 1901 that the Treasury would not sanction large-scale reforms, and in 1902 the C-in-C had to oppose an attempt

---

3   HPL Wolseley Papers WP 29/65: Wolseley to Lady Wolseley, 3 October 1900. As mentioned above, 'Hindoo' or 'Hindu' was a reference to Roberts's service in the Indian Army; 'old Cooley' may be a misreading on the present author's part, or a version of 'Coolie' originally meaning lower-class Indian. Wolseley apparently did not consider Roberts's service as C-in-C Ireland 1895–1899 sufficient acquaintance with the British Army at home.

4   Kochanski, 'Planning for War in the Final Years of *Pax Britannica*, 1889–1903', pp. 21–2; Hamer, *The British Army*, pp. 190–196.

5   Barnett, *Britain and Her Army*, pp. 355–7.

6   TNA WO 32/6260 'Composition of a Brigade of Cavalry', (1902), Memorandum by Roberts, 13 November 1901.

7   Wessels (ed.), *Lord Roberts and the War in South Africa 1899–1902*, pp. 174–5.

8   Barnett, *Britain and Her Army*, pp. 358–9.

to reduce the Army Estimates and cancel the next year's manoeuvres as an economy measure.[9]

Despite these much wider issues, Roberts treated the reform of the cavalry as a priority. In May 1901 he wrote to Lord Curzon as Viceroy of India about reform of the Indian Army, explaining the role that he envisaged for Smith-Dorrien, who was taking up the position of Adjutant-General in India, and criticising both the incumbent C-in-C India Sir Power Palmer (formerly of Hodson's Horse) and Sir George Luck, who after serving as Inspector-General of Cavalry in India 1887–1895, and then Inspector-General of Cavalry at home 1895–1898, was back in India commanding the Bengal Army:

> I am glad that Smith-Dorrien is coming to England on his way to take up his appointment, as I am most anxious to impress upon him the necessity for encouraging musketry throughout the Army in India.... The fact is that the older generation of Cavalry Officers cannot be made to understand that, under the present conditions of war, it is as essential for mounted, as it is for Infantry, men to be skilful in the use of their rifles, and it is unfortunate that both the Commander-in-Chief in India and the General Officer Commanding the Bengal Army Corps (in whose province the great Rifle Meetings have always been held) rose in the Cavalry. So long as Palmer and Luck are at the head of affairs, I fear there will be no improvement, a great misfortune for the Army in India.[10]

This letter may have been an attempt by Roberts to ease Kitchener's path in his cherished ambition to become C-in-C India, in which he succeeded in 1902. But Roberts, who was older than both Palmer and Luck, also postulated in this letter an 'older generation' of officers who neglected musketry because as cavalrymen they did not understand the realities of the new firepower. Based entirely on Roberts's view of the cavalry in South Africa when compared to the MI, this argument, that having risen through the cavalry disqualified a senior officer from understanding the new realities of warfare, would be repeated in various forms throughout the First World War and beyond. But in 1901 Roberts expected to find this attitude only in older cavalrymen, and not among 'men like Haig, Rimington, Allenby, Scobell, Bethune, &c', the rising stars of the cavalry.[11]

What made this phase of the debate about the cavalry unique was that it took place very much in public, with the normal confidential minutes and letters of official correspondence interacting with the opinion and letters columns of newspapers. 'The question is not demonstrated by names or authority', wrote one confident critic of the cavalry in *The Times*, 'and a correct solution can only be arrived at by an open mind duly considering the evidence of things.'[12] This scrutiny of the Army and its ways by civilians struck at the very basis of military organisation and discipline: the fundamental idea that senior officers held their posts and determined doctrine by virtue of their professional experience and expertise. It is notoriously difficult to judge

---

9 IWM Wilson Papers: Diary entries, 10 February and 3 May 1901; NAM Roberts Papers 124: Roberts to Brodrick, 10 October 1902.
10 Wessels (ed.), *Lord Roberts and the War in South Africa 1899–1902*, pp. 177–80.
11 NAM Roberts Papers 122: Roberts to Kitchener, 6 September 1901.
12 Letter Dalyell-Walton to *The Times*, 4 May 1903.

British mass public opinion and attitudes towards both the Army and the Boer War at this time.[13] But elite opinion was both reflected and to some extent shaped by the major daily newspapers, published in London (except for the *Manchester Guardian*, the organ of traditional Liberalism), and led as they had been for over a century by *The Times*, together with the small-circulation London evening 'clubland' press; and beyond these were the mass circulation newspapers and regional newspapers.[14] If the press is any guide, then in broad terms both the opinion-forming elites and middle classes (and very probably a majority of the working classes) largely supported the war if not always the Army's way of conducting it, while Roberts's own prestige was very high indeed.

More than any other senior officer, Roberts was aware of this power of the press and how to use it. Redvers Buller returned to Great Britain in November 1900, to a rapturous public welcome, and resumed his command at Aldershot with the prospect of further promotion. To counter this, Roberts rushed the publication of his South Africa dispatches, entrusting their drafting in part to Henry Wilson. Roberts's dispatches appeared on 8 February 1901, and dealt with the cavalry's role in ways that were highly misleading, implying that they had played a minor role in the relief of Kimberley, that they had not been responsible for stopping Cronjé at Paardeberg, and that despite the poor condition of the horses they should have done more at Poplar Grove.[15] What had been intended by Roberts as an attack on Buller also appeared as a denigration of French and the reformed cavalry. Buller's career was finally ended in October 1901, largely through a press campaign in which Amery played a prominent role.[16]

It is hard to ascribe a common attitude among cavalry officers towards these public criticisms, except a general resentment. Cavalry officers who had fought hard, and had seen friends killed or wounded, believed that they were entitled to some consideration from their country. There was also no shortage of former cavalry officers in influential positions who were more than willing to offer their support to the cavalry. As the war dragged on into its guerrilla phase, officers blamed newspaper editors for sensationalism or for criticising military operations from too great a distance. According to Major General Younghusband (late of the Guides), confronted with a headline 'ANOTHER BRITISH DISASTER – on reading further, one might

---

13 See Price, *An Imperial War and the British Working Class*; Pelling, *Popular Politics and Society in Late Victorian Britain*; Miller, 'In Support of the "Imperial Mission"?' pp. 691–711.

14 McEwan, 'The National Press during the First World War: Ownership and Circulation', pp. 459–86; Brown, *Victorian News and Newspapers*, pp. 26–74; Koss, *The Rise and Fall of the Political Press in Britain Volume 2: The Twentieth Century*, pp. 1–4.

15 NAM Roberts Papers 122: Lord Roberts's official despatches, printed in the *London Gazette* of 8 February 1901; IWM Wilson Papers: Diary entries, 8 January 1901 and 19 January 1901; Amery, *My Political Life Volume One*, pp. 153–6; Stirling, *Our Regiments in South Africa*, pp. 400–401.

16 Amery, *My Political Life Volume One*, pp. 153–9; Powell, *Buller: A Scapegoat?* pp. 194–205.

discover that a patrol of three men and a serjeant were missing.'[17] Kitchener wrote to Roberts that 'I only wish the English papers would take up a sounder line. They do all in their power to encourage the Boers and to dishearten our troops.'[18] Henderson also blamed the press for elementary mistakes about the British Army that had found their way into foreign accounts of the war.[19]

Those troops still fighting were surprised at Roberts's high popular image, fuelled by press support. One MI soldier wrote home in October 1900 that 'I wonder that people have not begun to carp at Lord Roberts and Lord Kitchener for their apparent inability to find an end to it, but the public and the papers seem to have unlimited faith in those two and nobody has yet raised a note of disapproval.'[20] Almost a year later, Allenby answered an obviously effusive letter from his wife with the guarded remark that 'Lord Roberts has been very genial to me. I don't know whether he is a great man or not.'[21] Allenby was one of several officers whose views on cavalry reorganisation and equipment were canvassed by Roberts between 1900 and 1902, although his own observation was that 'It is not so much reorganisation that the cavalry want as a little common sense.'[22]

Roberts's programme for Army reform, including reform of the cavalry, was publicised by a combination of his own authority as C-in-C, his exploitation of the press and manipulation of public opinion, and also by the actions of a number of officers and civilians whose views meshed with his, and saw either his patronage or the opportunities he offered as a way to advance their own careers. Roberts was curiously indifferent to the results that inevitably came from these more extreme pronouncements, which he encouraged without endorsing or repeating them in public. In May 1902 he wrote at length on the subject to Ian Hamilton:

> There have been so many references in the papers during the last year about my thinking that cavalry are no longer useful as cavalry that I must take an early opportunity of expressing [sic] that in my opinion cavalry will be more useful than ever in war. What I contend is that the rifle, and not the sword or lance, is the weapon on which cavalry will mainly depend.
>
> They must be taught to ride well and look after their horses for their principal work will be scouting, reconnoitring, making wide turning movements, and pursuing a disorganised enemy. I believe that knee to knee charges will seldom be possible, and when charges have to be made, they will be in some dispersed, not close, formation.[23]

This balanced pronouncement may be compared with the outspoken remarks of Churchill, who stood as a successful candidate in the 'Khaki Election' of October 1900. On his return to London, Churchill told the Royal United Service Institution

---

17 Younghusband, *Forty Years a Soldier*, p. 315; emphasis in the original; 'Serjeant' is an alternative spelling of 'sergeant' in use in some regiments both at this time and later.
18 NAM Roberts Papers 33: Kitchener to Roberts, 9 August 1901.
19 Henderson, in the preface to Sternberg, *My Experiences of the Boer War*, p. v.
20 LHCMA Ballard Papers: Ballard to his mother, 10 October 1900.
21 LHCMA Allenby Papers 1/2/113: Allenby to his wife, 14 September 1901.
22 TNA WO 32/6781 'Report on the Organisation and Equipment of Cavalry', (1902); Wavell, *Allenby*, pp. 95–6.
23 NAM Roberts Papers 124: Roberts to Ian Hamilton, 13 May 1902.

that within a month of the war's start cavalry shock tactics had 'vanished from the battlefield, as I hold, never to return'.[24] He also spread these views in a lecture tour around the country, before developing an unofficial alliance with Henry Wilson on the need to publicise Army reform.[25] Churchill's claims and behaviour require no very complex explanation. He was an eyewitness to the successful cavalry charges at Diamond Hill, but he had nearly suffered the wreck of his reporting career in South Africa through Roberts's hostility, he had only won Roberts over with difficulty, and as a young and ambitious politician he had learned to support Roberts's line regardless.[26]

The end of the war was also accompanied by an absolute deluge of books, so that by 1903 authors were almost apologising for the appearance of 'Still another book about the war!'[27] Sydney Goldmann's *With General French and the Cavalry in South Africa*, published in 1902 and drawing on the Cavalry Division's official records to detail its supply problems, became lost in the morass.[28] An example of how outspoken Roberts's supporters could be on the cavalry issue came from Conan-Doyle's best-selling account *The Great Boer War*, published in its first edition in 1900 with a further 16 editions by the war's end. Heavily influenced by Roberts's staff, and by his own propaganda work for Roberts while at Bloemfontein, Conan Doyle's account included a damning indictment of the cavalry: 'The simplest and most effective reform would be one which should abolish it altogether, retaining the household regiments for public functions.'[29] Like a number of other civilian critics of the cavalry, Conan Doyle in fact advocated mounted riflemen, but only if they were institutionally separate from the cavalry regiments, writing that 'lances, swords and revolvers have only one place – the museum' when opposed by skirmishing mounted riflemen.[30]

Leopold Amery's multi-volume *The Times History of the War in South Africa* also ensured that it would be Roberts's version of the cavalry's tactics, and of the cavalry's and MI's successes and failures in South Africa, that would enter public consciousness. As editor of these volumes (and author of most of them) Amery felt that 'unflinching frankness of criticism was needed in the public interest', and indeed was 'desired by the great body of officers who supplied me with information'.[31] Three of the five officers that he mentioned as particularly valuable as sources for his history were Roberts, Ian Hamilton, and Wilson; Rawlinson also lent Amery some material, and Hamilton may have provided help for Conan Doyle's history.[32] For

---

24 Churchill, 'Impressions of the War in South Africa', *Journal of the Royal United Service Institution*, Volume 45, 1900, pp. 835–48.
25 IWM Wilson Papers: Diary entry 9 May 1901.
26 Badsey, 'War Correspondents in the Boer War', pp. 187–202.
27 Stirling, *Our Regiments in South Africa*, p. ix.
28 Goldmann, *With General French and the Cavalry in South Africa*, especially pp. 438–41.
29 Conan Doyle, *The Great Boer War*, pp. 518–19.
30 Ibid., p. 591.
31 Amery, *My Political Life Volume One*, p. 152.
32 Ibid., pp. 192–3; the other officers mentioned by Amery were Evelyn Wood and Major Gerald Ellison, an advocate of German General Staff methods; NAM Rawlinson Papers 8:

Roberts and his men this was entirely a political exercise in controlling the public perception of the war: Hamilton even wrote to Sir George White advising him not to co-operate with Amery, to make sure White's version of events gained no publicity.[33] The early drafts of *The Times History* were sent for correction to Roberts, and to Wilson, who had begun to play an increasingly large role in Roberts's professional life despite his relatively junior rank and position.[34]

The first three volumes of *The Times History* of the war, all published by the end of 1905 (a year before the first volume of the War Office's *Official History* appeared) concluded that the cavalry charge in any form was obsolete, and in particular that at the critical battle of Poplar Grove the Boers had not panicked but had fought a skilful retreat as mounted riflemen, tactics with which a British cavalry trained to think only in terms of shock charges had been unable to cope. De Wet's evidence to the contrary was handled by the staggeringly simple method of declaring him mistaken.[35] The poor condition of the cavalry's horses in the advance from Modder River to Bloemfontein was blamed entirely on bad horsemanship, and in particular on French over-working the Cavalry Division on 16 February, just as Roberts had written to Lansdowne.[36] In 1904 the German General Staff also produced an official account of the war, which Amery claimed was essentially based on his own, and which enjoyed some attention in Great Britain. This history blamed the cavalry's failure in South Africa on lack of acclimatisation, overloading and poor horsemanship, and dismissed starvation as 'an ever-recurring excuse'.[37]

Haig had already outlined his own ideas on cavalry back in July 1900. Using some spare pages at the back of his personal diary for 1899, he produced a short memorandum headed 'Army Reorganisation', which set down that '*Cavalry as now arrived is a new factor in tactics.*'[38] In Haig's conception, in the fighting from Modder River to Diamond Hill the reformed cavalry, equipped with magazine carbines and trained to use both firepower and shock, had shown itself to be an entirely new arm, distinct from cavalry as the term was traditionally understood, and able to take and hold ground against dismounted irregulars. He recommended an increase in the new cavalry to make up 20–25 per cent of the Army, increasing the strength of the squadron as the basic tactical unit from 120 to 160 men in peacetime, and selecting cavalry officers from other arms for their ability and intelligence. The remainder of Haig's memorandum reflected the programme of reform that had already begun in the cavalry: recruiting lighter riders, reducing the weight on the horse, more tactical

---

'Orders and States, Rawlinson's Column, March 1901 to January 1902' includes a note of thanks from Amery on returning the document to Rawlinson; For Conan Doyle see LHCMA Hamilton Papers 2/3/11: Ian Hamilton to Lord Roberts, 9 January 1902.

33   Beckett, 'British Official History and the South African War', p. 35.

34   NAM Roberts Papers 1: Amery to Roberts, 25 November 1902; IWM Wilson Papers: Diary entry, 19 June 1904.

35   Amery, *The Times History of the War in South Africa*, Volume III, p. 562.

36   Ibid., p. 413.

37   Waters and du Cane (trans), *The German Official Account of the War in South Africa*, Volume II, p. 143; Amery, *My Political Life Volume One*, p. 219.

38   NLS Haig Papers 2b: Personal Diary for 1899, memorandum written in the back, 'Army Reorganisation', Pretoria, 3 July 1900; emphasis in the original.

training in musketry, a better carbine or short rifle, training in rapid dismounting, and a 'scientific' horse-breeding system. As an incidental point, Haig felt that the lance had not fitted well with the new tactics; 'Question whether the dragoon lancer is not a mistake!' he wrote, apparently using 'dragoon' in the older sense of mounted rifleman, 'His lance hampers him.'[39]

Haig's views on the future of cavalry were very close indeed to Roberts's official position as C-in-C. In August 1901 Roberts wrote to French, in a manner that, if it could not avoid raising some contentious issues about mounted tactics in the war, was far from being confrontational:

> It is quite clear, I think, that cavalrymen only require one weapon besides the rifle, should it be the lance or the sword, or should there be some of one kind and some of the other?... The Boers have no cavalry, but they have shown us more than once that the way to keep cavalry off is by dismounting and opening fire with the rifle. This they did effectively at Elandslaagte siding when you tried with Gordon's [cavalry] brigade to turn their right flank. Shock action may be possible in the future but in my opinion the side which dismounts and opens fire with the magazine rifle will prevent the other from getting near them. However, your experience is unrivalled, and I am most anxious to get your views on the subject, and on other important matters connected with cavalry equipment.[40]

Roberts had not been present at Elandslaagte, and in his letter he appeared to have confused Brigadier General James Gordon, commander of a cavalry brigade which was also not present at the battle, with the battalion of Gordon Highlanders under the command of Ian Hamilton (his military secretary when he wrote to French, perhaps a pointer to the source of the confusion). Although the battle had opened with a dismounted skirmish between the British cavalry and the Boers, the 'charge of the two Fifths' of which French had such fond memories had indeed turned the Boer right flank, and then shattered their retreat. What exactly French thought of this attempt by Roberts to re-write one of his own victories is not recorded. But his reply was a reproduction of the programme for the cavalry laid out in Haig's memorandum (quite possibly written for that purpose), a version of which he may already have sent to the War Office. Despite his enthusiasm for dismounted firepower, French insisted on the primacy of shock action:

> Cavalry like other arms will of course gain strength from the possession of an improved fire-arm, and (with greater attention paid to training in its use) will probably resort more frequently to dismounted action. Still I should [illegible] be averse to curtailing in any degree – either in training or in warfare – its power of offensive action as *Cavalry*. Some time ago, I sent the Military Secretary a short paper on this subject explaining my views – and General [Ian] Hamilton told me that you had seen this.
>
> My idea therefore is that *Hussars* and *Lancers* should retain all the arms they now carry, but that *the Lance* should be taken away from *Dragoon Guards* and *Dragoons* who should be armed like Hussars.
>
> So many lances become broken and damaged on service that if only half a regiment is armed with the thing they are apt to disappear very quickly indeed, and if that is the only

---

39 Ibid.
40 NAM Roberts Papers 122: Roberts to French, 19 August 1901.

weapon that cavalry soldiers have to rely on for mounted attack they run the risk of being without any at all after a certain time.[41]

French followed this up with a report on the cavalry's armament put together from the opinions of column commanders and other senior officers still serving in South Africa; reaching the War Office in November, this strongly recommended replacing the cavalry's carbine with a rifle.[42]

After writing to French, in September Roberts wrote to Evelyn Wood, then commanding at Salisbury, including a paragraph on the cavalry and its future:

> No-one can have a greater belief in cavalry than I have. It will, I am satisfied, be more required than ever in war time, and it is essential that the cavalry soldier should be a good rider, and skilful in the use of sword and lance... [But] opportunities for shock will seldom occur, and cavalrymen will have to mainly depend on their rifles. For this reason I would do all in my power to encourage musketry, and to make cavalrymen understand that they must not think it is in any way *infra dig* being trained to fight on foot.[43]

Wood's reply was unhelpful, managing to support Roberts while opposing him in the same sentence, 'As to the cavalry question', he wrote, 'I am glad to think we are absolutely of the same mind. My idea, put very roughly, is that the cavalry soldier should never dismount when he can overthrow the enemy on horseback with minimum loss.'[44] Unless this comment was the product of complete confusion on Wood's part, it may be read as a political signal to Roberts not to force the cavalry issue, but to let the small differences between them pass unremarked in exchange for Wood's wider support; much the same attitude could be deduced from French's reply.

Despite calls from Conan Doyle, Churchill and others for the abolition of cavalry or of the arme blanche, among military writers on the war the range of opinions was much narrower, mostly lying between Roberts's official position that the rifle should take precedence, and French's or Haig's position that dismounted action was critical for good cavalry but should not predominate over the mounted charge. One of the first theorists to publish, Major A.W. Andrew, an officer from an Indian lancer regiment (later the 20th Deccan Horse) who had served with the New Zealand Mounted Rifles in the war, began by claiming that 'Cavalry, as such, when opposed by modern rifles, can make no headway on the flat', (*cavalry, as such* meaning, presumably, a close-order charge), but reached conclusions that were similar to Denison's 30 years before, 'A force of cavalry and mounted rifles, with a preponderance of the latter, is the best combination for war. One regiment of cavalry to three of mounted rifles is ample.'[45] Andrew also called for the reduction of lance-carrying regiments to one-quarter of

---

41 NAM Roberts Papers 30: French to Roberts, 15 September 1901; emphasis in the original.

42 TNA WO 32/6781 'Report on the Organisation and Equipment of Cavalry', 8 November 1901.

43 NAM Roberts Papers 122: Roberts to Wood, 29 September 1901. Infra dig[nitatum] is Latin for 'beneath dignity'.

44 Ibid., 91: Wood to Roberts, 30 September 1901.

45 Andrew, *Cavalry Tactics of Today*, p. 109.

their existing number. Charles Callwell, the author of *Small Wars*, produced a short work *The Tactics of Today*, written (as he charmingly described it) 'while advancing with [Buller's] Natal Field Force from Laing's Nek to the Lydenburg district' but not published until 1903. In this he argued that 'mounted troops should now depend on their rifles and carbines rather than upon shock action', and that rifle fire had ended any possibility of a frontal knee-to-knee charge, although the effectiveness of envelopment from a flank by mounted troops had been greatly increased by their having rifles. Callwell also argued that the close-order charge remained valid as a tactic against 'ill-armed undisciplined warriors', so that 'it would be as unwise to deprive the trooper of the arme blanche as it would to rob the infantryman of his bayonet', although the cavalry sword should be considered very much an auxiliary weapon.[46] Colonel Maude, drawing on analysis going back to the Franco-Prussian War, offered his reasons why some cavalry charges had succeeded in South Africa:

> For practical purposes the Boer Mauser does not fire twice as many bullets in a minute as the Chassepôt. [Hence] if the fire of 5,000 Chassepôts to the mile of front failed to stop the Prussian cavalry [at Mars-la-Tour] there is no reason to suppose that 500 Mausers to the mile [at Diamond Hill] would have any better effect.[47]

Maude also pointed out the trend of all horsemen in the war, including the Boer commandos, to become much the same hybrid troop type after the fighting had lasted about a year, arguing that since the distinctions made in peacetime between mounted rifles, mounted infantry and cavalry were artificial and broke down in warfare then neither mounted rifles nor mounted infantry offered any advantage over cavalry.[48] Major General Sir Henry Hallam Parr, issuing in 1902 a revised version of his book on mounted infantry of the 1880s, took a traditionalist position in arguing that the war had confirmed that cavalry and mounted infantry were separate arms, and that both would continue to be necessary.[49] Rimington added his own authoritative voice to the argument in 1904. Despite the great reputation he had won through commanding his irregular 'Tigers', he still believed in the mounted charge, including among his reasons one not usually considered, 'It is generally conceded that once cavalry superiority is gained we may consider the difficulties of the forage supply as almost settled. One successful charge may mean this. No fire effect is likely to do so.'[50]

Lieutenant Colonel Henderson died in March 1903 while working on the start of the official *History of the War in South Africa 1899–1902*, and his posthumous collected essays, *The Science of War*, was published in 1905, edited by Captain Neil Malcolm (later chief staff officer of Fifth Army on the Western Front under Hubert Gough). Consisting of largely undated extracts from more than 20 years of lectures and articles, this book could be mined for almost any opinion on the cavalry and the mounted charge. Henderson's initial reaction to the war, first published in April

---

46 Callwell, *The Tactics of Today*, pp. 19–20 and p. 86.
47 Maude, *Cavalry: Its Past and Future*, p. 253.
48 Ibid., p. 269 and p. 274.
49 Hallam Parr, *The Further Training and Employment of Mounted Infantry and Yeomanry*, pp. 38–51.
50 Rimington, *The Horse in Recent War*, p. 15.

1901 and based on his experiences serving on Roberts's staff up to Paardeberg Drift, were that 'cavalry, armed, trained and equipped as the cavalry of the Continent, is as obsolete as the crusaders'.[51] But unlike many who came back from South Africa with such firm opinions, Henderson took time for reflection, studying the experiences of others, and placing the war in a wider context. The culmination of this process, and most representative of his final views, was an article originally written for the *Encyclopaedia Britannica* in 1902, based on evidence and arguments from the American Civil War onwards. In this Henderson argued for a mixed mounted force, made up of cavalry trained for the charge and of a larger number of supporting mounted rifles, and a tactical combination of mounted charges with dismounted firepower, including his assessment that 'there is no escaping the conclusion that really good cavalry must be trained with the lance as well as the sabre and rifle'.[52] Henderson's replacement as the principal author of the *Official History*, Sir Frederick Maurice, also expressed a preference for cavalry over mounted infantry, concluding as early as 1900 from his study of the cavalry's pursuit of Cronjé to Paardeberg Drift that 'the conditions of modern fighting still permit cavalry and Horse artillery to play a role of supreme importance in war'.[53] The views of two of the most prestigious theorists in the Army could not be easily dismissed as a blind or sentimental attachment to the cavalry or the charge.

Taking all these views together, from Roberts downwards a broad consensus existed both among British senior officers and influential military writers that the mounted troops in the future would depend on dismounted fire as well as on the mounted charge, that a large proportion of these mounted troops might be considered mounted riflemen, whether or not they carried arme blanche weapons, and that the value of the lance was in dispute chiefly because of the practical difficulties that it gave a horse soldier who needed to dismount. This not only reflected the real experience of mounted combat in the Boer War, it also fitted well with the existing structure of the mounted troops of the British Empire, made up of a highly trained regular cavalry that could both charge and shoot as the potential core of larger formations made up of mounted infantry, yeomanry, and colonial contingents which were chiefly mounted rifles, all of which might be expanded or further improvised in war. However much arguments might be made for mounted corps with separate specialisations, this combination of an elite regular cavalry supported by volunteer mounted corps around the Empire was the only practical solution given the underlying realities, including Treasury finance. Under Roberts, a proportionately larger share of the Army's budget was in fact directed to the infantry, and to the artillery which received a new generation of quick-firing field and horse guns, than to the cavalry: between 1900 and 1903 the cavalry's share of the Army Estimates declined from 6 per cent to just under 4.5 per cent.[54] Cavalry recruiting was halted altogether for a year in 1902, and over the five-year period 1899–1905 the number

---

51 Henderson, *The Science of War*, p. 372.
52 Ibid., p. 68.
53 Quoted in Luvaas, *The Education of an Army*, p. 198.
54 Figures derived from TNA WO 112 Army Estimates 1900/1901 to 1903/1904; Spiers, 'Rearming the Edwardian Artillery', pp. 167–76.

of cavalry declined by over 1,300 troopers, or from 8 per cent to 6.5 per cent of the regular Army.[55] As the Boer War came to a close, MI commanders, including Henry Rawlinson, begged Roberts to establish their battalions, which over two years' campaigning had become very good mounted riflemen, as permanent units in the Army.[56] But Brodrick's reorganisation scheme had neither the need nor the budget for so many mounted troops, and the considerable expertise of the mounted columns of 1902 was instead dispersed through the Army and the Empire as the MI battalions were disbanded. Huttton, as the foremost advocate of mounted infantry, was sent out to Australia once more in November 1901, to take charge of the new commonwealth's armed forces and promote mounted rifle ideas. But the disbanding and dispersal of the MI battalions was not necessarily a bad thing for Army doctrine: as Kipling's poem on the MI expressed it in 1903, 'we are the men that have been / Over a year at the business, smelt it an' felt it an' seen. / We 'ave got 'old of the needful – *you* will be told by and by; / Wait till you've 'eard the Ikonas, spoke to the old MI!'[57]

The potential existed in 1901 for Roberts and his senior staff officers to co-operate closely with the cavalry reformers under French in developing a unified doctrine for the mounted troops of the British Empire. Instead, during Roberts's tenure as C-in-C the issue of cavalry reform produced a major and often bitter row within the Army, which involved both Secretaries of State for War as well as King Edward VII, and gained wide press and public attention, centred largely on the relatively minor matter of the tactical value of the lance. Most of this feud was due to the rival interpretations of events in South Africa. Put bleakly, if French's view of the cavalry and the value of the shock charge were correct, then the failure to end the war at Poplar Grove had been Roberts's fault. Personalities certainly played a part in this argument, as did institutional Army politics, assertions of authority, and opinions made all the stronger by memories of the battlefield. Also, because Roberts began so positively in seeking reform, he gained the support of the cavalry reformers; later when his real views became clear, relationships were made correspondingly worse by a sense among the cavalry that they had been deceived. But those men who were most involved in this dispute were professional senior officers, not squabbling schoolboys; they may have disagreed on cavalry or on many other things, but they shared many common beliefs, of which the General Staff and the BEF of 1914 were to be the eventual product. The way in which they worked through their disagreements on the cavalry and its tactics offers a case study both of the manner in which much wider issues impacted on military doctrine, and also of how the Army of this period dealt with major institutional conflicts and changes within itself.

---

55 Figures derived from TNA WO 112 Army Estimates 1899/1900 to 1904/1905.

56 NAM Roberts Papers 61: Rawlinson to Roberts, 27 March 1902, and Roberts Papers 122: Dunne, 'A plea for the formation of a special corps out of the present Mounted Infantry in South Africa'.

57 Kipling, 'MI (Mounted Infantry of the Line)', in *The Five Nations*, p. 169; emphasis in the original. 'Ikonas' is an anglicised plural of the Boer word Ikona meaning 'friend', adopted by the British during the war.

While French, Haig and many of the reforming cavalrymen stayed in South Africa until the end of the war, Roberts as soon as he could moved his own men into key positions. Nicholson, his military secretary from South Africa, was made Director General of Mobilisation and Military Intelligence in May 1901.[58] Ian Hamilton, after serving as Roberts's military secretary at the War Office and then Kitchener's chief staff officer, returned to become Quartermaster General in 1903. Rawlinson first joined Robertson and Wilson at the War Office, and in May 1904, on Roberts's recommendation, he was made Commandant of the Staff College.[59] Some of these officers shared a conviction of the superiority of Indian methods that at times showed as open contempt, coupled with an arrogance that came from being kept away from the big prizes for too long by Wolseley and his Ring. They now controlled the central levers of Army power and patronage, including the distribution of honours for the war, the writing and publication of drill books and training manuals, and the setting and marking of promotion examinations.[60] 'They say the smell of curry all over the War Office is very overpowering' wrote Wolseley, spitefully.[61]

Whatever the merits of his more senior appointments, Roberts's rewarding of his 'friends' added to a general atmosphere of soreness and recrimination that found one of its outlets in the argument over the cavalry. The Duke of Cambridge let it be known that 'I was C-in-C for nearly forty years. There were, I know, some jobs done, but Lord Wolseley in four years did more jobs than I did in forty. Then came Lord Roberts, who in three years did more jobs than I and Wolseley put together.'[62] By the end of 1901 the phrase 'Bobs, Jobs, Snobs and Co.' began to be used to describe the War Office.[63] Although the identities of some of these 'jobs' remain open to speculation, they certainly included Wilson and Rawlinson, together described in unflattering terms by French: 'Now, both those fellows did much harm in Roberts' time. They are very clever and were R[oberts]'s special "Pets".'[64] Roberts also extended his patronage to other officers, including Lord Dundonald, Hubert Gough and de Lisle. Despite not serving under Roberts in the war, Dundonald in particular was just the sort of officer to attract his attention: competent, opinionated, well regarded by the press and politically well connected, and also a member of the nobility. (It cannot be ignored that two of Roberts's closest advisers, Ian Hamilton and Henry Rawlinson, also knew the real story of the relief of Ladysmith on which Dundonald's reputation largely rested.) At the same time, and in the same manner as

---

58 TNA PRO 30/57/28 Official Papers of Lord Kitchener, Roberts to Kitchener, 21 May 1903.

59 NAM Roberts Papers 122: Roberts to Knollys, 19 October 1903; Bond, *The Victorian Army and the Staff College 1854–1914*, pp. 196–99.

60 IWM Wilson Papers: Diary entries, 27 February 1901 and 14 June 1901.

61 HPL Wolseley Papers W/W.4 171: Wolseley to his brother George Wolseley, 6 February 1902.

62 AWM Bean Papers DRL 7953/34: Edmonds to Bean, 18 September 1929; Cambridge died in 1904; James Edmonds in this letter says that he verified the story with Cambridge's nephew, who in 1904 was Alexander of Teck and an officer of the 7th Hussars, and in 1929 was Earl of Athlone.

63 HPL Wolseley Papers W/W.4 164: Wolseley to George Wolseley, 6 November 1901.

64 Quoted in Holmes, *The Little Field Marshal*, p. 127.

the Wolseley Ring before it, as the Roberts Ring reached the apogee of its success, so its senior officers began to show greater independence while retaining great personal affection for Roberts as their 'Chief'. In particular, Ian Hamilton and Nicholson developed a rivalry that became outright hostility to each other by 1904.

The parcelling out of the Army's top posts to Roberts's men left only a few good positions for the other rising stars of the Army. No member of the Cavalry Division staff from South Africa (or indeed the staff of any of the infantry divisions) joined Roberts at the War Office. Hutton wrote to French in commiseration that 'the principle of keeping everything in the way of a *practical* reward for the Commander-in-Chief is new in the annals of military campaigns, introduced by the present Commander-in-Chief who can recognise no-one but Number One'.[65] Most of the successful cavalrymen went to regimental postings, including Allenby, Byng, and Hubert Gough. Haig took command of the 17th Lancers, first in South Africa and then in Edinburgh. French on his return was rewarded with Aldershot (with Archibald Murray as his chief staff officer), and Roberts was also keen to promote Haig and other rising cavalry officers to the rank of colonel.[66] In early 1902 Roberts asked Ian Hamilton for his assessment of a list of middle ranking officers, and Hamilton replied that Haig 'as you know, is one of the most thoughtful, educated, and large minded of our staff officers'.[67] Even Hutton regarded Haig as 'the best cavalry officer of the rising lot, without any comparison'.[68]

In 1902 Roberts entrusted Haig to write the new *Cavalry Training*, one of the series of manuals through which Roberts hoped to cement into Army doctrine the lessons of the Boer War. But Roberts at first refused, despite French's requests, to elevate Haig to a general's rank.[69] This may be contrasted with Ian Hamilton's accelerated promotion under Roberts from major before the war to lieutenant general, or de Lisle's promotion from captain to brevet lieutenant colonel. Hamilton also favoured de Lisle, writing to Roberts that 'I gather that several of the men who surround him have endeavoured to belittle de Lisle, with some success. I consider him quite the best man I had to work with.'[70] Thirteen years later, de Lisle would command the 29th Division under Hamilton at Gallipoli.

The lack of any agreed Army doctrinal terminology for mounted troops was now felt more than ever, as debates took place entirely at cross-purposes, or with confusingly vague phrases about the value of 'cavalry as cavalry'. There was also a strong suspicion among cavalry officers fearful for the future of their regiments that when Roberts claimed to want more 'cavalry' in the Army he had something else in mind. De Lisle, who transferred to the cavalry in 1902, advised Roberts that 'When cavalry object to becoming mounted infantry the term itself forms part of

---

65   BL Hutton Papers Add. 50086: Hutton to French, 4 November 1902; emphasis in the original.
66   NAM Roberts Papers 122: Roberts to Ian Hamilton, 31 August 1901; TNA PRO 30/57/20 Official Papers of Lord Kitchener, Roberts to Kitchener, 7 February 1902.
67   LHCMA Hamilton Papers 2/3/16: Hamilton to Roberts, 8 February 1902.
68   BL Hutton Papers Add 50086: Hutton to French, 1 April 1903.
69   NLS Haig Papers 6c: Haig to his sister, 7 August 1900.
70   LHCMA Hamilton Papers 2/3/16: Hamilton to Roberts, 8 February 1902.

the objection. Cavalry are taught, and rightly taught, to despise infantry, with a view to encouraging them, when the occasion arises, to charge broken and demoralised infantry with confidence and boldness.'[71] Roberts denied to Ian Hamilton that he was 'the one who turned, or wishes to turn, the cavalry into mounted infantry'.[72] But a great deal of the unpleasantness that followed was due to the cavalry's increasing lack of trust in Roberts's sincerity, their increasing anger at what they perceived as his attempts to shift the blame for failures in South Africa onto them, and their increasing dislike of his 'jobbing' and intriguing methods. What in early 1901 had been the potential for co-operation had by early 1904 become a breakdown into two opposing camps.

Roberts's reputation for jobbery certainly added to the general unease of the cavalry reformers on their return from South Africa. In April 1902 French, on taking up his post at Aldershot, told Haig that he wanted him to command the Aldershot Cavalry Brigade, but the appointment was not forthcoming.[73] Five months later Kitchener, secure in his own new post as C-in-C India, told Haig that he wanted him as his Inspector General of Cavalry, but there was a long delay over this appointment as well.[74] Ian Hamilton, whom Haig had believed would help him in his career, had tried to influence Kitchener's choice for the Indian cavalry appointment a few months earlier (in which direction is not clear), but felt that Kitchener 'has made up his own mind'.[75] Haig preferred the Aldershot Cavalry Brigade, but became increasingly convinced that this was being blocked by Roberts as one of his 'jobs', perhaps with the connivance of Lady Roberts, who had a particularly bad reputation for interfering in military appointments made by her husband.[76] In late August, Haig wrote to his sister that 'I fancy the excellent house at Aldershot in which the GOC Cavalry Brigade lives will oblige Lord Roberts to select the husband of "Dear Mrs" So & So because the nursery and rooms will so exactly suit the family!'[77] By the next month Haig was clearly worried about his future prospects, writing that 'I have heard nothing officially about either going to Aldershot as GOC Cavalry Brigade or to India as Inspector-General, so no doubt one of Roberts's pals (or ? Lady Roberts's pals) has been chosen for the former.'[78] This appears to be a case of Roberts's reputation generating suspicion over nothing: there is no evidence that he prevented Haig from

---

71 NAM Roberts Papers 223: Paper marked 'Cavalry Training' by de Lisle, not dated but probably 1902.

72 Ibid., 122: Roberts to Ian Hamilton, 4 April 1902.

73 NLS Haig Papers 6c: Haig to his sister, 25 April 1902.

74 Scott (ed.), *Douglas Haig: The Preparatory Prologue: Diaries and Letters 1861–1914*, p. 214.

75 LHCMA Hamilton Papers 2/3/31: Hamilton to Roberts, 1 June 1902. This letter refers to an enclosure listing Hamilton's preferences for the Inspector Generalship and asking Roberts to tear the list up once he has read it. It is possible to interpret Hamilton's letter as meaning that he recommended Haig to Kitchener but too late to affect his decision; or otherwise.

76 Beckett, 'Women and Patronage in the Late Victorian Army', pp. 463–80.

77 Scott (ed.), *Douglas Haig: The Preparatory Prologue: Diaries and Letters 1861–1914*, p. 213.

78 Ibid., p. 214.

getting the Aldershot Cavalry Brigade. Soon after Haig's letter to his sister, Roberts appointed Henry 'Harry' Scobell (5th Lancers), another of French's protégés who had established a reputation as a column commander in South Africa, to command the Aldershot Cavalry Brigade, with first Hubert Gough and later Vaughan as his brigade major, while Haig was given the Indian cavalry appointment.[79] In fact, Roberts prevented Haig from leaving for India because he found him too useful as a reformer. In March 1903 he wrote to Kitchener that 'Douglas Haig is being very helpful, as he was about reducing the expenses of polo tournaments, and I hope you will not object to his remaining in this country until the summer drills are over. I should like to keep him until the middle of September.'[80]

Following the Boer War, the issue of the expensive lifestyle expected of cavalry officers became both a major point of official and public criticism of the Army, and an important plank in Roberts's reform programme. Fairly typical was the acid comment from the 1902 Akers-Douglas Committee report into the education of officers, 'Our cavalry must be officered. We may require from the candidates either money or brains; the supply is most unlikely to meet the demand if we endeavour to extract both.'[81] Roberts noted that in the 1903 entrance examination for Sandhurst, those aspiring to join cavalry regiments fell almost entirely at or near the bottom of the list.[82] The Stanley Committee on officers' expenses also reported in 1902, confirming that it was regimental custom rather than any professional requirements that made life for officers in smart regiments so expensive. The report calculated that in the most modest of infantry regiments a young officer would require about £200 for initial expenditure and a private income of at least £60 for what it called 'legitimate expenses', and that for a cavalry regiment these costs were respectively £600 and £160–240.[83] Even to serve as a young officer in a native cavalry regiment in India required over £100 a year.[84] One best-selling critic foresaw that soon 'a monument erected to the memory of the departed British Empire', would read 'Wrecked by a cavalry subaltern with a thousand a year', and although Churchill

---

79 Gough, *Soldiering On*, pp. 91–2; Vaughan, *Cavalry and Sporting Memories*, p. 110; for some details of Scobell, whose sister divorced Repington of *The Times*, see Morris (ed.), *The Letters of Lieutenant Colonel Charles à Court Repington*, p. 6. In 1902 it was believed that Scobell had a heart complaint that would lead to his retirement; see LHCMA Hamilton Papers 2/3/16: Hamilton to Roberts, 8 February 1902, stating that 'his heart will never, I am told, enable him to take the field again'. Presumably the report was false or Scobell recovered, since Roberts continued to allow his promotion.

80 TNA PRO 30/57/28 Official Papers of Lord Kitchener, Roberts to Kitchener, 19 March 1903.

81 TNA CSC 3/319 'Report of Mr Akers-Douglas' Committee on the Education and Training of Army Officers', (1902) Appendix 42, p. 71; Bond, *The Victorian Army and the Staff College 1854–1914*, p. 186.

82 NAM Roberts Papers 124: Roberts to Haig, 10 January 1903.

83 TNA WO 32/8684 'Report of the Committee to Enquire into the Nature of Expenses Incurred by Officers of the Army', (Stanley Committee), (1902) pp. 7–10.

84 TNA WO 163/611 'Recommendations of Committees on Army Matters 1900–1920', p. 179; NLS Haig Papers 2d: Diary entry, 13 April 1904.

dismissed this as 'garbage', like all caricatures it contained an element of truth.[85] An IY sergeant offered a regular commission wrote resignedly to his father in 1900 that, 'I could not afford to stop in a cavalry regiment at home.'[86] De Lisle complained to Roberts that officers wanting to serve in cavalry regiments were often deterred because of the high costs, and that this 'ought to be made impossible'.[87] Costs in the cavalry affected even potential generals, as some officers returned from South Africa requesting postings to India because they could not afford the expenses involved in commanding a cavalry brigade at home. In addition to some health problems, Broadwood declined the Curragh Cavalry Brigade and took a post in India because, as he told Roberts, 'he could not afford to live in this country'.[88] The Akers-Douglas Committee recommended that social expenses in cavalry regiments should be curtailed to the point at which £200 a year would be enough for a subaltern or captain.[89] As a result, Roberts formed a committee of cavalry officers under Haig which met during the early months of 1903 to advise on ways of reducing costs, and as recounted he was pleased with the results.[90]

It has been suggested that before 1914 an officer serving in an exclusive cavalry regiment at home could hardly survive socially without at least two horses for hunting and three polo ponies.[91] While this appears to be an overstatement, as long as the government continued to recruit junior cavalry officers from a class that did not expect their official salary to cover their mess bills, some displays of personal wealth were almost unavoidable; and there were arguments to be made that polo and hunting were useful ways for officers to keep fit and train in horsemanship. In 1900 Alderson authored a book on the value of hunting in training mounted officers.[92] Kitchener told the Elgin Commission that 'hunting and polo are the best and quickest means of exercising and developing the qualities and muscles required in the field'.[93] In July 1903 Haig captained the 17th Lancers polo team to win the Inter-Regimental Tournament at Hurlingham.[94] (The cup was presented by Queen Alexandra, and present was her Maid of Honour Dorothy 'Doris' Vivian, the sister of Lord Vivian

---

85 Cairnes, *An Absent-Minded War*, p. 25; Churchill, 'Impressions of the War in South Africa', *Journal of the Royal United Service Institution*, Volume 45, 1900, pp. 835–48.

86 NAM Britten Papers: Britten to his father, 18 May 1900.

87 NAM Roberts Papers 223: Note 'Cavalry Training' by de Lisle, not dated but probably 1902.

88 TNA PRO 30/57/22, Official Papers of Lord Kitchener: Roberts to Kitchener, 24 January 1902, 31 January 1902 and 3 April 1903; NAM Roberts Papers 122: Roberts to Ian Hamilton, 11 January 1902.

89 TNA CSC 3/319 'Report of Mr Akers-Douglas' Committee on the Education and Training of Army Officers', p. 35 (1902).

90 TNA WO 30/57 Official Papers of Lord Kitchener: Roberts to Kitchener, 19 March 1903.

91 Baynes, *Morale*, p. 30.

92 Alderson, *Pink and Scarlet*; Alderson went on to command the 1st Mounted Division at home in 1914, and then Canadian forces on the Western Front.

93 *Elgin Commission Report*, p. 54; Riedi, 'Brains or Polo? Equestrian Sport, Army Reform and the Gentlemanly Officer Tradition, 1900–1914', pp. 236–53.

94 Cooper, *Haig*, Volume I, pp. 96–8; Terraine, *Douglas Haig*, pp. 36–7.

of Haig's regiment; although they did not meet formally on that occasion, Haig married Doris next year.) As a regimental commander, Haig's personal contribution to solving the problem of officer expenses was to pay for any subordinate officers that he asked to take part in sports with him, asking only that they should adopt the same practice if they ever reached his rank.[95] But the Haig Committee's suggestion that the government should pay for officers' riding horses was indignantly rejected, on the grounds that the Army had no intention of paying for officers to hunt in their leisure time.[96] One of the problems from which the cavalry suffered was that, although the overall numbers of riding horses in Great Britain and Ireland remained broadly constant, the heavier weight-carrying horses bred for riding to hounds were considered after the Boer War to be less suitable for the cavalry than slightly smaller chargers ('half-bred hunters') with greater endurance, and only the Household Cavalry continued to ride the larger type of horse.[97] The government also rejected a scheme to pay for the horses of the yeomanry cavalry, their single greatest expense.[98] Meanwhile, a string of Army Orders, mostly issued in 1903, cut back on displays of personal wealth by young cavalry officers, particularly on polo and hunting.[99] Although not completely successful, these restrictions meant that by 1904 a private income of no more than £300 was seen as adequate for a cavalry subaltern, and stayed so until 1914.[100]

One of Wolseley's last acts as C-in-C, in November 1900, was the decision that the cavalry and the yeomanry should both make the transition from the carbine to the rifle, 'All cavalry, including yeomanry, should be turned into "rifle cavalry", i.e. carry an Infantry rifle in the Namaqua bucket on the model of the famous "Bowers' Hants Horse"', the old 1st Hampshire Light Horse Volunteers.[101] Steering the yeomanry's tactics in this direction made sense since the yeomanry could be seen, however unofficially, as a source of recruits for the IY still fighting in South Africa. It was a policy that Roberts inherited, but he implemented it in a manner that seemed almost intended to provoke opposition, especially as the second contingent or 'new IY' leaving in early 1901 were regarded as being such poor quality. In January 1901 a War Office committee on the future organisation and equipment of the yeomanry reported to Roberts.[102] Of its seven members, six were yeomanry officers, plus Lord Dundonald as the regular cavalry representative. Five officers submitted a report

---

95 Cooper, *Haig*, Volume I, p. 96.
96 TNA WO 163/5 'Minutes and Précis', pp. 256–8; see also Alderson, *Pink and Scarlet*, p. 9.
97 Tylden, *Horses and Saddlery*, p. 37.
98 TNA WO 163/611 'Recommendations of Committees on Army Matters 1900–1920', p. 179.
99 TNA WO 123/45 Army Orders (War Office) 1903, AO 1/1903, AO 169/1903, Special AO 9/1903, and WO 123/47 Army Orders (War Office) 1903, AO 121/1903.
100 TNA WO 163/10 'Minutes of Proceedings and Précis Prepared for the Army Council', (1905), Précis Number 248, pp. 470–71; LHCMA Allenby Papers 1/5: Allenby to his wife, 11 December 1914.
101 HPL Wolseley Papers W/Misc/11: Memorandum by Wolseley, 11 November 1900.
102 TNA WO 163/611 'Recommendations of Committees on Army Matters 1900–1920', p. 459.

accepting conversion of the yeomanry to mounted rifles, to be armed with a rifle, a bayonet and a revolver; although three officers also submitted a minority report calling for the sword to be retained. But a second minority report, signed by only one yeomanry officer and by Dundonald, called for the yeomanry to be armed with the rifle alone, and to be renamed 'Imperial Yeomanry', so identifying them completely with the IY in South Africa. Roberts prevailed on Brodrick to accept Dundonald's minority report, so that what had been known as the home-service yeomanry or 'Yeomanry Cavalry' became the 'Imperial Yeomanry', with the resulting confusion that the same title was given to two (technically quite separate but in practice closely linked) branches of the Army. Dundonald also submitted a memorandum which called (as Haig's had done a year earlier) for cavalry officers to consist of the elite of the Army; but also arguing that since the cavalry would have to train the new rifle-armed yeomanry, then the cavalry itself must convert to being mounted rifles, with the lancer regiments alone being kept for the shock charge.[103]

On 17 May 1901, Brodrick spoke in the House of Commons in support of the change to yeomanry armament and doctrine, clearly drawing on information provided by Roberts:

> The Commander-in-Chief and a body of officers only yesterday rode over a considerable portion of the country, which might have to be defended, in the neighbourhood of London, and they decided – I believe without a single dissentient voice – that there was not one part of the 27 miles they travelled over in which cavalry, as cavalry, could possibly act, whereas mounted troops, armed and drilled as it is proposed to drill and arm the new yeomanry, would be invaluable.[104]

This was only a confirmation of the view expressed by Wolseley in 1895 and by French in *Cavalry Drill 1896*. But the problem for Roberts, having chosen such a radical policy for the yeomanry, was how to implement it without their agreement. Part of Roberts's influence and prestige came from his employment of aristocratic staff officers, and several of these had connections with the yeomanry, as well as the many peers and members of parliament serving with the IY in South Africa. Roberts had also lavished praise on the volunteers of the IY and CIV in the Boer War, to the anger of the regular cavalry (and the dominion mounted rifles) who knew how bad the IY had often been. It would be politically difficult now for him to criticise what were perceived to be essentially the same yeomanry regiments.[105]

Presumably in response to Brodrick's speech, in May 1901 the Duke of Beaufort as regimental colonel of the Royal Gloucestershire Hussars sought reassurance from Roberts on the yeomanry's future. Facing an influential member of the nobility, Roberts made an evasive reply:

---

103 Dundonald, *My Army Life*, pp.180–83; NAM Roberts Papers 223: Memorandum 'Opinion of the Earl of Dundonald on Yeomanry Armament'.
104 HPL, Wolseley Papers W/PR/116: 'Army Reorganisation: Mr Brodrick's speeches in the House of Commons on 9 March 1901 and 17 May 1901'.
105 Smith-Dorrien, *Memories of Forty Eight Years' Service*, pp. 247–50.

The Duke of Beaufort was speaking to him about having some weapon other than the rifle. Well, at present they had got the sword. What might happen in the future he did not know. They, themselves, might take it that some kind of sword, or a sword that went on a rifle, would be necessary.[106]

Adding ambiguity to unpopularity did not help Roberts's case, and almost at once the yeomanry officers sought to reverse his high-handed action. One of the ways available to them to challenge the C-in-C was to petition the monarchy. The Duke of Beaufort led the Royal Gloucestershire Hussars in a successful petition to King Edward VII to allow them to carry the sword on ceremonial parades (a careful distinction since in theory this did not affect their training); the Middlesex Yeomanry then petitioned successfully for the same privilege, followed by the Montgomeryshire Yeomanry; and petitions became so common that at the end of the year Roberts had to fight off a Royal request to make the carrying of swords by the yeomanry a general practice.[107] Roberts's objection was (according to an Army Council review three years later) 'It was feared that if a sword was issued to the yeomanry generally, the mounted infantry character which had been given to them on reorganisation would tend to be obscured.'[108] Instead, in 1903 the yeomanry were issued with an infantry bayonet to go with the new rifle with which all the British mounted troops were being equipped, the .303-inch Short Magazine Lee Enfield or SMLE (known to the Army for the rest of the century, in all its variants, as the 'Lee Enfield' or 'Smellie').[109]

Also in May 1901, Ian Hamilton suggested to Roberts that Hutton should write a new drill book for the yeomanry, 'in order that their training should be carried out on the right lines'.[110] In June Hutton's commission was changed to produce a manual for 'the Mounted Infantry regiments, and so be framed as to be useful for the Imperial Yeomanry'.[111] With the assistance of Lieutenant Colonel Alexander Godley (Scots Guards), Commandant of the Aldershot MI School, and Major Lord Charles Cavendish Bentinck (9th Lancers), Hutton completed the book in draft by November 1901, when he left for Australia. According to Hutton, he gave it to Roberts with a warning that it might prove too radical for Army opinion, and that Roberts should wait for French to return from South Africa before issuing it. Roberts instead immediately issued an amended version of Hutton's manual as *Imperial Yeomanry Training 1902*.[112] In his introduction, Roberts exhorted the newly-named Imperial Yeomanry, 'Not to aim at what they have not the time at their disposal to

---

106 Quoted in TNA WO 163/9 Army Council Decisions (1904), pp. 208–9.
107 Fox, *The History of the Royal Gloucestershire Hussars Yeomanry*, pp. 16–17; Stonham and Freeman, *Historical Records of the Middlesex Yeomanry*, p. 109; Williams Wynn, *The Historical Records of the Montgomeryshire Yeomanry*, Volume I, p. 82; NAM Roberts Papers 223: 'Memorandum on the Arming and Training of Yeomanry', not dated but probably 1909.
108 TNA WO 163/9 Army Council Decisions (1904), pp. 246–7.
109 NAM Roberts Papers 223: 'Memorandum on the Arming and Training of Yeomanry', not dated but probably 1909.
110 BL Hutton Papers Add. 50085: Roberts to Hutton, 5 May 1901.
111 Ibid., Wood to Hutton, 21 June 1901.
112 Ibid., Staff of the Adjutant General to Hutton, 12 September 1901; Hutton to Roberts 26 September 1902; Add. 50086: Hutton to French, 25 September 1901; Add. 50098: Hutton

become, i.e. an efficient cavalry, but to strive to perfect themselves in those duties for which the imperial yeomanry are eminently qualified.'[113] Told to accept a mounted infantry drill book and second-class status, the yeomanry both complained and suspected that Roberts was concealing his real views; and they were right to do so. Ian Hamilton wrote to Roberts that 'I have just read your preface to the Yeomanry Training Regulations, and I think you have skated over this thin ice with all your wonted skill, and that you have made your point with a minimum of disturbance to the preconceived ideas of those immediately concerned.'[114] Roberts, and even more Hamilton, in their handling of the disputes over cavalry doctrine believed that they were showing consideration and disguising their real opinions out of respect for the cherished but mistaken views of others, who would presumably eventually come round to their way of thinking. But in practice their disguise was completely transparent. As one yeomanry officer told the Royal United Service Institution in 1905, 'The real object of this halting policy was to discourage the cavalry tradition', and it 'paid very little attention to the powers of sentiment'.[115] By the time that Roberts left office in 1904, the cavalry sword had become a symbol for the yeomanry of their opposition to the way in which he had ignored and deceived them. In one extreme response, the South Nottinghamshire Hussars refused to carry the rifle, and in 1904 paid to equip the whole regiment with lances.[116] By 1905 the Inspector General of Cavalry was left repeatedly trying to convince the yeomanry of the value of dismounted rifle action, against the opposition of his own district inspectors and regimental adjutants (all regular cavalry officers) and of the yeomanry generally.[117]

Also in 1901 Roberts convened another committee, this time to investigate the weight carried on the horse in the mounted branches of the Army, chaired by Major General Henry Grant, who had succeeded Luck as Inspector General of Cavalry, with Ian Hamilton representing the mounted infantry, and Dundonald this time representing the yeomanry. On the issue of weight itself the committee did a good job: by juggling numbers and discarding equipment they managed to increase the rifle ammunition carried on cavalry horses from 30 to 50 rounds, while reducing the overall weight by over two stones, which was a substantial saving. But on the issue of how much weight could be saved by abandoning the arme blanche the committee failed, and could only submit three mutually opposing minority reports. Dundonald, clearly focused on his idea of the lancer regiments as the sole practitioners of the shock charge, revived the old notion of lancers discarding the sword as a weight saving. Grant partly agreed with this for the lancer regiments only, but still wanted

---

to Dundonald, 25 April 1904; Godley went on to command ANZAC forces in the First World War; Bentinck was the half-brother of the 6th Duke of Portland.

113 Preface to *Imperial Yeomanry Training 1902 (Provisional)*.

114 LHCMA Hamilton Papers 23/32: Hamilton to Roberts, 7 June 1902.

115 Le Roy Lewis, 'Imperial Yeomanry in 1905', *Journal of the Royal United Service Institution*, Volume 48, 1905, p. 1024.

116 Fellows and Freeman, *Historical Records of the South Nottinghamshire Hussars Yeomanry*, Volume I pp. 193–6.

117 TNA WO 27/508 'State and Efficiency of the Army and Defences. Reports by Inspector General of the Forces – submitted to the Army Council' (1903–1913), Report by Baden-Powell to the Duke of Connaught, 10 June 1905.

the dragoon and dragoon guard regiments to keep the lance for their front rank as well as the sword. Hamilton submitted a lengthy dissent from them both on the whole question of the arme blanche, making claims about its ineffectiveness that went far beyond the committee's remit, to which he added a concluding paragraph, perhaps with Conan Doyle's words in his mind:

> I do not mean the foregoing remarks to be read as an advocacy for the immediate relegation of all lances and swords to museums. I would leave the existing lancer regiments alone, and would retain the sword for hussars and dragoons:
> (1) Because it is always well to proceed with caution, and the feelings of the whole of the cavalry have to be considered.
> (2) Because I admit that the consciousness of an ability to meet a mounted charge without dismounting undoubtedly tends to boldness of movement in the field.[118]

It is one thing to show consideration for another's mistaken but treasured beliefs; it is quite another to tell him that you are doing so. Hamilton's condescending attitude, and the assumption that nothing but the traditionalist sentiment of the 'old school' was behind the desire to keep the sword and lance, only added to the opposition to Roberts's reforms.

In 1902 Dundonald went to Canada to command the militia, and as part of his reform programme he issued an order in September 1902 that any Canadian mounted militia regiments that had swords were to discard them, effectively turning the Canadian militia cavalry into mounted rifles. He followed this with a new training manual, *Cavalry Training Canada 1904*, emphasising the importance of dismounted shooting, for which he received Roberts's congratulations.[119] But *Cavalry Training Canada 1904* received a stinging review back in Great Britain in the *United Service Magazine*, written anonymously under the pen-name 'Reiver':

> It is all very well to write of 'coolly dismounting and forming up, and when the enemy gets within range' – (pray, what is that – fifteen or fifteen hundred yards?) – pouring in such a withering fire as will kill as many of the enemy as the same enemy with sword and lance would kill in five years of active service'. But what happens in war? We have not yet forgotten Botha's charge at Bakenlaagte and Kemp's charge in the Western Transvaal, both unsupported by artillery fire. What became of the coolness and accurate fire?[120]

The review ended with the sarcastic suggestion that Dundonald should read Prince Kraft's *Letters on Cavalry* for enlightenment. Dundonald was told, and seems to have had no difficulty believing, that the author of this piece was Douglas Haig, although the prose style does not bear much resemblance to Haig's known writings. Nevertheless, the review reflected the extent to which views on the issue of cavalry armament had come to depend on increasingly rival interpretations of the Boer War.

---

118 TNA WO 33/209 'Report of the Committee on the Weight on the Horse in the Mounted Branches' (1901).

119 Dundonald, *My Army Life*, p. 194; NAM Roberts Papers 122: Roberts to Dundonald, 22 April 1904.

120 'Reiver', 'Cavalry Training Canada 1904', *United Service Magazine*, Volume XXIX NS, pp. 414–18; Dundonald, *My Army Life*, p.194.

The Roberts Era 1902–1905

Despite their shared views on mounted tactics, Hutton had never met Dundonald or had any professional knowledge of him, nor was he willing to share his status as the grandmaster of the mounted infantry. When Dundonald hopefully sent him a copy of *Cavalry Training Canada 1904* Hutton dismissed it with contempt, on the sole grounds that it suggested that mounted riflemen should use a formation of two ranks when mounted rather than one.[121] Dundonald's wider relationship with the Canadian authorities also proved difficult, and his disagreements with them ended his career in 1904.[122]

By the time of his arrival in Australia, Hutton had developed a large vision of a 'force of mounted troops to be maintained in Canada and Australia available for Imperial military operations', arguing that these should be mounted riflemen or mounted infantry, since 'Cavalry, organised and equipped on the European model, require a long and careful training for both men and horses, a condition which is only possible in the case of regular troops, and which is impractical in the case of militia or volunteers.'[123] Given the experience of the Boer War, and the nature of any possible military threat to Australia, the new Commonwealth's Defence Act of 1903 allowed for a force of nine militia brigades, of which six were to be mounted rifles – to be known as 'Light Horse', with a cavalry regimental structure – and the remaining three infantry.[124] Rather than give the Australians *Imperial Yeomanry Training 1902*, Hutton adopted his own original drafts for the book to become the *Mounted Service Manual for Australian Light Horse and Mounted Infantry &c 1902*, with Roberts's authorisation, and with French's approval once he had seen it.[125] Hutton argued, very much as Haig had done earlier, that the new rifles had given mounted troops much greater importance, 'a power which, in the future, must materially modify, if it does not revolutionise, the tactics of the field of battle and the strategical combinations of the campaign'.[126] In a reflection of his own memorandum of 1901, Hutton's manual also argued that 'for operations against an enemy possessing cavalry trained upon the European model, it will be as desirable as hereforeto to possess a cavalry force trained in shock tactics and to [sic] offensive action mounted', arguing only that this was not an appropriate role for Australian or other dominion troopers.[127] He wrote to French, 'I trust that you will not give me the credit for [sic] being so narrow minded as to suppose that because we want our cavalry to have increased and more powerful

---

121 BL Hutton Papers Add. 50098: Hutton to Dundonald, 25 April 1904; Ibid., Add. 50081: Hutton to Minto, 26 May 1903 and 16 May 1904.

122 Dundonald, *My Army Life*, pp. 261–9; Morton, *A Military History of Canada*, pp. 119–23.

123 Ibid., Add. 50085: 'Proposal for a force of mounted troops to be maintained in Canada and Australia available for Imperial military operations.' Not dated but 1901.

124 Grey, *A Military History of Australia*, pp. 63–9.

125 BL Hutton Papers Acc. 50086: Hutton to French, 1 August 1903.

126 *Mounted Service Manual for Australian Light Horse and Mounted Infantry &c 1902*, p. ix; this paragraph is based largely on Bou, 'The Evolution and Development of the Australian Light Horse, 1860–1945, pp. 90–121.

127 *Mounted Service Manual for Australian Light Horse and Mounted Infantry &c 1902*, p. xi.

fire-power, that the days of "the Charge" are over.'[128] What Hutton now wanted as light horse doctrine was a fusion of MI firepower with cavalry spirit.

As in his earlier disputes with the New South Wales authorities, Hutton and the Australian politicians found difficulties with each other, and this time the quarrels ended his career.[129] He came home in 1904 hoping for further advancement, considering himself a serious candidate to succeed French at Aldershot Command in 1907 (for which he had already identified Rimington as his preferred commander of the Aldershot Cavalry Brigade). But in August 1906, while at Aldershot in temporary command of 3rd Division, Hutton quarrelled with French for reasons which are not known, and he retired from active service as a lieutenant general in 1907.[130] It is significant that both Hutton and Dundonald, strong supporters of Roberts's views on cavalry and mounted infantry, lost their positions of influence in 1904 at almost the same time as Roberts himself, and that exactly the same fault blighted the reforming efforts of all three men: an over-imperious insistence on their own way when they lacked the real power to enforce their wishes.

In January 1903, Grant retired as Inspector General of Cavalry, a post that would clearly be of critical importance in Roberts's plans for reforming the cavalry. The last two Inspectors General had transferred from holding the equivalent post in India, but Haig was due to take over as Inspector General of Cavalry in India in October, a post for which as a new colonel he was still relatively junior. This left Roberts with some talented and capable officers to choose from, including his cavalry brigade commanders, most obviously Rimington at the Curragh. Instead, evidently believing that none of these men would wholeheartedly support his own policies for the cavalry, Roberts made the highly unusual choice of Baden-Powell, who was then settling down as a major general commanding the paramilitary South African Constabulary.[131] Baden-Powell's regimental service with the 13th Hussars and 5th Dragoon Guards had been largely in India, he was not a graduate of the Staff College, and he felt himself to be out of touch with opinion within the British cavalry regiments. Also, despite his popular reputation in the Boer War as the defender of Mafeking, he had not made a good impression as a leader in the field: French and Kitchener thought him slow, Hutton thought him weak, Haig classed him as one of his own least favourite types, a 'self-advertiser', while Roberts's own damning judgement had been that as a colonel 'He is certainly not a General.'[132] Astonished at this sudden revival of his military career, Baden-Powell wrote gratefully to Roberts

---

128 BL Hutton Papers Add. 50086: Hutton to French, 1 August 1903.

129 Grey, *A Military History of Australia* pp. 66–7. See also Morton, *A Military History of Canada*, pp. 212–19 for a comparison of Hutton with Dundonald.

130 BL Hutton Papers Add. 50014: Comments by Hutton in the index to his papers, pp. 161 and 165. The two men were reconciled in August 1914, and Hutton briefly commanded the new 21st Division at home, but he retired again from illness in April 1915 without seeing active service.

131 Hillcourt, *Baden-Powell*, p. 163.

132 NAM Roberts Papers 122: Roberts to Ian Hamilton, 27 November 1901; Kitchener to Roberts 24 May 1901; and Roberts to Kitchener, 20 July 1901; BL Hutton Papers Add. 50081 Hutton to Minto, 27 March 1901; NLS Haig Papers 334a: French to Haig, 20 May 1901, and Ibid., 6c: Haig to his sister, 9 July 1900.

from South Africa that 'Your selection of me for the post of Inspector General of Cavalry has come to me as a great surprise, and as a great gratification, for it means that you have confidence in me', concluding that 'I will do everything in my power to carry out any designs you may have with regard to the development of cavalry.'[133]

Being unfamiliar with the intricacies of the cavalry's doctrinal debate, Baden-Powell was at first at a great disadvantage as their representative. In late 1902, when asked by the Elgin Commission about what arm cavalry should have beside the rifle, the very heart of the issue, Baden-Powell replied that 'I do not care much about that. I do not think it matters what they have, [but] a good sword-bayonet, which you can use as well as a bayonet, is as good a thing as any.'[134] Before the end of 1903 he had endorsed in a preface to a book by his brother (a serving Guards officer) the view that 'whereas formerly it was the golden rule for cavalry never to receive a charge at the halt, but to gallop forward to meet it, now it would almost invariably be preferable to dismount and receive the charge with a volley of musketry'.[135] Roberts's selection of Baden-Powell as a pliable tool suggests that, whatever he may have felt about the rising cavalrymen in 1901, two years later he was more concerned about getting his own way.

Despite Baden-Powell's indifference, the future of the cavalry and of its arme blanche weapons were major issues for the Elgin Commission, and every cavalry, yeomanry, and mounted infantry officer who gave evidence was asked for his views on the matter. In contrast, no member of the Army's Veterinary Department or the Remount Department was called to give evidence on the horse supply. Kitchener, who as Roberts's chief staff officer had, at least, nominal responsibility for the failure of the supply system during the advance from Modder River to Bloemfontein, sought to minimise its importance to the commissioners, giving evidence that:

> No doubt the war horse suffered to some extent from the shortness of the ration that he received in the field, especially the large animals that were so generally in use at the beginning of the campaign, but I consider that the falling off of condition was due more to the want of rest and the general hardships experienced from the heavy work and new climate, a condition on which an extra 6 lbs or 8 lbs of oats would have little or no effect.[136]

Despite the evidence of French and Rimington in particular about the condition of the horses on campaign, the Elgin Commission, faced with contradictory testimony from very senior officers, never fully appreciated the extent of the cavalry's collapse during late 1899 and early 1900. Its report concluded that:

> The evidence before us confirms the view that the chief cause for the loss of horses in the war was that they were for the most part brought from distant countries, submitted to a long and deteriorating sea voyage, when landed sent into the field without time for recuperation, and there put to hard and continuous work on short rations.[137]

---

133 NAM Roberts Papers 191: Baden-Powell to Roberts, 18 January 1903.
134 *Elgin Commission Report*, Evidence Volume II, p. 430.
135 Baden-Powell, *War in Practice*, p. 248.
136 *Elgin Commission Report*, Evidence Volume I, p. 9.
137 *Elgin Commission Report*, p. 98.

All these were certainly factors in the high rate of horse loss in the war. But the report failed to mention the overloading of horses and the standard of horsemastership, the two areas in which improvements could be made through peacetime training. Nor did the commissioners make the connection between all these factors and the debate over cavalry tactics: that all arguments depended on the fitness of the horses, and that it mattered very little what weapons or doctrines were adopted if the horse was dying underneath its rider and he did not know how to keep it alive. Fortunately, the committee under Grant had already taken the first steps to lessen the weight on the horse, while every column commander in South Africa had learned from sheer necessity to become a good horsemaster. French's evidence to the Commission (perhaps overstated) was that by 1902 'the horsemastership of the Cavalry is very nearly all that we can desire', and with the breakup of the mounted columns this knowledge was being disseminated in training throughout the cavalry, the yeomanry, and the dominion mounted rifle regiments as well as the mounted infantry.[138]

When witnesses before the Elgin Commission were asked about the weapons of the cavalry, and the ethos of the cavalry spirit that went with the arme blanche, their replies depended largely on the institutional positions that they held. Attitudes had hardened, and officers saw a threat to their regiments behind apparently innocent questions about tactics. French gave evidence broadly in defence of the doctrines that had prevailed before the war: that the cavalry depended on the sword for their morale, that the yeomanry should also keep their swords while being considered mounted rifles, and that the mounted infantry could never be anything other than a form of infantry transport, with no wider value as scouts or mounted rifles. Haig agreed, stressing that 'the ideal cavalry is that which can attack on foot and fight on horseback', apparently taking defence on foot for granted. Rimington wanted the mounted infantry disbanded and the mounted rifles converted into cavalry capable of the arme blanche charge.[139] Of the yeomanry commanders who gave evidence, Brabazon enlivened a dull day by explaining enthusiastically to the commissioners that it was not Anglo-Saxon nature to point with a sword as the training manuals required, and that the yeomanry should be equipped with a tomahawk instead; it was one of those episodes which seemed to confirm for civilians – especially Lord Esher – their worst suspicions about cavalry officers.[140] (Remarkably, a cavalry tomahawk or battleaxe was given a trial in the 1908 manoeuvres, where Haig dismissed it as 'absolutely useless'.)[141] Other yeomanry officers wanted a sword-bayonet or light sword for their men. The mounted infantry commanders were quite content with the existing improvised nature of their force, denouncing the sword as 'an absurdity'; and Godley as Commandant of the Aldershot MI School maintained that his troops were able not only to support the cavalry but 'in the absence of cavalry, to take its place'.[142]

---

138 Ibid., p. 47.
139 Ibid., Evidence Volume II, pp. 300–317, pp. 402–12 and pp. 27–31.
140 Ibid., Evidence Volume I, p. 294; Gooch, *The Plans of War*, p. 34.
141 NLS Haig Papers 2h: Diary entry, 23 August 1908.
142 *Elgin Commission Report*, Evidence Volume I, p. 300 and pp. 311–12, Volume II, p. 320 and p. 434.

Lord Roberts as C-in-C was a principal witness for the commissioners, and was called twice, in December 1902 and again in January 1903, to give evidence on a wide variety of topics, including the issue of mounted troops. Faced with such an important investigation Roberts again temporised on his position, giving evidence that the rifle should be regarded as the cavalry's main weapon, but that he was not certain whether the lance as well as the sword was needed. In the middle of his institutional fight with the yeomanry, Roberts's reply to a direct question on whether they liked their new training as mounted rifles was that he believed that they did. This was a rare case in the debate of an indisputable lie by Roberts on the record, and a reflection of how heated the issue had become.[143]

While Roberts gave evidence, Ian Hamilton as his military secretary sat beside him to prompt his chief; the association was a striking one, particularly as Hamilton had worked closely with both Roberts and Kitchener in the war. Hamilton had throughout his career been a champion of long-range rifle fire, he had made his reputation commanding mounted infantry, and he was now an important figure in the Army in his own right, at last moving out of Roberts's shadow. An astute political soldier, Hamilton was also developing close contacts with the Liberal opposition, being (quite unusually for a general of the time) more Liberal than Unionist in his convictions.[144] Whereas Roberts felt it necessary to be circumspect about mounted tactics to the commissioners, Hamilton was the very opposite. Giving evidence in February 1903 after Roberts, he lambasted and ridiculed the cavalry position on the value of the arme blanche:

> I have heard it said that if the Boers had possessed cavalry, in the European sense of the word, our men would have had a chance of showing the advantages of a boot-to-boot charge over a looser formation admitting of more individual initiative. It is difficult to answer this sort of argument. If both sides were to agree to carry out their fight with *punctilio* and a chivalrous disregard of the requirements of scientific arms, then no doubt there would still be suitable scope in warfare for old-world methods. [But] compared to the modern rifle, the sword or lance can only be regarded as a mediaeval toy.[145]

Again, when contrasted even with Hamilton's minority report for the Grant Committee in early 1901, this shows just how much his opinion had hardened in two years, or how much more he felt free to express himself. When challenged, Hamilton also could not resist adopting the same patronising tone towards the cavalry that had already done such damage:

> I think that the regular cavalry still ought to have a weapon of offence, because for hundreds of years it has been so intimately connected with every cavalry story, and their whole history that, morally, it gives them the idea that they can do things which they cannot, but still they think they can, and therefore it enables them to act with greater boldness than they otherwise would.[146]

---

143 *Elgin Commission Report*, Evidence Volume I, pp. 438–9 and Volume II, p. 66.
144 Lee, *A Soldier's Life*, pp. 70–73.
145 *Elgin Commission Report*, Evidence Volume II, p. 105, emphasis in the original.
146 Ibid.

Hamilton noted against this passage in his own copy of the Elgin Commission's report that 'This infuriated Haig and French beyond measure!' while Nicholson reportedly annotated another copy of the same passage with 'This man has a tile loose!'[147] Within two weeks of Hamilton giving his evidence, Roberts with Hamilton's support took the step that transformed the debate over the future of the cavalry into a public row: the abolition of the lance.

The Elgin Commission had weighty issues of national defence and preparedness for war on which to comment, and its civilian members were ill-equipped to understand a dispute on cavalry tactics. But if they did not understand the technical details, they did understand that there was a strong disagreement, and the implications of this for the Army's future. Their report when it appeared in August 1903 included a lengthy section on the cavalry:

> In the late war the Boer force consisted entirely of mounted riflemen... Most of the witnesses agree that in view of the great extension of the field of operations in modern warfare, an Army should contain a much larger proportion of mounted men than formerly. There was, however, much diversity of opinion as to what should be the nature and armament of these mounted forces.... In practice there was no real distinction between the use of 'Mounted Infantry', and 'Mounted Rifles', and in the latter part of the war the Cavalry were armed and employed in much the same way.[148]

Without setting the matter out in so many words, the commissioners signalled in their report that, while it was not their responsibility to resolve this dispute, it should be ended by compromise between the disputants. The report concluded its section on the issue with the following recommendations:

> (1) That regular cavalry should be armed with the sword, if not the lance, and trained in shock tactics, but should also be more carefully trained than heretofore to fight on foot and use the rifle, and
> (2) That there should be available a considerable force of mounted riflemen, not trained in shock tactics, or to the use of the sword, but well trained in horsemanship, horsemastership, shooting and working in loose formations.[149]

This force of mounted riflemen was to include the yeomanry, although the mounted infantry and the dominion mounted rifles and light horse were not specifically mentioned. This, together with the skilled politicians' ambiguity of the phrase 'the sword, if not the lance' may be treasured as a form of words designed to negotiate around the dispute, and to provide the grounds for an agreement within the Army.

With much goodwill, the compromise offered by the Elgin Commission might have worked, but Roberts had already set the seal on the hostility between himself and the cavalry. On 10 March, before either French or Haig had given evidence to the commissioners, Roberts issued Army Order 39 of 1903 as C-in-C, limiting the use of lances in lancer, dragoon and dragoon guard regiments to escort duties, parades and reviews; the lance was not to be carried on manoeuvres, nor was it to be

---

147 Quoted in Lee, *A Soldier's Life*, p. 75.
148 *Elgin Commission Report*, p. 49.
149 Ibid., p. 51.

taken to war. Along with this Army Order, Roberts issued a memorandum setting out reasons for his action, basing his decision largely on evidence from recent military history.[150] French believed that the real author of this memorandum was Hamilton, and as Roberts's military secretary he probably drafted it, as one of his last acts before taking up his post as Quartermaster General in April.[151] The memorandum listed the failed French cavalry charges in the Franco-Prussian War, explained that it was the timid orders of the French commander at Mars-la-Tour, Marshal Bazaine, rather than the Prussian 'Death Ride' charge that had halted the French advance, and contrasted these failures of cavalry trained in shock with the successful use of firepower by horsemen in the American Civil War. The memorandum's version of mounted combat in the Boer War was that already espoused by the Roberts Ring: the complete uselessness of the charge in the face of rifle fire. The conclusion to be drawn from this historical survey was that the rifle was the principal cavalry weapon; and from this it followed that the lance, which was conspicuous when scouting and made dismounting difficult, should be given up (just as Haig in 1900 had wondered about the practicality of the 'dragoon lancer'). Army Order 39 was binding on the cavalry regiments of the British Army in India just as anywhere else, but not on the Indian Army under Kitchener, to whom Roberts sent a copy of both the Army Order and his memorandum. Kitchener supported Roberts's policy, circulating copies of the memorandum to all commanding officers of cavalry regiments in India, where the 9th Lancers and 21st Lancers were also stationed.[152]

By coincidence, the rotation of units between home and overseas postings meant that in 1903 three of the six lancer regiments – the 5th Lancers, the 12th Lancers and the 16th Lancers – were brigaded together, forming the Aldershot Cavalry Brigade under Scobell, and so were uniquely placed to benefit from wider official and unofficial support. The response of these lancer regiments forms a further case study of the methods available to smart British Army regiments in protesting against the actions of a C-in-C. Just as Roberts had exploited the press and politics to establish his own version of the Boer War in the public consciousness, so the lancer regiments employed at least four inter-related means of protest. These were political protest through sympathetic members of parliament, public protest through letters to *The Times* and other newspapers by retired or senior officers, protests in an elite forum at the Royal United Service Institution, and direct petitions over the head of the C-in-C to the sovereign. All of these were seen as entirely legitimate means of challenging Roberts's authority.

In March 1903, just after Army Order 39 and the accompanying memorandum were issued, the matter of the lance was raised in a debate in the House of Commons. Herbert Jessel, a Liberal Unionist MP who had served as a young officer in the 17th Lancers, spoke against Roberts's actions, and later gave his view of the matter as,

---

150 TNA WO 32/6782 'Role of Cavalry and its Armament: Abolition of the Lance', 10 March 1903. The text of this memorandum was given wide circulation and can be found as 'Memorandum by Lord Roberts on Cavalry Armament', *Journal of the Royal United Service Institution*, Volume 43, 1903, pp. 575–82.

151 BL Arnold-Forster Papers, Add. Mss 50336: Diary entry, 29 February 1904.

152 NAM Roberts Papers 57: Pretyman to Roberts, 21 March 1903.

'on the initiative of Sir Ian Hamilton a movement was afoot to abolish cavalry and substitute mounted infantry'.[153] Trying to force the issue, Jessel and his colleagues argued that it was unreasonable to expect a soldier to carry and care for a weapon that he would never actually use; the lance must be either reinstated or abandoned altogether. This was followed from April onwards by letters appearing in *The Times* from former lancer officers and colonels of regiments which carried the lance, arguing that the lance was as a weapon superior to the sword (a point quite irrelevant to Roberts's argument), letters that were collected by Roberts in what became a special file in his papers on the whole cavalry question.[154]

Arguments about the lance continued into the following year, reaching a high point in early May 1904 when the Royal United Service Institution heard a paper on 'The lance as a cavalry weapon', delivered by Lieutenant Colonel G.B. Mayne of the Royal Engineers, which had been advertised in *The Times* beforehand as offering the definitive statement on the matter.[155] The meeting was chaired by Lieutenant General Sir Henry Wilkinson, regimental colonel of the 4th (Royal Irish) Dragoon Guards, who had commanded the Indian cavalry brigade in Egypt in 1882. The paper itself was delivered modestly and moderately enough: although attacking Roberts's memorandum as 'a bit of special pleading' that struck at 'the proud traditions of our cavalry' and as 'failing to grasp the true idea and spirit of cavalry action'; it concluded after a long historical review that there was in fact little to choose between swords and lances, so the loss of the lance was no great handicap. But then, in a remarkable scene, supporters of the lance led by the chairman stood up to declare its superiority over the sword in extravagant terms. For good measure Lieutenant General Wilkinson had a dismounted lancer perform full lance drill for the audience, including a manoeuvre called the 'round wave' which, he claimed, could account for many enemy at once.[156] This bizarre episode only reinforced the views of Roberts and his men that the opposition to them consisted of blind reaction and folly. Even when Evelyn Wood wrote, along with two other officers, calling for the lance's reinstatement, Roberts observed to Hamilton that it was 'rather amusing' that Wood should pose as an expert after having seen no active service for a quarter of a century.[157]

The cavalry reformers opposed Roberts's abolition of the lance for entirely different reasons. The lance itself meant comparatively little to them, as they had already made clear. French wrote to Roberts in March 1903 that 'I do not attach so

---

153 *Record of Parliamentary Debates* (Hansard) 4th Series, Volume 120, pp. 639–63; Scott (ed.), *Douglas Haig: The Preparatory Prologue: Diaries and Letters 1861–1914*, p. 225.

154 NAM Roberts Papers 221: Letters to *The Times* from Lieutenant General H.C. Wilkinson (Colonel, 4th Dragoon Guards), 23 April 1903; Lieutenant General Dunham-Massey (Colonel 5th Lancers), 26 April 1903; Compton, 4 May 1903; Howard, 24 December 1903; also 'Lance versus Sword by a very old cavalry officer' *Army and Navy Gazette*, 18 April 1903.

155 Letter, Hale to *The Times*, 4 May 1903.

156 Mayne, 'The Lance as a Cavalry Weapon', *Journal of the Royal United Service Institution*, Volume 49, 1903, pp. 118–40;

157 NAM Roberts Papers 122: Roberts to Ian Hamilton, 4 May 1904.

much importance to the question of sword versus lance as some people do, but I think that the lance should be retained in the existing lancer regiments, on the same principle that they are probably retained in the Russian Army by the Cossacks of the Don.'[158] When the Russo-Japanese War (also known as the Manchurian War) broke out in the following year, the use of lances by the Cossacks would itself become a matter of dispute; but French presumably meant that the Cossacks, who were principally mounted riflemen, retained their lances for occasional use in a pursuit or a charge. In April 1903, as commanding officer of the 17th Lancers, Haig demonstrated his lack of attachment to the lance by suggesting its replacement by 'a good hog spear' of the type used in India for wild boar hunting.[159] But Haig was also prepared to do his duty for his regiment. He was made an aide de camp to King Edward VII while at Edinburgh, and used the opportunity to raise the matter of the lance. In June 1903 Roberts wrote to Kitchener:

> I am glad to get your opinion about the lance as it helps me with the King, who is somewhat regretting that weapon having being done away with after he had some conversation with Haig in Edinburgh. Haig, I am sorry to say, still inclines to the lance, though he can have no experience of its use in war. I agree with you that a cavalry soldier must have a sword and be able to use it.[160]

Roberts's greatest error throughout the whole controversy was his belief that all opposition to his own views was based on sentiment rather than experience or reason. In Haig's case, he had forgotten about the successful lancer charges at Klip Drift, Elandslaagte and Omdurman. His second greatest error was the lack of consistency between his own pronouncements on the use or retention of the *arme blanche*, such as in his letter to Kitchener, and statements made by his supporters with his obvious authorisation and approval.

Perhaps the most revealing response to Roberts's order on the lance came in August from Hutton in Australia, where there were two regiments of New South Wales Lancers:

> I see by the War Office General Order that the lance has been abolished in the Army at Home. There are at present in Australia two regiments of Lancers and I think it would be most undesirable to make any change in their equipment at present.... The essential element however in the case of the Australian Militia Cavalry is that the retention of the lance establishes the principle, hitherto not recognised by Australian mounted men, that our Light Horse Regiments must be prepared to charge and close with the enemy whether armed with a lance or a pistol. I trust therefore your Lordship will not disapprove of the lance being retained in certain special regiments and in certain special squadrons. It is well to add that the feeling in favour of the lance is so strong in the two lancer regiments mentioned that had I abolished its use both regiments would have disbanded.[161]

---

158 Ibid., 221: Telegram from French to Roberts, 18 March 1903.

159 NLA Haig Papers 346a: Haig to Jessel, 23 April 1903.

160 TNA PRO 30/57/28 Official Papers of Lord Kitchener: Roberts to Kitchener, 30 June 1903. An *aide-de-camp* or ADC was the title of a junior officer employed to carry out tasks by a senior one; but in the context of a royal appointment the title was symbolic.

161 BL Hutton Papers Add. 50085: Hutton to Roberts, 19 August 1903.

Roberts's reply accepted that the lancers could keep their lances.[162] Hutton, who had given his professional life to the cause of the MI, had through his experience in the Boer War come to accept that the mounted charge was a necessity, and that symbols like the lance could inculcate a form of cavalry spirit even in mounted riflemen.

What the reforming cavalrymen could not accept was Roberts's position that in cavalry doctrine the rifle, rather than the arme blanche, should be seen as the principal weapon. But as was to become apparent over the next decade, the reformers had no great objection to any individual senior officer taking this view. Their real objection was to the argument that lay behind this position: if the rifle was the cavalry's principal weapon then when faced with the choice of charging mounted or dismounting to fire, the normal tactics of cavalry on the battlefield should be to dismount. The cavalrymen were convinced that this would lead to passivity and lack of enterprise. Closely linked to this was that the argument for the rifle was based on the interpretation of the Boer War being promulgated in public by Roberts and his supporters, which was that the cavalry had failed.

Haig's papers include a typewritten set of notes made in response to Roberts's memorandum, possibly only as an aid to thought, which listed and destroyed the memorandum's historical arguments. Roberts had cited the French cavalry failures of 1870 and not the various Prussian successes; 'What', Haig asked, 'does that prove? That German cavalry were better trained and better led than the French, and again the French, in having a better carbine, were better armed.' As for the interpretation of how successful the Death Ride had been at Mars-la-Tour in stopping the French advance, 'who can say? It is merely an *ex parte* statement.' On the issue of cavalry in the Civil War, Haig added:

> We do not wish to deny that the firearm is a useful weapon. What Lord Roberts says about the American Army in a matter of combination of fire and shock admits our entire contention. We maintain that shock action can produce important effects and particularly in combination with fire action that the sphere of usefulness of cavalry action is increased.[163]

Haig's history was in fact too good: he recognised that the use of trenches by infantry would render cavalry shock action much less effective, but (a year before the Russo-Japanese War) pointed out that no modern army fought from trenches or wished to do so. Despite the use of trenches in some battles of the Boer War, to the British Army of 1903 'the trenches' recalled the Crimea in 1854–1856 or Richmond in 1864–1865. Even more so than the other armies of Europe before the First World War, the British Army understood how important it would be for their infantry to seek cover and to entrench in the face of modern firepower; but (again like all the other armies) they did not plan for a slow-moving or static war of entrenchments

---

162 Ibid., Roberts to Hutton, 12 October 1903.
163 NLS Haig Papers 32a: Undated, unsigned typewritten paper with corrections in Haig's handwriting; the original has 'shot' not 'shock' which suggests that it might have been dictated or typed from notes. There is no indication of what use, if any, Haig made of these notes, but it might be speculated that they are in some way related to the officers' meeting of 25 September 1903, mentioned below.

and heavy artillery because this was exactly the kind of war they hoped to avoid, by using rapid manoeuvre to achieve a quick victory.[164]

Roberts's conversation with King Edward VII in June 1903 appears to have been the first time that the C-in-C discovered that Haig did not support his views on the cavalry. This was a genuine disappointment to Roberts, but he continued to value Haig's abilities highly. Roberts inspected the 17th Lancers in August (presumably with their lances being carried on parade, as allowed by his Army Order), and Haig served on Roberts's staff for the annual Army manoeuvres in September.[165] But Roberts was further dissatisfied with what he saw and heard from cavalry officers in these manoeuvres, and decided to have the matter out with them. 'We are having a great cavalry meeting at the War Office tomorrow, presided over by Lord Roberts', French wrote on 24 September, 'I hope good may come of it.'[166]

While these events were taking place, Haig gave to Roberts a draft of the part of the cavalry training manual that he was writing. This was the first appearance of the new *Cavalry Training*, which for the next nine years would be a political football between the Roberts Ring and the senior cavalrymen, going through three editions. Like similar training manuals for the other arms, *Cavalry Training* was structured in four parts, dealing in turn with general principles, individual training, unit training, and finally collective training with other arms. It was the collective training section that Haig had finished and gave to Roberts, and which seems to have partly prompted Roberts's decision to call the cavalry to order. Roberts wrote to Kitchener:

> I am to have a meeting tomorrow with all the senior cavalry officers about the proper method of training their branch of the service. Haig, I am surprised to find, clings to the old arme blanche system, and in the chapter for the revised edition of the drill book, which was entrusted to him, on collective training there is not a word about artillery or dismounted fire. Haig, supported by French and Scobell, insists on cavalry soldiers being taught to consider the sword their chief weapon, and the rifle as a kind of auxiliary one – a very different opinion to that held by the present Inspector General of Cavalry [Baden-Powell]. I am all in favour of cavalry soldiers being bold riders, and of endeavouring to overthrow their enemies [sic] mounted men, but I am convinced that in 99 cases out of a hundred this will be done more effectively by artillery and dismounted fire in the first instance. I hope you will keep Haig on the right lines, as I intend to keep Baden-Powell.[167]

Roberts's frustration was evident: he had searched as far as South Africa for a compliant Inspector General of Cavalry, only to find that the other senior cavalry officers were defying him; while the Canadians were opposing Dundonald, and Hutton in Australia was defending the lance. But the views that Roberts expressed to Kitchener in his letter were not very far from the views held by French or Haig, or any of the senior cavalrymen, if only they could have talked the matter through in an open manner. Instead, the meeting took place on 25 September in an atmosphere

---

164 Strachan, *European Armies and the Conduct of War*, pp. 108–29; Jones, *The Art of War in the Western World*, pp. 419–23; Howard, 'Men Against Fire', pp. 510–26.
165 NLS Haig Papers 2c: Diary entries, 10 August 1903 and 13 September 1903.
166 BL Hutton Papers Add 50086: French to Hutton, 24 September 1903.
167 NAM Roberts Papers 122: Roberts to Kitchener, 24 September 1903.

of hostility, with Roberts putting forward his position that the rifle was the principal cavalry weapon, and most of the senior cavalrymen replying that in their view it was not. Haig gave an account of the meeting in note form: 'Attended meeting of officers under presidency of Lord Roberts at War Office, *re.* cavalry question. I strongly maintain that chief method of action for cavalry is the mounted role. He hotly opposes me *re.* the principles laid down by me in Part IV Cav[alry] Drill "Collective Training"'.[168] A more vivid account of this meeting appears in de Lisle's memoirs, written many years later:

> I was ordered to attend, although only a major. He [Roberts] first made a short address to the effect that modern weapons made it necessary to reconsider the tactical employment of the cavalry, which in future must depend on the rifle and machine-gun as the primary weapons, and the sword and lance as secondary. He then turned to Major-General [sic] Sir John French on his right and asked for his views. French was very nervous. 'Well, my Lord', he said, 'well, my Lord, I fear I cannot agree. I think the *arme blanche* should still remain the first weapon of cavalry, and Douglas Haig agrees with me.' [Lieutenant] Colonel Haig, on French's right, was next called upon and endorsed French's statement, and so on all round the table... When Lord Roberts left the room he beckoned to me to accompany him, and said the result of the conference was much as he had expected, and added 'This is the last time I shall ever call a conference of cavalry officers. They are prejudiced and unable to think for themselves.'[169]

Haig left for India to take up his post as Inspector General of Cavalry a few days later, still working on *Cavalry Training*, and unaware that simultaneously a letter from Roberts to Kitchener was making the same journey, in which Roberts gave Kitchener a warning:

> The meeting of cavalry officers I told you [about] in my last letter was not altogether satisfactory, in as much as I found the majority bent on considering the sword as the principal weapon and the rifle as the auxiliary one... Haig is one of the strongest supporters of the sword and charging, and you will have to be very firm with him if your views on Cavalry Training agree with mine, as I believe they do.[170]

At least Roberts and the cavalrymen now understood each other's positions: they disagreed on the doctrinal issue of whether the rifle or the sword should be officially regarded as the cavalryman's principal weapon, but not on more radical matters that were still filling the press, such as whether the sword should be retained or the cavalry regiments abolished. Even then, there may have been a misunderstanding over *Cavalry Training*: Haig was certainly committed to dismounted fighting by the cavalry, but – as later events would show – he saw no point in using dismounted cavalry when infantry were available, and his draft on collective training may have simply reflected this.

---

168 NLS Haig Papers 2c: Diary entry, 25 September 1903.
169 de Lisle, *Reminiscences of Sport and War*, p. 122. French was a lieutenant general at this date.
170 NAM Roberts Papers 122: Roberts to Kitchener, 8 October 1903.

In an atmosphere in which each side was likely to take the worst view of any action by the other, yet more decisions were taken by the C-in-C that both antagonised the cavalry and appeared to confirm their fears. It was a major reform to standardise on the short Lee-Enfield rifle throughout the Empire, but to accompany this Roberts ordered the changing of the cavalry trumpet calls so that they were identical to those of infantry bugles. This apparently trivial and quite unnecessary order drew from Private Grainger in Rawalpindi the glum observation that 'Expect we shall soon be MI in peace as well as war.'[171] A similar lack of trust was evident when Roberts, with Baden-Powell's support, argued that the cavalry should carry the new Lee-Enfield slung across the soldier's back. This was a good way to carry the rifle, but the alternative was for the rifle to be carried in a long bucket on the saddle, partially counterbalancing the weight of the sword on the opposite side, and in the hostile atmosphere of the time Roberts's position was interpreted as a threat to the cavalry's swords. This argument lasted for most of 1904, until a bloc of senior cavalrymen including French, Scobell, Rimington, Byng, Broadwood and Haig prevailed with the new Army Council to let the rifle be carried in its bucket, a decision that was unanimously approved in 1906 by a committee under Haig.[172]

The motive behind Kitchener's request for Haig as his Inspector General of Cavalry was the transformation of the Indian Army so that it could dispatch a force capable of fighting a war outside India, a project which included the creation of a second branch of the Staff College at Quetta, and to which Haig returned when he became Chief of Staff to the C-in-C India in 1909–1912.[173] Along with a few British cavalry regiments that had remained in India during the Boer War, the Indian cavalry regiments needed to learn more about horsemastership, to make the transition to becoming rifle cavalry, and to adjust their tactics accordingly. In April 1903 Roberts wrote to Kitchener seeking support for his position regarding the lance and his Army Order 39.[174] 'I wish we had the new short rifle to try', Kitchener replied, 'Could you send me a few to try with the cavalry instead of lances?'[175] At Rawalpindi the 9th Lancers had kept the older long Lee-Metford or Lee-Enfield used in South Africa rather than reverting to carbines. The new short Lee-Enfield reached them in May 1904, prompting Private Grainger, who was already a skilled shot at 200 and 600 yards with the rifle, to contribute his usual jaundiced view:

Practising with the new rifles which came… They are about 6 inches smaller than at present, that is all the difference I could see. Someone else coining money – made enough

---

171 NAM Grainger Papers: Diary entry, 29 September 1903; TNA WO 163/114 'Army Council Decisions', (1909) number 608, pp. 424–5.

172 TNA WO 163/611 'Recommendations of Committees on Army Matters 1900–1920', p. 129; WO 163/9 Army Council Decisions (1904), pp. 342–4; NAM Roberts Papers 122: Roberts to French, 24 January 1904; NLS Haig Papers 2f: Diary entry, 13 March 1906.

173 Birdwood, *Khaki and Gown*, pp. 143–4.

174 TNA PRO 30/57/28 Official Papers of Lord Kitchener: Roberts to Kitchener, 17 April 1903.

175 NAM Roberts Papers 33: Kitchener to Roberts, 20 April 1903.

fuss about S[outh] A[frican] war and yet they are continually wasting money in the war department. Shall have to alter the rifle racks now as will not fit new rifle.[176]

The real difference between the long and short versions of the Lee-Enfield was the discovery that a rifle could be a few inches shorter in the barrel with only a slight loss of accuracy at extreme ranges, and therefore short enough not to hamper a soldier when mounted (and even this loss of accuracy was soon corrected by the introduction of new ammunition). Alone among the armies of the major powers in 1914, the British and Imperial mounted forces had their cavalry, and indeed their artillery and all branches of the Army, armed with exactly the same rifle as their infantry, and the short Lee-Enfield turned out to be one of the outstanding rifles of the twentieth century. Two of the best design features of the short Lee-Enfield, the flat-nosed fore-end covering the barrel almost up to the muzzle, and the curved rifle bolt enabling the shooter to stay on target while reloading, also allowed the rifle to be carried in the rifle bucket on horseback, and may have been designed with this in mind. Significantly, the much smaller US Army reached the same conclusion in issuing the short Model 1903 Springfield rifle to its cavalry as well as its other troops, and by 1911 the US Cavalry's ideal was once more a horse soldier 'equally efficient mounted or dismounted' with rifle and sabre.[177] The main exception within the Empire to equipping all troops with the short Lee-Enfield was the Canadian militia, which (including the cavalry and mounted rifle regiments), was armed in 1902 with the .303-inch Ross rifle, broadly comparable in shooting performance to the Lee-Enfield but mechanically far less reliable. The Mark III version of the Ross was replaced in the Canadian forces by the Mark III Lee-Enfield in the course of the First World War.[178] To provide greater fire support for the cavalry, the new 13-pounder QF horse artillery gun (essentially a smaller version of the 18-pounder QF field artillery) was introduced in 1904, together with the Maxim machine-gun.[179] That the British and their Empire were virtually unique in the First World War in having rifle cavalry, with almost the same intrinsic artillery and machine-gun support as the infantry, helped to transform the nature of these troops, their tactics, and their value in combat.

In addition to circulating Roberts's Army Order and its accompanying memorandum on the lance, in the course of 1903 Kitchener also removed the lance from three of his Indian cavalry regiments.[180] But Kitchener was much more sensitive than Roberts to his own army and its attitudes. On 10 May 1903 he wrote to Roberts that he was reluctant to force the issue since 'The natives seem to cling

---

176 NAM Grainger Papers: Diary entry, 11 May 1904.

177 Theodore F. Rodenbough, quoted in Phillips, 'Douglas Haig and the Development of Twentieth Century Cavalry', p. 149; Urwin, *The United States Cavalry*, pp. 176–80.

178 Seely, *Adventure*, pp. 158–9; Reynolds, *The Lee-Enfield Rifle*.

179 TNA WO 163/611 'Recommendations of Committees on Army Matters 1900–1920', p. 47; Spiers, 'Rearming the Edwardian Artillery', pp. 167–76; Bidwell and Graham, *Fire-Power*, pp. 13–21

180 TNA PRO 30/57/29 Official Papers of Lord Kitchener: Kitchener to Roberts, 20 April 1903.

to the lance, for show and *izzat* [Urdu: 'honour'] as much as anything.'[181] The matter was further complicated by the Indian Cavalry's *silladar* system. In 1912 Lieutenant Colonel George Barrow, commanding the 35th Scinde Horse, took the view that under the *silladar* system his authority over his regiment extended to determining its armament, and ordered lances to be made and issued to his troopers to go with their swords and rifles. But although the C-in-C India objected, the only action taken against Barrow was the demand that the lances should be put back in store.[182]

On Haig's arrival in India in late 1904, Kitchener (having been well-primed by Roberts) was intent on making sure that he did not stray too far from Army doctrine on the importance of the rifle and dismounted action for the cavalry. But as it turned out, the great confrontation between Kitchener and Haig on cavalry doctrine was a damp squib: Kitchener accepted the importance of the shock charge, just as Haig accepted dismounted rifle action; their views were very close, and it was only a question of how long it took them to realise this. They met on 3 November, with Haig recording in his diary that 'Have interview with the Chief who is quite at one with me regarding method of cavalry action, namely *offensive tactics*.'[183] Kitchener's version of this first meeting, as recounted to Roberts, was significantly different:

> Haig has arrived and I have had one talk with him and mean to have another; he seems to have a wrong idea that the morale of the cavalry will be injured by dismounted training. I have told him that I disagree with this; that while I do not wish in any way to injure the dash or power of shock tactics of cavalry, they must understand that whereas in old days the carbine was the adjunct to the sword or lance in all training, now the sword or lance must be the adjunct to the rifle and its practice.[184]

The second meeting took place on 9 November, again to Haig's satisfaction; he wrote in his diary that Kitchener 'quite agrees as to the need for impressing on cavalry the importance of offensive action mounted, while insisting on the necessity of being able to act dismounted with effect'.[185] Both Kitchener and Haig could be notoriously inarticulate speakers, and it is quite possible that they were simply failing to communicate either their meanings or their differences properly. But the important result for Haig's work for the Indian Cavalry was that the two men at least believed they were in agreement, and could follow a common plan for cavalry reform.

Haig was at first unimpressed by both the British and Indian cavalry training that he saw in India. Presumably with memories of similar episodes in the Boer War, he wrote that:

> From what I see there is a risk of making our cavalry act on the *defensive* too much; at the Punjab manoeuvres it struck me on several occasions that commanders dismounted

---

181 TNA PRO 30/57/28 Official Papers of Lord Kitchener: Kitchener to Roberts, 10 May 1903. For *izzat*, which was a fundamental concept among soldiers in the Indian Army of the time, see Morton Jack, 'The Indian Army on the Western Front 1914–1915', p. 336.

182 Barrow, *The Fire of Life*, pp. 131–5.

183 NLS Haig Papers 2c: Diary entry for 3 November 1903; emphasis in the original.

184 TNA PRO 30/57/28 Official Papers of Lord Kitchener: Kitchener to Roberts, 5 November 1903.

185 NLS Haig Papers 2c: Diary entry, 9 November 1903.

180   *Doctrine and Reform in the British Cavalry 1880–1918*

their men to hold positions *passively*, when the military situation demanded an *energetic offensive* at once. On one occasion I saw a cavalry brigade attacked by infantry when holding a village, and eventually [they] were outflanked and surrounded![186]

An officer serving in India who would come to be closely associated with Haig as his chief of intelligence in the First World War, John Charteris, later wrote in enthusiastic terms of Haig's response:

> The Indian cavalry under the influence of many of its officers who had served in South Africa with mounted infantry units was permeated with the new doctrine and looked for approval from the new Inspector-General. There was a rude awakening. Haig would have none of it. Both at his inspections of regiments, and still more by means of his training memoranda and staff rides, he taught unceasingly to his cavalry in India that warfare still offered scope for horse and man and bare steel.[187]

Charteris was right in the sense that Haig taught that cavalry should be willing to charge, if and when the opportunity arose. Haig's diary for 1904 includes at the front a note written as an aid to memory, 'Cf. von Bredow at Mars-la-Tour. He checked a whole corps. With dismounted fire at most he could have restrained one regiment!'[188] But otherwise, Charteris gave an exaggerated impression of Haig focusing on mounted charges to the neglect of dismounted fire. Both Haig's diary and his notebooks as Inspector General reveal his preoccupation with raising efficiency overall in the Indian cavalry, with concern over the 'principle of the charge not understood', but also a staff ride to 'consider action of cavalry holding a position until the arrival of infantry'; with 'thorough instruction of every horseman in skirmishing – they already shoot well', and 'higher training of officers in the tactical use of the rifle'.[189]

One of the Indian Army staff officers that Haig employed to help him organise his 'staff rides' (training exercises on horseback for commanders and staff officers, in which the existence and location of troops was imagined) was George Barrow, then serving as a major with the Indian 4th Cavalry (one of the regiments that had lost its lances under Kitchener, having been the 4th Lancers a year previously). Barrow had been a junior contemporary of Haig and Allenby at the Army Staff College; and although refused permission to serve in the Boer War, he had seen active service elsewhere. His memoirs, although not particularly favourable to Haig, record that 'His instruction was more practical and realistic than anything the cavalry in India had known previously.'[190] Smith-Dorrien, by 1904 commanding 4th (Quetta) Division and with his long experience of mounted infantry, also recalled that Haig inspected the cavalry under his command, 'and shortly afterwards I submitted to him

---

186 LHCMA Edmonds Papers 2/4: Haig to Edmonds, 29 December 1903, emphasis in the original.

187 Charteris, *Field Marshal Earl Haig*, pp. 27–8.

188 NLS Haig Papers 2d: Haig Diary 1904, note in the front of the diary, presumably as an aid to memory.

189 Ibid., 2d: Diary entries, 23 January 1904 and 26 February 1904; Ibid., 40c–l: Notebooks on Manoeuvres 1903–1906.

190 Barrow, *The Fire of Life*, p. 104.

my scheme for cavalry training and manoeuvres, which he returned remarking that he could not improve on it'.[191]

While in India, Haig continued to work on the various sections of *Cavalry Training* for about a month, incorporating the ideas of Austrian and German cavalry theorists.[192] Meanwhile back in London the draft collective training section of the manual was given by Roberts to a trio of cavalry officers: de Lisle, Rimington and Hubert Gough, with some input from Wilson, presumably to ensure that the result reflected Roberts's views.[193] A version of the manual was completed by the first week of January 1904 and copies circulated. Also in the first week of January, a series of articles on 'The Future of Cavalry' appeared in the Conservative daily *The Morning Post* by its military correspondent H.F. Prevost Battersby, clearly well briefed to report favourably on Roberts's position.[194]

Inevitably, this version of the *Cavalry Training* manual affirmed that the rifle was the principal weapon of the cavalry, and that the sword was the auxiliary. But otherwise, even the requirement for the cavalry to sacrifice themselves if necessary had been retained, and the manual taught the need for the charge in either close or open order to be retained as a tactic:

> When the chance of a charge arises, it should be seized without a moment's delay, and the attack delivered with the full determination of riding the enemy down by sheer force and impetus. It should, as a rule, be assisted by the fire of horse artillery and dismounted men.[195]

Again, this was a basis on which reformed cavalry doctrine might have been agreed, but Roberts chose otherwise by asserting his authority as C-in-C in a way that served no purpose except to antagonise the cavalry even further. From October 1903 onwards the position of C-in-C of the Army had been marked for abolition under the Esher Committee's plans to reorganise the War Office and create a true General Staff. Roberts was seriously ill over the winter and inclined to leave his post quietly, but by 3 January 1904 he had recovered sufficiently to want to fight on.[196] On 9 January, Baden-Powell wrote to Roberts pointing out that the C-in-C had planned to provide a preface to the new *Cavalry Training*, but that this had been delayed due to his illness, and it was now needed. Three days later Roberts provided his preface: it was a précis of his memorandum on the abolition of the lance, which would now

---

[191] Smith-Dorrien, *Memories of Forty Eight Years' Service*, p. 326.

[192] NLS Haig Papers 2c: Diary entry, 8 November 1903; NAM Roberts Papers 221: Newspaper clippings, article 'Obsolete Theories in Tactics', *The Standard*, 13 April 1910.

[193] NAM Roberts Papers 122: Roberts to Kitchener, 28 January 1903; Ibid., 221: Hubert Gough to Roberts, 1 December 1903; and undated, unsigned paper 'The following is suggested as a substitute for Col. Haig's introduction to Part IV'; Callwell, *Field Marshal Sir Henry Wilson*, Volume I, p. 56.

[194] NAM Roberts Papers 221: Newspaper clippings, *Morning Post*, 'The Future of Cavalry' by Prevost Battersby, 30 December 1903, 4 January 1904, 5 January 1904, and 6 January 1904.

[195] *Cavalry Training 1904 (Provisional)*, p. 201.

[196] Hamer, *The British Army: Civil Military Relations 1885–1905*, pp. 223–44.

be incorporated into the official *Cavalry Training* manual.[197] The effect was like a deliberate slap in the face for the cavalry reformers.

Roberts officially approved the *Cavalry Training* manual on 1 February for issue on 1 March, in what was quite probably the last decision on doctrine ever taken by a C-in-C of the British Army. On 11 February, he was removed from his post in the precipitate action taken by Esher to implement the interim report of his committee; Wilson wrote in his diary that Roberts was 'dismissed & is more hurt & angry than I ever saw him, & no wonder'.[198] By way of some compensation, Roberts was offered a salaried post on the CID.

On 18 February, the day after the formal announcement creating the Army Council appeared, French came up from Aldershot to see Arnold-Forster as Secretary of State for War, ostensibly to talk about a new sword planned for the cavalry, but also to discuss *Cavalry Training*. Arnold-Forster's diary records that this meeting took place on his initiative rather than French's, which may be true or perhaps a credit to French's own political skills. Arnold-Forster went on:

> I said I had heard how much he had been concerned to hear of recent decisions with regard to the use of cavalry. It appears to me that as a sort of 'by-product' it has been decided that we should cease to have any cavalry, in the ordinary Continental sense. As a civilian I did not know if this were right or wrong, but it seemed to me far too important a question to be decided off-hand. He entirely agreed. I suggested that he, as the only Cavalry Officer commanding an Army Corps, should write a full statement of the case for submission to the A[rmy] C[ouncil].[199]

A week later, after taking soundings from other officers, Arnold-Forster decided to delay publication of *Cavalry Training* until the Army Council membership was complete, and in order to give French the opportunity to submit a formal paper to the Army Council explaining his opposition to the manual. 'There will of course be a hideous row', Arnold-Forster noted, 'but after all it is our Council and not Lord R[oberts] which is now responsible.'[200] Unfortunately, as Roberts told Ian Hamilton, 'this piece of impertinence was too much' for him.[201] On 26 February Lord Lansdowne, now Foreign Secretary, lunched with Arnold-Forster, who noted in his diary:

> [Lansdowne] told me that Lord Roberts was exceedingly upset by the postponement of the issue of the new Cavalry Drill Book, threatened to give up the Committee of [Imperial] Defence, indeed to throw up everything and to make a violent attack upon the government in general and the Prime Minister in particular for their supposed bad treatment of him.[202]

---

197 NAM Roberts Papers 6: Baden-Powell to Roberts, 9 January 1904 and 12 January 1904.
198 IWM Wilson Papers: Diary entry, 11 February 1904.
199 BL Arnold-Forster Papers, Add. Mss. 50336: Diary entry, 18 February 1904.
200 Ibid., Diary entry, 23 February 1904.
201 NAM Roberts Papers 122: Roberts to Ian Hamilton, 28 February 1904.
202 BL Arnold-Forster Papers, Add. Mss. 50336: Diary entry, 26 February 1904.

It is clear from the phrasing in his diary that Arnold-Forster had only the most general idea of the nature of the debate over cavalry doctrine, and there is a strong note of puzzlement in his account: how could a delay in publishing a cavalry training manual result in a public denunciation of the government by the Empire's premier soldier? He looked quickly for a compromise: Lansdowne could inform Roberts that the manual would be published as planned, with the agreement of the Army Council, but with provisional status for the time being. Roberts accepted this 'with gratitude' and a relieved Arnold-Forster explained the position to French on 28 February.[203] On the same day, Roberts wrote to Kitchener in the hope of securing support in what he now saw as his battle for reform against a faction of reactionary cavalrymen headed by French at Aldershot and Haig in India:

> The revised Cavalry Training is getting on, and I hope it will be published next month. A good deal of it was started by Haig, with some of whose ideas about cavalry I do not agree, and consequently much of the work has had to be re-written. I am most anxious that the manual should be really sound and practical... I consider it quite a misfortune that Haig should be of the old school in regard to the role of cavalry in the field. He is a clever, able fellow and his views have a great effect on French and Scobell and some other senior officers. Had I known this sooner, I should have hesitated to appoint Scobell to command of the Cavalry at Aldershot. I only hope that you may be able to get Haig to change his mind, or as Inspector General of Cavalry he may do a great deal of mischief.[204]

Haig and French shared comparable views on the cavalry, rather than one man influencing the other, and there is no evidence to suggest that Haig had any great influence on Scobell. What Roberts could not accept was that the cavalry reformers were not of 'the old school', and that there was a genuine consensus among cavalry officers opposing his own behaviour.

At this point King Edward VII, who had already been consulted over the issue of the lance, became involved in the *Cavalry Training* affair, telling Roberts on 3 March of French's fears that Roberts and his supporters were intent on turning the cavalry into mounted rifles. The King's words appear to have been prompted by Lord Esher, whose support French had invoked in his fight with Roberts, and who he thanked on 11 March for 'putting those papers before the King. I think he is on our side.'[205] These may have included French's memorandum for the Army Council on *Cavalry Training*, which was not formally submitted until 7 March, since a copy was sent to the Royal household, probably in advance.[206] After listening to the King, Roberts at once wrote to French:

> Nothing could be further from my views... There is nothing in the training that I advocate which could possibly interfere with the dash and confidence which it is so essential for a cavalry soldier to possess. On the contrary, I believe that it will increase the true Cavalry Spirit and give the cavalry soldier infinitely more reliance on his own powers....

---

203 Ibid., Diary entries, 26 February, 27 February and 28 February 1904.
204 NAM Roberts Papers 122: Roberts to Kitchener, 28 January 1904.
205 French, *The Life of Field Marshal Sir John French*, p. 141.
206 Holmes, *The Little Field Marshal*, pp. 157–8 and p. 383, note 20.

It distresses me to think that your views and mine are at variance on a matter which is of such importance to the cavalry.[207]

Although Roberts still carried immense prestige and influence both in the Army and the country, he now had no official power, and French's reply reminded him of this:

As I tried to explain to you the other evening I have only made the same representations on the subject to the Army Council as I have repeatedly made to you as Commander-in-Chief. Nothing can make me alter the views I hold on the subject of cavalry, and I am sure they are nothing like so much at variance with yours as you appear to think.[208]

French also let Esher know on 22 March that Evelyn Wood had promised 'strong and substantial support in the "Cavalry" matter. I am going to make this a real "Casus Belli"'.[209]

Much of the *Cavalry Training 1904* affair may be explained by Roberts's indignation at being removed from office so precipitously by the Esher reforms. There were certainly genuine doctrinal differences between Roberts and French, but as both men had signalled to each other, these could have been overcome. On 23 March, French submitted his memorandum to the Army Council: as before, he absolutely agreed that cavalry soldiers needed to be 'the best possible shots' with their new rifles, but not that the rifle should be their principal weapon or 'we shall soon find that we have no cavalry in the British Army worthy of the name'. Writing for an Army Council that included civilians, French then made a brave attempt to define the indefinable:

It is difficult to define what one means by the 'cavalry spirit', but it is a power which is *felt* and *realised* by those who have served much in that arm. Its attributes are 'dash', 'élan' a fixed determination always to take the offensive and secure the initiative. Such a spirit can never be created in a body of troops whose first idea is to abandon their horses and lie down under cover in the face of a swiftly charging mass of horsemen.[210]

For French, an often emotional man of action and violence rather than philosophy and wordplay, this was about as close as he could come to explaining what lay at the heart of motivation in mounted combat.

Over the next few days the Army Council received opinions from several senior officers supporting French's memorandum, including Evelyn Wood and even Baden-Powell as Inspector General of Cavalry, who wrote that 'I fully agree with

---

207 NAM Roberts Papers 122: Roberts to French, 4 March 1904.
208 Ibid., 30: French to Roberts, 6 March 1904.
209 Quoted in French, *The Life of Field Marshal Sir John French*, p. 141. French seems to have made a common error in thinking that the Latin expression 'casus belli' means something like 'cause for war'; in fact it means 'the occasion for war' and is a legal concept referring to an incident that provokes a war rather than its underlying cause, e.g. the assassination of Archduke Franz Ferdinand. Nevertheless, his meaning is clear.
210 TNA WO 36/6782 Army Organisation, Cavalry (Code 14(D)): 'Role of Cavalry and its Armament: Abolition of the Lance: Memorandum by Sir John French to the Army Council', 7 March 1904; emphasis in the original.

General Sir J. French's remarks as regards the role of cavalry' (without necessarily endorsing his views on its armament).[211] Roberts argued to the Army Council that the opposition to him came from a relatively small and reactionary clique, and that his own views were shared by the great majority of cavalry officers, but he could produce no evidence for this conviction. A few years later, Roberts would use the identical argument that he alone knew and spoke for the real views of the Army and its officers against its leaders on the much wider and more public issue of peacetime conscription, and with as little evidence.[212]

The response of the Army Council to the cavalrymen's concerns over *Cavalry Training* was to agree to the provisional publication of the manual with Roberts's preface (this was a foregone conclusion following his earlier deal with Arnold-Forster), and it appeared a few days later as *Cavalry Training 1904 (Provisional)*. But the Army Council rejected a call by French, Scobell and Rimington for the reinstatement of the lance for war, and instead announced an intention to abolish the lance altogether, with the new Quartermaster General, Herbert Plumer, asking the delicate question as to whether regiments without lances should retain the title of 'Lancers'. This suggestion prompted a further Royal intervention, when on 5 May the Army Council were told that King Edward VII would not sanction the outright abolition of the lance, and there the matter temporarily stuck.[213]

While Roberts was locked in dispute with the Army Council over *Cavalry Training 1904*, the Russo-Japanese War broke out in February 1904, and Ian Hamilton travelled out to the theatre of war as an official British Army observer. As the first information became available, one of the war's greatest surprises was that in the apparently poor cavalry country of southern Manchuria and Korea, the Japanese cavalry with a limited but firm doctrine of shock action was holding its own against about ten times its own number of Russian cavalry and Cossacks, reputedly the best mounted riflemen in the world.[214] Something very strange in terms of cavalry tactics was happening, and General Sir Neville Lyttelton, the new Chief of the General Staff, advised Roberts that no further decision would be taken on *Cavalry Training 1904* until further information was received on the performance of the Russian and Japanese mounted troops. Roberts at once let Hamilton know what he wanted to hear about the Japanese cavalry and why, 'I gather they are really mounted riflemen riding ponies chiefly', explaining that he needed this assessment in detail in order to help his case with the Army Council.[215] Foreign reports on the performance of mounted troops on both sides in the Russo-Japanese War were accompanied by ambiguities and disputes, but even so, Hamilton was unique among British observers in concluding that the arme blanche had failed completely in the war. To Roberts, who by the end

---

211 Ibid., 'Role of Cavalry and its Armament: Abolition of the Lance: Memorandum by Major General Sir Robert Baden-Powell, Inspector-General of Cavalry', 10 March 1904.

212 Strachan, *The Politics of the British Army*, pp. 110–11.

213 TNA WO 163/10 'Minutes of Proceedings and Précis Prepared for the Army Council', (1905), Précis Number 170, pp. 118–38 and Précis Number 218, pp. 374–5.

214 Cadell, 'Some Lessons from the Russo-Japanese War', *United Service Magazine*, Volume XXX, New Series, p. 115.

215 NAM Roberts Papers 122: Roberts to Ian Hamilton, 4 May 1904.

of 1904 was claiming that both French and Haig were obsessed with knee-to-knee charges and neglecting musketry, Hamilton's letters were a vindication.[216]

Cavalry Training 1904 (Provisional) reached India in early April, prompting a further episode involving Kitchener and Haig which showed conclusively that the issue dividing Roberts and the cavalrymen was not ultimately one of doctrine. On 11 April Haig submitted a report on *Cavalry Training 1904 (Provisional)* to Kitchener, and after reading it Kitchener felt able to put out an Army Order that day supporting the manual. Not knowing this, Roberts wrote to Kitchener on 13 April asking him for a letter of support and warning Kitchener about Haig's opposition.[217] When Roberts received a copy of Kitchener's Army Order he was delighted, writing back that 'what you have said in that order is exactly what I want'.[218] But what is striking is that Kitchener's order was also quite acceptable to Haig, who recorded in his diary:

> Had a long talk with Lord K[itchener] re new Cavalry Drill Book. He read me his remarks in letter [sic] which he had sent to Lord Roberts on the subject. He takes a middle course, thinking exact drill re training for charge necessary, but putting efficiency in rifle first.[219]

A puzzled Kitchener wrote to Roberts that 'someone must have given you the wrong impression about Haig', as 'he quite agrees with what I wrote in the enclosed A[rmy] O[rder] and told me so more than once'.[220] Unless Haig was being entirely deceitful even in his own diary, the doctrinal compromise between those who believed in the primacy of the rifle for the cavalry and those who believed in the primacy of the arme blanche was there for the taking. In 1904 the main issue at stake was not the cavalry's tactics but the personality and methods of Lord Roberts: the cavalry simply did not trust him. Kitchener realised this in his conversations with Haig, 'Although he agrees with my views he always seems to hark back as if something more was intended than was said', he wrote to Roberts, 'the cavalry are, I think, evidently very nervous that more is intended than is written down'.[221] Behind everything that was said to them remained one of the cavalry officers' greatest fears: that to accept becoming regiments of mounted riflemen meant eventually to accept becoming the mounted battalions of infantry regiments.

Roberts saw French again on the cavalry issue in June 1904, and came away with much the same impression, that French no longer trusted anything that was said to him. But Roberts's letter about this meeting to Kitchener only underlined how remote from understanding the cavalry he had become: 'I am afraid that our conversations will not result in much good, although French promised me to disabuse Scobell, Haig *and the few other officers who agree with them*, that there is not the slightest wish

---

216 Ibid., 122: Roberts to Ian Hamilton, 7 December 1904.
217 Ibid., 122: Roberts to Kitchener, 13 April 1904. Haig's report to Kitchener is not in the Haig Papers and does not appear to have survived.
218 TNA PRO 30/57/28 Official Papers of Lord Kitchener: Roberts to Kitchener, 4 May 1904.
219 NLS Haig Papers 2d: Diary entry, 14 May 1904.
220 NAM Roberts Papers 122: Kitchener to Roberts, 12 May 1904; NLS Haig Papers 2d: Haig Diary entry, 11 May 1904.
221 NAM Roberts Papers 122: Kitchener to Roberts, 12 May 1904.

to turn them into mounted rifles.'[222] In keeping with his habitual behaviour, Roberts also sought the support of the press, asking Amery to write a series of articles in favour of his case for *The Times*.[223] A few days after Roberts's meeting with French, Amery wrote to Roberts:

> I went down to Aldershot last night to stay with General French and he, Scobell and myself talked cavalry tactics hammer and tongs from nine till midnight, and we had some more at breakfast this morning. It was all very interesting, and I was glad to get their point of view, but I confess I heard nothing that would induce me to go over to their camp. Their chief point is that the man who doesn't dismount is much more mobile than the one who does and can therefore always choose the point where he will break through. But they omit from their consideration the mobility of the bullet, which is the greatest factor of all.[224]

Roberts was very pleased with Amery's articles, drawing Kitchener's particular attention to them.[225]

Roberts was now retired as C-in-C, and despite his efforts *Cavalry Training 1904* remained provisional. In January 1905 the manual was re-issued without its preface, removing the offence as far as most of the senior cavalrymen were concerned. Roberts's response to this removal was to write to Prime Minister Arthur Balfour (through his personal secretary), a long, rambling, and in some ways sad letter of complaint that reflected his own anger and perceived humiliation rather than the realities of the Boer War and subsequent cavalry reform:

> The officers' reports have now been received and I understand that they are unanimous as to the usefulness and practicality of the new regulations... I know that in some commands, particularly Aldershot, the training is being carried out very much as it was before the war. Very little attention is being paid to dismounted work... [In the Boer War] General French would never go anywhere without some Mounted Infantry to assist him because his cavalry could not cope with the Boers when fighting with the rifle... We must not allow the sensitivities of some of the more senior cavalry officers – some of whom cling to the traditions of bygone days – to prevent [the] necessity for changes in the future being pointed out.[226]

This letter achieved nothing except to reinforce for the future the critics' perspective on the cavalry reformers: that they were reactionaries, driven by sentiment for tradition, and unwilling to admit the realities of modern warfare.

Having made his point in this letter to Balfour, Roberts seems to have undergone a change of heart (although it would be a temporary one), or to have recognised that his dispute with French was bad for the Army. In February 1905 he used the occasion of the Kimberley Reunion Dinner 'to dispel any notion that I am not favourably disposed towards the cavalry branch' and made his peace with French, writing 'I lay

---

222 Ibid., Roberts to Kitchener, 3 June 1904; emphasis added.
223 Ibid., 1: Amery to Roberts, 11 May 1904.
224 Ibid., 1: Amery to Roberts, 14 June 1904.
225 Ibid., 122: Roberts to Kitchener, 3 June 1904 and 10 June 1904.
226 Ibid., 122: Roberts to Sanders, 12 January 1905.

more stress on the rifle, you on the sword. The cavalry soldier must be able to use both weapons skilfully.'[227] French's reply was under the circumstances a generous one, probably fuelled by the emotion of the reunion:

> It seems an impertinence of me to hold any difference of opinion on any military subject whatever to you, Sir; but you have so encouraged us all to speak our minds quite freely and have so taught us to regard you as a friend in whom we may confide as well as our great commander, that we never seem to hesitate in explaining our views. Really, sir, the one point upon which you think we differ is a very small one. No one more fully realises the value of the rifle in the hands of the cavalry soldier than I do. And as to the *employment* of cavalry, I *know* your views are mine exactly.[228]

This was the doctrinal middle way that all senior officers but Roberts himself (and also Ian Hamilton) had already adopted more than a year earlier. The employment of cavalry on which there was firm doctrinal agreement was as an increasingly independent force operating as an advance guard or to the flank, with the 'Jeb Stuart ride' into the enemy rear as its greatest achievement.

The effect on the regular cavalry regiments and on their officers of three years of public argument about their lifestyles, competence and military value was exactly what might have been expected. Criticised and ridiculed in the press and in books (with what they rightly believed was the connivance of the C-in-C), they had been insulted by Roberts over tactical reform, they had seen their regiments threatened, they had been told to accept that their proudest achievements in South Africa were lies that had never happened, and they had seen their opportunities to enjoy themselves in peacetime and to show off their wealth forcibly curtailed. Voluntary resignations among cavalry officers in 1903, according to one estimate, were triple what they had been in 1898; and replacements were not forthcoming.[229] 'Young men with private incomes of £400–£1,000 a year are ceasing to join the British Cavalry', Baden-Powell was told, 'while young men with smaller incomes cannot afford to join.'[230] A War Office inquiry into the shortage of cavalry officers in 1905 gave three main reasons: the low pay compared to expenses, the cutting of social activities and long leave, and the ridicule to which the cavalry had been subject in the press.[231] At the end of 1904, Major General Charles 'Sunny Jim' Douglas, as Adjutant General, issued a strongly-worded memorandum on officers' expenses in the cavalry, and addressed the Army Council in words which echoed the Akers-Douglas Committee's recommendations:

---

227 Ibid., 122: Roberts to French, 16 February 1905.

228 Letter from Sir John French to Lord Roberts, 20 February 1905, quoted in French, *The Life of Field Marshal Sir John French, First Earl of Ypres*, p. 143; emphasis in the original. This letter could not be traced in either the French or Roberts Papers.

229 'Mrs Clarke' (pseudonym), 'Jobbery Under Arms', *United Service Magazine*, Volume XXX, New Series, p. 538.

230 NLS Haig Papers 2c: Carbon of a letter, undated, unsigned, possibly from Haig, to Baden-Powell c.1903–1905.

231 TNA WO 163/611 'Recommendations of Committees on Army Matters 1900–1920', p. 179.

The monied classes must be eliminated from the cavalry and a poorer class of officer sent in, letting the officer commanding know that if the young officer with, say £200 a year, cannot live in the regiment, the officer commanding will be removed. Although hunting and polo may improve cavalry officers, he considered that the choice between money and brains must be made, and if we elect for brains the hunting and polo must go.[232]

However 'the monied classes' might be defined, the repeated standard of a private income of £200 showed clearly that still no social revolution was intended. But in response, Baden-Powell took his officers' side, passing on their complaints that:

They were seldom, if ever, consulted or taken into the confidence of their legislators, with whom they were altogether out of touch (even up to date: a typical example being the recent unfortunate memorandum on the expenses of cavalry officers). This feeling of discouragement has not merely been confined to the senior officers, but has in a measure extended down to all.[233]

Neither the Army Council nor the government would face the basic issue: most cavalry officers were expected to follow a lifestyle that needed a private income to supplement their pay, and as long as this was true their views had to be taken into account. As Vaughan remembered, the officers of the 4th Hussars and 10th Hussars (both serving in India) circumvented the new attempts to limit their sporting pleasures with ease, and with the connivance of sympathetic local military authorities.[234]

With such disagreements about the cavalry at the Army's higher levels, it was to be expected that junior officers would become uncertain in making decisions. The dispute over of the cavalry's tactics was not only felt within the cavalry regiments, but also affected the way that cavalry and its role were understood throughout the Army. In 1901 examiners for promotion of junior officers were impressed by their understanding of mounted troops, much of it presumably learned in a practical fashion on the veldt. But by 1904 'the mobility of mounted troops was not always sufficiently considered'.[235] A year later the handling of cavalry was considered a weak point among junior officers, and it remained so until the start of the First World War.

Despite the row created over *Cavalry Training 1904*, cavalry reform in more general terms continued to make progress. In 1904 the Cavalry School was established at Netheravon with Byng as its first commandant, and with horsemastership and veterinary science as important parts of its training.[236] Shortly afterwards, an

---

232 TNA WO 163/10 'Minutes of Proceedings and Précis Prepared for the Army Council' (1905), Précis Number 191 p. 238, and appendix containing memorandum dated 15 December 1904, pp. 251–2.

233 TNA WO 27/508 'State and efficiency of the Army and Defences. Reports by Inspector General of the Forces – submitted to the Army Council' (1903–1913), Summary of cavalry winter training by Baden-Powell, 18 April 1905.

234 Vaughan, *Cavalry and Sporting Memories*, pp. 115–16.

235 CUL Official Publications Room: 'Reports on the examination of officers of the regular forces, militia and volunteers', May 1901 captains; November 1904 captains; May 1905 lieutenants; December 1913 captains.

236 Smith, *A History of the Royal Army Veterinary Corps 1796–1919*, pp. 226–7.

equivalent Cavalry School was founded at Saugor (modern Sagar) in north-central India, largely at Haig's instigation.[237] In 1908 the chief instructor at the Netheravon Cavalry School was Tom Bridges of the Royal Field Artillery (and late of the Imperial Light Horse), who transferred to the 4th Dragoon Guards in the following year. At Baden-Powell's recommendation a standing Cavalry Committee was formed to investigate technical problems; and in 1905 in an important development *The Cavalry Journal* was first published, with Goldmann as editor, as a forum for debate.[238] In the first issue Broadwood answered the contentious question 'Is the rifle or sword the principal weapon of cavalry?' with the new orthodoxy, 'Whichever you like to call so, provided that you are equally prepared to use either.'[239]

So, with the departure of Roberts from the post of C-in-C and the instigation of these reforms, the cavalry doctrinal debate became once more something internal to the Army, something for captains and majors to write articles about. Although it would become public once more before the start of the First World War, it would never again be as bitter or as intense. But its consequences would be felt for years to come.

---

237 For comparison, the School of Musketry at Hythe was created in 1854, but the School of Artillery at Larkhill not until 1920, although a School of Gunnery for Royal Horse Artillery and Royal Field Artillery did exist before 1914.

238 TNA WO 163/19 Army Council Decisions 1905, Number 177, pp. 167–9 and Number 216, p. 373.

239 Broadwood, 'The Place of Fire Tactics in the Training of British Cavalry', *The Cavalry Journal*, Volume 1, Number 1, p. 90.

Chapter 5

The Haldane Era 1905–1914

In 1878 a British War Office report on the Russo-Turkish War noted the unusual nature of the Russian Army's Cossack regiments, horsemen armed with lance, sword and rifle, but trained to fight mainly on foot.[1] Six years later, it was strongly emphasised that Russian cavalry, of which the Cossacks formed a considerable part, 'now differs in type, training and equipment from all other European cavalry, and is avowedly intended to act as mounted infantry rather than regular cavalry'.[2] In 1901 the British military attaché in Pekin (as the capital city of China was then known), although chiefly concerned with the cavalry of other nationalities, noted that both Russian Cossacks and Japanese cavalry in China 'appear to be very good mounted infantry'.[3] British soldiers cramming for promotion examinations in 1903 learned that 'the Russians alone have mainly armed their cavalry with the rifle as their sole [sic] weapon'.[4] In his *Small Wars*, Callwell distinguished the 'Russian dragoon' as 'a cavalry soldier trained especially to fight on foot and provided with a rifle and a bayonet'.[5] The point, at least for the British War Office, was not in dispute. The majority of British officers reporting on the Russo-Japanese War (some of them cavalry officers) confirmed that the Russian cavalry, including the Cossacks, were trained primarily to fight on foot with a carbine or rifle.[6] Even in 1910, in *War and the Arme Blanche*, his denunciation of British cavalry doctrine and of the new *Cavalry Training 1907* that had replaced Roberts's 1904 manual, Erskine Childers had to argue hard that the Russian experience had not undermined his case that mounted riflemen were the superior form of cavalry.[7] Childers contacted Ian Hamilton, now serving as Adjutant General, for an explanation for the poor Russian cavalry performance, and Hamilton wrote back (in a letter that he copied to Roberts and to Churchill) with a long discourse on the history of cavalry tactics, ending with the Russo-Japanese War:

---

1 TNA WO 33/31 'The Russo-Turkish War 1877: Operations in Europe' (1878).
2 Chenevix-Trench, *Cavalry in Modern War*, p. 14.
3 TNA WO 33/184 'Notes Regarding the French, German and American Cavalry in China' (1901).
4 Moores, *Summary of Tactics for Military Operations*, p. 173.
5 Callwell, *Small Wars*, p. 422.
6 TNA WO 33/337 Report on the Russo-Japanese War up to 15 August 1904, (1905); 'How Not To Do It', *The Cavalry Journal*, Volume 1, Number 3, p. 316; Zalesskij, 'The Russian Cavalry in the War with the Japanese', *The Cavalry Journal*, Volume 8, Number 32, p. 404.
7 Childers, *War and the Arme Blanche*, pp. 334–7.

Next came the Manchurian War. Extremely awkward for the framers of the 1907 Cavalry Training, even you must admit... The upholders of the arme blanche have been driven, in discussing it, to invent the astonishing theory that Russian cavalry and Cossacks are not cavalry at all but merely mounted infantry... In their complete adherence to shock tactics and the arme blanche the Russian regular cavalry are second only to the British. As for Cossacks, a Cossack off his horse is like a duck out of water.[8]

Following Hamilton's letter, Childers's next book, *German Influence on British Cavalry* announced that Cossacks were swordsmen totally ignorant of both the rifle and dismounted action.[9] This was the divisive level to which the British Army's debate about cavalry had once again sunk.

It is quite possible that British assessments of the Cossacks before the Russo-Japanese War had placed too much emphasis on their capability to act dismounted, which was an unusual feature when compared to other European cavalry of the time. But descriptions by British observers and military critics of cavalry of both sides in the Russo-Japanese War may have been influenced by their own continuing arguments more than by any objective analysis. The ensuing debate consisted of little more than contradictory assertions on the nature of the Cossacks (a term sometimes used generically by the British to include all Russian cavalry) and their Japanese opponents.[10] Since the Cossacks had been praised for some years as the ideal mounted riflemen, this produced the strange result among theorists that General Count Carl Gustav von Wrangel in Austria condemned the Cossacks for their obsession with dismounted work, while General François de Négrier in France insisted that they owed such successes as they had achieved to their dismounted skills, and General Ian Hamilton in Great Britain blamed their failures on their total lack of such skills.[11]

Much as had happened after the Boer War and earlier wars, the first arguments over the value of the arme blanche and the charge failed to include other factors which might have influenced the tactics of both Russian and Japanese mounted troops. The terrain of the principal land theatre of southern Manchuria was considered too broken and irregular for the use of large masses of cavalry; Hamilton called it 'five squadron country'.[12] Both sides, particularly the Russians, were fighting at the end of long supply lines and lacked the ability to protect their horses properly against the often freezing weather, or to provide them with enough food.[13] But these conditions did not explain the failure of the Cossacks to dominate their numerically much inferior

---

8 LHCMA Hamilton Papers 5/1/8: Hamilton to Childers, 30 October 1910.

9 Childers, *German Influence on British Cavalry*, p. 145.

10 The best account of British interpretations of the Russo-Japanese War remains Towle, 'The Influence of the Russo-Japanese War on British Military and Naval Thought'. See in particular pp. 165–90 and p. 385.

11 von Wrangel, *The Cavalry in the Russo-Japanese War*, p. 55; de Négrier, *Lessons of the Russo-Japanese War*, p. 8 and p. 72.

12 Hamilton, *A Staff Officer's Scrap Book*, Volume 1, p. 191.

13 TNA WO 33/337 'A Report on the Russo-Japanese War up to 15 August 1904', p. 152.

Japanese opponents, who fought as mounted riflemen trained to charge mounted only in extreme circumstances.

Most British observers blamed the general quality of the Cossacks as troops for their poor performance. Colonel W.H.H. Waters, late of the Royal Artillery (and translator of the German official history of the Boer War), attached to the Russian forces in Manchuria, reported that 'Even with very inferior numbers, the cavalry of any other great Power would literally have walked round the numerous Cossack squadrons, either in shock tactics or in shooting.'[14] Another officer considered the Cossacks to be 'very nearly useless – badly led, badly drilled and very often wanting in courage'.[15] Rawlinson, watching Russian exercises shortly after the war, concluded that his 8th MI from the Boer War would have routed twice their number of Cossacks.[16]

Many British cavalrymen, locked in their doctrinal debate, preferred to believe that faulty Russian doctrine had produced bad troops, 'that excessive dismounted work and dependence on fire effect destroy that true cavalry spirit without which any army in the field is deprived of its eyes and ears'.[17] This interpretation was particularly favoured by traditionalist cavalry officers, their feathers already badly ruffled by their experiences under Roberts. A colonial veteran of the Boer War, who arrived in London in 1904, was startled by what he was told:

> I met several cavalry officers whom I had met during the war, and was surprised to learn from them that if a squadron leader wishes to get on now, spit and polish, knee to knee drill, and a studious avoidance of useful dismounted work was the way to do it. On the other hand, if he studied individuality, Boer tactics, mounted or dismounted, concealed outposts, common-sense ideas in combination with sufficient close cavalry drill, he was at once classed as a —— Mounted Infantryman, and thus a marked man.[18]

Perfecting mounted charging in all its forms still took up a considerable amount of time, about four-fifths of all British cavalry training according to de Lisle.[19] But since as Rimington put it, 'a good swordsman on a perfectly trained horse should account for any three of ordinary ability on average horses', this devotion still made sense if mounted charging was a valid tactic.[20]

The British Army's assessment of mounted combat in the Russo-Japanese War strongly echoed the early British interpretations of mounted action in the American Civil War: that the horsemen of both sides were made cautious by over-reliance on firearms. The behaviour of both the Russians and the Japanese after the war gave

---

14 TNA WO 33/350 'Reports on the Campaign in Manchuria 1904 with Photographs: Report of Colonel Waters', p. 42.

15 TNA WO 33/337 'A Report on the Russo-Japanese War up to 15 August 1904', p. 6.

16 Maurice, *The Life of General Lord Rawlinson of Trent*, p. 93.

17 Holbrook, 'The Russo-Japanese War IV: Mistchenko's Cavalry Raid', *United Service Magazine*, Volume XXX, New Series, p. 382.

18 'The British Cavalry and the Lessons of 1899 to 1902 by a Colonial', *United Service Magazine*, Volume XXIX, New Series, p. 420.

19 NAM Roberts Papers 223: de Lisle to Roberts, 7 June 1910.

20 Rimington, *Our Cavalry*, p. 193.

support to this interpretation. In what seems something of an act of desperation, the Russians took away their Cossacks' rifles temporarily in order to emphasise their need to rediscover the charge.[21] The Japanese response to the war was to double their number of cavalry regiments and to issue new regulations that 'the weapons of cavalry are the sword when mounted and the rifle on foot. As a general rule cavalry will fight mounted.'[22] British defenders of the reformed cavalry welcomed this support of their views; opponents of the cavalry charge saw it only as proof that idiotic, sentimental cavalrymen were not confined to the western hemisphere.[23]

Particularly in *The Cavalry Journal*, 'lessons' were almost ruthlessly extracted from the few mounted and dismounted actions in Manchuria, which had been seldom more than of squadron size.[24] George Barrow, making the first of a series of contributions to *The Cavalry Journal*, wrote that 'If we go below the surface and seek the reason why the Russian cavalry played so subordinate a part in this titanic struggle, we will find that it lies in the fact that for many years the Russians have been teaching their men to look upon their rifles as the principal thing.'[25] The views at this time of men like Vaughan, Barrow, and Home, who each went on to serve as chief staff officer of the Cavalry Corps in 1914–1915, are important as representing something close to the average for good cavalry officers. British military theorists studying the Russo-Japanese War were also struck by the renewed importance of infantry and artillery, suggesting that the experience of the Boer War had indeed been unusual and that future armies were not, after all, going to contain a high proportion of mounted troops. The failure of mounted raids to penetrate deep into the enemy rear areas also called that idea into question. But the observers and theorists were also struck by the need, and the ability, of infantry to close with their enemies in bayonet charges and fight hand-to-hand, just as the cavalry sometimes also charged home, and by the evident battle fatigue appearing in troops who had endured very intense combat for days, rather than the one-day battles of earlier wars.[26] Haig was one of those impressed by the idea that the cavalry might have to wait behind the main fighting line while the infantry and artillery wore down the enemy; writing in 1909 that 'cavalry, of itself, cannot produce this state of moral and physical decadence in the enemy in a general engagement' and that it must 'keep

---

21 Stone, *The Eastern Front 1914–1917*, p. 17; TNA WO 33/419 'The Military Resources of the Russian Empire' (1907).

22 'The New Japanese Cavalry Regulations', *The Cavalry Journal*, Volume 3, Number 11, p. 218.

23 NAM Roberts Papers 223: Newspaper clippings, Letters from Colonel Charles à Court Repington to *The Times*, 26 March 1910, and Erskine Childers to *The Times*, 17 May 1910.

24 'Minor Tactics in Manchuria', *The Cavalry Journal*, Volume 2, Number 5, p. 64; 'How cavalry might have been used in the Russo-Japanese War', *The Cavalry Journal*, Volume 2, Number 8, p. 477; Birkbeck, 'The Russo-Japanese War', *The Cavalry Journal*, Volume 3, Number 12, p. 501.

25 Barrow, 'The Spirit of Cavalry', *The Cavalry Journal*, Volume 1, Number 1, p. 22.

26 'The Value of the Arme Blanche From Actual Instances in the Russo-Japanese War', *The Cavalry Journal*, Volume 6, Number 23, p. 322.

close to the other arms who attack the infantry and prepare the way for the decisive action of the cavalry'.[27]

Any debates about cavalry soon became subordinated to the major reorganisation of the Army under Richard Burdon Haldane, the new Liberal government's Secretary of State for War 1905–1912, the biggest and most far-reaching changes to the Army's structure since 1886. Coming on the heels of the creation of the new General Staff, with Lyttelton becoming the first Chief of the Imperial General Staff (CIGS) in 1909, the Haldane reforms created the British Army with which the country entered the First World War. Haig returned to Great Britain at Haldane's request in 1905 to participate in these reforms, being replaced as Inspector General of Cavalry in India by Rimington. In addition to being Haldane's closest military adviser, Haig also held key posts in the War Office to help oversee the implementation of his plans, as Director of Military Training (DMT) 1905–1907 and then Director of Staff Duties (DSD) 1907–1909.[28]

Building on the work of Brodrick and Arnold-Forster, and working from the Army's first priority to provide troops to garrison the Empire including India, Haldane was still able to create the new BEF, based in Great Britain and Ireland and ready for overseas deployment. Intended to be commanded on mobilisation for war by the CIGS, the BEF consisted of six regular infantry divisions plus a cavalry division, and was supplemented by the new Territorial Force (TF), created from the old militia, volunteers and yeomanry (often known unofficially as the Territorial Army), and intended for home defence.[29] As originally planned, the regular cavalry were to provide the regiments (including a composite Household Regiment) for the BEF's Cavalry Division, while the yeomanry regiments were to provide 14 mounted brigades for the TF, each commanded by a regular cavalry officer, and also the divisional mounted troops for each of the planned 14 TF infantry divisions. With some variation, the minimum strength of a yeomanry regiment was fixed in 1908 at 450 all ranks to give them the necessary strength for this role.[30]

Haldane inherited from his predecessors the basic strategic problem that the BEF or any one of its divisions – including of course the cavalry – might have to fight against almost any opponent virtually anywhere in the world, and to adjust its tactics accordingly. But a European war undoubtedly figured greatly in Haldane's reforms, as well as in the reforms to the Indian Army in which Haig participated; while the probability of the BEF's involvement in a war against Germany increased

---

27 Quoted in Gooch, *The Plans of War*, p. 117.

28 The best account of the Haldane reforms is Spiers, *Haldane*; see also Gooch, *The Plans of War*, pp. 132–64; Beckett, 'Selection by Disparagement', pp. 53–6; Terraine, *Haig*, pp. 37–45.

29 The BEF was commanded in 1914 by French, who had resigned as CIGS a few months earlier over the Curragh Incident, apparently on the understanding that he would remain as designated GOC-in-C BEF, and his appointment was made directly by Prime Minister Herbert Asquith. See Holmes, *The Little Field Marshal*, pp. 166–96; Jeffrey, *Field Marshal Sir Henry Wilson*, pp. 118–29. 'Territorial Force' is an exact translation of *Landwehr*, the German Army's title for its reserve formations; the title was changed officially to Territorial Army in 1922.

30 Verdin, *The Cheshire (Earl of Chester's) Yeomanry 1898–1967*, p. 25.

considerably as a result of Henry Wilson's staff talks with the French as Director of Military Operations (DMO) from 1911 onwards.[31] Even so, the next major war for the British Empire might easily have occurred elsewhere and against very different opponents. This meant letting large parts of doctrine be dictated by circumstances, as Haig explained in 1911:

> While the German General Staff preaches the doctrine of envelopment, and the French General Staff advocates a large general reserve with a view to a concentrated blow at a decisive point of the enemy's battle order, the critics urge [complain] that the British General Staff hesitates to publish and to teach a clear line of action. The reasoning appears to be that unless some such definite doctrine is decided and inculcated in peace, action in war will be hesitating and mistakes will be made. The critics seem to lose sight of the real nature of war, and the varying conditions under which the British Army may have to take the field. It is neither necessary nor desirable that we should go further than what is so clearly laid down in our regulations. If we go further, we run the risk of tying ourselves to a doctrine that may not be always applicable, and gain nothing in return. An army trained to march long distances, to manoeuvre quickly, and to fight with the utmost determination, will be a suitable instrument in the hands of a competent commander whether the situation is to be solved by 'envelopment' or 'penetration'.[32]

In the case of the cavalry this meant being able to carry out a close-order charge, perhaps even of divisional size, against a primitive and ill-equipped enemy, or in European war against an enemy cavalry division that had placed itself in isolation as an advance guard or flank guard; but also being able to fight mounted and dismounted using more sophisticated tactics.

The Cavalry Division of the BEF consisted of four brigades each of three regiments. A fifth independent cavalry brigade was created in 1908, initially as part of a force based round a putative 7th Infantry Division for possible deployment to Egypt.[33] The Cavalry Division had no permanent peacetime existence: for exercises the four brigades came together under the Inspector General of Cavalry as divisional commander, with the divisional troops and a headquarters being made up of officers and men coming from various peacetime appointments. In the same way, on mobilisation in 1914 Allenby as the designated GOC Cavalry Division simply commandeered Barrow to be his Intelligence Officer.[34] Following the training structures laid down in the field manuals, the culmination of staff rides or cavalry manoeuvres remained the 'cavalry fight', the massed charge of all four brigades

---

31 Jeffrey, *Field Marshal Sir Henry Wilson*, pp. 85–105; Strachan, 'The British Army, its General Staff, and the Continental Commitment, 1904–14', pp. 75–94.

32 The report on Haig's last staff ride as chief of staff in India in 1911, quoted in Charteris, *Field Marshal Earl Haig*, pp. 55–6. For the continuation of this tradition of a 'problem solving' approach to doctrine into the Second World War, particularly in the Canadian Army, see Copp, *Fields of Fire*, pp. 3–32.

33 TNA WO 32/7084 'Organisation of a force for operations in Egypt. Increase in Establishments. Formation of 7th Division and 5th Cavalry Brigade', Memorandum by the Director of Military Operations, 31 July 1908.

34 Wavell, *Allenby*, p. 118; Barrow, *The Fire of Life*, pp. 140–42; Home, *The Diary of a World War I Cavalry Officer*, p. 13.

together against a mounted enemy. But although the German Army, as the most likely future enemy, included the massed divisional charge in its cavalry repertoire, this did not mean that the British expected the Germans to use these tactics. While the 1909 German cavalry regulations, the last version to appear before the First World War, maintained that 'Mounted action is the predominant way in which cavalry fights', senior officers including Count Alfred von Schlieffen had raised doubts about the viability of the close-order mass cavalry charge.[35] Assessments made in 1914 were that German cavalry doctrine stressed 'vigorous offensive action by small cavalry detachments'.[36] After the First World War, the semi-official German account of their cavalry in 1914 stated that 'The fighting on foot of large bodies' of cavalry had 'not sufficiently been taken care of' in training.[37]

Rather than spending much of its time perfecting the massed charge, after the 1910 manoeuvres the BEF's cavalry assembled only once more to train as a complete division: in 1912 in the Corps manoeuvres in East Anglia in which Grierson's forces were judged to have defeated Haig's.[38] There was one final training exercise before the BEF went to war, a map scheme in autumn 1913 with French taking the part of the General Officer Commanding-in-Chief (GOC-in-C) of a BEF of four divisions and a cavalry division, and Grierson his chief staff officer. Haig, who also took part, was not impressed by French's battle plans, which he considered 'impractical', and on going to war next year, Haig in an early diary entry recorded his pessimistic view of French's abilities in the 1913 exercise. Throughout the war, Haig provided his wife Doris with regular copies of this diary, in a similar system of indirect political communication to that which he had used through his sister Henrietta.[39]

Many years later, Edmonds recalled asking Haig why four brigades were needed for the BEF's cavalry division, when French and German cavalry divisions had only three brigades. According to Edmonds, Haig replied that two brigades were needed for the first line of a divisional charge, one brigade for the second line and one brigade for the third or reserve line. It is entirely possible that Haig gave Edmonds this answer as a justification, but the real reasons for the size and structure of the Cavalry Division were institutional rather than tactical. The five cavalry brigades simply conformed to five military districts within the United Kingdom. In 1913 it was proposed to create a second BEF cavalry division (each division of three brigades) by withdrawing to Great Britain two cavalry regiments then in South Africa, but the Treasury would not sanction the extra cost of the artillery and other troops needed.[40]

---

35 Quoted, with Schlieffen reference, in Guderian, *Achtung – Panzer!*, p. 31.
36 Quoted in Anglesey, *A History of the British Cavalry Volume 7*, pp. 82–5.
37 von Poseck, *The German Cavalry 1914 in Belgium and France*, p. 222; the grammar of the original, which is that of the US Army translators, has been retained in this quotation.
38 Charteris, *Field Marshal Earl Haig*, pp. 65–6; French, *The Life of Sir John French*, pp. 184–9; Wavell, *Allenby*, p. 118.
39 Sheffield and Bourne (eds), *Douglas Haig: War Diaries and Letters 1914–1918*, p. 58.
40 TNA WO 163/18 'Army Council Decisions 1913 No. 734', pp. 446–8; Edmonds quoted in Gardener, *Allenby*, p. 75; Steiner, *Britain and the Origins of the First World War*, p. 194. Before 1914 the United Kingdom was divided into seven military commands or districts: Aldershot (with two infantry divisions), Southern, Eastern, Western, Northern,

Vaughan, who served as chief staff officer to the Cavalry Division on the outbreak of war in 1914, later wrote that he and Allenby 'both knew from manoeuvres that three brigades were enough for a Division, but we never dared say so lest the politicos would seize the opportunity and disband three cavalry regiments'.[41] Given Haig's role in the creation of the BEF, it is significant that he did not insist on the two cavalry divisions that he had told Lonsdale Hale in 1900 were essential (for example, at the expense of having TF troops make up part of the sixth infantry division), and neither did French. Despite the arguments made during and after the Boer War that the Army needed a higher proportion of mounted troops, including the recommendations of the Elgin Commission, the BEF's structure shows a complete absence of any high ranking conspiracy to promote the cavalry's interests. The Haldane reforms, like every other attempt at reform going back to Cardwell, failed to provide the Army with a properly organised cavalry force.

Henry Wilson was fond of saying at the time of the Haldane reforms that there was no military problem to which the solution was six divisions.[42] The BEF was a product of many factors, of which its military suitability for any given role was only one. Its single Cavalry Division of – in practice – 5 brigades or 15 regiments was excellently equipped, as the only cavalry of a major power to be entirely rifle-armed and also trained for the mounted charge (excluding the Russian Cossacks, the Japanese cavalry, and the cavalry of the United States, all of which also carried rifles). The troopers were supported by two brigades (four six-gun batteries) of 13-pounder guns, and by two Maxims for each regiment for both cavalry and yeomanry, changing to the lighter .303-inch Vickers machine-gun after 1912, issued to the cavalry before the infantry. In numbers the Cavalry Division was about twice the size of a French or German cavalry division, and its brigades had a higher proportion of machine-guns and artillery to troops than either. But dismounted it fielded only the equivalent of about two weak brigades of infantry, with less than a quarter of the artillery firepower of an infantry division, and no intrinsic heavy artillery.[43] The cavalry regiments were equipped with entrenching tools just before the outbreak of war, carried on one packhorse for each troop.[44]

The Haldane reforms made no great change to the number or the cost of the cavalry, which remained broadly consistent with policy dating back to the Cardwell-Childers era. In absolute terms, the number of regular cavalrymen (including Household, line and depot troops) serving in the Army increased slightly from 14,000 in the 1880s to just over 15,000 in 1914, while the percentage of cavalry in the Army as a whole declined from almost ten per cent in the 1880s to just over eight per cent in 1914. Despite all the complaint about officers' extravagancies, for an arm that provided a

---

Scottish and Irish. The equivalent of one cavalry brigade with each of these districts would have provided two cavalry divisions (each of three brigades) plus the divisional cavalry for six infantry divisions.

41   Vaughan, *Cavalry and Sporting Memories*, p. 161.
42   Jeffrey, *Field Marshal Sir Henry Wilson*, p. 86.
43   Charrington, *Where Cavalry Stands Today*, pp. 25–6; Badsey, 'Cavalry and the Development of Breakthrough Doctrine', pp. 138–74.
44   Vaughan, *Cavalry and Sporting Memories*, p. 151.

notional 14 per cent of the combat power of the BEF (one division out of seven) the regular cavalry was also quite cheap, its cost declining from seven per cent of the total cost of the Army in the 1880s to about five and a half per cent in 1914. When corrected for real prices, the Army Estimates more than doubled between 1871 and 1914, but the amount spent on the cavalry increased by only eighteen per cent.[45]

A belief which certainly existed at the time was that between 1904 and 1914 the cavalry branch provided a disproportionate number of senior officers for the British Army, and that their views in turn exercised undue influence. Haig's work, both with Haldane and later, led to his appointment as GOC Aldershot Command in 1912. French, who had held the same appointment 1902–1907, was respected by Haldane if not as closely involved with his reforms as Haig, and also well connected with Esher; in 1907 French was appointed Inspector General of the Forces in succession to the Duke of Connaught, and in 1912 he became CIGS.[46] The phenomenon of two cavalry officers who had worked closely together throughout their careers holding such influential posts inevitably led to French and Haig being viewed as some kind of two-man cavalry conspiracy, and certainly both men's views of the cavalry had to be taken into account in dealing with either of them. French made no secret of his continued commitment to the cavalry, habitually wearing a cavalry stock around his neck with his general's uniform, and carrying a riding whip.[47] As early as 1906 Henry Wilson, with remarkable cynicism, took the precaution of telling French that the cavalry should be an elite within the Army, getting the pick of the Sandhurst and Woolwich for its officers, and that French should himself succeed Kitchener as C-in-C India. To Wilson's delight, French responded that 'I must never fear living on half-pay, and he would see me given command of a brigade.'[48] This was the start of an increasingly close association between French and Wilson, of which Wilson's perspective was that he was dominating or controlling French.[49] To Roberts, whom he still habitually called his 'Chief', Wilson continued to show contempt for French both as a general and as a cavalry theorist.[50] In 1907 Wilson succeeded Rawlinson as Commandant of the Staff College, after some controversy about his suitability, but with support from both French and Roberts.[51]

In 1908 Haig reached an agreement with Wilson that there should be a specialist cavalry instructor at the Staff College, and requested Barrow from India.[52] According to Barrow's memory, on arrival he was told on Wilson's authority (Wilson himself not being present) that only three lectures a year would be given on cavalry, and those by the artillery specialist. This might just have been Wilson's idea of a joke, but Barrow tried to resign from his new post, only to be told by Haig that he wanted him in this

---

45   All these figures derive from TNA WO 112 Army Estimates 1871/2 to 1913/14; for detailed figures see the appendices of tables in Badsey, 'Fire and the Sword'.
46   Holmes, *The Little Field Marshal*, pp. 123–36.
47   Ibid., p. 151.
48   IWM Wilson Papers: Diary entry, 1 August 1906.
49   Ibid., Diary entries, 19 March 1912 and 22 September 1914.
50   NAM Roberts Papers 223: Wilson to Roberts, 27 March 1910.
51   Bond, *The Victorian Army and the Staff College*, pp. 244–6; Jeffrey, *Field Marshal Sir Henry Wilson*, pp. 64–6; IWM Wilson Papers: Diary entry, 9 October 1906.
52   IWM Wilson Papers: Diary entry, 31 March 1908.

position of influence precisely to counter what he saw as a negative view of the cavalry in Staff College thinking.[53] Within a year Barrow's entire teaching schedule at the Staff College was occupied with cavalry matters, and it was presumably from him that Staff College students in 1908, including Captain R.E. Cecil of the 21st Lancers, learned of the need for cavalry 'training in all arms so as to be independent in emergency, e.g. strategic cavalry pushed well to the front: must be able to cross rivers etc.'[54]

Although French and Haig continued to work together, and although both of them had influence to exert in the Army of the time, there is little in the pattern of appointments and promotions between 1904 and 1914 to suggest a dominant faction of cavalrymen. In 1905 Byng and Allenby were given 2nd and 4th Cavalry Brigades respectively, with Byng moving across to command 1st Cavalry Brigade at Aldershot in 1907.[55] In the same year, French secured for Scobell the position of Inspector General of Cavalry. As part of the Aldershot manoeuvres that year, for one two-day exercise French commanded the attacking troops against a notional defending force (represented chiefly by flag marking) commanded by Hubert Gough, who was only a lieutenant colonel. Gough boasted about the experience to his father:

> As a matter of fact I don't think it was a very difficult task to defeat Sir John. He knows, to my mind, *nothing* of the art of Grand Tactics – of combining the operations of any large masses. He still talks of the artillery duel and artillery preparation, which are worse than useless. The preparation for the decisive struggle *must* be done by both Infantry and Artillery. The Infantry *must* advance and *threaten* assault in order to force the defenders to expose themselves to artillery fire. His fronts were absurdly extended and he kept no reserves, and never settled on any one point that was decisive and then took pains to mass a preponderating [sic] force there. The result was that I could always hold him in the defensible localities and by massing beforehand a large reserve in some spot that I had *previously* selected, I could walk right through his Army. He always thought the defence of a position was one's only object, and not the defeat of the enemy, and he was perforce surprised when I suddenly assumed the *offensive*!!! His employment of cavalry, too, was very poor. In my last battle, I intended to break his centre and then finish off his left wing.[56]

This gives only Gough's perspective on the manoeuvres, but he was not the only officer of the period who thought that French was poor at commanding infantry, dispersing his troops and failing to keep a reserve as if he were still leading cavalry.[57] Gough's letter is also a valuable snapshot of Army training of the time: a promising

---

53 Barrow, *The Fire of Life*, pp. 111–12. But note that, writing in 1941, Barrow places the publication of Childers's *War and the Arme Blanche* as at the same time as this event, i.e. in 1908, rather than correctly in 1910, and his memory of events cannot be taken as exact.

54 NAM Cecil Papers: Staff College notebook c.1907–1908, p. 77.

55 Hughes, 'Edmund Allenby', p. 15; Gardner, 'Julian Byng', p. 55.

56 NAM Gough Papers 446: Hubert Gough to Charles Gough, not dated but posted 23 September 1907, emphasis in the original. In these exercises large bodies of troops were represented by a few soldiers carrying flags marking the corners and edges of the notional formations, who moved keeping the correct distances from each other.

57 BL Hutton Papers Add. 50086: Hutton to Wood, 26 November 1903.

middle-ranking officer like Gough was allowed notional command of a Corps, some eight years before he would command a Corps in reality on the Western Front. Although a cavalry officer, Gough had his own ideas on combined tactics, and great confidence in his own abilities; his identification of a decisive point is particularly important, as being identical to the German *Schwerpunkt* ('point of main effort'), a critical concept in later manoeuvre war theory.[58]

The new Cavalry Division came together for the first time for manoeuvres in 1908, but Scobell's attempt at handling it was so unenterprising that French as Inspector General of the Forces gave him a poor report, ending Scobell's career despite a long friendship.[59] One of French's criticisms of Scobell was that he had got the balance wrong between mounted and dismounted action, and that the Cavalry Division 'were worked too much like infantry'.[60] Hubert Gough, commanding the 16th Lancers as part of the 1st Cavalry Brigade, was particularly unimpressed with Scobell's approach.[61] Haig concurred, showing his disapproval of using cavalry dismounted for its own sake. 'The Cavalry Division dismounted with three brigades', Haig wrote, 'and formed for attack like infantry with "the object of deceiving the enemy". Question whether the risk was worth the results likely to be obtained; no commander would be likely to risk his reserve at the sight of a thousand men!'[62] Scobell's progress represents the closest thing to a case of French advancing the career of a cavalry officer out of 'friendship' or jobbery; but it had a clear limit when it conflicted with military competence. French's patronage of Haig was clearly based on professional competence as well as personal friendship. Even Edmonds, who seldom lost an opportunity to denigrate the cavalry, absolved Haig completely in the 1920s of pushing or promoting the careers of cavalry officers solely out of 'friendship' rather than competence.[63]

After Scobell's removal, Haig while continuing as DSD also took over as temporary Inspector General of Cavalry until his departure for India, with Allenby becoming Inspector General of Cavalry in 1910.[64] Hubert Gough doubled as Haig's chief staff officer for the 1909 cavalry manoeuvres (Hubert's brother John became Haig's chief staff officer at Aldershot Command in 1912), and Barrow also served on Haig's staff for these manoeuvres. Haig certainly helped advance Hubert Gough's career, but again only within the cavalry, and only as far as a brigade command before the First World War. Gough's views on the cavalry and the charge, given in early 1914, place him rather further in the traditionalist camp than Haig or French:

---

58 See e.g. Leonard, *The Art of Maneuver*, pp. 51–2.
59 NLS Haldane Papers 6109: French to Haldane, copied to Knollys, 16 September 1908; Holmes, *The Little Field Marshal*, pp. 129–30;
60 TNA WO 27/510 'State and efficiency of the Army and Defences. Reports by Inspector General of the Forces – submitted to the Army Council' (1904–1913), Inspection of the Cavalry Division 21–28 August 1908.
61 Gough, *Soldiering On*, pp. 91–2; Vaughan, *Cavalry and Sporting Memories*, p. 110.
62 NLS Haig Papers 2h: Diary entry, 28 August 1908.
63 AWM Bean Papers DRL 7953/34: Edmonds to Bean, 26 June 1929.
64 NLS Haig Papers 2i: Diary entry, 11 July 1909; Gough, *Soldiering On*, p. 95.

The rifle is a weapon which cavalry should know how to use, and I may say that the British cavalry certainly do know how to use it, but it is not the weapon with which they must normally seek their decisions. The decision can only be arrived at by closing with the enemy, and when cold steel comes into play.[65]

Haig also valued Henry Horne of the Royal Horse Artillery from their experiences together in the Boer War, but there is little to suggest that Haig played any real part in advancing Horne's career before 1914.[66] Another important gunner with the Cavalry Division of 1914 was the commander of an artillery brigade, Brigadier General Noel 'Curly' Birch, a Royal Horse Artillery officer and the author of a book on horsemanship. According to Barrow, Birch 'probably knew more about a horse at the beginning of the war than he did about any gun larger than a fifteen-pounder', (the guns that had been replaced by 13-pounders in the horse artillery).[67] Birch was to succeed Barrow in 1915 as chief staff officer of the Cavalry Corps under Allenby, before becoming chief artillery adviser to Rawlinson's Fourth Army for the Battle of the Somme in 1916 and then for Haig at GHQ. Another horse gunner who, with Birch and others, shaped the British artillery on the Western Front was Herbert Uniacke, whose first combat experience was in command of V Brigade RHA 1914–1915.[68]

Haig's report as acting Inspector General of Cavalry from his first cavalry staff ride in March 1909 taught that 'Occasions for charging will be few, but they occur – and the results from such actions will be immense. The mounted attack, therefore, must always be our ideal, our final objective.'[69] In his second staff ride in June, Haig added that on the specific issue of the close-order charge of cavalry against cavalry there was 'only one positive doctrine relative [relevant?] to the cavalry fight and that is: *Attack in close order, at the right time* and *against the right objective*. The rest will take care of itself.'[70] This 'right' time and objective would be inculcated in officers and troopers by training and by the shared doctrine of 'cavalry spirit', but everything else would remain the decision of the commander on the spot. According to Barrow, part of his duties was to write up these notes to reflect Haig's views. Barrow also commented after the war on the importance of these exercises, including the mass charge, not so much for their tactical value but for their importance in cultivating a shared doctrine:

The four cavalry brigades moving over the plain on a summer's day made up a superb picture that bore no resemblance to war as we came to know war not long afterwards. Not that these manoeuvres were wasted: they had the inestimable value of uniting staffs,

---

65 Gough, introduction to the English edition of Monsenergue, *Cavalry Tactical Schemes*, p. xvi.

66 Gough, *Soldiering On*, p. 95; Robbins, 'Henry Horne', pp. 97–9; Beckett, *Johnnie Gough VC*.

67 Barrow, *The Fire of Life*, pp. 145 and 154; Bidwell and Graham, *Fire-Power*, pp. 81–2.

68 Marble, 'Command of Artillery: the Case of Herbert Uniacke', pp. 195–212.

69 NLS Haig Papers 82: 'Report on a Cavalry staff ride held by the Director of Staff Duties 1st–6th March 1909'.

70 Ibid., 79: 'Report on the second cavalry staff ride held by the DSD 21–26 June 1909', p. 46, emphasis in the original.

commanders and regimental officers in continuity of method and mutual understanding, and strengthening the bond of comradeship that was a marked feature in the old pre-war cavalry and does so much towards lightening the load along the road to success.[71]

In September, just before leaving for India, Haig ran a last training exercise at the Cavalry School at Netheravon, after which French as Inspector General of the Forces summed up, paying what Haig recorded in his diary as something of a backhanded compliment:

> Attended meeting at 10.30 a.m. for brigadiers and c[ommanding] o[officer]s with Insp[ector] Gen[eral] of the Forces] (Sir J. French). Latter v[ery] complimentary to me – said I had nothing to gain from the extra work which I had undertaken in training the Cav[alry] Div[ision] etc etc, but gave vent to some terrible heresies such as chief use of Cav[alry] Div[ision] in battle is their rifle fire; led horses to be moved and men need not be close to them. Cavalry should *always* go for its adversary![72]

Unless Haig misunderstood French's remarks, this suggests that French was coming round to the view that dismounted action would prevail on the battlefield. Despite his personal compliments to Haig, in his report as Inspector General of the Forces at the end of 1909 French criticised the cavalry's dismounted work, and ordered that:

> Cavalry officers require also to familiarise themselves with the methods to be employed in a fire-fight.... I do not think [the cavalry] realise fully that the enormous advances in modern firearms have, to a large extent, modified, if not revolutionised, the methods to be adopted by cavalry when supporting other arms... [I hope] a somewhat wider and more far-reaching view may be taken of the possible action and tactics of dismounted men.[73]

This also suggests that by 1909 French's views on cavalry and their dismounted action had changed from the position that he had adopted in his dispute with Roberts. There does not appear to be any one moment at which French came to his new viewpoint; rather it seems to have emerged over time, possibly with Wilson as a contributory influence.

Rather than a pre-war Army dominated by cavalrymen, it was the associations originally formed within the Roberts Ring that continued as its single most significant group. But although Roberts remained politically highly active and influential, without his patronage as C-in-C the careers of some of his Ring members suffered, and it was natural for some of them to attribute their difficulties to 'the cavalrymen' who Roberts had already demonised. Rawlinson went to an infantry brigade at Aldershot in 1906, which after the heights of commanding the Staff College counted as a backwards step in his career. In 1907 de Lisle complained to Roberts that his candidacy for the post of Commandant of the Cavalry School was being blocked,

---

71 Barrow, *The Fire of Life*, pp. 117–18.

72 NLS Haig Papers 2i: Diary entry, 1 September 1909; emphasis in the original. In this context 'commanding officers' means lieutenant colonels commanding the cavalry regiments.

73 TNA WO 27/510 'State and Efficiency of the Army and Defences. Reports by Inspector General of the Forces – submitted to the Army Council' (1904–1913), Report for 1909.

he believed by Haig; he was appointed instead as second-in-command and then commanding officer of the 1st (Royal) Dragoons in India, itself a remarkable thing for an officer who had transferred so late from an unfashionable infantry regiment.[74] In 1909 de Lisle returned to Great Britain as chief staff officer of the 2nd Division; 30 years later he recounted in his memoirs (with what accuracy it is hard to judge) a story of how he had first asked for a cavalry brigade and been refused by French as Inspector General of the Forces, on the grounds that as a believer in the rifle rather than the arme blanche he might damage the cavalry, only to have Smith-Dorrien act as his patron in securing his staff appointment (not that French or Smith-Dorrien actually had this authority).[75] In 1907 Robertson's job at the War Office ended, and he also made a surprising request for the command of a cavalry brigade. Robertson had begun his career in the 16th Lancers as a private in 1877 and had been commissioned into the 3rd Dragoon Guards in 1888, but since 1891 all his appointments had been on the staff, and he had no real connections with the cavalry. He was instead given another staff appointment, as assistant quartermaster general at Aldershot. Robertson never referred to the matter again, and Wilson attributed Robertson's failure to get his cavalry brigade to Lyttelton as CIGS, rather than to the influence of any cavalry general.[76] Ian Hamilton's career continued to progress very well: after serving as GOC Southern Command on his return from Japan, he became Adjutant General in 1909. But Hamilton was by then very much his own man, his final break with Roberts coming in 1911 when he publicly opposed peacetime conscription, of which Roberts with his National Service League was the leading advocate.[77] The same era saw the rise to prominence of officers who had no particular connection either with the old Roberts Ring or with the cavalry, including Plumer, who recovered from the near-wreck of his career in 1905 to become GOC Northern Command in 1911, and Grierson, who became DMO in the Esher reforms and GOC Eastern Command in 1912.

One of the most significant appointments for the future of the BEF was that of Smith-Dorrien to Aldershot Command in 1907, recommended (or so he believed) by both French and Kitchener.[78] Smith-Dorrien's skills in training troops complemented those of French and Haig, but he continued to hold quite different views on cavalry. After Scobell's 1908 manoeuvres, Smith-Dorrien wrote to Roberts that 'I think that at the Aldershot manoeuvres the cavalry got in some most excellent reconnaissance as well as a lot of dismounted work and that they proved themselves most capable of doing it', an opinion which contrasts very sharply with the criticisms of Scobell made

---

74 NAM Roberts Papers 221: de Lisle to Roberts, 25 November 1907; de Lisle, *Reminiscences of Sport and War*, p. 122.

75 de Lisle, *Reminiscences of Sport and War*, pp. 214–16; according to de Lisle, French offered him an infantry brigade instead.

76 IWM Wilson Papers: Diary entries, 11 October 1906 and 31 December 1906; Robertson's own memoirs make no mention of a cavalry brigade but say that he expected to become the chief staff officer at one of the Home commands, see Robertson, *From Private To Field Marshal*, pp. 152–3.

77 Adams and Poirier, *The Conscription Controversy in Great Britain 1900–18*, pp. 44–5.

78 Smith-Dorrien, *Memories of Forty Eight Years' Service*, p. 339.

by French, Haig and Gough.[79] But this story is complicated by later contradictory evidence from Smith-Dorrien. The hand-over of Aldershot Command from French to Smith-Dorrien, two men of mercurial temperament, was always likely to produce some difficulties, but Smith-Dorrien had forgotten about his letter praising Scobell's manoeuvres when, many years later, he claimed in his memoirs:

> I was, therefore, not at all pleased to find that the Cavalry Brigade at Aldershot were low down on the annual musketry courses, and further, on fields days and manoeuvres, hardly ever dismounted, but delivered perfectly carried out, although impossible, knee to knee charges against infantry in action. So, on 21st August 1909, ordering all cavalry officers to meet me in the 16th Lancers Mess, I gave them my views pretty clearly, with the result that dismounted work was taken up seriously, and the improvement in musketry was so marked that the cavalry went nearly to the head of the lists in the Annual Musketry.[80]

There is more than a hint in this passage of Smith-Dorrien settling old scores. He neglected to mention Haig's work as Inspector General of Cavalry, and it is also a factor that in 1909 the commander of the 1st Cavalry Brigade was Byng and the commanding officer of the 16th Lancers was Hubert Gough, both of whose careers as Army commanders on the Western Front flourished after Smith-Dorrien's removal. A reasonable assessment is that between them – and whatever their differences – all these men helped improve the cavalry's standards. De Lisle, back in Great Britain from India and about to take over as chief staff officer of 2nd Division, considered that at the 1909 cavalry manoeuvres 'I saw a marked advance in training to anything I had previously witnessed.'[81]

On the eve of the First World War, cavalrymen held the two most important field commands that the Army had to offer: French as designated GOC-in-C of the BEF and Haig as GOC Aldershot Command. But otherwise, there was nothing to suggest a domination of the Army by cavalrymen. Of the former Roberts Ring members, Ian Hamilton was Inspector General of Overseas Forces, Wilson held the influential position of DMO, and Rawlinson was GOC 3rd Division (going on half-pay in May 1914). Grierson was still at Eastern Command, Plumer at Northern Command, and Smith-Dorrien had moved to Southern Command. Of the outstanding cavalrymen of the Boer War, Allenby was Inspector General of Cavalry and designated GOC Cavalry Division, and Rimington was Inspector General of Cavalry in India, but Byng was given a TF division in 1910 and made C-in-C Egypt in 1912. Broadwood was put on half pay in 1913, as was Charles 'Black Jack' Kavanagh, who had established a good reputation serving under French in South Africa and who had succeeded Byng in command of the 10th Hussars and then in command of 1st Cavalry Brigade.[82] Of the five brigades of the Cavalry Division in 1914, three were commanded by Beauvoir de Lisle, Hubert Gough, and Charles Briggs (the last commander of the

---

79 NAM Roberts Papers 223: Smith-Dorrien to Roberts, 26 September 1908.
80 Smith-Dorrien, *Memories of Forty Eight Years' Service*, p. 359.
81 NAM Roberts papers 223: de Lisle to French, 12 October 1909.
82 For French's opinion of Kavanagh see Wessels (ed.), *Lord Roberts and the War in South Africa 1899–1902*, pp. 228–9.

Imperial Light Horse in the Boer War), and the remaining two by Cis Bingham and Philip Chetwode.

In the Army as a whole in 1914, also, there was also nothing to suggest any domination by cavalrymen. Excluding honorary appointments, of 8 field marshals only 2 were cavalrymen, John French and Evelyn Wood (who had long since retired).[83] Of 18 serving full generals just one, Haig, was a cavalryman; of 27 lieutenant generals 3 were cavalrymen, and of 114 major generals 8 were cavalrymen: 7 per cent of the total, which was entirely consistent with the proportion of cavalry in the Army and in the BEF.[84] This should be compared with the 2 generals, 3 lieutenant generals and 19 major generals in 1914 who had served at some point in their careers in the mounted infantry.[85]

At first after Roberts's departure as C-in-C in early 1904, a conscious effort was made to maintain the consensus reached by senior officers about the cavalry's tactics, and to repair the damage done to its morale by the arguments of the previous years. Ian Hamilton as GOC Southern Command in particular had come to appreciate that the cavalry, given contradictory rulings in training exercises, had become uncertain and hesitant in their behaviour. 'The fact is that they are afraid of umpires', Hamilton acknowledged after the 1907 manoeuvres, 'If they charge, some umpires will declare them all dead men. If they dismount and use their rifles, other umpires will accuse them of having lost the Cavalry Spirit, which in peacetime seems to them even worse than annihilation.'[86] This was true; an infantry officer serving as an umpire at the same manoeuvres complained at what seemed to him to be the cavalry's inappropriate addiction to mounted charges:

> What impressed me as an infantryman was the number of times squadrons advanced against entrenched positions mounted. These tactics seemed impossible, dismounted action being the only chance of success against entrenchments held by modern rifle fire, and where dismounted action was used it was generally successful, but the cavalry soldier seemed very loath to leave his horse.[87]

Unfortunately, this account did not expound on whether the cavalry used supporting fire, extended formations, or manoeuvred to attack these entrenchments from a flank; some cavalry charges against entrenched infantry certainly succeed in the First World War. One aggrieved cavalry officer hit back in *The Cavalry Journal* at the insistence that dismounted action was the only realistic battlefield tactic for the

---

83 Evelyn Wood was 75 years old in 1914, but remained on the active list like all field marshals, and he was a marginal case as a 'cavalryman' having served in several regiments. Curiously, both Wood and John French had begun their careers in the Royal Navy as midshipmen.

84 These figures are derived from the *Army List* for 1913–1914, and from TNA WO 112 Army Estimates 1912/13 to 1913/14; see also Terraine, *The Smoke and the Fire*, pp. 161–9; Badsey, 'Cavalry and the Development of Breakthrough Doctrine', pp. 138–74.

85 'The passing of the old MI', *The Cavalry Journal*, Volume 9, Number 34, pp. 209–11.

86 NAM Roberts Papers 223: 'Copy of notes on Manoeuvres 1907 by Sir Ian Hamilton, 1 September 1907'.

87 Letham, 'Impressions of an Infantry Officer at the Cavalry Manoeuvres 1907', *The Cavalry Journal*, Volume 3, Number 9, p. 55.

cavalry, 'to such pernicious and absurd lengths has this so-called lesson (sic!) of South Africa been carried, that our cavalry officers will now throw themselves off their horses at once on seeing, or even *hearing* of an enemy'.[88] The new Maxim or Vickers machine-guns, sometimes grouped together at brigade level, were a particular source of stories about bewildered young officers who had somehow failed to read their superiors' minds on exercise, including the celebrated (if perhaps apocryphal) rebuke by one commanding officer, 'Can't you see I'm busy? Take the damn things to a flank and hide them!' which was of course the correct thing to do.[89] Lieutenant (Edward) Louis Spiers of the 11th Hussars recalled that in one exercise at Aldershot as 1st Cavalry Brigade machine-gun officer he simulated firing all six machine-guns at the brigade, stationary and mounted in close order, for ten minutes at 1,000 yards, while they sat and ignored him. When Lieutenant Spiers informed Brigadier General Kavanagh that he had just wiped his command out twice over, he was denounced for lack of cavalry spirit (or possibly for interfering in the middle of a complicated exercise) and forced to walk home as a punishment.[90]

This uncertainty among officers about what the correct role of cavalry was, and what was expected of them from their superiors, spread throughout the rest of the Army. By 1910 the examiners for promotion of junior officers to the rank of captain complained that in the answers to one tactical problem:

> Scarcely any of the candidates appeared to realise that the cavalry are meant to fight just as much as the artillery or the infantry. When the advance guard commenced its attack, orders were sent to the cavalry to... do everything except to attack the enemy in conjunction with the other arms.[91]

Barrow, back in India in 1912 to command the 35th Scinde Horse, complained that on manoeuvres 'Nobody seemed to know what to do' with the cavalry, 'and got out of the difficulty by giving it a free hand.'[92] This perhaps encouraged initiative and cavalry spirit, but did little to promote understanding of what was expected of the cavalry. When Barrow's command of the regiment ended in 1914 he was succeeded by John Shea.

Barrow had given up his post as cavalry instructor at the Staff College in 1911 because, with a larger family, he could not afford the expense of remaining at Camberley, and had to return to India.[93] The shortage and rapid turnover of cavalry

---

88 'Further Letters on Cavalry: Not by Prince Kraft', *The Cavalry Journal*, Volume 5, Number 18, p. 152.
89 Holmes, *Riding the Retreat*, p. 58.
90 Spears, *The Picnic Basket*, p. 79 (Spiers later changed his name to Edward L. Spears). If taken literally, Spiers's claim involved firing six guns at their standard rate of fire of 250 rounds a minute, or 15,000 rounds in ten minutes, quite enough to cause over 2,000 casualties to mounted troops stationary and closed up at a known range of 1,000 yards. However, a cavalry brigade coming under fire from grouped machine-guns at 1,000 yards would have opened out and charged the guns from several directions at once, which was perhaps Kavanagh's point.
91 CUL Official Publications Room: 'Reports on the results of examinations held of officers of Regular Forces.' 1910, Captains, p. 26.
92 Barrow, *The Fire of Life*, p. 130.
93 Ibid., p. 121.

officers persisted, closely linked to poor morale following Roberts's attacks on the cavalry and the subsequent confusion over doctrine. In 1904 in cavalry regiments, up to 70 per cent of troop officer posts, supposed to be held by a lieutenant, were being held instead by non-commissioned officers.[94] Next year the cavalry were allowed the expedient of 'probationer' officers: following a custom that was well-established in the Guards and Household regiments but frowned upon by reformers, this allowed civilian nominees of officers already serving in cavalry regiments to be commissioned directly into those regiments without prior training, and to serve for two years before taking any formal examination.[95] Rather than having a choice even of money or brains, the Army was forced to accept these cavalry officers solely on the basis of who their 'friends' were. This removed almost any incentive for junior cavalry officers to pass through Sandhurst, where by 1912 a cavalry subaltern was thought 'as rare as a black pearl'.[96] At the time of the Curragh Incident in March 1914 the regiments of 3rd Cavalry Brigade involved – the 16th Lancers, 4th Hussars and 5th Lancers – had respectively 16, 19 and 20 officers serving, against an authorised higher establishment of 26 officers and a lower establishment of 23 officers.[97]

A factor highlighted by the Curragh Incident was that almost all the cavalry officers involved were not only independently minded by inclination but financially in a position to quit their jobs if they chose to do so (although some expected to be compensated or expressed concerns about their pensions). This point was made exactly by Tom Bridges of the 4th Dragoon Guards when he wrote that many officers were threatening to resign their commissions over the incident, and 'the Cavalry should take the lead – not only because they should be more ready to take risks but it is not a question of bread and butter to them and they can afford to be scapegoats if necessary'.[98] This financial independence continued to be a powerful restraining influence on any attempts at reform that did not have the support of the regiments.

In 1906 the third and final edition of *Small Wars* by Charles Callwell, now a colonel, appeared, with a preface by Lyttelton as Chief of the General Staff giving it considerable official authority, although in a manner characteristic of British doctrine, Lyttelton's preface 'recommended' the book while stipulating that 'it is not to be regarded as laying down inflexible rules for guidance, or as an expression of official opinion'.[99] In this 1906 edition, Callwell continued to insist on the unusual fighting characteristics of the Boers, and provided a critical interpretation of mounted

---

94 TNA WO 27/509 'State and Efficiency of the Army and Defences. Reports by Inspector General of the Forces – submitted to the Army Council' (1903–1913), Report for 1904.

95 'T.M.P.' 'A Proposal for Officering Cavalry Regiments', *United Service Magazine*, Volume XXXIII, New Series, pp. 503–8; TNA WO 163/10 'Minutes of Proceedings and Précis Prepared for the Army Council', (1905), Précis Number 191, pp. 236–42; TNA WO 163/611 'Recommendations of Committees on Army Matters 1900–1920', p. 179.

96 'F.O.', 'Military Officers' Education', *United Service Magazine*, Volume XLV, New Series, pp. 188–92.

97 Beckett, *The Army and the Curragh Incident, 1914*, pp. 79–80; Grierson, *Scarlet into Khaki*, p. 44.

98 Quoted in Beckett, *The Army and the Curragh Incident, 1914*, p. 274.

99 Lyttelton, preface (no pagination) to Callwell, *Small Wars*, 1906 edition.

operations in South Africa with which few of the cavalry participants would have agreed:

> [The Boers] were mounted rifles who fought dismounted, and the result of months of warfare in which some of the finest cavalry in the world was pitted against them, was that they, irregulars as they were, and to all extents and purposes untrained in the art of war, compelled the cavalry to transform itself into mounted rifles.[100]

But Callwell had retreated somewhat from the position that he had put forward in 1903 in *The Tactics of Today*, and in *Small Wars* he walked a careful line in maintaining the new consensus. He managed to support *Cavalry Training 1904* as applicable to colonial warfare, while insisting that, whatever might be happening in 'regular warfare' the value of the cavalry shock charge remained very high 'against irregular warriors'.[101] Callwell also continued to recommend the importance for the cavalry of combining mounted and dismounted fighting in irregular warfare, and co-operation between cavalry and mounted rifles.

In 1907 a new *Cavalry Training* was issued, in an attempt to put behind the cavalry the 1904 manual and the bad feelings associated with it. *Cavalry Training 1907* kept most of the previous manual, and included a statement on the nature of mounted and dismounted combat which reflected the consensus within the Army:

> In modern war numerous difficulties will present themselves which cannot be overcome by mounted action, and which demand the employment of rifle fire. The employment of mounted action is, for example, precluded against an enemy posted behind entrenchments or occupying intersected or broken ground... As it may be beyond the power of cavalry to achieve success in such operations by shock action, squadrons must be able to attack on foot *when the situation imperatively demands it*... [T]horough efficiency in the use of the rifle and in dismounted tactics is an absolute necessity. At the same time, the essence of the cavalry spirit lies in holding the balance correctly between fire power and shock action, and while training troops for the former they must not be allowed to lose confidence in the latter.
>
> Experience in war and peace teaches us that the average leader is only too ready to resort to dismounted action which often results in acting defensively. It is of importance to lay stress during peace training on the necessity for *offensive* tactics for cavalry even when fighting on foot.[102]

But this was followed by a passage which, taken both from this context, and from the wider context of the attempts to revive the cavalry's morale and establish a coherent doctrine, became notorious:

> It must be accepted as a principle that the rifle, effective as it is, cannot replace the effect produced by the speed of the horse, the magnetism of the charge, and the terror of cold steel. For when opportunities for mounted action occur, these characteristics combine to produce such dash, enthusiasm, and moral ascendancy that cavalry is rendered irresistible.

---

100 Callwell, *Small Wars*, pp. 412–13.
101 Ibid., p. 404.
102 *Cavalry Training 1907*, pp. 186–7, emphasis in the original.

It is this which explains the success of many of the apparent 'impossibilities' of cavalry action in the past.[103]

The author of these passages is not known, but the responsibility undoubtedly lay with Haig as DMT, and *Cavalry Training 1907* shows several hints of his writing style and personal ideas. As an evocation of cavalry spirit it bears comparison to Roberts's supposed exhortation prior to the relief of Kimberley, and was evidently written with much the same intention of restoring the cavalry's battered self esteem. It might not have attracted much attention, except that the sentence beginning 'It must be accepted...' was seized upon by Erskine Childers as the opening text for his book *War and the Arme Blanche*, as the epitome of everything that was at fault with the cavalry.[104] Subsequently this passage has been repeated out of context by historians who have viewed it (from the other side of the trench deadlock of the Western Front) either with humorous disbelief as their proof that Haig and all other British cavalry officers were incompetent fools, or with sad apology if they have understood better the realities of the tactical debate prior to 1914.[105] It was a massive overstatement, the cavalry's reaction to all they had endured including repeated inaccurate claims about the obsolescence of the charge. But it was also a temporary expedient that was removed from Army doctrine well before the First World War.

The new *Cavalry Training 1907* was accompanied by a series of small changes reversing some of Roberts's decisions, made with the aim of restoring cavalry morale, but also undertaken with restraint so as not to outrage or alienate those officers who had sided with Roberts. Over a period of six years, the lance was reintroduced for lancer regiments as a weapon of war. First, in 1906 ten lances were allowed per squadron 'for recreative purposes'. Then in the 1907 manoeuvres French let the lancer regiments of the 1st Cavalry Brigade at Aldershot, by then commanded by Byng, collectively defy orders by carrying their lances, and the Duke of Connaught as Inspector General of the Forces expressed his sympathies with their action. Eighteen months later the Army Council was invited to reconsider the matter, and a new drill was put forward which made it easier for lancers to dismount, leaving the lance in the rifle bucket as they did so. The lance was officially re-introduced for peacetime training in 1909, but not as part of wartime equipment until 1912.[106] As evidence that this restoration of the lance was a matter of morale rather than tactics, dragoon guard and dragoon regiments serving with the BEF were allowed to give up the lance altogether rather than retaining it for their first rank. It is not entirely clear even from regimental records which regiments actually gave up the lance; the 5th Dragoon Guards expressed a certain relief to be rid of this weapon, but dragoon

---

103 Ibid., p. 187.
104 Childers, *War and the Arme Blanche*, pp. 1–3.
105 Luvaas, *The Military Legacy of the Civil War*, p. 197; Ellis, *Eye Deep in Hell*, p. 84; Holmes, *Riding the Retreat*, p. 61 describes the passage as 'Not quite the folly it seemed.'
106 TNA WO 123/48 Army Orders (War Office) 258 (1906); WO 123/51 158 (1909); WO 123/54 (1912); WO 27/510 'State and Efficiency of the Army and Defences. Reports by Inspector General of the Forces – submitted to the Army Council' (1904–1913), Report for 1907; WO 163/14 Army Council Decisions, (1909), Number 419, pp. 71–2.

guard and dragoon regiments serving in India appear to have kept the Indian Army practice of maintaining one lancer squadron out of four in the regiment.[107]

In 1903, after the experience of the Boer War, a committee under French had proposed a new cavalry sword, but this had been turned down by Roberts on grounds of cost, at the time an apparently ominous decision. In 1906 a second committee under Scobell agreed on a better sword design: officially introduced as the 1908 pattern cavalry sword (with slight differences between the designs for officers and troopers) and intended principally for thrusting, this turned out to be one of the better swords ever designed for warfare.[108] As a final gesture, even the cavalry trumpet calls were re-introduced in 1909.[109]

As well as the new *Cavalry Training*, in 1907 Haig published his *Cavalry Studies*, a book based on his staff rides while Inspector General of Cavalry in India. This was written with the assistance of Lonsdale Hale, and contained borrowings from a number of military writers including some from France; Barrow also later wrote that part of the book was copied directly from the notes that he wrote up for Haig on his staff rides. This use of surrogates was not unusual for a busy senior officer, and *Cavalry Studies* may be taken as a fair statement of Haig's views, if not entirely the product of his own original thinking.[110] At the start of the book, Haig argued that 'the role of cavalry will always go on increasing', giving his reasons in list form:

1. The extended nature of the modern battlefield means that there will be a greater choice of cover to favour the concealed approach of cavalry.
2. The increased range and killing power of modern guns, and the great length of time during which battles will last, will augment the moral exhaustion, which will affect the men's nerves more, and produce more demoralisation amongst the troops. These factors contribute to provoke panic, and to render troops (short service soldiers nowadays) ripe for attack by cavalry.
3. The longer the range and killing power of modern arms, the more important will rapidity of movement become, because it lessens the relative time of exposure to danger in favour of the cavalry.
4. The introduction of the small-bore rifle, the bullet from which has little stopping-power against a horse.[111]

If Haig had written 'mobile troops' instead of 'cavalry', later generations would have viewed this as nothing but a reasonable prediction of future war. As it was, it

---

107 Pomeroy, *The Story of a Regiment of Horse*, Volume I, p. 270.

108 *Elgin Commission Report*, p. 94; TNA WO 163/10 'Minutes of Proceedings and Précis Prepared for the Army Council', (1905), Précis Number 156, p. 72; TNA WO 163/611 'Recommendations of Committees on Army Matters 1900–1920', 1908, p. 11.

109 TNA WO 163/14 Army Council Decisions, 1909, Number 608, pp. 424–5.

110 See Barrow, *The Fire of Life*, p. 105; Anglesey, *A History of the British Cavalry Volume 4*, p. 389. One example is that Haig, *Cavalry Studies*, pp. 66–9 are part of the English translation of a series of lectures given to the French Ecole de Guerre: TNA WO 33/54 'Digest of Colonel Cherfils' Lectures on Cavalry Tactics at the Ecole de Guerre, 1892–1893'. These papers would have been available to Haig at some time in his career, possibly at the Army Staff College, Camberley.

111 Haig, *Cavalry Studies*, p. 8.

has become another of the passages repeatedly cited as evidence of Haig's stupidity, or his irrational attachment to the horse, or at best his lack of a clear vision of the future.[112] But in 1907 no other forms of mobile troops were realistically available, in Great Britain or India. Haig's statement was not an arme blanche fanatic's fantasy; it was a summary of the case for the tactics that the cavalry were still developing: the use of cover for comparatively small units to advance, the use of surprise, the use of speed, and the fact that in practice a charging horse was a hard thing to kill.

After the 1908 manoeuvres Ian Hamilton explained to Southern Command (with difficulty as he swallowed his personal views), some of the reasoning behind this new consensus in doctrine, and why there might still be a role for mounted tactics:

> Without for a moment touching on the controversial question of cavalry being capable or incapable of 'getting home' against modern fire-arms, it will be admitted on all sides that they will do well, whenever they have the option, to choose the lesser of two evils and not the greater. Now although the modern rifle may be taken for general purposes to be several times as effective as it was in 1870, still, when the increased resisting power of infantry against cavalry shock tactics is brought under discussion, there are several saving clauses which must be placed on the other side of the balance. Thus, taking the rifle itself, there is good reason to believe that the present .303 bullet, with its complete cupro-nickel envelope, is less capable of stopping a horse than the .577 or .45 leaden bullet which preceded it. Again, it is unquestionable that, since the days of the Franco-Prussian War, infantry have been forced by other considerations to weaken their powers of resistance to shock and run some serious risks in respect of the dangers of a charge. Firing lines, for instance, are much less in hand than formerly; extensions are infinitely wider and, the depth of formations also being greater, formed supports are considerably further from the front than they used to be.[113]

Whatever his real opinion, Hamilton certainly shared the common desire to restore the cavalry's morale and officer recruiting levels. He noted with pleasure at the same manoeuvres that the cavalry had lost its tendency to hang back uncertainly, and saw reason to hope that 'the heated controversies of the past few years as to the respective merits of fire and shock tactics are at last cooling down to the sensible conclusion that there may be room on the battlefield for either or both'.[114] This was while supposedly, as Childers put it with characteristically exuberant overstatement, Hamilton 'drives or is trying to drive a coach and pair through the [1907] cavalry drill book – all honour to him!'[115] De Lisle also expressed the same view as Hamilton in 1908, in one of a series of articles:

> Some of our best officers… fearing that modern reformers were attacking the principal weapon of the cavalry, felt obliged to defend the future importance of the sword,

---

112 See J.F.C. Fuller, introduction to Wolff, *In Flanders Fields*, p. xiii; Marshall-Cornwall, *Haig as Military Commander*, p. 65; Anglesey, *A History of the British Cavalry Volume 4*, p. 389.

113 'Tactical Training', *United Service Magazine*, Volume XXXVIII, New Series, pp. 302–3.

114 'Notes' in *The Cavalry Journal*, Volume 3, Number 9, p. 117.

115 NAM Roberts Papers 222: Childers to Roberts, 10 August 1909.

sometimes perhaps beyond their own convictions. The dispute is now happily at an end, and a sensible mean has been reached to which both parties in the encounter were aiming, namely, a proper appreciation of both weapons, fire and steel, and an equal ability to use the right one at the right time.[116]

French entirely agreed with these sentiments. Chairing a talk at the Royal United Service Institution in 1906 by Brigadier General Edward Bethune (late of the 16th Lancers and Bethune's Mounted Infantry in the Boer War), French warned that 'one amateur centaur would dash the sword and lance entirely out of the cavalryman's hand, while another (Beau Sabreur) would throw the horseman's splendid fire-arm to the wind'.[117]

The establishment of this new consensus on cavalry tactics among senior officers (at least in public and in front of their men) did not mean the end of the controversy, or anything like the end. The issue was still a very lively one in the military press as a fresh generation of officers discovered it and aired their views, particularly in *The Cavalry Journal*. But little had changed, or could change, about the basic arguments since the 1880s: firepower and ranges had increased massively, cavalry charges sometimes worked and sometimes did not, and in practice there were too many variables involved in each separate episode for anyone to say why. There was the same tendency from both sides to overstate a good case or employ provocation, the same emphasis from the cavalrymen on the value of examples from actual combat rather than theoretical models, the same arguments about the preservation of mobility, aggression and morale through the arme blanche against the realities of firepower – and, rapidly, the same complaints about an overworked subject. The consensus among those publishing in *The Cavalry Journal* was very much in favour of the doctrinal compromise, emphasising the importance of dismounted action and how much it helped the cavalry's attacking power. In typical passages, one officer wrote only that it was possible to use the rifle well 'without losing the cavalry spirit', while another went further in arguing that 'Cavalry will only succeed on condition that it knows how to make best use of all its means, and does not confound *Cavalry Spirit* with the unreasoning obstinacy of wishing only to fight mounted.'[118] At the same time, as another argued, 'Cavalry which is taught in peace to have a belief in mounted action, the *arme blanche* and shock tactics, will be likely, *now and then*, to take a reasonable risk to achieve a great end.'[119]

---

116 Ibid., 223: Article by de Lisle, 'Letters of an Old Cavalry Officer to his son – 4'.

117 French in discussion of E.C. Bethune, 'Uses of Cavalry and Mounted Infantry in Modern War', *Journal of the Royal United Service Institution*, Volume 50, p. 633. 'Beau Sabreur' is a French expression very difficult to translate, meaning literally 'Handsome Swordsman'.

118 'A rough British military summary by an Indian Army officer', *United Service Magazine*, Volume XXXVIII, New Series, p. 80; Review of 'Cavalry in Action in Wars of the Future', *The Cavalry Journal*, Volume 1, Number 2, p. 194.

119 'Notrofe' [pseudonym], *Cavalry Taught by Experience*, p. 62; emphasis in the original. This book, which is based on the format of the much better known (and better written) Swinton, *The Defence of Duffer's Drift*, has been attributed to Haig, but apparently without any reason;

The spirit of aggression, enterprise and sacrifice shared by all these writers and their brother officers was not just rhetoric. According to Barrow, writing in 1906, 'According to theories of trajectory, energy, penetrative intensity, rapidity of fire and ballistics, there should long ago have ceased to be any place for cavalry on the battlefield', adding that, 'Cavalry must be prepared to face heavy losses, to suffer annihilation, if victory is gained thereby.'[120] In 1910 in *The Cavalry Journal*, in a passage which does much to convey just what cavalry spirit meant to the average officer, breathless scorn was poured by one major (a Staff College graduate) on the whole notion of analysing combat when compared to the glories of the charge, 'The theories of today are oft the falsehoods of yesterday! War oft makes of them lasting heresies! Damn theories, let us remain practical! Attack – attack quickly – attack persistently and tenaciously. Keep on the "attack" and chance the casualties'.[121] Extravagant as such an outburst may appear, and evidence of the inarticulate dogmatism for which the cavalry were so often blamed, it was also a reflection of the high morale that the cavalry would need in the event of a European war. On mobilisation in 1914 Briggs as GOC 1st Cavalry Brigade at Aldershot told his regimental commanders that they must expect to suffer 50 per cent casualties in the first week of fighting.[122] It was very well understood that a cavalry charge against European troops, particularly if made in close order, carried with it the likelihood of high casualties whether it succeeded or failed. But the response of many traditionalist cavalry officers to this amounted to a shrug of the shoulders; they would genuinely rather have risked death than be seen to fail the traditions and ethos of the cavalry, and on the Western Front they had the chance to prove it.

In 1911, editorship of *The Cavalry Journal* became one of the duties of the commandant of the Netheravon Cavalry School. As the idea of a future war in which Great Britain would be allied to France and opposed to Germany (although of course this was not officially British government policy) began to permeate through Army thinking, so writers became increasingly concerned about the nature of the cavalry's task in such a war. There was a strong argument to be made that, since the British cavalry would be very inferior in numbers to its enemies, it should concentrate on scouting. As Hubert Gough pointed out, 'if the cavalry failed in every other duty but reconnaissance and did get information, they would be a most valuable arm'.[123] But the preservation of the cavalry for scouting also implied an approach favouring dismounted action. 'Are our two or three brigades of cavalry to go on charging and annihilating division after division of German cavalry', one officer wanted to know,

---

the present British Library catalogue identifies 'Notrofe' as Ernest Frederick Orton (name and initials reversed).

120 Barrow, 'The Spirit of Cavalry', *The Cavalry Journal*, Volume 1, Number 1, p. 19.

121 Haag, 'Contact Squadron', *Cavalry Journal*, Volume 5, Number 19, p. 313. The author was Major Emil Haag of the 18th Hussars.

122 Lumley, *The History of the Eleventh Hussars*, p. 22.

123 Gough quoted in *The Question of Mounted Infantry – by a Rifleman*, p. 13. The author of this book is identified by Holmes, *Riding the Retreat*, p. 62 as Major F.M. Crum, who served with the King's Royal Rifle Corps, including its mounted infantry contingent in the Boer War.

reasonably enough, 'and still remain a serviceable arm?'[124] There was no easy or obvious answer to this question.

Although the British still studied the French cavalry and their doctrines, they were more than a little suspicious of a French approach that seemed predicated on charging mounted regardless, and of the Ecole de Guerre teachings that it did not matter what weapons the defending infantry carried 'if they can no longer use them and fear conquers the soul'.[125] When Spiers translated one French theorist with the sole object of establishing a reputation for himself, he was mildly rebuked in the *United Service Magazine* for subscribing to the more extreme French arme blanche cult.[126] When in 1909 the French announced that it was only by means of their 13 cuirassier regiments, complete with helmet, breastplate, and sword (but no firearm other than a pistol), 'that we shall be able to give ourselves elbow room' for manoeuvre, British officers writing in *The Cavalry Journal* noted carefully that 'this remains to be seen', and looked askance at the French 'robust and perhaps fanatical faith in the importance of shock tactics'.[127] At least in print, no British officers agreed with two French light cavalrymen that dismounted action was fit only for cavalrymen 'too scared, old or worn out to gallop'.[128] Nor did any British general echo the observation in 1912 to his troops by General Sordet (whose cavalry corps was to play an important role in co-operation with the BEF in 1914) that the only cavalry tactic of which infantry needed to be afraid was the charge.[129] However, all these pronouncements from a major European power and potential ally were more than welcome to any traditionalist cavalrymen who continued to believe in the mounted charge as their foremost if not their only tactic.

British attitudes towards German ideas on cavalry were much more respectful. In 1914 the German cavalry still practised divisional-sized charges against infantry, and rather than giving their cavalry rifles relied on Jäger infantry battalions accompanying their cavalry divisions to provide firepower.[130] The idea of dismounted firepower and a balance between fire and shock had made some headway in the German Army in the early 1900s, particularly through the writings of General Frederick von

---

124 'The British Cavalry: by One of Them', *United Service Magazine*, Volume XXXIII, New Series, p. 315; Buckley-Johnson, 'Cavalry Organisation – a Suggestion', *The Cavalry Journal*, Volume 2, Number 7, p. 339.

125 TNA WO 33/629, 'Cavalry Tactics', translation of the Ecole de Guerre Lectures 1913, Volume I, p. 13. The Ecole de Guerre ('War School') was broadly the French equivalent of the Staff College.

126 Spears, *The Picnic Basket*, p. 73; Review of 'Tactical Schemes', *United Service Magazine*, Volume XLVIII, New Series, p. 691.

127 Lowther, 'The French Cavalry', *The Cavalry Journal*, Volume 4, Number 14, p. 196; 'Cavalry in France and Germany 1909', *The Cavalry Journal*, Volume 5, Number 18, p. 222.

128 Quoted in *The Cavalry Journal*, Volume 8, Number 29, p. 94 from a French journal – the original in French sounds even better: 'plus timides, agés ou fatigués qu'ils ne gallopent plus'.

129 'French Manoeuvres in 1912', *The Cavalry Journal*, Volume 9, Number 33, p. 107.

130 Hensman, 'Some impressions of German manoeuvres', *United Service Magazine*, Volume XXXIV, New Series, p. 33; 'German Cavalry Training 1909', *The Cavalry Journal*, Volume 4, Number 15, pp. 371–8.

216 *Doctrine and Reform in the British Cavalry 1880–1918*

Bernhardi, chief of the war historical section of the German General Staff 1898–1901 and later a Corps commander, whose works achieved celebrity status among senior British officers.[131] French wrote the preface to the English edition of Bernhardi's book *Cavalry in Future Wars*, which was published in 1906 in a translation by the cavalry's old associate Sydney Goldmann, while Childers identified what he perceived as Bernhardi's sinister German influence in *Cavalry Training 1907*.[132]

As a reflection of the lack of centralised written doctrine, debate about the cavalry and mounted infantry within the British Army was still complicated by the absence of any agreed or official terminology. In 1908 the military pundit and writer Captain Cecil Battine told the Royal United Service Institution that 'we hear a lot of talk about mounted infantry, but I don't think anyone could really tell you what was the difference between a mounted infantry corps and a cavalry corps'.[133] Two years later, a major who had served with the MI in South Africa complained that there were no clear Army definitions of such fundamental terms as 'cavalry', 'mounted troops', and 'mounted rifles'.[134] A new *Mounted Infantry Training* manual appeared provisionally in 1906, but being based on *Regulations for Mounted Infantry 1899* rather than Hutton's revision it was out of date before it was published.

The clear doctrinal statement on cavalry and mounted infantry did not come until 1909, with the publication of *Field Service Regulations (FSR)*, in two volumes, intended to establish fundamental principles for the Army. *FSR Part I Operations* and *FSR Part II Administration* both had a long gestation period stretching back to 1904, and contributions from many authors, including Rawlinson and Wilson, but both volumes were seen through to publication by Haig as DSD before his departure for India. Haig saw *FSR Part I Operations* in particular as his own legacy.[135] In a letter written to Wilson as CIGS in September 1918, at the height of his last victories on the Western Front, Haig quoted a key passage from its first page:

[W]e have a surprisingly large number of *very capable* generals. Thanks to these gentlemen and to their 'sound military knowledge built up by study and practice until it has become an instinct' and to a steady adherence to the principles of our Field Service Regulations Part I are our successes to be chiefly attributed.[136]

This may have been Haig's idea of a joke, as either he or Wilson might have been the author of the passage about 'sound military knowledge' from *FSR Part I Operations*

---

131 For Bernhardi's importance see e.g. TNA WO 279/496 'Report of a conference of General Staff officers at the Staff College under the direction of CIGS, 17–20 January 1910', pp. 7–15; NAM Roberts Papers 223: Article by de Lisle, 'Letters of an Old Cavalry Officer to his son – 4'.

132 French, preface to Bernhardi, *Cavalry in War and Peace*; NAM Roberts Papers 223: Newspaper clippings 'Obsolete Theories in Tactics', *The Standard*, 13 April 1910.

133 Cecil Battine, 'The Uses of the Horse Soldier in the Twentieth Century', *Journal of the Royal United Service Institution*, Volume 152, p. 315.

134 *The Question of Mounted Infantry – by a Rifleman*, p. 9.

135 Cooper, *Haig*, Volume I, pp. 106–7; Gooch, *The Plans of War*, p. 28.

136 Quoted in Terraine, *To Win a War*, pp. 150–51 emphasis in the original; *Field Service Regulations Part I Operations* (1909), p. 11.

The Haldane Era 1905–1914

that he quoted. In a section headed 'Cavalry and other Mounted Troops', *FSR Part I Operations* made, for the first time, the Army's official distinction between cavalry and mounted infantry:

> 1. Ability to move rapidly and to cover long distances in a comparatively short time gives cavalry power to obtain information and to combine attack and surprise to the best advantage. The fact that it is armed with a long-range rifle has endowed it with great independence, and extended its sphere of action; for cavalry need no longer be stopped by difficulties which can only be overcome by the employment of rifle fire.
> 2. Mounted infantry acts by fire. When co-operating with cavalry, it assists the latter to combine fire with shock action; when co-operating with other arms, its mobility enables a commander to transfer it rapidly from one portion of the field to another, and thus to turn to account opportunities which he would be otherwise unable to seize.[137]

The emphasis in both cases was on the importance of mobility, and no specific mention was made of the arme blanche weapons of the cavalry. It was this, rather than *Cavalry Training 1907*, that represented both Haig's real view and the British Army's cavalry doctrine before the First World War.

While the cavalry got used to their new rifles, and recovered their lances and trumpet calls, the MI without a patron to support them were gradually phased out of existence. This was a relatively slow process, suggesting changing circumstances rather than any deliberate intent. The experience of the Boer War had shown beyond any reasonable consideration that good horsemen capable of the wider duties of cavalry such as scouting could not be improvised quickly. Even so, when in 1905 the Army Council considered making the MI a permanent force, this was rejected not only on grounds of cost but because the MI commanders themselves opposed the idea, preferring for their battalions to remain temporary and improvised formations, and part of the infantry.[138] Presumably they were concerned that if the MI ceased to be infantry they would leave the institutional protection of the regimental system. Next year the Duke of Connaught as Inspector General of the Forces reported that due to the rotation of contingents through the MI Schools, one-fifth of the troops of the MI battalions were untrained at any one time, and 'the principle is all wrong'.[139] As even Roberts admitted, the arming of the cavalry with the new Lee-Enfield removed most of the argument that MI were needed with cavalry formations to provide long-range fire. Instead, in the Haldane reforms the MI were made the divisional mounted troops of the BEF, with two companies permanently attached to each infantry division.[140]

In 1908 and 1909 the MI Schools in India and Egypt were closed down as no longer necessary; and when it proved impossible to form the proposed second cavalry division in 1912, the two cavalry regiments returning from South Africa

---

137 *Field Service Regulations Part I Operations*, General Staff, War Office, p. 12.

138 TNA WO 163/10 'Minutes of Proceedings and Précis Prepared for the Army Council' (1905), Précis Number 160, pp. 78–80.

139 TNA WO 27/510 'State and Efficiency of the Army and Defences. Reports by Inspector General of the Forces – submitted to the Army Council' 1904–1913, Report on troops and defences in South Africa, January and February 1907.

140 Roberts, 'The Army As It Was and Is', *The Nineteenth Century and After*, Volume LVII, p. 21.

took instead the MI's last remaining role by contributing a squadron to each of the BEF's six infantry divisions, forming the divisional mounted troops together with six companies of infantry cyclists. French as CIGS advised the Army Council on this decision:

> It would not be possible to provide on mobilisation even the twelve companies of Mounted Infantry [two for each infantry division] without incorporating a large percentage of reservists. The presence of such men in the ranks of the Mounted Infantry would undoubtedly be a source of danger in the event of a European campaign.[141]

This was not perhaps a sincere argument given the dependency of the entire BEF on reservists, including the cavalry who went to war with about 30 per cent of its other ranks recalled from the reserves. How well the MI would have fought in the First World War is a question that can never be answered, although as infantry of the BEF it may be assumed that they would have fought well; during the retreat from Mons there were accounts of infantrymen with MI training taking spare horses and joining in with the cavalry.[142] But the MI had only ever been intended as an expedient to cover both a shortage of regular cavalry and a lack of mobile firepower, both of which had been addressed with the establishment of the BEF's Cavalry Division. The MI were, in a phrase coined in 1913 by Lieutenant Colonel Charles à Court Repington of *The Times*, 'the cavalry of poverty', and with the Haldane reforms their usefulness was at an end.[143]

By 1908 there was an agreement among senior officers that the arguments over the cavalry were all in the past – but only two years later the whole debate burst open in public once again. The agreement was certainly a fragile one, with Ian Hamilton and Horace Smith-Dorrien barely able to conceal their real opinions on the mounted charge. When Hamilton became Adjutant General in 1910 he felt able to express his views openly once more; while the antipathy between Smith-Dorrien and French, the product of powerful personalities but also of real differences on cavalry tactics and other military issues, had grown until by 1910 it was an open secret within the Army.[144] It may also have been a factor that Haig was out of the country, having taken up his post as Chief of Staff in India. But the most important role in re-opening the public argument was once again played by Lord Roberts.

The trigger for this remarkable episode was the behaviour of the yeomanry, aggrieved after their treatment by Roberts and with much less reason than the regular cavalry to accept slow changes for the sake of harmony. Barely had Roberts left office in 1904 when a majority of yeomanry regimental commanders petitioned the Army Council that they should be allowed once more to carry the sword, now the

---

141 TNA WO 163/18 Army Council Decisions 1913, Number 734, pp. 446–8; WO 32/7084 'Organisation of a force for operations in Egypt. Increase in establishments. Formation of 7th Division and 5th Cavalry Brigade', memorandum by the Director of Military Operations, 31 July 1908; *The Question of Mounted Infantry – by a Rifleman*, p. 5.
    142 Anglesey, *A History of the British Cavalry Volume 7*, p. 131.
    143 Quoted in Luvaas, *The Education of an Army*, p. 316.
    144 Holmes, *The Little Field Marshal*, pp. 132–3.

symbol of their grievance.[145] Even so, the re-issue of *Cavalry Training 1904* in early 1905 (without Roberts's offending preface) was accompanied by a short pamphlet *Instructions for Training of Imperial Yeomanry 1905* which maintained the position taken by *Imperial Yeomanry Training 1902* in ordering the yeomanry to accept an inferior status and subordinate role to that of the cavalry:

> Imperial Yeomanry should be so trained as to be capable of performing all the duties allotted to cavalry except those connected with shock action. In carrying out their training commanding officers will adhere to the principles contained in 'Cavalry Training 1904' (except as modified in this pamphlet) as far as they are applicable to their arm, but in doing so they must exercise considerable discretion, bearing in mind the short period available for training, the fact that the Yeomanry are not armed with a weapon suitable for shock action, and that they drill in single rank [rather than the double ranks of cavalry]. During the annual course of training particular attention should be devoted to instruction in scouting, reconnaissance, fire action dismounted, and detached duties; but that precision in drill required of troops employing shock action should not be aimed at.[146]

Although they had the option of volunteering for overseas service in case of war, by 1910 only six per cent of yeomen had done so, a considerably lower percentage than the yeomen who had joined the IY for South Africa in 1899–1900.[147] Within the TF they were intended only for home defence, either as divisional mounted troops or as mounted brigades of 'protective cavalry', rather than the more important and glamorous 'independent cavalry' role reserved for the regulars. As one officer grumbled in *The Cavalry Journal* in 1908, 'Armed with a rifle only and precluded from taking part in mounted combats, yeomanry must be content to abandon all idea of a strategic role.'[148] But the creation of the TF brought important changes for the yeomanry, as the word 'Imperial' was quietly dropped from the regimental titles and they became once more just 'the yeomanry' or 'Territorial mounted' troops. The idea of their being used as drafts for a European war on the model of the IY of the Boer War was never officially stated, but it was widely assumed, and the yeomanry believed that in order to cope with European-style cavalry they would need swords and the skill to charge mounted.

The enduring problem, stated very clearly in *Instructions for Training of Imperial Yeomanry 1905*, was that the yeomanry did not have the training time to reach a high enough standard to make the mounted charge a worthwhile tactic. Although with the formation of the TF annual training was increased to 15 days, only 8 days were needed for a pass certificate. For the gentlemen of leisure who rode as yeomanry officers, or even sometimes as troopers, training was carefully timed to come between the mayfly season and the autumn's hunting, and the same horses were shipped round

---

145 TNA WO 163/9 Army Council Decisions 1904, Number 93, pp. 246–7.

146 *Instructions for Training of Imperial Yeomanry*, p. 5.

147 TNA WO 122 Army Estimates 1910/11 quoting a speech by Haldane as Secretary of State for War.

148 'The Training of a Yeomanry Brigade', *The Cavalry Journal*, Volume 3, Number 12, p. 547.

the country for different regiments to ride in rotation.[149] A yeoman might easily turn up on Salisbury plain for training riding a horse he had met only a few days before, and carrying a rifle he had never fired.[150]

Since his removal as C-in-C, Roberts's main political concern had become the need for peacetime conscription and a mass British Army, an issue over which he had left the CID at the end of 1904 and accepted the presidency of the National Service League, and he had become highly critical of the TF as inadequate to British military needs.[151] The problems in training the yeomanry made a very good case for what the League considered as the inadequacies of Haldane's scheme. Roberts's first move was to write to Amery asking 'about the question of swords for yeomanry', suggesting that Amery or Childers 'should ferret out incidents in the South African war which help to confirm your [Roberts's] view that swords are needless'.[152] Amery, who had a developing political career of his own, passed the letter on to Childers, whose outspoken views on the primacy of mounted riflemen over cavalry were already well known from his authorship of the fifth volume of the *Times History*, covering the period in the Boer War from May 1901 onwards. There was already a story circulating, dated by Charteris to Haig's period as Inspector General of Cavalry in India 1903–1905, that at the newly founded Cavalry School at Saugor there was a 'Childers Road': a cul-de-sac leading to the cemetery.[153] Childers replied to Roberts's letter in characteristic fashion:

> I am only too glad to fall in with your suggestion, for my studies have led me inevitably to your conclusion. Personally (if without presumption I may say so) I go further and would like to see the arme blanche totally abolished in the regular service and all our mounted troops trained to act as mounted riflemen... I believe it is mainly the weight of old cavalry tradition which perpetuates the present system.[154]

Childers gathered the material for his book over the following year, keeping in close written contact with Roberts as he did so. *War and the Arme Blanche* was published in March 1910 with an introductory preface by Roberts, who also helped circulate copies in draft form and to orchestrate a promotional campaign for the book both in the press and among senior officers.

Childers's book was written as an extended critique of Bernhardi's *Cavalry in Future Wars*, openly criticising French for his support of Bernhardi, and portraying him as an unreformed believer in the arme blanche who had promoted Bernhardi's views as 'a conclusive answer to the English critics of shock manoeuvre with the

---

149 Verdin, *The Cheshire (Earl of Chester's) Yeomanry 1898–1967*, p. 25; Carton de Wiart, *Happy Odyssey*, p. 43; NAM Roberts Papers 221: Memorandum from the DAAG to the Adjutant General on Yeomanry, 1 January 1904.

150 Knox, 'Yeoman Hopkins, One Asset in our Armour', *The Nineteenth Century and After*, Volume LXIX, p. 560.

151 James, *The Life of Lord Roberts*, pp. 411–63; Adams and Poirier, *The Conscription Controversy in Great Britain 1900–18*, pp. 1–48.

152 NAM Roberts Papers 222: Childers to Roberts, 4 November 1908.

153 Charteris, *Field Marshal Earl Haig*, p. 29.

154 NAM Roberts Papers 222: Childers to Roberts, 4 November 1908.

arme blanche'. What French had actually written was that he supported Bernhardi's emphasis on the charge as part of an antidote to 'the increasing tendency of umpires and superior officers to insist on cavalry at manoeuvres and elsewhere being ultra-cautious', a preoccupation of the 1907 and 1908 manoeuvres.[155] This was only one of many misleading or contentious statements in *War and the Arme Blanche*, but Childers, who openly described himself in the book as 'a controversialist', was presenting a polemical case rather than a factual treatise, and was intent on provoking a reaction.[156] He dismissed arguments supporting the value of the mounted charge with swords with grandiose contempt. As a typical example of his style, when citing a passage from Bernhardi which advocated dismounted action under the appropriate circumstances, Childers could not resist the opportunity both to mock and to let his own anti-German attitudes show through:

> The logical hiatus, so familiar in all writers on shock, is complete. There is no attempt made to bridge it. One can almost hear the ghost of Frederick the Great whispering in the impious General's ear, 'What is all this despicable talk about dismounting? Betray the steel? Never!'[157]

Childers enjoyed himself so much that his book was taken, both at the time and later (even by one of his own biographers) as an argument for the abolition of cavalry.[158]

In company with his irreverent tone, Childers deliberately targeted all the sensitive spots in the senior cavalrymen's psychology: their belief in the authority of cavalry officers of other nationalities as sharing with them the status of experts; the value of historical examples of the charge; and the value of the arme blanche in promoting morale. He rejected the evidence of all previous wars except for the Boer War and the Russo-Japanese War; aimed his book at 'all thinking men, whether professional soldiers or not'; and dismissed any defence of the arme blanche as 'the incalculable influence of purely sentimental conservatism upon even the ablest cavalry soldiers', stretching the definition considerably to include Henderson.[159]

Childers concluded without hesitation that if mounted charges against dismounted British troopers or Boer commandos had succeeded, then cavalry charges against European infantry should also succeed. But his conclusion from episodes like the Klip Drift charge was not that the cavalry could adjust their tactics according to circumstances, but – going further even than Haig in 1900 – that mounted troops would be the all-conquering weapon of the future, overcoming both infantry and artillery:

> Mounted men not only can pass a fire-zone unscathed, but make genuine destructive assaults upon riflemen and guns… [But] the mounted men who do these things must be

---

155 Childers, *War and the Arme Blanche*, p. 9; French, preface to Bernhardi, *Cavalry in Future Wars*, p. xxvii.
156 Childers, *War and the Arme Blanche*, p. 129.
157 Ibid., p. 309.
158 Barrow, *The Fire of Life*, p. 111; Boyle, *The Riddle of Erskine Childers*, p. 136.
159 Childers, *War and the Arme Blanche*, p. 3, p. 8, and p. 14; NAM Roberts Papers 222: Childers to Roberts, 8 March 1910.

mounted riflemen, trained to rely on rifle and horse combined, and purged of all leanings towards *shock*.[160]

Having no other explanation, Childers attributed the success of these tactics to the morale effect of saddle fire, particularly in the guerrilla phase of the war, and rejected the idea of 'shock', which he interpreted in the purely physical sense as the collision of mounted troops with their enemies, as fundamentally unfeasible. Childers also rejected completely the idea that any mounted troops could become proficient with both swords and rifles, since 'the cavalry spirit, in its inmost essence, means the spirit of fighting *on horseback* with a steel weapon, in contradistinction to the spirit of fighting on foot with a firearm'.[161] As far as he was concerned, there were only two possible troop types: on the one hand an obsolete cavalry obsessed with the arme blanche and the knee-to-knee charge, and on the other hand mounted riflemen.

Judged as part of the history of the cavalry debate, *War and the Arme Blanche* was actually an anachronism, a throwback to the discredited theories of writers such as Havelock, fervently denying the possibility of cavalry that could both charge and shoot, and linking the regular cavalry regiments utterly with the arme blanche in order to condemn both. In fact, with the public revival of interest in the cavalry, Denison in Canada issued a revised version of his *A History of Cavalry* in 1913, proclaiming that the intervening years had not 'varied my views, or modified them in any way', and citing Childers as a fellow authority.[162]

At the start of 1910, Roberts supplied advance copies of *War and the Arme Blanche* to the Staff College, where Wilson was completing his time as commandant. Among those who commented on the book for Roberts was one unidentified officer serving in the War Office, who observed that 'the tone, for an unknown civilian, is too didactic and absolute. A very little change in the wording would do away with this and would prevent the *writer* arousing angry and hostile feelings at the outset.'[163] Childers's reply to Roberts unconsciously confirmed the point:

> I am sorry to hear that cavalry officers seem likely to take offence at certain passages. I have taken... the utmost care to prevent this... [But] the whole history of the subject so far is that of tentative over-deferential advocacy of change which is sneered down without argument at once by *ex cathedra* pronouncements of the arme blanche school.[164]

On 29 January 1910, Roberts visited the Staff College seeking Wilson's help in writing a preface for *War and the Arme Blanche*, in which Roberts proposed contrasting *Cavalry Training 1904* with *Cavalry Training 1907*. Despite a warning from Rawlinson, who was unhappy about Roberts's decision to support Childers

---

160 Childers, *War and the Arme Blanche*, p. 105; emphasis in the original.

161 Ibid., p. 37; emphasis in the original.

162 Denison, *A History of Cavalry*, 2nd edition, 1913, p. xv; Luvaas, *The Military Legacy of the Civil War*, p. 113.

163 NAM Roberts Papers 223: file of papers on the publication of *War and the Arme Blanche*, undated unsigned notes on War Office notepaper, apparently referring to the pre-published version of the book; emphasis in the original.

164 Ibid., 222: Childers to Roberts, 2 February 1910; ex cathedra ('from the throne') means with an air of infallibility.

in this way, Wilson became deeply involved in the publication of the book and the subsequent public affair. This episode throws a significant light on the support that Wilson gave Roberts over conscription during the same period, and on his relationship with French.[165] On 4 February, Wilson told John Gough, his chief staff officer, that he felt Childers had made 'an unanswerable case' in his book.[166] Next day, Wilson took over the project from Roberts, in his own mind attempting to tone down what he saw as a personal attack by Roberts on French:

> I think I persuaded the Chief to entirely alter his preface and instead of comparing the present Cavalry Training with his own of 1904 to strike a higher note and to ask his brother officers to read Childers's book and either refute or agree. I am sure this is the wisest course. To me there is something distasteful in the Chief crossing swords with a man like French, his inferior immeasurably in every way.[167]

Two days later Roberts showed Wilson his revised attempt at a preface, which had adopted Wilson's suggestions, and Wilson then worked on re-writing and polishing it to his own satisfaction, so that by 20 February he considered it to be 'in grand shape'. Although published in Roberts's name, the finished preface certainly had Wilson's fingerprints on it:

> I call upon my brother officers, in whatever part of the Empire you may be serving, whether in the mounted or dismounted branches... to study the facts for yourselves, weigh the arguments, follow the deductions, note the conclusions and then do one of two things. Either traverse [sic] the facts, refute the deductions, and upset the conclusions, *or* admit the facts, agree with the arguments, acknowledge the deductions, and accept the conclusions.[168]

All the cavalry's suspicions of Roberts when he had been C-in-C seemed to be confirmed by this preface, which opened with a brief comparison between *Cavalry Training 1904* and *Cavalry Training 1907*, and then added that:

> My opinion on the subject with which it deals is already so well known throughout the army that I need not labour to say how entirely I agree with the author's main thesis; indeed, anyone who will take the trouble to read 'Cavalry Training' (1904) will see that I anticipated the arguments which he has so ably developed.[169]

But despite Childers's absolute rejection of any form of arme blanche for mounted troops, Roberts's preface stated that it was 'desirable' for cavalry to keep a sword-bayonet for use as a short sword in mounted charges, 'at night, in a mist, or on other occasions when a fire-fight might be impossible or inadvisable'. Perhaps Roberts – or Wilson – had not really absorbed Childers's arguments, or quite possibly read

---

165 IWM Wilson Papers: Diary entries, 29 January and 31 January 1910; Jeffrey, *Field Marshal Sir Henry Wilson*, pp. 75–7.
166 IWM Wilson Papers: Diary entry, 4 February 1910.
167 Ibid., Diary entry, 5 February 1910.
168 Roberts [Wilson], preface to Childers, *War and the Arme Blanche*, p. xvi; emphasis in the original
169 Ibid., p. v.

his book in its entirety.[170] It is hard to escape the conclusion that between Erskine Childers on one side and Henry Wilson on the other, *War and the Arme Blanche* had somewhat escaped away from Roberts's original intentions.

On publication in March 1910 Roberts sent advance copies of *War and the Arme Blanche* to selected senior officers, military correspondents of influential newspapers, and to some civilians including Lord Esher and the Oxford University historian Sir Charles Oman, with a covering letter that contained a hint of apology:

> I trust that neither you nor any cavalry officer will look upon this book 'War and the Arme Blanche' about to be published as an attack on the cavalry service, but will recognise it as an earnest desire to induce all ranks to realise that, under the conditions of modern warfare, the rifle and not the sword is the weapon upon which they must mainly depend.... The question of the relative value of the two weapons is put in very plain language... [I] would ask you not to let this disconcert you.[171]

Almost all major national newspapers reviewed Childers's book, although favourable reviews largely reflected the extent of each newspaper's support for Roberts's wider positions on military issues. Roberts's old supporter, the military correspondent of the *Morning Post* H.F. Prevost Battersby, wrote in almost messianic terms of the cavalry officer, 'to be freed from the fatal consequences of the so-called "Cavalry Spirit" he must be delivered from its paralysing faith, and Mr Childers has written to bring him deliverance'.[172] Colonel Repington of *The Times* considered that 'the question of the armament of cavalry is one which can only be determined by cavalry officers with much experience in peace and war', and other reviewers also fell back on the authority of cavalry officers rather than criticise either French or Roberts openly.[173] These first reviews were followed by many letters to the newspapers (all of them collected by Roberts), including from Conan Doyle in broad support of Childers, and from Childers himself joining enthusiastically into the fray, which between them kept the matter in the public eye throughout the summer. In August the Liberal *Westminster Gazette* commented that 'There is no public journal of any standing that has not had something to say on a question which has clearly attracted public attention to a quite remarkable degree.'[174]

Because of the nature of Childers's book and Roberts's preface, the questions debated were entirely concerned with the relative merits of the rifle and the sword, rather than the role and value of cavalry. There was also little discussion of the real problems faced by the cavalry in the early phase of the Boer War under Roberts, neatly summed up in one letter to *The Spectator*, apparently written by a veteran:

> In South Africa mounted action was not so often used as it might have been because (1) the horses were starved (2) the English press advocated making war without risks

---

170 Ibid., p. xii.
171 NAM Roberts Papers 223: Covering letter for *War and the Arme Blanche* (six copies).
172 Ibid., 223: File of newspaper clippings on *War and the Arme Blanche*, review in the *Morning Post*, 29 March 1910.
173 Ibid., review in *The Times*, 26 March 1910.
174 Ibid., review by the *Westminster Gazette*, 2 August 1910.

(3) the higher commanders had never studied the use of cavalry (4) the Boers would not chance it in the open when there were swords and lances about.[175]

Never before had the debate on the cavalry been brought on such a scale to the attention of the newspaper-reading British public, those people who were most likely to be impressed by Childers's rhetoric and Roberts's reputation. While there is no way of measuring the impact of *War and the Arme Blanche* on public opinion, it seems entirely plausible that many who perhaps never read Childers's book had their views of the cavalry as incompetent or reactionary either established or confirmed by these public events.

To the Army, which had already dealt to its own satisfaction with the cavalry debate, *War and the Arme Blanche* was something of an embarrassment. Senior officers who were sent copies of the book by Roberts were placed in the difficult position of not wishing to offend the distinguished field marshal, but also not wanting to be drawn into the argument. Of those who are known to have been sent copies of *War and the Arme Blanche* by Roberts, most responded with a polite acknowledgement, including Douglas as GOC Southern Command, his chief staff officer Richard Haking, Rawlinson as GOC 3rd Division, Launcelot Kiggell, who had replaced Haig as DSD at the War Office, and Allenby as the designated Inspector General of Cavalry, who responded that 'I certainly do not look upon the book as an attack on the cavalry service.'[176] Ian Hamilton as Adjutant General wrote that he had not yet read the book but that 'never, as long at any rate as I am here, will the Territorial Mounted men be given back the sword', which was at least the point of Roberts's original action.[177] Robertson, still in his staff appointment at Aldershot, claimed to see no improvement at all in the cavalry since he had served as a trooper in the 1880s:

> Cavalry are, indeed, very loath and slow to adjust their tactics to modern requirements, and I doubt if much improvement will be made as long as the brigades are automatically pooled together in a division and trained on Salisbury plain.... Why the so-called 'Cavalry Spirit' should suffer by practising dismounted duties I cannot conceive. At present cavalry regiments are encouraged, rather, to continue on the same lines as 40 years ago.[178]

It is not apparent why Robertson held this view of the cavalry, but it would have considerable consequences six years later, when he was CIGS working with Haig as GOC-in-C of the BEF. The most aggressive disagreement with Childers in a letter to Roberts came from Hubert Gough, who argued that 'fire *must* be the means of preparation, but that for the final *decision*, the resolute advance to close quarters will often be necessary'.[179] Wilson was the most proactive of Roberts's correspondents, suggesting that Roberts should also write to Allenby and Douglas, to all the cavalry

---

175 Ibid., letter by 'Common Sense' to *The Spectator*, 16 June 1910.
176 Ibid., 223: Allenby to Roberts, 23 April 1910; correspondence from other officers mentioned is collected in the same file.
177 Ibid., Ian Hamilton to Roberts, 10 March 1910.
178 Ibid., Robertson to Roberts, 10 March 1910.
179 Ibid., Hubert Gough to Roberts, 10 March 1910, emphasis in the original.

brigade commanders, and to a few cavalry commanding officers who he presumably regarded as potentially sharing Roberts's views, including Vaughan and Chetwode, and also de Lisle, who in response politely pointed out to Roberts the central problem with Childers's analysis:

> I am sure the book will do good... [but] he builds all his arguments on the assumption that the cavalry cannot be taught the tactical use of two weapons. It is true that cavalry officers both at home and abroad think the same. At present our cavalry leaders are persistent in their refusal to acknowledge the value of the rifle, and for any brigadier to declare other views means the loss of his command.[180]

De Lisle's assumption about the attitude of 'cavalry leaders' was a common one, but hardly reflected the pronouncements and behaviour of French, Haig or Allenby. In fact, with Allenby yet to take up his appointment and Haig still in India, the only cavalryman holding a senior position on the General Staff at the time was French as Inspector General of the Forces.

On publication of *War and the Arme Blanche*, three reviews all carrying a degree of official status challenged Childers's argument. In *The Cavalry Journal*, an anonymous review attributed to Allenby maintained that 'It is the sharp point of the steel weapon in the hands of the skilled rider that counts in shock tactics', and that 'all cavalry leaders who have seen war know that only confidence in the steel weapon can keep alive the spirit of the eager offensive'.[181] In the same issue of *The Cavalry Journal* a commentary on Childers's book issued in the name of the General Staff stressed the professional expertise of British cavalry generals and pointed out the shortcomings of the rifle charge, while conceding that the principal value of the arme blanche was to encourage a desire to close with the enemy. 'It seems to us', wrote the reviewers, 'that it would be more difficult for cavalry to pull up and dismount in the open, under close rifle fire, than to charge home led by its officers.'[182] In the same month, Battine delivered an almost identical denunciation of Childers's book at the Royal United Service Institution, observing in his talk that the consensus of agreement was 'very satisfactory'; Allenby, who chaired the meeting, added that 'everyone nowadays agrees that the rifle will be the main arm of the cavalry in war', but that this was no reason to give up the sword.[183]

For good measure, *The Cavalry Journal* published a review of *War and the Arme Blanche* by Bernhardi, who predictably dismissed Childers's book as 'amateurish and illogical', concluding that Roberts must have supported him from some unfathomable personal motive. Bernhardi attributed the success of the Boer rifle charges to the shortcomings of the British 'militia' who 'lost their heads completely'

---

180 Ibid., de Lisle to Roberts, 29 April 1910, and Wilson to Roberts, 9 March 1910.

181 Review of Childers, *War and the Arme Blanche*, *The Cavalry Journal*, Volume 5, Number 19, pp. 283–7. The attribution of this to Allenby was made in the *Westminster Gazette*, 2 August 1910.

182 Comment by the General Staff on Childers, *War and the Arme Blanche*, *The Cavalry Journal*, Volume 5, Number 19, p. 408.

183 Battine, 'The Proposed Changes in Cavalry Tactics', *Journal of the Royal United Service Institution*, Volume 54, p. 1416 and p. 1443.

(a phrase often used in military German of the time, and less insulting than it appears in English) when faced by a charge. Childers's reply was equally combative, railing against the German for daring to accuse British troops of 'cowardice' rather than poor tactics.[184]

To cap the whole story of *War and the Arme Blanche*, back in January 1910, just as the book was about to appear, Roberts had been told that the General Staff was changing its cavalry doctrine so as to render most of Childers's criticisms of the cavalry out of date before they appeared, and Wilson also knew that this was happening when he re-wrote Roberts's preface. One of the Staff College innovations under Wilson was an annual conference of General Staff officers to discuss a major military topic, and for 17–20 January 1910 the subject was cavalry tactics.[185] The conference was hosted by Wilson assisted by John Gough, and included Nicholson as CIGS, Murray as DMT and Sir Spencer Ewart as DMO, plus the chief staff officers of the major military commands including Aldershot. No senior cavalrymen attended this conference, although Barrow as Wilson's cavalry specialist led one discussion. As a handwritten note on Roberts's own notepaper (possibly dictated from a telephone message) shows, Roberts was informed at the time of the General Staff's conclusions:

> It was agreed the other day at the General Staff Conference that cavalry might have to attack like infantry (though not on such a large scale) and the regulations are about to be revised to this effect. In fact the whole book 'Cavalry Training' is being revised, and the General Staff are trying to formulate a definite policy for the training and arming of all mounted troops, including mounted infantry, mounted rifles and yeomanry.[186]

Although Haig was in India, the decision that dismounted cavalry should be taught infantry tactics in attack as well as in defence went back to his recommendation to the Elgin Commission in 1903, and addressed the problem of how cavalry could attack entrenchments if a mounted charge was not feasible. Roberts did not tell Childers of these decisions, and it was not until July 1910 at the height of the public controversy that Childers learned that cavalry doctrine was been changed. He wrote to Roberts following one discussion that 'The cavalry officers present were of course on the wrong side, but they were very mild in their criticism and they made no real attempt to make out any strong case for shock. I gather they are going to publish a new Cavalry Training revised in favour of fire.'[187]

Having constructed for the purpose of his book a demon in the form of a large clique of reactionary cavalry officers obsessed with the arme blanche, Childers was quite surprised when he talked to cavalry officers and discovered their real views.

---

184 Bernhardi, Review of Childers, *War and the Arme Blanche*, *The Cavalry Journal*, Volume 5, Number 20, pp. 466–83; Letter by Erskine Childers in *The Cavalry Journal*, Volume 6, Number 22, pp. 234–9.

185 TNA WO 279/496 Report of a Conference of General Staff officers at the Staff College under the Direction of CIGS, (1910).

186 NAM Roberts Papers 223: File of material relating to *War and the Arme Blanche*, undated and unsigned handwritten notes; the handwriting is not that of Roberts himself.

187 Ibid., 222: Childers to Roberts, 15 July 1910.

As the review of *War and the Arme Blanche* in the *United Service Magazine* pointed out:

> In one respect this book might have been written immediately after the South African War, since the author writes as though the defects then noticed in our cavalry training, and now once more brought forward, still existed – that no improvement had since taken place, that the fire-action of our horsemen was as ineffective today as it admittedly was ten years ago.[188]

Whatever Roberts's wider motives might have been for promoting a public controversy through a book which he knew in advance was based on a false premise, once his own point had been made he let the matter rest. In July 1910 another book by Bernhardi appeared, *Cavalry in War and Peace*, translated by Bridges and with an introduction by French, in part replying to Childers's criticisms. It was soon after this, in October 1910, that Ian Hamilton wrote his letter about the Russo-Japanese War to Childers, who was preparing his own next book, *German Influence on British Cavalry*. But by the time that this book appeared in 1911 Childers's relationship with Roberts had largely ended; Roberts gave Childers's new book no support, and it made no impact. Despite his continued polemical tone, Childers had also modified his views by the time that *German Influence on British Cavalry* appeared:

> The lance should go altogether. Whether the sword is retained, as the American cavalry retain it, rather as a symbol than as a factor in tactics, or is dispensed with altogether, as our divisional mounted troops [mounted infantry and yeomanry] and our Colonial mounted riflemen dispense with it, is a matter of very small moment, provided that the correct principle be established and worked out in practice. It was because I doubted the possibility of establishing the correct principle in this country without abolition that in my previous book I advocated abolition, on the precedent of the South African War.[189]

This 'matter of very small moment' had been the core of Childers's case; with this second book his position became virtually indistinguishable (other than on the matter of the lance) from that of official British Army cavalry doctrine. In turn, after several years' argument, that doctrine had shifted gradually from an insistence that the arme blanche must be seen as the more important of the cavalry's weapons to an agreement that the rifle was probably the more important, and certainly the more likely to be used.

Next year *Cavalry Training 1912*, a revised manual with altogether more stress on practical issues than *Cavalry Training 1907*, laid down that:

> The rifle endows cavalry with great independence in war, and numerous situations will occur when it can be used with greater effect than sword or lance. But a bold leader will find frequent opportunities for mounted attack which will produce more rapid and decisive results than can be gained by even the most skilful use of the rifle. It is, however,

---

188 Review of Childers, *War and the Arme Blanche*, in the *United Service Magazine*, Volume XLI, New Series, p. 234.

189 Childers, *German Influence on British Cavalry*, p. 215; Bernhardi (translated Bridges), *Cavalry in War and Peace*.

by no means necessary when an attack is made that only one of the two methods should be employed, for fire-action can create favourable opportunities for shock action.[190]

This passage was accompanied by a diagram showing a squadron attacking advancing enemy troops by encircling them, using a 'fire attack' from one flank to accompany a mounted charge from the other.

The authors of *Cavalry Training 1912* are not known, although the responsibility lay with Murray as DMT, and with Allenby, who as Inspector General of Cavalry reviewed the proofs; and the manual certainly had echoes of Haig, including its statement that:

> cavalry can seldom hope to reduce the enemy to a state of moral and physical degeneration. This condition must be produced by the attacks of the other arms. Cavalry must therefore keep in close touch with the other arms and take advantage of their progress, offering them such help as it can with its guns and rifles, and supplementing their decisive attack by sweeping the battlefield with its squadrons.[191]

Haig would return to this doctrine in his preparations for the Battle of the Somme four years later.

Cavalry Training 1912 set out a wide range of cavalry tactics, including small mounted charges supported (usually from a flank) by dismounted firepower from rifles, machine-guns or artillery, building up to the full divisional charge if needed. While accepting that a divisional charge was unlikely to achieve surprise, the manual argued that massed cavalry might 'achieve great results against troops which are worn out, demoralised, and obliged to leave their fighting positions'.[192] It advocated not a choice between firepower and shock action but a combination of the two using fire from other arms and from the cavalry's own artillery, machine-guns and rifles, since 'a well-executed combination of the two methods will often present the greatest chance of success'.[193] Vaughan described the practical application of this doctrine in an exercise that he undertook for Haig in India in 1910, in which he routed an enemy cavalry screen by using a mixture of manoeuvre and firepower:

> I had no horse artillery battery in my scratch lot, so I made up for it with my good machine gunners. I expected that the enemy would probably send out only one squadron on Advanced Guard or reconnaissance, so I put two squadrons of the Tenth [Hussars] with orders to gallop everything they saw, on the same duty. They soon chased the [enemy] 17th Lancers patrols back on their main position. This was a ridge running North and South, with subsidiary ridges running out to the West, like a man's knuckles and fingers, the tips of which, as they merged with the plain we were crossing, might be 600 or 800 yards apart. But on every one of these tips had galloped, with the troop that had seized

---

190 *Cavalry Training 1912*, p. 268 and diagram on p. 270
191 *Cavalry Training 1912*, p. 240; LHCMA Allenby Papers 2/5: Allenby to Vaughan, 2 March 1919.
192 *Cavalry Training 1912*, p. 241.
193 Ibid., p. 268.

it, one or two Vickers guns. The enemy ... tried to send out fresh reconnaissances, but as soon as our tom-toms beat [simulating machine-gun fire] the umpires sent them home.[194]

The lessons that Vaughan identified from these manoeuvres were '(1) Machine guns must be mobile and inconspicuous until they open fire. (2) Contain your enemy in the front and stalk him in flank.'[195] A description by Major Winwood of the 5th Dragoon Guards, part of the 1st Cavalry Brigade at Aldershot, of a squadron exercise for an attack against enemy artillery in April 1912 shows that the same ideas of fire and manoeuvre had permeated down to squadron level:

> Attack on guns. Advance too long. Halt anywhere under cover, make fresh plans, send one troop off at the guns, another at the flank, to kill the gunners, another to the led horses, and have the other for the escort. Mounted attack, rally a troop under its commander then each troop come to the squadron.[196]

By this date Vaughan had returned to become Commandant of the Cavalry School at Netheravon.

Despite the progress made, uncertainties and differences of opinion about the cavalry still remained. At the 1912 East Anglia manoeuvres Douglas, who had succeeded French as Inspector General of the Forces, made the infantryman's complaint that 'Our cavalry commanders are inclined to employ shock action whenever possible regardless of circumstances.'[197] French as CIGS also felt that the cavalry still had much to learn about co-operation with the other arms, and in particular in adopting the tactics of deliberately showing itself to the enemy both mounted and dismounted, so as to confuse them as to the location of the main body of the BEF. The standard of the training of individual cavalry brigades gave greater cause for satisfaction, notably at Aldershot, where Douglas considered Kavanagh's 1st Cavalry Brigade as 'liable to render a good account of itself in war, for which it is, in my opinion, in a state of preparedness'.[198]

In the few years before the First World War, the British cavalry regiments achieved a quite remarkable standard of shooting with their rifles, in many cases either equal or superior to that of the infantry battalions with which they served. By 1913, Spiers's 11th Hussars made a point of pride in having no third-class shots and only 80 second-class shots; all the rest were first-class shots or marksmen; the 14th Hussars, serving in India, had an almost comparable record with four third-class shots, 35 second-class shots, 212 first-class shots, and 354 marksmen.[199] Although

---

194 Vaughan, *Cavalry and Sporting Memories*, pp. 132–3.
195 Ibid., p. 133.
196 NAM Winwood Papers: Diary entry, 13 April 1912.
197 TNA WO 27/511 'State and efficiency of the Army and Defences. Reports by Inspector General of the Forces – submitted to the Army Council' (1904–1913), Report for 1912; French, *The Life of Field Marshal Sir John French*, p. 187.
198 TNA WO 27/511 'State and efficiency of the Army and Defences. Reports by Inspector General of the Forces – submitted to the Army Council' (1904–1913), Report for 1913.
199 Spears, *The Picnic Basket*, p. 77; Lumley, *The History of the Eleventh Hussars*, p. 10; Holmes, *Riding the Retreat*, p. 63; the exact number of marksmen etc. of course varied

attitudes to the rifle continued to vary between regiments, its importance was increasingly widely accepted: Private Maitand remembered that the 19th Hussars hated musketry, but also that 'daily, we are taught that the rifle is our best friend'; while the 1st Life Guards enjoyed their 'glorious outings' to the rifle ranges.[200]

But if the cavalry had adapted the rifle to cavalry spirit (rather than the other way around), the yeomanry, which continued to be well represented in parliament, (including at least one cabinet minister, Winston Churchill of the Queen's Own Oxfordshire Hussars) remained incorrigible, insofar as while accepting training with the rifle they had simply refused to give up their swords.[201] On exercise in 1911 a yeomanry brigade even charged mounted uphill against a dismounted cavalry brigade waiting to receive them with rifle-fire.[202] In 1912 French as CIGS convinced the Army Council to accept reality: the official position was changed so that the yeomanry would be issued swords in the event of mobilisation for war, and in the interval (although the government would not pay for their swords) they were to be allowed to practise swordsmanship in peacetime if they wished.[203] This reality was recognised by the new *Yeomanry and Mounted Rifle Training 1912*, which was also meant to cover mounted infantry, and the light horse and mounted rifle regiments of the Empire including Australia, (although not the Canadian Mounted Rifles, still covered by *Cavalry Training Canada 1904*). This manual was very close to *Cavalry Training 1912* but was issued with Parts I and II bound together in one volume, and a note that Part III, containing the training instructions for mounted combat, would be issued as a second volume (in fact Part III was never issued, the war intervening). In recognition of the fact that in practice the various types of mounted troops tended to blur together, *Yeomanry and Mounted Rifle Training 1912* gave the following definitions:

> The term *mounted troops* in this manual is to be understood to include cavalry, yeomanry, mounted rifles, and mounted infantry.
>
> *Yeomanry and mounted rifles* are cavalry soldiers, enlisted or enrolled as such, who are trained to use the rifle as their principal offensive or defensive weapon. Their training is to be directed, in the first instance, solely to the subjects dealt with in Parts I and II of this manual, and until they have been fully trained in these subjects they are not to be permitted to receive instruction in the elements of shock action mounted....
>
> By *mounted infantry* is meant fully trained infantry soldiers, mounted solely for the purpose of locomotion. Such troops are not to be regarded as horse-soldiers, but as infantry possessing special mobility.[204]

---

with each year and new test, see Browne and Bridges, *Historical Record of the 14th (King's) Hussars, Volume II, 1900–1922*, pp. 251–272 which shows that the regiment averaged about 95 per cent marksmen or first class shots 1908–1915.

200 Maitland, *Hussar of the Line*, p. 29; Lloyd, *A Trooper in the Tins*, p. 23.

201 Holmes, *Tommy*, p. 128.

202 Knox, 'Yeoman Hopkins, one Asset in our Armour', *The Nineteenth Century and After*, Volume LXIX, p. 565.

203 TNA WO 163/17 Army Council Decisions (1912), Number 595, pp. 37–40.

204 *Yeomanry and Mounted Rifle Training Parts I and II, 1912*, p. 1.

In training in July 1914 squadrons of the Middlesex Yeomanry and Warwickshire Yeomanry taking part in a 'cavalry fight' misjudged the critical moment at which to pull up, and actually charged full-tilt into each other; 12 horses were knocked over in the collision but, as the Middlesex's historian wrote, 'fortunately swords were not drawn'.[205] For ten years, the yeomanry had successfully defied attempts by the War Office to prevent their training for the arme blanche charge.

Once again, the argument over the relative merits of rifle and sword in this period distracted attention away from the very real reforms taking place in the cavalry, and misled or confused other arms about what the cavalry could do. The most important of these reforms was the creation of a new strength and preparedness in depth through the introduction of the cavalry divisional structure, even if that division had no permanent headquarters and seldom trained as a unit. The number of trained troop horses serving with the cavalry regiments, the basic determinant of how tactically mobile the regiment was in reality, increased from barely 50 per cent in the 1880s to over 80 per cent in 1914, with the expectation that a reserve of horses could bring the regiments up to full strength quickly in wartime.[206] In 1909, following the recommendations of a committee chaired by Haig, a plan was created for entire 'reserve regiments' to be formed in the event of a major war, and six training depots formed throughout the country. An Army Council decision that it was too expensive to keep the cavalry at optimum regimental strength in peacetime meant that the shortage of trained horses continued until 1911, when a system was introduced of boarding out cavalry horses to civilians, so that on mobilisation in 1914 there was no noticeable horse shortage and 115,000 horses were impressed for service in 12 days.[207]

Despite all these reforms, a sense of unreality about the cavalry debate continued to grow within the Army, and among the wider public. Great Britain was the most industrialised country in the world, and a further decline in its agriculture was accompanied by inventions in communications and transport that were very obviously transforming the industrialised world, and were expected to transform the wider world in the course of the twentieth century. This was an age in which telegraph messages were sent round the Empire in a matter of hours, and radio transmissions were sent across the Atlantic; in which both steam railway engines and motor cars had exceeded 100 miles an hour; and in which heavier-than-air powered aircraft flew across the English Channel. The horse population of Great Britain was judged to have declined by over 11 per cent between 1904 and 1910 as motor vehicles took over a variety of horses' roles, the greatest decline coming in riding horses suitable

---

205 Stonham and Freeman, *Historical Records of the Middlesex Yeomanry 1797–1927*, p. 126.

206 TNA WO 27/511 'State and efficiency of the Army and Defences. Reports by Inspector General of the Forces – submitted to the Army Council' (1904–1913), Report for 1913'; Badsey, 'Fire and the Sword', p. 367.

207 TNA WO 163/611 'Recommendations of Committees on Army Matters 1900–1920', (1909) p. 8; WO 163/14 Army Council Decisions (1909), Number 418, p. 43; Speech by the Secretary of State for War (Haldane) quoted in WO 112 Army Estimates 1910/11 p. 2; WO 33/576 'Report of the Committee on the Shortage of Trained Horses for the Cavalry Division on Mobilisation' (1909); James, *British Regiments 1914–18*, pp. 13–15.

as cavalry chargers rather than heavier horses for haulage.[208] It was this recognition that produced in many writers and artists, and quite a few members of the rural upper and middle classes, a nostalgic sense of a pastoral age coming to an end. Their objection was not only to industrialisation and motorisation, but to the rise of modernism in its widest sense.[209] This objection to an increasingly industrial future was shared by many of the polo-playing, foxhunting sons of the shires officering the cavalry regiments. Vaughan in 1914 was looking forward to commanding 4th Cavalry Brigade at Canterbury, 'where I knew there was good dry-fly fishing in the Stour and hunting with three packs, drag, stag and fox'.[210] On 1 September 1915, Home, by then chief staff officer to 1st Cavalry Division, plaintively asked his diary 'why am I not shooting partridges?' rather than fighting a war.[211] One career cavalry officer killed on the Western Front in 1915 was Julian Grenfell, eldest son of Lord Desborough and one of the more controversial of the 'trench poets' for his views of the redemptive powers of war and violence. Grenfell had joined the 1st (Royal) Dragoons in India in 1910, just after de Lisle had left as their commanding officer, and served with them as part of the Meerut Cavalry Brigade in France. Although by definition a poet is not a typical soldier, Grenfell's best-known poem 'Into Battle', with its fatalism and conviction that 'he is dead that will not fight / and who dies fighting has increase' may be understood as one of the most intelligent and powerful evocations of pre-war cavalry spirit.[212]

Particularly after the Boer War, the Army had to struggle with the problem that, in a predominantly urban country, both cavalry horses and recruits who knew how to ride were in increasingly short supply. In 1902 the Adjutant General's staff noted that 'a large number of yeomanry are really townspeople with no intimate knowledge of, or feeling for, horses'.[213] Whereas in 1876 about 76 per cent of yeomen came with their own horses, and 70 per cent in 1899, by 1903 the figure was down to 50 per cent.[214] Rimington considered that only one-sixth of cavalry recruits were natural riders, while traditionalist cavalrymen scoffed at the idea that 'townbred men can be taught to scout like Buffalo Bill and ride like Cossacks', a function which it was increasingly expected would be filled by the mounted rifles and light horse of the Empire.[215] In 1908 it was suggested in *The Cavalry Journal*, rather desperately, that

---

208 'The Scarcity of Horses in the British Empire', *The Cavalry Journal*, Volume 6, Number 24, pp. 472–84. Whether the total number of horses, as opposed to those suitable for the Army, was declining during this period has been disputed by Winton, 'Horsing the British Army 1878–1923', pp. 212–14.

209 Fussell, *The Great War and Modern Memory*, pp. 3–7; Barnett, *The Collapse of British Power*, pp. 424–35; see also Eksteins, *Rites of Spring*.

210 Vaughan, *Cavalry and Sporting Memories*, p. 157.

211 Home, *The Diary of a World War I Cavalry Officer*, p. 82.

212 Grenfell, 'Into Battle', quoted in Gardner, *Up the Line to Death*, pp. 34–6; Stephen, *The Price of Pity*, pp. 84–7; Reader, *'At Duty's Call'*, pp. 130–32.

213 TNA WO 33/246 'Report of Committee on provision of horses for the Imperial Yeomanry' (1902) p. 3.

214 Beckett, *The Amateur Military Tradition 1558–1945*, p. 190.

215 Rimington, *Our Cavalry*, p. 18; 'Cavalry Training by XYZ', *United Service Magazine*, Volume XXXIII, New Series, p. 192.

the government should artificially restrict the number of motor cars and lorries in order to preserve the country's horse population.[216]

The justification for having cavalry in the Army was that the horse provided both greater mobility for functions like scouting, and greater speed in attack and defence. As civilian life became more urbanised and mechanised, the idea of these functions being carried out by men with machines naturally followed. This included such well-known stories as H.G. Wells's *The Land Ironclads* of 1903, which envisaged giant fighting tractors to overcome a future stalemate, although a large and slow-moving fighting vehicle was the last thing the Army needed for its planned war of manoeuvre. Wells also made an impact on popular consciousness with his novel *The War in the Air* of 1908; although perhaps more influential on the Army was Ernest Swinton's 'A Joint in the Harness' of 1907, a tale of a 'cavalry' raid to destroy a crucial bridge behind enemy lines by primitive bomber aircraft.[217] These and many other stories and novels all predicted a future war of technology. As the First World War approached, the cavalry with its horses, swords and lances seemed increasingly to come from another age, both more romantic and more primitive, and to symbolise a military unwillingness to recognise the impact of industrialisation.

In the course of the First World War the argument was made, including by Churchill and particularly by Fuller as the first chief staff officer of the Army's new Tank Corps, that the Army might be (or retrospectively might have been before 1914) remodelled to be based on mechanisation, particularly on tanks and aircraft, and that it was only military conservatism and institutional loyalty to the hierarchy of regiments that had prevented this. Fuller's vision was almost certainly not a practical option even at the height of the First World War, since neither dependable military vehicles nor the industrial base to support them existed on the required scale.[218] Cost also featured in the prevailing attitude towards motor vehicles, as did a reluctance to disturb the Army structure further following the Haldane reorganisation. Even so, and in a manner typical of their ethos, at least one yeomanry regiment carried out experiments with motor cars as early as 1906.[219]

Much before 1904, by far the most practical alternative to the horse for mobile troops was the humble bicycle. By 1914 the military uses of bicycles were well explored, and the savings in terms of cost and maintenance when compared to the horse were obvious. On its creation in 1908 the TF absorbed ten battalions of Volunteer cyclists.[220] But the drawbacks of the bicycle when compared to horse-mounted troops were equally obvious: the soldier had to supply his own motive

---

216 'The Provision of Horses in War', *The Cavalry Journal*, Volume 3, Number 11, p. 341.

217 Travers, 'Future Warfare: H.G. Wells and British Military Theory 1895–1916', pp. 67–87; Harris, *Men, Ideas and Tanks*, pp. 4–10; Swinton, *The Green Curve Omnibus*, pp. 95–118; Clarke, *Voices Prophesying War*, pp. 57–92.

218 Churchill, *The World Crisis*, Volume II, pp. 1219–21; Trythal, *'Boney' Fuller*, pp. 41–96; Holden Reid, *J.F.C. Fuller: Military Thinker*, pp. 30–80; Terraine, *The Smoke and the Fire*, pp. 148–60; Travers, *How the War was Won*, pp. 175–82.

219 French, *Military Identities*, pp. 262–3.

220 'The Future of Cavalry by a Cavalryman', *United Service Magazine*, Volume XLIII, New Series, p. 655.

power, wind and rain could more than halve his average speed, and movement was largely restricted to roads or to level ground, although men could carry their bicycles for short distances.[221] The relative cheapness of bicycles, and the difficulties in providing sufficient trained riders and horses for the yeomanry, led the Adjutant General's staff in 1904 to suggest converting the yeomanry into a force of military cyclists, a suggestion which, given the yeomanry's reaction to giving up their swords, perhaps fortunately never became public.[222] But on the creation of the TF, yeomen who could not provide their own horses were told that they might bring bicycles instead, and the yeomanry brigades were in fact a mixture of mounted rifles and cyclists.[223] Haig in 1906 pressed for a special cyclist unit to serve with the cavalry division, the idea was revived in 1913, and a committee under Allenby was studying it when the First World War broke out.[224] Meanwhile, with the abolition of the MI, the BEF's infantry divisions were each given a cyclist company (taken from the infantry battalions) as well as a cavalry squadron to make up their divisional mounted troops: a signal that the Army regarded fully-trained cyclists as complementary to cavalry. The BEF had fewer than 150 motorcycles, and they were considered too noisy for scouting and awkward to ride with a rifle, a weak argument which suggests that cost was the real explanation.[225]

In military terms the motor vehicle hardly made an impact before the very end of the nineteenth century, but by the outbreak of the First World War it had long ceased to be regarded as some kind of sporting toy. Between 1904 and 1914 the number of private cars registered in Great Britain tripled to 26,238, part of an estimated 132,000 motor vehicles in total.[226] In 1903 the Army created a reserve of 1,500 hired cars, which were considered something of a luxury by the Treasury since their main role was to transport officers.[227] Permanent motorised transport columns were created for the BEF only in 1912, and the cavalry division possessed just 15 staff cars. But the idea of armoured cars was opposed not by the cavalry but by the motor reserve itself. In 1909 one of its senior officers wrote in *The Cavalry Journal*:

---

221 Trapman, 'Cyclists in Conjunction with Cavalry', *The Cavalry Journal*, Volume 3, Number 11, p. 353; Gill, 'Lessons from the Volunteer Cyclist Manoeuvres of 1906', *United Service Magazine*, Volume XXXIV, New Series, p. 106.

222 NAM Roberts Papers 221: Memorandum on Yeomanry by DAAG to Adjutant General, 1 January 1904.

223 Verdin, *The Cheshire (Earl of Chester's) Yeomanry 1898–1967*, p. 40.

224 TNA WO 279/42 'Report of a Conference of General Staff Officers at the Staff College, 9–12 January 1912', pp. 19–29; WO 279/45 'Report of a Conference of General Staff Officers at the Staff College, 13–16 January 1913', pp. 40–46; WO 32/4737 'Army Organisation: Cavalry (Code 14(D)): Provision of cyclists for employment with a Cavalry Division', (1913).

225 TNA WO 33/3026 'Report of the Advisory Committee on Motor Cyclists (Technical Reserve)', (1911), pp. 3–7.

226 Bird, *The Motor Car 1765–1914*, p. 79, p. 119, and pp. 150–200.

227 TNA WO 279/25 'Conference of General Staff Officers at the Staff College 18–21 January 1909', p. 63; Barnes, *The British Army of 1914*, p. 30.

Armoured machine-gun wagons have of course been talked of, although we are not aware that any such vehicles have been built in this country; their advantages are small and their practical disadvantages many. If the machine-guns are to be fired from the car they are confined to the road, if not, the armour is superfluous.[228]

It is both noteworthy and disappointing that there was no major advocate of motorised troops among the British Army's senior officers in the period 1908–1914, which must be considered a blind-spot in military thinking. Soon after the outbreak of the First World War, the Rolls-Royce Silver Ghost (among other cars) was converted to make an excellent armoured car, while lorried machine-gunners became one of the features of the war, followed by increasingly heavily armoured vehicles to protect infantry and machine-gunners as the century progressed. On the other hand, it is also fair to recognise the short time frame, less than a decade before 1914, in which motor vehicles established themselves as a serious challenge to some of the horse's functions. The motor vehicle's serious emergence as a weapon of war came just as the great changes of the Haldane reforms had been agreed and were being carried through.[229]

The same was largely true of the emergence of the aeroplane as a vehicle for scouting. Tethered balloons for observation dated back to before the middle of the nineteenth century, and they had been used (not very successfully) in the Boer War and the Russo-Japanese War; but the first powered heavier-than-air flight took place in 1903, with the tentative emergence of military aviation over the next five years. In 1908 one of the Army's specialists on aeronautics, Major H. Bannerman-Philips, wrote that while balloons and airships had a practical future, heavier than air machines, while they evoked admiration for the courage of their pilots, 'remain interesting toys, of little or no practical value for purposes of war', largely due to their extreme fragility.[230] It was only during the following 12 months that military airpower revealed itself to be both practical and of immense potential, including in the crossing of the English Channel by Louis Blériot in a heavier-than-air machine in 1909, and the establishment of a civil airline in Germany for the giant Zeppelin rigid airships.[231] Also in 1909, one frequent contributor to the *United Service Magazine* reflected:

> It seems conceivable that the aeroplane may revolutionise the functions of the mounted man in war, or even that the 'airman' may in time entirely supersede the horseman. The wheeled motor, or, indeed, the more antiquated man-driven cycle, would have already to a great extent have taken the place of the saddle-horse if only either mechanism could have been made to leap fences and negotiate the varieties of rough and soft 'going'. But the cross-country cycle and 'auto' have failed to materialise, and it may be assumed that

---

228 Mayhew, 'Motor Cars with the Army', *The Cavalry Journal*, Volume 4, Number 16, pp. 438–42.

229 Brown, *British Logistics on the Western Front 1914–1919*, pp. 17–40.

230 H. Bannerman-Phillips, 'The Future of Airships in War', *United Service Magazine*, Volume XXXVII, New Series, p. 589.

231 Buckley, *Air Power in the Age of Total War*, pp. 22–34.

at least the fag end of the pre-aviation era is still in the future as far as military men are concerned.[232]

The two aeroplanes which scouted for the 1910 manoeuvres (together with a successful reconnaissance by an airship) convinced Bannerman-Phillips of their value in war, but still he insisted that:

> It would be fatuous to suppose for a moment that the time has come, or ever will come, when the air-scout by reason of his elevated position will be able to take the place of the reconnoiterer on terra firma, or that cavalry will no longer be employed for reconnaissance.[233]

In a further article dedicated to the issue of aircraft in co-operation with cavalry, Bannerman-Phillips assured his readers that weather conditions in Great Britain and Europe would keep aircraft grounded for two days out of three.[234] Once more, it was the early aviators themselves who expressed doubts about the utility of their aircraft, rather than the cavalry who opposed the idea of air reconnaissance.

It was part of the mythology of air power in the First World War that the scout or pursuit aircraft became the cavalry or knights of the air, and certainly cavalrymen played a willing role in the establishment of the fledgling airpower of the British Army. The Royal Flying Corps came into existence in 1912 with its Military Wing commanded by Major Frederick Sykes of the 15th Hussars, and its Number 3 Squadron took part in the Cavalry Division's training in autumn 1912, prior to the Army manoeuvres held in East Anglia.[235] One of the factors in Grierson's victory over Haig in the 1912 manoeuvres was his more effective use of aircraft for reconnaissance; although both sides used aircraft in conjunction with cavalry.[236] Grierson argued after the manoeuvres for the need for a fight to establish air superiority at the start of a campaign, in much the same way that theorists had argued for the mounted charge to establish cavalry superiority:

> Personally, I think there is no doubt that, before land fighting takes place, we shall have to fight and destroy the enemy's aircraft. It seems to me impossible for troops to fight while hostile aircraft are able to keep up their observation. That is to say, warfare will be impossible unless we have mastery of the air.[237]

This idea of air superiority was taken up very rapidly indeed by the Army, although the War Office position, announced just before the 1912 manoeuvres, was that the

---

232 'Patrick Perterras', (pseudonym of Colonel Henry Pilkington) 'Reflections on the Future of Cavalry', *United Service Magazine*, Volume XLI, New Series, p. 396.

233 Bannerman-Phillips, 'Progress in Aeronautics', *United Service Magazine*, Volume XLIII, New Series, p. 92. Terra firma is Latin for solid ground.

234 Bannerman-Phillips, 'Aircraft in Co-Operation with Cavalry', *The Nineteenth Century and After*, Volume LXIX, p. 80.

235 Mead, *The Eye in the Air*, pp. 40–46.

236 Whitmarsh, 'British Army Manoeuvres and the Development of Military Aviation, 1910–1913', pp. 325–46.

237 Quoted in Ibid., p. 346.

cavalry and the air arm were complementary to each other in the reconnaissance role, rather than rivals.

Following the innovative use of scouting aircraft in the 1912 manoeuvres, Colonel Callwell of *Small Wars* fame proclaimed nothing less than a revolution in warfare:

> The reconnaissance service is of such vital importance that the virtual sacrifice of the mounted troops in its interest is fully justified so long as no other means of obtaining the information exists; but if that service can be carried out by a totally different arm, the whole scheme falls to the ground. The hussar and lancer have no reason to regard their supplantment by flying *corps* as a dire calamity. Rather would such a development in the art of war tend to relieve them of duties which are apt to virtually banish them from the battlefield.[238]

In Colonel Repington's vivid phrase, the cavalry were both the eyes and the fists of the Army, and the tension between these two functions – the past roles of light cavalry and heavy cavalry – had been a major factor in their deliberations for decades; it now looked as if this might change.[239] If their scouting role was diminishing or gone, then almost the only thing that the cavalry had to justify their existence was their battlefield role, and that meant the arme blanche as well as the rifle. But, as one reflective soldier noted in 1910, 'We see that its reconnaissance duties will be lessened, its shock action must be of infrequent occurrence, its protective duties can be carried out by less expensive branches, while envelopment is considered a waste of strength, power and cohesion. What, therefore, is left to our cavalry?'[240]

Only the experience of the next war could reveal whether the cavalry's doctrines had been misconceived, and how well they would perform. Theorists writing in *The Cavalry Journal* before the First World War invited their readers to 'picture the state of two armies, each consisting of five or six corps, after three or four days' desperate strife on the banks of the Meuse'.[241] While the infantry and artillery fought, the cavalry would be held in reserve until 'the *right* moment' when the enemy's ammunition was low, his reserves were all committed and used up, his soldiers were numb with battle fatigue, and a weak point could be created for the cavalry to break through and complete the rout; 'This may not come, remember', wrote one cautious theorist, 'for two or three days.'[242]

---

238 Callwell, 'A Revolution in Land Warfare', *Blackwood's Magazine*, Volume CXCII, p. 652.

239 Repington to *The Times*, 26 March 1910; see also Bidwell and Graham, *Fire-Power*, pp. 32–4.

240 Fraser, 'Military Aircraft in the Light of Experience', *United Service Magazine*, Volume XLIII, New Series, p. 653.

241 'Cavalry in France and Germany 1909', *The Cavalry Journal*, Volume 5, Number 18, p. 225.

242 'Eques', 'Cavalry on the Battlefield', *The Cavalry Journal*, Volume 3, Number 10, p. 143; emphasis in the original.

Chapter 6

The First World War 1914–1918

On 11 August 1914, as the Cavalry Division left for France as part of the BEF, Allenby received a letter from Lord Roberts including a final barbed comment about the cavalry:

> I congratulate you most warmly on having such a splendid command, and I shall look forward with interest to the doings of the cavalry in the war. May I say how earnestly I hope that the men may be made to understand that they should never be on their horses when they can be off them. I issued an order to this effect both during the Boer War and when I was Commander-in-Chief at home – but I fear the custom is never to dismount except by order.[1]

Roberts was still fighting his outdated battle against an imaginary enemy: dismounting on the march and walking alongside the horses in order to rest them had long been standard practice. In November, Roberts died from pneumonia while visiting the troops of the Indian Corps on the Western Front, but his legacy continued to affect the relationships between British generals. Rawlinson, on half-pay at the start of the war, wrote:

> The appointment of [William] Pulteney to command the III Army Corps [of the BEF] and the selection of [Charles] Monro to command the 2nd Division in place of [Archibald] Murray were clear indications that I was not in favour with Sir John [French]. However, when on August 4th it seemed likely that Lord K[itchener] would be appointed Secretary of State for War my hopes revived, and altogether I was not sorry to find myself working under his direct orders.[2]

Rawlinson's belief that he would be working directly under Kitchener was significant: Kitchener's appointment as Secretary of State for War was a political one, but as a field marshal he remained on the active list and he was senior to French, who felt that Kitchener was behaving too much like an old C-in-C.[3] Despite French's complaints, in October Kitchener gave Rawlinson a Corps-sized independent command in an unsuccessful attempt to relieve Antwerp.[4] Kitchener had already asserted his authority over French when in August Grierson, GOC of II Corps, died of a heart attack as the BEF deployed. Ian Hamilton, who like Haig was a full general, put himself forward to Kitchener for the post, and Kitchener asked for French's view. Significantly, French did not request a cavalryman in preference to Hamilton, (and

---

1   LHCMA Allenby Papers 1/5: Roberts to Allenby, 11 August 1914.
2   CAC Rawlinson Papers RAWL 1/1: Diary entry, 7 September 1914.
3   French, *The Life of Field Marshal Sir John French*, p. 221.
4   Maurice, *The Life of General Lord Rawlinson of Trent*, pp. 98–107.

there were none remotely senior enough, except perhaps Allenby), but asked instead for Plumer. Kitchener's response was to insist, in the face of French's objections, on appointing Smith-Dorrien.[5] Kitchener also employed Hamilton as a military-style chief staff officer at the War Office, and in November he appears to have suggested to the French Army's higher command that Hamilton should replace French as GOC-in-C of the BEF, a suggestion soon known to French through Henry Wilson.[6] In all this, the notoriously uncommunicative Kitchener appears to have been trying to rebuild a familiar team of subordinates; but these were also the men who under Roberts had been strong critics of the cavalry, and who in most cases had clashed with French. At BEF General Headquarters (GHQ) Wilson, whose relationship with Kitchener was very bad, held an anomalous position serving as 'sub-chief of staff' in rivalry to Murray as the BEF's chief staff officer (a situation comparable to that which had existed between French, Haig and Erroll in the Cavalry Division of February 1900).[7] Wilson never changed his low opinion of the cavalry as an institution or as an instrument of war: in 1918 Home as chief staff officer of the Cavalry Corps wrote of Wilson simply that 'he hates the cavalry'.[8]

The senior cavalrymen of 1914 were in no sense a united clique or faction within the Army. In August 1914 Haig told King George V of his 'doubts' about French's ability to command the BEF, and his real view was that both French and Murray were unfit for their positions.[9] Hubert Gough made no secret of his hatred of Allenby, and French's view of Gough was at best ambivalent after the Curragh Incident.[10] There is little hard evidence for Haig's and Allenby's views about each other before 1914, although Vaughan thought them good friends, but they became rivals as the war progressed. On Allenby's appointment as GOC Third Army in October 1915, Haig did not hesitate to refer to the cavalry's lack of activity on the Western Front in condemning the decision:

> Allenby (who was given command of the 5th Corps about two months ago [recte: May 1915]) and has done nothing, has been given command of the 3rd Army, and [Hew] Fanshawe (comm[anding the] Cavalry Corps) who has not seen a shot fired this war, has been appointed to succeed him. There seems to be considerable feeling regarding these appointments in the Army. Fanshawe was French's adjutant when he commanded the 19th Hussars and Allenby is an old friend.[11]

---

5   Holmes, *The Little Field Marshal*, pp. 209–10; Lee, *A Soldier's Life*, pp. 128–33.

6   Holmes, *The Little Field Marshal*, pp. 254–5; Magus, *Kitchener*, pp. 287–305. Hamilton was instead given command of the Gallipoli expedition by Kitchener in early 1915.

7   Jeffrey, *Field Marshal Sir Henry Wilson*, pp. 132–40.

8   Home, *The Diary of a World War I Cavalry Officer*, p. 178.

9   Sheffield and Bourne (eds), *Douglas Haig: War Diaries and Letters 1914–1918*, pp. 56–8.

10   See Hughes, 'Edmund Allenby', pp. 12–32 and Sheffield and McCartney, 'Hubert Gough', pp. 75–96.

11   NLS Haig Papers 103: Diary entry, 24 October 1915.

Allenby's loyalty to French lasted beyond the grave: in 1931 he wrote eulogistically that it was to French's influence and example 'that I personally owe every success which has come to me in my military career'.[12]

Because of these rivalries between senior cavalry officers, in the politics of high command in the First World War the importance of the cavalry issue should not be exaggerated, although its occasional prominence did obscure the cavalry's real value as a fighting arm. Given the limitations from which they suffered before 1914, including the failure by successive governments to provide an adequate cavalry force, the cavalry may be reasonably said to have succeeded in the war beyond expectation. Allenby, who from his first wartime appointment as GOC of the Cavalry Division to his last as GOC-in-C of the Egyptian Expeditionary Force (EEF) commanded more successful cavalry operations than any other senior British officer, offered this assessment at the war's end:

> Armed with modern weapons of precision, rifle and machine-gun, in addition to its old-time equipment of sword and lance, cavalry can adapt itself to any conditions. We used to hear, especially in peace manoeuvres, that such or such a tract of country was suited to cavalry action. The truth is that cavalry can and will fit its tactics to any country. This has been shown repeatedly during the war just ended – in the wire-enclosed fields of Flanders, the holding clay of Picardy, the deserts of eastern and western Egypt, the alluvial areas of Mesopotamia, the rocky hills of Judea, the plains of the Palestine coast, the deep valley of the River Jordan, and the mountains of Moab.[13]

Haig, who from December 1915 as GOC-in-C of the BEF commanded the largest British cavalry force assembled in any one theatre, three British and two Indian cavalry divisions (until March 1918), gave a similar opinion:

> Cavalry has been, is, and will continue to be indispensable in modern warfare… It is my considered opinion that had I had at my disposal a much larger force of cavalry the fruits of victory would have been more rapidly gathered…. In rearguard actions, when fighting becomes loose and units scattered, the value of cavalry has been constantly proved both in the retreat from Mons [in August 1914] and during the retirement of the Fifth Army in the Spring of the present year… In open country, such as the theatre of war in which General Allenby's forces were operating, cavalry may well still exercise a decisive influence.[14]

These statements came from senior officers associated with the cavalry who hoped to see it continue in existence after the war; but they were not by any means outright falsehoods. In any consideration of the British cavalry of the First World War, it should never be forgotten that by far the largest cavalry operations in history (using 'cavalry' to mean horse soldiers) took place in the Second World War, and that cavalry continued successfully in military service in some parts of the world beyond

---

12 Allenby, foreword to French, *The Life of Field Marshal Sir John French*, p. xxi.
13 Quoted in the US Cavalry School Monograph, *The Palestine Campaign*, p. 277.
14 NLS Haig Papers 134: Haig to Prothero, 1 December 1918.

the end of the twentieth century. To predict in 1918 that cavalry had a future was to be accurate.[15]

Isolating the contribution of the British cavalry (including the yeomanry and the Indian and dominion mounted forces) from the totality of the First World War and its battles poses much greater problems than for the Boer War. In a war on such a scale with its many theatres, there was scarcely a British battle in which cavalry did not participate, and a history of cavalry operations in the war would be little more (or less) than an appendix to these battles.[16] In addition to the Western Front and Palestine, the British also used the equivalent of a division of Indian cavalry in Mesopotamia, two brigades of yeomanry in Salonika, and at least a regiment of mounted troops in virtually every theatre in which they fought.[17] At Gallipoli, where the nature of the ground made mounted action impossible, British and Australasian troopers fought dismounted in a way that would have been impossible for European cavalry of even 30 years before.[18]

Before 1914, the British Army's aim had been to produce a regular cavalry arm of high quality, with the doctrines and equipment to fight in a European war, but also capable of fighting a colonial war, possibly in collaboration with Indian cavalry and with volunteer British and dominion mounted troops. The great test of British cavalry doctrine and reform came in the first battles on the Western Front of August to December 1914. Then the cavalry faced the problem of the continuing deadlock on the Western Front, the theatre of war where conditions were least favourable to mounted troops. During this period of deadlock, the cavalry's role was comparable to that of any other auxiliary arm in the British effort, which was dominated by infantry, artillery and combat engineering. The cavalry also played a role in the restoration of semi-mobile warfare to the Western Front in 1918, in part contrast to the German doctrinal approach which, although similar, did not employ cavalry (or tanks) to any great extent. Finally the British campaign which most closely resembled a colonial war, fought in Palestine in 1917 and 1918 with British yeomanry, Indian cavalry, and dominion mounted troops against the Ottoman Turkish Empire, formed the last great test of cavalry doctrine and of all the reforms that had taken place since the 1880s.

The cavalry's contribution to the 1914 campaign on the Western Front was also a test of how well the wider British Army understood the use of the new cavalry. The effort that had gone into the arguments about the cavalry's weapons produced superbly confident tactics, but only a hesitant use of cavalry by GHQ. Problems

---

15 Phillips, 'Scapegoat Arm', pp. 37–74; Piekalkiewicz, *The Cavalry of World War II*; Glantz and House, *When Titans Clashed*.

16 A summary of British cavalry on the Western Front can be found in Badsey, 'Cavalry and the Development of Breakthrough Doctrine', pp. 138–74. Although inevitably that article and this chapter cover some of the same issues and draw on some of the same evidence, they are intended as complementary to each other. To list general histories of the First World War would be redundant, but of recent one-volume histories Stevenson, *1914–1918: The History of the First World War* is the best, while to judge from its first volume, Strachan, *The First World War: Volume I: To Arms*, this multi-volume history will be definitive.

17 Anglesey, *A History of the British Cavalry Volume 6*, pp. 175–6.

18 Phillips, 'Scapegoat Arm', pp. 50–55; Badsey, 'Cavalry and the Development of Breakthrough Doctrine', pp. 151–2.

also occurred between Allenby's improvised Cavalry Division headquarters and the cavalry brigades.[19] Both the British cavalry's doctrine of manoeuvre within brigades, and the wide dispersal often employed, meant that throughout the war the brigade, rather than the division, was the basic tactical unit for mounted combat.

At least part of the British hesitancy in 1914 came from the knowledge that they were seriously outnumbered. Potentially, 15 British cavalry regiments with their supporting artillery and machine-guns faced both the German II Cavalry Corps of three divisions and I Cavalry Corps of two divisions, or 30 larger cavalry regiments with ten Jäger battalions between them, deployed to cover the gap between First and Second Armies.[20] But even before the British encountered the Germans, an early episode revealed the limitations of German cavalry doctrine, which failed badly on 12 August when II Cavalry Corps repeatedly tried to force the line of the River Gette at Haelen against dismounted Belgian cavalry, where its mounted charges suffered heavy losses.[21] Mauled in Belgium and unable to penetrate the opposing French cavalry screen, both I and II Cavalry Corps were held back between First Army and Second Army. By the time that they first encountered the BEF, the German cavalry were very reluctant to risk themselves, and fought 'chiefly at long range, with artillery' as Allenby noted.[22]

In September, Eric von Falkenhayn, the German War Minister and later Chief of the Great General Staff, announced that 'The dismounted cavalryman should be able to fight exactly as an infantryman; cavalry charges no longer play any part in warfare.'[23] At the end of 1914 German cavalry were issued with bayonets, and in July 1915 their swords were withdrawn, leaving them with lances, pistols and carbines. Although German infantry divisions continued to include a squadron of divisional cavalry, from late 1914 until late 1916 all German cavalry divisions were relocated to the Eastern Front (with the exception of one division used in a policing role in Belgium), and in the course of the war most cavalry divisions were dismounted. This was partly in response to the failure of German cavalry doctrine in the face of the new firepower, but largely a consequence of other factors. As a semi-official German account commented enviously (if not entirely accurately) after the war:

> A shortage of both horses and men had forced us to utilise almost the entire cavalry as dismounted troops. Our enemies, on the other hand, not being cut off by any blockade from fresh supplies and from sources of fresh levies could afford to retain a large part

---

19 These are discussed most critically in Gardner, *Trial By Fire*, although other accounts including Holmes, *The Little Field Marshal*, pp. 195–240 should be read as correctives.

20 The German cavalry divisions were each three brigades of two regiments; for a detailed order of battle see Becke, *Nery, 1914*, pp. 366–8. This short book was reprinted from an original article of the same name in the *Journal of the Royal Artillery*, Volume LIV, Number 3, 1927, pp. 307–69. The five battalions with I Cavalry Corps included the Guard Jäger and the Guard Schützen battalions.

21 von Poseck, *The German Cavalry in 1914 in Belgium and France*, pp. 21–8; Becke, *Nery, 1914*, pp. 307–8; Guderian, *Achtung – Panzer!*, pp. 26–33.

22 LHCMA Allenby Papers 1/5: Allenby to his wife, 30 August 1914.

23 Quoted in translation in the Editor's Notes for the *United Service Magazine*, Volume LI, New Series, p. 226.

of their cavalry for the final deciding battles. As a matter of fact, the entente cavalry was frequently thrown into battle and fought mounted during our retreat in 1918.[24]

Three German cavalry brigades from two divisions helped cover the retirement to the Hindenburg Line in early 1917, but otherwise these two divisions were used dismounted in the Vosges, and German cavalry did not play any significant part in their offensives on the Western Front in 1918.

Characteristically and revealingly, the British misinterpreted the German cavalry's lack of aggression in 1914, attributing it to a pre-war doctrine of cavalry reliance on dismounted fire-action and neglect of the arme blanche, rather than the opposite.[25] Because of this German failure, the mass charge of cavalry division against cavalry division in advance of the closing armies, for which the British had practised the close-order divisional charge, never took place. Instead, British cavalry achieved domination over their German enemies by many small-scale actions, combining mounted charges with dismounted firepower and artillery. But this was not what the public expected or understood, or often what they were told. Allenby wrote to his wife in September that 'The great charges, captures of guns, etc., are mostly inventions of the reporters, none of whom have been nearer [the front] than Paris.'[26]

The early discovery that the German cavalry was tactically inferior to the British removed considerable pressure from Allenby. If he had wrecked the Cavalry Division in an ill-judged mass charge he could have lost the scouting and screening force on which the BEF depended in about ten minutes. As it was, the cavalry brigades spread out for scouting (with Chetwode's independent 5th Cavalry Brigade attached to Haig's I Corps), and by the morning of 21 August they had identified the threat posed by the arriving Germans, only to have their reports rejected by GHQ.[27] Most of the BEF's credible scouting information both before and after the Battle of Mons came from aircraft, which rapidly took the main reconnaissance role, as had been predicted before the war.[28]

As in previous wars, good cavalry doctrine and training could not guarantee success in battle, particularly for an arm whose chief value lay in quick decisions taken in confused circumstances. What might have happened to the whole Cavalry Division, and with what consequences for the BEF, was shown at Audregnies on 24 August (the day after Mons), when under disputed circumstances de Lisle as GOC 2nd Cavalry Brigade ordered – or at least failed to restrain – a mass charge with artillery support by the 9th Lancers and two squadrons of the 4th Dragoon Guards for almost a mile over unreconnoitred ground, in the general direction of two German divisions and at least nine batteries. Well short of contact with the enemy, the charge was halted by pre-war wire enclosures and a railway embankment. The main

---

24 von Poseck, *The German Cavalry 1914 in Belgium and France*, p. 221.

25 Nash, *German Army Handbook April 1918*, pp. 63–6. The original of this handbook was written by War Office Intelligence; a reproduction with an introduction by David Nash was published in 1977.

26 LHCMA Allenby Papers 1/5: Allenby to his wife, 26 September 1914.

27 Edmonds, *Official History France and Belgium 1914, Volume I*, p. 514; Barrow, *The Fire of Life*, pp. 143–4.

28 Mead, *The Eye in the Air*, pp. 52–8.

effect was to scatter most of the brigade, although only 169 men became casualties. De Lisle's special brigade order praised the 'true cavalry spirit of the 9th Lancers in daring to charge unbroken infantry in order to save neighbouring troops'.[29] A lieutenant in the brigade's third regiment, the 18th Hussars, wrote that 'We all think the General played the fool and we all thought each other dead', although he was surprised, after seeing the two regiments vanish into shellfire, how few losses had been taken.[30]

The consequences of this charge continued to be felt next day, as with most of 2nd Cavalry Brigade still scattered, the BEF's cavalry screen failed. Allenby lost all contact with Gough's 3rd Cavalry Brigade, and advised Smith-Dorrien that night that he did not have enough troops to screen II Corps on the following day, leading to Smith-Dorrien's decision to stand and fight at Le Cateau on 26 August.[31] Many years later, Chetwode and Barrow both contended that Gough had deliberately taken his brigade 'as far away from the Bull [Allenby] as possible' to give himself an independent command.[32] The allegation was not merely that Gough had disobeyed orders, but that he was allowed to profit from it largely because his brother John was Haig's chief staff officer: 3rd Cavalry Brigade never came back under Allenby, and Hubert Gough was given effective command of the new 2nd Cavalry Division (initially just 3rd and 5th Brigades) from 5 September onwards. Gough was utterly unrepentant, later claiming that he had received no orders and had exercised his own initiative as a cavalry officer should.[33]

After Le Cateau the BEF was never seriously troubled by the Germans in the retreat from Mons, as their First Army advanced south-westward with most of II Cavalry Corps conforming to the advance rather than pursuing southwards, partly since the Germans assumed that the BEF had already been largely destroyed, an assessment shared by the French and even briefly by GHQ.[34] For more than a week the British cavalry regiments prevented the Germans from properly locating the BEF, fighting in a highly dispersed fashion and often out of touch with their higher

---

29 IWM Fraser Papers: 'Official Report of the Action at Audregnies on 24 August 1914 by Lieutenant Colonel D.G.M. Campbell, commanding 9th Lancers', and 'report by Brigadier General H. de B. de Lisle' including 'Special Brigade Order 28 August 1914'; Coleman, *From Mons to Ypres with French*, p. 7.

30 NAM Haslam Papers: Haslam to his parents, 4 September 1914; Anglesey, *A History of the British Cavalry Volume 7*, pp. 119–25.

31 See in particular Smith-Dorrien's own version: BL Smith-Dorrien Papers [Add. Mss. 52777]: MS Account, Volume I, pp. 31–3.

32 LHCMA Allenby Papers 6/6: Chetwode to Wavell, 20 June 1938, and 6/6: Barrow to Wavell, not dated; Wavell, *Allenby*, pp. 136–8.

33 Gough, *The Fifth Army*, pp. 8–33. This version of Gough's memoirs was ghost written for him in 1931 by Bernard Newman, the novelist and travel writer, at the instigation of Basil Liddell Hart; see Newman, *Speaking From Memory*, p. 62 and correspondence between Newman and Liddell Hart in LHCMA: Liddell Hart Papers 1/543: 'Newman' File. The designation of 2nd Cavalry Division for Gough's command became official on 13 September 1914.

34 Anglesey, *A History of the British Cavalry 1816–1919 Volume 7*, pp. 143–7; Becke, *Nery, 1914*, pp. 308–9; Doughty, *Pyrrhic Victory*, pp. 78–9.

headquarters, so that only on 30 August did the three remaining brigades come back under the Cavalry Division's control.[35] Although not all encounters with German cavalry in the retreat were automatic British successes, their many small victories had a strong cumulative effect. At Cerizy on 28 August, 5th Cavalry Brigade overwhelmed the advancing German 2nd Guard Dragoons in a combined fire-and-charge manoeuvre that might have been taken directly from the diagrams in *Cavalry Training 1912*; while at Nery early on 1 September, 1st Cavalry Brigade with its horse artillery, surprised in bivouacs by the German 4th Cavalry Division, turned a perilous situation around by defeating the Germans with superior firepower; a rare case of a dismounted defence becoming a British cavalry legend.[36]

As the British moved onto the offensive in the Battle of the Marne and the Battle of the Aisne, the cavalrymen and their horses were already understrength and close to exhaustion, and like all other combatants in 1914 they were discovering that defence was easier than attack. There was also the same uncertainty at GHQ on how much to risk the cavalry. Haig was scathing about what he saw as missed opportunities, writing on 7 September that:

> I saw the Aldershot [1st] Cavalry Brigade for the first time since we left Aldershot. Horses looked well but thin. I saw Gen[eral] Allenby and Colonel [John] Vaughan (the GSO1 Cav[alry] Div[ision]). I thought they were not doing much, in fact our infantry was in front of their left, and eventually the Cavalry Division bivouacked *behind* my right flank.[37]

Although some of the cavalry's problems appear to have come from GHQ's orders, they remained in continual contact with the retreating Germans in the advance from the Aisne, scoring several minor tactical victories. An infantry regimental officer wrote admiringly a month later of how 'our cavalry always ride sword in hand or lance at the "carry", and charge at sight at any hostile mounted bodies within charging distance'.[38]

In this war of movement the British enjoyed two considerable advantages over their German enemies and their French allies, both of them products of their tactical reforms before the war. The first was a considerably superior standard of horsemastership, and consequently much fitter horses able to charge. With the short distances involved to the theatre of war, acclimatisation was not an issue as it had been in the Boer War, and fodder was not seen as a problem partly because of the competence of Wully Robertson as the BEF's Quartermaster General.[39] In contrast the Germans suffered severe supply problems, and by 4 September Colonel General

---

35 The claim has been made that the Cavalry Division 'disintegrated' during the retreat; but this is to misunderstand British cavalry tactics of the period; see Gardner, 'Command and Control in the "Great Retreat" of 1914', pp. 29–54.

36 Becke, *Nery, 1914*, pp. 324–44; Anglesey, *A History of the British Cavalry 1816–1919 Volume 7*, pp. 136–55; von Poseck, *The German Cavalry 1914 in Belgium and France*, pp. 81–2; Holmes, *Riding the Retreat*, pp. 213–19 and pp. 253–7.

37 NLS Haig Papers 98: Diary entry, 7 September 1914, emphasis in the original.

38 Terraine (ed.), *General Jack's Diary*, p. 63; see also Anglesey, *A History of the British Cavalry Volume 7*, pp. 180–196; Gardner, *Trial By Fire*, pp. 73–108.

39 Robertson, *From Private to Field Marshal*, pp. 206–13.

Helmut von Moltke, Chief of the Great General Staff, advised that they had 'hardly a horse in the army that can go out of a walk'.[40] Where the British outshone both the French and Germans was in having less weight on the horses and resting them whenever possible. In November a trooper of the composite Household Regiment described some captured German cavalry horses as 'reduced to skin, bone and sores. The saddlery was superior to our officers' [saddlery]. The wallets were huge, and contained more odds and ends than a whole troop of ours. No wonder the much vaunted Uhlan is a poor cavalryman.'[41] Lieutenant Spiers of the 11th Hussars, serving as a liaison officer with the French, remembered that 'there were thousands of animals with sore backs' in the French cavalry, from overloading and poor horsemastership, and 'the smell of some units, owing to this cause, was painful'.[42]

The second advantage enjoyed by the British cavalry was not simply the superiority of their Lee-Enfield rifles over German and French carbines, but the training that went with these rifles and the willingness to fight dismounted and even entrench that had been established before the war. The French Berthier carbine, a worse firearm even than its German Mauser equivalent, was habitually described by the British as a 'toy' or 'pop-gun'. In September the commanding officer of the composite Household Regiment wrote home, 'I regret I cannot say much good for the [French] cavalry. They do nothing but sit on their horses and retire directly an advance is made on them. In fact they are not worth a Damn. They carry what looks like toy rifles over their shoulders, a long lance, and a sword.'[43] Mostly, the British regarded the French cavalry as brave but hopelessly compromised by their pre-war arme blanche doctrines. Spiers recalled French regiments in October 1914 near Béthune actually charging dismounted with lances in lieu of any better tactics.[44] Of the German cavalry Allenby wrote to his wife in October 1914 that 'We seldom get in touch with their mounted men. They won't face us, but [rely?] on machine guns and artillery, to which they are little more than an escort. They fight a little on foot, but depend for that chiefly on infantry or bicycles.'[45]

By the middle of October Allenby's command had grown to a Cavalry Corps through the addition of the 3rd Cavalry Division under Byng. Allenby wrote to his wife that 'The French are much struck by the all-round work of our cavalry; but they are rather shocked to see them in the trenches, as they think that's derogatory to the Cavalry Spirit! They admit, too, that we look after our horses better than they do, and make them last longer.'[46] Vaughan described how on 12 October early in the First Battle of Ypres his 3rd Cavalry Brigade captured the Mont des Cats using tactics rehearsed in peacetime, 'Off galloped the 16th [Lancers] in three lines well extended. Dismounted and charged the trenches on foot. Of course, played on by

---

40 Quoted in Barnett, *The Swordbearers*, p. 81; see also van Creveld, *Supplying War*, pp. 124–5.
41 Lloyd, *A Trooper in the Tins*, p. 99.
42 Spears, *Liaison 1914*, p. 101.
43 IWM Cook Papers: Cook to his home, 20 September 1914.
44 Spears, *Liaison 1914*, p. 100.
45 LHCMA Allenby Papers 1/5: Allenby to his wife, 14 October 1914.
46 Ibid., 1/5/25: Allenby to his wife, 7 October 1914.

machine-guns at close range, the Huns could not put their heads up and the 16th had only seven casualties.'[47]

The cavalry's willingness to fight in any way necessary culminated in the emergency of First Ypres in their largely using dismounted tactics on Messines ridge, sometimes in ways for which they had no pre-war training. Given that by October a dismounted cavalry division was not much stronger than an infantry battalion, Home thought that 'no other nation could do it, it is a game of pure bluff, that is all', adding that at Messines village 'The cavalry have had to do most things but street fighting with bayonets is quite new.'[48] Haig recorded how in the crisis of the battle on 31 October two regiments of 6th Cavalry Brigade advanced to seal the gap between his hard-pressed infantry formations, 'with much dash, partly mounted and partly dismounted'.[49] At the end of the battle French addressed the cavalry, laying 'special emphasis on the fact that in 48 hours, on the 30th–31st October, the Cavalry Corps held a front of seven miles against the attacks of a whole German Army Corps – a record feat for cavalry'.[50] With characteristic cavalry insouciance, a captain in the 5th Lancers wrote to his parents that 'We really only did what the infantry always do, except for the fact that we knew we had no supports or big guns.'[51]

The fighting from Mons to First Ypres ('Wipers') was as costly for the cavalry as for the rest of the pre-war BEF, with losses almost on the scale predicted before the war. By December 1914, 1st Cavalry Division (now only two brigades) had two regiments below half strength, and four regiments below two-thirds strength; in other regiments losses of 200 or 300 men were not uncommon, and the Household Regiment used up the entire line cavalry reserve of trained men to replace their losses.[52] The Cavalry Corps was brought up to its full strength of 27 regiments over winter 1914–1915 only by the Household Regiment expanding to field its three parent regiments as a brigade, and by the addition of five yeomanry regiments.[53] In October 1914, as a consequence of pre-war planning, the Indian Cavalry Corps commanded by Rimington (two divisions including six British regiments), arrived in France to accompany the Indian Corps.[54] So, with little thought as to strategy beyond the urgent need for troops at the war's start, five cavalry divisions came to serve on the Western Front by spring 1915.

The wider context of what happened to the British cavalry for the next three years was the creation, operational deployment, and maintenance in combat of almost 70

---

47 Vaughan, *Cavalry and Sporting Memories*, p. 171; Vaughan had moved to take command of 3rd Cavalry Brigade by this date.
48 Home, *The Diary of a World War I Cavalry Officer*, pp. 30–33.
49 NLS Haig Papers 99: Diary entry, 31 October 1914.
50 LHCMA Allenby Papers 1/5: Allenby to his wife, 12 November 1914.
51 NAM Talbot-Rice Papers: Talbot-Rice to his parents, 4 November 1914.
52 Home, *The Diary of a World War I Cavalry Officer*, p. 44; Lloyd, *A Trooper in the Tins*, p. 75; for casualties see Badsey, 'Cavalry and the Development of Breakthrough Doctrine', p. 140; Anglesey, *A History of the British Cavalry Volume 7*, p. 215.
53 Details of the organisation of the cavalry divisions and any changes are in Becke, *Order of Battle of Divisions Part 1 – The Regular British Divisions*, pp. 1–24.
54 See Grimshaw, *Indian Cavalry Officer*, pp. 201–2; Corrigan, *Sepoys in The Trenches*, pp. 23–7.

British, Indian and dominion infantry divisions, an effort to which all other troop considerations were secondary.[55] The yeomanry regiments volunteered for overseas service along with the rest of the TF, and eventually 20 yeomanry regiments were used as divisional cavalry (Indian divisions at first had an Indian cavalry squadron instead). Most, but not all, infantry divisions that served on the Western Front were given divisional cavalry squadrons, although from early 1915 most of these squadrons were grouped back together as Corps cavalry regiments.[56] The yeomanry serving overseas were issued with swords (if they did not have them already), and as the war progressed the cavalry and yeomanry were given hand grenades, steel helmets, trench mortars and other equipment identical to that of the infantry, except that the cavalry were given the more portable .303-inch Hotchkiss light machine-guns rather than Lewis guns; by 1916 it was doctrine that every man in a squadron should know how to fire its machine-guns.

In the entire course of the war, no new British regular cavalry regiments were created, nor were the line cavalry regiments expanded, the replacements for the cavalry coming at first from the reserve regiments at home and later from the yeomanry.[57] The need for yeomanry regiments to serve on the Western Front put an end to the pre-war TF mounted brigade structure, and instead those regiments not serving overseas were consolidated into first two and then three large mounted divisions, with a cyclist battalion for each brigade to regularise the position of the yeomanry cyclists.[58] The yeomanry of 2nd Mounted Division were sent to Egypt for the war against the Ottoman Empire, intended at first as a general reserve, and then used dismounted at Gallipoli in 1915, in company with two brigades of Australian Light Horse and one of New Zealand Mounted Rifles.[59] Back in Great Britain, 1st Mounted Division functioned principally as a training division, while second line yeomanry regiments were created in the same way as for the infantry of the TF, and 2/2nd Mounted Division established in May 1915.

Despite all pre-war concerns, the dismounted British and Australasian troopers at Gallipoli made good infantry, although there were the same problems as at Ypres with units that were too small and lacked adequate firepower when compared with infantry battalions and divisions. Since they left their horses behind in Egypt, acclimatisation was not a major issue later in the Sinai or the Palestine campaigns. British cavalry horses remained the half-bred hunter type supplied from Ireland, while the Australians, New Zealanders and Indians used Walers supplied from their own countries; the typical fully equipped trooper in Palestine rode at about 21

---

55 The best account of this remains Simkins, *Kitchener's Army*; see also Middlebrook, *Your Country Needs You*.

56 The most famous example of an infantry division without a cavalry squadron was 63rd (Royal Naval) Division, which gave rise to the myth of the 'Royal Naval Hussars'; see Jerrold, *The Royal Naval Division*, p. 48.

57 Beckett, 'The Territorial Force', pp. 132–46.

58 Becke, *Order of Battle of Divisions Part 2a – The First-Line Territorial Divisions*, pp. 1–34.

59 Steel and Hart, *Defeat at Gallipoli*, p. 225 and pp. 287–92; Travers, *Gallipoli 1915*, pp. 271–4.

stones, and the comparative absence of horse exhaustion was a tribute to their high standards of horsemastership.[60]

After Gallipoli, the Australian and New Zealand infantry were sent to the Western Front, and elements of three mounted regiments were sent with them to act as divisional cavalry. Patrols of the 13th Light Horse, the divisional cavalry of I ANZAC Corps, played a useful part in the Battle of the Menin Road Ridge in September 1917 as part of the Third Battle of Ypres (Passchendaele), and later used 'bold mounted tactics' during the general advance and exploitation of September 1918.[61] Meanwhile, 2nd Mounted Division was broken up in Egypt, and some of its yeomanry brigades used for operations in Egypt and Sinai. In March 1916 the EEF's first mounted division was formed, the ANZAC Mounted Division of four brigades under the Australian Major General Harry Chauvel, who had served with the Queensland Mounted Infantry in the Boer War. Chauvel thought that his light horse troopers came from 'a different class of men altogether' from the Australian infantry, echoing British recruiters before the war.[62] But while the characteristic British officers' opinion of dominion infantry was that they were brave but reckless and needed discipline, British cavalrymen considered that their dominion mounted troops at first lacked the enterprise that came from cavalry spirit. In May 1917, after Allenby had succeeded to command of the EEF, his chief staff officer wrote that 'The Chief is of the opinion that Chauvel and Co. are a bit fond of digging in and walking on their flat feet instead of using their horses to the utmost.'[63]

Unlike the Australians, in late 1914 and 1915 the Canadians largely converted their militia mounted rifle regiments into infantry battalions for service on the Western Front. An exception was the Corps cavalry regiment of the Canadian Corps, the Canadian Light Horse, which also contrived a very small but successful mounted charge by a patrol on 12 April 1917 during the Battle of Arras, briefly reported by the Germans at the time as 'a strong force of English cavalry has broken through'.[64] The two peacetime Canadian cavalry regiments formed the Canadian Cavalry Brigade, first brigaded with King Edward's Horse and then with the re-founded Fort Garry Horse, and the brigade served on the Western Front from 1916 onwards. There were no appreciable doctrinal difficulties in assimilating the Canadians, although there

---

60 Preston, *The Desert Mounted Corps*, p. 95.

61 Monash, *The Australian Victories in France in 1918*, p. 178; Lee, 'Command and Control in Battle: British Divisions on the Menin Road Ridge, 20 September 1917', pp. 132–3. The organisational and name changes were as complex for the ANZAC formations as for the British Army, but it appears that the first ANZAC divisional cavalry were squadrons of the 4th Light Horse (which was later brought back up to full strength with the EEF), the 13th Light Horse, and the Otago Mounted Rifles from New Zealand, designed as the I ANZAC Corps Mounted Regiment; by 1916 this had been disbanded, so that the reformed 13th Light Horse acted as the Corps cavalry to I ANZAC Corps and later for the Australian Corps, while II ANZAC Corps Mounted Regiment was formed from elements of 4th Light Horse and the Otago Mounted Rifles and acted as divisional cavalry for II ANZAC Corps and later for XXII Corps.

62 AWM Chauvel Papers Folder 5: Chauvel to his wife, 7 January 1916.

63 IWM Chetwode Papers: Lynden-Bell to Chetwode, 30 May 1917.

64 Quoted in Williams, *Byng of Vimy*, pp. 161–3.

were considerable criticisms from all sides of 'Galloper Jack' Seely as their brigade commander (a considerable step down from his previous position as Secretary of State for War until the Curragh Incident forced his resignation), and the brigade was felt to improve when in May 1918 the invalided Seely was replaced by a Canadian officer, R.W. Paterson.[65]

Many doctrinal pamphlets were published by the BEF during the war, but *Cavalry Training 1912*, reprinted in 1915 to incorporate some minor additions including a short section on the importance of cavalry in pursuit, remained the cavalry's only published doctrine; and at the war's end Allenby argued that it needed no further revision.[66] Although there were additions to cavalry doctrine, particularly between 1915 and 1917, they were not published or disseminated beyond the Cavalry Corps, possibly because they were not universally accepted within it. The pre-war idea of waiting while the infantry and artillery fought soon adopted a name from the Army's 'Bingo' system of map reading (before the grid system of map references was introduced early in 1915), in which lettering on a shared map was treated as if it existed physically on the ground (*Field Service Regulations Part 1: Operations* gave the example of 'crossroads ½ mile S.W. of the second E in HASELEY').[67] This became a catchphrase: the cavalry were waiting until the infantry and artillery made a gap in the enemy lines, and then they would 'Ride for the G in GAP', otherwise known as 'putting the cavalry through'.[68] With its overtones of cavalry élan and dash, but also its implications of uselessness, the 'Gap Scheme' shaped perceptions of the cavalry's role considerably. By June 1915 it was already a sour joke among the cavalry staffs: they could plan endlessly for how to ride through the 'Gap', but someone would have to make it first.[69]

Although the Gap Scheme was the cavalry ideal, plans for other forms of cavalry exploitation on a smaller scale were in circulation by December 1914. Home, who was very unimpressed, had no doubt as to their historical origin:

> Talked very wildly about a Cavalry Raid – what on I wonder? The Kiel Canal and the German Fleet? We are an extraordinary nation – times are quiet so men at once commence casting about and someone remembers the word 'raid' having probably read the American Civil War. So at once they say what a good thing it would be – they forget the essential of a 'raid': quick movement, secrecy, surprise.... Such talk is childish, it is absolute lack of knowledge. Let the Infantry burst a hole in the German lines first so as to let the Cavalry through, then something might be done.[70]

---

65 Home, *The Diary of a World War I Cavalry Officer*, p. 125; Grodzinski and McNorgan, 'It's a Charge, Boys, It's a Charge!', pp. 241–50; Morton, *A Military History of Canada*, pp. 137–72.

66 LHCMA Allenby Papers 2/5: Allenby to Vaughan, 2 March 1919; *Cavalry Training 1915*, p. 242. The author expresses his gratitude to Vivian John for this point.

67 *Field Service Regulations Volume I: Operations*, p. 20; see also Bidwell and Graham, *Fire-Power*, p. 102; Holmes, *Tommy*, pp. 454–5.

68 This expression was so widespread so early in the war that any search for its point or date of origin appears futile; see e.g. Wavell, *Allenby*, p. 143.

69 Home, *The Diary of a World War I Cavalry Officer*, p. 73.

70 Ibid., pp. 43–4.

Despite Home's criticisms, the idea of a raid behind enemy lines became and remained a feature of British battle plans. While a Gap Scheme implied a major German collapse, on the Western Front a Cavalry Raid implied only making a temporary hole through which a body of cavalry could be passed to create mayhem in the enemy rear before regaining the safety of British lines quickly, in contrast to the deep raids of earlier wars.

In addition to the Gap Scheme and the Cavalry Raid, First Ypres had established the value of the cavalry as a mobile reserve of firepower, in attack or defence. Home, who became chief staff officer to the Cavalry Corps in August 1915, noted that 'A Cavalry Division [of three brigades] dismounted produces 1,500 rifles or two weak battalions. On the other hand, 1,500 rifles plus the mobility of the horse (i.e. to put in quickly at the most favourable place) are equal to 4–5,000 infantry put into that place 24 hours later.'[71] In January 1915, Hubert Gough invited his brother John (late of the Rifle Brigade and still Haig's chief staff officer at First Army until he was fatally wounded a month later) to 'come over today to criticise and help us in practising the infantry attacks and tactics. We had the 5th [Cavalry] Brigade trying to fight its way through a thick wood in the morning and the other two [brigades] attacking a village in the afternoon.'[72] In May 1915, Home recorded a difference of opinion between officers like himself who felt that 'cavalry spirit' was best expressed by a willingness to undertake any form of fighting that was needed, and more traditional officers with what he considered 'a bad and rotten attitude' of being content to sit behind the lines and wait for the 'Gap' to be made.[73] Other than acting as a mobile reserve and holding trenches, while out of the line the cavalry tried to keep their horses fit and up to the demands of sudden hard work in all weathers (which was a full-time occupation), and carried out a variety of duties including even trench digging. 'No doubt this was necessary work', one officer complained, 'but nothing could have been devised to dampen the spirits of cavalrymen more.'[74] Wully Robertson, promoted to chief staff officer at GHQ, voiced concern in September 1915 that the cavalry 'might lack push after all our trench work'.[75]

Very quickly, a further doctrinal debate emerged from the deadlock, over nothing less than the cavalry's continued presence on the Western Front. Although this was not a continuation of the arguments after the Boer War, the attitudes formed before 1914 played some part in it. Once more the dispute reached the highest political levels, and once more the opinions expressed ran the full gamut including suggestions of abolishing the cavalry outright. In June 1915, a captain serving with the 2nd Indian Cavalry Division, who had experienced nothing but trench duty, gave voice to what seems to have been a fairly typical point of view:

> I hear there is some talk of breaking up the Cavalry Corps. I am not surprised. At present one sees the absurd situation of a body of troops requiring more mechanical transport to feed it than would suffice to move the man personnel [sic] of it almost any distance in

---

71 Ibid., p. 45.
72 Quoted in Beckett, *Johnnie Gough VC*, p. 197.
73 Home, *The Diary of a World War I Cavalry Officer*, p. 71.
74 Lumley, *The History of the Eleventh Hussars*, p. 258.
75 Cited in Home, *The Diary of a World War I Cavalry Officer*, p. 83.

one third of the time their horses could do. So far as I can ascertain, there is nothing that the Cavalry has so far accomplished, that Infantry in armoured busses could not have achieved.... A large force of Cavalry consumes immense quantities of fodder that are required for gun teams [instead]. When the men dismount, 25 per cent have to remain with the horses and the latter block the road to a degree not often appreciated by the uninitiated. Mechanical transport possesses none of these drawbacks. I can quite understand that in uncivilised countries, or semi-civilised ones, Cavalry are invaluable... [But] surely it is better to put one's money into guns and aircraft rather than into Cavalry?[76]

For the next three years, the future of the cavalry on the Western Front would be argued over largely in those terms: whether their presence justified the supplies and transport needed to maintain them and their horses; whether 'armoured busses' or the equivalent offered a practical alternative; and whether or not British attacks should include provision for a breakthrough and the employment of the cavalry for exploitation. Just as the arguments after the Boer War had been caricatured as taking place between believers in the rifle and believers in the mass knee-to-knee charge, so arguments over cavalry on the Western Front were represented as taking place between believers in a methodical form of infantry attack, and believers in a massed charge for the 'Gap'. As on the previous occasions, both sides often preferred hypothetical arguments and asserted appeals to self-evidence to any real attempt to analyse the cavalry's contribution to the battlefield. With each successive British failure, the cavalry waiting in the rear took on a symbolic importance that went far beyond the facts. Already over-sensitive to criticism after the Boer War, the cavalry became increasingly defensively minded, seeing insults and plots against them where they did not exist, as well as where they certainly did.

On 7 March 1915, Gough visited First Army, where Haig briefed him on his plans for the forthcoming battle of Neuve Chapelle, his expectations of breaking the German lines, and his hopes for Gough's 2nd Cavalry Division, recording next day that 'I urged that the cavalry must go through the gap when made by our infantry and guns!'[77] French appears to have allowed for the possibility of all five cavalry divisions pouring through a rupture in the German lines, while at the same time cautioning Rimington of the Indian Cavalry Corps 'against risking his troops mounted too close to the enemy. He is not experienced in this kind of warfare and thinks he may be able to do some dashing cavalry work'.[78] Preceded by a short bombardment, the battle took place 10–13 March, but with no opportunity for the cavalry. On the second day, Haig attached an infantry brigade to Gough's cavalry division to exploit any local advance, and an armoured car unit under the Duke of Westminster was also made ready to support the cavalry against machine-gun nests. After the failure to break through, Haig made what was to become a repeated complaint in Western Front battles: that as the local commander he had not been given command of a cavalry force early enough to exploit a potential situation, 'Had I had a cavalry brigade

---

76 Grimshaw, *Indian Cavalry Officer 1914–15*, p. 79.

77 Sheffield and Bourne (eds), *Douglas Haig: War Diaries and Letters 1914–1918*, p. 108; NLS Haig Papers 100: Diary entry, 8 March 1915.

78 Quoted in Holmes, *The Little Field Marshal*, pp. 273–4; Home, *The Diary of a World War I Cavalry Officer*, p. 59.

on the spot, I would have pushed it at once through the village, where our troops were completely successful.'[79] The Cavalry Corps felt that the battle plan for Neuve Chapelle had not been communicated properly beforehand. 'This sort of thing does not give one a great deal of confidence', Home wrote, 'In cavalry work the carrying out of orders intelligently means making decisions on the spot without being able to refer to higher formations for orders. In the case of cavalry ordered forward this applies specially', but without knowledge of the wider plan these decisions could not be made.[80]

One officer who faced serious criticism after Neuve Chapelle was Rawlinson, whose IV Corps had made the attack together with the Indian Corps. Rawlinson at first tried to shift the blame onto one of his divisional commanders, but was unsuccessful, and further damaged his own reputation in the attempt.[81] On 14 March he rehearsed a second line of self-defence in his diary:

> [Haig] looked for too much. He expects to get the cavalry through with his next push, but I very much doubt that he will succeed in doing more than kill a large number of gallant men without effecting any very great triumph. I should be content with capturing another piece out of the enemy's line of trenches and waiting for the counter attack. I am not a believer in the cavalry raid, which even if it comes off will not effect very much.[82]

This was the first of several assertions by Rawlinson that were to be important for the future of cavalry doctrine on the Western Front. Next day he told Wilson that 'Haig was still obsessed with the idea of pushing the cavalry through and that he was going to renew the attack', but that Haig 'will only lose life' if he tried.[83] Rawlinson returned to the theme a week later:

> I think D[ouglas] H[aig] would have been better advised to content himself with the capture of the village... I advised him to do this in the first instance but he and Sir John were so obsessed with the cavalry idea that he would not listen. Had he been content with the village we should have gained as much ground and reduced our casualties by three quarters.[84]

This entry was also a rehearsal for an attempt to convince someone else; next day Rawlinson wrote to Kitchener:

> Douglas Haig was very anxious to get the cavalry through the line to raid behind the German front, but on this occasion it never looked as if the cavalry would be able to penetrate the line for the hole was never large enough. Later on when we have more troops

---

79 NLS Haig Papers 100: Diary entries, 8–14 March 1915, quotation from the entry 11 March; Home, *The Diary of a World War I Cavalry Officer*, p. 58.

80 Home, *The Diary of a World War I Cavalry Officer*, p. 60.

81 Sheffield and Bourne (eds), *Douglas Haig: War Diaries and Letters 1914–1918*, pp. 110–16.

82 CAC Rawlinson Papers RAWL 1/1: Diary entry, 14 March 1915.

83 IWM Wilson Papers: Diary entry, 15 March 1915.

84 CAC Rawlinson Papers RAWL 1/1: Diary entry, 22 March 1915.

and more guns available we shall be able to make a larger hole and then perhaps pass the cavalry through supported by a strongish force of infantry.[85]

Two days later, Rawlinson wrote to King George V through his aide-de-camp Colonel Clive Wigram, setting out his own alternative doctrinal approach:

> What we want to do now is what I call 'bite and hold'. Bite off a piece of the enemy's line, like Neuve Chapelle, and hold it against counter-attack. The bite can be made without much loss, and, if we choose the right place and make every preparation and put it quickly in a state of defence there ought to be no difficulty in holding it against the enemy's counter attacks and inflicting on him at least twice the loss that we have suffered in the bite.[86]

This statement of 'bite and hold' has been taken as Rawlinson's definitive contribution to the doctrinal issue. But a week later he wrote to Kitchener, still blaming French and Haig as cavalry officers for the failure at Neuve Chapelle, but also still with a significantly different emphasis from that in his letter to Wigram:

> If we had not tried to do too much our losses would have been one quarter of what they were and we should have gained just as much ground, but the idea of pushing through the cavalry which has been seized upon by our leaders, all cavalry officers, was the origin of our heavy losses. Cavalry against unbeaten infantry will do no good and will suffer heavy loss. When the enemy infantry is defeated of course cavalry will have great success but the German infantry is not yet sufficiently shaken to warrant you charging them with the cavalry.[87]

Rawlinson did not deny the value of the mass use of cavalry to exploit a gap in the German lines, arguing simply that its time had not yet come. This was reflected in his approach in planning battles in 1916 and again in 1918: he saw no point in using cavalry on a small scale, and only fully employed the cavalry as part of his battle plan when ordered to do so by Haig at Amiens in August 1918.

On 11 April 1915, the chief staff officer of the Indian Cavalry Corps visited Haig at First Army to talk about Neuve Chapelle, bringing significant news:

> Brigadier General [Henry 'Harry'] MacAndrew and Major [Harry] Baird (Indian Cavalry Corps) came to dinner. MacAndrew very amusing about the orders issued to the cavalry during the Neuve Chapelle operations by the Field Marshal [French], and of course he was very critical. Allenby and [Philip] Howell ([chief] staff officer now) of [the] Cavalry Corps seem to be despondent regarding the possibilities of cavalry action in future. MacAndrew thinks that if these two had their way, cavalry would cease to exist as such.

---

85   TNA PRO 20/57 Official Papers of Lord Kitchener WB/17: Rawlinson to Kitchener, 23 March 1915.

86   NAM Rawlinson Papers 17: Rawlinson to Wigram, 25 March 1915; Prior and Wilson, *Command on the Western Front*, p. 78.

87   TNA PRO 20/57 Official Papers of Lord Kitchener WB/17: Rawlinson to Kitchener, 1 April 1915.

In their opinion, the war will continue and end in the trenches. I told them that we cannot hope to reap the fruits of victory without a large force of mounted men.[88]

There appears to be no direct evidence from Allenby or his staff which would collaborate the idea that he gave up a belief in a breakthrough and cavalry exploitation on the Western Front so early. But if so, then Allenby had reached this conclusion in a way that Rawlinson never did, and he was not the only cavalry general to do so. In May 1917 Byng, by then the experienced commander of the Canadian Corps, wrote to Chetwode in Palestine about the recently failed Nivelle Offensive that 'great expectations were centred on the French push and they talked about "breaking through", we gave up that catchword some time ago'.[89]

After the unsuccessful Battle of Aubers Ridge on 8 May 1915 (fought on essentially the same ground as Neuve Chapelle), Haig concluded that German defences were so strong that 'in order to demolish them a *long methodical bombardment* will be necessary by heavy artillery', giving up any idea of surprise.[90] French still saw the cavalry breakthrough as his ideal, writing (in a private letter) after the unsuccessful attack was repeated on 15 May in the Battle of Festubert, 'How I should love to have a real good "go" at them in the open with lots of cavalry and horse artillery. Well! it may come.'[91] French told a planning meeting in August for the Battle of Loos that 'he proposed to throw his Cavalry Corps and the Conneau Corps', (the French cavalry corps under General Conneau), 'through any gap made, and keep the Indian Cavalry Corps in support'.[92] Even so, it has been disputed whether either French or Haig actually believed that a British breakthrough was possible at the Battle of Loos, which began on 25 September 1915 and lasted until 18 October but achieved only a limited advance.[93] It was Rawlinson who remained guardedly optimistic, writing in his personal diary on 27 September that 'There is yet a chance that all may be well and the cavalry may get through, but if the enemy are allowed to collect again they may still be able to hold us up.'[94]

Again the failure to break through at Loos was accompanied by an argument over the use of reserves (in this case not involving the cavalry), which became a factor in French's replacement by Haig in December. In almost all of their offensive battles of 1915–1917, British commanders argued among themselves about whether a gap in the German line could have been created and exploited by a cavalry advance. This was not a fantasy of higher commanders, but extended down on occasions to brigade

---

88 Sheffield and Bourne (eds), *Douglas Haig: War Diaries and Letters 1914–1918*, pp. 114–15; as can be seen from Sheffield and Bourne's edition, this is one of the passages in Haig's diaries that he re-worked between the first written version and the completed entry, but the re-working does not change the meaning.

89 IWM Chetwode Papers: Byng to Chetwode, 30 May 1917.

90 Quoted in Bristow, *A Serious Disappointment*, p. 164, emphasis in the original.

91 Quoted in Holmes, *The Little Field Marshal*, p. 294.

92 NLS Haig Papers 102: 'Proceedings of a Meeting Held at Beauquesne 4 p.m. 26th August 1915'.

93 French, *British Strategy and War Aims 1914–1916*, pp. 111–12; Gooch, *The Plans of War*, pp. 316–27.

94 CAC Rawlinson Papers RAWL 1/7: Diary entry, 27 September 1915.

or battalion level, where experienced combat veterans recorded that a properly co-ordinated reinforcement by cavalry could have transformed a weak spot in the German lines into a real break.[95] The merits of these counterfactual arguments have attracted surprisingly little attention, and at least part of this neglect has come from a belief that the cavalry was capable only of a massed charge pouring through the gap if the entire German line collapsed, which was a virtual impossibility.[96] Rather, at Loos and again in later battles, the British cavalry had a range of options for exploiting an opportunity if one occurred. Haig issued orders for Loos that 'Corps commanders must also have the mounted troops of divisions, machine guns and cyclists ready to exploit the success', and accordingly Rawlinson's IV Corps put together a 'Corps Pursuit Force' of three yeomanry squadrons, three cyclist companies and some armoured cars with machine-guns.[97] French also placed a cavalry division (less one brigade) directly under Haig's command rather than under GHQ for the attack if a wider hole appeared.[98] As Home wrote after Loos, 'There can be no question of putting our Cavalry through the gap and then allowing it to be pinched. An advance through the gap should be a systematic operation of war: i.e. unless there is a debacle and that may sometimes happen.'[99] In what has every appearance of a return to the principles of *Cavalry Training 1912*, the doctrine was beginning to develop of cavalry fighting their way forward to create or widen a gap in conjunction with the infantry, rather than waiting for a perfect gap to be cleared.

Meanwhile, early in October 1915 the Cavalry Corps, searching for a way to show that, in Home's words 'in all events we are doing our bit', put forward a plan to place their horses in stables and to use the troopers to form a Dismounted Division, structured like a weak infantry division 8,200 strong.[100] This was approved by French and later by Haig, and from late 1915 onwards the Dismounted Division was used for trench-holding, either during the winter or on occasions that an extra division was needed and there was no immediate plan to employ the cavalry mounted. The three British regular cavalry divisions saw enough active service in the war to lose 16,227 troopers as casualties (not counting men of other arms who served in them), or about two-thirds of their front-line strength.[101] But unlike many infantry divisions the cavalry's losses were never so great as to destroy their original character. Even in 1918 Home could describe them as 'made of the old stuff and properly officered', the last of the old BEF.[102]

---

95 Griffith, *Battle Tactics of the Western Front*, pp. 160–62.

96 The exception being Loos, for which the issue has been whether Haig was correct to criticise French over the handling of the reserves, rather than whether their employment could have created a gap; see Travers, *The Killing Ground*, pp. 16–19 and de Groot, *Douglas Haig 1861–1928*, pp. 207–9.

97 NLS Haig Papers 102: Diary entry, 8 September 1915; Pease, *The History of the Northumberland (Hussars) Yeomanry 1819–1923*, p. 122.

98 NLS Haig Papers 102: Diary entry, 18 September 1915.

99 Home, *The Diary of a World War I Cavalry Officer*, p. 82.

100 Ibid., p. 89.

101 *Statistics of the Military Effort of the British Empire During the Great War 1914–1920*, p. 249.

102 Home, *The Diary of a World War I Cavalry Officer*, p. 168.

The key to attacking – or defending – successfully on the deadlocked Western Front was the co-ordination of artillery with infantry, including the use of reserves. Artillery tactics made particular advances during the war, and the British played a major part in developing them.[103] But while new technology became increasingly important, victory in battle was determined even more by new concepts in command and staffwork which enabled forces to co-operate together on an unprecedented scale.[104] In the middle period of the war the British, like all other armies, were grappling with a problem for which not even a vocabulary would exist for some decades: the doctrinal concept known to later military thought as 'the operational level of war', and the related 'operational art'. In the context of the First World War, operational art was the technique of employing Army-sized and Corps-sized formations, an intermediary level of thinking that lay between tactics as used by front-line combat formations and strategy as used by nations.

The concept of the operational level dates back at least to Napoleonic times, appearing in the writings of Jomini, who used both 'operations' and 'grand tactics' to describe 'the art of making good combinations preliminary to battles, as well as during their progress'.[105] It was a particular feature of the military thought of the German Field Marshal Helmut von Moltke 'the Elder' in the middle nineteenth century, although in the First World War some senior German officers rejected it in favour of attritional tactics and firepower: in his planning for the March 1918 Kaiserschlacht offensive, First Quartermaster General Erich Ludendorff ordered that, 'I do not want to hear the word "operation". We hack a hole [into the enemy front]. The rest comes on its own.'[106] Although the term 'grand tactics' was still used other than in Germany, any specific meaning for 'operations' seems to have fallen into disuse well before the First World War, in the British case possibly through the attention paid to smaller colonial wars to which Corps-sized manoeuvre was not relevant. The concept was only taken up again systematically in the 1920s, in the military doctrine of the new Soviet Union, and continued to develop throughout the twentieth century. As late as the middle 1980s there was no agreed definition of the operational level of war or of operational art among the countries of the North Atlantic Treaty Organisation (NATO).[107]

---

103 Bailey, 'The First World War and the Birth of Modern Warfare', pp. 132–53; Griffith, *Battle Tactics of the Western Front*, pp. 135–58; Bidwell and Graham, *Fire-Power*, pp. 61–148.

104 See in particular Sheffield and Todman (eds), *Command and Control on the Western Front: the British Army's Experience 1914–18*; Robbins, *British Generalship on the Western Front 1914–18*; and Simpson, *Directing Operations*.

105 Jomini, *The Art of War*, p. 178; Handel, *Masters of War*, pp. 37–8 suggests that Jomini also used 'strategy' to mean what would now be called the operational level.

106 This version of Ludendorff's remark is quoted in Geyer, 'German Strategy in the Age of Machine Warfare 1914–1945', p. 552; other versions or translations use 'strategy' rather than 'operation'. For Moltke see Hughes (ed.), *Moltke on the Art of War*, Introduction pp. 11–12; Foley, *German Strategy and the Path to Verdun*.

107 Triandafillov, *The Nature of the Operations of Modern Armies*; Gat, *A History of Military Thought*, pp. 636–9; Simpkin, *Race to the Swift*, pp. 23–4.

The First World War 1914–1918

It is therefore something of an anachronism to discuss the operational art of the British Army in the First World War, or to criticise its generals for failing to employ operational art properly. But although British doctrine did not have the words, it did have at least some of the concepts, and recent attention has been paid to this in understanding Army-level and Corps-level command on the Western Front.[108] By 1918 the Army had made considerable advances in developing a common doctrine at the operational level. As expressed by Lieutenant General Sir John Monash, GOC Australian Corps:

> A perfect modern battle is like nothing so much as a score for an orchestral composition, where the various arms and units are the instruments, and the tasks they perform are their respective musical phrases. Each individual unit must make its entry precisely at the proper moment, and play its phrase in the general harmony. The whole programme is controlled by an exact time-table, to which every infantryman, every heavy or light gun, every mortar and machine-gun, every tank and aeroplane, must respond with punctuality; otherwise there will be discords which will impair the success of the operation and increase the cost of it.[109]

The doctrinal basis of this fixity was that poor communications across no-man's land made it impractical to co-ordinate the artillery bombardment with the infantry advance, and the solution was to make the attacking infantry conform to the artillery timetable rather than the other way around. At first appearance, there was no place in such a doctrine for the improvisation and seizing of opportunities typified by cavalry spirit. But Monash also distinguished between these 'set-piece' operations, as he called them, and battles in which events changed from hour to hour and improvisation was essential, or even battles which began as 'set-pieces' and then became improvisations, including 'the second phase' of the first day of the Battle of Amiens.[110] Monash also described how during the last great advances on the Western Front from late August 1918 onwards, 'nothing in the nature of a detailed time-table was possible' at GHQ and that 'it was therefore necessarily left to the commanders of the armies to conform to a general policy of the attack, the time and method being left to their own decision or recommendation. And they in turn relied upon their corps commanders, to seize the initiative in the pursuit of such a policy.'[111] This was operational art or something very close to it.

One major problem which only operational art could solve, and that beset British battles from 1915 onwards, was how to pass reserves safely and swiftly from the rear through an existing front line and into combat, often during the height of a battle, a technique that was much easier when defending than when attacking. This also had its origins in Napoleonic warfare if not earlier, in a notoriously difficult battlefield

---

108 The first suggestion that Corps level might be the most important level of command on the Western Front appears to come in Prior and Wilson, *Command on the Western Front*, pp. 392–4.
109 Monash, *The Australian Victories in France in 1918*, p. 38.
110 Ibid., pp. 203–5.
111 Ibid., pp. 130–31.

manoeuvre used to replace battalions in the firing line called the 'passage of lines'.[112] Between spring 1917 at Arras and summer 1918 at Amiens, British and dominion staffs learned how to 'leap frog' the combat troops of entire divisions through each other in an attack.[113] The procedures for moving cavalry up from reserve and into action in this way were not intrinsically different from those for moving any other troops, except that cavalry occupied considerable road space, and their effective use depended on rapid deployment. This promoted an argument, which was never entirely resolved, as to whether delays in getting the cavalry into action were due to poor staffwork by the infantry divisions and higher formations, or whether the likely results of getting the cavalry into the battle were simply not worth the effort required.

The failure at Loos, and dissatisfaction with the progress of the war, led to French being replaced by Haig as GOC-in-C of the BEF in December 1915, with Robertson moving to become CIGS, replacing Murray. Although political circumstances made Haig almost the inevitable choice as French's successor, other names were put forward. Bridges suggested that 'Plumer would probably have had the Army's vote', a significant judgement from a cavalryman.[114] One of French's strongest political allies, Colonel Repington of *The Times*, lobbied Andrew Bonar Law, Colonial Secretary in the Asquith coalition, strongly against Haig's appointment. Deploying any arguments that he could find, Repington condemned Haig as 'a cavalry officer, of whom we already have too many in high command and in a war that mainly concerns other arms', a criticism that he extended to Allenby, but not to French, nor to Robertson who he recommended as French's successor, nor to Gough who he placed with Lord Cavan as the best of the 'younger men'. While condemning Haig as a cavalryman, Repington also characterised him as an 'excellent staff officer' who in contrast to French 'has not the great qualities of character needed for the Commander in Chief'.[115] This was probably the first occasion on which Haig was condemned simultaneously as an ignorant cavalryman *and* an unimaginative staff officer, ideas which then grew with some vigour among his critics.

The replacement of one cavalry general with another in command of the BEF was certain to attract comments like Repington's, particularly as Robertson was also perceived to be a cavalryman. If the case for the Army of 1904–1914 being dominated by cavalrymen appears weak, the same cannot be said of the Army of 1914–1918. By the war's end, although Henry Wilson had replaced Robertson as CIGS, Allenby had replaced the infantryman Murray as GOC-in-C of the EEF, and otherwise infantrymen commanded (or had commanded) only the sideshows: Ian Hamilton at Gallipoli, John Nixon and Percy Lake in Mesopotamia, Plumer in Italy, and the gunner George Milne in Salonika. On the Western Front, of ten men who at some time held Army commands, Haig, Allenby, Gough, Byng and Birdwood

---

112 Griffith, *Rally Once Again*, pp. 63–7; van Creveld, *Command in War*, pp. 155–88.

113 Monash, *The Australian Victories in France in 1918*, pp. 61–2; Nicholls, *Cheerful Sacrifice*, pp. 24–5.

114 Bridges, *Alarms and Excursions*, p. 138.

115 Morris (ed.), *The Letters of Lieutenant Colonel Charles à Court Repington*, pp. 239–40.

were cavalrymen and Horne was a horse gunner, while only Smith-Dorrien, Plumer, Rawlinson and Monro (who briefly commanded by First Army and Third Army) were infantry. Even Haig's chief staff officer in 1918, Herbert Lawrence, came from the 17th Lancers. The Cavalry Corps of 1914 produced a theatre commander in Allenby, and three Army commanders in Gough, Byng and Horne. It also produced de Lisle, who commanded first XIII Corps and then XV Corps on the Western Front; Chetwode who commanded XX Corps in Palestine; and Briggs who commanded XVI Corps in Salonika. The Indian Cavalry Corps contributed Hew Fanshaw, late of the 19th Hussars, who rose from commanding 2nd Indian Cavalry Division in 1914 to command V Corps 1915–1916.[116] Among the cavalry majors and lieutenant colonels of 1914, Bridges commanded 19th (Western) Division from December 1915 until wounded in June 1917 and ended the war as a lieutenant general; Home served as chief staff officer of 46th (North Midland) Division and then IX Corps in 1916 before returning to the Cavalry Corps; Barrow served as chief staff officer of X Corps and then of First Army before taking command of 7th Division in January 1917, followed by the Yeomanry Division in Palestine; and Shea, once Barrow's successor in command of the 35th Scinde Horse, commanded 30th Division on the Western Front, and then 60th Division in Palestine.[117]

The allegation that these appointments represented not only a domination of the Army by cavalry officers but also an intentional cavalry conspiracy has been subject to repeated historical investigation, most recently as part of a comprehensive study by Simon Robbins of 700 British 'war managers' (mostly serving officers) who commanded and controlled the BEF.[118] As a first finding, neither French nor Haig had the undisputed right to appoint Army commanders or members of their own

---

116 Haig may have seen Fanshawe (not to be confused with his brother Edward) as being too close to French. He was demoted to command 58th (2/1st London) Division in 1916, before commanding 18th Indian Division in Mesopotamia 1917–1918.

117 Details of individual appointments may be found in the five volumes of Becke, *Order of Battle of Divisions*; see also Barrow, *The Fire of Life*, pp. 157–65; Home, *The Diary of a World War I Cavalry Officer*, pp. 103–19. The usual quibbles exist over whether an officer should be regarded as a 'cavalryman'. Griffith, *Battle Tactics of the Western Front*, p. 217 says that 'the 1914 cavalry' produced five Corps commanders; Terraine, *The Smoke and the Fire*, p. 163 says that there was only one cavalryman commanding a Corps in 1918; Robbins, *British Generalship on the Western Front 1914–18*, pp. 210–14 lists ten Corps commanders on the Western Front as cavalrymen including two serving in 1918, and 27 divisional commanders, although this appears to include both commanders of cavalry divisions and generals who held divisional commands before being promoted. The most contentious case is Horne of First Army, who deserves to be counted with the cavalrymen through his long association with them. But if Horne is included, a case could be made for including other officers of the Royal Horse Artillery such as Birch. Officers like Shea, de Lisle and Bridges did not begin their careers in the cavalry, but all were so closely associated with cavalry before 1914 as to deserve inclusion. Birdwood is usually listed as Indian Army, but he began his career in the cavalry and continued in the Indian cavalry; and so on.

118 Robbins, *British Generalship on the Western Front 1914–18*, especially pp. 188–217; Badsey, 'Cavalry and the Development of Breakthrough Doctrine', pp. 138–74 and Badsey, 'Fire and the Sword', pp. 295–301 and pp. 372–5; Terraine, *The Smoke and the Fire*, pp. 161–8.

staff. Like Smith-Dorrien's appointment to Second Army, Horne's appointment to First Army in 1916 was a compromise after Haig had attempted to promote Richard Haking, an infantryman; while Lawrence was imposed on Haig rather than being his own choice.[119] Both Byng and Birdwood, when promoted to Army command, had extensive Corps experience, including political skills in command of the Canadian Corps and ANZAC Corps respectively. In both their cases also, their promotion opened the way for Canadian and Australian officers to succeed them.[120] Only in the case of Gough in 1916 is it evident that Haig elevated a trusted cavalryman to Army command, and that was because he hoped for Gough's Reserve Army to function as a breakout and pursuit force. As a further point, having a cavalryman as an Army commander did not guarantee a sympathetic attitude to the cavalry. In August 1918, when the Cavalry Corps was much in demand, Horne thought that Third Army staff under Byng had little understanding of how to work with cavalry, and that Rawlinson's Fourth Army staff were much better.[121]

In September 1914 the cavalry numbered 7.72 per cent of the Army's ration strength and 9.28 per cent of its combat strength, although this proportion sank rapidly as the Army expanded, to 3.88 per cent of combat strength in September 1915, and 2.77 per cent in September 1917.[122] Looked at another way, the Cavalry Division was one out of seven divisions in the BEF of 1914, or just over 14 per cent of its divisional strength, and it had six command appointments (Allenby and five brigade commanders) out of 34 in the whole BEF, or 17–18 per cent.[123] On this basis, as the Army expanded cavalrymen should have continued to hold about eight per cent of its middle-level command appointments such as divisional command, and about twice that number of higher commands. The promotion pattern for cavalrymen is very consistent with this statistical average, especially on the Western Front. According to the *Army List* and other sources, at the end of the war 18 cavalrymen held the rank of major general, or 7 percent of the total number, while in the course of the war 27 cavalrymen, or 14 per cent, held or had held divisional commands. By 1918 the Army had 23 Corps (17 of them on the Western Front) and one Cavalry Corps, not including dominion forces. Of 56 generals who commanded these Corps, between 9 and 11 may be described as cavalrymen, or 18–19 per cent, figures slightly inflated by cases in which the same general commanded more than one Corps.

If cavalrymen were slightly over-represented in Corps command, they were correspondingly slightly under-represented among senior staff officers. Lawrence as Haig's chief staff officer stood out in a GHQ that out of 326 officers in its first echelon

---

119 Sheffield and Bourne, *Douglas Haig: War Diaries and Letters 1914–1918*, pp. 216–18; Robbins, 'Henry Horne', pp. 122–40; Robbins, *British Generalship on the Western Front 1914–18*, pp. 119–20.

120 Gardner, 'Julian Byng', pp. 54–74; Birdwood, *Khaki and Gown*, pp. 249–339; Williams, *Byng of Vimy*, pp. 168–70.

121 Horne, *The Diary of a World War I Cavalry Officer*, pp. 180–81.

122 *Statistics of the Military Effort of the British Empire During the Great War 1914–1920*, p. 65.

123 This calculation is based on one GOC-in-C (French), three Corps commands, 7 divisional commands and 21 infantry brigade commands.

contained just 22 cavalrymen at the war's end.[124] Other than Barrow, no British or Indian cavalry officer ever headed the staff of an Army; only 5 cavalrymen headed the staff of a Corps on the Western Front, and 22 cavalrymen headed the staff of a division, or 8 per cent of the total in both cases.[125] All the Army commanders on the Western Front had passed the Staff College except Horne, together with rather more than half of all BEF Corps and divisional commanders, those that were cavalrymen coming out slightly better than average. Almost all chief staff officers of Armies and Corps had also passed the Staff College, together with about four-fifths of the chief staff officers of divisions; and again the record of cavalry officers holding these positions was a little better than average.[126]

All this suggests that the prevalence of cavalrymen in the very highest British commands in the First World War was either a statistical anomaly or attributable to other factors; and various possibilities suggest themselves, all strongly interlinked. First, in addition to the cavalrymen, several higher ranking officers came from smart or socially exclusive regiments, including Rawlinson of the Coldstream, Ian Hamilton of the Gordon Highlanders, and Wilson of the Rifle Brigade, although Smith-Dorrien, Plumer, Monro and Murray began their careers in relatively unfashionable infantry regiments.[127] Most of the generals who held senior command positions at the end of the war had begun by serving either in the original BEF or in three (out of five) regular divisions formed on the war's outbreak: 7th Division (commanded by Gough in 1915), 27th Division, and 29th Division (commanded by de Lisle 1915–1918).[128] All commanders of brigadier general's rank or higher in the Cavalry Corps survived First Ypres, and as the Army expanded it was evidently policy to promote officers who were Staff College qualified, or who had commanded anything larger than a battalion in 1914, regardless of their branch of service. This slightly favoured cavalry generals, because being trained in staffwork and infantry tactics they could take infantry commands, while no ambitious infantry officer would have wanted a cavalry command. In March 1915 the BEF consisted of four Corps plus a Cavalry Corps, a total of 19 higher command positions of which four (or 21 per cent) were exclusive to cavalrymen, not including the Indian Corps of two divisions and the Indian Cavalry Corps of two divisions.[129] This small advantage at the start of the Army's expansion may partly account for the proportion of cavalrymen who went on to hold much higher rank.

---

124 NLS Haig Papers 220j: 'Composition of Headquarters of British Armies in France, 1 February 1919'.

125 Simpson, *Directing Operations*, pp. 210–11 and 227–8; Badsey, 'Fire and the Sword', p. 373; Terraine, *The Smoke and the Fire*, p. 163. Again, it is impossible to avoid anomalies in these calculations: e.g. Gough's temporary command of Reserve Corps in 1916 has been omitted since it almost immediately became Reserve Army.

126 Robbins, *British Generalship on the Western Front 1914–18*, pp. 210–11.

127 This point is dealt with in more detail in Badsey, 'Cavalry and the Development of Breakthrough Doctrine', pp. 142–3. Monro was commissioned into the Queen's (Royal West Surrey Regiment).

128 Griffith, *Battle Tactics of the Western Front*, pp. 214–17.

129 This calculation is based on one GOC-in-C, two Army commands, five Corps commands including the cavalry and 11 divisional commands including the cavalry.

A further, if presently thoroughly heretical, possibility is that the officer corps of the late nineteenth and early twentieth century cavalry, with its unusual social structure and opportunities for independent thought and action, produced a crop of good officers, militarily competent and politically astute, who deserved their promotions on merit as this was understood by the Army of the time. Ian Hamilton's reaction to Byng's appointment to command IX Corps at Gallipoli in 1915 was not dismay at getting a cavalryman but that 'Byng will make everyone happy; he never spares himself'.[130] Cavalry officers were given the same Staff College training as all others, and in planning battles drew on the same manuals including *Training and Manoeuvre Regulations 1909*.[131] It is possible that the extra confidence and initiative required by cavalry spirit gave its officers an advantage, as Chetwode claimed after the war, writing that 'The average British officer, unless he has been trained in the cavalry or is a very exceptional man, enters an operation, whether in peace or war, without having made up his mind what he intends to do.'[132]

The contrary view was first put forward by Rawlinson after Neuve Chapelle: that cavalry spirit was not an appropriate doctrine for the conditions of trench deadlock, and that its emphasis on initiative and trying to achieve the utmost produced plans that were unrealistically optimistic and unnecessarily costly in life.[133] In this conception, Haig as GOC-in-C exercised a malign influence by promoting a doctrine of cavalry spirit throughout the BEF, reflected not only in battle plans based on putting cavalry through a 'Gap', but more generally in demanding more than could realistically be achieved in all aspects of planning. In addition to Rawlinson's 'bite and hold' strictures, cavalry spirit or its equivalent has been held at least partly responsible for the poor results achieved by Fifth Army under Gough in the early stages of Third Ypres, in contrast to the deliberate 'step by step' or 'set-piece' tactics used by Plumer's Second Army. Although the actual results of the two Armies' attacks were not very different in terms of ground gained and casualties lost, Gough's style – like Haig's very often – promised much and failed to deliver, whereas Plumer's did neither.[134]

Haig's as GOC-in-C has often been described as a 'thruster', a term in use on the Western Front as early as June 1915. A thruster was an officer of any rank, who took aggressive risks not only with his own life but those of his troops also. The term could be a compliment or an insult depending on the viewpoint of the speaker, but the opposite of being a thruster was to be 'sticky', a definite criticism. Thruster doctrine had two main strands, one of which applied to day-to-day trench warfare and the other to major battles. The daily routine version was based on a belief that even in the deadlock of the trenches it was better to attack the enemy frequently on

---

130 Williams, *Byng of Vimy*, p. 93.
131 Garsia, *A Key To Victory*, pp. 28–33.
132 LHCMA Liddell Hart Papers I/166/2: Chetwode to Liddell Hart, 11 March 1930.
133 Robbins, *British Generalship on the Western Front 1914–18*, pp. 68–82 equates cavalry spirit directly with 'the cult of optimism'.
134 Lee, 'Command and Control in Battle: British Divisions on the Menin Road Ridge, 20 September 1917', pp. 119–40; Terraine, *The Road to Passchendaele*, pp. 211–335; Prior and Wilson, *Passchendaele: The Untold Story*, pp. 113–39; but for an important criticism of Plumer's tactics at Third Ypres see Thompson, 'Mud, Blood and Wood', pp. 237–56.

a small scale, through activities such as artillery or mortar bombardments and trench raids. Thruster doctrine held that such attacks provided training, information, and other benefits, and raised morale while lowering that of the enemy, so making major attacks more effective when they came. This aspect of thruster doctrine has never been either proved or disproved (and it is hard to see how it could be); and it has been criticised for actually lowering morale through apparent callousness towards men and wasting lives, but it had its supporters.[135]

In planning battles, thruster doctrine has been characterised as relying on bravery and determination to overcome enemy defences including firepower, and has been closely linked with breakthrough doctrine; both have also been linked to cavalry spirit and with any approach to battle on the Western Front which treated the cavalry's mobility as a significant factor.[136] In this argument, since a military staff took its style and behaviour very much from its commander, a cavalryman in a high position could have a disproportionate effect on the way that battles were planned.[137] Undoubtedly there were many similarities between the thruster approach and cavalry spirit. It was claimed that the veteran cavalryman Robert Broadwood, who returned to active service on the Western Front as GOC 57th (2nd West Lancashire) Division, felt so disgraced by criticisms that he lacked 'fighting spirit' that in June 1917 he deliberately found death in battle.[138] But not all thrusters were cavalrymen, including several officers promoted by Haig; while if Gough appears as almost the definition of a thruster, the appellation does not sit easily on Byng or some other cavalry generals. Allenby showed thruster traits both in command of the cavalry in 1914–1915 and again in Palestine in 1917–1918, but was criticised by Haig in the Battle of Arras in 1917 for lack of thruster qualities.[139] Also, rather than being exclusive to the cavalry, the thruster philosophy of human factors and morale overcoming enemy firepower could be found throughout the pre-war Army. In his polemical book *Compulsory Service* of 1910 (written in opposition to Roberts's campaign to introduce peacetime conscription), the cavalry's greatest critic Ian Hamilton wrote that 'War is essentially the triumph, not of a line of men entrenched behind wire entanglements and fire-swept zones over men exposing themselves in the open, but of one will over another weaker will.'[140] The association of thruster behaviour with cavalry generals was largely one of perception. While a thruster who risked his own life might earn respect, the same attitude could appear unattractive in a senior officer who might only rarely be in personal danger, especially if accompanied by the languid manner cultivated by some cavalrymen.

---

135 By far the best study of this idea of the 'thrusters' and their impact remains Ashworth, *Trench Warfare 1914–1918*, especially pp. 86–96.

136 In particular by Travers, *The Killing Ground*, pp. 54–5 and pp. 134–5.

137 For this phenomenon see Holden Reid, 'The Commander and his Chief of Staff', p. 23.

138 Quoted in Davies and Maddocks, *Bloody Red Tabs*, pp. 48–50; the original claim was made by Basil Liddell Hart in 1937 on the basis of anecdotes passed to him.

139 Travers, *The Killing Ground*, pp. 10–11; Terraine, *Douglas Haig*, pp. 289–90.

140 Hamilton, *Compulsory Service*, pp. 121–2; and see Travers, *The Killing Ground*, pp. 44–5, and Howard, 'Men Against Fire: the Doctrine of the Offensive in 1914', pp. 510–26.

It is also important that a belief in morale, and in human will dominating the enemy, was not exclusive to the military thinking of the First World War, and far less an outdated relic of the nineteenth century. Although first and best codified by the German military theorist Carl von Clausewitz in 1831, it has continued as a commonplace of all subsequent western military thinking. A case has been made for understanding Clausewitz's ideas as a product of the German Romantic variant of the Enlightenment, but there was nothing in their adoption that was inherently hostile to new technology or to the realities of firepower.[141] United States Marine Corps doctrine in 1989 was that 'war is a clash between opposing human wills'; British Army doctrine in 1996 (which quoted Clausewitz repeatedly) was that conflict 'is a struggle or a clash between opposing forces or contending wishes' and Australian Army doctrine in 1998 was that 'The Army's will to fight, sometimes called its morale, is provided mostly by the moral component of fighting power.'[142] The idea that the thruster-like approach and belief in morale were hostile to technology in the First World War has also been debunked; Haig in particular was receptive to new military technologies, including tanks and aircraft, while continuing to believe that 'the man who controls the machine has more than anything to do with gaining success'.[143]

Just as warfare itself and the nature of battle changed between Waterloo in 1815 and the Somme in 1916, so within the last generation considerable changes have taken place in understanding how the British Army fought on the Western Front, (including the contributions of the Canadian and Australian forces), and in the wider politics and strategy of the First World War.[144] So much new evidence has emerged that historians are now seeking to understand why the impression of the First World War that prevailed until about 40 years ago (and continues to prevail in much popular culture), could ever have come into existence, when compared to real events of the war.[145] The interpretation that the deadlock and the heavy casualties of the Western Front were entirely due to military incompetence has long been discredited. But

---

141 Lynn, *Battle*, pp. 179–218; Heuser, *Reading Clausewitz*, pp. 24–43.

142 *Warfighting: The US Marine Corps Book of Strategy*, p. 12; *Design for Military Operations: The British Military Doctrine*, p. 3–1; *Land Warfare Doctrine 1: The Fundamentals of Land Warfare*, p. 5–5; see also e.g. Handel, *Masters of War*, pp. 81–90.

143 Haig made this comment about the new Fokker monoplane in 1916, see NLS Haig papers 105: Haig Diary, entry for 11 April 1916; see also Crawshaw, 'The Impact of Technology on the BEF and Its Commander', pp. 155–75; Harris, *Men, Ideas and Tanks*, pp. 54–68.

144 For a summary of the present position see Sheffield, *Forgotten Victory*; otherwise the literature is massive and growing, with among the more important recent works being Robbins, *British Generalship on the Western Front 1914–18*; Griffith, *Battle Tactics of the Western Front*; Simpson, *Directing Operations*; Schrieber, *Shock Army of the British Empire*; and Bond and Cave (eds), *Haig: A Reappraisal 70 Years On*. Comparatively little equivalent work has yet been done on the German and French armies. For an eccentric view which argues that in a cultural sense the Germans were victorious see Mosier, *The Myth of the Great War*.

145 For a summary of the present position in another rapidly growing field, Todman, *The Great War: Myth and Memory* is excellent, and should be read together with Bond, *The Unquiet Western Front*.

a variation on Fuller's views remains among historians who argue that failings in the conduct of British battles may be explained by a cultural bias among generals towards a romanticised pre-industrial view of war, and that cavalry generals and Haig in particular showed this fault.[146] The need to provide an Army that could fight both European and colonial wars, and the dominance of colonial warfare in the personal experiences of its generals, may have made a transition to industrialised warfare difficult. But it is equally possible that British officers trained in cavalry doctrines had an advantage in facing the problems of the Western Front, particularly after their experience before 1914 in working through so successfully the complex problem of what cavalry doctrines were needed for the future. It is certainly something of a paradox that while German Auftragstaktik has been so universally praised as part of the solution to trench deadlock, its closest British equivalent cavalry spirit has been just as universally condemned.

For the Battle of the Somme in 1916 Haig planned and hoped – and never ceased to plan and hope in all his subsequent offensives – for the possibility that the German front would collapse. But Haig also emphasised, starting with an Army Commanders' Conference on 8 January 1916, that future operations would consist of 'Preliminary operations to wear out the enemy and exhaust his reserves' only then followed by 'a decisive attack made with the objective of piercing the enemy's lines of defence'.[147] As part of the much greater issues involved in planning for the Somme, two distinct views of the cavalry prevailed in British high command at this time. The first view was that the cavalry would be valuable only if the German front collapsed completely, and this was so unlikely as to make it unnecessary to plan for such an event. This view was held by Rawlinson and probably the majority of senior officers; an experienced Corps staff officer's opinion that 'pushing cavalry through the gap' was 'all nonsense' appears typical.[148] The second view, shared by the Cavalry Corps staff, by Haig, and probably by Gough, was that small numbers of cavalry should join in the attack immediately behind the first lines of infantry, combining with and supporting the infantry at battalion and brigade level, leading to further opportunities for larger cavalry formations to join in and exploit, and so help create the conditions for a breakthrough. As far as Haig was concerned, divisional cavalry were fighting troops to be used in battle, and at an Army Commanders' Conference on 18 March he 'called attention to the training of the divisional cavalry and cyclists with machine-guns etc. Some GOC Divisions [sic] are using them as orderlies, sharpshooters, etc., and neglecting their tactical training. This must be seen to at once, in order to be ready.'[149]

---

146 See especially Travers, *The Killing Ground*, pp. 89–95, and Travers, *How the War was Won*; also Gardner, *Trial By Fire*, pp. 1–32; Prior and Wilson, *Command on the Western Front* and *The Somme*; and de Groot, *Douglas Haig 1861–1928*. It is perhaps significant that, just as technological determinism is more a feature of US than British military historical writings, so none of these authors is British.

147 NLS Haig Papers 104: Records of the Army Commanders Conference, 8 January 1916.

148 Brigadier General Lord Loch, chief staff officer of VI Corps, quoted in Brown, *The Imperial War Museum Book of the Western Front*, p. 160.

149 NLS Haig Papers 105: Diary entry, 18 March 1916.

Beyond these debates on the cavalry's tactics was the larger issue of their future on the Western Front. Over winter 1915–1916 the British government debated whether the country could afford the economic cost of expanding the Army and continuing the war, and one of the many products of this debate was that the military value of five cavalry divisions on the Western Front came into question.[150] From early 1916 onwards British strategy depended heavily on the close alliance between Haig as GOC-in-C of the BEF and Robertson as CIGS, but the cavalry was one of the few areas in which Robertson did not support Haig wholeheartedly. Although as Home noted Robertson 'loves people to think that he is a Cavalry Soldier', he had little real connection with the cavalry, and he had reached the view that the cavalry were a drain on manpower.[151] If Haig had truly been obsessed with the cavalry, then this would have divided the two men long before Robertson's resignation in February 1918. As it was, Haig kept his belief in the value of the cavalry, but he was prepared to accept changes and reductions in their numbers.

On 31 December 1915, Robertson complained to Haig that 'no fewer than 17 fat mounted Brigades have for long been allocated for Home defence', and started planning to reduce their numbers.[152] In response, Haig advised that, 'I hear indirectly that there is a proposal at home to abolish the second line yeomanry. I think this would be a mistake because, in my opinion, we shall want every mounted man we can put into the field as soon as we get moving.'[153] By January 1916 the issue had become not the cavalry reserves at home but Haig's cavalry in the BEF. Robertson wrote:

> There is a good deal of talk in the War Committee and elsewhere about your having more Cavalry than you need. This is because of the various investigations now proceeding as to the directions in economy that can be effected. I have represented that the proportion of Cavalry that you have to other arms is very much below the normal proportion although of course the conditions are not at present normal. I have always added that they may become normal some day. I should be glad to have your views on this matter. I did not think that you would care to decrease the amount of Cavalry you have, but on the other hand you may be of a different opinion and think that you can dispense with some or the whole of the Indian Cavalry Corps.[154]

The BEF on the Western Front, like all armies in the First World War, was dependent for its transport on horses and mules; and although motorised transport expanded to become an essential supplement, it was never their replacement. The cavalry's requirements made up only a small fraction of the Army's demands, which included 5,919,427 tons of oats and hay shipped across the English Channel during the war compared with 5,269,302 tons of ammunition, and the purchase of 1,248,323 horses

---

150 French, *British Strategy and War Aims 1914–1916*, pp. 116–81.

151 Home, *The Diary of a World War I Cavalry Officer*, p. 93.

152 Woodward, *The Military Correspondence of Field Marshal Sir William Robertson*, p. 25. It is hard to square Robertson's claim with the existence of only three mounted divisions at home; it may include mounted troops at all levels of training.

153 NLS Haig Papers 104: Haig to Robertson, 3 February 1916.

154 Woodward, *The Military Correspondence of Field Marshal Sir William Robertson*, p. 28.

and mules, of which only 174,665 were riding horses.[155] But even this small number attracted the attention of politicians who were already highly critical of the war's conduct, and who were familiar with the cavalry only through popular stereotypes, most recently the *War and the Arme Blanche* affair. On 19 May Robertson informed Haig of a War Committee decision on the previous day to reduce the cavalry in order to save on horses, although adding that since this fell within his remit as CIGS 'I am unable at present to agree to any further reduction being made in these units either in France or elsewhere.'[156] Haig wrote back in real or feigned incomprehension, asking what the War Committee expected to reduce, since 'it can hardly be the number of units in the field, nor can it be the establishment of horses in these units'.[157] Robertson replied at the end of May that, 'In a few weeks *we must consider the reduction in the number of cavalry divisions*', but that 'I can, at a pinch, always find you some cavalry from England, who meanwhile are useful there.'[158] Haig at once responded that:

> As to reducing the cavalry, I have already given orders to consider how we can reduce the cost of their keep in the coming winter. If we can't effect economy then some of them must go, but I have an inward feeling that events will make us regret the reduction in mounted troops. It seems to me that [German] troops and materiel are so imbedded in trench warfare, that a general retreat will be most difficult. We ought therefore be prepared to exploit a success along the lines of 1806.[159]

This appears to be a Staff College-like reference to Napoleon's victory at the Battle of Jena in 1806, after which the French had exploited so rapidly, led by their cavalry, that they had overwhelmed their slower moving enemies, leading to the complete collapse and surrender of Prussia. This 'inward feeling' certainly represented Haig at his most optimistic.

Even a few days before the opening of the Battle of the Somme, the matter of reducing the cavalry was not allowed to rest. At the start of June, Haig was in London for discussions with the War Committee and visited Buckingham Palace, where King George V had been prevailed upon to pass on a message. 'He thought the cavalry should be reduced on account of the cost of maintenance', Haig recorded, replying with arguments similar to those of his Jena allusion, 'I protested that it would be unwise, because in order to shorten the war and reap the fruits of any success, we must make full use of the mobility of the cavalry.'[160] But Haig's authority over the Indian cavalry was less clear-cut than over British troops, and in mid-June an Indian

---

155 *Statistics of the Military Effort of the British Empire During the Great War 1914–1920* p. 397 and p. 521; the horse supply to the British Army during the war is examined in detail in Winton, 'Horsing the British Army 1878–1923', pp. 342–439.
156 NLS Haig Papers 106: Robertson to Haig, 19 May 1916.
157 Ibid., Haig to Robertson, 20 May 1916.
158 Woodward, *The Military Correspondence of Field Marshal Sir William Robertson*, p. 53; the emphasis is in the original and depicts underlining, apparently by Haig.
159 Ibid. The author is grateful to Elizabeth Greenhalgh for this reference, and for some clarification about its use.
160 NLS Haig Papers 106: Diary entry, 7 June 1916.

cavalry brigade was withdrawn from the BEF and sent to Mesopotamia, being replaced in 2nd Indian Cavalry Division by the Canadian Cavalry Brigade.

From these exchanges the idea took hold that Haig had some kind of cavalry obsession. David Lloyd George, in his memoirs published in 1934 with help from Basil Liddell Hart, gave an account of his tour of the Western Front as Secretary of State for War, and his meeting with Haig and General Joseph Joffre a few days before the attack of 15 September on the Somme, including their visit to the headquarters of XIV Corps under Lord Cavan:

> On my way to this rendezvous I had driven through squadrons of cavalry clattering proudly to the front. When I asked what they were for, Sir Douglas Haig explained that they were to be brought up as near the front line as possible, so as to be ready to charge through the gap which was to be made by the Guards [Division] in the coming attack. The cavalry were to exploit the anticipated success and finish the German rout... When I ventured to express to Generals Joffre and Haig my doubts as to whether cavalry could ever operate successfully on a front bristling for miles behind the enemy lines with barbed wire and machine-guns, both Generals fell ecstatically upon me, and Joffre in particular explained that he expected the French cavalry to ride through the broken German lines on his front the following morning. You could hear the distant racket of the massed guns which were at that moment tearing a breach for the French horsemen. Just then a Press [official] photographer, of whose presence we were unaware, snapped us.[161]

The photograph of Haig and Joffre arguing with Lloyd George became one of the most famous of the war. Whether the conversation took place as Lloyd George described it is impossible to say.

As early as the end of February 1916, Haig began to make major changes in the structure and doctrine of his cavalry force. He disbanded the headquarters of both the Cavalry Corps and the Indian Cavalry Corps (so ending the careers of their GOCs, Bingham and Rimington), distributing one cavalry division to each of his four Armies, and at first keeping one division as the nucleus of a new Reserve Corps under Gough. At an Army Commanders' Conference on 18 March Haig explained the purpose of these changes, and the future employment of divisional cavalry:

> We cannot expect to [exploit an opening] by at once pushing mobile troops through the breech to operate *at any great distance* beyond it. The first gap will probably not be wide enough to pass great forces through, even if they are immediately available; while small forces, however mobile, pushed through beyond supporting distance would, under the existing conditions of the enemy's reserves, certainly be held up, and eventually enveloped by superior numbers.[162]

Haig's new doctrine was for mobile forces of all arms to be pushed forward a short distance into a gap, with the main objective of any deeper advance being at first

---

161 Lloyd George, *War Memoirs of David Lloyd George*, Volume I, p. 323; for Liddell Hart's role as a consultant to Lloyd George for this book see Danchev, *Alchemist of War*, p. 66; also Blake, *The Private Papers of Douglas Haig 1914–1919*, pp. 165–7.

162 NLS Haig Papers 105: Records of an Army Commanders Conference 18 March 1916, Paper 32(b).

to slow or deflect enemy reinforcements while the gap was being widened. 'The operations to be undertaken', he concluded, 'will entail both attack and defence, mounted and dismounted, and the closest co-operation between the cavalry and the other arms will be essential.'[163] Haig repeated this doctrine to Rawlinson at Fourth Army headquarters on 27 June, just before the battle started. 'I told him to impress on his Corps commanders the use of their Corps cavalry and mounted troops', who were mostly yeomanry, Haig recorded, 'and if necessary supplement them with regular cavalry units.'[164]

To this end, Haig gave Gough the portentous additional title of 'Temporary Inspector General of Cavalry Divisions' in order to supervise their training. 'Above all', Haig wrote in April, 'he is to spread the "doctrine" and get cavalry officers to believe in the power of their arm when acting in co-operation with guns and infantry. I am told there are some officers who think that cavalry are no longer required!'[165] Particular emphasis was placed on a new form of combat engineering developed for the cavalry under the conditions of the Western Front, first seen at Neuve Chapelle, and called 'Cavalry Tracks'. Because cavalry took up so much road space but were more mobile across country than infantry or artillery, the troopers were required to construct and clear their own cross-country routes, about two horsemen wide, before the battle, including improvised bridges, to get them to the front more quickly; this was an advance in doctrine, but often heavy work for the cavalry involved.[166] Gough also ran special training and co-operation courses for divisional cavalry and mobile troops, and presided over an exercise using 25th Division on how an infantry division could capture the third and final enemy line of entrenchments to free the way for a cavalry breakthrough.[167]

At the start of May, Gough put forward his proposals to Haig for the role of his Reserve Corps in the initial attack on 1 July, for which he planned to deploy two cavalry brigades each with a horse artillery battery, one behind the northern sector of the British line and one behind the southern sector, to help widen a gap should one occur, plus a cavalry division in reserve in the north to be used as a single formation if the opportunity presented. Kiggell as Haig's chief staff officer noted that Haig considered this too ambitious, 'One cavalry division in all is the utmost that can be allotted or that could be used. In such ground masses of cavalry cannot be employed.'[168] By the middle of June, when Gough's force was renamed Reserve Army, it consisted only of 1st and 3rd Cavalry Divisions and 2nd Indian Cavalry Division, but plans existed to strengthen it with 25th Division and also with II Corps to give Gough the all-arms force for exploitation that Haig envisaged.

---

163 Ibid.
164 Ibid., 106: Haig Diary, 27 June 1916.
165 Ibid., 105: Haig Diary, 9 April 1916.
166 Anglesey, *A History of the British Cavalry Volume 8*, pp. 26 and 46–7; later for the Battle of Cambrai in 1917 a 'Cavalry Track Battalion' was improvised from Indian troopers for the Cavalry Corps, see ibid., p. 113.
167 The evidence for this training and its implications is discussed in more detail in Badsey, 'Cavalry and the Development of Breakthrough Doctrine', pp. 153–5.
168 TNA WO 158/245 Reserve Army File, marginal note to Memorandum, Gough to Kiggell, 1 May 1916.

At the same time, Haig never lost sight of the *possibility* that the enemy front might collapse on 1 July, and that the cavalry divisions would need to be ready to exploit this. On 15 June he issued orders to Fourth Army that 'if the enemy's defence breaks down', then Rawlinson should 'push detachments of cavalry to hold Bapaume and work northwards with the bulk of the cavalry and other arms so as to widen the breech in the enemy's line.'[169] Three days later Haig returned to this grandiose plan for cavalry exploitation, repeating that it would apply only 'in case the enemy's defence broke down on the first day', and summarised it in a further note to Rawlinson before putting Reserve Army under Fourth Army on 21 June.[170]

The plans for the Battle of the Somme, and the manner in which different versions were passed back and forth between Haig's GHQ and Rawlinson's Fourth Army from April onwards, have attracted considerable analysis.[171] What has emerged is that major disagreements between Haig and Rawlinson, over in the tactics of the artillery and infantry as well as those of the cavalry, were not resolved before the start of the battle on 1 July. Haig repeatedly made his cavalry doctrine clear to Rawlinson; when one Fourth Army plan in April proposed holding a mass of cavalry in reserve he wrote firmly that, 'This seems to indicate the use, intentionally too, of the cavalry as *one* unit. This is not my view of its employment *during* the fight.'[172] Rawlinson either somehow never grasped this tactical doctrine, or more probably deliberately rejected it. On 22 June, the day after Gough was placed under him, Rawlinson briefed his Corps commanders:

> An opportunity may occur to push the cavalry through, in order to confirm success, and in this connection I will read you the orders which I have received on the subject from the Commander-in-Chief this morning. But before I read them I had better make it quite clear that it may not be possible to break the enemy's line and put the cavalry through in the first rush. In the event of our not being able to capture the green [first] line until the afternoon, it would not be possible to send the cavalry through on the first day at all. A situation may supervene later when the attack on the brown [second] line takes place for pushing the cavalry through; but until we can see what is the course of the battle, it is impossible to predict at what moment we shall be able to undertake this, and the decision will rest in my hand to say when it can be carried out.[173]

Haig's orders to which Rawlinson referred began by pointing out that the British would enjoy considerable numerical advantage 'during the first six days' of the offensive. Haig continued that 'If the first attack goes well every effort must be made to develop the success to the utmost by, firstly opening a way for our cavalry and then as quickly as possible pushing the cavalry through to seize Bapaume and

---

169 NLS Haig Papers 106: Diary entry, 15 June 1916.

170 Ibid. Diary entry, 18 June 1916 and 'Note of C-in-C's instructions in amplification to No. OAD 12 issued 16 June 1916'.

171 Particularly by Prior and Wilson, *Command on the Western Front*, pp. 137–70 and *The Somme*, pp. 41–69.

172 TNA WO 158/233 'Fourth Army', marginal note by Haig, 23 April, to Rawlinson's plan, 19 April 1916, emphasis in the original.

173 IWM Rawlinson Fourth Army Papers: Volume 6, 'Report of the Army Commander's Remarks at a Conference Held at Fourth Army Headquarters, 22 June 1916'.

establish itself in good positions in that neighbourhood', and that it was 'for the above purpose' that he had placed Gough's force (which he described as 'the cavalry in GHQ Reserve') under Rawlinson, on the understanding that 'the advance of the cavalry should be supported by such divisions of Fourth Army as may be necessary. It is considered that these supporting troops also should be placed under General Gough's orders when he advances.'[174] II Corps also was kept by Haig as part of GHQ Reserve rather than being allotted to Rawlinson. Haig was not necessarily thinking solely of a German collapse on the first day, but of a major breakthrough that could develop over a few days from a good opening.

In maintaining that a breakthrough and German collapse was possible but unlikely and that his Corps commanders should not base their approach on its taking place, Rawlinson's speech to his Corps commanders was within the letter of these orders by Haig, but not within their spirit. Rawlinson repeated his views in his personal diary on the evening of the attack, writing that 'the cavalry are in the best of form and dying to get at the Boches but I shall not let them go unless there is a really good chance for them'.[175] On 1 July, Rawlinson gave no orders at all to Gough and the Reserve Army, noting in his diary at 12.14 p.m. that 'there is of course no hope of getting cavalry through today'.[176] In the southern British sector some advance had been made, and further progress was far from impossible, but this was to be yet another occasion in which commanders close to the front felt that a chance to exploit a German weakness had been missed.[177] Whether a more decisive advance at the start of the battle would have made any difference to its conduct or eventual outcome is an open-ended debate. But there is some evidence that, for a variety of reasons, German popular support for the war wavered in autumn 1916, and it may certainly be argued that a greater advance or victory on the Somme could have contributed to tipping Germany towards a negotiated peace that year.[178]

The next major attack on the Somme, towards High Wood on 14 July, produced a cavalry episode which, although also very controversial, provided some evidence that Haig's concept of using the cavalry early and in small numbers had the potential to succeed. Following the infantry night attack, at 7.40 a.m. Rawlinson was sufficiently pleased with progress to call for 2nd Indian Cavalry Division to move forward along its pre-dug cavalry tracks, with High Wood as its objective. 'If they get possession

---

174 Ibid., Volume 1, 'War Diary of Fourth Army Feb 5 1916 to July 13 1916', OAD 17 from GHQ, 21 July 1916. In keeping with British Army staff practice proper names including Bapaume are capitalised in the original.

175 CAC Rawlinson Papers RAWL 1/5: Diary entry, 30 June 1916. 'Boches' was a slang French term for Germans, adopted by the British.

176 Ibid., Entry 1 July 1916.

177 This possibility is discussed in Badsey 'Cavalry and the Development of Breakthrough Doctrine', pp. 155–6 and in Sheffield, *The Somme*, pp. 65–8. Unfortunately both these accounts include a small error (which the present author deeply regrets passing on uncorrected to Professor Sheffield) based on a misdating of a document in the Haig Papers by another author. A corrective in both our names was published in the *Journal of the Society for Army Historical Research*, Summer 2004, Volume 82, Number 330, pp. 179–81.

178 Stevenson, *1914–1918: The History of the First World War*, pp. 223–4 and pp. 276–82.

of this', Rawlinson wrote, 'we shall be on the high road to a big success.'[179] In keeping with Haig's ideas, the leading Secunderabad Cavalry Brigade was organised as an all-arms formation of three cavalry regiments (two Indian and one British), a squadron of Canadian cavalry with special equipment for bridging trenches, a field troop of Royal Engineers, two armoured cars, the brigade machine-gun section, and a battery of horse artillery.[180] At 1.30 p.m. Rawlinson recorded that 'A report is just in that the hostile guns in front of the III Corps have stopped firing. I fear they are off. Oh! If we could get the cavalry through to charge them.'[181] But although the squadrons of the 7th Dragoon Guards and 20th Deccan Horse made their successful charge south of High Wood, bringing up their machine-guns and dismounting to hold the ground they had taken, they were not given orders to attack until about 6.25 p.m., too late in the evening for any major opportunity to develop. Almost all accounts have explained the failure to get 2nd Indian Cavalry Division properly into action in terms of the delays they faced in moving up into position, including Rawlinson's comment in his diary that 'The cavalry found the ground so slippery from the wet that they could not get along and did not go through the line.'[182] Recent research by David Kenyon has shown that, on the contrary, the entire Secunderabad Cavalry Brigade was in position on the old British front line and ready to advance by 9.30 a.m., but received no orders until it was far too late.[183] What was worrying for the cavalry themselves was that no-one in the brigade had taken the initiative and acted with cavalry spirit. Doctrine, as still taught at the Netheravon Cavalry School in August 1916, was that 'It is better to act quickly and chance a mistake than not to act at all – It is necessary too, to always have a desire to assume the offensive, to attack or counterattack – The chief arm of the cavalry soldier is his horse.'[184]

The charge of these two squadrons at High Wood was the first of a number of small cavalry actions that took place on the Western Front between 1916 and the end of the war.[185] In each case the tactics were similar: anything between a few troopers and more than a regiment advancing at the gallop, accompanied by their machine-guns, and supported by as much fire as possible, with the objective of taking a critical piece of enemy territory and holding it dismounted. The result of these tactics was to project a force of riflemen and machine-gunners several hundred yards forward in a matter of minutes. In the process of the men dismounting, and quite usually entrenching, the horses would either be scattered back to friendly lines or simply treated as expendable, and casualties among horses were invariably greater

---

179 CAC Rawlinson Papers RAWL 1/5: Diary entry, 14 July 1916.
180 Norman, *The Hell They Called High Wood*, p. 81.
181 CAC Rawlinson Papers RAWL 1/5: Diary entry, 14 July 1916.
182 Ibid., Diary entry, 14 July 1916.
183 This research is cited with due acknowledgement in Holmes, *Tommy*, pp. 440–42.
184 NAM Bateman Papers: Cavalry School Netheravon Course exercise book, August 1916
185 This paragraph is based almost entirely on research undertaken and information supplied by David Kenyon, a generous act so close to submission of his own doctoral thesis, for which the present author is duly grateful.

than among men.[186] Charges that resulted in actual contact and the use of the arme blanche were rare enough to draw comment, but far from unique; the most recent research has identified at least 20 British cases of arme blanche charges and combat on the Western Front 1916–1918. Cavalry commanders certainly understood the risks involved and the likely consequences of failure to support the charge properly with fire, such as the disastrous charge of the 6th (Inniskilling) Dragoons on 1 December 1917 during the German counterattack at Cambrai, made despite repeated protests.[187] Even when a charge was successful, such as the capture of Monchy-le-Preux village during the Battle of Arras, heavy losses resulted if the infantry could not get forward to reinforce the advance quickly; Byng's mordant observation was that 'it seems a pity to lose all those chaps who were perfect cavalrymen for the sake of a village which is a complete shell-trap for the British side'.[188] The use of cavalry on such a small scale could not in any way be decisive, but such charges gave them an additional role, and paved the way for developments later in the war.

On 2 July 1916, Gough with Reserve Army headquarters was given command of the northern part of the British line on the Somme, leaving the cavalry divisions under GHQ's command. On 7 September the Cavalry Corps headquarters was re-established with most of its old staff, including Home as chief staff officer once more, and all five cavalry divisions put under it, the two Indian divisions being renamed 4th Cavalry Division and 5th Cavalry Division. The new choice of Lieutenant General Charles Kavanagh to command the Cavalry Corps was a curious one. Home thought him 'a real leader of men and knows his job, has a mind of his own', but Kavanagh's implied bluntness was taken by some others for stupidity.[189] His position was unusual in that the normal use of the cavalry was as dispersed formations, for which the Cavalry Corps headquarters had a training and administrative function, like the Royal Flying Corps or the Machine Gun Corps; but in the event of a German collapse Kavanagh might have to command all five cavalry divisions together in battle. Also, the Cavalry Corps came directly under GHQ, so that Kavanagh enjoyed a unique privilege as a Corps commander in attending Army Commanders Conferences, and his staff regularly attended GHQ meetings.[190]

Haig's reasons for re-forming the Cavalry Corps as one body may have been institutional and political, as this made it slightly harder to detach the Indian divisions from the BEF, and gave the cavalry a centre for doctrine. For the forthcoming attack of 15 September on the Somme, including the first use of tanks, Haig had great hopes

---

186 Searching for a comparison in order to make these tactics more comprehensible on battlefield tours, the author took to describing this kind of cavalry charge as very 'short-range paratroops', seizing a position and then holding it until relieved by the infantry in the manner of paratroopers in the Second World War. This expression, duly acknowledged as his, was published by Sheffield, *Forgotten Victory*, p. 144 and p. 259, so now the present author is stuck with it.

187 Badsey, 'Cavalry and the Development of Breakthrough Doctrine', pp. 160–61.

188 IWM Chetwode Papers: Byng to Chetwode, 30 May 1917.

189 Home, *The Diary of a World War I Cavalry Officer*, p. 119; Sheffield and Bourne (eds), *Douglas Haig: War Diaries and Letters 1914–1918*, pp. 228–9.

190 Robertson, *From Private to Field Marshal*, p. 206; Gardner, *Trial By Fire*, pp. 42–3; Home, *The Diary of a World War I Cavalry Officer*, p. 143.

that 'the crisis of the battle is likely to be reached, and the moment might possibly be favourable for cavalry action'.[191] But although they shared the excitement, there was a strong sense at Cavalry Corps headquarters that if the cavalry were not used this time they could well be disbanded or sent elsewhere.[192] There were no cavalry or mounted divisions left in reserve: between July and September Robertson, bowing to War Committee pressure, authorised the conversion of the three mounted divisions at home into cyclists and then their breaking up, leaving a single Cyclist Division at home by January 1917. One yeomanry regiment facing conversion to cyclists erected a mock tombstone 'Sacred To the Memory of Spurs'.[193]

For the renewed attack on 15 September, Rawlinson agreed with Kavanagh that if an opportunity arose then 'the leading regiment must settle the moment for the cavalry to go through', perhaps trying to correct the error at High Wood.[194] Rawlinson's own views had not changed significantly. On 10 September he briefed his Corps commanders including 'the employment of the cavalry which has quite a reasonable chance of coming off', but on the eve of the attack he was 'a little anxious lest Kavanagh act prematurely and thus compromise the actions of the other arms', rather than accepting that cavalry could participate in the all-arms battle.[195] On the day of the attack the cavalry again received no orders and were left, in the frustrated words of one junior officer, 'Still waiting about in the mud'.[196]

With the failure of the Battle of the Somme to achieve any obvious gains except for a small amount of territory, Haig's position was increasingly politically vulnerable, and his support of the cavalry was an obvious point to attack. At the War Committee meeting of 9 November 1916, Lloyd George criticised the cavalry, claiming that there were 54,828 cavalry horses on the Western Front, 45,900 of them with the cavalry divisions:

> It was his intention at the proper time to raise the question of whether we needed these cavalry in France. Was there... the slightest chance the cavalry could be used for a breakthrough? He was told that on the Eastern Front, where the cavalry had several times gone through, they had invariably been roughly handled and driven back often badly shattered by a few machine-guns.[197]

In the wider context of British politics and strategy this was one of several periods of high drama, with the Asquith coalition within weeks or even days of collapse. At the same meeting, the War Committee received its first warnings of the German plan to re-introduce unrestricted submarine warfare early in 1917. Nevertheless, once

---

191 Sheffield and Bourne (eds), *Douglas Haig: War Diaries and Letters 1914–1918*, pp. 228–9.
192 Home, *The Diary of a World War I Cavalry Officer*, pp. 119–20.
193 Rogers, *The Mounted Troops of the British Army 1066–1945*, pp. 233–4; Badsey, 'Cavalry and the Development of Breakthrough Doctrine', pp. 169–70.
194 CAC Rawlinson Papers RAWL 1/5: Rawlinson Diary entry for 11 September 1916.
195 Ibid. Diary entries 10 and 14 September 1916.
196 NAM Talbot-Rice Papers: Talbot-Rice to his parents, 20 September 1916.
197 TNA CAB 22/65 Minutes of a Meeting of the War Committee, 9 November 1916, pp. 4–5.

again, cavalry tactics, and such weighty issues as whether bicyclist troops might be used instead, came to occupy the country's highest political leadership.[198] First, the War Office asked Haig to consider withdrawing the bulk of the cavalry back to Great Britain until the spring.[199] On 23 November Haig appeared before the War Committee to reply, armed with a memorandum from his GHQ staff citing figures and calculations showing that of 420,000 horses with the BEF only 37,000 or six per cent belonged to the five cavalry divisions, and that any such move, or any change in the existing cavalry dispositions, would only *cost* shipping. Haig then repeated his belief in victory on the Western Front in 1917, and the place of the cavalry in his strategy, claiming Robertson's support:

> The point was, was there a reasonable possibility of using the cavalry: had the enemy's *moral* been so shaken that there was a chance of breaking through and letting the cavalry get to work? They [Haig and Robertson] were satisfied that the *moral* of the enemy had been so far reduced that there appeared to be a reasonable prospect of the use of cavalry. He reminded the Committee that the cavalry were the only force left which consisted of seasoned soldiers.[200]

According to Haig, the three British cavalry divisions consumed about 100 tons of all types of supplies a day, which in this context was a trivial amount. Lord Curzon as Chairman of the Shipping Control Board raised the idea of sending the 11 Indian cavalry regiments serving with 4th and 5th Cavalry Divisions to Egypt, since 'the consequent saving would be eight ships of 4,000 tons for two months and eight ships a year for forage. This might appear almost a negligible quantity, but he wished the Committee to realise that we had come to such a pass that we had literally to *scrape up* ships.'[201] On this occasion Robertson supported Haig, pointing out flaws in Curzon's assumption that transporting the Indian cavalry to Egypt would produce any saving, and the Committee agreed to leave the cavalry as they were.

The first few months of the subsequent Lloyd George coalition was a period of unusually sustained crisis both in British domestic politics and in the management of the war. Conscription had been introduced in January 1916 (except in Ireland), but when unrestricted submarine warfare began exactly a year later in January 1917, the manpower crisis was already at its most acute, with about 50,000 fewer replacements reaching the BEF each month than were needed to maintain its strength.[202] This was accompanied by a further crisis within the alliance with the first Russian Revolution and the failure of the Nivelle Offensive in April 1917, producing a drift in British political leadership that led both to Third Ypres and to a half-formed strategy of

---

198 French, *The Strategy of the Lloyd George Coalition 1914–1918*, pp. 40–44; Woodward, *Lloyd George and the Generals*, pp. 116–32.

199 NLS Haig Papers 109: Diary entry, 19 November 1916.

200 TNA CAB 22/73 War Committee Meeting 23 November 1916, p. 3, emphasis in the original.

201 Ibid., p.5; NLS Haig Papers 109: Diary entry, 19 November 1916; and 214h: GHQ Memorandum from QMG to C-in-C, 14 November 1916, emphasis in the original.

202 Millman, *Pessimism and British War Policy 1916–1918*, p. 83; Grieves, *The Politics of Manpower 1914–1918*, pp. 90–148.

a new importance for the EEF and the war against the Ottoman Empire in rivalry to the Western Front.[203] Meanwhile in the course of 1917 the yeomanry, the only trained cavalry reserve, were run down to just over half their previous numbers, until between August and October 1917 Robertson halted cavalry and yeomanry recruiting altogether, and it was not resumed for the rest of the war.[204] After June 1917 the British mounted troops of the EEF received no remounts at all, partly due to shipping problems.[205]

In consequence, for the next year there would be times in which British grand strategy, balancing the Western Front with Palestine, would hinge on the existence and deployment of one or two understrength cavalry divisions. With Lloyd George as Prime Minister, the issue of the cavalry on the Western Front became much less about military realities and shipping calculations, and much more of a way to illustrate Haig's lack of fitness for command. Facing an increasing shortage of manpower, the view from Whitehall – including Robertson as CIGS – was that the cavalry on the Western Front were a waste of rations, fodder and shipping. In early 1917 the War Office took to sending out trained cavalrymen as part of the drafts of replacements for infantry formations. In February, after representations by Kavanagh, GHQ began identifying these men and diverting them back into the cavalry instead; until in May Haig was rebuked by the Army Council for diverting at least 1,000 soldiers in this way.[206]

For almost two years, as the Army expanded and promotion opportunities including commissions appeared in the infantry and other branches, the cavalry had been losing their battle to keep up to strength, and to retain good officers and men. But despite the promotion of outstanding majors like Bridges, it was generally not Army policy to promote cavalrymen to command infantry brigades, leading to a block in promotion within the cavalry below brigade level. Comparing the Army List of January 1915 with that of January 1918, of 21 new cavalry regimental commanders, in 15 cases the new appointee was the regiment's senior major, and in 5 of the remaining 6 cases he was the senior major of the next regiment in line.[207] As early as October 1915, Home had complained that 'we all get restless, young officers feel that they are not pulling their weight and want to go where there is more fighting. It is only natural – yet one does not want to lose the best cavalry soldiers we have got.'[208] The cavalry were highly conscious of this problem, including many officers and men lost to the Royal Flying Corps and to the new Tank Corps, some as volunteers and some simply posted to branches considered to have a higher priority. At the end of 1916 Haig issued a circular order to the cavalry that 'in future no

---

203 Hughes, *Allenby and British Strategy in the Middle East 1917–1919*, pp. 23–42; French, *The Strategy of the Lloyd George Coalition 1916–1918*, pp. 67–93.

204 *Statistics of the Military Effort of the British Empire During the Great War 1914–1920*, p. 208; Terraine, *The Road to Passchendaele*, p. 235.

205 Preston, *The Desert Mounted Corps*, p. 317

206 NLS Haig Papers 110: Diary entry, 1 February 1917 and Note 79 OAD 291/2 Minutes of a Meeting 3 February 1917; TNA WO 32/11355 'Dismounting of One Cavalry Division', Army Council to Haig, 12 May 1917.

207 Badsey, 'Fire and the Sword', p. 297, comparing the monthly Army List.

208 Home, *The Diary of a World War I Cavalry Officer*, p. 90.

applications for transfers of officers or NCOs to other branches of the service are to be entertained'.[209] By November 1917, during the Battle of Cambrai one Corps commander observed that 'I fear the Cavalry have lost their thrusters, they have gone to the Tanks, the Flying Corps and the Infantry.'[210]

Haig's plans for 1917 were drastically revised by the change in British grand strategy that accompanied the replacement of Joffre by Robert Nivelle and that led to the Battle of Arras. When Allenby, whose Third Army was to make the attack (in conjunction with First Army) came to see him on 23 December 1916, Haig recorded that Allenby was 'anxious to push the cavalry right through to Monchy-le-Preux', an advance of about 7,000 yards rather than a complete breakout, and that 'I consider that the cavalry should first co-operate with the infantry in widening gaps in the line.'[211] For the first time in the war, the doctrine of using the cavalry in small units as early as possible was to be employed between a GOC-in-C and an Army commander who both understood and accepted it. Following his previous practice, Haig made allowance in his plans for Arras possibly being a major success followed by a cavalry exploitation, but issued firm orders applying to all the cavalry divisions:

> The Field Marshal Commanding-in-Chief wishes it to be clearly understood by Army Commanders that the efficiency of the Cavalry Divisions is to be preserved, and that these divisions should be carefully handled so that their value may remain unimpaired. It is essential that the Cavalry Corps should be in a condition to deliver an effective blow against the enemy after battle [sic]. This moment has not yet arrived.[212]

Any plans for a deep cavalry exploitation at Arras were given up after the German retirement to the Hindenburg Line in February, which Cavalry Corps headquarters understood had rendered any such advance unfeasible.[213] Instead, Allenby's plan for 9 April was for a limited advance, with the cavalry moving in co-operation with the infantry. Two cavalry divisions were held about 4,000 yards behind the British front while the first infantry attack attempted to drive 5,000 yards into the German positions. If this had worked completely, then the cavalry moving in brigades would have 'galloped' a further 5,000 yards to the River Sensée where they would have held their positions until relieved by the infantry, and then advanced a further 5,000 yards to complete a penetration of about eight miles through the German defences.[214] The problem of the attack was greatly magnified by the dreadful weather before and during the battle, including snowstorms and slush, which affected the horses of the cavalry very badly. A trooper with 1st Life Guards remembered that on the first morning, 'what with the freezing night which had weakened the horses and our combined weight, many of them just collapsed and died' as the regiment mounted

---

209 Quoted in Anglesey, *A History of the British Cavalry Volume 7*, p.105; see also Badsey, 'Cavalry and the Development of Breakthrough Doctrine', pp. 144–5.
210 Crozier, *A Brass Hat in No Man's Land*, p. 193.
211 NLS Haig Papers 109: Diary entry, 23 December 1916.
212 Ibid., 111: Note 337 OAD 347, 20 March 1917.
213 Home, *The Diary of a World War I Cavalry Officer*, p. 133.
214 Edmonds, *Official History, France and Belgium, 1917, Volume I*, pp. 100–104.

up.[215] But although the infantry attack did not go perfectly and there were difficulties in getting the cavalry forward in time, several regiments saw action during the first few days, including the capture of Monchy-le-Preux by the 8th Cavalry Brigade on 11 April.

It has been recognised that in the Battle of Arras the British Army showed improvements over the Battle of the Somme in many branches and aspects, including improved staffwork and a grasp of operational art.[216] This was just as true of the cavalry as of any other arm. Haig's doctrine of using mobile troops at divisional level as early as possible, followed by regular cavalry advancing in dispersed formations, worked after a fashion, despite some frustrating delays. The cavalry showed that once they could get into action they could manoeuvre on a battlefield in regimental and even brigade strength, although at a heavy price: the 10th Hussars, one of the regiments that fought at Monchy, suffered 189 casualties.[217] The consensus among senior officers was that early in the battle there *might* have been a chance to get a small cavalry force, between a regiment and a brigade, through the German defences, where – if it had followed doctrine – it would not have charged blindly and been wiped out, but would have reached a defensive position, dug in, and hoped for reinforcements. Even so, a comment made 20 years later by one officer involved, Sir Charles Fergusson GOC XVII Corps, 'I doubt whether one [cavalry] brigade, let loose onto the Douai plain *without any definite objective*, would have done more than create some temporary discomfort and local confusion', reveals a disturbing lack of interest or understanding of cavalry doctrine.[218] While Allenby maintained close control and liaison with his subordinate Corps in planning the battle, the Cavalry Corps was the exception, being very much allowed to go its own way.[219]

At Arras the cavalry had finally played a part in the all-arms battle, in contrast to waiting for the 'Gap' at Neuve Chapelle. But they were so heavily associated with the Gap Scheme and the breakout that this limited success in accordance with the overall plan was widely interpreted as their failure, including by the cavalry themselves. There was also a strong sense that, just as the cavalry had volunteered for new roles to protect themselves institutionally and to feel useful, so Haig's doctrine was chiefly a device for justifying the existence of the cavalry against the day when the German front would finally collapse.

One of the issues raised for the first time in preparation for Arras was the co-operation of cavalry with tanks. The chief staff officer of the Heavy Branch Machine Gun Corps (later the Tank Corps), Lieutenant Colonel J.F.C. Fuller, drew up a vague plan for the tanks to function as a mobile blockhouse line for the cavalry to base its operations on, and for forming bridgeheads or seizing and holding points of tactical importance for the cavalry. But no actual co-operation between the tanks and the

---

215 Trooper Sam Bailey, quoted in Nicholls, *Cheerful Sacrifice*, p. 132.
216 Griffith, *Battle Tactics of the Western Front*, pp. 65–100; Simpson, *Directing Operations*, pp. 61–86; Rawlins, *Surviving Trench Warfare*, pp. 87–113.
217 Brander, *The 10th Royal Hussars*, p. 97; see also Nicholls, *Cheerful Sacrifice*, pp. 137–47
218 Quoted in Hughes, 'Edmund Allenby', pp. 24–6, emphasis added.
219 Simpson, *Directing Operations*, p. 70.

cavalry took place in the battle, and there the matter rested for a few months.[220] The Tank Corps' lack of enthusiasm may in part be explained by the argument used in the origin and development of the tanks that personnel and resources could be found for the new arm by cutting back on the cavalry or abolishing them altogether.[221]

Haig next began planning for the Third Battle of Ypres, although the cavalry issue continued to cause trouble for him. On 12 May, an official letter from the Army Council under Robertson (one military authority that he could not defy) ordered Haig that, due to the need to maintain infantry reserves and save on shipping, he was to dismount one of his five cavalry divisions, convert the men into four infantry battalions, and send the horses to Egypt. Haig almost certainly had advanced warning of this decision, since his answer was that the Cavalry Corps had just formed its Dismounted Division and taken over part of the line, that to withdraw it would seriously disrupt his plans, and that he could not discuss the matter for at least another six weeks, (the Dismounted Division carried out ten regimental-sized trench raids between May and July, nine of them deemed successful).[222] There then followed discussions between Haig and Lord Derby, the new Secretary of State for War, and Haig's visit to London on 19 June to defend his planned offensive before the War Cabinet. Along with these much greater matters, Haig made it clear that he was not about to disband his cavalry divisions on the eve of what he believed would be his decisive breakthrough battle, and it seemed unlikely that the cavalry regiments would convert to infantry without an institutional fight.[223]

The Army Council was not to be put off so easily. On 27 June it ordered Haig to free 3,000 horses for Egypt by dismounting 12 Corps cavalry regiments of yeomanry, using line cavalry regiments from the cavalry divisions as replacements. Next day Haig wrote back again refusing to break up his cavalry divisions, even temporarily, and explaining his doctrine that 'even under existing conditions, opportunities arise in every battle for the tactical use, locally, of small bodies of cavalry'.[224] For a major offensive his minimum needs were 6 Corps cavalry regiments (18 squadrons) with the Army making the main attack, and two regiments each with the other Armies, or 14 regiments in all; he was therefore prepared to disband 6 of the 20 Corps cavalry yeomanry regiments then with the BEF. On 11 July the Army Council replied insisting on its original demand for dismounting the equivalent of a cavalry division *plus* the six yeomanry regiments. On 14 July Haig offered (under protest) a further six Cops cavalry regiments instead, to be selected by the Army Board, and this was accepted on the same day. The result, in the largest British Army in history, was reminiscent of Wolseley's struggles over a few hundred horses 30 years before. On 30 July – the day before the opening of the Ypres offensive – Haig wrote to the

---

220 Hammond, 'The Theory and Practice of Tank Co-Operation with Other Arms on the Western Front in the First World War', p. 100.

221 Harris, *Men, Ideas and Tanks*, pp. 130–33.

222 TNA WO 32/11355 'Dismounting of One Cavalry Division', Army Council to Haig 12 May 1917 and Haig to the Army Council, 14 May 1917. Home, *The Diary of a World War I Cavalry Officer*, pp. 141–6.

223 Sheffield and Bourne (eds), *Douglas Haig: Diaries and Letters 1914–1918*, pp. 300–301.

224 TNA WO 32/11355 'Dismounting of One Cavalry Division', Army Council to Haig 27 June 1917 and Haig to Army Council, 28 June 1917.

Army Council that the 12 dismounted regiments had yielded an average of 419 men each for conversion to infantry, but only 350 fit horses each or 2,100 altogether. He undertook to send the balance to Egypt in due course, but pointed out tartly that 'on the 25th July the number of fit Cavalry horses in Remount Depots in France over and above outstanding demands amounted to 51'.[225]

On 2 July Haig issued orders that two weeks later the Cavalry Corps headquarters and two divisions would concentrate behind Gough's Fifth Army, which would make the initial attack on 31 July to begin the Third Battle of Ypres. The orders for the cavalry's employment were issued on 22 July, stating that 'Nothing more than Corps cavalry should, however, be employed in local exploitation unless the opportunity is judged favourable for a larger force', for which 1st Cavalry Division was held ready on the first day, but that 'we must be prepared subsequently to employ at once two cavalry divisions to exploit success in the attack on the Passchendaele-Westroosebeek portion of the ridge', the delay between the first attack and the chance to use the cavalry being 'perhaps by three or four days or even more'.[226] This assumption that the cavalry's role in the battle, for which Haig had insisted for a year that they must be preserved, would start after the seizure of the Passchendaele ridge in only a few days proved ridiculously optimistic, as the fight for the ridge consumed three months of bitter fighting. While this was not the cavalry's fault, even before the battle started they had become the symbol of the massive disparity between British hopes for a breakthrough and the reality of each new offensive. On 20 July, one loyal but hard-bitten infantry battalion commander preparing for the battle wrote that:

> Our cavalry are assembling in the vicinity for the battle. High Command, with their incurable faith in their luck, continue to expect that the infantry assaults will burst a gap through and create havoc in the enemy's rear. The 10th [Hussars], which lost some two thirds of their men [sic] last Spring, do not appear to share this belief... But should the German defences be widely and completely broken, cavalry, supported by tanks and artillery, might get an opportunity of routing disorganised forces. The bare possibility of this justifies the readiness of the Cavalry Corps.[227]

On 24 September Haig ordered Kavanagh to train the cavalry in co-operation with tanks, but there was again little enthusiasm from the Tank Corps, which simply resurrected Fuller's memorandum from before Arras as a basis for training. These ideas about how tanks might co-operate with cavalry gradually transferred from the planning for Third Ypres to the planning for Cambrai, but there is no official Corps record that any joint training actually took place.[228] After the main effort was transferred from Gough to Plumer's Second Army, Haig also gave orders in response to the success of Plumer's attacks along the Menin Road ridge, that 'in order to

---

225 Ibid., Haig to Army Council, 30 July 1917.
226 NLS Haig Papers 115: Note 1 OAD 532, 2 July 1917; and Note 111 OAD 563/1 'Note on possible employment of the Cavalry Corps during the forthcoming operations', 22 July 1917.
227 Terraine (ed.), *General Jack's Diary*, p. 229.
228 NLS Haig Papers 117: Diary entry, 24 September 1917; Hammond, 'The Theory and Practice of Tank Co-Operation with Other Arms on the Western Front in the First World War', pp. 179–80; Simpson, *Directing Operations*, p. 117.

exploit our [expected] success, there must be *fresh* troops available, also Tanks and Cavalry'.[229]

Four days before Plumer's attack on 4 October, Haig consulted Kavanagh on using the Cavalry Corps to support the next attack, which he envisaged as following a few days later if the attack on 4 October went well. Haig saw this as a real chance for cavalry exploitation, issuing orders next day that 'When a favourable moment for Cavalry action arises, one or both of the two leading divisions will move forward under cover of their advance guards'.[230] Home, who was present at the meeting, loyally recorded that 'I think there is a chance. We shall lose heavily; on the other hand we ought to make a big bag of guns and men. It is for the Chief to decide whether it is worthwhile.'[231] There is little doubt that if this attack had gone ahead and succeeded, then the Cavalry could have got into position up on the ridges and at least as far as their planned start lines, since at this date the front line artillery and infantry were being supplied principally by convoys of big mules of comparable size and carrying capacity to the Cavalry's horses. Nevertheless, there is something both moving and frightening in an experienced officer like Home loyally facing his own probable death and that of many of his comrades in this way.

In the event, the attack of 4 October achieved little success, and became the last British effort before the heavy rains turned the battle into another month's fight for Passchendaele ridge. On 12 October Home wrote that 'The weather has really broken', and 'I do not now think there is a chance of using the cavalry this year.'[232]

Among the many factors in the British failure to reach the Passchendaele ridge except after three months' hard fighting was their first major encounter with the new German tactics of defence in depth, holding a front line thinly and spreading back often more than 10,000 yards to include a battle zone and a rear zone, plus counterattacking reserves.[233] Defence in depth marked an important doctrinal advance, and in various forms it was to become the accepted method of defence in industrialised warfare throughout the twentieth century. But during 1918, under conditions that were very different to those on the Ypres ridges, this style of defence would also provide both the opportunity and the necessity for British cavalry to play a larger role on the Western Front.

There could scarcely be a greater contrast in October 1917 than between the mud and pillbox bunkers of the Ypres ridges and the rocky desert facing the EEF under Allenby as it prepared for the Third Battle of Gaza. But for the cavalry the Western Front and Palestine were connected both by the transfer of senior personnel and by exchanges of troops and of doctrine. Before Allenby's arrival in June the mounted troops had been mostly grouped into the Desert Column under Chetwode. Promoting him to command XX Corps, Allenby gave the Desert Column to Chauvel, expanding it to become what was originally intended as II Cavalry Corps, but was instead

---

229 NLS Haig Papers 117: Diary entry, 28 September 1917.
230 Ibid., OAD 646, 2 October 1917.
231 Home, *The Diary of a World War I Cavalry Officer*, p. 150.
232 Ibid., p. 151.
233 Prior and Wilson, *Passchendaele: The Untold Story*, pp. 71–3; Griffith, *Forward Into Battle*, pp. 78–80.

named the Desert Mounted Corps in August, consisting of three mounted divisions and three independent brigades. The ANZAC Mounted Division (reduced to two Australian Light Horse brigades and one New Zealand Mounted Rifles brigade) went to the New Zealander Major General Sir Edward Chaytor. The Australian Mounted Division (originally formed in January 1917 as the Imperial Mounted Division) with two light horse brigades and one yeomanry brigade served under Major General Sir Henry Hodgson (15th Hussars); and the resurrected 2nd Mounted Division, renamed the Yeomanry Division (three yeomanry brigades), served under Barrow (35th Scinde Horse). The Corps also included an independent yeomanry brigade, an Imperial Service Cavalry Brigade (raised and equipped by some Indian princes) and an Imperial Camel Corps Brigade. The Corps cavalry for XX Corps and XXI Corps were provided by yeomanry regiments.[234]

British strategy regarding Palestine remained vague, and Allenby's appointment was not in any sense the deliberate placing of a cavalry general in command of a large mounted force, or in a theatre in which experience in mobile warfare might be of value. Allenby was at least the second, and possibly the fifth, choice as a replacement for Murray as GOC-in-C of the EEF, and he considered it a demotion from his command of Third Army. It was also Murray and not Allenby who had requested Barrow to command the new Yeomanry Division. If anyone was the driving force behind the reorganisation, as well as the plan for Third Gaza, it appears to have been Chetwode.[235] But the great differences from the Western Front were that the EEF was appreciably stronger than the opposing Turkish forces (although Allenby's intelligence over-estimated Turkish strength by about half); the Turks were resolute in defence and equipped with modern weapons, and had already repeatedly defeated British attacks on several fronts, but they did not have the fighting abilities of the Germans; the Turkish entrenchments were also much weaker than on the Western Front, their strongpoints at Gaza and Beersheba being interspersed with light entrenchments; and the ratio of troops to frontage was such that there was an open flank to the east of Beersheba. Drawing on British doctrine going back to *Small Wars*, this was an opportunity for an Imperial – rather than simply British – Army to show how it could fight in such conditions.[236]

Before Allenby's arrival there had been suggestions that the yeomanry should give up their swords as a weight saving, as in the Boer War.[237] At the same time,

---

234 Preston, *The Desert Mounted Corps*, pp. 7–9; *A Brief Record of the Advance of the Egyptian Expeditionary Force under the Command of General Sir Edmund H.H. Allenby G.C.B., G.C.M.G., July 1917 to October 1918, Compiled From Official Sources* (hereafter *The Advance of the Egyptian Expeditionary Force*), pp. 37–73.

235 NLS Haig Papers 112: Robertson to Haig, 15 April 1917 mentions four other candidates for GOC-in-C EEF; see also Hughes, 'Edmund Allenby', p. 12 and p. 28; Hughes, *Allenby and British Strategy in the Middle East 1917–1919*, pp. 42–6; Barrow, *The Fire of Life*, pp. 166–7.

236 Preston, *The Desert Mounted Corps*, pp. 3–5; Kearsey, *A Summary of the Strategy and Tactics of the Egypt and Palestine Campaigns*, pp. 17–28; Sheffy, *British Military Intelligence in the Palestine Campaign 1914–1918*, pp. 286–8.

237 McMunn and Falls (ed. Edmonds), *Official History Egypt and Palestine, Volume I*, p. 123.

the Desert Mounted Corps had followed with interest the evolution of mounted tactics on the Western Front and the success of small mounted charges in 1916 and 1917. According to Major Lord Hampton of the Worcestershire Hussars, 'for some months previous to the advance, the possibility of having to carry enemy trenches at the gallop had been urged upon us'.[238] Even before Gallipoli, both the Australians and New Zealanders had practised mounted charges, and they habitually referred to themselves as cavalry in official documents.[239] The British assessment in January 1917 was that they were good, but not yet up to British cavalry standards. Major General Sir Robert Whigham, the Deputy CIGS, wrote sympathetically to Chetwode that 'The ANZAC Mounted troops must be fine fellows but I can well imagine your regret at their not having the flexibility and cohesion of regular Cavalry.'[240] But Chetwode was capable of being disingenuous in such matters; in April 1917 he wrote of his mounted troops including the yeomanry that they were 'not cavalry, they are high-class mounted rifles, ready to undertake purely infantry work at any moment', but only because he was arguing against an attempt to replace their 18-pounder field artillery with less powerful 13-pounder horse guns.[241] The Desert Mounted Corps' semi-official history described the state of Corps doctrine in August 1917 as follows:

> There was considerable divergence of opinion in the cavalry as to the best method to be employed in a mounted attack. As there were no reliable precedents in modern warfare, with its machine guns and quick firing artillery, brigadiers had been given a free hand to develop the tactics they favoured, subject to the principle that fire support should always be provided if available, and that the line of fire and the direction of the mounted attack should be as near as possible at right angles to one another.... If more than one regiment took part in the attack, the machine guns, of course, moved on the outer flanks of the regiments.... The wisdom of accompanying a mounted attack by one or two machine guns was generally recognised, and in most cases where a charge was made deliberately and after due preparation, and the guns were available, this method of support was employed. Where a mounted attack had to cover a considerable distance of open ground before reaching charging distance, the most usual formation was in column of squadrons in line of troop columns. Our own gunners were of the opinion that this formation offered the most difficult target to artillery, provided the interval between troops was not less than 25 yards, and the distance between squadrons was not less than 100 yards. The experience of the campaign seemed to point to the fact that cavalry also suffered less from machine gun fire in this formation than in any other, at any rate at ranges beyond 1000 yards.[242]

---

238 IWM Hampton Papers: Memoirs 1917, p. 11; Preston, *The Desert Mounted Corps*, pp. 55–6.

239 AWM 4 153 War Diary 3rd Australian Light Horse Brigade, 4 May 1915; AWM 4 151 War Diary 1st Australian Light Horse Brigade, Brigade Order 63 of 15 March 1915 records a rifle lost by the Auckland Mounted Riles during a cavalry charge at divisional manoeuvres.

240 IWM Chetwode Papers: Whigham to Chetwode, 17 January 1917.

241 Ibid., Memorandum by Chetwode, 20 April 1917.

242 Preston, *The Desert Mounted Corps*, pp. 55–6; the idea of a mounted charge supported by fire at right angles or close appears in several Desert Mounted Corps war diaries, e.g. AWM 4 154 War Diary 4th Light Horse Brigade, entry 18 March 1918.

The opposing Turkish cavalry was inferior in numbers, and thought less aggressive by Chauvel's troopers; only one case was recorded of a Turkish successful mounted charge, early in the campaign.[243] In contrast, the Desert Mounted Corps history lists 14 significant mounted charges in the 1917–1918 campaign, (fewer than on the Western Front 1916–1918 but usually involving larger formations), of which three were shot down by artillery and machine guns, and the rest succeeded.

Placing Chauvel as an Australian in command of a mixed Corps of eleven horsed brigades, five of them yeomanry, four Australian, one New Zealander, and one Indian, was unique in the war. But just as tactical ideas were shared among the brigades, so the Desert Mounted Corps was more homogenous than it appeared. Chauvel deliberated in June 1917 whether to transfer to the regular British Army as a career move, and he had pre-war ties of family friendship with Hodgson. His chief staff officer Lieutenant Colonel Richard Howard-Vyse, 'the best staff officer in the British Army' according to Allenby, was a Staff College graduate from the Royal Horse Guards, and had been Chetwode's brigade major (chief staff officer) in 1914.[244] In Barrow's Yeomanry Division, all the brigade commanders and five of the nine regimental commanders were pre-war regular cavalry or Indian cavalry officers. Artillery for all three divisions was British, other divisional troops varied in nationality, and staffs were a mixture of nationalities. Into this framework the Australian and New Zealand troopers fitted as their predecessors had into the mounted columns of the Boer War.

What later became the most famous charge of the war under British command, the capture of Beersheba on 31 October 1917, was carried out by the 4th Light Horse and 12th Light Horse of the Australian Mounted Division, many brandishing their bayonets in accordance with Hodgson's standing orders.[245] The Third Battle of Gaza, which began on 28 October, was planned as a classic cavalry flank manoeuvre in conjunction with a frontal infantry attack, using the ANZAC Mounted Division and the Australian Mounted Division to turn the Turkish positions from the east by capturing the town of Beersheba with its critical water supply. Allenby's briefing notes for the battle show the style in which it was fought, including the emphasis on initiative: '*Lessons.* Thorough *preparation – Deception – reinforce where winning and accept losses – Trust your luck – Cavalry and Beersheba? Water!*'[246] The reference to reinforcing where the Army was winning rather than allowing itself to be held up, a fundamental concept in later manoeuvre war theory, is particularly noteworthy. After the Australian Mounted Division had turned the open Turkish desert flank, late in the afternoon of 31 October the 4th Light Horse Brigade's leading two regiments put in a mounted charge in successive lines of squadrons, about 300 yards between lines, through artillery and machine-gun fire and over the Beersheba entrenchments

---

243 Preston, *The Desert Mounted Corps*, p. 22.

244 AWM Chauvel Papers Folder 8: Chauvel to his wife, 3 June 1917; Ibid., Folder 7: Chauvel to his wife, 27 January and 7 April 1917; Allenby quoted by Hill, *Chauvel of the Light Horse*, p. 123.

245 As with all mounted charges, the broad outline of events at Beersheba is clear but the details are disputed. The evidence is summarised by Anglesey, *A History of the British Cavalry Volume 5*, pp. 148–62.

246 LHCMA Allenby Papers 3/7: Manuscript notes for the briefing, October 1917; emphasis in the original.

to capture the town. Hodgson wrote in a private letter that 'the light was going, so I decided to gallop it – and sent the leading brigade at it in four lines'; the brigade commander later claimed to have acted on his own initiative, although his report described the order to charge as coming from Hodgson 'and also direct instructions' from Chauvel, who believed that he had ordered the charge.[247] What does not seem disputed is that there was no wire defending the Turkish trenches, the Australian casualties were comparatively light, and that no other course of action could have captured the town by nightfall.[248]

The capture of Beersheba unhinged the Turkish line, forcing a retreat northward, and opening the way for a pursuit by the whole Desert Mounted Corps involving more mounted charges, including the one made by the Warwickshire Yeomanry and Worcestershire Hussars at Huj, initiated by Shea commanding 60th Division. 'We had to mourn the loss of many a good yeoman whom we could ill spare', wrote Lord Hampton, 'but they had at least upheld the traditions of British cavalry, they had accomplished the end-all of a cavalryman's training.'[249] Barrow described a charge at El Mughar that he ordered personally as 'a complete answer to the critics of the mounted arm'.[250] The pursuit was slowed by the need for water, and yeomanry regiments recorded between 56 and 72 hours of thirst, but sore backs and horse exhaustion were almost unknown. As one yeoman said, 'These men do not want telling how to make things easy for "the old oss" [horse], they have learned by experience and a genuine sympathy for horses.'[251] As the Turks retreated into the Judean hills the troopers dismounted to continue the pursuit until fought to a standstill or relieved by infantry, who continued the attack until Jerusalem fell on 9 December. No matter what their tactics, casualties from prolonged fighting would always be high for such weak formations called upon to undertake perilous tasks without heavy artillery support, and in its dismounted defensive battle in the hills in front of Jerusalem 20–28 November the Yeomanry Division suffered 499 casualties, or more than 41 per cent of its remaining front-line strength.[252] French wrote to Allenby that 'I regard the capture of Jerusalem as the finest feat of the war.'[253]

Both at the time and later, Chetwode's plan for Third Gaza as implemented by Allenby was criticised for being flawed at the operational level. The argument was one of logistics: that only the coastal road northwards through Gaza provided a combination of good going and an open supply route that would have allowed the Desert Mounted Corps to get behind the retreating Turks and cut them off, rather than just driving them northwards. But whatever the shortcomings of the decision to attack Beersheba, it does not automatically follow that an attack at Gaza, which had

---

247 IWM Hodgson Papers 66/145/1: Hodgson to his brother, 8 February 1918; Hill, *Chauvel of the Light Horse*, pp. 125–8; Hughes (ed.), *Allenby in Palestine*, pp. 72–4; AWM 4 154 War Diary 4th Australian Light Horse Brigade, Report on Operations (Attack on Beersheba).

248 Jones, 'Beersheba: The Light Horse Charge and the Making of Myths', pp. 26–37.

249 IWM Hampton Papers: Memoirs, p. 22.

250 Barrow, *The Fire of Life*, p. 169.

251 Quoted in Tylden, *Horses and Saddlery*, p. 42.

252 Barrow, *The Fire of Life*, p. 187.

253 LHCMA Allenby Papers 1/8: French to Allenby, 23 December 1917.

already failed twice, would have succeeded in cutting off the Turks. Allenby, whose worst-case plans had allowed for six months to capture Jerusalem, was astonished by the scale and speed of his own victory; but although he was aware that a chance had been missed, he would not let any blame fall on the mounted divisions.[254]

This involves the argument over Third Gaza in a controversial theory belonging to operational art, often known as the 'Collapse Theory', for which the terminology was only developed 50 years later in the 1967 Arab–Israeli War. This is the view that massive surprise and sudden defeat on the battlefield may combine to produce a much larger version at the operational level of the 'shock' that in 1917 was still associated with cavalry charges, causing enemy command chains to react like a body in paralysis, and enemy units to fragment into leaderless mobs. Some versions of this theory that have appeared since 1967 argue that some armies are particularly vulnerable to this kind of operational shock, either because of their military culture or their parent civilian culture, and this argument helped encourage later twentieth-century theories of manoeuvre war.[255] One of the earliest appearances of these ideas came just after the First World War in the writings of J.F.C. Fuller, who described the possibility of 'strategic paralysis' afflicting an army through a sudden violent attack.[256] But Fuller's contempt for the cavalry led him to neglect the importance of Third Gaza and the subsequent pursuit. In Palestine, as well as being tactically innovative, the cavalry were – if perhaps unintentionally – among the leading exponents of new operational art.

The capture of Jerusalem helped promote a change in Lloyd George's strategic thinking over winter 1917–1918, to a belief that victory for any side on the Western Front was impossible, and that with the collapse of Russia the best British strategy was to stake out imperial gains in Ottoman Turkey.[257] A British Imperial army had demonstrated that given sufficiently favourable circumstances, including a less than overwhelming numerical superiority, it could shatter the defending forces of a second-class power; and the new rifle-armed cavalry had shown its value and tactical flexibility in attacking and maintaining a pursuit both mounted and dismounted.

While this was happening, the British launched their last offensive of the year on the Western Front at the Battle of Cambrai, starting on 20 November with an attack by III Corps and IV Corps of Byng's Third Army, with VII Corps in support, and followed by a German counterattack that lasted until 7 December. At the time, Cambrai was hailed as a triumph for the Tank Corps, with the first mass use of 324 fighting tanks (476 in total) over open ground that had not been churned up by a long preliminary bombardment. More recently, the battle has come to be seen as the

---

254 Garsia, *A Key To Victory*, pp. 153–235; Hughes, *Allenby and British Strategy in the Middle East 1917–1919*, pp. 55–9; Hill, *Chauvel of the Light Horse*, p. 137.

255 For differing views on 1967 see Luttwak and Horowitz, *The Israeli Army*, pp. 282–92; van Creveld, *The Sword and the Olive*, pp. 180–99. See also Scales, *Certain Victory*, pp. 106–8.

256 Holden Reid, *J.F.C. Fuller: Military Thinker*, pp. 50–53; Trythal, *'Boney' Fuller*, pp. 60–62.

257 French, *The Strategy of the Lloyd George Coalition*, pp. 193–212; Millman, *Pessimism and British War Policy 1916–1918*, pp. 112–54; Hughes, *Allenby and British Military Strategy in the Middle East 1917–1919*, pp. 60–70.

first major British test of several interconnecting military technologies, including the operational art of combining artillery, airpower, tanks and infantry. Of these, by far the most important was the development during 1917 of the ability to assemble in secret enough artillery to fire a mass 'hurricane' bombardment against enemy strongpoints and artillery, using only maps and calculations without the need for prior registration firing. This when coupled with new infantry weapons and tactics of infiltration made it possible for the first time since Neuve Chapelle for an attacker to achieve surprise, the key element in restoring mobility to the Western Front. Since there was no preliminary bombardment, the enemy's barbed wire had to be flattened or hauled out of the way by the tanks, which became their most important function in the battle.

The British attack was made broadly north-easterly towards the high ground at Bourlon Wood 8,000 yards away, bounded to the west by the incomplete Canal du Nord and to the north-east by the Canal de l'Escault, beyond which was the town of Cambrai itself.[258] The plan called for three cavalry divisions to be used on the first day, 1st Cavalry Division with IV Corps to advance northwards along the British side of the Canal de l'Escault, while 2nd and 5th Cavalry Divisions with III Corps crossed the canal and then rode north of Cambrai in a circle from east to west to regain the British lines, a 'Raid' of about ten miles compared to the eight-mile advance planned for Arras. As always with Haig's plans, there was also an option to leave these two divisions north and east of Cambrai and to reinforce them with the two remaining cavalry divisions, if the German line collapsed completely.[259]

This employment of the cavalry faced three major problems. One was the British command structure, which was too elaborate for a battle that would be fast moving by Western Front standards. Both the Tank Corps and the Cavalry Corps were given some command functions in association with III Corps and IV Corps, but the lines of command were far from clear. Although 1st Cavalry Division was attached to IV Corps in the centre, formal orders had to go from IV Corps through the Cavalry Corps and back down again; while the Cavalry Corps with its two leading divisions was superimposed on III Corps area to the east. Too many critical decisions ended up being taken by informal gatherings on the battlefield of officers answerable to different headquarters.[260] Another problem was the Canal de l'Escault, since as Seely of the Canadian Cavalry Brigade complained, 'Horses can cross almost

---

258 The waterway to the east and north-east of the battlefield forming a principal British objective began as the St Quentin Canal, which was joined for part of its length by the River l'Escault flowing in parallel, then the Schelde stream, before becoming the l'Escault Canal; in accounts of the battle it is usually referred to throughout as the Canal de l'Escault.

259 The British official history of the Battle of Cambrai is, in a controversial series, well-written: see W. Miles (ed. Edmonds), *Official History France and Belgium 1917, Volume III*; for the origins of the plan for Cambrai see Hammond, 'The Theory and Practice of Tank Co-Operation with Other Arms on the Western Front in the First World War', pp. 178–225; Williams, *Byng of Vimy*, pp. 171–92 and Harris, *Men, Ideas and Tanks*, pp. 79–119; Griffith, *Battle Tactics of the Western Front*, pp. 164–9; see also three dated but useful accounts, Cooper, *The Ironclads of Cambrai*; Smithers, *Cambrai*; Woolcombe, *The First Tank Battle*.

260 Woolcombe, *The First Tank Battle*, pp. 127–31; Simpson, *Directing Operations*, pp. 116–18.

anything, they can even swim broad rivers, as they have often done in war. But the one thing that they cannot get over, unless they can bridge it, is a canal with perpendicular banks. They can get in but they can't get out.'[261] This meant that for the cavalry everything would depend on co-operation with the tanks, which would need to capture bridges across the canal. Back in August, in one of the proposals that led to Cambrai, Tank Corps headquarters had suggested 'a Tank attack on some other part of the line [than Ypres] in conjunction with Cavalry'; but once the battle was agreed upon they showed no interest at all in this co-operation.[262] Although 12 wire-clearing tanks were attached to 1st Cavalry Division, once more Tank Corps headquarters simply dusted off Fuller's suggestion that advancing tanks could be used as mobile blockhouses for the cavalry, while one tank commander summed up his understanding of his role as 'we go straight in and sit on the Germans until the Cavalry come'.[263]

True to his own doctrine, Haig recommended to Byng the formation of 'detachments of all arms, lightly equipped', to lead the initial attack, although there is no evidence that this advice was followed; the Cavalry Corps did issue its own notes for co-operation on 15 November, in which it characterised the tanks as slow-moving equivalents of armoured cars with machine-guns.[264] The first day of the attack went very well, an advance of 4,000–6,000 yards for relatively light British casualties. But it was comparatively easy for the Germans to destroy the bridges before the tanks could reach them, bringing up reserves to defend the canal. One tank commander later recalled approaching his target bridge:

> Then there was a heavy thump, a cloud of dirty white dust, and the bridge had gone. So I was beaten by only a few minutes and only a few yards.... Then a most ludicrous thing happened, there was a great deal of clattering, galloping and shouting and a lot of our mediaeval horse soldiers came charging down the street; I yelled to them that the bridge was gone but they took no notice of me and went right up to it, one m[achine-]g[un] would have wiped out the lot, and then they turned about and with a very pious air trotted back the way they had come.[265]

In his evident contempt for the cavalry, this officer clearly did not consider that he had failed in his principal mission. The troopers were not the effete British stereotype of his imagination but Canadians of the Fort Garry Horse, who found another small bridge undefended. With about half an hour of daylight remaining, one squadron crossed the canal and raided successfully through the German rear positions until, having lost half their numbers, they stampeded their horses and re-crossed the canal.

---

261 Seely, *Adventure*, pp. 273–4.

262 Quoted by Hammond, 'The Theory and Practice of Tank Co-Operation with Other Arms on the Western Front in the First World War', p. 179.

263 Miles (ed. Edmonds), *Official History France and Belgium 1917, Volume III*, p. 29; Hammond, 'The Theory and Practice of Tank Co-Operation with Other Arms on the Western Front in the First World War', pp. 197–9.

264 NLS Haig Papers 119: Haig to Byng, 3 November 1917; Anglesey, *A History of the British Cavalry Volume 8*, pp. 106–7.

265 Major Philip Hamond, F Battalion Tank Corps, quoted in Woolcombe, *The First Tank Battle*, pp. 84–5.

But blocked all along the canal, the cavalry failed to find other bridges that were undefended and crossable.[266] In the centre, IV Corps headquarters was convinced that a genuine 'Gap' did exist and that 1st Cavalry Division could have passed through if only it had shown enough enterprise; a squadron of the 4th Dragoon Guards did find its way forward and charged in the pouring rain through the German rear, returning with 50 prisoners for the loss of 15 men and 30 horses, but once again it was only one squadron that made it into action, out of the entire division.[267] Haig ordered the attack to continue next day, northwards towards the high ground at Bourlon Wood rather than trying to cross the defended canal; but both surprise and momentum had been lost, and on 27 November Byng closed the battle down. The cavalry continued to fight valiantly, both in the attack and in defence against the German counterattack when it came, until the battle ended.

Within a month of the battle, all three infantry Corps commanders involved at Cambrai had been dismissed.[268] But in a reflection of cavalry spirit, the cavalry did not blame others for giving them an almost impossible objective and then letting them down so badly; they blamed themselves for failing to carry out their intended role in the wider plan; and for having a chance but failing to grasp it. The British could not know, at the time, that they were attempting what was to become in the course of the century one of the most notoriously difficult manoeuvres in warfare: trying to move an exploitation force as large as a division or larger rapidly through a slower moving force, against enemy opposition in the middle of a battle. The British Army would suffer similar traffic jams trying to get armoured divisions forward in battles throughout the Second World War.[269] Haig was sent a number of confidential reports, all of which (in addition to criticising IV Corps heavily) told the same story of failure of cavalry spirit. One complained that:

> When the infantry gained their first objective with hardly a casualty the dreamed-of 'Gap' was there… Why did the cavalry fail? For fail they did to justify their traditions. Reasons –
> 1. Incredulity on the part of many senior officers…
> 2. Lack of enthusiasm… due to the stagnation which now obtains in the cavalry; due to slow promotions – boredom – and the waning of the fire which must always burn in good cavalry…
> 3. Lack of 'Drive'….
> It was the one chance the Cavalry has had in this war from the start, to date, of carrying out its legitimate offensive role, and it failed from lack of offensive spirit, amongst the leaders, not amongst as a rule the regimental officers… it failed because the offensive has entirely given way to the defensive spirit and because failure is not visited with the drastic penalty it deserves.[270]

---

266 Williams, *Byng of Vimy*, pp. 202–3.
267 Ibid., pp. 187–90; Woolcombe, *The First Tank Battle*, pp. 126–39.
268 Williams, *Byng of Vimy*, p. 205; Simpson, *Directing Operations*, p. 230.
269 Cases which have been well studied include Operation Goodwood in Normandy, July 1944 and Operation Lightfoot at El Alamein, October 1942; see e.g. d'Este, *Decision in Normandy*, pp. 352–99; Barr, *The Pendulum of War*, pp. 307–82.
270 NLS Haig Papers 119: Note 111 'Private: 1st Cavalry Division – Cavalry Operations November 20th–26th 1917'.

MacAndrew, now GOC 5th Cavalry Division which included Seely's Canadians, expressed his opinion of 1st Cavalry Division's problems in no uncertain terms:

> Our failure here that day, to get any further than the above line, appeared, to an observer, to be due to the following causes:
> 1. Complete lack of liaison between the leading [Cavalry] Brigade and Infantry
> 2.   "   "   "   "   "   "   "   " and Tanks
> 3.   "   "   " vigour and determination on the part of [Cavalry] Brigade commanders
> 4.   "   "   "   "   "   "   "   "   "   " C[ommanding] O[fficer]s [of cavalry regiments][271]

Haig minuted 'There is much truth in what Harry MacAndrew has written above.'[272] Home at Cavalry Corps headquarters recorded his view that 'There were two points that affected us: the first was that the Boche had two Divisions in Reserve behind the line [of the canal] where we hoped he had none; secondly the want of confidence in some of the Infantry in the powers of the Tank', blaming IV Corps in particular, and ending 'It had been a good day's work: a little more and I think that the Cavalry would have got through.'[273] Vaughan, who commanded 3rd Cavalry Division at Cambrai, believed that 'bad staff work is responsible', and that 'The Cavalry had, in fact, been concentrated in too large formations and located too far back to deploy effectively and come into action on a short winter's day.'[274] The consistent view was that doctrine for getting the cavalry into action in brigades and divisions rather than squadrons was now correct, and that any failures at Cambrai were due to departures from it.

At the end of December Byng showed Home his own report for Haig, in which he expressed frustration that the cavalry's chance for greater success had been missed. Home noted that a complete overhaul of British strategy was clearly coming, and that 'it is right that they should do so and on it hangs the future of the cavalry'.[275] The consequences of the fall of Jerusalem, the failure at Cambrai, and the change in British grand strategy away from the Western Front soon became apparent. At a meeting of the War Cabinet Committee on Manpower in December, Lloyd George argued from the chair that cavalry on the Western Front were useless, and (taking up an idea of Churchill's) that its personnel should be transferred to aircraft, tanks and armoured cars, a suggestion with which Lloyd George stated that Robertson was 'in substantial agreement'.[276] On 7 January Haig defended his cavalry before the War Cabinet in terms which he would never have used before 1914:

---

271 Ibid., Note 115 Comment on 'Personal Narrative of an officer attached to 2nd Cavalry Brigade 20th November 1917'.
272 Ibid., marginal note by Haig.
273 Home, *The Diary of a World War I Cavalry Officer*, p. 156.
274 Vaughan, *Cavalry and Sporting Memories*, p. 190.
275 Ibid., p. 160.
276 TNA CAB 23/13 War Cabinet Minutes Meeting 7 January 1918, p. 187; CAB 27/14 Manpower (1917), pp. 3–4 of 4th Meeting, p. 14 of report; CAB 1/25/26 Manpower (1917) Memorandum by Churchill, p. 4.

Sir Douglas Haig stated that he considered the value and importance of cavalry to be very great not only in offensive but in defensive operations. This was due to their superior mobility and the ease with which cavalry could be moved from one sector to another and then used dismounted. He pointed out that the British Cavalry resembled highly trained mobile infantry rather than the old cavalry arm.

The Prime Minister pointed out that the cavalry question vitally affected shipping, and that, in view of the shortage of shipping, he hoped that every effort would be made to economise the requirements of the Army in the matter of horses and their maintenance. It would be most helpful if some of the ships now utilised for the transport of horses and hay could be used for the purpose of bringing over American troops.

Lord Curzon added that it would appear that the character of warfare during the ensuing few months would present few opportunities for the use of cavalry.

Sir Douglas Haig stated that once the cavalry had been disbanded it would be difficult to build up again so highly trained and technical an arm, and it would be many months before the cavalry, once dissipated, could be re-created.[277]

The logical way to reduce the BEF's cavalry would have been to disband one or more of the divisions outright, but the institutional and regimental politics both of the cavalry and of the Indian Army made this problematic. Instead, Haig was told on 13 January of the War Cabinet decision to send the Indian cavalry regiments to Palestine, in exchange for yeomanry from Palestine to be converted to machine-gunners, a decision which began an almost ridiculously lengthy and elaborate process. At the end of March 1918, 5th Cavalry Division (intact except for its British cavalry regiments) and the Indian cavalry regiments from 4th Cavalry Division embarked for Palestine, where the Yeomanry Division was broken up and its troops used to reform 4th and 5th Cavalry Divisions. The nine yeomanry regiments left over from this process, including the independent brigades, were converted into machine-gun battalions and sent to France, not to arrive until May. Haig accepted the reasoning underlying these moves, writing in February that 'owing to the lack of tonnage we are doing everything possible to reduce the number of horses with the Army'.[278] But although Robertson did not oppose these moves, he was fully aware that in reality they represented no saving in shipping, and in the event they took place just as the German Kaiserschlacht offensive struck.[279] Their farcical nature was emphasised when in June the Imperial War Cabinet, faced with the problems of keeping the EEF supplied, only narrowly decided against sending the Australian Mounted Division to France.[280]

Of the regiments in France released from 4th and 5th Cavalry Divisions, the Canadian Cavalry Brigade joined 3rd Cavalry Division, while the four British line cavalry regiments, three Household regiments (which with their bigger horses presented a persistent problem) and two Corps cavalry regiments that had escaped disbanding were earmarked for conversion to cyclists or machine-gunners.[281] The

---

277 CAB 23/13 War Cabinet Minutes Meeting 7 January 1918, p. 187.
278 NLS Haig Papers 123: Diary entry, 12 February 1918.
279 Robertson, *From Private to Field Marshal*, p. 324.
280 TNA CAB 23/44 Imperial War Cabinet Meetings 21 June–16 August 1918, pp. 2–6.
281 The original plan was to reduce the Household brigade to a composite regiment once more; see NLS Haig Papers 123: Diary entry, 15 January 1918.

result was 20 regiments of cavalry fewer with the BEF for two more with the EEF, and neither command could have been said to benefit. The reaction of the yeomanry associations (led by the Earl of Warwick, with Sidney Peel among those involved) to converting their last remaining regiments on the Western Front to cyclists was to organise a deputation to the War Office; however their object was not to prevent their regiments being dismounted, which they accepted as inevitable, but to keep the yeomanry titles and regimental structure as far as possible.[282] The Household also were prepared to give up their horses to keep their regimental identities.

The Household and the yeomanry had just surrendered their horses, and the Indian cavalry had begun to sail, when the Germans attacked on 21 March. In the emergency most of the yeomanry regiments regained their horses, and since Haig had given Gough's Fifth Army his three remaining cavalry divisions as a reserve, these fought a skilful mobile defence against the Germans, both mounted and dismounted, including the Canadian charge at Moreuil Wood. One high point of this was a determined dismounted action by 1st Cavalry Division (constituted as a 'Dismounted Division 24–26 March) alongside Monash's 3rd Australian Division, which produced favourable comments from both sides.[283] The German doctrine of attack by hurricane bombardment and infiltration was similar to that of the British, but conducted almost without tanks and also without cavalry. Haig, Gough and Home all felt that this lack of cavalry to exploit the attack was an error, and there were cases in which British troops fell back in response to false reports of German cavalry attacking; 'It was a crowning mercy that they had no cavalry', wrote one veteran British infantry officer later, 'Cavalry was the one factor that would have smashed the morale of the defence in a twinkling.'[284] After the crisis was over, the three Household regiments were converted into two motorised machine-gun battalions in lorries, still as part of the Cavalry Corps; but the yeomanry regiments were disbanded to make up the numbers of the severely depleted cavalry, with the single exception of the Oxfordshire Hussars which remained part of 2nd Cavalry Division.

Even before the German offensive, Haig had begun work to revitalise the cavalry. On 15 January, Kavanagh asked Haig that MacAndrew should replace R.L. Mullens as GOC 1st Cavalry Division rather than go to Palestine as GOC 5th Cavalry Division; Haig and Kavanagh also discussed replacing W.H. Greenly as GOC 2nd Cavalry Division with Home, and replacing Vaughan as GOC 3rd Cavalry Division; in the event only the last of these changes was carried out, as the first two divisional commanders did well enough against the German offensive to keep their posts.[285] Next day the Cavalry Corps held a conference at which Kavanagh 'spoke

---

282 IWM Home Papers 2: Folder 3, 'Report of Conference and Deputation'.

283 Monash, *The Australian Victories in France in 1918*, pp. 14–15.

284 Captain Sidney Rogerson, 2nd West Yorkshires, quoted in Terraine, *To Win a War*, p. 72; see also Boraston (ed.), *Sir Douglas Haig's Despatches*, p. 328; Gough, *The Fifth Army*, pp. 322–3; Home, *The Diary of a World War I Cavalry Officer*, p. 163.

285 NLS Haig Papers 123: Diary entry, 15 January 1918; Vaughan, *Cavalry and Sporting Memories*, pp. 191–2.

his mind very freely' on the need for improvements.[286] Haig consulted Gough for his opinion on the state of the cavalry after Cambrai, and on 18 March Gough replied scathingly that 'the cavalry divisions are not really efficient and don't know what modern war, with all its casualties, really requires to achieve success'.[287] Following Gough's recommendations, next day Haig told Kavanagh that he was being sent home in April in order to unblock promotions within the cavalry, adding that the War Office had suggested the outright abolition of the Cavalry Corps.[288] In the event it was Gough who was dismissed from Fifth Army during the German offensive, and Kavanagh who kept his post.[289] Despite the great events in which he was involved, Haig continued to keep an eye on the cavalry and its tactics, telling Kavanagh in August that 'The training of the "troop" under its "leader" is of first importance' for his next battle.[290]

The great test on the Western Front of cavalry doctrine, and the extent that cavalry could be integrated into the new technological all-arms warfare, came at the Battle of Amiens on 8 August.[291] Home at Cavalry Corps headquarters was at least as concerned about the cavalry's institutional survival as its success:

> The Cavalry are about to go to war again, this time under the 4th Army. It is once more a Scheme with a [limited ?] objective or GAPS Scheme. I never like them, it will either be a walkover or the very devil. If the Boche does not reinforce this front, all will be well. Secrecy is going to be the guiding factor. I fancy we are being pushed into it as another determined attack is being made by our friends at home on the Cavalry. The proposal is to abolish the Corps, turn one division into machine guns, one Division into Corps Cavalry and keep one Division mounted. This savours of Henry Wilson as he hates the Cavalry. People really go mad sometimes. If we make peace with the Boche on the Hindenburg line, then we don't want any Cavalry; but if we are going to beat him, we shall need every bus, car, horse, mule and donkey we can raise.[292]

The German defenders opposite Rawlinson's Fourth Army were in a weakened state. In accordance with their own doctrines for this period of the war they had adopted a defence in depth, stretching back from a weakly held front line to battle positions further in the rear; but these positions were significantly weaker than those that the British had faced at Ypres. Also, and in contrast to the Somme two years earlier, Haig was in a position to insist on his own way regarding the cavalry, and Rawlinson seems to have at least grudgingly accepted that their time might have come. Only

---

286 Home, *The Diary of a World War I Cavalry Officer*, p. 161.
287 NLS Haig Papers 124: Diary entry, 18 March 1918.
288 This suggestion was made by letter on 21 February 1918; see NLS Haig Papers 130: Note 232 Extract from War Office Letter.
289 Ibid., Diary entry, 19 March 1918; a cryptic and compressed reference to Gough's attempt to remove Kavanagh is in Home, *The Diary of a World War I Cavalry Officer*, p. 162.
290 NLS Haig Papers 130: Diary entry 1 August 1918.
291 Most accounts of Amiens still neglect or disparage the cavalry's role; for a clear account of the cavalry's part in the battle see Anglesey, *A History of the British Cavalry Volume 8*, pp. 230–48.
292 Home, *The Diary of a World War I Cavalry Officer*, p. 178.

three days before the battle, Haig was still demanding that Rawlinson should plan to 'advance as rapidly as possible' and give the cavalry a greater role, 'I said that the cavalry must keep in touch with the battle and *be prepared to pass through anywhere between the R[iver] Somme and the Roye-Amiens Road.*'[293] Rawlinson employed the cavalry to follow up the first infantry attacks and to gallop forward to hold positions while the reserve infantry caught up, extending the day's advance from about 5,000 to 10,000 yards, clean through the depth of the German defences into open country. On the way the cavalry delivered several successful charges of regimental size, overrunning both guns and machine-guns. The Cavalry Corps was withdrawn into reserve on 12 August, with losses of about 1,000 men and 1,800 horses for the battle, having taken at least 1,300 prisoners. Rawlinson wrote in his diary on 8 August that the cavalry had 'done splendid work'; while Haig noted with pride the achievement of his old regiment the 17th Lancers, who had reached their objective 'four hours before the infantry came up. The latter were able to advance 5,000 yards without a shot being fired at them in consequence'.[294] Home's laconic comment was 'The result of the day's operations was that all our objectives were gained and that the absolute necessity for good and well trained cavalry was proved.'[295]

Once again, a major problem for the cavalry was in getting any co-operation from the Tank Corps, particularly in the first use of the Medium A Whippet tanks, armed with machine-guns and perfect for eliminating enemy machine-gun nests, but with a cross-country speed about half that of cavalry horses. In this case also, the British did not know that they were dealing for the first time with a problem in tactical doctrine that would endure throughout the twentieth century: how to fight and co-ordinate an all-arms battle that was also mobile. That the cavalry and Whippets moved at different speeds, and had different levels of protection, was a problem to be solved by proper tactics, not an insuperable objection to their being used together.[296] The Cavalry Corps after-action report suggested that a troop of Whippets should be attached permanently to each cavalry squadron as a less vulnerable replacement for machine-guns carried on pack horses, concluding that 'The use of Whippet tanks with the cavalry is in its infancy, and if successful co-operation is to be achieved, both must train and practise together'; the Tank Corps report did not even mention the cavalry's existence.[297]

Already in July, Fuller (who was serving back at home) had advocated the outright abolition of the BEF's cavalry.[298] When Wilson visited the front as CIGS on 11 August, Kavanagh tackled him directly on the future of the Cavalry Corps, and despite the success of Amiens, Wilson appears to have confirmed that he planned to

---

293 NLS Haig Papers 130: Diary entry, 5 August 1918, emphasis in the original.

294 CAC Rawlinson Papers RAWL 1/11: Diary entry, 8 August 1918; NLS Haig Papers 130: Diary entry, 13 August 1918.

295 Home, *The Diary of a World War I Cavalry Officer*, p. 179.

296 Surprisingly, several historians have accepted unquestioningly the Tank Corps' interpretation of these events; see e.g. Johnson, *Breakthrough!* p. 263; Terraine, *To Win a War*, p. 111; Prior and Wilson, *Command on the Western Front*, p. 307.

297 IWM Rawlinson Fourth Army Papers Volume 65: Cavalry Corps Narratives August–October 1918; Tank Corps Narratives August–October 1918.

298 Johnson, *Breakthrough!*, pp. 136–7.

break the Corps up.[299] Home's comments show how little had really changed about the Army since the nineteenth century:

> The Cavalry had the chance of doing a job and carried it out splendidly. In the papers a great deal of credit is given to the tanks, especially the Whippets, they being the latest toy. We shall have to get a tame correspondent and have the South African business once more: nothing but advertisement... If they split up the Divisions, they will ruin the spirit which now exists; each Division will go its own way. The Corps Commander has built this spirit up in the last two years and the credit is his and his alone.[300]

On the one side was the Cavalry Corps, an arm that was institutionally powerful but in decline, looking for ways to remain part of the battle; on the other was the Tank Corps, a new arm still fighting for its institutional independence. The result was an emerging doctrinal conflict that would occupy much of the British Army's time for the next two decades.

Amiens proved that, by using the right tactical doctrine and staffwork, horsed cavalry could be successfully integrated into the industrialised all-arms battles of the early twentieth century. The more difficult question was whether this should be done at all. After the war, Monash summarised (with some wariness) the case against keeping the cavalry on the Western Front:

> The utility of cavalry in modern war, at any rate in a European theatre, has been the subject of endless controversy. It is one into which I do not propose to enter. There is no doubt that, given suitable ground and an absence of wire entanglements, cavalry can move rapidly and undertake important turning or enveloping movements. Yet it has been argued that the rarity of such suitable conditions negatives [sic] any justification for superimposing so unwieldy a burden as a large body of cavalry – on the bare chance that it might be useful – upon already overpopulated areas, billets, watering places and roads.[301]

The argument that, however many small successes the cavalry won, these could have always been won more cheaply without them, was made repeatedly and more emphatically in the *Official History* by Edmonds (since all cavalry officers have been accused of thinking alike, it is fair to mention that Monash and Edmonds were both trained engineers).[302] The counter-argument was set out just as clearly by Haig in his final dispatch in April 1919, in a paragraph that came just before his arguments in favour of tanks and aircraft:

> From time to time as the war of position dragged on and the enemy's trench system remained unbroken, while questions of man power and the shortage of shipping became acute, the wisdom or necessity of maintaining any large force of mounted men was freely

---

299 Home, *The Diary of a World War I Cavalry Officer*, p. 180; there is no mention of this discussion in the Wilson Papers.
300 Ibid., p. 180.
301 Monash, *The Australian Victories in France in 1918*, p. 54.
302 Badsey, 'Cavalry and the Development of Breakthrough Doctrine', pp. 140–41. Edmonds was commissioned into the Royal Engineers; Monash was a qualified and experienced civilian engineer first commissioned into the Garrison Artillery of the militia in Australia, later serving as an infantry officer.

discussed. In the light of the full experience of the war the decision to preserve the Cavalry Corps has been completely justified. It has been proved that cavalry, whether used for shock effect under suitable conditions or as mobile infantry, still have an indispensable part to play in modern war... throughout the whole period of trench fighting they constituted an important mobile reserve.... [In 1918] our cavalry, pressing hard on the enemy's heels, hastened his retreat and threw him into worse confusion. At such a time the moral effect of cavalry is overwhelming and is in itself a sufficient reason for the retention of that arm.[303]

These arguments were not about tactics, but about operational art and the closely related art of logistics. Above them loomed the still larger debates about grand strategy and national warfighting capabilities, in which any discussion of the cavalry was hopelessly compromised by pre-war perspectives and prejudices about its nature and capabilities.

On 19 August 1918, Haig noted that for an attack by Third Army 'Byng had only arranged to use about a brigade of cavalry. I told him that the Cavalry Corps is now 100 p[er] c[ent] better than it was at Cambrai. *He must use the cavalry to the fullest extent possible.*'[304] Although Byng declined to change his planned attack to a more ambitious one, Haig impressed upon him 'to detail a cavalry regiment to each Corps taking part in the attack, because the enemy's "line of resistance" may have been withdrawn some distance from our front trenches, and it will be necessary to push forward *Advance Guards of all arms to reconnoitre*'.[305] Haig's response to the German defence in depth was to use the dash and mobility of the cavalry to push on through. 'Reinforce where we are winning', he ordered one Corps commander (echoing Allenby before Third Gaza) 'Not where we are held up!'[306]

A large part of Haig's problem was that for these last battles the Cavalry Corps was very weak, and that its regiments had to double as Corps cavalry as well as perform their normal role with the cavalry divisions. On 1 March 1918, the strength of the British cavalry arm in all combat theatres was 15,755 in total, or 1.65 per cent of all fighting troops. By 1 July the absolute numbers had declined slightly to 15,262. For illustration, this compares with a strength on 1 March 1918 for the Royal Flying Corps of 31,092 or 3.24 per cent of all combat troops, and for the Tank Corps of 10,072 or 1.05 per cent.[307] The Cavalry Corps of late 1918 may have been weaker on certain days than the single Cavalry Division of 1914. But like the rest of the BEF, the Cavalry Corps had also come to rely heavily on firepower. From late August onwards it included a cyclist battalion, the two Household battalions of motorised machine-gunners, an attached infantry brigade in buses, and a mixed artillery brigade including four 18-pounders and two lorry-towed 4.5-inch howitzers.[308] For the last few weeks of fighting, Haig tried to keep a balance between using the cavalry

---

303 Boraston (ed.), *Sir Douglas Haig's Despatches*, pp. 327–8.
304 NLS Haig Papers 130: Diary entry, 19 August 1918, emphasis in the original.
305 Ibid., emphasis in the original.
306 Ibid., 130: Diary entry, 21 August 1918.
307 *Statistics of the Military Effort of the British Empire During the Great War 1914–1920*, p. 65.
308 NLS Haig Papers 130: Diary entry 28 August 1918.

in detached divisions and brigades to assist in the repeated short breakthroughs by which the British Army maintained its advance, and trying to preserve the Cavalry Corps in case the Germans did collapse and the advance became a rout. On 1 September he told Byng:

> I therefore wished the Cavalry Corps to be kept as strong as possible, and at the same time merely to detach the minimum number of squadrons necessary for divisional and Corps requirements. By this procedure I hope to have an efficient Cavalry Corps ready to act vigorously when the decisive moment comes, and reap the fruits of victory.[309]

On the same day Haig wrote formally to Wilson:

> Our shortage of cavalry is daily becoming noticeable, and there is no doubt that your predecessor committed a serious error in sending off to Palestine two cavalry divisions last February. I hear that they are doing little or nothing there. I am going to ask officially for an Australian Mounted Brigade for the Australian Corps. A few more mounted men would save many of the railways, bridges, etc., etc.[310]

On 17 September Haig took a day away from his headquarters to watch a major training exercise for the Cavalry Corps in locating bridges across waterways in the face of enemy rearguards of machine-guns and infantry.[311]

The total German collapse never came, but the cavalry in dispersed formations continued to take part in the advance up to the Armistice. At the end of September an infantry brigade commander attacking down the Menin Road with the 9th (Scottish) Division recorded that:

> This day, for the first (and last) time, scattered groups of cavalry followed the leading battalions. Although conditions here are all against mounted troops, I think that small, resolute bodies, able quickly to charge or disperse, presenting too, a fleeting, difficult mark, do not run undue risks and may get occasional chances of rounding up parties of the enemy, or at any rate hurrying up his retirement with the gleam of their lances.[312]

The Cavalry Corps got its last chance on 8 October, with 3rd Cavalry Division reaching as far as Le Cateau in a successful combined action by all three of its brigades, before the Corps was pulled into reserve two days later.[313] Even at this late date, Haig was far from being the only one who believed in cavalry spirit. Lieutenant Colonel George Franks commanding the 19th Hussars briefed his regimental sergeants for the advance on 8 October with the words, 'I am the man to drop the flag, and off we go to *Death or Glory*', causing one of those listening to write 'if successful it will be a bigger thing than the Palestine affair!' Sadly, Franks was killed attempting a regimental charge against field artillery and machine-guns.[314]

---

309 Ibid., 131: Diary entry, 1 September 1918.
310 Ibid., 131: Haig to Wilson, 1 September 1918.
311 Ibid., 131: Diary entry, 17 September 1918.
312 Terraine (ed.), *General Jack's Diary*, pp. 275–6.
313 Terraine, *To Win a War*, pp. 191–3.
314 Light Dragoons Museum Brunton Papers: Diary of Sergeant D. Brunton, 19th Hussars, 8 November 1918; Holmes, *Tommy*, pp. 447–8.

'All Corps commanders are asking for more cavalry', Haig wrote on 9 November; and even Edmonds in the *Official History* conceded that 'the absence of mounted troops was severely felt' at the war's end.[315] The matter continued to rankle with Haig even after the war. In 1922 two of his former staff officers published *Sir Douglas Haig's Command*, his authorised account in all but name. A chapter of this book, sarcastically entitled 'Cavalry Studies' after Haig's pre-war publication, firmly blamed the War Cabinet decisions of January 1918 for the problems faced by the British Army in exploiting success on the Western Front from September 1918 onwards. In Haig's opinion, the loss or removal of the two Indian cavalry divisions and 20 yeomanry regiments of Corps cavalry had prevented his doctrine of exploitation from being implemented as he had intended, resulting in unnecessary British casualties and a less decisive victory.[316]

The Hundred Days campaign on the Western Front from Amiens to the Armistice was matched almost exactly by the Battle of Megiddo in Palestine, begun by the EEF on 19 September north of Jerusalem and resulting in the complete disintegration of the opposing Turkish forces, a pursuit to first Damascus and then Aleppo by 25 October, and an armistice six days later. Although in this campaign the cavalry got the recognition that they never received on the Western Front, the key to the EEF's crushing victory was once more surprise and the co-ordination of all arms including airpower, plus a small overall numerical superiority. Very early on the first day, XXI Corps attacked the Turkish line at its western or coastal edge, bending it back to release 4th and 5th Cavalry Divisions and the Australian Mounted Division deep into the enemy rear areas.[317] In Palestine, the British had no agreed doctrinal and staff procedures for passing a cavalry division rapidly through a Corps attack, and Barrow commanding the 4th Cavalry Division had to come to a local agreement with Major General Sir Vere Fane commanding 7th Meerut Division (an Indian Army officer who had served earlier in his career in the 1st Punjab Cavalry), to disregard what they both saw as an unworkable Corps plan.[318]

As representative of several mounted charges made by his 4th Cavalry Division, Barrow described the charge by the 2nd Lancers near Afuleh on 20 September with machine-gun support:

> At 5.30 a.m., fire was suddenly opened… from a position about two miles from where the road debouches from Leffun onto the plain. Captain Davidson, commander of the advance guard, was prompt to act. Without a moment's hesitation he ordered a mounted attack. The enemy kept up a heavy rifle and m[achine-]g[un] fire until the Lancers were

---

315 NLS Haig Papers 133: Diary, entry 9 November 1918; Edmonds (ed.), *Official History France and Belgium 1918, Volume V*, p. 535.

316 Dewar and Boraston, *Sir Douglas Haig's Command*, Volume II, pp. 44–8.

317 There are many accounts of the Battle of Megiddo, also known as the Armageddon campaign, and surprisingly few controversies. See Preston, *The Desert Mounted Corps*, pp. 202–94; Kearsey, *A Summary of the Strategy and Tactics of the Egypt and Palestine Campaigns*; Wavell, *Allenby*, pp. 272–89; and for modern perspectives Woodward, *Hell in the Holy Land*, pp.190–206; Hughes, *Allenby and British Strategy in the Middle East 1917–1919*, pp. 97–100.

318 Barrow, *The Fire of Life*, pp. 192–5.

among them, when, as must inevitably happen when distance no longer intervenes, fire weapons must surrender to cold steel. As already had occurred and was to occur again in this theatre of the Great War, the *arme blanche* showed that, given the proper conditions, it was still effective as in the days of Joshua. The upshot of this combat was 46 Germans and Turks killed and wounded (mostly by the lance) and 470, with three m[achine-]g[un]s captured, together with consequences greatly transcending the merely local results. The road to Beisan was now practically clear. Our losses were one man wounded and twelve horses killed.

The depot regiment, the force encountered by the advance guard, had not been previously engaged and its *morale* had not suffered from defeat or retreat. What was it that enabled this small, tired, mounted force to override a fresh infantry battalion at so small cost to itself? It was the result of a happy combination of the principles of surprise, fire, movement and co-operation.[319]

The 4th Cavalry Division continued its advance for 70 miles over 34 hours for the loss of 26 horses. The ability of the troopers to keep going in this way was also a tribute to their horsemastership, especially compared to the accompanying French colonial cavalry regiment, which arrived at Damascus crippled with sore-backed horses.[320]

Also on 20 September, Harry Chauvel as GOC Desert Mounted Corps wrote to his wife in a letter which, however unintentionally, provided an elegant commentary on the cavalry doctrinal debate:

I have had a glorious time. We have done a regular Jeb Stuart ride. I wrote to you two days ago from just north of Jaffa, when I had my whole Corps, except Chaytor [ANZAC Mounted Division], hidden in the orange groves, and I am writing now from a hill close to Leffun (Megiddo) overlooking the plain of Armageddon which is strewn with Turkish dead 'harpooned' by my Indian cavalry this morning, and from my tent door I can see Nazareth.... We have been fighting what I can only hope will be the last 'Battle of Armageddon' all day. MacAndrew [5th Cavalry Division], after a wild ride during which he had to shed all his wheels, including his guns, took Nazareth with nearly two thousand prisoners early this morning. Barrow [4th Cavalry Division] took El Afule with nearly 1,500 prisoners and I have just heard that one of H[odgson]'s, Australian Mounted Division] brigades, [L. C.] Wilson's [3rd Australian Light Horse Brigade]has taken Jenin with another thousand prisoners, having got into them with the sword, for, tell it not in Gath or to Curly Hutton, I have armed all of H[odgson]'s col[umn] with that weapon at their own request! All this miles behind the enemy's front line, through which B[ulfin's XXI Corps] made a gap for us on the coast and which he and P[hilip] C[hetwode's XX Corps] are now attacking. It is the first time in this war that the G in Gap Scheme has really come off and I am feeling very pleased with myself.[321]

---

319 Ibid., p. 201.
320 Preston, *The Desert Mounted Corps*, pp. 318–19; the French contingent consisted of two squadrons of 1st Spahis and two squadrons of 4th Chasseurs d'Afrique.
321 AWM Chauvel Papers Folder 10: Chauvel to his wife 20 September 1918. 'Tell it not in Gath', is from the King James Version of the Bible, Second Samuel Chapter 1 Verse 20, and at that time had proverbial status meaning jokingly 'don't repeat this but....'. For the adoption of swords by the Light Horse see also Bou, 'The Evolution and Development of the Australian Light Horse 1860–1945', pp. 185–220.

In terms of cavalry doctrine the most significant feature of EEF operation in 1918 was that, following Beersheba and with Hodgson's prompting, the Australian Mounted Division successfully petitioned in August to be given swords and trained for the close-order charge, which was used repeatedly by troopers of all three divisions in the advance. The Australians were particularly impressed by the Indian lancers 'harpooning' Turkish infantry. The ANZAC Mounted Division, which performed an important auxiliary role, did not request swords and remained mounted riflemen, a split in Australian mounted doctrine that in the context of the battle did not matter at all.

A case may certainly be made that the weakness and poor morale of the Turkish forces contributed both to the overall success of the Megiddo campaign, and to the success of mounted charges which would have probably failed against more determined opponents. One uphill charge on 23 September by the Indian 29th Lancers, again with machine-gun support, overran and captured 800 Turks with 25 machine-guns.[322] The German General Otto Liman von Sanders who commanded the Turkish forces opposite Allenby laid great stress on his troops' weakness, and on this occasion British intelligence had a clear picture of just how feeble their opponents were.[323] Although these criticisms qualify some claims about the tactical effectiveness of the mounted charge, as for Third Gaza and for Amiens they also serve to highlight the effectiveness of mounted – or mobile – shock troops used in this manner, and in a way that would continue to occur throughout the twentieth century.

---

[322] Preston, *The Desert Mounted Corps*, p. 230.

[323] Liman von Sanders, *Five Years in Turkey*, pp. 268–305; Sheffy, *British Military Intelligence in the Palestine Campaign 1914–1918*, pp. 316–19.

Conclusion

'THE OUTSTANDING LESSONS OF THE GREAT WAR', wrote Lieutenant Colonel H.V.S. Charrington (late 12th Lancers) in 1927, writing in capitals for emphasis as Harry Havelock had done exactly 60 years before, 'ARE THE VALUE OF MOUNTED TROOPS ACTING IN SMALL DETACHMENTS IN CLOSE CO-OPERATION WITH OTHER ARMS AND THEIR LIMITATIONS WHEN ACTING INDEPENDENTLY IN LARGE FORMATIONS.' Those limitations were determined largely by whether or not the cavalry was facing a first-class industrialised European enemy.[1] For several decades, the British, along with other armies, had looked for ways to bridge the gap created in the traditional spectrum of land forces by the new vulnerability of horses to firepower. While the changes in firepower and the size of armies between 1880 and 1918 were radical and revolutionary, adjustments to the tactics, training and equipment of horsed soldiers could only ever be incremental. An infantry weapon could evolve from a musket into a machine-gun, but ultimately a horse was a horse and a sword was a sword. The eventual solution to the problem was the development of armoured vehicles with cross-country speed and capabilities at least as great as that of horsed soldiers, and this did not happen until some years after the First World War.[2] In the interval, the British doctrinal solution based on horsed cavalry was not a bad one.

Attractive as it may have appeared both to some theorists and to some generals between 1880 and 1918, the idea of restricting the cavalry regiments to the mounted charge alone, and creating an institutionally separate arm for mounted firepower, was virtually doomed to fail. It was in direct opposition to two of the strongest and most consistent British government policies for the Army throughout this period. One of these was the government demand that the cost of the Army to the Treasury should be held to the lowest possible level. The other was that the political stability of the Army and its recruiting should be made dependent on a regimental system of loyalties, including an officer corps recruited largely from the privileged classes, and therefore with a considerable voice in its own institutional future. A further important factor was that the British Army might have to fight either a war in Europe, or a colonial war, or a wider war with aspects of both. Within the context of British politics and defence policy, the doctrinal solutions reached by the British cavalry between 1880 and 1918 were practical, and just as important they were successful in war.

Too much cannot be claimed for the officers who developed British cavalry doctrine between 1880 and 1918, except that broadly they got it right when many got it wrong, and at a time when many errors were made in forming other military doctrines. In French's case, it would be enough to note that the continuing belief that

---

1 Charrington, *Where Cavalry Stands Today*, p. 53.
2 For the wider implications of this to the deadlock on the Western Front see Sheffield, *Forgotten Victory*, pp. 102–3.

while in command of the BEF he remained what Edmonds called '*un beau sabreur* of the old fashioned sort', obsessed with a cavalry breakthrough, is quite false.[3] But if French at his best was a skilled practitioner of cavalry tactics rather than a military thinker, the importance of the military thought of other British officers between the Boer War and the First World War has been remarkably neglected by historians. By the middle of the twentieth century, the two most significant British military theorists of this period were considered to be the civilian Spencer Wilkinson and Colonel Repington, although some credit was also given to Henderson.[4] Since that time, British officers of the period have either been ignored outright or disparaged by historians of military thought, in Haig's case certainly because of his enduring reputation as a stupid cavalryman.[5] This is not to suggest that as a military thinker Haig, any more than Ferdinand Foch or Erich Ludendorff, was necessarily right, but simply that for an era in which Great Britain was the strongest power in the world, and the British Army was among the most consistently successful, the military thought of such British officers is too important to ignore.

All these conclusions are so far removed from the traditional image of the British cavalry that an explanation is required. Although the cavalry and their generals became scapegoats for the perceived wider failings of the British Army on the Western Front, this process took several years to reach its final form. In 1920, Churchill in his foreword to the history of the 4th Hussars did not disappoint his old regiment, although he could not quite bring himself to mention Haig's final victory:

> The vitally important cavalry work of the Retreat from Mons was succeeded by a prolonged period when the trenches stretched from the sea to the Alps, when there were no flanks for the cavalry to turn and no war of movement for their manoeuvring capacity. As the British Army grew, division by division, from the small original Expeditionary Force to a total strength of about two million men, no proportionate increase was made in the cavalry. On the contrary, it became actually smaller, and a single cavalry corps sufficed in the last phase of the war for all the requirements of a British Army of nearly sixty divisions. This unique body of horsemen, with their power of intensely rapid movement across country, became the one mobile reserve on which Lord French and Lord Haig in turn counted to throw into any gap that might be made in the front by a sudden attack of the enemy. As such, the cavalry rendered services of the utmost importance in each successive year of the war. In addition, they took their turn in the trenches whenever it was possible to spare them from their paramount duty.[6]

But by the time Churchill wrote his memoirs *The World Crisis* between 1923 and 1927 he was ready to claim that in British and French planning for battles in late 1915 'In the absurd misconceptions of the Staff, large masses of cavalry were

---

3   Quoted (with approval) by Robbins, *British Generalship on the Western Front 1914–18*, p. 118; as before, 'Beau Sabreur' is a French expression meaning 'Handsome Swordsman'.
4   Luvaas, *The Education of an Army*, pp. 191–2 and pp. 249–333.
5   See Gat, *A History of Military Thought*, pp. 684–8, Paret, *Makers of Modern Strategy*, and Handel, *Masters of War* for a neglect of British military thought at the height of Empire.
6   Quoted in Anglesey, *A History of the British Cavalry Volume 8*, p. 283.

brought up to press the victory to a decisive conclusion.'[7] Like many critics of the cavalry, Churchill also employed ridicule, noting that on the Somme on 14 July 1916 'the world was eagerly informed that a squadron of the 7th Dragoon Guards had actually ridden their horses as far as High Wood'.[8] The partial success of a cavalry squadron that had adjusted its tactics to the Western Front was an occasion for laughter, whereas the partial success of a handful of tanks two months later at Flers-Courcelette was depicted as a war-changing event. In 1930, Churchill also published *My Early Life*, in which he significantly revised his account of the charge of the 21st Lancers at Omdurman, adding the assessment that 'There one could see the futility of the much vaunted *Arme Blanche*', something for which there is no justification in his contemporary writings.[9]

A critical period in forming the popular image of the war was the era of the Great Depression, when any benefits from winning the war seemed distant, and which included the unsavoury 'Battle of the Memoirs' between senior politicians and generals or their respective champions.[10] Critics of the British conduct of the war on the Western Front and of British generalship found it particularly taxing to balance their image of the cavalry general as the ultimate incompetent with the achievements in Palestine. In his book *Reputations* written in 1928, Liddell Hart looked among Allenby's victories in 1917 and 1918 for 'the brain of a Staff Officer behind the form of the Commander – to ask who was Allenby's Weygand, if not his Ludendorff', finally concluding that Allenby evolved from 'the bad General of 1914–15 to the great General of 1918', rather than that conditions in the two theatres were significantly different.[11] But undoubtedly the classic statement on British cavalry generals came from Lloyd George in 1934:

> It is not too much to say that when the Great War broke out our Generals had the most important lessons of their art to learn. Before they began they had much to unlearn. Their brains were cluttered with useless lumber, packed into every niche and corner. Some of it was never cleared out to the end of the War. For instance, take their ridiculous cavalry obsession. In a war where artillery and engineering and trench work were more in demand than in any war in history, we were led by soldiers trained in the cavalry. Haig was persuaded to the end of the War that a time would come when his troopers would one day charge through the gap made by his artillery and convert the German defeat into a headlong scamper for the Rhine. Needless to say, that chance never came.[12]

---

7   Churchill, *The World Crisis*, Volume II, p. 893.
8   Ibid., Volume II, p. 1078.
9   Churchill, *My Early Life*, p. 206.
10 The first historian to suggest this appears to be Barnett, *The Collapse of British Power*, pp. 426–38; for the 'Battle of the Memoirs', see the section with that title in Bond (ed.), *The First World War and British Military History*, consisting of the contributions by Beckett, 'Frocks and Brasshats', pp. 89–112, Holmes, 'Sir John French and Lord Kitchener', pp. 113–40, and Simpson, 'The Reputation of Sir Douglas Haig', pp. 141–62. See also Todman, *The Great War: Myth and Memory*, pp. 73–94; Bond, *The Unquiet Western Front*, pp. 27–50.
11 Liddell Hart, *Reputations*, p. 238 and pp. 259–60. Maxime Weygand was Ferdinand Foch's deputy for most of the First World War.
12 Lloyd George, *War Memoirs of David Lloyd George*, Volume II, p. 2038.

Lloyd George was not the only widely-read author of the time to equate belief in the tactical value of cavalry, or past service in a cavalry regiment, with military incompetence. The poet and memoirist Siegfried Sassoon described Rawlinson as an 'old cavalryman'.[13] C.S. Forester's novel *The General*, published in 1936, which portrayed the typical Western Front general as a stupid and ignorant cavalryman, continued to be cited as evidence in histories of warfare almost to the end of the twentieth century.[14] Although Edmonds had earlier absolved Haig of favouritism towards other cavalrymen, in 1947 in the volume of his *Official History* dealing with the last months of the war he listed the cavalrymen in high command on the Western Front with the comment that 'what the Army called "cavalry spirit" led to pressure for haste and to expectation of ground gained incompatible with siege warfare'.[15] Three years later Edmonds asserted as a fact that Haig had obtained the post of GOC-in-C only by continuing French's policy of promoting cavalrymen to Army commands.[16] Lloyd George had written that 'The Army chiefs were mostly horsemen – Lord French and Sir Douglas Haig were both cavalry men and had won their reputations as cavalry generals', and by 1963 in A.J.P. Taylor's best-selling *The First World War: An Illustrated History* this had become 'most British generals were cavalry men'.[17] The process was essentially complete when Sassoon's fellow poet and memoirist Robert Graves wrote on the 50th anniversary of the Armistice in 1968:

> All our generals were cavalrymen.... And, blind to change, Generals French, Haig, Plumer, [Lord] Cavan and the rest still thought of war as a succession of heroic cavalry charges: their territorial gains consolidated by slow-marching infantry. They made a point of opposing every mechanical innovation that might disturb this dream. They loved horses: they excelled in polo; they hated motor-cars and lorries – nasty, smelly things at which horses shied.[18]

By the last quarter of the twentieth century, the term 'cavalryman' in the context of the First World War had become little more than a vague expression of abuse.

This perception of the cavalry general and the cavalry charge has taken on the qualities of what are sometimes called zombie myths: those that will not die no matter how many times they are destroyed. In 1941, George Orwell in his desire to insult the English ruling elites of the inter-war era (and despite his stated opposition to stale or tired imagery), resorted to what was already a cliché when he wrote that 'They dealt with Fascism as the cavalry generals of 1914 dealt with the machine gun

---

13 Sassoon, *Memoirs of an Infantry Officer*, p. 136.

14 Forester, *The General*; Messenger, *The Art of Blitzkrieg*, p. 11; Dixon, *On the Psychology of Military Incompetence*, p. 307; Cohen and Gooch, *Military Misfortunes*, p. 11.

15 Edmonds, *Official History France and Belgium 1918, Volume V*, p. 605.

16 Travers, *The Killing Ground*, p. 10 and endnote 26, p. 30.

17 Lloyd George, *War Memoirs of David Lloyd George*, Volume I, p. 76; Taylor, *The First World War: An Illustrated History*, p. 23.

18 Graves, 'The Kaiser's War: A British Point of View', in Panichas (ed.), *Promise of Greatness: the War of 1914–1918*, p. 6; Lord Cavan began his regimental career in the Grenadier Guards.

– by ignoring it.'[19] Even distinguished modern historians have dismissed without investigation the idea of cavalry being able to charge effectively as a fantasy, the product of a distorted system of personal values, or even a form of mental disorder on the part of the generals involved, 'prattling about the nobility of the horse and the magnetism of the charge'.[20] Like Orwell before him, in 1972 Correlli Barnett in search of an image to describe the shortcomings of politicians of the 1919–1939 era wrote that 'English statesmen were like Victorian cavalry generals trying to conduct a great tank battle.'[21] The metaphor of an uncomprehending cavalry general ordering his obsolete troopers to charge to their doom has spread beyond military studies, into the general vocabulary of historians and readers of history, as a touchstone of all that is reactionary, foolish and futile. It is probably too well established ever to be removed.

---

19 'England Your England', originally published 1941, in Orwell, *Inside the Wale and Other Essays*, p. 81.

20 van Creveld, *Technology and War*, p.175; see also Kiernan, *Colonial Empires and Armies 1815–1960*, p. 182; Dixon, *On the Psychology of Military Incompetence*, especially pp. 86–94, pp. 115–18 and pp. 249–51; but also for recent correctives see Edgerton, *The Shock of the Old*, pp. 138–59, and Phillips, 'Scapegoat Arm'.

21 Barnett, *The Collapse of British Power*, p. 451.

Appendix

British and Imperial Cavalry Regiments 1914–1918

Regimental titles are those used in 1914, unless otherwise stated. British regular regiments are given according to the Order of Precedence, which was based partly on the original date of foundation of a regiment, partly on its continuous existence, partly on its numbering, and partly on its function (heavy guard cavalry took precedence over other cavalry), and was often disputed by the regiments themselves. Otherwise the order follows numerical or alphabetical sequence, except for the Canadian cavalry where it follows order of foundation.

British Cavalry

1st Life Guards
2nd Life Guards
The Royal Horse Guards (The Blues)
1st (King's) Dragoon Guards
2nd Dragoon Guards (Queen's Bays)
3rd (Prince of Wales's) Dragoon Guards
4th (Royal Irish) Dragoon Guards
5th (Princess Charlotte of Wales's) Dragoon Guards
6th Dragoon Guards (Carabiniers)
7th (Princess Royal's) Dragoon Guards
1st (Royal) Dragoons
2nd Dragoons (Royal Scots Greys)
3rd King's Own Hussars
4th (Queen's Own) Hussars
5th (Royal Irish) Lancers
6th (Inniskilling) Dragoons
7th (Queen's Own) Hussars
8th (King's Royal Irish) Hussars
9th (Queen's Royal) Lancers
10th (Prince of Wales's Own Royal) Hussars
11th (Prince Albert's Own) Hussars
12th (Prince of Wales's Royal) Lancers
13th Hussars
14th (King's) Hussars
15th (The King's) Hussars

16th (The Queen's) Lancers
17th (Duke of Cambridge's Own) Lancers
18th (Queen Mary's Own) Hussars
19th (Queen Alexandra's Own) Hussars
20th Hussars
21st (Empress of India's) Lancers

All British cavalry regiments saw active service in the First World War, although in the case of the 21st Lancers this was limited to a single squadron as part of the Corps cavalry regiment of XIV Corps on the Western Front 1916–1917.

British Special Reserve Mounted

North Irish Horse
South Irish Horse
King Edward's Horse (The King's Overseas Dominions Regiment)

All special reserve regiments saw active service during the First World War; King Edward's Horse served briefly in 1915 as part of the Canadian Cavalry Brigade. As given below, the Scottish Horse, and the Welsh Horse (which was formed in August 1914 after the outbreak of the war), were yeomanry rather than special reserve.

Yeomanry

Ayrshire Yeomanry
Bedfordshire Yeomanry
Berkshire Yeomanry
Royal Buckinghamshire Hussars Yeomanry
Cheshire Yeomanry (Earl of Chester's)
Denbighshire Yeomanry
Derbyshire Yeomanry
Royal 1st Devon Yeomanry
Royal North Devon Yeomanry
Dorset Yeomanry (Queen's Own)
Essex Yeomanry
Fife and Forfar Yeomanry
Glamorgan Yeomanry
Queen's Own Royal Glasgow Yeomanry
Gloucestershire Yeomanry (Royal Gloucestershire Hussars)
Hampshire Yeomanry (Carabiniers)
Herts Yeomanry
Royal East Kent Yeomanry (The Duke of Connaught's Own Mounted Rifles)
West Kent Yeomanry
Lanarkshire Yeomanry
Lancashire Hussars Yeomanry

Duke of Lancaster's Own Yeomanry
Leicestershire Yeomanry (Prince Albert's Own)
Lincolnshire Yeomanry
City of London Yeomanry (Rough Riders)
1st County of London Yeomanry (Middlesex Duke of Cambridge's Hussars)
2nd County of London Yeomanry (Westminster Dragoons)
3rd County of London Yeomanry (Sharpshooters)
Lothians and Border Horse Yeomanry
1st Lovat's Scouts Yeomanry
2nd Lovat's Scouts Yeomanry
Montgomeryshire Yeomanry
Norfolk Yeomanry (The King's Own Royal Regiment)
Northamptonshire Yeomanry
Northumberland Yeomanry (Hussars)
Nottinghamshire Yeomanry (Sherwood Rangers)
Nottinghamshire Yeomanry (South Nottinghamshire Hussars)
Oxfordshire Yeomanry (Queen's Own Oxfordshire Hussars)
Pembroke Yeomanry (Castelemartin)
Scottish Horse
Shropshire Yeomanry
North Somerset Yeomanry
West Somerset Yeomanry
Staffordshire Yeomanry (Queen's Own Royal Regiment)
Suffolk Regiment (The Duke of York's Own Loyal Suffolk Hussars)
Surrey Yeomanry (Queen Mary's Regiment)
Sussex Yeomanry
Warwickshire Yeomanry
Welsh Horse Yeomanry
Westmoreland and Cumberland Yeomanry
Royal Wiltshire Yeomanry (Prince of Wales's Own Royal Regiment)
Worcestershire Yeomanry (The Queen's Own Worcestershire Hussars)
Yorkshire Dragoons (Queen's Own)
Yorkshire Hussars Yeomanry (Alexandra Princess of Wales's Own)
East Riding of Yorkshire Yeomanry

This order of precedence for the yeomanry is by alphabetical order of counties as they existed in 1914. Some counties had no yeomanry regiment.

Indian Cavalry

1st Duke of York's Own Lancers (Skinner's Horse)
2nd Lancers (Gardner's Horse)
3rd Skinner's Horse
4th Cavalry
5th Cavalry

6th King Edward's Own Cavalry
7th Hariana Lancers
8th Cavalry
9th Hodson's Horse
10th Duke of Cambridge's Own Lancers (Hodson's Horse)
11th King Edward's Own Lancers (Probyn's Horse)
12th Cavalry
13th Duke of Connaught's Lancers (Watson's Horse)
14th Murray Jat Lancers
15th Lancers (Cureton's Multanis)
16th Cavalry
17th Cavalry
18th King George's Own Lancers
19th Lancers (Fane's Horse)
20th Deccan Horse
21st Prince Albert Victor's Own Cavalry (Frontier Force) (Daly's Horse)
22nd Sam Browne's Cavalry (Frontier Force)
23rd Cavalry (Frontier Force)
25th Cavalry (Frontier Force)
26th King George's Own Light Cavalry
27th Light Cavalry
28th Light Cavalry
29th Lancers (Deccan Horse)
30th Lancers (Gordon's Horse)
31st Duke of Connaught's Own Lancers
32nd Lancers
33rd Queen Victoria's Own Light Cavalry
34th Prince Albert Victor's Own Poona Horse
35th Scinde Horse
36th Jacob's Horse
37th Lancers (Baluch Horse)
38th King George's Own Central India Horse
39th King George's Own Central India Horse
Queen Victoria's Own Corps of Guides (Frontier Force) (Lumsden's) Cavalry

In the reorganisation of 1901–4 the regimental number for 24th Cavalry was left intentionally blank for the 4th Punjab Cavalry, which had been disbanded in 1882. The Corps of Guides had no regimental number.

Canadian Cavalry

The Royal Canadian Dragoons
Lord Strathcona's Horse (Royal Canadians)
The Fort Garry Horse

The first two of these regiments had a permanent pre-war existence as cavalry. The Fort Garry Horse had its origins in a mounted rifle militia regiment, the 34th Fort Garry Horse, which remained at home during the war as a training unit providing troops chiefly for Canadian infantry battalions; other Canadian mounted rifle regiments did the same, or were themselves converted to infantry battalions. The Canadian Cavalry Brigade was formed in 1915 for service on the Western Front, and later that year King Edward's Horse was replaced as its third regiment by the newly-formed Fort Garry Horse.

Australian Light Horse

1st to 13th Light Horse Regiments

New Zealand Mounted Rifles

Auckland Mounted Rifles
Canterbury Mounted Rifles
Otego Mounted Rifles
Wellington Mounted Rifles

Bibliography

PRIMARY SOURCES

Collections Of Official Papers

Australian War Memorial (AWM) Canberra

AWM 4 Series

Cambridge University Library (CUL) Cambridge

Material held in the Official Publications Room
Record of Parliamentary Debates (Hansard)

The National Archives (TNA), Kew, London

Cabinet Office Series (CAB)
Command Series (Cd)
Civil Service Commission Series (CSC)
Public Record Office Series (PRO)
War Office Series (WO)

Collections of Private Papers

Australian War Memorial (AWM) Canberra

Bean Papers [AWM 38 DRL 7953/34]: Papers of Charles Bean, the Australian official historian of the First World War.
Chauvel Papers [AWM PROO535]: Papers of General Sir Henry Chauvel.

British Library (BL), London

Arnold Forster Papers [Add. Mss. 50336]: Diary of Hugh O. Arnold-Forster MP.
Dilke Papers [Add. Mss. 43908]: Papers of Emelia Francis, wife of Sir Charles Wentworth Dilke.
Hutton Papers [Add. Mss. 50078–114]: Papers of Lieutenant General Sir Edward Hutton.
Smith-Dorrien Papers [Add. Mss. 52767–77]: Bound account by General Sir Horace Smith-Dorrien in response to Sir John French's book *1914*.

Churchill Archive Centre (CAC), Churchill College, Cambridge

Rawlinson Papers [RWLN]: The Diary of General Lord Rawlinson 1914–1918 and associated papers.

Hove Public Library (HPL), Hove

Wolseley Papers: Papers of Field Marshal Lord [Garnet] Wolseley.

Imperial War Museum (IWM), London

Fraser Papers [72/60/1]: Papers of Major General W.A.K. Fraser relating to his service as a captain in the 16th Lancers during the First World War.
French Papers [PP/MCR/C32]: Papers of Field Marshal Sir John French, 1st Earl of Ypres. This includes a copy of French's diary for the Boer War, of which the original is in the Brenthurst Library, Houghton, South Africa.
Chetwode Papers [P183 and PP/MCR/C1]: Papers of Field Marshal Sir Philip Chetwode, 1st Baron Chetwode, for the First World War.
Hampton Papers [DS/MISC/82]: Memoirs of Major Lord Hampton, 1/1st Queen's Own Worcestershire Hussars Yeomanry, Palestine, 1917.
Home Papers [82/18/2]: Diary and Papers of Brigadier General Sir Archibald Home for the First World War.
Rawlinson Fourth Army Papers: The War Diary of Fourth Army 1916–1918 originally deposited at the Staff College Camberley in the name of General Lord Rawlinson by his former staff officers.
Wilson Papers [DS/MISC/80 and HHW2]: Papers of Field Marshal Sir Henry Wilson.

Liddell Hart Centre for Military Archives (LHCMA), Kings College, London

Allenby Papers: Papers of Field Marshal Lord Allenby.
Ballard Papers: Papers of Captain (later Brigadier General) Colin Robert Ballard.
Edmonds Papers: Papers of Brigadier General Sir James Edmonds.
Hamilton Papers: Papers of General Sir Ian Hamilton.
Liddell Hart Papers: Papers of Sir Basil Liddell Hart.

Light Dragoons (15th/19th Royal Hussars) Museum

Brunton Papers: Diary of Sergeant D. Brunton, 19th Hussars, 1914–1918.

National Army Museum (NAM) London

Bateman Papers [7910–87]: Papers of Lieutenant W.R. Bateman, Buckinghamshire Yeomanry, 1916.
Bellew Papers [5707–18]: Diary of Captain Robert Bellew, 16th Lancers, for the Boer War.

Britten Papers [7812–34]: Papers of Sergeant R.S. Britten, Buckinghamshire Imperial Yeomanry, for the Boer War.
Broadwood Papers [7508–34]: Papers of Lieutenant General Robert G. Broadwood.
Carew Papers [7711–117]: Diary of Lieutenant G.A.L. Carew, 7th Hussars, for his service in India 1887–1888.
Cecil Papers [7501–20]: Notebooks of Captain R.E. Cecil, 21st Lancers, at the Army Staff College Camberley c. 1907–1908.
Cobb Papers [7802–4]: Papers of Squadron Sergeant Major F. Cobb, 7th Dragoon Guards, for the Boer War.
Davies-Cook Papers [7104–25]: Diary of Lieutenant P.T. Davies-Cook, 10th Hussars, for the Boer War.
Fergusson Papers [6807–269]: Papers of Private F. Fergusson, 20th Hussars, serving in Egypt 1884–1885.
Gough Papers [8304–32]: Papers of Sir Charles Gough VC, Viscount Gough.
Grainger Papers [7104–31]: Diary of Private P.Y. Grainger, 9th Lancers, serving in India 1903–4.
Haslam Papers [7612–21]: Letters of Lieutenant P.L.C. Haslam, 18th Hussars, for the First World War.
Paterson Papers [7208–8]: Scrapbook/Diary of Corporal Paterson of the 17th Ayrshire IY Company for the Boer War.
Rawlinson Papers [5201–33]: Papers of General Lord Rawlinson for the Boer War and the First World War.
Roberts Papers [7101–23]: Papers of Field Marshal Lord Roberts.
Talbot-Rice Papers [7511–80]: Papers of Captain J.A. Talbot-Rice, 5th Lancers, for the First World War.
Winwood Papers [7105–3]: Papers of Captain William Q. Winwood, 5th Dragoon Guards, 1898–1913.

National Library of Scotland (NLS) Edinburgh

Haig Papers [Acc. 3155]: Papers of Field Marshal Sir Douglas Haig, Earl Haig of Bemersyde.
Haldane Papers [Mss. 5901–6109]: Papers of Richard Burdon Haldane, Lord Haldane.

British (And Imperial) Army Training Manuals Etc 1880–1918

Cavalry Drill Volume II (London: HMSO, 1896 – reissued 1898).
Cavalry Training 1904 (Provisional) (London: HMSO, 1904).
Cavalry Training 1907 (London: HMSO, 1907).
Cavalry Training 1912 (London: HMSO, 1912).
Cavalry Training 1915 (London: HMSO, 1915).
Cavalry Training Canada 1904 (Ottawa: Government Printing Bureau, 1904).
Field Service Regulations Part I: Operations, 1909 (London: HMSO, 1909).

Imperial Yeomanry Training 1902 (Provisional) (London: HMSO, 1902).
Instructions for Training of Imperial Yeomanry (London: HMSO, 1905).
Mounted Service Manual for Australian Light Horse and Mounted Infantry &c (Sydney: Cunninghame, 1902).
Regulations and Field Service Manual for Mounted Infantry (London: HMSO, 1889).
Regulations for the Instruction and Movement of Cavalry 1876 (London: HMSO, 1876).
Yeomanry and Mounted Rifle Training: Parts I and II, 1912 (London: HMSO, 1912).

Journals and Magazines 1880–1918

Blackwood's Magazine
The Cavalry Journal
Colburn's United Service Magazine – *later* the United Service Magazine
Journal of the Royal United Service Institution – *later* the Royal United Services Institute
The Nineteenth Century – *later* The Nineteenth Century and After

Books and Articles

[Anon], *A Brief Record of the Advance of the Egyptian Expeditionary Force under the Command of General Sir Edmund H.H. Allenby G.C.B., G.C.M.G., July 1917 to October 1918, Compiled From Official Sources* (London: HMSO, 1919).
[Anon.], *Design for Military Operations: The British Military Doctrine* (London: Ministry of Defence, 1996).
[Anon.], *Land Warfare Doctrine 1: The Fundamentals of Land Warfare* (Canberra: CATDC, 1998).
[Anon], *Notes on Cavalry Tactics, Organisation etc, by a Cavalry Officer* (London: Beccles, 1878).
[Anon.], *The Palestine Campaign*, (Fort Riley KS: US Army Cavalry School, n.d.).
[Anon], *The Second Afghan War: Abridged Official Account – Produced in the Intelligence Branch, Army Headquarters, India* (London: John Murray, 1908).
[Anon.], *Statistics of the Military Effort of the British Empire During the Great War 1914–1920* (London: HMSO, 1921).
[Anon.], *Warfighting: The US Marine Corps Book of Strategy* (New York: Doubleday, [1989] 1994).
Adderley, H.A., *History of the Warwickshire Yeomanry Cavalry* (Warwick: Smith, 1896).
Alderson, Edwin, *Pink and Scarlet, or Hunting as a School for Soldiering etc.* (London: William Heinemann, 1900).
Amery, L.S., *My Political Life Volume One: England Before the Storm 1896–1914* (London: Hutchinson, 1953).

Amery, L.S. (ed.) *The Times History of the War in South Africa 1899–1902*, seven volumes (London: Samspon, Lowe, Marsden, 1900–1909).

Andrew, A.W., *Cavalry Tactics of Today* (Bombay: Thacker, 1903).

Arthur, George (ed.), *The Letters of Lord and Lady Wolseley* (London: William Heinemann, 1922).

Baden-Powell, B.F.S.,*War in Practice: Some Tactical and Other Lessons of the Campaign in South Africa, 1899–1902* (London: Isbister, 1903).

Baden-Powell, R.S.S., *Cavalry Instruction* (London: Harrison and Sons, 1885).

Barrow, George de S., *The Fire of Life* (London: Hutchinson, 1942).

Becke, A.F., *Nery, 1914: The Adventure of the German 4th Cavalry Division on the 31st August and the 1st September* (London: Naval and Military Press, n.d.).

——, *Order of Battle of Divisions Parts1 –5a* (London: HMSO, 1935).

Bernhardi, Frederick von (trans. Sydney Goldmann), *Cavalry in Future Wars* (London: Murray, 1906).

——, (trans. G.T.M. Bridges), *Cavalry in War and Peace* (London: Hugh Rees, 1910).

Birdwood, William, *Khaki and Gown: An Autobiography by Field-Marshal Lord Birdwood* (London: Ward Lock, 1941).

Blake, Robert (ed.), *The Private Papers of Douglas Haig 1914–1919* (London: Eyre and Spottiswoode, 1952).

Bonie, Jean Jacques (trans. C.F. Thompson), *The French Cavalry in 1870: With its Tactical Results* (London: Mitchell, 1873).

Boraston, J.H. (ed.), *Sir Douglas Haig's Despatches (December 1915–April 1919)* (London: J.M. Dent, 1919).

Bridges, Tom, *Alarms and Excursions: Reminiscences of a Soldier* (London: Longman Green, 1938).

Browne, J. Gilbert and E.J. Bridges, *Historical Record of the 14th (King's) Hussars Volume II, 1900–1922* (London: RUSI, 1932).

[Cairnes, W.E.], *An Absent-Minded War: Being Some Reflections on our Reverses and the Causes which Have Led to Them – by a British Staff Officer* (London: John Milne, 1900).

[Cairnes, W.E.], *Social Life in the British Army – by a British Officer* (London.: Long, 1900).

Callwell, C.E., *Field Marshal Sir Henry Wilson*, 2 Volumes (London: Cassell, 1927).

——, *Small Wars: Their Principles and Practice* (London: Greenhill [1906] 1990).

——, *The Tactics of Today* (Edinburgh: Blackwood, 1903).

Carton de Wiart, Adrian, *Happy Odyssey* (London: Cape, 1950).

Charrington, H.V.R., *Where Cavalry Stands Today* (London: Hugh Rees, 1927).

Charteris, John, *Field Marshal Earl Haig* (London: Cassell, 1929).

——, *Haig*, Great Lives Series (London: Duckworth, 1933).

Chenevix-Trench, Frederick, *Cavalry in Modern War* (London: Military Handbooks, 1884).

Chesney, C.C., *A Military View of the Recent Campaigns in Virginia and Maryland* (London: Smith Elder, 1863).

Chesney, C.C. and H. Reeve, *The Military Resources of France and Prussia* (London: Longman, 1870).

Childers, Erskine, *German Influence on British Cavalry* (London: Edward Arnold, 1911).

——, *In the Ranks of the C.I.V.* (Staplehurst: Spellmount, [1901] 1999).

——, *War and the Arme Blanche* (London: Edward Arnold, 1910).

Churchill, Winston S., *Ian Hamilton's March* (London: Longman, 1900).

——, *My Early Life: A Roving Commission* (London: Macmillan, 1930).

——, *The World Crisis 1911–1918*, Revised Edition 2 Volumes, (London: Odhams, 1938).

Clery, C.F., *Minor Tactics* (London: H.S. King, 1875).

Coleman, Frederick, *From Mons to Ypres with French* (London: Sampson Low, Marston, 1916).

Compton, H. (ed.) [Edwin Mole], *A King's Hussar: Being the Military Memoirs for twenty-five years of a Troop Serjeant-Major of the 14th (King's) Hussars (E. Mole)* (London: Cassell, 1893).

Conan Doyle, Arthur, *The Great Boer War* (London: Smith Elder, 1900).

Crozier, Frank, *A Brass Hat in No-Man's Land* (London: Jonathan Cape, 1930).

[Crum, F.M.], *The Question of Mounted Infantry – by a Rifleman* (London: Rees, 1909).

Denison, George T., *A History of Cavalry from the Earliest Times: With Lessons for the Future* (London: Macmillan, [1877] 1913).

——, *Modern Cavalry: Its Organisation, Armament and Employment in War* (London: Bosworth, 1868).

Dewar, A.B. and J.H. Boraston, *Sir Douglas Haig's Command: December 19, 1915 to November 11, 1918*, 2 Volumes, (London: Constable, 1922).

Duke, Basil, *A History of Morgan's Cavalry* (Bloomington IL: Indiana University Press, [1867] 1960).

Dundonald, Lord, *My Army Life* (London: Arnold, 1926).

Edmonds, James E. (general ed.), *The History of the Great War Based on Official Documents: Military Operations*, multiple volumes, (London: Macmillan, 1922 etc.).

Fellows, George and Benson Freeman, *Historical Records of the South Nottinghamshire Hussars Yeomanry, 1794 to 1924*, 2 Volumes (Aldershot: Gale and Polden, 1928).

Forbes, Archibald, *Memories and Studies of War and Peace* (London: Cassell, 1895).

Forester, C.S., *The General* (London: Penguin, 1936).

Fox, Frank, *The History of the Royal Gloucestershire Hussars Yeomanry 1898–1922* (London: P. Allen, 1923).

Fremantle, Arthur, *Three Months in the Southern States* (Edinburgh: Blackwood, 1863).

Garsia, Clive, *A Key to Victory: A Study in War Planning* (London: Eyre and Spottiswode, 1940).

Gilmore, Harry, *Four Years in the Saddle: In the Confederate Army During the American War* (New York: N.P., 1866).

Goldmann, C.S., *With General French and the Cavalry in South Africa* (London: Macmillan, 1902).

Goodenough, W.H. and J.C. Dalton, *The Army Book for the British Empire* (London: HMSO, 1893).

Gough, Hubert, *The Fifth Army* (London: Hodder and Stoughton, 1931).

——, *Soldiering On: Being the Memoirs of General Sir Hubert Gough* (London: Arthur Barker, 1954).

Greene, F.V., *Report on the Russian Army and Its Campaigns in Turkey 1877–8* (London: W.H. Allen, 1879).

[Grierson, James Moncrieff], *Scarlet into Khaki: The British Army on the Eve of the Boer War* (London: Greenhill, [1899] 1988).

Grimshaw, Roly (eds J. Wakefield and J.M. Weippert), *Indian Cavalry Officer 1914–15* (Tunbridge Wells: Costello, 1986).

Guderian, Heinz (trans. Christopher Duffy), *Achtung – Panzer! The Development of Armoured Forces, Their Tactics and Operational Potential* (London: Arms and Armour, [1937] 1992).

Haig, Douglas, *Cavalry Studies* (London: Hugh Rees, 1907).

Hallam Parr, Henry, *The Further Training and Employment of Mounted Infantry and Yeomanry*, 3rd Edition (Aldershot: Gale and Polden, 1902).

Hamilton, Ian, *Compulsory Service: A Study of the Question in the Light of Experience* (London: John Murray, 1910).

——, *The Fighting of the Future* (London: Kegan Paul, 1885).

——, *A Staff Officer's Scrap Book – During the Russo-Japanese War*, 2 Volumes (London: Edward Arnold, 1905).

Hamley, Edward Bruce, *Operations of War* (Edinburgh: Blackwood, 1866).

Hancock, W.R. and Jean van der Poel (eds), *Selections from the Smuts Papers Volume I June 1886–May 1902* (Cambridge: Cambridge University Press, 1966).

Harington, Charles, *Plumer of Messines* (London: John Murray, 1935).

Hatton, S.F., *The Yarn of a Yeoman* (London: Hutchinson, n.d.)

Havelock, Henry, *Three Main Military Questions of the Day* (London: N.P, 1867).

Henderson, G.F.R., *The Battle of Woerth* (Camberley: Gale and Polden, 1911).

——, *The Science of War* (London: Longman Green, 1905).

——, *Stonewall Jackson and the American Civil War* (London: Longman Green, 1898).

Home, Archibald, *The Diary of a World War I Cavalry Officer* (London: Costello, 1985).

Hozier, H.M., *The Seven Weeks' War: Its Antecedents and Incidents*, 2 Volumes (London: N.P., 1867).

Hughes, Daniel J. (ed.), *Moltke on the Art of War: Selected Writings* (Novato CA: Presidio, 1993).

Hughes, Matthew (ed.), *Allenby in Palestine: The Middle East Correspondence of Field Marshal Viscount Allenby* (London: Army Records Society, 2004).

Hutton, E.T.H., *Five Lectures on Mounted Infantry* (Aldershot: Gale and Polden, 1891).

Ismay, Lord, *The Memoirs of General The Lord Ismay* (London: Heinemann, 1960).

Jackson, E.S., *The Inniskilling Dragoons: The Records of an Old Heavy Cavalry Regiment* (London: Arthur L. Humphreys, 1909).
Jerrold, Douglas, *The Royal Naval Division* (London: Privately Published, 1923).
Jomini, Antoine Henri, *The Art of War* (London: Greenhill, [1838] 1992).
Kearsey, A., *A Summary of the Strategy and Tactics of the Egypt and Palestine Campaigns with Details of the 1917–18 Operations Illustrating the Principles of War* (Aldershot: Gale and Polden, 1931).
Kipling, Rudyard, *The Five Nations* (London: Methuen, 1903).
Kraft, Prince Karl August Eduard Friedrich zu Hohenlohe-Ingelfingen (trans. N.L. Walford), *Letters on Cavalry* (London: E. Stanford, 1889).
Liman von Sanders, [Otto], *Five Years in Turkey* (Nashville Tenn.: The Battery Press, 1928).
de Lisle, Beauvoir, *Reminiscences of Sport and War* (London: Eyre and Spottiswoode, 1939).
Lloyd, Robert A., *A Trooper in the Tins: Autobiography of a Life Guardsman* (London: Hurst and Blackett, 1938).
Lloyd George, David, *War Memoirs of David Lloyd George*, 2nd Edition, 2 Volumes (London: Odhams, [1935] 1938).
Lumley, L.R., *The History of the Eleventh Hussars (Prince Albert's Own) 1908–1934* (London: RUSI, 1936).
Lyttelton, Neville, *Eighty Years: Soldiering, Politics, Games* (London: Hodder and Stoughton, 1925).
Maitland, Frances, *Hussar of the Line* (London: Hurst and Blackett, 1951).
Malet, Harold, *The Historical Memoirs of the XVIII Hussars* (London: Simpkin, 1907).
Marling, Percival, *Rifleman and Hussar* (London: John Murray, 1931).
Maude, F.N., *Cavalry: Its Past and Future* (London: William Clowes, 1903).
Maurice, Frederick, *History of the War in South Africa 1899–1902*, 4 Volumes (London: Hurst and Blackett, 1906–10).
——, *The Life of General Lord Rawlinson of Trent* (London: Cassell, 1928).
Maurice J.F., *Military History of the Campaign of 1882 in Egypt* (London: HMSO, 1887).
Monash, John, *The Australian Victories in France in 1918* (Sydney: Angus and Robertson, 1936).
Monsenergue [Colonel] (trans. E.L. Spiers), *Cavalry Tactical Schemes: A Series of Practical Exercises* (London: Hugh Rees, 1914).
Moores, Samuel (revised J. Markham Rose) *Summary of Tactics for Military Operations*, 4th Edition (Portsmouth: W.H. Barrell, 1903).
Morris, A.J.A. (ed.) *The Letters of Lieutenant-Colonel Charles à Court Repington CMG, Military Correspondent of The Times 1903–1918* (London: Army Records Society, 1999).
Mosby, John S. (Charles Wells Russell ed.), *The Memoirs of Colonel John S. Mosby* (Boston: Little Brown, 1917).
Nash, David (ed.), *German Army Handbook April 1918* (London: Arms and Armour [1918] 1977).

de Négrier, François (trans. E.L. Spiers), *Lessons of the Russo-Japanese War* (London: Rees, 1906).
'Notrofe' (pseud. of Ernest Frederick Orton), *Cavalry Taught by Experience: A Forecast of Cavalry under Modern War Conditions* (London: Hugh Rees, 1910).
Orwell, George, *Inside the Wale and Other Essays* (London: Penguin, [1962] 1977).
Patry, Leonce (trans. Douglas Fermer), *The Reality of War: A Memoir of the Franco-Prussian War and the Paris Commune 1870–1871 by a French Officer* (London: Cassell, 2001).
Pease, Howard, *The History of the Northumberland (Hussars) Yeomanry 1819–1923* (London: Constable, 1924).
Peel, Sidney, *OC Beds Yeomanry* (Oxford: Oxford University Press, 1935).
——, *Trooper 8008 IY* (London: Arnold, 1901).
Pember Reeves, Maud, *Round About a Pound a Week* (London: Virago, [1913] 1979).
Pomeroy, R.L., *The Story of a Regiment of Horse: Being the Regimental History from 1685 to 1922 of the 5th Princess Charlotte of Wales' Dragoon Guards*, 2 Volumes, (Edinburgh, Blackwood, 1924).
Ponsonby, Frederick, *Recollections of Three Reigns* (London: Eyre and Spottiswoode, 1951).
von Poseck, Max, (trans. Alexander Strecker et al), *The German Cavalry 1914 in Belgium and France* (Berlin: Mittler, 1923).
Preston, R.M.P., *The Desert Mounted Corps* (London: Constable, 1921).
Reitz, Deneys, *Commando* (London: Faber, 1929).
Rimington, Michael F., *The Horse in Recent War* (Dublin: Military Society of Ireland, 1904).
——, *Our Cavalry* (London: Macmillan, 1912).
[Roberts, F.J.], *The Wipers Times: The Complete Series of the Famous Wartime Trench Newspaper* (London: Little Books, 2006).
Roberts, Lord, *Forty One Years in India: From Subaltern to Commander in Chief* (London: Macmillan, [1897] 1911).
Robertson, William, *From Private to Field Marshal* (London: Constable, 1921).
——, *Soldiers and Statesmen, 1914–1918*, 2 Volumes (New York: Charles Scribners's Sons, 1926).
Robson, Brian (ed.), *Roberts in India: The Military Papers of Field Marshal Lord Roberts 1876–1893* (London: Army Record Society, 1993).
Sampson, Phillip J., *The Capture of De Wet: the South African Rebellion, 1914* (London: Edward Arnold, 1915).
Sassoon, Siegfried, *Memoirs of an Infantry Officer* (London: Faber and Faber, 1930).
von Schmidt, Carl (trans. C.W.B. Bell), *Instructions for the Training, Employment and Leading of Cavalry* (London: HMSO, 1881).
Scott, Douglas (ed.), *Douglas Haig: The Preparatory Prologue: Diaries and Letters 1861–1914* (London: Pen and Sword, 2006).
Seely, J.E.B., *Adventure* (London: William Heinemann, 1930).
Shaw, George Bernard, *Plays Pleasant* (London: Penguin, [1898] 2003).

Sheffield, Gary and John Bourne (eds), *Douglas Haig: War Diaries and Letters 1914–1918* (London: Weidenfeld and Nicholson, 2005).

Sheridan, Philip H., *The Personal Memoirs of P.H. Sheridan, General United States Army* (New York: C.L. Webster, 1888).

Smith, Frederick, *A History of the Royal Army Veterinary Corps 1796–1919* (London: Balliere, Tindall and Cox, 1927).

——, *A Veterinary History of the War in South Africa* (London: H.W. Brown, 1919).

Smith, Michael W., *Drill and Manoeuvres of Cavalry* (London: Longman, 1865).

——, *Modern Tactics of the Three Arms* (London: privately published, 1869).

Smith-Dorrien, Horace, *Memories of Forty Eight Years' Service* (London: John Murray, 1925).

Spears, Edward L., *Liaison 1914: A Narrative of the Great Retreat* (London: Eyre and Spottiswoode, [1930] 1968).

——, *The Picnic Basket* (London: Secker and Warberg, 1967).

Sternberg, Count (trans. G.F.R. Henderson), *My Experiences of the Boer War* (London: Longmans Green, 1901).

Stirling, John, *Our Regiments in South Africa* (Edinburgh: Blackwood, 1903) reprinted Uckfield: Naval and Military Press, 2006.

Stonham, Charles and Benson Freeman, *Historical Records of the Middlesex Yeomanry, 1797–1927* (London: Privately Printed, 1930).

'Backsight Forethought' [Swinton, Ernest], *The Defence of Duffer's Drift* (London: William Clowes, 1904).

'Ole-Luk-Oie' [Swinton, Ernest], *The Green Curve Omnibus* (London: Faber and Faber, 1942).

Tennant, E., *The Royal Deccan Horse in the Great War* (Aldershot: Gale and Polden, 1939).

Terraine, John (ed.), *General Jack's Diary: The Trench Diary of Brigadier General J.L. Jack DSO* (London: Cassell [1964] 2000).

Triandafillov, V.K. (trans. William A. Burhans), *The Nature of the Operations of Modern Armies* (London: Routledge, 1994).

Vaughan, John, *Cavalry and Sporting Memories* (Bala: The Bala Press, 1954).

Verdin, Richard, *The Cheshire (Earl of Chester's) Yeomanry 1898–1967: The Last Regiment to Fight on Horse* (Chester: Privately Printed, 1967).

Verner, Willoughby, *The Military Life of H.R.H. George Duke of Cambridge*, 2 Volumes, (London: John Murray, 1905).

Waters, W.W.H. and Hubert du Cane (trans.), *The German Official Account of the War in South Africa: Prepared in the Historical Section of the Great General Staff* (London: John Murray, 1904).

Wessels, André (ed.), *Lord Kitchener and the War in South Africa 1899–1902* (London: Army Records Society, 2006).

——, *Lord Roberts and the War in South Africa 1899–1902* (London: Army Records Society, 2000).

Western, J.S.E, *Reminiscences of an Indian Cavalry Officer* (London: Allen and Unwin, 1922).

de Wet, Christiaan Rudolf, *Three Years War* (Westminster: Archibald Constable, 1902).
Williams Wynn, R.W., *The Historical Records of the Yeomanry and Volunteers of Montgomeryshire. 1803–1908,* 2 Volumes (Oswestry: Woodall, 1909),
[Wolseley, Garnet] Rawley, James A. (ed), *The American Civil War: An English View* (Charlottesville, University Press of Virginia, 1864).
Wolseley, Garnet, *The Story of a Soldier's Life*, 2 Volumes (London: Constable, 1903).
Wood, Evelyn, *Achievements of Cavalry – with a Chapter on Mounted Infantry* (London: George Bell, [1897] 1900).
——, *From Midshipman to Field Marshal*, 2 Volumes (London: Methuen, 1906).
——, 'Mounted Riflemen', Royal United Service Institution Pamphlet, 1874.
Woods, Frederick (ed.), *Young Winston's Wars: the Original Despatches of Winston S. Churchill* (London: Sphere, 1972).
Woodward, David R. (ed.), *The Military Correspondence of Field Marshal Sir William Robertson, Chief of the Imperial General Staff December 1915–February 1918* (London: Army Records Society, 1989).
von Wrangel, Count Carl Gustav (trans. Joseph Montgomery), *The Cavalry in the Russo-Japanese War* (London: Hugh Rees, 1907).
von Wright, C.H. and H.M. Hozier (trans), *The Campaign of 1866 in Germany: Compiled by the Department of Military History of the Prussian Staff* (London: N.P., 1872).
Younghusband, George, *Forty Years a Soldier* (London: Herbert Jenkins, 1923).
——, *A Soldier's Memories in Peace and War* (London: Herbert Jenkins, 1917).

SECONDARY SOURCES

Unpublished University Theses

Badsey, S.D., 'Fire and the Sword: the British Army and the *Arme Blanche* Controversy 1871–1921', PhD, Cambridge University, 1982.
Bou, J., 'The Evolution and Development of the Australian Light Horse, 1860–1945', PhD, University of New South Wales, Australia, 2005.
Hammond, C.B., 'The Theory and Practice of Tank Co-Operation with Other Arms on the Western Front in the First World War', PhD, University of Birmingham, 2005.
Holmes, E.R., 'The Road to Sedan: The French Army 1866–70', PhD, University of Reading, 1975.
Towle, P.A., 'The Influence of the Russo-Japanese War on British Military and Naval Thought 1904–14', PhD, University of London, 1973.
Winton, G.R., 'Horsing the British Army 1878–1923', PhD, University of Birmingham, 1997.

Books and Articles

Adams, R.J.Q. and Philip P. Poirier, *The Conscription Controversy in Great Britain 1900–18* (Columbus OH: Ohio State University Press, 1987).

Addington, Larry H., *The Patterns of War Since the Eighteenth Century* (Bloomington IN: Indiana University Press, 1984).

Anglesey, The Marquis of, *A History of the British Cavalry 1816–1919*, 8 Volumes (London: Leo Cooper, 1973–1998).

Ascoli, David, *A Companion to the British Army 1660–1983* (London: Book Club Associates, 1984).

Ashworth, Tony, *Trench Warfare 1914–1918: the Live and Let Live System* (London: Macmillan, 1980).

Babington, Anthony, *Military Intervention in Britain: From the Gordon Riots to the Gibraltar Incident* (London: Routledge, 1990).

Badsey, Stephen, 'The Boer War (1899–1902) and British Cavalry Doctrine: A Re-Evaluation', *The Journal of Military History*, Volume 71, Number 1, January 2007.

——, 'Cavalry and the Development of the Breakthrough Doctrine', in Griffith, Paddy (ed.), *British Fighting Methods of the Great War* (London: Frank Cass, 1996).

——, 'The Doctrines of the Coalition Forces', in Pimott, John and Stephen Badsey (eds), *The Gulf War Assessed* (London: Arms and Armour, 1992).

——, *The Franco-Prussian War 1870–1871* (Oxford: Osprey, 2003).

——, 'The Impact of Communications and the Media on the Art of War Since 1815', in Jensen, Geoffrey and Andrew Wiest (eds), *War in the Age of Technology: Myriad Faces of Modern Armed Conflict* (New York: New York University Press, 2001).

——, 'New Wars, New Press, New Country? The British Army, the Expansion of the Empire, and the Mass Media 1877–1918', in Ian F.W. Beckett (ed.), *The Society for Army Historical Research Special Publication No. 16*, 2007.

——, 'The Road to Stalemate 1899–1914', in Trew, Simon and Gary Sheffield (eds), *100 Years of Conflict 1900–2000* (Thrupp: Sutton, 2000).

——, 'War Correspondents in the Boer War', in Gooch, John (ed.), *The Boer War: Direction, Experience and Image* (London: Cassell, 2000).

Bailey, Jonathan, 'The First World War and the Birth of Modern Warfare', in Knox, MacGregor and Williamson Murray (eds), *The Dynamics of Military Revolution 1300–2050* (Cambridge: Cambridge University Press, 2001).

Baker, Anthony, *Battles and Battlefields of the Anglo-Boer War 1899–1902* (Milton Keynes: The Military Press, 1999).

Barnes, R. Money, *The British Army of 1914: Its History, Uniforms and Contemporary Continental Armies* (London: Seely Service, 1968).

Barnett, Correlli, *Britain and Her Army: A Military, Political and Social Survey* (London: Allen Lane, 1970).

——, *The Collapse of British Power* (London: Eyre Methuen, 1972).

——, *The Swordbearers: Studies in Supreme Command in the First World War* (London: Eyre and Spottiswoode, 1963).

Barr, Niall, *The Pendulum of War: The Three Battles of El Alamein* (London: Jonathan Cape, 2004).

Barthorp, Michael, *Blood-Red Desert Sand: The British Invasions of Egypt and the Sudan 1882–1898* (London: Cassell, 2002).

Baynes, John, *Morale: A Study of Men and Courage* (London: Leo Cooper, 1967).

Beales, Derek, *From Castlereagh to Gladstone 1815–1885* (London: Sphere, 1971).

Beckett, Ian F.W., *The Amateur Military Tradition 1558–1945* (Manchester: Manchester University Press, 1991).

——, *The Army and the Curragh Incident, 1914* (London: Army Records Society, 1986).

——, 'British Official History and the South African War', in Wilcox, Craig (ed.), *Recording the South African War: Journalism and Official History 1899–1914* (London: Sir Robert Menzies Centre for Australian Studies, 1999).

——, 'Buller and the Politics of Command', in Gooch, John (ed.), *The Boer War: Direction, Experience and Image* (London: Cassell, 2000).

——, 'Frocks and Brasshats', in Bond, Brian (ed.), *The First World War and British Military History* (Oxford: Clarendon Press, 1991).

——, *Johnnie Gough VC: A Biography of Brigadier-General Sir John Edmond Gough VC, KCB, CMG* (London: Tom Donovan, 1989).

——, 'King George V and His Generals', in Hughes, Matthew and Matthew Seligmann (eds), *Leadership in Conflict 1914–1918* (London: Leo Cooper, 2000).

——, '"Selection by Disparagement": Lord Esher, the General Staff and the Politics of Command 1904–1914', in French, David and Brian Holden Reid (eds), *The British General Staff: Reform and Innovation 1890–1939* (London: Frank Cass, 2002).

——, 'The Territorial Force', in Beckett, Ian F.W. and Keith Simpson (eds), *A Nation in Arms: A Social Study of the British Army in the First World War* (Manchester: Manchester University Press, 1985).

——, *The Victorians at War* (London: Hambledon and London, 2003).

——, 'Women and Patronage in the Late Victorian Army', *History*, Volume 35, Number 279, July 2000.

Beckett, Ian F.W. and Steven J. Corvi (eds), *Haig's Generals* (London: Pen and Sword, 2006).

Belfield, Eversley, *The Boer War* (London: Leo Cooper, 1975).

Bennett, Ian, *A Rain of Lead: The Siege and Surrender of the British at Potchefstroom* (London: Greenhill, 2001).

Bennett, Will, *Absent Minded Beggars: Volunteers in the Boer War* (London: Leo Cooper, 1999).

Belich, James, *The New Zealand Wars and the Victorian Interpretation of Racial Conflict* (London: Penguin, [1986] 1988).

Bellamy, Christopher, *The Evolution of Modern Land Warfare: Theory and Practice* (London: Routledge, 1990).

Bidwell, Shelford and Dominick Graham, *Fire-Power: British Army Weapons and Theories of War 1904–1945* (London: George Allen and Unwin, 1982).

Bird, Anthony, *The Motor Car 1765–1914* (London: Batsford, 1960).
Bond, Brian, 'Doctrine and Training in the British Cavalry 1870–1914', in Howard, Michael (ed.), *The Theory and Practice of War: Essays Presented to Captain B.H. Liddell Hart on his Seventieth Birthday* (London: Cassell, 1965).
——, *The Unquiet Western Front: Britain's Role in Literature and History* (Cambridge: Cambridge University Press, 2002).
——, *The Victorian Army and the Staff College 1854–1914* (London: Eyre Methuen, 1972).
——, *Victorian Military Campaigns* (London: Tom Donovan, 1967).
——, *War and Society in Europe 1870–1970* (Thrupp: Sutton, [1984] 1998).
Bond, Brian and Nigel Cave (eds), *Haig: A Reappraisal 70 Years On* (London: Leo Cooper, 1999).
Bou, Jean, 'Cavalry, Firepower, and Swords: The Australian Light Horse and the Tactical Lessons of Cavalry Operations in Palestine, 1916–1918', *The Journal of Military History*, Volume 71, Number 1, January 2007.
Bourke, Joanna, *An Intimate History of Killing: Face-to-Face Killing in Twentieth Century Warfare* (London: Granta, 1999).
Bourne, J.M., *Patronage and Society in Nineteenth Century England* (London: Edward Arnold, 1986).
Bourne, John, 'Charles Monro', in Beckett, Ian F.W. and Steven J. Corvi (eds), *Haig's Generals* (London: Pen and Sword, 2006).
Bowling, A.H., *Indian Cavalry Regiments 1880–1914* (London: Almark, 1971).
Boyle, Andrew, *The Riddle of Erskine Childers* (London: Hutchinson, 1977).
Brander, M., *The 10th Royal Hussars* (London: Leo Cooper, 1969).
Bristow, Adrian, *A Serious Disappointment: The Battle of Aubers Ridge 1915 and the Munitions Scandal* (London: Leo Cooper, 1995).
Brown, Ian Malcolm, *British Logistics on the Western Front 1914–1919* (Westport CT: Praeger, 1998).
Brown, Lucy, *Victorian News and Newspapers* (Oxford: Clarendon Press, 1985).
Brown, Malcolm, *The Imperial War Museum Book of the Western Front* (London: Sidgwick and Jackson, 1993).
Bruce, George, *Six Battles for India: The Anglo-Sikh Wars 1845–6, 1848–9* (London: Arthur Barker, 1969).
Buckley, John, *Air Power in the Age of Total War* (London: UCL Press, 1999).
Cannadine, David, *The Decline and Fall of the British Aristocracy* (London: Papermac, 1992).
Carman, W.Y., *Light Horse and Mounted Rifle Volunteers 1860–1901* (London: Arrow, 1995).
Clarke, I.F., *Voices Prophesying War: Future Wars 1763–3749* 2nd Edition (Oxford: Oxford University Press, 1992).
Cohen, Eliot A. and John Gooch, *Military Misfortunes: The Anatomy of Failure in War* (New York: The Free Press, 1990).
Cook, Chris and John Stevenson, *The Longman Handbook of Modern British History 1714–1980* (London: Longman, 1983).
Cooper, Bryan, *The Ironclads of Cambrai: the First Great Tank Battle* (London: Cassell, 1967).

Cooper, [Alfred] Duff, *Haig*, 2 Volumes (London: Faber and Faber, 1935).
Copp, Terry, *Fields of Fire: The Canadians in Normandy* (Toronto: University of Toronto Press, 2003).
Corrigan, Gordon, *Sepoys in the Trenches: The Indian Corps on the Western Front 1914–15* (Staplehurst: Spellmount, 1999).
Crawshaw, Michael, 'The Impact of Technology on the BEF and Its Commander', in Bond, Brian and Nigel Cave (eds), *Haig: A Reappraisal 70 Years On* (London: Leo Cooper, 1999).
van Creveld, Martin, *Command in War* (Cambridge MA: Harvard University Press, 1985).
——, *Supplying War: Logistics from Wallenstein to Patton* (Cambridge: Cambridge University Press, 1977).
——, *The Sword and the Olive: A Critical History of the Israeli Defense Force* (New York: Public Affairs, 1998).
——, *Technology and War: From 2000 B.C. to the Present* (London: Brassey's, 1991).
Cull, Nicholas J., David Culbert and David Welch (eds), *Propaganda and Mass Persuasion: A Historical Encyclopedia 1500 to the Present* (Santa Barbara CA: ABC-Clio, 2003).
Danchev, Alex, *Alchemist of War: The Life of Basil Liddell Hart* (London: Weidenfeld and Nicholson, 1998).
David, Saul, *The Indian Mutiny 1857* (London: Viking, 2002).
Davidson, Apollon and Irina Filatova, *The Russians and the Anglo-Boer War 1899–1902* (Cape Town: Human and Rousseau, 1998).
Davies, Frank and Graham Maddocks, *Bloody Red Tabs: General Officer Casualties of the Great War 1914–1918* (London: Leo Cooper, 1995).
Dean, Eric T. Jr., *Shook Over Hell: Post-Traumatic Stress, Vietnam and the Civil War* (Cambridge MA: Harvard University Press, 1997).
Derry, T.K. and Trevor I. Williams, *A Short History of Technology* (Oxford: Oxford University Press, [1960] 1970).
Dixon, Norman, *On the Psychology of Military Incompetence* (London: Pimlico, 1976).
Doughty, Robert A., *Pyrrhic Victory: French Strategy and Operations in the Great War* (Cambridge MA: Belknap Press, 2005).
Dunlop, John K., *The Development of the British Army 1899–1914* (London: Methuen, 1938).
Duxbury, George R., *David and Goliath: The First War of Independence 1880–1881* (Johannesburg: South African Museum of Military History, 1981).
Edgerton, David, *The Shock of the Old: Technology and Global History Since 1900* (London: Profile, 2006).
Eksteins, Modris, *Rites of Spring: The Great War and the Birth of the Modern Age* (London: Black Swan, 1990).
Ellis, John, *Eye Deep in Hell: The Western Front 1914–18* (London: Book Club Associates, 1979).
——, *The Sharp End of War: The Fighting Man in World War II* (London: David and Charles, 1980).

——, *The Social History of the Machine Gun* (London: Croom Helm, 1975).
Evans, Roger, *The Story of the Fifth Royal Inniskilling Dragoon Guards* (Aldershot: Gale and Polden, 1951).
D'Este, Carlo, *Decision in Normandy: The Unwritten Story of Montgomery and the Allied Campaign* (London: Pan, [1983] 1984).
Falls, Cyril, *The Art of War* (Oxford: Oxford University Press, 1961).
Farwell, Byron, *Queen Victoria's Little Wars* (London: Wordsworth, [1973] 1999).
Fergusson, Niall, *Empire: How Britain Made the Modern World* (London: Penguin, [2003] 2004).
——, *The Pity of War* (London: Allen Lane, 1998).
Foley, Robert T., *German Strategy and the Path to Verdun: Erich von Falkenhayn and the Development of Attrition, 1870–1916* (Cambridge: Cambridge University Press, 2005).
Förster, Stig and Jörg Nagler (eds), *On the Road to Total War: The American Civil War and the German Wars of Unification 1861–1871* (Cambridge: Cambridge University Press, 1997).
French, David, *British Strategy and War Aims 1914–1916* (London: Allen and Unwin, 1986).
——, *Military Identities: The Regimental System, the British Army & the British People c. 1870–2000* (Oxford: Oxford University Press, 2005).
——, *The Strategy of the Lloyd George Coalition, 1916–1918* (Oxford: Clarendon Press, 1995).
French, David and Brian Holden Reid (eds), *The British General Staff: Reform and Innovation 1890–1939* (London: Frank Cass, 2002).
French, Gerald, *The Life of Field Marshal Sir John French, First Earl of Ypres* (London: Cassell, 1931).
Fuller, J.F.C., *The Conduct of War 1789–1961* (London: Methuen, [1961] 1972).
Fussell, Paul, *The Great War and Modern Memory* (Oxford: Oxford University Press, 1979).
Gardner, Brian, *Allenby* (London: Cassell, 1965).
Gardner, Brian (ed.), *Up the Line to Death: The War Poets 1914–1918* (London: Magnum, 1977).
Gardner, Nikolas, 'Command and Control in the "Great Retreat" of 1914: the Disintegration of the British Cavalry Division', *The Journal of Military History* Number 63, January 1999.
——, 'Julian Byng', in Beckett, Ian F.W. and Steven J. Corvi (eds), *Haig's Generals* (London: Pen and Sword, 2006).
——, *Trial By Fire: Command and the British Expeditionary Force in 1914* (London: Praeger, 2003).
Gat, Azar, *A History of Military Thought: From the Enlightenment to the Cold War* (Oxford: Oxford University Press, 2001).
Geyer, Michael, 'German Strategy in the Age of Machine Warfare 1914–1945', in Paret, Peter (ed.), *Makers of Modern Strategy: From Machiavelli to the Nuclear Age* (Oxford: Clarendon Press, 1990).
Glantz, David M. and Jonathan House, *When Titans Clashed: How the Red Army Stopped Hitler* (Lawrence KA: University Press of Kansas, 1995).

Glover, Michael, 'The Purchase of Commissions', *The Journal of the Society for Army Historical Research*, Volume LVIII, Number 236, 1980.
Gooch, John, 'Attitudes Towards War in Late Victorian and Edwardian England', in Bond, Brian and Ian Roy (eds), *War and Society: A Yearbook of Military History* (New York: Holmes and Meier, 1975).
——, *The Plans of War: The General Staff and British Military Strategy c.1900–1916* (London: Routledge & Kegan Paul, 1974).
Gooch, John (ed.), *The Boer War: Direction, Experience and Image* (London: Cassell, 2000).
Grey, Jeffrey, *A Military History of Australia* (Cambridge: Cambridge University Press, 1999).
Grieves, Keith, *The Politics of Manpower 1914–1918* (Manchester: Manchester University Press, 1988).
Griffith, Paddy, *Battle Tactics of the Western Front: The British Army's Art of Attack 1916–18* (New Haven: Yale University Press, 1994).
——, *Forward Into Battle: Fighting Tactics from Waterloo to Vietnam* (Chichester: Anthony Bird, 1981).
——, *Military Thought in the French Army 1815–51* (Manchester: Manchester University Press, 1989).
——, *Rally Once Again: Battle Tactics of the American Civil War* (Marlborough: Crowood, 1987).
Grimsley, Mark, 'Surviving Military Revolution: The US Civil War', in Knox, MacGregor and Williamson Murray (eds), *The Dynamics of Military Revolution 1300–2050* (Cambridge: Cambridge University Press, 2001).
Grodzinski, John R. and Michael R. McNorgan, '"It's a Charge, Boys, It's a Charge!" Cavalry Action at Moreuil Wood, 30 March 1918', in Graves, Donald E. (ed.), *Fighting for Canada: Seven Battles 1758–1945* (Toronto: Robin Brass Studio, 2000).
de Groot, Gerard J., 'Educated Soldier or Cavalry Officer? Contradictions in the pre-1914 Career of Douglas Haig', *War and Society*, Volume 4, Number 2, September 1986.
——, *Douglas Haig 1861–1928* (London: Unwin Hyman, 1988).
Grossman, David (ed.), *On Killing: The Psychological Cost of Learning to Kill in War and Society* (New York: Little, Brown, 1996).
Hagerman, Edward, *The American Civil War and the Origins of Modern Warfare: Ideas, Organisation and Field Command* (Bloomington IN: Indiana University Press, 1992).
Hall, Darrell (eds Fransjohan Pretorius and Gilbert Toriage), *The Hall Handbook of the Anglo-Boer War* (Pietermaritzburg: University of Natal Press, 1999).
Hamer, W.S., *The British Army: Civil Military Relations 1885–1905* (Oxford: Clarendon Press, 1970).
Hamilton, Ian B.M., *The Happy Warrior: A Life of General Sir Ian Hamilton* (London: Cassell, 1966).
Hancock, W.K., *Smuts: Volume I: The Sanguine Years 1870–1919* (Cambridge: Cambridge University Press, 1962).

Handel. Michael I., *Masters of War: Classical Strategic Thought* (London: Frank Cass, 2001).

Harries-Jenkins, Gwyn, *The Army in Victorian Society* (London: Routledge and Kegan Paul, 1977).

Harris, J.P., *Men, Ideas and Tanks: British Military Thought and Armoured Forces 1903–1939* (Manchester: Manchester University Press, 1995).

Haythornthwaite, Philip J., *The Armies of Wellington* (London: Arms and Armour, 1994).

Headrick, Daniel R., *The Tools of Empire: Technology and European Imperialism in the Nineteenth Century* (Oxford: Oxford University Press, 1981).

Heathcote, T.A., *The Afghan Wars 1839–1919* (Staplehurst: Spellmount, [1980] 2003).

——, *The British Field Marshals 1736–1997: A Biographical Dictionary* (London: Leo Cooper, 1999).

——, *The Indian Army: The Garrison of British Imperial India 1822–1922* (London: David & Charles, 1974).

Heuser, Beatrice, *Reading Clausewitz* (London: Pimlico, 2002).

Hill, A.J., *Chauvel of the Light Horse: a Biography of General Sir Harry Chauvel* (Melbourne: Melbourne University Press, 1978).

Hillcourt, William (with Olave, Lady Baden-Powell), *Baden-Powell, The Two Lives of a Hero* (London: Heinemann, 1967).

Hills, Reginald, *The Life Guards* (London: Leo Cooper, 1971).

Hobsbawm, Eric, *The Age of Empire 1875–1914* (London: Weidenfeld and Nicholson, 1987).

Holden Reid, Brian, 'The Commander and his Chief of Staff: Ulysses S. Grant and John A. Rawlins 1861–1865', in Sheffield, G.D. (ed.), *Leadership and Command: The Anglo-American Experience since 1861* (London: Brassey's, 1997).

——, *J.F.C. Fuller: Military Thinker* (London: Macmillan, 1987).

——, *The Origins of the American Civil War* (London: Longman, 1996).

Holmes, Richard, *Firing Line* (London: Penguin, 1987).

——, *The Little Field Marshal: Sir John French* (London: Jonathan Cape, 1981).

——, *Riding the Retreat: Mons to the Marne 1914 Revisited* (London: Jonathan Cape, 1995).

——, *Sahib: The British Soldier in India 1750–1914* (London: Harper, 2006).

——, 'Sir John French and Lord Kitchener', in Bond, Brian (ed.), *The First World War and British Military History* (Oxford: Clarendon Press, 1991).

——, *Tommy: The British Soldier on the Western Front 1914–1918* (London: HarperCollins, 2004).

Howard, Michael, *The Franco-Prussian War* (London: Granada, [1961] 1979).

——, 'Men Against Fire: the Doctrine of the Offensive in 1914', in Paret, Peter (ed.), *Makers of Modern Strategy: From Machiavelli to the Nuclear Age* (Oxford: Clarendon Press, 1990).

Hughes, Matthew, *Allenby and British Strategy in the Middle East 1917–1919* (London: Frank Cass, 1999).

——, 'Edmund Allenby', in Beckett, Ian F.W. and Steven J. Corvi (eds), *Haig's Generals* (London: Pen and Sword, 2006).

Morton Jack, George, 'The Indian Army on the Western Front 1914–1915: A Portrait of Collaboration', *War In History*, Volume 13, Number 3, 2006.
James, David, *The Life of Lord Roberts* (London: Hollis and Carter, 1954).
James, E.A., *British Regiments 1914–18* (London: Naval and Military Press, 1978).
Jeffrey, Keith, *Field Marshal Sir Henry Wilson: A Political Soldier* (Oxford: Oxford University Press, 2006).
Jenkins, Robin, '"One of the Human Atoms": a Soldier's View of the South African War 1899–1902', *The Journal of the Society for Army Historical Research*, Volume 85, Number 341, Spring 2007.
Johnson, Hubert C., *Breakthrough! Tactics, Technology and the Search for Victory on the Western Front in World War I* (Novato CA: Presidio, 1994).
Jones, Archer, *The Art of War in the Western World* (New York: Barnes and Noble, 1987).
Jones, Ian, 'Beersheba: The Light Horse Charge and the Making of Myths', *The Journal of the Australian War Memorial*, No. 3, October 1983.
Judd, Denis, *Empire: The British Imperial Experience from 1765 to the Present* (London: HarperCollins, 1996).
Judd, Denis and Keith Surridge, *The Boer War* (London: John Murray, 2002).
Keegan, John, *The Face of Battle* (London: Jonathan Cape, 1978).
Kennedy, Greg (ed.), *Imperial Defence: The Old World Order 1856–1956* (London: Routledge, 2007).
Kennedy, Paul M., *The Rise and Fall of British Naval Mastery* (London: Allen Lane, 1976).
Kiernan, V.G., *Colonial Empires and Armies 1815–1960* (Thrupp: Sutton, [1982] 1998).
Knight, Ian and Ian Castle, *The Zulu War Then and Now* (London: After the Battle, 1993).
——, *Zulu War* (Oxford: Osprey, 2004).
Kochanski, Halik, 'Planning for War in the Final Years of *Pax Britannica*, 1889–1903', in French, David and Brian Holden Reid (eds), *The British General Staff: Reform and Innovation 1890–1939* (London: Frank Cass, 2002).
——, *Sir Garnet Wolseley: Victorian Hero* (London: Hambledon, 1999).
Koss, Stephen, *The Rise and Fall of the Political Press in Britain*, 2 Volumes (London: Hamish Hamilton, 1984).
Koss, Stephen (ed.), *The Pro-Boers: The Anatomy of an Anti-War Movement* (Chicago: University of Chicago Press, 1973).
Laband, John, *The Transvaal Rebellion: The First Boer War 1880–1881* (London: Pearson, 2005).
Labuschagne, Pieter, *Ghostriders of the Anglo-Boer War 1899–1902: The Role and Contribution of the Agterryers* (Pretoria; University of South Africa, 1999).
Leckie, William H., *The Buffalo Soldiers: A Narrative of the Negro Cavalry in the West* (Norman OK: University of Oklahoma Press, 1967).
Lee, Emanoel, *To the Bitter End: A Photographic History of the Boer War 1899–1902* (London: Penguin, 1986).
Lee, John, 'Command and Control in Battle: British Divisions on the Menin Road Ridge, 20 September 1917', in Sheffield, Gary and Dan Todman (eds), *Command*

and Control on the Western Front: the British Army's Experience 1914–18 (Staplehurst: Spellmount, 2004).

———, *A Soldier's Life: General Sir Ian Hamilton 1853–1947* (London: Macmillan, 2000).

Lehman, Joseph, *The First Boer War* (London: Buchan and Enright, [1972] 1985).

Leonard, Robert, *The Art of Maneuver: Maneuver-Warfare Theory and AirLand Battle* (Novato CA: Presido, 1991).

Liddell Hart, B.H., *Reputations* (London: John Murray, 1928).

Liddle, Peter H., *Voices of War 1914–1918: Front Line and Home Front* (London: Leo Cooper, 1988).

Lock, Ron and Peter Quantrill, *Zulu Victory: The Epic of Isandlwana and the Cover-Up* (London: Greenhill, [2002] 2005).

Lunt, James, *Charge to Glory! A Garland of Cavalry Exploits* (London: Heinemann, 1961).

Luttwak, Edward and Dan Horowitz, *The Israeli Army* (London: Allen Lane, 1975).

Luvaas, Jay, *The Education of an Army: British Military Thought 1815–1945* (Chicago: University of Chicago Press, 1964).

———, *The Military Legacy of the Civil War: The European Inheritance*, Revised Edition (Lawrence KA: University Press of Kansas, [1959] 1988).

Lynn, John A. *Battle: A History of Combat and Culture* (Boulder CO: Westview, 2003.

McCracken, Donal P., *MacBride's Brigade: Irish Commandos in the Anglo-Boer War* (Dublin: Four Courts Press, 1999).

Macdonald, Lyn, *Somme* (London: Macmillan, 1983).

McEwan, John M., 'The National Press during the First World War: Ownership and Circulation', *Journal of Contemporary History*, Volume 17, Number 3, July 1982.

McFarland, E.W., '"Empire-Enlarging Genius": Scottish Imperial Yeomanry in the Boer War', *War in History*, Volume 13, Number 3, July 2006.

McGregor, Malcolm, *Officers of the Durham Light Infantry, 1758–1968*, (Esher: Privately Printed, 1989).

McLaughlin, Greg, *The War Correspondent* (London: Pluto Press, 2002).

Magnus, Philip, *Kitchener: Portrait of an Imperialist* (London: John Murray, 1958).

Marble, Sanders, 'Command of Artillery: the Case of Herbert Uniacke', in Sheffield, Gary and Dan Todman (eds), *Command and Control on the Western Front: the British Army's Experience 1914–18* (Staplehurst: Spellmount, 2004).

Marix Evans, Martin, *The Boer War: South Africa 1899–1902* (Oxford: Osprey, 1999).

Marshall-Cornwall, James, *Haig as Military Commander* (London: Batsford, 1973).

Mason, Philip, *The English Gentleman: The Rise and Fall of an Ideal* (London: Pimlico, 1993).

Mead, Peter, *The Eye in the Air: History of Air Observation and Reconnaissance for the Army 1785–1945* (London: HMSO, 1983).

Messenger, Charles, *The Art of Blitzkrieg* (London: Ian Allen, 1976).
Middlebrook, Martin, *Your Country Needs You: From Six to Sixty Five Divisions* (Barnsley: Leo Cooper, 2000).
Miller, Carman, *Painting the Map Red: Canada and the South African War 1899–1902* (Montreal: Canadian War Museum, 1993).
Miller, Stephen M., 'In Support of the "Imperial Mission"? Volunteering for the South African War 1899–1902', *The Journal of Military History*, Volume 69, Number 3, July 2005.
——, *Lord Methuen and the British Army: Failure and Redemption in South Africa* (London: Frank Cass, 1999).
——, 'Slogging Across the Veldt: British Volunteers and the Guerrilla Phase of the South African War, 1899–1902', *The Journal of the Society for Army Historical Research*, Volume 84, Number 338, Summer 2006.
Millman, Brock, *Pessimism and British War Policy 1916–1918* (London: Frank Cass, 2001).
Mollo, Boris, *The Kent Yeomanry* (Stroud: Tempus, 2006).
Morton, Desmond, *A Military History of Canada: From Champlain to Kosovo* (Toronto: McClelland and Stewart, 1999).
——, *When Your Number's Up: The Canadian Soldier in the First World War* (Toronto: Random House, 1993).
Morris, Donald R., *The Washing of the Spears: a History of the Rise of the Zulu Nation under Shaka and its Fall in the Zulu War of 1879* (London: Jonathan Cape, 1966).
Mosier, John, *The Myth of the Great War: A New Military History of World War One* (New York, HarperCollins, 2001).
Nasson, Bill, 'Africans at War', in Gooch, John (ed.), *The Boer War: Direction, Experience and Image* (London: Cassell, 2000).
——, *Britannia's Empire: A Short History of the British Empire* (London: Tempus, 2006).
——, *The South African War 1899–1902* (London: Arnold, 1999).
Newman, Bernard, *Speaking From Memory* (London: Jenkins, 1960).
Nicholls, Jonathan, *Cheerful Sacrifice: The Battle of Arras 1917* (Barnsley: Pen and Sword, [1990] 2005).
Norman, Terry, *The Hell They Called High Wood* (London: William Kimber, 1984).
Packenham, Thomas, *The Boer War* (London: The Folio Society, [1979] 1999).
Palazzo, Albert, *Seeking Victory on the Western Front: the British Army and Chemical Warfare in World War I* (Lincoln NA: University of Nabraska Press, 2000).
Panichas, George A. (ed.), *Promise of Greatness: the War of 1914–1918* (London: Cassell, 1968).
Paret, Peter (ed.), *Makers of Modern Strategy: From Machiavelli to the Nuclear Age* (Oxford: Clarendon Press, 1990).
Pelling, Henry, *Popular Politics and Society in Late Victorian Britain* (London: Macmillan, 1968).
Pemberton, W. Baring, *Battles of the Boer War* (London: Pan 1964).

Phillips, Gervase, 'Douglas Haig and the Development of Twentieth Century Cavalry', *Archives: The Journal of the British Records Association*, Volume 28, Number 108, April 2003.

——, 'The Obsolescence of the *Arme Blanche* and Technological Determinism in British Military History', *War in History*, Volume 9, Number 39, 2002.

——, 'Scapegoat Arm: Twentieth Century Cavalry in Anglophone Historiography', *The Journal of Military History*, Volume 70, Number 1, January 2007.

Piekalkiewicz, Janusz, *The Cavalry of World War II* (London: Orbis, 1979).

Pooley, Colin and Jean Turnbull, *Migration and Mobility in Britain Since the 18th Century* (London: Lancaster University Press, 1998).

Powell, Geoffrey, *Buller: A Scapegoat? A Life of General Sir Redvers Buller VC 1839–1908* (London: Leo Cooper, 1994).

——, *Plumer: The Soldiers' General – A Biography of Field Marshal Viscount Plumer of Messines* (London: Pen and Sword [1990] 2004).

Pretorius, Fransjohan, *The Great Escape of the Boer Pimpernel: Christiaan de Wet, the Making of a Legend* (Pietermaritzburg: University of Natal Press, 2001).

——, *Life on Commando during the Anglo-Boer War, 1899–1902* (Cape Town: Human and Rousseau, 1999).

Price, Richard, *An Imperial War and the British Working Class: Working Class Attitudes and Reactions to the Boer War 1899–1902* (London: Routledge and Kegan Paul, 1972).

Prior, Robin and Trevor Wilson, *Command on the Western Front: The Military Career of Sir Henry Rawlinson* (Oxford: Blackwell, 1992).

——, *Passchendaele: The Untold Story* (New Haven NJ: Yale University Press, 1996).

——, *The Somme* (New Haven NJ: Yale University Press, 2005).

Rawling, Bill, *Surviving Trench Warfare: Technology and the Canadian Corps 1914–18* (Toronto: University of Toronto Press, 1992).

Reader, W.J., *'At Duty's Call': A Study in Obsolete Patriotism* (Manchester: Manchester University Press, 1988).

Reid, Walter, *Architect of Victory: Douglas Haig* (Edinburgh: Berlinn, 2006).

Reynolds, E.G.B. *The Lee-Enfield Rifle* (London: Herbert Jenkins, 1960).

Riedi, Eliza, 'Brains or Polo? Equestrian Sport, Army Reform and the Gentlemanly Officer Tradition, 1900–1914', *Journal of the Society for Army Historical Research*, Volume 84, Number 339, Autumn 2006.

Rickey, Don Jr., *Forty Miles a Day on Beans and Hay: the Enlisted Soldier Fighting the Indian Wars* (Norman: University of Oklahoma Press, 1963).

Robbins, Simon, *British Generalship on the Western Front 1914–18: Defeat Into Victory* (London: Routledge, 2005).

——, 'Henry Horne', in Beckett, Ian F.W. and Steven J. Corvi (eds), *Haig's Generals* (London: Pen and Sword, 2006).

Rodger, N.A.M., *The Wooden World: An Anatomy of the Georgian Navy* (London: Fontana, [1986] 1988).

Rogers, H.C.B., *The Mounted Troops of the British Army 1066–1945* (London: Seely Service, 1959).

Samuels, Martin, *Command or Control? Command, Training and Tactics in the British and German Armies, 1888–1918* (London: Frank Cass, 1995).
Sandys, Celia, *Churchill Wanted Dead or Alive* (London: HarperCollins, 1999).
Scales, Robert H., *Certain Victory: The US Army in the Gulf War* (Washington DC: Brassey's, 1994).
Schreiber, Shane B., *Shock Army of the British Empire: The Canadian Corps in the Last 100 Days of the Great War* (London: Praeger, 1997).
Searle, G.R., *A New England? Peace and War 1886–1918* (Oxford: Oxford University Press, 2004).
Selby, John, *The Boer War: A Study in Cowardice and Courage* (London: Barker, 1969).
Sheffield, G.D., *Leadership in the Trenches: Officer–Man Relations, Morale and Discipline in the British Army in the Era of the First World War* (London: Macmillan, 2000).
Sheffield, Gary, *Forgotten Victory – The First World War: Myths and Realities* (London: Headline, 2001).
——, *The Somme* (London: Cassell, 2003).
——, 'The Impact of Two Revolutions 1789–1898', in Trew, Simon and Gary Sheffield (eds), *100 Years of Conflict 1900–2000* (Thrupp: Sutton, 2000).
Sheffield, Gary and Helen McCartney, 'Hubert Gough', in Beckett, Ian F.W. and Steven J. Corvi (eds), *Haig's Generals* (London: Pen and Sword, 2006).
Sheffield, Gary and Dan Todman (eds), *Command and Control on the Western Front: the British Army's Experience 1914–18* (Staplehurst: Spellmount, 2004).
Sheffy, Yigal, *British Military Intelligence in the Palestine Campaign 1914–1918* (London: Frank Cass, 1998).
Showalter, Dennis, 'The Prusso-German RMA 1840–1871', in Knox, MacGregor and Williamson Murray (eds), *The Dynamics of Military Revolution 1300–2050* (Cambridge: Cambridge University Press, 2001).
Simkins, Peter, *Kitchener's Army: The Raising of the New Armies, 1914–16* (Manchester: Manchester University Press, 1988).
Simpkin, Richard, *Race to the Swift: Thoughts on Twenty-First Century Warfare* (London: Brassey's, 1985).
Simpson, Andy, *Directing Operations: British Corps Command on the Western Front 1914–18* (Stroud: Spellmount, 2006).
Simpson, Keith, 'The Reputation of Sir Douglas Haig', in Bond, Brian (ed.) *The First World War and British Military History* (Oxford: Clarendon Press, 1991).
Skelley, Alan Ramsey, *The Victorian Army at Home: The Recruitment and Terms and Conditions of the British Regular 1859–1899* (London: Croom Helm, 1977).
Smith, Neil C., *Men of Beersheba: a History of the 4th Light Horse Regiment 1914–1919* (Melbourne: Mostly Unsung Military History Research and Publications, 1993).
Smithers, A.J., *Cambrai, The First Great Tank Battle* (London: Leo Cooper, 1992).
Spence, Iain G., '"To Shoot and to Ride": Mobility and Firepower in Mounted Warfare', in Dennis, Peter and Jeffrey Grey (eds), *The Boer War: Army, Nation and Empire* (Canberra: Army History Unit, 2000).

Spiers, Edward M., 'Campaigning under Kitchener', in Spiers, Edward M. (ed.) *Sudan: The Reconquest Reappraised* (London: Frank Cass, 1998).
——, *Haldane: An Army Reformer* (Edinburgh: Edinburgh University Press, 1980).
——, *The Late Victorian Army 1868–1902* (Manchester: Manchester University Press, 1992).
——, 'Rearming the Edwardian Artillery', *Journal of the Society for Army Historical Research*, Volume LVII, Number 231, 1979.
——, *The Victorian Soldier in Africa* (Manchester: Manchester University Press, 2004).
Spiers, Edward M. (ed.) *Sudan: The Reconquest Reappraised* (London: Frank Cass, 1998).
Starr, Stephen Z., *The Union Cavalry in the Civil War*, 3 Volumes, (Baton Rouge LA: Louisiana University Press, 1979–85).
Stephen, Martin, *The Price of Pity: Poetry, History and Myth in the Great War* (London: Leo Cooper, 1996).
Steiner, Zara S., *Britain and the Origins of the First World War* (London: Macmillan, 1977).
Stevenson, David, *1914–1918: The History of the First World War* (London: Allen Lane, 2004).
Stewart, A.T.Q., *The Pagoda War: Lord Dufferin and the Fall of the Kingdom of Ava 1885–6* (Newton Abbot: Victorian and Modern History Book Club, 1974).
——, *The Ulster Crisis* (London: Faber and Faber, 1967).
Stone, David, *First Reich: Inside the German Army During the War with France 1870–71* (London: Brassey's, 2002).
Stone, Norman, *The Eastern Front 1914–1917* (London: Hodder and Stoughton, 1975).
Strachan, Hew, 'The British Army, its General Staff and the Continental Commitment, 1904–14', in French, David and Brian Holden Reid (eds.), *The British General Staff: Reform and Innovation 1890–1939* (London: Frank Cass, 2002).
——, *European Armies and the Conduct of War* (London: George Allen and Unwin, 1983).
——, *The First World War: Volume I: To Arms* (Oxford: Oxford University Press, 2001).
——, *From Waterloo to Balaclava: Tactics, Technology and the British Army 1815–1854* (Cambridge: Cambridge University Press, 1985).
——, *The Politics of the British Army* (Oxford: Clarendon Press, 1997).
——, *Wellington's Legacy: The Reform of the British Army 1830–54* (Manchester: Manchester University Press, 1984).
Steel, Nigel and Peter Hart, *Defeat at Gallipoli* (London: Papermac, [1994] 1995).
Surridge, Keith Terrance, *Managing the South African War, 1899–1902: Politicians v. Generals* (London: The Royal Historical Society, 1998).
Taylor, A.J.P., *The First World War: An Illustrated History* (London, Penguin, [1963] 1966).
Terraine, John, *Douglas Haig: the Educated Soldier* (London: Leo Cooper, 2nd Edition, 1990).

——, *The Road to Passchendaele – The Flanders Offensive of 1917: A Study in Inevitability* (London: Leo Cooper, 1977).

——, *The Smoke and the Fire: Myths and Anti-Myths of War 1861–1945* (London: Leo Cooper, 1980).

——, *To Win a War: 1918 The Year of Victory* (London: Cassell, 2003).

——, *White Heat: The New Warfare 1914–18* (London: Book Club Associates, 1982).

Thompson, Rob, 'Mud, Blood and Wood: BEF Operational and Combat Logistico-Engineering during the Battle of Third Ypres 1917', in Doyle, Peter and Matthew R. Bennett (eds), *Fields of Battle: Terrain in Military History* (London: Kluwer, 2002).

Todman, Dan, *The Great War: Myth and Memory* (London: Hambledon and London, 2005).

Travers, T.H.E., 'Future Warfare: H.G. Wells and British Military Theory 1895–1916', in Bond, Brian and Ian Roy (eds), *War and Society: A Yearbook of Military History* (New York: Holmes and Meier, 1975).

Travers, Tim, *Gallipoli 1915* (Stroud: Tempus, 2001).

——, *How the War was Won: Factors that Led to Victory in World War One* (London: Pen and Sword, 2005).

——, *The Killing Ground: The British Army, The Western Front and the Emergence of Modern Warfare 1900–1918* (London: Unwin Hyman, 1990).

Trythall, Anthony John, *'Bony' Fuller: the Intellectual General 1878–1966* (London: Cassell, 1977).

Tylden, G., *Horses and Saddlery* (London: J. Allen, 1965).

Urwin, Gregory J.W., *The United States Cavalry: An Illustrated History* (Poole: Blandford, 1983).

Vagts, Alfred, *A History of Militarism: Civilian and Military* (London: Hollis and Carter, 1959).

van der Waag, Ian, 'South Africa and the Boer Military System', in Dennis, Peter and Jeffrey Grey (eds), *The Boer War: Army, Nation and Empire* (Canberra: Army History Unit, 2000).

Wavell, Archibald, *Allenby: A Study in Greatness – The Biography of Field Marshal Viscount Allenby of Megiddo and Felixstowe* (London: George G. Harrap, 1940).

Wawro, Geoffrey, *The Austro-Prussian War: Austria's War with Prussia and Italy in 1866* (Cambridge: Cambridge University Press, 1996).

——, *The Franco-Prussian War: The German Conquest of France in 1870–1871* (Cambridge: Cambridge University Press, 2003).

Wessels, André, 'Afrikaners at War', in Gooch, John (ed.), *The Boer War: Direction, Experience and Image* (London: Cassell, 2000).

Whitmarsh, Andrew, 'British Army Manoeuvres and the Development of Military Aviation 1910–1913', *War in History*, Volume 14, Number 3, 2007.

Wilkinson, Glenn R., *Depictions and Images of War in Edwardian Newspapers, 1899–1914* (London: Palgrave Macmillan, 2003).

Wilkinson-Latham, R.J., *From Our Special Correspondent: Victorian War Correspondents and their Campaigns* (London: Hodder and Stoughton, 1979).

Williams, Geoffrey, *Byng of Vimy: General and Governor General* (London: Leo Cooper, 1983).

Wolff, Leon, *In Flanders Fields* (London: Longmans, Green, 1959).

Woodhall, Robert, 'The Abolition of Purchase in the British Army', *History Today*, Volume XXIX, October 1979.

Woodham Smith, Cecil, *The Reason Why* (London: Constable, 1953).

Woodward, David, *Hell in the Holy Land: World War I in the Middle East* (Lexington KY: University Press of Kentucky, 2006).

——, *Lloyd George and the Generals* (Newark NJ: University of Delaware Press, 1983).

Woolcombe, Robert, *The First Tank Battle: Cambrai 1917* (London: Arthur Barker, 1967).

Index

Note: bold entries indicate figures

Afghan War, Second (1878–80)
    9, 38, 53–4, 58
Afghanistan 5, 64
aircraft 236–8, 244
Akers-Douglas Committee 158, 159, 188–9
Alderson, Edwin 56, 113, 159
Aleppo 300
Alexander the Great 4
Alexander of Teck, see Athlone, Earl of
Alexandra, Queen 159
Allan-Williams, A.C. 29
Allenby, Edmund
    and Boer War 88, 103, 122, 128
    post-Boer War and Roberts era
        145, 147, 156, 180
    under Haldane 198, 200, 201, 202, 205
        and *War and the Arme Blanche*
            episode 225, 226
    pre-First World War 229, 235
    and First World War 196,
        241, 260, 261, 262
        commencement of 239, 240–41
        Palestine 283–8 *passim*,
            298, 302, 305
        Western Front (1914) 242–7 *passim*
        Western Front (deadlock)
            250, 251, 255–6, 280
American Civil War (1861–65) 23n99, 24,
    42–7, 65–6, 67, 122, 171, 174
    Shenandoah Valley campaign (1862) 42
Amery, Leopold 81, 97, 107, 111, 116,
    122, 146, 148–9, 187, 220
Andrew, A.W. 151
Antwerp 239
Arabi, Said Ahmed (Pasha) 58, 59
Arnold-Forster, H.O. 144, 182–3, 185, 195
Ashanti Ring, see Wolseley Ring
Ashanti War (1873–74) 35, 38
Asquith, Herbert 195n29, 260, 276
Athlone, Earl of 155n62
Auftragstaktik 21, 267
Australia 37, 38
Austro-Prussian War (1866) 36, 47–8

BATTLES
    Custoza (1866) 47, 48
    Königgrätz (1866) 47, 48
        Stresetice, charge at 47
automobiles 235–6

Babington, James 100
Baden-Powell, Baden 167
Baden-Powell, Robert 61, 69
    and Boer War 87
    post-Boer War and Roberts era 166–7,
        175, 177, 181, 184, 188, 189, 190
Baird, Harry 255
Balfour, Arthur 187
Bankkop, see Boer War: BATTLES
    (Onverwacht [1902])
Bannerman-Philips, H. 236–7
Bapaume 272
Barnett, Correlli 307
Barrow, George 77
    post-Boer War and Roberts era 179, 180
    and Russo-Japanese War 194
    under Haldane 199–200, 201,
        202, 207, 211, 214, 227
    and First World War 196, 261, 263,
        284, 286, 287, 300, 301
Basutoland 84
Battersby, H.F. Prevost, see Prevost
    Battersby, H.F.
Battine, Cecil 216, 226
Bazaine, François-Achille 171
Beaufort, Duke of 161–2
Beersheba, Battle of, see First World
    War: Palestine: BATTLES
    (Gaza, Third Battle of [1917])
Belgium 243
Bentinck, Charles (Lord) 162, 163n112
Bernhardi, Frederick von 215–16,
    220–21, 226–7, 228
Bethune, Edward
    and Boer War 93n59
    post-Boer War and Roberts era 145
    under Haldane 213

bicycles 76–7, 234–5, 236
Bingham, Cecil 72, 103, 206, 270
Birch, Noel 202, 261n117
Birdwood, William 11, 58
   and Boer War 85, 93, 107, 124
   and First World War 260, 261n117, 262
Blériot, Louis 236
Bloemfontein 85, 91, 97, 105, 106,
      108, 110–11, 113, 114–15,
      118, 119, 148, 149, 167
Boer War (1899–1902) 1n2, 7, 12, 16, 20,
      26, 29, 37, 81, 171, 187, 236
   planning for 82–3
   theatre of 84–5
   early battles of 87–8, 89, 91–2, 224–5
   guerrilla phase 122–7
   reactions to/interpretation
      of 147–53, 224–5
   BATTLES
   Bakenlaagte (1901) 128, 164
   Bakenlop (1900) 116
   Belmont (1899) 92
   Blood River Poort (1901) 128
   Boschmanskop (1902) 129
   Colenso (1899) 26, 92–3, 96
   Diamond Hill (1900) 81, 121,
      122, 148, 149, 152
   Elandslaagte (1899) 29, 89,
      92, 120, 150, 173
   Graspan (1899) 92
   Kimberley, siege and relief of
      (1899–1900) 81, 87, 97, 100,
      101–5, 107, 109, 110, 111,
      115, 117, 118, 146, 210
      Klip Drift, charge at (1900) 16,
         89, 102–4, 105, 173, 221
   Ladysmith, siege and relief of
      (1899–1900) 87, 90, 92,
      97, 107–8, 111, 155
   Lindley (1900) 111
   Mafeking, siege and relief of
      (1899–1900) 87, 122
   Magersfontein (1899) 92
   Modder River (1899) 92,
      99–100, 101, 122
   Onverwacht (1902) 129
   Paardeberg Drift (1900) 104–8,
      110, 116, 146, 153
   Poplar Grove (1900) 108–9, 110,
      115, 116, 117, 146, 149, 154
   Reddersburg (1900) 113

   Rooiwal (1902) 129
   Spion Kop (1900) 92
   Stormberg (1899) 92
   Talana Hill (1899) 89, 114
   Tweebosch (1902) 129
   Vlakfontein (1901) 128
   Zand River (1900) 119–21
Boer War, First (1880–81), see
      Transvaal War
Bonar Law, Andrew, see Law,
      Andrew Bonar
Bond, Brian 15
Bower, J. 13
Brabazon, John 100, 111, 122, 168
Brackenbury, Henry 40, 62, 65, 73, 75
Bredow, Friedrich von 17, 75, 180
Bridges, G.T.M. 93, 190, 208,
      228, 260, 261, 278
Briggs, Charles 205, 214, 261
Broadwood, Robert
   and Boer War 101, 104, 117
   post-Boer War and Roberts
      era 159, 177, 190
   under Haldane 205
   and First World War 265
Brodrick, St John 195
   and Boer War 124, 126
   post-Boer War and Roberts
      era 144, 154, 161
Buller, Redvers 54, 71, 74–5, 77
   and Boer War 83, 84, 87, 90, 92–3,
      97, 99, 107, 111, 118, 119
   post-Boer War and Roberts era 146, 152
Burma 71
Burmese War, Third (1885–86) 38
Butler, Lady 17
Byng, Julian 60
   and Boer War 84, 108, 122, 123
   post-Boer War and Roberts
      era 156, 177, 189
   under Haldane 200, 205, 210
   and First World War 260, 261, 262, 264
      Western Front (1914) 247
      Western Front (deadlock) 256,
         265, 275, 288, 290, 291, 292
      Western Front (Hundred Days
         campaign) 298, 299

Callwell, Charles 39, 152, 191, 208–9, 238
Cambridge, Duke of 8, 40, 50, 51,
      52, 59, 60, 62, 74, 76, 155

Canada 37, 38
Cape Colony 13, 37, 84, 87, 89,
    91, 110, 117, 123
Cape Frontier Wars (1779–1877) 14
Cape Town 57, 85, 88, 90, 96,
    97, 100, 106, 111
Cardigan, Lord 22
Cardwell, Edward 5, 21, 36,
    37, 39, 40, 52, 59
  see also Cardwell–Childers reforms
Cardwell–Childers reforms 5, 21,
    36–7, 39, 40, 50–53, 59, 67
Carnarvon Commission 37
Carnoy Valley **136**
cars, see automobiles
cavalry raid 5, 43, 46, 48, 69, 106,
    194, 234, 251–2, 254
Cavalry Schools
  Netheravon 189–90, 203, 214, 230, 274
  Saugor 190, 220
Cavalry Tracks 271
Cavan, Lord 260, 270, 306
Cecil, R.E. 200
Chamberlain, Joseph 83–4
charges 5, 11, 14, 15–20, 41,
    72–3, 75, 116, 173
  and American Civil War
    42–7, 65, 171, 174
  and Austro-Prussian and Franco-
    Prussian wars 47–8, 66,
    152, 171, 174, 180
  in Egyptian Expedition 59, 62
  in Gordon Relief Expedition 60, 62
  in Boer War 89, 103–5, 120–22,
    127–9, 148, 150, 152, 164,
    171, 173, 221, 226
  post-Boer War and Roberts era 147,
    149, 151–3, 154, 166, 168, 169,
    171, 173, 174, 180, 181, 186
  and Russo-Japanese War 192–4, 221
  disputes under Haldane **134**, 196–7,
    202, 210, 214–15, 218–20
  and *War and the Arme Blanche*
    episode 220–28
  pre-First World War **134**, 229
  in First World War **137**, 206,
    243–5, 274–5, 286, 287,
    294, 296, 299, 300–302
  accounts of 26–34
  formations in 17–18

knee-to-knee 15, 18, 77–8, 116,
    147, 152, 186, 222
  and Yeomanry 218–20, 232
Charrington, H.V.S. 303
Charteris, John 180, 220
Chauvel, Harry 112, 113
  and First World War 250,
    283, 286, 287, 301
Chaytor, Edward 284, 301
Chelmsford, Lord 55
Chesham, Lord 111
Chesney, C.C. 43
Chetwode, Philip 22–3, 72
  under Haldane 206
  and *War and the Arme
    Blanche* episode 226
  and First World War 256, 261, 264
  Palestine 283–7 *passim*, 301
  Western Front (1914) 244, 245
Childers, Erskine
  and Boer War 116–17, 120, 128
  and Russo-Japanese War 191, 192
  under Haldane 210, 212, 216
  and *War and the Arme
    Blanche* 220–28
Childers, Hugh 5, 36, 39, 40
  see also Cardwell–Childers reforms
Churchill, Winston 18, 19, 68, 191
  and Boer War 97, 100, 107–8,
    115–16, 121, 122
  post-Boer War and Roberts era
    147–8, 151, 158–9
  pre-First World War 231
  and First World War 234, 292, 304–5
CID, see Committee for Imperial Defence
Clausewitz, Carl von 266
Clery, Francis 41, 49
Cochrane, Lord, see Dundonald, Earl of
Colenso 85
  see also under Boer War: BATTLES
Colesburg 85, 89
Collapse Theory 288
Colley, George Pomeroy, see
    Pomeroy-Colley, George
Committee for Imperial Defence
    (CID) 144, 182, 220
Commonwealth Defence Act (1903) 165
Conan Doyle, Arthur 93, 97,
    148, 151, 164, 224
Connaught, Duke of 8, 50, 199, 210, 217
Conneau (General) 256

Crimean War (1854–56) 22,
    23n99, 36, 48, 51, 174
  BATTLES
    Balaklava (1854), charge of the
      Light Brigade at 17, 18, 22, 27
Cronjé, Piet 100, 101, 104–6, 111, 146, 153
Curragh Incident (1914) 195n29,
    208, 240, 251
Curzon, Lord 145, 277, 293

Damascus **137**, 300, 301
Dardanelles, *see* First World War:
    Gallipoli campaign
De Aar Junction 85, 88, 98
de la Rey, J.H. 'Koos' 129
Denison, George 44–5, 65, 222
Derby, Lord 281
Desborough, Lord 233
doctrine
  definition of 3–4
  military history and 4
  see also structure and organisation,
    tactics, weaponry
Douglas, Charles 188, 225
  pre-First World War 230
Dundonald, Earl of (Lord Cochrane) 61, 69
  and Boer War 92–3, 107–8, 112, 124
  post-Boer War and Roberts era 155,
    160–61, 163, 164–5, 166, 175
Durban 85

East India Company 10, 11
Edmonds, James 16, 32, 197, 201,
    297, 300, 304, 306
Edward VII, King 8, 11, 12, 154,
    162, 173, 175, 183, 185
Egypt 6, 11–12, 196
  Egyptian Expedition (1882) 7,
    18, 19, 38, 39, 58–60, 172
  Gordon Relief Expedition (1884–85)
    39, 60–62, 71
  and First World War 249,
    250, 277, 281, 282
Egyptian Expedition (1882) 7, 18,
    19, 38, 39, 58–60, 172
  BATTLES
    Kassassin (1882) 18, 59
    Mahsama (1882) 19
    Tel-el-Kebir (1882) 59
Elgin, Lord 81

Elgin Commission 81, 98, 122, 127,
    144, 159, 167–70, 198, 227
Enslin, Battle of, *see* Boer War:
    BATTLES (Graspan [1899])
Erroll, Earl of 240
  and Boer War 101, 105, 111
Esher, Lord 168, 183–4, 199, 204, 224
Esher Committee 144, 181–2
Ewart, Spencer 227

Falkenhayn, Eric von 243
Falls, Cyril 22
Fane, Vere 300
Fanshawe, Hugh 240, 261
Fergusson, Charles 280
First World War
  cavalry contribution in 26,
    27–8, 241–2, 303–7
  senior officers 260–64
  commencement of 239–41
  Eastern Front 243, 276
  Gallipoli campaign 156, 240n6,
    242, 249, 260, 264
  Mesopotamia 242, 260
  Palestine 16, 20, 28, 29, 242,
    249, 256, 261, 278, 283–8,
    293, 299, 300–302, 305
  BATTLES
    El Mughar, charge at (1917) 287
    Gaza, Third Battle of (1917) **139**,
      283, 284, 286–8, 298, 302
    Huj, charge at (1917) 29, 34, 287
    Jerusalem, capture of (1917)
      287, 288, 292
    Megiddo (1918) 300–302
      Afuleh, charge at 300–301
  Salonika 242, 260, 261
  Western Front
    Armistice 299, 300, 306
    British performance on
      21, 23, 264–70
    cavalry's contribution on 16, 30–34,
      240, 242, 262, 263, 303–7
    1914 campaign 242–8
    deadlock 248–60, 268–70,
      270–76, 276–83, 288–92
    Hundred Days campaign
      295–300
    Germans on 21, 30–31, 242
    1914 campaign 243–8 *passim*

deadlock 275, 279, 283, 288, 290, 291
Kaiserschlacht offensive 23, 32–4, 258, 293, 294, 295
Hundred Days campaign 295, 299
Hindenburg Line 244, 279, 295
BATTLES
Aisne (1914) 246
Amiens (1918) 31–2, 255, 259, 260, 295–7, 300, 302
Arras (1917) 250, 260, 265, 275, 279–80, 282, 289
Monchy-le-Preux 275, 279, 280
Aubers Ridge (1915) 256
Audregnies, charge at (1914) 244
Béthune, charge near (1914) 247
Cambrai (1917) 275, 279, 282, 288–92, 295, 298
Cerizy, charge at (1914) 246
Festubert (1915) 256
Haelen (1914) 243
Le Cateau (1914) 245, 299
Loos (1915) 256, 257, 260
Marne (1914) 246
Mons, Battle of and Retreat from (1914) 218, 241, 244, 245, 248, 304
Moreuil Wood, charge at (1918) 32–4, 294
Nery (1914) 246
Neuve Chapelle (1915) 253–6 *passim*, 264, 271, 280, 289
Nivelle Offensive (1917) 256, 277
Somme (1916) 1, 25, 31, 202, 229, 266–76 *passim*, 280, 295, 305
Flers-Courcelette 305
High Wood 30–31, 34, 273–4, 276, 305
Ypres, First Battle of ('Wipers') (1914) 247–8, 249, 252, 263
Messines 248
Mont des Cats 247
Ypres, Third Battle of (Passchendaele) (1917) 250, 264, 277, 281–2, 283, 295
Menin Road Ridge 250, 282
Flowerdew, Gordon 33–4
Foch, Ferdinand 304
Forbes, Archibald 27
Forester, C.S. 306

France 196, 214
Franco-Prussian War (1870–71) 17, 36, 42, 47–8, 66, 152, 171, 174, 269
BATTLES
Gravelotte (1870) 47, 48
Mars-la-Tour (1870) 27, 47
Prussian 'Death Ride' charge at 17, 47, 50, 75, 171, 174, 180
Metz, siege of (1870) 47
Sedan (1870) 48
Franks, George 299
Fraser, James Keith 15, 60, 61, 64, 65–7, 71, 73, 74, 77
French, John 3, 16, 26, 29, 51, 61, 71–2, 74–5, 77
and Boer War 82, 83, 89, 92, 99, 100–101, 101–104, 105, 106–7, 108–9, 110, 113–16, 117–20, 122–4
post-Boer War and Roberts era 146, 149, 150–51, 154–8 *passim*, 161, 162, 165–73 *passim*, 175–6, 177, 182–5, 186–8
under Haldane 197, 198, 199–206 *passim*, 210, 213, 216, 218
and *War and the Arme Blanche* episode 221–2, 223, 224
pre-First World War 230, 231
and First World War 260, 261, 287, 303–4, 306
commencement of 239–41
Western Front (1914) 248
Western Front (deadlock) 253, 254, 255–6, 257
Froneman, C.C. 103
Fuller, J.F.C. 4
and First World War 234, 267, 280, 282, 288, 290, 296

Gap Scheme 251–2, 253, 256, 257, 264, 270–71, 280, 295, 301
Gatacre, William 92
General Staff 40, 50, 70, 97, 154, 181
under Haldane 195, 196, 226, 227
and *War and the Arme Blanche* episode 226
George V, King 240, 255, 269
Germany 39, 195–6, 214, 273
Godley, Alexander 162, 163n112, 168
Goldmann, Charles S. 118, 148, 190, 216
Gordon, James 150

Gordon Relief Expedition (1884–85)
39, 60–62, 71
BATTLES
Abu Klea (1885) 61
Gough, Hubert 21, 23, 77, 152
and Boer War 93, 107–8, 122, 128–9
post-Boer War and Roberts era
155, 156, 158, 181
under Haldane 200–201, 205, 214
and *War and the Arme
Blanche* episode 225
and First World War 260, 261, 262, 263
commencement of 240
Western Front (1914) 245
Western Front (deadlock)
252, 253, 264, 265, 267,
270–73, 275, 282, 295
Western Front (Kaiserschlacht
offensive) 294, 295
Gough, John 201
and First World War 245, 252
and *War and the Arme Blanche*
episode 223, 227
Grainger, P.Y. 10, 143, 177
Grant, Henry 163, 166, 168
Grant Committee 163, 168, 169
Graves, Robert 306
Greenly, W.H. 294
Grenfell, Julian 233
Grierson, James 18
and Boer War 96–7
under Haldane 197, 204, 205
pre-First World War 237
and First World War 239

Haig, Dorothy (Lady) 159–60, 197
Haig, Douglas 3, 12, 18, 19, 26,
29, 51, 71–3, 74–5, 77
and Boer War 83, 88, 89–90, 92,
100–101, 103, 105, 106–7, 110, 113,
114, 116, 118, 119, 122–3, 127
post-Boer War and Roberts era 145,
149–50, 151, 155, 156–8, 159, 160,
161, 164, 165, 166, 168, 170, 173,
174–7, 179–81, 183, 186, 190
under Haldane 194, 195–206 *passim*,
210, 211–12, 216–17, 218, 220
and *War and the Arme Blanche*
episode 221, 225, 226, 227
pre-First World War 229, 232, 235

and First World War **141**, 229, 241,
260–62 *passim*, 304, 305, 306
commencement of 239–40
Western Front (1914) 244–8 *passim*
Western Front (deadlock) 253–7
passim, 264–70 *passim*, 270–74,
275–83 *passim*, 289–95 *passim*
Western Front (Kaiserschlacht
offensive) 294, 295
Western Front (Hundred Days
campaign) 295–300 *passim*
Haig Committee 160
Haking, Richard 225, 262
Haldane, Richard Burdon (Lord) 36, 71
reforms under 195–9, 217–18, 234, 236
Hale, Lonsdale 107, 198, 211
Hallam Parr, Henry 152
Hamilton, Ian 3, 26, 70, 265
and Boer War 85, 89, 97, 110–11,
113, 115–16, 117, 118, 120,
121, 123, 124, 126, 128
post-Boer War and Roberts era
147, 148–9, 150, 155, 156–7,
162, 163, 164, 169–70, 171,
172, 182, 185–6, 188
and Russo-Japanese War 191–2, 228
under Haldane 204, 205, 206,
212, 218, 225, 228
and War and the Arme
Blanche episode 225
and First World War 260, 263, 264
commencement of 239–40
Hamley, Edward 45
Hampton, Lord 285, 287
Hannay, Ormelie 104
Hart, Basil Liddell, *see* Liddell Hart, Basil
Hartington Commission 40
Havelock, Harry 14, 44–5, 222, 303
Henderson, G.F.R. 1, 3, 4, 48,
49, 70, 221, 304
and American Civil War 42, 45–6
and Boer War 82, 104
post-Boer War and Roberts
era 147, 152–3
Hodgson, Henry 28, 284, 286–7, 301, 302
Home, Archibald 31, 240
and Boer War 129
post-Roberts 194
pre-First World War 233
and First World War 261, 262
Western Front (1914) 248

Western Front (deadlock) 251–2, 254, 257, 268, 275, 278, 283, 292, 294
Western Front (Kaiserschlacht offensive) 294
Western Front (Hundred Days campaign) 295, 296, 297
Horne, Henry
  and Boer War 85, 122
  under Haldane 202
  and First World War 261, 262, 263
Howard-Vyse, Richard 286
Howell, Philip 255
Hutton, Edward 13, 56, 59, 60, 62, 63, 65–7, 74, 301
  and Boer War 84, 88, 113–14, 119–20, 123
  post-Boer War and Roberts era 154, 156, 162, 165–6, 174–5
  under Haldane 216

India 5, 6, 10–11
  garrisoning of 35, 40, 144, 195
Indian Mutiny (1857–59) 14, 35, 101
Italy 260

Jackson, Thomas 'Stonewall' 42
Jameson, Henrietta 19, 71, 90, 92, 103, 110, 113, 118, 119, 157–8, 197
Jenin 301
Jerusalem 300
Jessel, Herbert (Lord) 171–2
Joffre, Joseph **141**, 270, 279
Johannesburg 81, 85, 119
Jomini, (Antoine) Henri 3, 258

Kavanagh, Charles
  under Haldane 205, 207
  pre-First World War 230
  First World War
    Western Front (deadlock) 275–6, 278, 282–3, 294, 295
    Western Front (Kaiserschlacht offensive) 295
    Western Front (Hundred Days campaign) 296
Keith Fraser, James, *see* Fraser, James Keith
Kelly-Kenny, Thomas 108, 119
Kemp, J.C.G. 128, 129, 164
Kenyon, David 274
Kerry, Earl of 111

Kiggell, Launcelot 225, 271
Kimberley 85, 92
  see also under Boer War: BATTLES
Kipling, Rudyard 97, 98, 154
Kitchener, Herbert 12, 19, 51, 52, 79, 81
  and Boer War 88, 92, 96, 97, 98, 99, 101, 104–6, 107, 117, 118, 119, 124, 125–6, 128, 129
  post-Boer War and Roberts era 145, 147, 155, 157, 158, 166, 167, 169, 171, 173, 175–80 *passim*, 183, 186–7
  under Haldane 199, 204
  and First World War
    commencement of 239–40
    Western Front (deadlock) 254, 255
Kraft, Karl (Prince) 50, 164
Kroonstadt 112
Kruger, Paul 110, 115

Ladysmith 85
  see also under Boer War: BATTLES
Laing's Nek 85, 152
  see also under Transvaal War: BATTLES
Lake, Percy 260
Lansdowne, Lord
  and Boer War 93–4, 96, 97, 99, 102, 105, 106, 109, 110, 111, 114, 116, 117
  post-Boer War and Roberts era 149, 182–3
Law, Andrew Bonar 260
Lawrence, Herbert 261, 262
Liddell Hart, Basil 270, 305
Liman von Sanders, Otto 302
Lisle, (Henry) Beauvoir de 21, 69, 72
  and Boer War 113, 121, 124
  post-Boer War and Roberts era 155, 156, 159, 176, 181
  post-Roberts 193
  under Haldane 203–4, 212, 233
  and *War and the Arme Blanche* episode 226
  and First World War 244–5, 261n117
Lloyd George, David **141**, 270, 276, 277, 278, 288, 292, 293, 305–6
Localisation Act (1872) 36
Luck, George 67, 75, 77
  and Boer War 101
  post-Boer War and Roberts era 145, 163
Ludendorff, Erich 258, 304

Lunt, James 21
Lyttelton, Neville 26, 185, 195, 204, 208

MacAndrew, Harry 255, 292, 294, 301
Mafeking 85, 166
   see also under Boer War: BATTLES
Mahdi, the, *see* Mohammed Ahmed
Maitland, Frances 10, 231
Majuba Hill 85
   see also under Transvaal
      War: BATTLES
Malcolm, Neil 152
Marlborough, Duke of 111
Maude, F.N. 3, 20, 26
   and Boer War 86
   post-Boer War and Roberts era 152
Maurice, Frederick 82, 153
Mayne, G.B. 172
Melgund, Viscount, *see* Minto, Earl
Methuen, Lord 85, 87, 92, 99
Milne, George 260
Minto, Earl 66
   and Boer War 113, 114, 119, 123
Modder River 92, 98, 102, 104, 108, 110–11, 117, 149, 167
   see also under Boer War: BATTLES
Mohammed Ahmed (the 'Mahdi') 60
Mole, Edwin 57
Moltke, Helmut von ('the Elder') 258
Moltke, Helmut von ('the Younger') 246–7
Monash, John 259, 294, 297
Monro, Charles 124, 239, 261, 263
Morris, William 43
Mounted Infantry Schools 62, 63, 66, 162, 168, 217
Mullens, R.L. 294
Murray, Archibald 156, 227, 229
   and First World War 260, 263
      commencement of 239, 240
      Palestine 284

Napoleonic Wars (1792–1815) 17, 22, 23, 258, 259, 269
   BATTLES
      Jena (1806) 269
      Waterloo (1815) 1, 17, 25, 266
Natal 37, 54, 55, 56, 84, 85, 87, 89, 90, 92
National Service League 204, 220
Nazareth 301
Négrier, François de 192
New Zealand 37, 38

Nicholson, William
   and Boer War 97
   post-Boer War and Roberts
      era 155, 156, 170
   under Haldane 227
Nivelle, Robert 279
Nixon, John 260
Nolan, (Edward) Lewis 18
Norfolk, Duke of 111
North Atlantic Treaty Organisation (NATO) 258

officers 8–9, 21–3, 67–70
   and Cardwell–Childers
      reforms 50–53, 67
   post-Boer War and Roberts
      era 158–60, 188–9
   under Haldane 207–8
Oman, Charles 224
operational art 258–60, 280, 288, 289
Orange Free State 81, 83, 84, 85, 108, 110
Orange River Colony 81, 110
Orwell, George 306–7
Ottoman Turkish Empire 242, 249, 278, 288

Paget, A.H. 116
Paget, George (Lord) 27
Palmer, Power 145
Parr, Henry Hallam, *see* Hallam Parr, Henry
Passchendaele, *see* First World War:
      Western Front: BATTLES
      (Ypres, Third Battle of [1917])
Paterson, R.W. 251
Peel, Sidney 22, 294
Peninsula War, *see* Napoleonic
      Wars (1792–1815)
Plumer, Herbert 70
   post-Boer War and Roberts
      era 84, 124, 185
   under Haldane 204, 205
   and First World War 260, 261, 263, 306
      commencement of 240
      Western Front (deadlock) 264, 282–3
Pole-Carew, Reginald 97, 100
Pomeroy-Colley, George 56–7
Pretoria 81, 85, 86, 98, 111, 115, 116, 117, 119, 121, 122, 126
Pretyman, George 97
Prevost Battersby, H.F. 181, 224
Prussia 17, 36, 269

Index

Pulteney, William 239

raid, *see* cavalry raid
Rawlinson, Henry 3, 70, 71, 79
   and Boer War 96–7, 111,
      118, 119, 124, 127
   post-Boer War and Roberts era
      144, 148, 154, 155
   and Russo-Japanese War 193
   under Haldane 199, 202, 203, 205, 216
      and *War and the Arme Blanche*
         episode 222, 225
   and First World War 261, 262, 263, 306
      commencement of 239
      Western Front (deadlock) 254–7,
         264, 267, 271–4, 276
      Western Front (Hundred Days
         campaign) 295–6
Red River Expedition (1870) 38
Regulation of the Forces Act (1871) 52
Repington, Charles 218, 224, 238, 260, 304
Rhodes, Cecil 106
Richardson, Wodehouse 99, 107
Riet River 101, 102
Rifle Volunteer movement 13
Rimington, Michael
   and Boer War 91, 98, 103, 109
   post-Boer War and Roberts era 145,
      152, 166, 167, 168, 177, 181, 185
   post-Roberts 193
   under Haldane 195, 205
   pre-First World War 233
   and First World War
      Western Front (1914) 248
      Western Front (deadlock) 253, 270
Robbins, Simon 261
Roberts, Frederick (Lord) 1, 5, 15–16,
   53, 57, 70–1, 73, 77, 79
   and Boer War 81, 92, 94, 96–101,
      101–2, 105–7, 108–19, 122–3,
      124, 125, 126, 127, 128
   as C-in-C
      abolition of C-in-C 181–2
      abolition of the lance 170–74
      Cavalry Training (1904) 175–82
      and Elgin Commission 169
      key appointments 155–8, 166–7
      and officers 158–60
      post-Boer War 143–9,
         150–51, 153–4
      and Yeomanry 160–63

   post C-in-C 181–7, 191, 199,
      203, 204, 210, 217
      and *Cavalry Training* (1904) 182–7
      and commencement of First
         World War 239, 240
      and *War and the Arme
         Blanche* 220–28
      and Yeomanry 218–19
Roberts, Lady 143, 157
Roberts Ring 70–71, 79, 97, 156,
   171, 175, 203–4, 205
Robertson, William 51, 68, 70
   and Boer War 96, 98, 124
   post-Boer War and Roberts era 155
   under Haldane 204
   and *War and the Arme
      Blanche* episode 225
   and First World War 260
      Western Front (1914) 246
      Western Front (deadlock) 252,
         276, 277–8, 281, 292, 293
Royal Military Academy Woolwich
   65n156, 199
Royal Military College Sandhurst
   11n47, 65, 199
Royal United Service Institution 24, 43, 65,
   147, 163, 171, 172, 213, 216, 226
Russell, Baker 53, 70, 77
Russia 288
   see also Soviet Union
Russo-Japanese War (1904–1905) 173,
   174, 185, 191–5, 228, 236
Russo-Turkish War (1877–78) 43, 48, 191

Sadowa, Battle of, *see* Austro-Prussian War:
   BATTLES (Könnigrätz [1866])
Sassoon, Siegfried 306
Schlieffen, Count Alfred von 197
Schmidt, Carl 48–9
School of Artillery, Larkhill 190n237
School of Gunnery 190n237
School of Musketry, Hythe 26, 190n237
Schwerpunkt 201
Scobell, Henry
   post-Boer War and Roberts era 145, 158,
      171, 175, 177, 183, 185, 186–7
   under Haldane 200, 201, 204–5, 211
scouting 4–5, 11, 14, 43, 44, 48–9,
   147, 214, 219, 244
   and mechanisation 234–8
Second World War (1939–45) 241, 291

Seely, J.E.B. 32–3
   and Boer War 95
   and First World War
      Western Front (deadlock)
         251, 289, 292
Seven Weeks War, see Austro-Prussian War
Shaw, George Bernard 2
Shea, John 11, 207, 261, 287
Sheridan, Philip 45–6
Sikh War, First (1845–46) 22
   BATTLES
      Aliwal (1846) 22
Sinai 249, 250
Smith, Frederick 88, 91, 99, 115
Smith, Michael 4
Smith-Dorrien, Horace 3, 71, 72, 77
   and Boer War 109, 115, 124, 127
   post-Boer War and Roberts era 145, 180
   under Haldane 204–5, 218
   and First World War 261, 262, 263
      commencement of 240
      Western Front (1914) 245
Smuts, Jan Christiaan 87, 127
Sordet (General) 215
South Africa 6, 37, 55, 79
South African Anglo-Boer War, see
      Boer War (1899–1902)
South African Republic, see
      Transvaal Republic
Soviet Union 258
Spears, Edward, see Spiers, (Edward) Louis
Spiers, (Edward) Louis 207, 215, 230, 247
Staff College 1, 17, 42, 43, 45, 51, 70,
      71, 72, 96, 100, 155, 166, 177,
      180, 199–200, 203, 207, 211n110,
      214, 222, 227, 263–4, 269, 286
Stanhope, Edward 40
Stanhope Memorandum (1891) 40
Stanley, Lord (Earl of Derby) 111
Stanley Committee 158
Starr, Stephen Z. 45
Steyn, Marthinus 110, 115
structure and organisation (cavalry) 5–14, 74
   pre-Boer War 35–41
      and Cardwell–Childers reforms
         21, 36–7, 39, 40, 50–53
      and Egyptian Expedition 59–60
      and Gordon Relief Expedition 60–61
   and Boer War 83–4, 92–7,
      99–101, 111, 113–15
   post-Boer War and Roberts
      era 144, 149, 153–6
   under Haldane 195–9
      Mounted Infantry 216–18
      senior officers 199–206
   pre-First World War 228–38
      and mechanisation 232–8
   and First World War
      commencement of 239–41
      Palestine 283–4, 286
      Western Front (deadlock) 257,
         268–70, 276–8, 281–2, 293–5
      Western Front (Kaiserschlacht
         offensive) 293–5
      Western Front (Hundred Days
         campaign) 298–9
Stuart, J.E.B. 'Jeb' 45, 46, 102, 188, 301
Suakin 37, 61–2
Suakin Field Force (1884–85) 61–2, 72
Sudan 37, 38
   Gordon Relief Expedition (1884–85)
      39, 60–61, 71
   Sudan (1884) 60–62
      BATTLES
      El Teb (1884) 60
   Reconquest of (1896–98)
      12, 38, 39, 71–2
      BATTLES
      Atbara (1898) 19
      Omdurman (1898) 18, 19–20,
         26, 27, 64, 173, 305
      Tamai (1884) 60, 61
Swinton, Ernest 213n119, 234
Sykes, Frederick 237

tactics (cavalry) 15–20, 41–2,
      63–7, 72–4, 75, 77–8
   and American Civil War 42–7
   and Austro-Prussian and Franco-
      Prussian wars 47–50
   and Russo-Turkish War 191
   Second Afghan War 53–4
   Zulu War 55, 58
   Transvaal War 56–7, 58
   Gordon Relief Expedition 61
   Boer War 89, 91–3, 94, 101–3, 104–5,
      108–9, 116, 119–22, 123–4, 127–30
   post-Boer War and Roberts era
      150–53, 154, 165, 168–71, 174,
      175–6, 179–81, 186–8, 189
   and Russo-Japanese War 191–5

under Haldane **134**, 195, 196–7, 202–3,
  206–7, 208–10, 211–16, 218–20
  and *War and the Arme Blanche*
    episode 220–28
  pre-First World War **134**, 228–38
  and mechanisation 232–8
  First World War
    and operational art 258–60
    Palestine 284–6, 288, 301–2
    Western Front (1914) 242–8
    Western Front (deadlock)
      251–60, 264–70, 270–76,
      279–81, 282–3, 289–92
    Western Front (Hundred Days
      campaign) 295–9
  see also charge
Taylor, A.J.P. 306
Tennyson, Alfred (Lord) 22
Thorneycroft, Alec 93n59
thruster doctrine 264–5
Tirah Expedition (1897) 64, 85
Transvaal Republic 54, 55–7, 79, 81,
  83, 84, 85, 110, 129, 164
  Jameson Raid (1895–96) 83
  see also South Africa
Transvaal War (1880–81) 26,
  54, 55–8, 87, 128
  BATTLES
  Laing's Nek (1881) 56
  Majuba Hill (1881) 26, 57, 87, 96, 105
Tulloch, Alexander 18

Uniacke, Herbert 202

Valentine, R. 29
Vaughan, John
  and Boer War 101, 103, 106, 110, 120
  post-Boer War and Roberts era 158, 189
  post-Roberts 194
  under Haldane 198
    and *War and the Arme
      Blanche* episode 226
  pre-First World War 229–30, 233
  and First World War
    commencement of 240
    Western Front (1914) 246,
      247, 292, 294
Victoria, Queen 50, 96, 101
Viljoen, B.J. 'Ben' 29
Vivian, Lord 159
Vosges 244

Warwick, Earl of 294
Waters, W.H.H. 193
weaponry (cavalry) 6–7, 14–15, 24–6,
  27–8, 41–2, 64, 66, 78
  and American Civil War 42–7
  and Austro-Prussian and Franco-
    Prussian wars 47–8
  and Russo-Turkish War 191
  Second Afghan War 54
  Zulu War 55
  Gordon Relief Expedition 61
  Boer War 83–4, 89, 120, 125, 127–8
  post-Boer War and Roberts era 143,
    147, 150–52, 153, 154, 160–64,
    167–74, 175–9, 181, 185, 188, 190
    abolition of lance 170–74, 185
  and Russo-Japanese War 191–5
  under Haldane 210–11, 212–13, 218–20
    reintroduction of lance 210–11
    and *War and the Arme Blanche*
      episode 220–28
  pre-First World War 228–9, 230–31, 232
  First World War 247, 302
Wellington, Duke of 22
Wells, H.G. 234
Westminster, Duke of 253
Wet, Christiaan de 86, 101, 102, 105,
  108–9, 110, 112, 116, 126, 149
Whigham, Robert 285
White, George 87, 149
Wigram, Clive 255
Wilkinson, Henry 172
Wilkinson, Spencer 111, 304
Wilson, Henry 3, 17, 51, 68, 71
  and Boer War 90, 107, 111, 117, 124
  post-Boer War and Roberts era
    146, 148–9, 155, 181, 182
  under Haldane 196, 198, 199,
    203, 204, 205, 216
    and *War and the Arme Blanche*
      episode 222–4, 225, 227
  and First World War 260
    commencement of 240
    Western Front (deadlock) 254
    Western Front (Hundred Days
      campaign) 295, 296, 299
Wilson, L.C. 301
Winwood, W.Q. 230
Wolseley, Garnet (Lord) 35, 40, 51, 52,
  69, 79, 143, 155, 160, 281

and American Civil War 42, 44, 45
and Zulu War 55
and Egyptian Expedition 58
and Gordon Relief Expedition 60
made C-in-C 50, 82–3
and Boer War 82–3, 90, 94, 96, 100, 101
on mounted infantry 62–7, 75, 78
on Yeomanry 76, 78, 94, 160, 161
Wolseley Ring 35, 38, 53, 56, 70, 71, 75, 79, 96, 100, 155, 156
Wood, Evelyn 12, 27, 51, 54, 63, 65, 66, 68, 71, 73–4, 77
   Boer War communications from Haig 90, 103, 118
   post-Boer War and Roberts era 151, 172, 184
   under Haldane 206
Wrangel, Carl Gustav von 192
Wyndham, George 93

Xenophon 4

Younghusband, George 18, 146
Ypres, Earl of, *see* French, John

ZAR, *see* Transvaal Republic
Zeppelins 236
Zulu 28, 54–5
Zulu War (1879) 27, 28, 54–5, 58
   BATTLES
      Isandlwana (1879) 55, 71
      Ulundi (1879) 27, 28, 55
Zululand 54–5, 90

ARMED FORCES

British

Aldershot District (later Command) 77
   pre-Boer War 39, 62–3, 64, 66, 73–4
   and Boer War 83
   post-Boer War and Roberts era 144, 146, 156, 157, 162, 166, 168, 182, 183, 187
   under Haldane 199, 200, 201, 203, 204, 205, 207, 210, 225, 227, 230
   and First World War
      commencement of 214
      Western Front (1914) 246
Army Remount Department 9, 62, 87, 167

Boer War 87
Army Service Corps 56
   in Boer War 99
Army Veterinary Department (later Corps) 88, 167
   Boer War 87
   Zulu War 55
Cavalry
   Household Cavalry 6, 7, 8, 9, 74
      and Egyptian Expedition 59
      Gordon Relief Expedition 60, 61
      and Boer War 82, 99, 109, 121, 124
      post-Boer War and Roberts era 160
      under Haldane 195, 208
      and First World War 247, 248, 293, 294, 298
   Dragoon Guards 6, 72
      post-Boer War and Roberts era 150, 164, 170
      under Haldane 210–11
   Dragoons 6, 72, 74
      post-Boer War and Roberts era 150, 164, 170
      under Haldane 210–11
   Hussars 6, 74
      post-Boer War and Roberts era 150, 164
   Lancers 6, 74
      post-Boer War and Roberts era 150, 163, 170–74, 185
      First World War **135**
Eastern Command
   under Haldane 204, 205
Flying Column
   Gordon Relief Expedition 61, 71
Guards (Foot Guards) 6, 7, 8
   Gordon Relief Expedition 60
Imperial Yeomanry (IY) 160–63
   in Boer War 93n60, 94–5, 97, 98, 111–12, 115, 116–17, 122, 124, 125, 126, 129, 160–61, 219
Machine Gun Corps
   in First World War 275
mounted infantry 14, 18, 19, 62–7, 75, 78
   in American Civil War 43–7, 65–6, 67
   in Transvaal War 56
   in Egyptian Expedition 59–60
   in Gordon Relief Expedition 60, 61
   in Boer War 90, 91, 92–6, 104–5, 106, 109, 110, 111–16, 120, 122, 126, 170

post-Boer War and Roberts era 152,
153–4, 156–7, 163, 165, 168, 170
and Russo-Japanese War 191–5
under Haldane 216–18, 227
pre-First World War 231
see also Mounted Infantry (MI)
Mounted Infantry (MI) 62–7, 78
in Boer War 90, 97–8, 99, 104–5,
106, 109, 110, 111, 113–16, 120,
123–4, 125, 127, 128, **132**, 187
post-Boer War and Roberts era
144, 154, 162, 166
under Haldane 216–18, 235
mounted rifles and Light Horse 13–14,
15, 17, 19, 44, 75, 92–6
in Boer War 90, 91, 92–6, 97–8, 99,
106, 111–13, 115, 116–17, 121–2,
123–4, 125, 126, 129, **133**, 170
post-Boer War and Roberts era
151, 153–4, 161, 164, 165,
168–9, 170, 174, 183
under Haldane 209, 222, 227
pre-First World War 231, 233
Northern Command
under Haldane 204, 205
Royal Artillery 7, 8, 39, 66, 193
in Boer War 125
Royal Field Artillery 190
in Boer War 93, 116
in First World War 7n24
Royal Horse Artillery (RHA) 7,
190n237, 202, 261n117
in First World War 7n24
Royal Engineers 8, 172
in First World War 274
Royal Flying Corps 237
in First World War 275, 278, 298
Royal Marines
Gordon Relief Expedition 60, 62
Salisbury District 151
Southern Command
under Haldane 204, 205, 206, 212, 225
Special Reserve
in First World War 13
Tank Corps
in First World War 278, 279, 280–81,
282, 288–9, 290, 296–7, 298
Territorial Force 13
under Haldane 195, 198, 219–20, 225
pre-First World War 234–5
and First World War 205, 249

Yeomanry 12–13, 17, 36, 76–7, 78, 163
and Boer War 83, 93–6, 122, 125, *see
also* Imperial Yeomanry (IY)
post-Boer War and Roberts era
153, 160–63, 168–9, 170
under Haldane 195, 198, 218–20, 227
pre-First World War 231–2, 233, 234–5
and First World War 300
Egypt 249, 250
Gallipoli 249
Palestine 242, 261, 284,
285, 286, 287, 293
Salonika 242
Sinai 250
Western Front (1914) 248
Western Front (deadlock)
249, 257, 268, 271, 276,
278, 281, 293, 294
Volunteers 13–14, 37–8
see also mounted rifles and Light
Horse, Yeomanry, Territorial Force

UNITS
British Expeditionary Force (BEF)
7, 24, 107, 154, 195, 304
under Haldane 195–9, 201, 204,
205, 206, 210, 217–18, 230
pre-First World War 235
and First World War 251, 257
Western Front (1914) 215,
239, 240, 243, 244, 245
Western Front (deadlock) 241,
260, 261, 262, 263, 264,
268, 270, 275, 277, 281
Western Front (Kaiserschlacht
offensive) 293, 294
Western Front (Hundred Days
campaign) 296, 298

Egyptian Expeditionary Force (EEF)
(First World War) 241, 250, 260,
278, 283–4, 293, 294, 300, 302

Armies (First World War)
First Army 252, 253, 255, 261, 262, 279
Second Army 262, 264, 282
Third Army 240, 261, 262,
279, 284, 288, 298
Fourth Army 202, 262,
271–3 *passim*, 295

Fifth Army 23, 152, 241,
  264, 282, 294, 295
Reserve Army 262, 263n125,
  271, 272–5 passim

Corps (First World War)
  Cavalry Corps 31, 194, 202, 240, 247,
    248, 251, 252, 254, 255, 256, 257,
    261–3, 267, 270, 275–6, 279–83,
    289, 290, 292, 294–9, 304
    as the Dismounted
      Division 257, 281
  Desert Mounted Corps 284–7, 301
    Desert Column 283
  I Corps 244
  II Corps 239, 245, 271, 273
  III Corps 239, 274, 288–9
  IV Corps 254, 257, 288–9, 291, 292
  V Corps 240, 261
  VI Corps 267n148
  VII Corps 288
  IX Corps 261, 264
  X Corps 261
  XIII Corps 261
  XIV Corps **141**, 270
  XV Corps 261
  XVI Corps 261
  XVII Corps 280
  XX Corps 261, 283, 284, 301
  XXI Corps 284, 300, 301
  XXII Corps 250n61
  Reserve Corps 263n125, 270

Divisions (First World War except
  where indicated)
  The Cavalry Division 40, 64, 66, 73, 75
    Egyptian Expedition 7, 58
    Boer War 7, 16, 72, 83, 85, 99,
      100–103, 105–9, 110, 113–14,
      115, 118–19, 148, 149, 156
    pre-First World War 144, 195–8,
      201–2, 205, 218, 232, 235, 237
    First World War 7, 239–46
      passim, 262, 298
    see also 1st Cavalry Division
  1st Cavalry Division 233, 248, 271,
    282, 289, 290, 291, 292, 294
    as a Dismounted Division 294
  2nd Cavalry Division 32,
    245, 253, 289, 294

3rd Cavalry Division 32, 247,
  271, 292, 293, 294, 299
4th Cavalry Division 275,
  277, 293, 300–301
5th Cavalry Division 275, 277,
  289, 292, 293, 294, 300–301
  see also 2nd Indian
    Cavalry Division
Mounted Infantry Division
  Boer War 113, 115, 116
1st Mounted Division 159n92, 249
2nd Mounted Division 249, 250, 284
  see also Yeomanry Division
2/2 Mounted Division 249
Imperial Mounted Division 284
  see also Australian
    Mounted Division
Yeomanry Division 261,
  284, 286–7, 293
2nd Division 239
  pre-First World War 204, 205
3rd Division
  pre-First World War 166, 205, 225
7th Division 261, 263
  pre-First World War 196
9th (Scottish) Division 299
19th (Western) Division 261
21st Division 166n130
25th Division 271
27th Division 263
29th Division 156, 263
30th Division 261
46th (North Midland) Division 261
57th (2nd West Lancashire)
  Division 265
58th (2/1st London) Division 261n116
60th (2/2nd London) Division 261, 287
63rd (Royal Naval) Division 249n56
Cyclist Division 276

Brigades
  1st Cavalry Brigade
    Boer War 107
    pre-First World War (Aldershot)
      74, 157–8, 166, 171, 200–201,
      205, 207, 210, 214, 230
    First World War 246
  2nd Cavalry Brigade
    Boer War 101, 104, 121
    pre-First World War (Tidworth) 200
    First World War 244–5

3rd Cavalry Brigade
   pre-First World War
     (Curragh) 159, 208
   First World War 33, 245, 247
4th Cavalry Brigade
   pre-First World War
     (Canterbury) 200, 233
5th Cavalry Brigade
   pre-First World War (York) 196
   First World War 244–6, 252
6th Cavalry Brigade
   First World War 248
8th Cavalry Brigade
   First World War 280
1st Mounted Brigade
   Boer War 104, 113
Heavy Cavalry Brigade
   Crimean War 22
Light Cavalry Brigade
   Crimean War 17, 18, 27

Camel Corps
   Gordon Relief Expedition 60–61
   Imperial Camel Corps Brigade 284

Cavalry regiments
   The (Composite) Household Regiment 6
     Egyptian Expedition 59
     Boer War 82, 99, 121
     pre-First World War 195, 198
     First World War 247, 248
   1st Life Guards 6, 231
     First World War 279
   2nd Life Guards 6, 60, 61, 69, 92
   Royal Horse Guards (The
     Blues) 6, 68, 286
   1st (King's) Dragoon Guards
     Zulu War 55
   2nd Dragoon Guards (Queen's Bays)
     Boer War 129
   3rd (Prince of Wales's) Dragoon
     Guards 4, 204
   4th (Royal Irish) Dragoon Guards
     6n22, 68, 172, 190, 208
     First World War 244, 291
   5th (Princess Charlotte of Wales's)
     Dragoon Guards 6n22,
     72n197, 166, 210, 230
     Boer War 29
   6th Dragoon Guards (Carabiniers) 6
   7th (Princess Royal's) Dragoon Guards
     Boer War 88
     First World War 30, 32, 274, 305
   1st (Royal) Dragoons 6, 7, 92, 204, 233
     Boer War 92
   2nd Dragoons (Royal Scots Greys) 6
   4th (Queen's Own) Hussars 11,
     18, 68, 100, 189, 208
   5th (Royal Irish) Lancers 6,
     21n86, 158, 171, 208
     Sudan (1884) 62n140
     Boer War 29, 127
     First World War **135**, 248
   6th (Inniskilling) Dragoons 6, 8,
     41n35, 72n197, 107n131
     Transvaal War 57
     Boer War 88, 91
     First World War 275
   7th (Queen's Own) Hussars
     68, 73, 77, 155n62
     Boer War 101, 129
   8th (King's Royal Irish) Hussars
     Boer War 120
   9th (Queen's Royal) Lancers 7,
     10, 69, 143, 162, 171, 177
     Second Afghan War 54
     First World War 244–5
   10th (Prince of Wales's Own
     Royal) Hussars 6, 7, 8, 9, 69,
     107n131, 189, 205, 229
     Second Afghan War 53
     Sudan (1884) 60
     Boer War 88
     First World War 280, 282
   11th (Prince Albert's Own)
     Hussars 207, 230
     First World War 129, 247
   12th (Prince of Wales's Royal)
     Lancers 11, 58, 171, 303
     Boer War 101, 121
   13th Hussars 7, 51, 61, 70, 166
     13th Light Dragoons 51
     Second Afghan War 53
     Boer War 92
   14th (King's) Hussars 57, 230
   15th (The King's) Hussars 57–8, 67, 237
     Second Afghan War 58
     First World War 28, 284
   16th (The Queen's) Lancers 21n86, 77,
     100, 171, 201, 204, 205, 208, 213
     First Sikh War 22
     Boer War 89, 93, 104

First World War **135**, 247–8
17th Lancers (Duke of Cambridge's
    Own) 5–6, 27, 156, 159,
    171, 173, 175, 229
  Zulu War 27, 28, 55
  First World War i, 261, 296
18th (Queen Mary's Own) Hussars
  Boer War 89, 114, 127
  First World War 245
19th (Queen Alexandra's Own) Hussars
    10, 18, 22, 72, 74, 231, 240, 261
  Egyptian Expedition 58
  Sudan (1884) 60
  Gordon Relief Expedition 61
  First World War 299
20th Hussars
  Sudan (1884) 60, 62n140
21st (Empress of India's)
    Lancers 6, 7, 171, 200
  21st Hussars 6
  Reconquest of Sudan 18,
      19–20, 27, 305

Infantry regiments
  Coldstream Guards 71, 263
  Durham Light Infantry 69
  Gordon Highlanders 70, 150, 263
  King's Royal Rifle Corps
      (60th Rifles) 8, 13, 70
  Rifle Brigade 7, 8, 68, 71, 252, 263
  Royal Irish Regiment 11
  Royal Scots Fusiliers
    Boer War 93n59
  Royal Scots 7n26
  Yorkshire and Lancashire Regiment 70

City Imperial Volunteers (CIV)
    Mounted Infantry
  Boer War 111, 116, 161

Mounted Volunteers
  1st Hampshire Light Horse Volunteers
      (Bower's Hants Horse) 13, 44, 160
  Mounted Infantry Volunteers 13
  Mounted Rifle Volunteers 75

Mounted Infantry
  2nd Corps Mounted Infantry 122n200
  Guards Mounted Infantry
    Boer War 124
  Royal Artillery Mounted Infantry
    Boer War 125
  1st Mounted Infantry
    Boer War 104n117
  2nd Mounted Infantry
    Boer War 124
  3rd Mounted Infantry
    Boer War 104n117
  5th Mounted Infantry
    Boer War 104n117
  6th Mounted Infantry
    Boer War 124
  7th Mounted Infantry
    Boer War 104n117
  8th Mounted Infantry
    Boer War 124, 127, 193

Imperial Yeomanry (IY) (Boer War)
  8th Imperial Yeomanry Battalion 95n68
  13th Imperial Yeomanry Battalion 111
  16th Imperial Yeomanry Battalion 95n68
  18th 'Sharpshooters' Imperial
      Yeomanry Battalion 95
  20th 'Rough Riders' Imperial
      Yeomanry Battalion 95
  41st Imperial Yeomanry Company 95

Royal Field Artillery 38th Battery
  Boer War 116
Royal Horse Artillery (FHA) V Brigade
  First World War 202

Yeomanry regiments (including
    Special Reserve)
  Bedfordshire Yeomanry
    First World War 22
  Cheshire Yeomanry (Earl
      of Chester's) 13
  City of London Yeomanry
      (Rough Riders) 12
  Hampshire Yeomanry
    Boer War 95
    41st (Hampshire) Company
      Boer War 95n72
  King Edward's Horse
    First World War 13, 250
  Middlesex Yeomanry 162, 232
  Montgomeryshire Yeomanry 162
  Nottinghamshire Yeomanry 107n131
  Oxfordshire Yeomanry (Queen's Own
      Oxfordshire Hussars) 12, 231
    Second World War 294

Index   357

40th (Oxfordshire) Company
   Boer War 95n72
Royal 1st Devon Yeomanry 12
Royal Buckinghamshire
   Hussars Yeomanry
   37th (Buckinghamshire) Company
      Boer War 95n72
   38th (Buckinghamshire) Company
      Boer War 95n72
Royal East Kent Yeomanry
   Boer War 93n60
Royal Gloucestershire Hussars 161–2
   First World War **137**
South Nottinghamshire Hussars 163
Warwickshire Yeomanry 232
   First World War 29, 287
West Kent Yeomanry 12
   Boer War 93
Worcestershire Hussars Yeomanry
   First World War 29, 285, 287
Yorkshire Dragoons Yeomanry
   Boer War 95n72
   11th (Yorkshire Dragoons) Company
      Boer War 95n72
Yorkshire Hussars Yeomanry
   9th (Yorkshire Hussars) Company
      Boer War 95n72

British Imperial

Australia and New Zealand

ANZAC (First World War)
   163n112, 242, 249, 285
Australian mounted troops 12, 37, 66
   and Boer War 95–6, 113, **133**
   post-Boer War and Roberts era
      154, 165, 166, 170, 173, 175
   pre-First World War 231, 233
   and First World War
      Gallipoli 242, 249
      Palestine 28, 249, 284, 285, 286,
         287, 293, 300, 301, 302
      Western Front 250, 293, 299
New Zealand mounted troops 12
   and Boer War 95–6, 113
   and First World War
      Gallipoli 249
      Palestine 249, 284, 285, 286
      Western Front 250

UNITS (ANZAC)
   ANZAC Corps 262
   I ANZAC Corps 250
   II ANZAC Corps 250n61
   ANZAC Mounted Division 250,
      284, 285, 286, 301, 302
   I ANZAC Corps Mounted
      Regiment 250n61
   II ANZAC Corps Mounted
      Regiment 250n61
UNITS (Australian)
   Australian Corps (First World War) 259, 299
   Australian Mounted Division (First World
      War) 28, 284, 286, 293, 300, 301–2
   Mounted regiments
      Australian Light Horse (First
         World War) 249, 284, 301
      3rd Light Horse 301
      4th Light Horse 250n61, 286
      12th Light Horse 286
      13th Light Horse 250
      New South Wales Lancers 37, 173
         Boer War 83, 96, 99
      New South Wales Mounted Rifles
         Boer War 104n117
      Queensland Mounted Infantry
         Boer War 112, 113, 250
      West Australian Mounted
         Infantry 122n200
         Boer War 121
UNITS (New Zealand)
   Mounted regiments
      New Zealand Mounted Rifles
         151, 249, 284
         Boer War 89
         First World War 249, 284
      Otago Mounted Rifles
         First World War 250n61

Canada

Canadian mounted troops 12, 66
   influence of American Civil War on 44
   and Boer War 84, 95–6, 113
   post-Boer War and Roberts era
      164, 165, 175, 178
   pre-First World War 231
   and First World War 262
      Western Front 32–4, **140**,
         159n92, 250, 256, 270, 274,
         289, 290, 292, 293, 294

UNITS
Canadian Corps (First World
  War) 250, 256, 262
Canadian Cavalry Brigade 95
  First World War 32, 250, 270, 293
Cavalry and Mounted regiments
  Canadian Light Horse
    First World War 250
  Canadian Mounted Rifles 231
    Boer War 96, 113
    see also Royal Canadian Dragoons
  2nd Canadian Mounted Rifles
    Boer War 96n73
  Fort Garry Horse
    First World War 32–3, 250, 290
  Governor General of Canada's
    Bodyguard 44
  Lord Strathcona's Horse 37
    Boer War 96, 112
    First World War 32–3
  Royal Canadian Dragoons 37
    Boer War 96
    First World War 32–3
    1st Canadian Mounted Rifles
      Boer War 96n73
North West Mounted Police ('Mounties')
  Boer War 96

India

Indian Army 35, 38, 39, 53, 70, 74,
  143n1, 145, 171, 177
Indian Cavalry 10–11, 15, 41–2, 58, 72, 77
  and Second Afghan War 53, 54
  and Egyptian Expedition 18, 59
  post-Boer War and Roberts era 145,
    157, 158, 172, 177, 178–81
  under Haldane 195, 211
  and First World War 261, 263, 300
    Mesopotamia 242, 271
    Palestine 242, 249, 286,
      293, 294, 301
    Sudan (1884) 61
    Western Front (1914) 248
    Western Front (deadlock) 31, 252,
      253, 254, 255, 256, 270, 271,
      273–4, 275, 277, 293, 294
UNITS
Bengal Army Corps 145
Indian Corps (First World War)
  239, 254, 263

Indian Cavalry Corps (First World War)
  248, 255, 256, 261, 263, 268, 270

2nd Indian Cavalry Division
  First World War 252, 261, 270, 271, 273
4th (Quetta) Division
  pre-First World War 180
7th (Meerut) Division
  First World War 300
18th Indian Division
  First World War 261n116

Imperial Service Cavalry Brigade
  First World War 284
Meerut Cavalry Brigade 233
Secunderabad Cavalry Brigade
  First World War 274

Cavalry regiments
  1st Punjab Cavalry 300
  2nd Lancers
    First World War 300
  4th Cavalry 180
  4th Lancers 77, 180
  5th Punjab Cavalry
    Second Afghan War 53, 70
    see also 25th Cavalry
  9th Bengal Cavalry
    Sudan (1884) 62n140
  9th Hodson's Horse 145
    Sudan (1884) 62n140
  10th Duke of Cambridge's Own
    Lancers (Hodson's Horse) 10–11
  11th Bengal Lancers 11
    Boer War 93
  11th Prince of Wales's Own Lancers 11
  15th Bengal Lancers 11
  15th Lancers 11
  16th Cavalry 10
  18th Bengal Lancers **131**
  20th Deccan Horse 151
    First World War 20, 30, **136**, 274
  25th Cavalry 53
  28th Light Cavalry 10
  29th Lancers
    First World War 302
  35th Scinde Horse 179, 207, 261, 284
  Queen Victoria's Own Corps
    of Guides (Frontier Force)
    (Lumsden's) Cavalry 10, 18

Index

Rhodesia

Rhodesia Regiment 84
    Boer War 84

South Africa

South African mounted troops 12, 37
Mounted regiments
    Bethune's Mounted Infantry 213
        Boer War 93
    Cape Mounted Rifles 13, 37
    Frontier Light Horse
        Zulu War 54
    Grahamstown Volunteer
        Mounted Infantry
            Boer War 105n117
    Imperial Light Horse 90, 190, 206
        Boer War 93
    Kitchener's Horse
        Boer War 97, 104n117, 110, 124
    Natal Carbineers 37
        Boer War 84, 93
    Natal Mounted Police 37
        Zulu War 54
        Transvaal War 56
        Boer War 93
    Natal Native Horse
        Zulu War 54
    Rimington's Guides (Tigers) 152
        Boer War 91, 102, 104n117
    Roberts's Horse
        Boer War 97, 104n117, 110, 124
    South African Light Horse 108
        Boer War 84, 93
    Thorneycroft's Mounted Infantry
        Boer War 93

Other Nationalities

Afghan cavalry 53
Austrian Army 29
Austrian cavalry 47
Belgian cavalry 243
Boers 76, 81n1, 208–9
    and Transvaal War 56
    and Boer War 26, 29, 147, 149, 150, 152, 164, 169, 170, 187, 208–9, 225, 226
    early phase 84, 85–7, 89, 91–2
    middle phase 100, 101, 103–4, 105, 108–10, 111–12, 116–17, 119–21
    final phase 122–9
Confederate Army (American Civil War) 42, 43, 44, 46
'foot cavalry' 24, 42
Egyptian cavalry 11–12, 19
French Army 62, 196
    Chasseurs à Pied 24
    Franco-Prussian War 47
    First World War 269
French cavalry 63, 72–3, 174, 197, 198, 215
    Franco-Prussian War 17, 27, 47–8, 171
    and First World War
        Palestine 301
        Western Front 243, 247, 256, 270
    'Conneau' Corps 256
German Army 39, 62, 196, 197, 276
    and First World War 21, 242
        Western Front (1914) 243–8 *passim*
        Western Front (deadlock) 30–31, 34, 275, 279, 283, 288, 290, 291
        Western Front (Kaiserschlacht offensive) 23, 32–4, 258, 293, 294, 295
        Western Front (Hundred Days campaign) 295, 299
    First Army 243, 245
    Second Army 243
    IV Corps 31
    23rd (Saxony) Infantry Division 32
    243rd (Württemberg) Infantry Division 32
    101st (Saxony) Grenadier Regiment 33
    122nd (Württemberg) Fusilier Regiment, 1st Battalion 33
German cavalry 2, 47, 48–9, 63, 72–3, 174, 181, 197, 198, 214, 215–16
    and First World War (Western Front) 21, 242, 243–8 *passim*
    I Cavalry Corps 243
        Guard Jäger 243n20
        Guard Schützen 243n20
    II Cavalry Corps 243, 245
    4th Cavalry Division 246
    2nd Guard Dragoons 246
Italian Army 47

Japanese cavalry 185, 191–5, 198
Prussian Army
  Army of the North German
    Federation 48n69
  cavalry of 17, 47–8, 50,
    66, 152, 171, 174
Russian Army
  cavalry of 45, 185, 191–5
  Cossacks 173, 185, 191–5, 198
Turkish Army
  and First World War 29–30, 242, 249,
    278, 284–8 *passim*, 300–302 *passim*
  cavalry of
    First World War 286
Union Army (American Civil
    War) 43, 44, 45–6
United States Army, cavalry of 42,
    43, 46–7, 178, 198

Printed in Great Britain
by Amazon